创意城市·共享遗产：
无界论坛论文选
（2012—2020）

主　编：丁　援
执行主编：许　颖

东南大学出版社
·南京·

图书在版编目(CIP)数据

创意城市·共享遗产：无界论坛论文选（2012—2020）/ 丁援主编. — 南京：东南大学出版社，2021.1
ISBN 978-7-5641-9296-9

Ⅰ.①创… Ⅱ.①丁… Ⅲ.①文化遗产-保护-世界-文集 Ⅳ.①K103-53

中国版本图书馆CIP数据核字(2020)第260373号

创意城市·共享遗产：无界论坛论文选(2012—2020)
Chuangyi Chengshi·Gongxiang Yichan: Wujie Luntan Lunwenxuan(2012—2020)

主　　编：	丁　援
执行主编：	许　颖
出版发行：	东南大学出版社
社　　址：	南京市四牌楼2号　邮编：210096
出 版 人：	江建中
责任编辑：	杨　凡
责任印制：	周荣虎
封面设计：	王金科　吴莎冰
网　　址：	http://www.seupress.com
经　　销：	全国各地新华书店
印　　刷：	上海雅昌艺术印刷有限公司
版　　次：	2021年1月第1版
印　　次：	2021年1月第1次印刷
开　　本：	889 mm×1194 mm　1/16
印　　张：	24.25　彩插16页
字　　数：	882千字
书　　号：	ISBN 978-7-5641-9296-9
定　　价：	268.00元

本社图书若有印装质量问题，请直接与营销部联系。电话(传真)：025-83791830

关于促进文化交流、保护共享遗产的武汉倡议
(代序)

2020年伊始,新冠疫情给世界带来了巨大挑战。在令人焦虑和充满不确定性的时刻,文化提供了慰藉、鼓励和希望。

文化遗产作为文化的载体,是人类文明的结晶,也是人类共同的财富。当今时代,人类生活于一个文化多元和文化共融的"地球村",共享文化、共享遗产、共同承担传承与发展责任,在全球交往受阻的背景下,正是我们需要共同面对的挑战和使命。

在此,我们共同发出倡议:

• 相互尊重,相互包容,相互理解和信任,这是文化与遗产共享的前提;各界人士须秉持平等、团结的精神,以敬畏的心态、传承的责任、无界的情怀,共享不同文化的价值,感悟不同文化的魅力。

• 文化和遗产的共享有赖于科学的手段,而文化科技的融合,为人类的共享共融创造了更好的技术保障,为共享遗产的保护与发展提供了坚实的依靠,同时,也为文化与遗产价值的传播提供了更加广阔的天地。

• 各方建立更加紧密的合作,积极推动公众参与,实现工程与文化的相互促进,大学与城市的相互促进,推动社区间、城市间、地区间、国家间的文化交流,用文化遗产提升地区形象,营造良好的社会氛围。

我们重申,促进和平、推动交流是我们的共同责任,也是遗产保护的根本目的。提升人类幸福水平,共筑人类友谊金桥是我们的共同愿望!

徐麟祥大师签名　　　　　　葛修润院士签名　　　　　　徐恭义大师签名

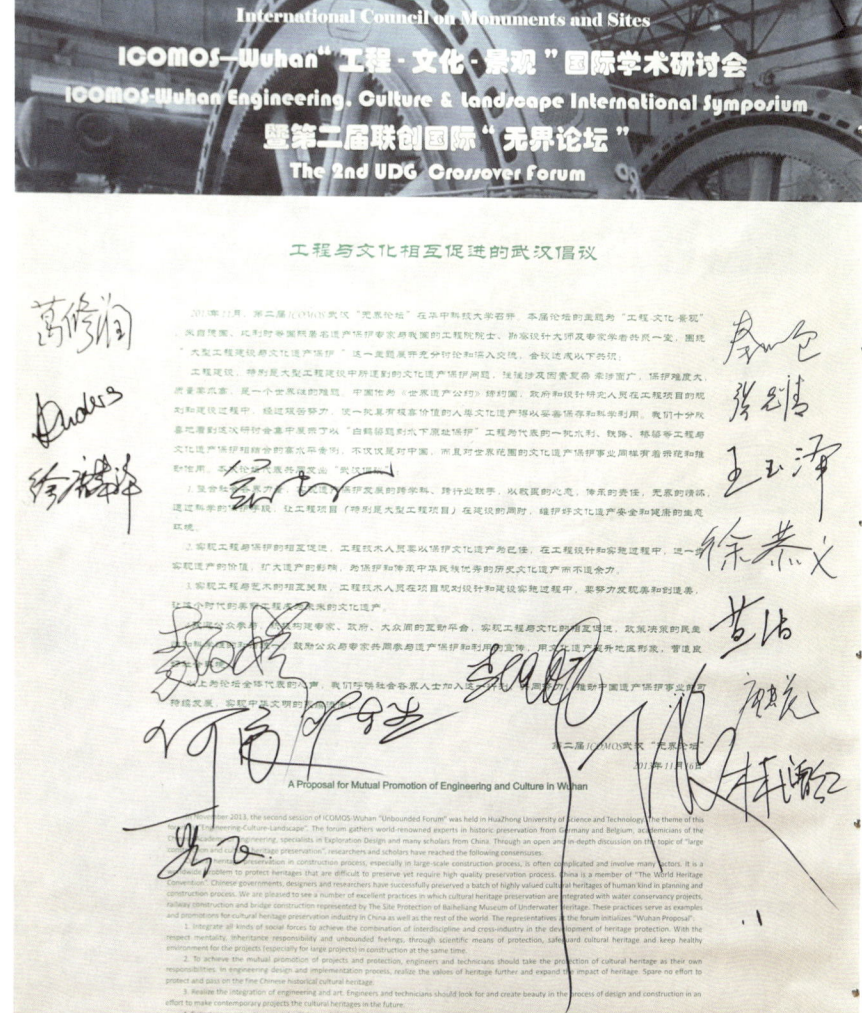

《工程与文化相互促进的武汉倡议》签名板

秦顺全院士签名　　　　　　张光清副市长签名　　　　　　李保峰教授签名

唐良智市长参加无界论坛并与ICOMOS专家互赠礼物

张光清副市长、安德斯主席、秦顺全院士、葛修润院士为共享遗产研究中心揭牌

吴良镛院士在无界论坛视频发言　　　　　　　　　　　赵宝江副部长与阮仪三教授场下交流

邵新宇院士在无界论坛发言　　　　　　　　　　　　　常青院士在无界论坛发言

中国建筑设计研究院陈同滨总规划师　　　华中科技大学何依教授　　　　　东南大学陈薇教授
在无界论坛发言　　　　　　　　　　　　在无界论坛发言　　　　　　　　在无界论坛发言

全国工程勘察设计大师周俭（同济大学教授）、王玉泽（铁四院总工程师）、张杰（清华大学教授）发言（从左至右）

武汉大学·第四届无界论坛现场

武汉会议中心·第七届无界论坛现场

武汉会议中心·第八届无界论坛现场

华中科技大学·
第二届无界论坛现场

华中师范大学·
第三届无界论坛现场

华中科技大学·第九届无界论坛现场

无界对话:"80后"对话"90后"

无界对话:当东方遇见西方

无界对话:女性与文化遗产

无界对话：联合国教科文组织教席与二类中心负责人对话

无界对话：文化线路与长江大保护

无界对话：遗产保护与城市发展

无界对话：国际视野下的文化遗产保护与公众参与

无界行走：李述永与UNESCO原文化副总干事班德林在汉口历史文化风貌区

无界沙龙：李晓红院士主持万里茶道沿线城市申遗座谈会

无界沙龙：武汉申报联合国教科文组织创意城市网络"设计之都"圆桌会议

无界沙龙：翟雅阁维修及利用

无界行走：东湖绿道

冯天瑜教授向阮元后人阮仪三教授赠送阮元书法作品

瑞普教授与青少年无界论坛获奖选手交流

无界行走：原UNESCO世界遗产中心副主任敏佳杨等国际专家参观考察武汉大学

无界行走：ICOMOS共享遗产委员会主席安德斯教授等国际专家参观考察汉口历史文化风貌区

无界行走：丁援博士陪同英国首相"第一先生"参观考察汉口历史文化风貌区

UNESCO特使、世界遗产中心原副主任 特纳教授在无界论坛发言

UNESCO遗产研究教席持有人阿尔伯特教授在无界论坛发言

ICOMOS秘书长菲利普在第二届青少年无界论坛点评选手发言

无界论坛合影·第一届至第四届

无界论坛合影·第五届至第八届

无界论坛花絮·武汉市领导与国内外专家场外交流

万勇市长致辞

无界论坛花絮·励小捷、张世华、陈邂馨场外交流

法国驻汉总领事贵永华致辞

UNESCO原文化副总干事班德林先生致辞

青少年无界论坛颁奖仪式

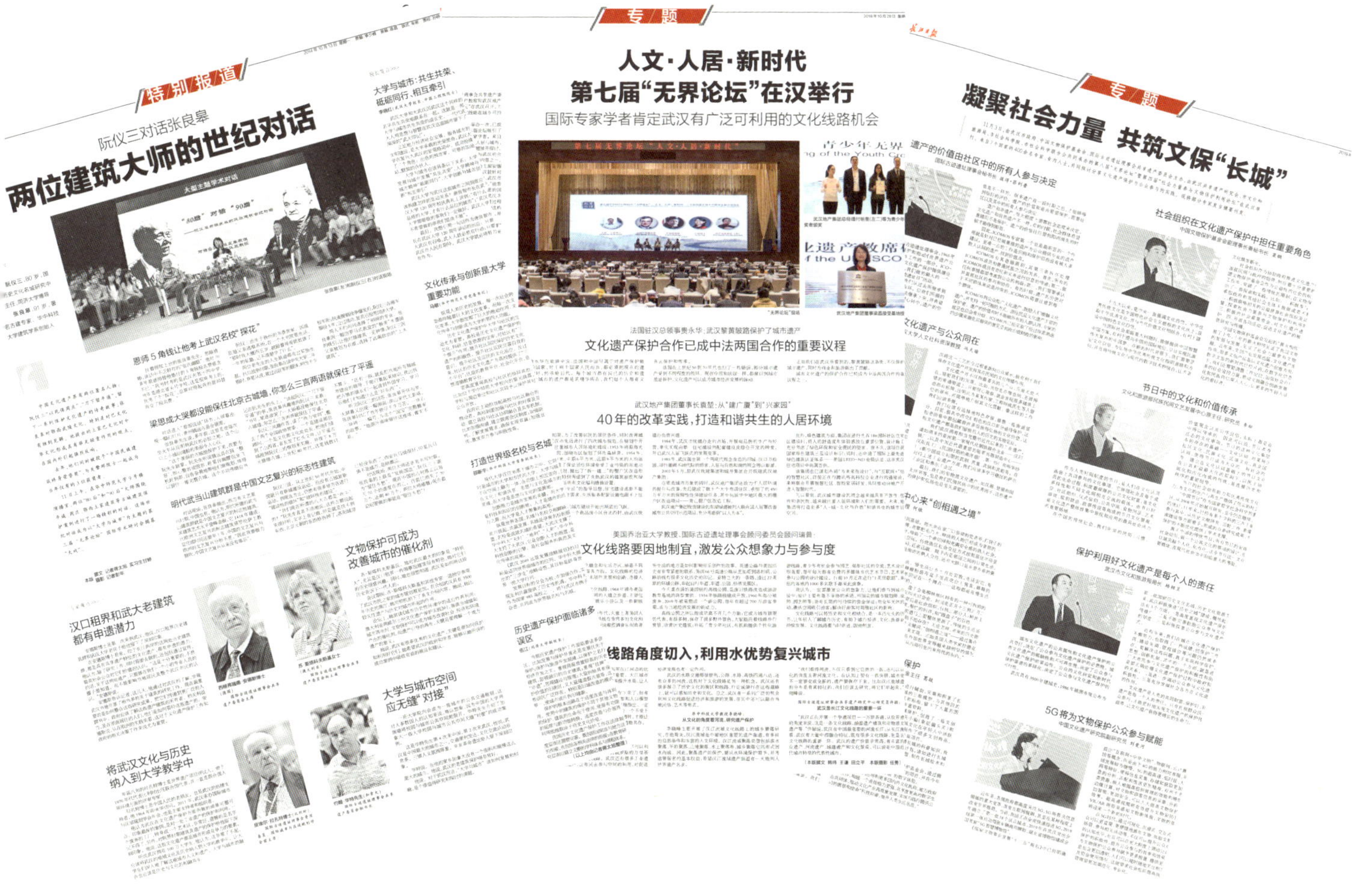

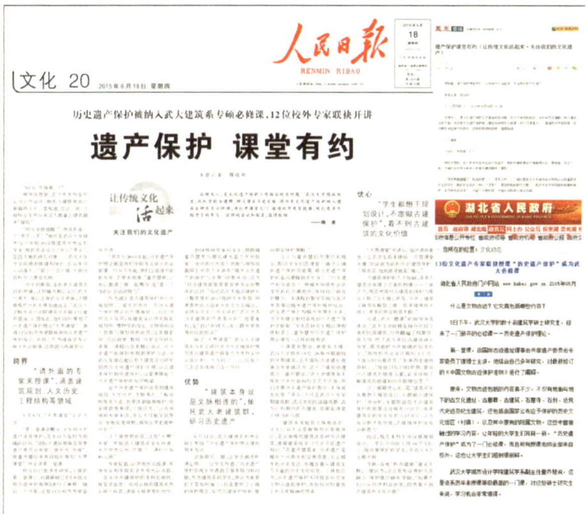

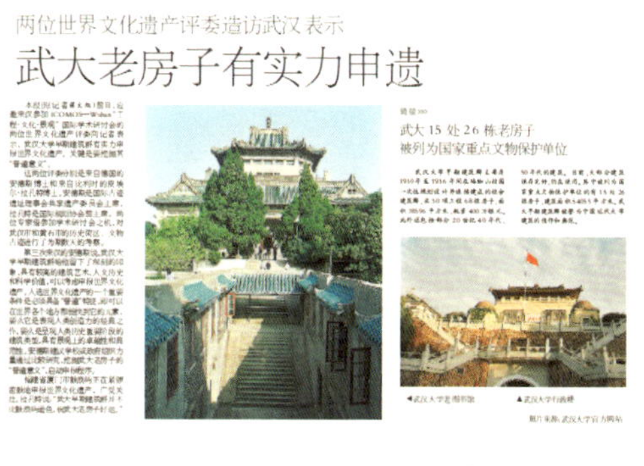

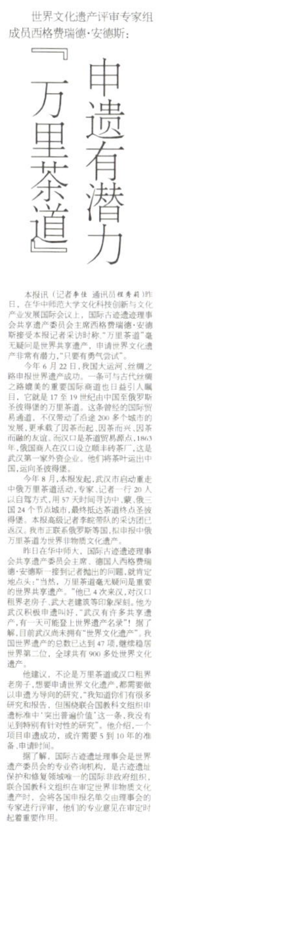

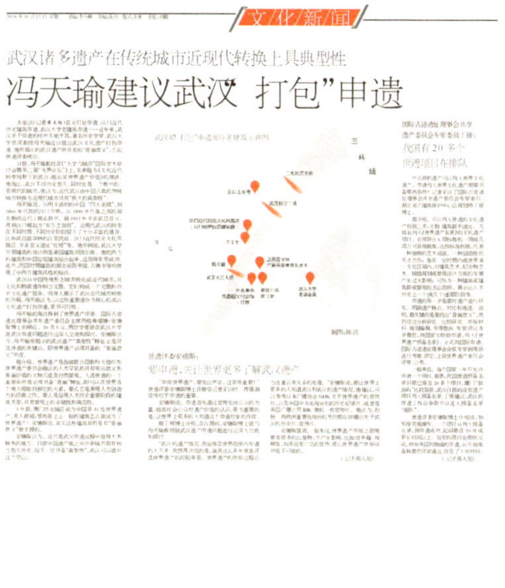

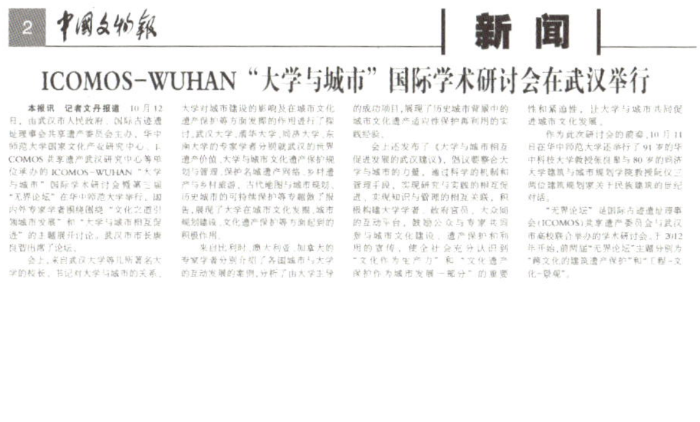

第九届无界论坛·武汉市长周先旺致辞

第九届无界论坛·长江灯光秀

第三届青少年无界论坛合影

第九届无界论坛

目 录

论文篇：无界论坛论文精选

跨文化遗产的保护与发展

论坛组委会：共享遗产与无界论坛 ··· 3

唐惠虎：近代武汉社会转型的文化路径及遗址 ··· 5

丁援：武汉近代遗产"无形文化线路"研究 ··· 13

冯天瑜，西格弗里德·安德斯：关于武汉申遗的珞珈山对话 ·· 20

敏佳杨：文化遗产作为城市发展指导原则的重要意义 ·· 25

张杰：系统认识名城价值，保护城市遗产网络 ·· 28

苏珊·杰克森-斯塔波夫斯基：澳大利亚ICOMOS《巴拉宪章》及其在"环境"与"背景"中的应用 ······ 31

童乔慧：澳门城市规划发展历程研究 ·· 37

西格弗里德·安德斯：共享建筑遗产：委员会、城市及案例 ··· 42

大学与城市

论坛组委会：大学与城市相互促进的武汉建议 ··· 56

伍江：上海城市历史文化遗产保护制度概述 ··· 58

黄永林：反思当代中国城市建筑追高崇洋逐奇现象 ·· 63

张松：城市历史环境的可持续保护 ··· 66

皮埃尔·拉孔特：比利时鲁汶大学新大学城：向鲁汶历史文化遗产的城市空间创新致敬 ················ 72

玛丽-塞莱斯·阿尔伯特：遗产研究：为新一代学者创建的一个研究领域 ··································· 83

王国恩：武汉大学早期优秀建筑保护与校园规划 ·· 88

周俭：乡村遗产与乡村旅游 ·· 94

董卫：基于历史地图的城市历史环境保护研究——以当涂老城为例 ·· 98

李晓红，马敏，邵新宇：大学与城市：校长们的话 ··· 104

阮仪三，张良皋："80后"对话"90后"：阮仪三教授与张良皋教授的民族建筑世纪对话 ················ 106

创意城市与文化遗产

联合国教科文组织：为什么是创意？为什么是城市？（节选） ··· 110

西格弗里德·安德斯：城市与遗产管理的工具：IBA——一个德国的城市发展项目与政策 ············· 112

克劳斯-皮特·艾希特：IBA1989—1999：德国埃姆舍公园国际建筑展的实践与影响 127

皮埃尔·拉孔特：IBA2006—2013：德国汉堡国际建筑展的实践与影响 133

郭粤梅：IBA、HUL与武汉的老城新生 136

高安亭：20世纪末期旧有建筑改造的探索与实践 140

洛伦佐·巴里奥努艾奥：武汉文化遗产保护中的西班牙理念启示 142

詹姆斯·瑞普：创意城市、可持续发展与世界遗产：一个观点与理念汇聚的时代 146

弗雷德里克·奥克莱尔：来自过去与未来的灵感之源：让生态性与包容性转型在当下成为可能 152

阮仪三：留住乡愁：新常态下的文化遗产保护 155

冯天瑜，皮埃尔·拉孔特，周婕：当东方遇见西方 157

时间与空间：城市更新中的文化遗产

《四维城市》序言节选 163

常青：对建筑遗产基本问题的认知 165

陈薇：历史城市保护方法二探：让地层说话——以扬州城址的保护范围和特色保护策略为例 176

张之平：阿巴和加—布达拉—天安门 182

郭粤梅：城市发展与遗产保护二元架构的思考 185

高曼士："遗产化"：一个发展中的复杂进程 188

李振宇：从Loft到社区：上海中心城区"城中厂"居住化更新的特征研究 191

张松：从历史风貌保护到城市景观管理——基于城市历史景观（HUL）理念的思考 197

何依：城市空间的时间性研究 203

文化·城市·未来：文化遗产在城市可持续发展中的角色

联合国教科文组织：《文化·城市·未来：文化促进城市可持续发展全球报告》节选 210

赵宝江：中国历史文化名城制度建立35年的回顾与思考 212

阮仪三：古民居保护的思考 217

迈克尔·特纳：UNESCO历史性城镇景观建议：面向可持续城市的理论与实践 219

杨华：中国古代礼制与城市空间设计 232

李晓峰：聚落认知与乡建误区 237

兰德：中国城乡遗产的未来：现场工作坊、国际交流与分享式学习 239

邵甬：历史性城镇景观视角下历史文化街区的保护与复兴 243

郑路：扬州可持续的古城保护 246

文化·大众化·数字化：新时代的文化遗产保护与公众参与

梁钢：文保社会组织在新时代文化遗产保护中的实践与思考 250

彼得·菲利普：谁的遗产？国际古迹遗址理事会视野下的文化遗产保护与公众参与 254

冯天瑜：文化遗产与公众同在 ··· 258

杨相卫：新时代文化遗产保护与公众参与 ··· 260

迈克尔·特纳：公众参与和城市遗产的物质与非物质价值 ······························ 263

葛燄：科技＋文化·腾讯的长城文保实践 ·· 273

帕梅拉·杰罗姆：赖特"流水别墅"的数字化 ·· 275

李松：认同与参与——节日文化景观中的大众参与和文化传承 ······················· 278

西尔万·肖恩巴尔特：波尔多月亮港的公众参与反馈 ··································· 280

刘爱河：5G时代下的文物保护公众参与 ··· 286

西蒙尼·里卡：遗产与社群——来自亚洲的范例 ··· 289

李晓武：信息时代的文化遗产保护：数字监测技术的应用与发展 ···················· 294

西格罗尼·查尔斯：城市建设中的本地声音与公众参与——以法国的小城市为例 ··· 302

贺艳：中国文化遗产数字化 ·· 306

詹姆斯·瑞普：美国的遗产保护与公众参与 ·· 310

菲利普，杰罗姆，里卡，等：国际视野下的文化遗产保护与公众参与 ·············· 322

视频篇：精选摘要

工程·文化·景观

葛修润：白鹤梁古水文题刻原址水下保护研究与工程实践 ······························ 331

王玉泽：高速铁路选线与古遗迹保护——以京沪高速铁路安徽凤阳段选线与明皇陵保护为例 ········ 332

徐麟祥：三峡工程文化遗产保护与利用 ··· 333

徐恭义：桥梁工程与文化环境协调统一的设计实践 ······································ 334

万敏：活态桥梁遗产及其在我国的发展 ··· 335

邓东生：南水北调大型水利工程与文化遗产保护——武当山遇真宫保护工程 ····· 336

吕晓应：城市轨道交通设计与文化遗产保护 ··· 337

皮埃尔·拉孔特：工业废弃地，明日城市的宝贵资源——国际最佳实践对中国的启示 ···· 338

秦顺全：关于"工程·文化·景观"的思考 ··· 339

段飞：传承与发展：汉正街历史风貌区的城市更新研究 ································ 340

人文·人居·新时代——文化线路在城乡可持续发展中的角色

武汉地产集团：从"建广厦"到"兴家园" ··· 342

张振山：联合国人居署的文化、人居、线路思考 ·· 343

陈同滨：丝绸之路的文化线路思考与实践 ·· 344

吴晨：北京的城市复兴 ··· 345

李晓峰：汉江流域文化线路上的城乡聚落研究 ··· 346

詹姆斯·瑞普：ICOMOS的文化·人居·线路的经验与思考——以纽约高线公园为例 ··· 347

克里斯托弗·沃罗：从文化线路中阅读欧洲历史——以克吕尼修道院及其欧洲网络为例 ··· 348

卡尔·万增：河流与遗产 ··· 349

弗莱塔斯：文化遗产与城市发展——澳门历史城区面临的挑战 ··· 350

特别篇：面向未来的共享遗产

共享遗产：文化的声音，交流的力量

常青：再生：建成遗产的活化途径 ··· 353

杨相卫：让文化遗产成为武汉疫后重振的重要力量 ··· 354

董志向：重塑老汉口历史风貌，传承大武汉城市文脉 ··· 355

杭侃：作为资源的文化遗产——源流运动的实践 ··· 356

邵甬：文化遗产与城市可持续发展——上海的实践与思考 ··· 357

何依：武汉：城市文本与当代阅读 ··· 358

陈曦：当代遗产价值的保护与阐释 ··· 359

吴琛瑜：网师园的传统与现代 ··· 360

施春煜：疫情之下文化遗产价值的思考 ··· 361

拉尼奥：地标建筑的复活 ··· 362

弗莱塔斯：遗产网络与遗产地 ··· 363

西格弗里德·安德斯，艾希特，詹姆斯·瑞普，等：共同未来，共享遗产 ··· 364

许颖，丁援：共享遗产：从认知到方法 ··· 373

后记 ··· 379

论文篇

无界论坛论文精选

跨文化遗产的保护与发展

CONSERVATION & DEVELOPMENT OF SHARED HERITAGE

共享遗产与无界论坛

国际古迹遗址理事会(International Council on Monuments and Sites，ICOMOS)是世界遗产委员会的专业咨询机构，执行联合国教科文组织世界遗产方面的评估、提名，并对已列入《世界遗产名录》的遗产地的保护状态给出相应的建议。作为国际文化遗产保护领域最有影响的非政府组织，ICOMOS是以1964年5月份在威尼斯举办的"第二届国际建筑师与历史建筑专家大会"和著名的《威尼斯宪章》为起点发展起来的。2012年起，ICOMOS共享遗产委员会与武汉市人民政府共同组织召开"无界论坛"，并于2013年起在武汉设立研究中心，推动共享遗产的研究与保护。

共享遗产委员会(Shared Built Heritage，SBH)是ICOMOS的29个科学委员会之一，主要致力于跨文化遗产的研究和保护。自2008年以来，共享遗产委员会在世界各大洲进行年度会议，探讨文化遗产保护的政策问题，并成功地在欧洲(格但斯克，波兰，2009)、南美洲(帕拉马里博，苏里南，2010)、非洲(开普敦，南非，2011)和亚洲(中国，2012；马来西亚和印度尼西亚，2014)举办学术研讨会。在中国，很多城市都可以找到共享遗产，而这些地方大都是源起于殖民、贸易，或者其他经济方面原因而引起的迁移，比如中国的澳门、香港、广州、厦门、上海、南京、武汉、北京、天津、青岛。

"无界论坛"为有识之士提供了登高一呼的场所，"无界"暗示了"国际与国内""社会科学与自然科学""工程与文化""科技与艺术"的结合与"共享"。文化遗产的保护与发展是一个世界性的难题，不仅武汉，威尼斯、罗马、京都、北京、上海这些城市同样面临困境与选择，同样需要跨学科专业人士的共同努力，需要国际、国内的赤诚合作。"无界论坛"在理论上和技术方法上的探索，若是能有所突破，其意义将不止于中国。

论坛组委会

SHARED HERITAGE AND THE CROSSOVER FORUM

ICOMOS, the International Council on Monuments and Sites, is an advisory body to the World Heritage Committee for the implementation of the UNESCO World Heritage Convention. As such, it evaluates World Heritage nominations for the cultural properties and advises on the state of conservation of properties already inscribed on the World Heritage List. As the most influential NGO (Non-Governmental Organiazation) in the field of protection of cultural heritage in the world, ICOMOS is the output of the famous Second International Congress of Architects and Specialists of Historic Buildings held in May of 1964 in Venice, Italy where the famous *Venice Charter* was inaugurated. Since 2012, the Crossover Forums has been jointly organized by ICOMOS International Committee on Shared Built Heritage and Wuhan Municipal People's Government, and a research center was set up in Wuhan in 2013 to promote the research and protection of shared built heritage.

As one of the 29 scientific committees of ICOMOS, ISC-SBH is the committee that represents ICOMOS in matters of shared built heritage across the world. Since 2008, SBH has adopted the policy of shedding light on the issues of shared built heritage across the globe by conducting its annual meeting/symposium in every continent of the world. After successful SBH symposia/conferences in Europe in 2009(Poland), in South America in 2010 (Suriname) and in Africa in 2011(South Africa), SBH annual meetings were held 2012 in China and 2014 in Malaysia and Indonesia. Shared Built Heritage in China could be found in places where migration caused by for instance colonization, trading or other economic issues. In China, Macao, Hong Kong, Guangzhou, Xiamen, Shanghai, Nanjing, Wuhan, Beijing, Tianjin and Qingdao are good examples for this development.

As a place for scholars, experts and professionals to exchange ideas and make public appeals, Crossover Forum uses the keyword of "crossover" to imply the union and sharing between international and domestic, social science and natural science, engineering and culture, technology and art. Heritage conservation and development is a worldwide issue, not only for Wuhan, but also for cities such as Venice, Rome, Kyoto, Beijing and Shanghai. To address this issue, we need to call for joint efforts of interdisciplinary professionals and international collaboration. The breakthroughs in both theoretical and technical aspects, which are to be achieved by Crossover Forum, will surely have a universal significance.

The Forum Organizing Committee

近代武汉社会转型的文化路径及遗址
CULTURAL ROUTES AND HERITAGE OF SOCIAL TRANSFORMATION IN MODERN TIMES IN WUHAN

唐惠虎　博士
武汉市政府原副秘书长
武汉市国家历史文化名城保护委员会办公室原主任
Dr. Tang Huihu
Former Deputy Secretary General of Wuhan Municipal Government
Former Office Director of Wuhan Protection Committee of National Famous Historical & Cultural Cities

Explaining the social transformation in Wuhan against the backdrop of the whole Chinese society in modern times, the speaker evaluates the role played by urbanization, concession development, industrialization as well as the 1911 Revolution which left the city an abundance of cultural heritage, hence proposes a cultural-route approach of heritage interpretation and presentation.

在中国近代史迹型国家历史文化名城中,武汉是唯一一座自12世纪以来一直是中国南土封疆大吏驻地的城市,君主专制制度发育十分完善。故武汉的近代社会文化转型,具有更为典型的普泛意义。

明清以来,武昌是国家君主专制制度和传统文化近现代化的转型要地之一;1861年,汉口开埠,17个国家在汉经营现代金融、工业、贸易,20个国家领事机构驻汉,汉口成为中国第二大工商城埠;1889—1907年,湖广总督张之洞督鄂湘18年,在武昌、汉阳、汉口兴新政、练新军、办工业、重教育、建市政,武汉成为晚清洋务运动的高地;1911年,辛亥革命武昌首义,推翻中国历时2 132年的封建制度,全球四分之一人口由此步入共和制国家,实质性推动中国近现代化;1927年,武汉国民政府对内争民权、对外争主权,体现民族的不屈;1938年,武汉成为抗日战争时期的"战时首都","武汉会战"聚歼日军精锐部队十余万人;1954年,武汉再次成为国家中心城市,成为重要工业基地、科学教育基地和综合性交通枢纽,成为促进社会文化转型的国家智库之一。

历史学家冯天瑜认为,中国社会及文化的现代转型,是亿万中国民众在长达三个世纪间经历着的伟大社会实践。近代武汉的这些重大事件,显示了明清之际中国内陆的近代因子和在欧美工业强国侵略下中华民族复兴的艰难历程。武汉是中国近代历史中比较完整的社会转型范本,同时有着十分明晰的社会转型文化线路。

一、近代文化转型的背景

从公元前2世纪到公元18世纪,中国一直是强大的封建帝国,农本经济发达,君主专制制度完备,典章文物成熟。进入19世纪中期,尚处于"天朝上国"的清朝,遭到西方工业强国坚船利炮的入侵,中国被迫卷入世界资本主义市场经济体系,成为半封建半殖民地国家,中国人民从此进行了百年艰苦奋斗。

中国近现代社会转型,源于明清之际开端的早期启蒙思想中的近代因子。中国本位变革模式的唯内因说,或者"冲击-反应"外因变革说,均有失偏颇。将中国近代社会转型定为"鸦片战争为起点",不符合整个18、19世纪,变革中国农本经济和传统文化的现代转换,成为朝野的核心动力;19世纪中期,洋务运动成为朝野改革主流;甲午海战后的清光绪二十一年(1895)公车上书始,变革国家君主专制制度,成为社会思想文化主流。西方工业强国对中国的侵略与西方政治、经济、社会制度的传入,增强了中华民族的民主意识,促进了工业崛起。革命派、立宪派、维新派变革封建君主专制制度的努力,最终在武昌爆发辛亥首义,推翻了中国封建君主专制制度,建立了共和制度。

近代社会转型的历史进程,浓缩在武汉市域的数百平方公里内,表现为:湖广总督、湖北巡抚的政体、经济制度改良,汉口五国租界(图1)及近代金融、工业兴起,中国近代工业在武汉三镇的崛起和推翻封建帝制的辛亥武昌首义。其中,以变革封建君主专制制度为中心的辛亥武昌首义,影响了世界五分之一的人口,彻底改变了中国历史。

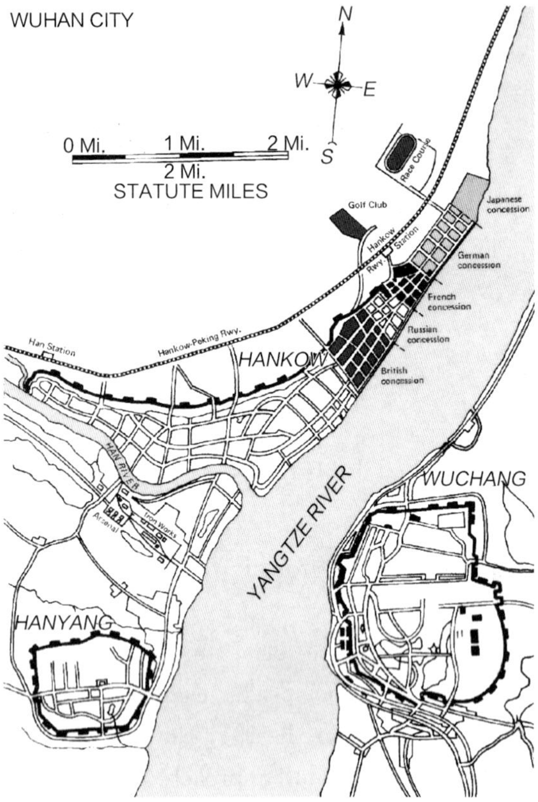

二、近代武汉社会转型的文化线路

作为近代社会转型的典范,武汉在社会转型中的文化路线是明晰的。

图1 汉口原五国租界

丁援博士认为,武汉社会转型路线为汉口五国租界区、汉阳工业遗产区、武昌首义遗产区三部分。这是很有见识的。鄙见认为,若在首位增加明末清初以来清廷湖广总督府等在武昌、汉阳、汉口内生革新部分,则转型线路将更显完整。

(一) 武昌、汉口的近代城镇化

1274年,元世祖忽必烈率军攻克鄂州(今武汉市武昌),派兵4万驻守,新设湖广行省,辖湖南、广西及湖北大部、广东、贵州一部,行省府署驻武昌。由此,武昌成为明清两朝中央政府治理南中国或华中的重镇。

清朝国土面积逾1 000万平方公里,清末设9个总督府和2处直属机构,以利统治。

清朝9个总督府基本情况

总督府名	驻地	管辖省域
直隶总督府	保定	河北、河南、内属蒙古、山东一部、山西等
两江总督府	江宁	江苏、安徽、江西等
湖广总督府	武昌	湖北、湖南
两广总督府	广州	广东、广西
闽浙总督府	福州	福建、浙江等
四川总督府	成都	四川
陕甘总督府	兰州	陕西、甘肃、新疆

续表

总督府名	驻地	管辖省域
云贵总督府	昆明	云南、贵州
东三省总督府①	盛京	黑龙江、吉林、奉天及内属蒙古一部②③

清顺治元年(1644),清廷设湖广总督府于武昌长街(今武昌解放路),辖湖北、湖南。农本时代,鄂湘两省在清朝占有重要的经济地位,所谓"湖广熟,天下足"。同年,清廷又置湖北巡抚,设府于武昌忠孝门外(今武昌小东门)。

城镇化是近代化的重要载体。在长达2000余年的中国封建时代,中国无"市"建制,总督府、巡抚府、知府府和县府均设于城埠,城埠多为县府以上衙门驻地,街道呈棋盘状纵横排列。对汉阳府汉阳县汉口镇的越制发展,甚至城埠规模超过省城武昌和清朝多数总督府署驻地的状况,湖广总督府、湖北巡抚府给予宽容和支持。

武昌、汉口的城镇近代化,深层次表现在传统社会群体的规模性流动、农本经济的转型、近代金融、手工业的重构,以及社会管理观念的转变等方面。其中,手工业、商业行会成为汉口社会自治的主体机构,一改传统的朝廷皇帝钦派制。

汉口早期部分商业行会(1678—1871)

年代	行会名称	行业在全国地位
清康熙十七年(1678年)	汉口米业公会	全国四大米市之一
清嘉庆二十五年(1820年)	汉口药材贸易行会	全国主要出口地
清道光元年(1821年)	汉口盐业公所	淮盐运输销售中心之一
清同治四年(1865年)	两湖会馆(木材为主)	全国最大木材交易市场
清同治十年(1871年)	汉口茶叶公所	全国三大茶市之一
清同治十年(1871年)	汉口钱业公会	全国主要金融中心之一④

明清之际,武汉三镇已出现近代化城市雏形,武昌、汉口成为手工业、农业深加工等早期工业企业集中地,运输能力大大加强。汉阳县汉口镇号称"人烟数十里,贾户数千家"。直隶学者刘献廷(1648—1695)在《广阳杂记》中称:"天下有四聚,北则京师,南则佛山,东则苏州、西则汉口。"这些中国最重要的"财货人口辐辏之地",已具备金融、贸易、运输、生产等近代城市功能。欧美传教士对汉口的繁华十分震惊。清乾隆二年(1737),英国耶稣会传教士罗宾报告称,汉口人口达到260万~300万,其中包括居住在长江、汉江旁的40万从事水运的人口。这显然是夸大的数字。

鸦片战争前,湖广总督中不乏与时俱进之人。清道光十七年(1837),林则徐就任湖广总督,极重农耕,一改江河管理旧制,提出"修防并重",使江汉平原数千里江堤安澜无事。他敢于抵制西方强国的掠夺,在武昌、汉阳、汉口收缴和焚烧大批从英国进口的鸦片,堪称中国最早的反鸦片群众运动;他也略通英语,任职禁烟钦差大臣后,组织翻译大批西方工业国家的科技、工业、军事、商业等书籍及报刊,被誉为"睁开眼睛

---

① 清朝初期设8个总督府。光绪三十三年(1907),清廷改盛京将军府为东三省总督府,辖奉天省(今辽宁省)、吉林省、黑龙江省,驻地盛京系今沈阳。
② 清朝另设驻藏大臣,颁布《钦定内藏章程》,与达赖、班禅共同管理西藏;设外藩蒙古,由清廷理藩院统管蒙古事务;设台厦道台湾府,管理台湾等。
③ 1982年国务院批准南京(江宁)、广州、成都为第一批国家历史文化名城,为历史古都型。1986年国务院批准保定、武汉(武昌系江南部分)、沈阳(盛京)为第二批国家历史文化名城,为近代史迹型。
④ 彭雨新,江溶.十九世纪汉口商业行会的发展及其积极意义:《汉口——一个中国城市的商业和社会(1796—1889)》简介[J].中国经济史研究,1994(4):143-153.

看世界第一人"。

(二) 西方工业列强的冲击——汉口五国租界

鸦片战争打断了中国近代转型的渐进历程。西方列强通过战争和签署不平等条约,直接将中国卷入全球资本主义经济体系。它们在攫卷中国财富和资源的同时,将近代西方社会制度、工业技术、商业贸易、市政建设、军事技术等传入中国。武汉成为受欧美近代化影响最大的中国内陆城市。

图 2　历史文化街区中的里分建筑

汉口的繁华和面向华西、华中的贸易辐射能力,引起西方列强的窥视。清道光二十二年(1842)英国军舰在舰长柯林逊率领下由上海驶向汉口,为西方列强抵汉首艘军舰。次年,海洋强国瑞典、挪威的商人进入汉口经商。其后,英国议会、基督教伦敦会等相继派员考察汉口。清道光三十年(1850),传教士 S. 威尔士·威廉姆斯在给基督教英国伦敦总部的报告中说:"只有伦敦、江户(东京)才能与汉口相比。"咸丰十一年(1861),《英国议会公报》记载汉口是"中华帝国的大商业中心";同年,传教士霍恩在给基督教伦敦总会的报告中称"汉口是中华帝国最大的商业中心,也是世界最大的商业中心之一"。

1861年3月,英国4艘军舰、火轮驶抵汉口,依照《中英天津条约》要求汉口开埠。同年,设英国驻汉口总领事馆,同时划定英国租界。此后,俄国、法国、德国、日本按"利益均沾"的殖民原则,在汉口分别建立租界,实际占地约2.2平方公里,建有数千栋欧式建筑或英式联排住宅的里分建筑(图2)。在中国的9个有租界的城市中,汉口租界国家数居全国第二,面积数居全国第三,居住的外国人数居全国第三。其对武汉近代化进程造成的影响不能低估。

1. 领事机构。20个国家设立驻汉领事机构。其中,英国、法国、美国、俄国、日本、德国、比利时、意大利8国设驻汉口总领事馆;葡萄牙、荷兰、丹麦、瑞典、挪威、墨西哥、芬兰、瑞士8国设立驻汉口领事馆;奥地利、西班牙、菲律宾、刚果等4个国家设立领事机构。这些领事机构负责中国中西部的本国事务,享有领事权和超越中国法律的法治权、经济权,直至干预中国内政。英、法、德、日等国在汉驻有军队,最多时长江武汉江段有18艘外国军舰。英、法、美、德、俄、日、瑞等国领事馆至今保护完好。其中,建于1895年的德国驻汉口领事馆为全国重点文物保护单位。

2. 海关。1862年清廷成立汉口江汉关,现与上海江海关、广州粤海关同为百年海关。1866—1927年61年间,江汉关有46年对外贸易量居中国第二位,仅次于上海。清廷海关官署总税务司、江汉关等税务司均为外国人出任,海关税收最大支出为偿还西方列强战争赔款。1890年清廷成立上海、汉口两个商务局,汉口商务局联络中国中西部七省对外贸易。竣工于1924年的江汉关为中国第一座采用欧洲古典建筑风格和英国钟楼形式建造的海关大楼,现为全国重点文物保护单位。建于1905年的清廷江汉关监督署大楼为武汉市文物保护单位。

3. 金融。武汉是中国近代金融中心之一,外国17家银行在武汉设立分行,1家设总行,其中英国汇丰、法国东方汇理、美国花旗、德国德华、法国与俄国合资的华俄道胜、日本横滨正金等13家外资银行在武汉发行货币,长江中游数省流通使用,发行数总额约1亿元。1919年成立的汉口证券交易所是中国最早的三个证交所之一,晚于北京一年、早于上海一年。现英国汇丰银行大楼、日本横滨正金银行大楼等为全国重点文物保护单位。

4. 进出口贸易。鼎盛时,汉口聚集了250多家外国贸易洋行,垄断了中国中西部的茶叶、皮革、桐油、苎麻、芝麻、蛋制品、肠制品等的出口贸易和机械、五金、煤油、棉布、火柴等的进口贸易。英、美、日相继垄断长江中下游航运。德国美最时洋行、西门子洋行、英国怡和洋行、法国立兴洋行等为省、市重点文物保护单位。

5. 宗教及社会事务。1673年天主教传入武昌,1861基督教传入汉口。武汉为基督教中国信义会总部和最高学府所在地。在数十年时间里,中国流传的基督教中文教材80%由基督教汉口圣教书局翻译出版。武汉建有20多座教会学校,建有一批小型医院、英日文报馆和西商跑马场。现天主教上海路堂、汉口东正教堂、美国海军青年会、英商赞育药房、英文《楚报》馆、法国德明饭店等,为省、市文物保护单位。

6. 近代工厂。武汉是外国银行、洋行在中国内陆的最大投资地。1910年前英、美、德、法、俄、日、瑞等国在武汉建有39家大中型工厂,主要为农产品深加工、日用品生产和租界供电等,其规模在全国居前。英国汉口电灯厂、和利冰厂等均为湖北省文物保护单位。

7. 城市市政建设。汉口五国租界引入近代城市道路、人行道和雨水分离下水道理念;建设公园、电影院等公共设施;通过税收杠杆迫使租界内必须建设欧式风格或现代风格建筑;英、德、法、俄、日等国在汉口成立建筑设计公司,设计了大批欧洲古典主义风格建筑及南亚殖民建筑风格建筑,故时称汉口是"万国建筑博物馆"。

8. 铁路。经湖广总督张之洞奏请清廷,借用外国部分贷款修建铁路得到批准。1906年,北京—汉口的京汉铁路通车;1936年,历时36年建设的广州—武昌的粤汉铁路通车;中国形成以武汉为交汇点、贯穿南北的近代交通大动脉网。这亦使沿途的石家庄、郑州由县城成为省会。1903年修建的汉口大智门火车站是国家重点文物保护单位。

一方面,汉口租界是西方列强殖民化中国的产物,是中国的"国中之国",中国人对此备感屈辱。另一方面,租界又引入了西方的政治、经济、社会管理制度,展示了西方文明,对武汉三镇走出中古城埠故道发挥了重要作用。同时,拥有"治外法权"的汉口租界也成为清朝末年反封建知识分子的庇护所和革命报刊的基地。

(三) 民族觉醒和近代工业的诞生——汉阳、武昌工业遗址

中国沦为半殖民地和国家主要税收流入西方列强国家的状况,使中国朝野痛下改革决心,洋务运动在北京、上海、天津、武汉、宁波等地迅速发展。在不涉及封建君主专制制度的前提下,洋务运动大力提倡引入西文、西技。张之洞在鄂、湘兴新政、练新军、重工业、办教育、建市政,武汉三镇成为晚清洋务运动的高地。改变科举考试制度、借外资兴建铁路、引进欧洲工厂成套设备、引进西方教育制度、反对西方列强鲸吞中国利权等等奏折,均由张之洞等在武昌或发出或实施,极大影响了中国近代文化的走向。

兴工业是张之洞洋务之举的重中之重,中国近代重工业在汉阳诞生。

张之洞在武汉主持创办的工业企业(1889—1907)

工业行业	建设时间	厂名
钢铁业	1891—1894	汉阳铁厂(湖北铁厂)①、贝色麻钢厂、西门士钢厂、钢轨厂、铁货厂、熟铁厂、铸铁厂、打铁厂、机器厂、造鱼片钩丁厂、汉冶萍煤铁股份有限公司(1908)②等
军工业	1892—1898	汉阳兵工厂(湖北枪炮厂)③、造枪厂、枪弹厂、铸炮厂、炮弹厂、钢罐厂、火药厂
纺织业	1890—1898	湖北织布局、湖北纺纱局、湖北缫丝局、湖北制麻局④
冶炼制币业	1893—1905	湖北银元局、武昌铜币局(扩建)
轻工业	1890—1907	白沙洲造纸厂、度支部造纸厂⑤、南湖制革厂、下新河毡呢厂、兰陵湖北模范工厂等

---

① 汉阳铁厂时为亚洲最早最大规模炼钢炼铁厂。
② 汉冶萍煤铁股份公司时为全国最大股份制工业公司。
③ 汉阳兵工厂时为全国规模最大枪炮工厂。
④ 武昌的湖北纺织四局,时为仅次于上海的第二大纺织基地。
⑤ 武昌白沙洲造纸厂、度支部造纸厂(湛家矶造纸厂),时为全国最大规模专业造纸厂之一。

此外，武汉建有一批机械、轻工业、医药、农产品深加工等民营大中型工厂：燮昌火柴厂时为亚洲规模第一；官方参股10%的汉镇既济水电有限公司，1906年建造的既济发电厂装机容量1 500千瓦，占全国华商电厂装机总量4 450千瓦的三分之一强，1908年投产的既济自来水厂时为全国规模之首；民营周恒顺机器厂时为重要工业装备制造厂。

中国近代四大工业城市比较(1895—1913年)①

城市	大中型厂矿数/家	厂矿资本总额/万元
上海	83	2 387
汉口	28	1 724
天津	17	472
广州	16	579

（四）创建共和制度的首义之地——辛亥武昌首义遗址区

变革封建君主专制制度，是中国近代社会转型的中心主题。迫于内外压力，清光绪三十二年(1906)朝廷颁发《宣示预备立宪谕》。此刻，中国的生产关系和社会阶层已发生很大的变化，知识分子因取消了科举考试而政治主张比较激进。维新派、立宪派、革命派均力图以政治主导文化。

推翻2 132年历史的封建君主专制制度的辛亥革命1911年10月10日在武昌爆发，有着深刻的社会背景和经济因素。

湖北武昌的宪政派在中国举足轻重。清宣统二年(1910)朝廷召开各省咨议局联合会第一次会议，湖北咨议局议长汤化龙被推选为会议主席。他抨击皇族内阁，主张实行宪政。

武昌是近代革命派的高地。作为中国近代教育发源地之一，武昌也是中国输出留学生最多的城埠之一，其中到日本留学者达5 000余人，大多以法政、军事为专业。大批具有民主意识的知识分子成为清朝湖北新军的支柱。其中湖北共进会、武昌文学社成员，更是辛亥革命武昌首义的中坚。黎元洪能出任鄂军都督，成为辛亥首义功臣，与其平日善待新军中的革命派有关。

武昌、汉口成为政治主导文化潮流的先驱。1873年中国人创办的第一份中文报纸《昭文新报》在汉口创刊。自此武汉与京津、沪宁、穗港一样为近代中国4个报业基地之一。武汉报章喜发表时政评论，政治小说占据报刊的重要版面，翻译或著述书作亦多着眼于政治，光绪帝、慈禧太后数度下谕封查。辛亥前夕，汉口《大江报》刊发黄侃的《大乱者救中国之妙药也》一文，震惊朝野。

武昌成为共和制度的诞生地。1911年10月11日，湖北革命党人入驻湖北谘议局大楼，成立鄂军都督府，并以鄂军都督黎元洪的名义发出第一号布告，宣布废除清朝帝制，建立"中华民国"。在1911年10月至1912年元月期间，鄂军都督府实际代行"中央政府"的作用，导引了全国17省起义；鄂军都督府并颁布了中国第一份具有资产阶级宪法性质的文件——《鄂州公约法》。

汉口商界支持辛亥武昌首义的自觉常被忽略，这实际上是商绅争取权利的政治觉醒。辛亥起义时，汉口总商会出钱出米出人，承担上万革命军官兵的生活物资。阳夏战争中，清军冯国璋下令焚烧汉口四天四夜。除汉口五国租界外，汉口城焚毁一半以上，几十万人流离失所，仅银行、洋行、商铺票据损失就达3 000余万两。次年元月中华民国一成立，汉口华商即主导重建城市，借鉴1866年伦敦大火、1871年芝加哥大火城市重建的经验，在中国的华埠中最早系统建设柏油马路、人行道、上下水道，装电灯、电话和种植行道树，建设公园、图书馆、电影院、厕所等公共设施，成为全国城市市政建设典范。1927年1月国民政府迁都

---

① 清朝宣统三年(1911)出版的《最近汉口工商业一斑》第五章"工业"中记载的清廷统计数据显示："自光绪二十九年至三十四年计六年间，我国工场禀部立案之数凡一百二十有六，而汉口附近占其四十，约当三分之一。又工场之资本额，其报部总数共四千八百余万两，而汉口附近实占其最多数，即汉冶萍制铁一业，已占却二千万两。可见汉口近年工业渐进之端倪也。"

汉口,宣布将武昌、汉口、汉阳三个城镇合为武汉市,成立京兆区。现汉口江汉路及中山大道为国务院批复的武汉城市总体规划中的历史文化街区。

三、武汉近代社会文化转型的遗产

近代武汉的社会文化转型遗产丰富,保护完好,种类较全,轨迹清晰。在三镇短短二十几公里的距离内,集中展示了中国近代的政治、经济、社会的转型轨迹。

1. 从一个角度反映了近代中国历史变革的规律

传统农本文明—明清之际城埠近代化—西方列强的殖民化—中华民族的复兴

2. 展示了武汉的近代城市发展轨迹

中古城埠—国际贸易港—中国近代工业发源地之一—清末民初政治中心之一

3. 保护及可观赏性

武汉市政府对"中国近代文化转型遗产线路"的保护十分重视,专门制定地方法规及配套文件,同时,在4个遗产区建有多座博物馆:(1)湖北省博物馆、武汉博物馆;(2)汉口五国租界区现有38处国家、省、市级文物保护单位,建有武汉中共中央机关旧址纪念馆、江汉关博物馆、八七会址纪念馆、湖北电力博物馆等;(3)汉阳工业遗址区建有张之洞及汉阳铁厂博物馆、龟北工业遗址博物馆;(4)辛亥武昌首义遗址区,现有35处国家、省、市级文物保护单位,建有辛亥革命纪念馆、辛亥革命博物馆。

历史学家耿云志等认为,中国文化近代转型所要克服的两大对象是"宗法礼教""君主专制"。主宰清末十几年的思想文化的中心问题,是对于君主专制制度的挑战与应战。

历史学家冯天瑜认为,变革君主专制制度是近代文化的大主题。中国文化的近代转型是一个学术价值深厚的课题,同时这一转型过程至今尚未完成。

这些论断,更突显了武汉在中国近代社会文化转型中的历史地位。

附:武汉近代社会转型文化线路及遗址

1. 明末清初遗址

(1) 全国重点文物保护单位

武昌古城中和门(明建,后名起义门)、明楚王墓(明)、木兰山古建筑群(明、清)、古德寺(清)等。

(2) 省、市级文物保护单位

九女墩(1856)、汉口汉正街药帮巷(清)、汉阳永丰闸(1839)等。

(3) 历史文化地段

武昌昙华林片。

(4) 历史地段[①]洪山片。

(5) 传统特色街区[②]

汉口汉正街片、汉阳显正街片。

2. 汉口五国租界旧址

(1) 全国重点文物保护单位

德国驻汉口领事馆(1896)、英国汇丰银行(1920)、日本横滨正金银行(1921)、江汉关新泰大楼[③](1924)。

(2) 湖北省重点文物保护单位

---

① 历史文化地段、历史地段为法定概念,由建设部、国家文物局审核申报,国务院批复。
② 传统特色街区为武汉市政府批准。
③ 全国重点文物保护单位名称为"汉口俄商新泰大楼",建筑实际上为英商1924年重建。

英国麦加利银行(1865)、上海路天主堂(1876)、汉口东正教堂(1876)、华俄道胜银行旧址(1898)、美国驻汉口总领事馆(1905年)、平汉铁路局(1911)、英国和利冰厂(1911)、美国海军青年会旧址(1913)、法商德明饭店(1919)、汉口景明大楼(1921)等。

(3) 武汉市重点文物保护单位

英国驻汉口总领事馆(1861)、德国美最时洋行(1896)、法国东方汇理银行(1901)、法国立兴洋行(1901)、俄国巡捕房(1902)、日本驻汉口总领事馆(1902)、平和打包厂(1905)、汉口日清洋行旧址(1913)、基督教信义公所大楼(1923)、亚细亚火油公司大楼(1924)等。

(4) 历史文化街区

汉口青岛路片、八七会址片、一元路片。

3. 三镇民族工业遗产遗址

(1) 全国重点文物保护单位

大智门火车站候车厅(1903)、汉口水塔(1909)、詹天佑故居(1912)。

(2) 省、市级文物保护单位

汉阳铁厂矿砂码头旧址(清末)、武昌路隧道(1904)、武泰闸(1906)、既济宗关水厂旧址(1908)、大清银行旧址(1915)、武昌第一纱厂旧址(1919)、汉口总商会旧址(1921)、汉口璇宫饭店(1921)、汉口总商会旧址(1921)、汉口华商总会旧址(1922)等。

(3) 传统特色街区

汉阳汉钢片、龟山北片

4. 武昌辛亥首义遗址

(1) 全国重点文物保护单位

中华民国军政府鄂军都督府(1911)、起义门(1911)等。

(2) 省、市文物保护单位

湖北共进会旧址(1902—1911)、庚子革命烈士墓(1910—1912)、楚望台军械库(1911)、工程八营旧址(1911)、黄兴拜将台遗址(1911)、三烈士亭(1911)、汉阳辛亥铁血将士公墓(1911)、汉口辛亥首义烈士公墓(1911)、武昌辛亥首义烈士墓(1911)、黎元洪墓(1935)、武昌黎元洪公馆(民国)等。

(3) 历史地段武昌首义片。

参考文献

[1] 冯天瑜. 中国文化近代转型管窥[M]. 北京:商务印书馆,2010.
[2] 耿志云. 近代中国文化转型研究[M]. 成都:四川人民出版社,2008.
[3] 罗威廉. 汉口:一个中国城市的商业和社会(1796—1889)[M]. 江溶,鲁西奇,译. 北京:中国人民大学出版社,2005.
[4] 丁援. 文化线路:有形与无形之间[M]. 南京:东南大学出版社,2011.
[5] 武汉地方志编纂委员会. 武汉市志(28卷本)[M]. 武汉:武汉大学出版社,1999.
[6] 汉口租界志编纂委员会. 汉口租界志[M]. 武汉:武汉出版社,2003.
[7] 武汉市国家历史文化名城保护委员会办公室. 武汉:国家历史文化名城通览[M]. 武汉:武汉出版社,2014.

武汉近代遗产"无形文化线路"研究

A Study on the Intangible Cultural Route of Modern Heritage in Wuhan

丁援 博士
中信建筑设计研究总院有限公司副总规划师
Dr. Ding Yuan
Deputy Chief Planner,
CITIC General Institute of Architectural Design and Research Co., Ltd

Cultural Routes represent a new approach in the currently evolving and quickly expanding process that affects the conceptual universe of cultural heritage, but it is based on the geographical diffusion theory, which has been seen as a fragile theory in the field of Anthropology. However, the idea of Intangible Cultural Routes (ICR), which came from the theory of Enculturation and Cultural Routes, offers new perspectives and tools for preserving cultural heritage. As a city gradually emerged in China's colonial period, Wuhan is the subject of the research to develop the idea that modern heritage, especially the heritage introduced in the intercultural communication, could be promoted, protected and managed with the concept of ICR. The intangible line, Chinese cultural reorientation, is linking the three parts of Wuhan to be the representation of the outstanding value. With the help of the ICR study, not only could the heritage of Wuhan be promoted, but also the concept of Cultural Routes could go out of its traditional types, which is defined in the grid of "Physical Representations in Physical Route", and can be identified with its Commemorative Integrity.

1 问题的提出

作为理论上的前沿概念,"文化线路"介绍和代表了一种新的对文化遗产保护概念定性的方法。然而,随着对众多线路遗产的深入研究,越来越显露出了基于"文化"概念的复杂性而来的"文化线路"概念的不确定性。从现有的众多"文化线路"实例来看,"线路"与"文化"常常形成矛盾:有形的线路往往无法完全涵盖文化交流的影响范围,而"文化"的发展本质上遵循着自身的非实体的文化濡化发展的线索。——这些在理论上,为进一步丰富"文化线路"的概念,给一些看似分散、实质相联的非线形遗产提供了整体保护的思路。

武汉是中国中部地区最大的城市,又是国务院公布的第二批国家历史文化名城,然而20世纪80年代以来,武汉大量的优秀文化遗产乏人问津,不仅来旅游的外地游客的人均消费额"低于全国平均水平",甚至还被一些中央媒体评选为全国"最市民化的城市"、描述为"被遗忘的江湖大佬"。——如何运用"文化线路"理论,特别是无形文化线路的观点,重新阐释武汉的近代历史文化遗产和武汉在中国文化发展变迁中的意义,彰显武汉的城市特色,是本文要解决的问题。

2 从"文化线路"到"无形文化线路"

2.1 "文化线路"概念的提出和发展

总的来说,"文化线路"是在案例实践和理论论证的二重奏中逐步进入高潮的。一方面,在此过程中,圣地亚哥朝圣线路起到了关键性的起步作用,而丝绸之路、北美淘金线路等来自不同大陆的典型遗产线路的研究,则从实践中逐步挖掘了"文化线路"概念的独特内涵和外延。从另一方面看,真正让"文化线路"作为一种新的遗产类型,进而形成独特理论力量的,是以国际研讨会为主要形式的各国专家间的理论论证。从1994年在西班牙马德里举办的"文化线路"国际会议到2005年西安国际古迹遗址理事会科学研讨会"文化线路"专题,各国专家正是以系列国际研讨会为平台,形成了对"文化线路"概念和理论的基本共识。

1993年圣地亚哥路线被列为世界遗产,其理论概念、研究方法,以及组织形式在当时还没有先例。敏锐的西班牙学者于1994年11月在马德里举行了名为"作为我们文化遗产一部分的文化线路"的会议。会议集中讨论了这个新的世界遗产,并邀请联合国教科文组织和ICOMOS的代表参加了会议。1994年以后,"文化线路"的研究越来越受到世界各国的重视,出现了各种类型的"文化线路"模式。其中《世界遗产名录》录入的运输线路、贸易线路、宗教线路和线型遗产等四种不同类型的线路遗产,因其得到联合国教科文组织的认可,成为各国寻找文化线路的重要样本。

此外,"文化线路"的概念在欧洲得以确认后,也影响了北美、亚洲、非洲等不同大陆,产生了强调自然遗产的北美克朗代克淘金线路,摒弃文化传播主义的欧亚"对话之路",以及跨越亚非欧的海上丝绸之路等不同于圣地亚哥线路的遗产线路。

文化线路概念的意义在于,它并不冲突或重叠于其他类别或类型,并且通过创新的科学视角,支持世界范围内遗产保护工作间的相互了解、交流与合作,从而于一个一体的、跨学科的、共享的框架内认可和提升这些分散的遗迹的价值。

2.2 "文化线路"概念的普遍性问题

然而,随着对众多线路遗产的深入研究,越来越显露出了"文化线路"仍然是一个发展中的概念,它需要文化学理论养分和遗产保护理论的进一步结合,以补充现在的"文化线路"概念的不足。如何界定文化线路的外延,如何确立文化线路的内涵?

在界定文化线路的外延的问题上,正如有学者指出的:"任何文化遗产都不是孤立的,从某一时期行政统治网络的角度,或者从某一时期经济联系网络的角度,我们都可以把一定时期的全部相关遗产编制在这个网络中。例如,我们可以按照《唐代交通图考》将所有唐代的城市遗址、寺塔雕塑等遗产编织成线路网络,也可以按照任何一本明清时期的供客商参考的书籍来串联明清的遗产。这些网络中的遗产不仅由一条存在的驿路联系起来,而且每条线路都发生过数不清的历史事件,它们很容易被归入文化线路这个遗产类型中。"

然而,从"文化线路"概念产生和发展研究看,"文化线路"在概念的确立上存在一定的先天不足,所谓"文化线路"的网络化结果在产生这个概念的圣地亚哥线路中就有所反映。由于文化线路所要求的是历史上文化现象的反映,而文化现象不可能仅仅在线性的范围内显现,这就使得"文化线路"具有流动性强、边界模糊、交融的特点,造成了"文化线路"原真性确认的难度;而由于在历史维度中的文化功能和概念的复杂性,也令线路的文化认同在今天难以为继。

从概念的内涵上看,"文化线路"比"遗产线路"等相似概念更应该强调遗产的文化认同,而以文化认同为纽带的遗产系列往往并非线型的。

2.3 "无形文化线路"概念的提出和界定

文化濡化首先是由美国文化人类学家赫斯科维茨(Melville J. Herskovits)提出的,即"在文化交流过程中,一种文化吸收或采纳了另一种文化元素,并且使之与主体文化协调起来,最终成为主体文化中的一部分"。

文化线路以文化交流理论为基础,而文化交流中的两种过程和途径——文化传播、濡化,应该成为广义的"文化线路"概念的两个组成部分。

基于此,提出"无形文化线路"的概念,界定如下:

无形文化线路是一定时期内,根据与不同人群在一定空间(线路)上发生的合目的性流动交往行为同时产生的跨文化碰撞与整合作用所形成的在有形和无形遗产基础上以文化濡化过程为线索的,具有一定类型特征的文化意象和文化遗产的统一体。

它具有动态的和历史性功能的特点,且符合以下四个条件:

第一,它不必以实体线路为绝对依托,但必须在文化变迁的变化发展中产生,并反映这种变迁。濡化过程不同于地理传播过程,很难找出一条明确的交通线路连缀其中。它更多的是依赖于一条文化认同(Cultural Identity)的心理线索。

第二,它必须是文化整合的体现。无形文化线路要展现在一定历史时期内,个人、国家、地区或大陆间,多维的、连续的,在物质、思想、知识和价值等方面的文化遗存。而在这个过程中,文化的发展要达到相对的完整和稳定。

第三,它必须在一定的空间和时间内,呈现出不同文化层面的影响,并反映在其有形和无形的遗产上。文化线路是一个融历史联系和文化遗存为一体的动态系统,而无形文化线路在历时态的维度中会有不同的文化的"遗存聚落",共同构成线路的各个环节。在一般以交通线路为纽带的文化线路中,文化层特点的突出必然和线路特点的鲜明形成矛盾,造成文化线路的点、线、面的含糊。无形文化线路是以文化濡化的虚线引导文化遗产的点和面,突出了遗产精神和价值上的统一。

第四,它是文化遗产类型和研究方法。无形文化线路联系在特定时间、区域内的文化遗产为一个统一整体,这样"化零为整"的统一整体可以作为一种文化遗产的类型,而联系这种类型的思路,则是一种总体性把握文化遗产价值的研究方法。在方法论上对文化线路的探讨,往往可以避开文化线路在外延界定上的困扰,而深入到文化遗产保护的本质和意义。

由文化濡化的发展过程分析,可以得出相应的"文化线路"模式,即文化转型遗产线路模式。提出"无形文化线路"概念的意义,本质上是在基于遗产的"文化显著性"的理解上的"纪念性完整"的维护。

3 武汉无形文化线路

3.1 武汉无形文化线路的形成基础

武汉的历史可以追溯到千年以前,然而,武汉的城市崛起和城市认同的形成是在近代,不仅同步于中国近代文化转型,而且集中见证了这个历史性的过程。

"武汉"成为一个城市的名称正式始于1927年元旦,作为一个独立的行政区始于1927年4月。根据最新的考证,之所以国民政府最终能将武昌、汉口、汉阳三镇合组为"京兆区",是因为当时认为"三镇合设一市长办事便利"。而在这个实用主义的"办事便利"背后,最终的原因还是在于原汉口、武昌、汉阳三镇在长期比邻、彼此磨合之后,特别是随着中国近代化的发展,形成了共同的地区依靠和认同。

1861年汉口开埠后,汉口在明清的传统商业基础上迅速崛起,政治、经济、文化等方面的影响力日益显著。

汉阳则是在建立汉阳铁厂等工业企业后,与武昌、汉口两地联系日益紧密,形成了治府在武昌、生产在汉阳、运输在汉口的局面。虽然没有形成统一的行政建制,但人们已经将汉阳、汉口联称为"阳夏",将武昌、汉阳联称为"武阳",或将武昌、汉阳、汉口联称为"武阳夏"。地区认同逐渐磨合、融会。

1911年武昌首义,一下子使得当时的三镇成为全国焦点和影响中国发展的关键地区,从此这个地区成为中国近代的大舞台。1926年秋,国民革命军攻克武昌三镇。次年初,国民政府将汉口市(辖汉阳县)与武昌合并,划为京兆区,作为首都,并建立统一的武汉市政府,此时,"武汉"才取得了作为政区、市区的称谓。

"武汉"正式作为政区、市区的称谓,不仅标志了一个新的城市的诞生,也从形式上固化了武汉认同。此后,武昌、汉阳、汉口时分时合,直到解放后,政务院将汉口、武昌、汉阳(县府所在地及邻近地区)合并为武汉市(原汉阳县治所迁至蔡甸,保留县的建制),武汉市人民政府设在汉口。至此,武汉三镇才又名副其实地合三为一。

进一步看,武汉的崛起过程同时也是武汉早期现代化的过程。对于武汉的初步近代化和城市地位的崛起,张之洞无疑是最重要的推动者。而从文化研究的角度看,张之洞是中国近代文化史上一个典型的过渡型人物,其"生命的节律与中国近代历史大体共始终"。张之洞作为历史过渡性人物的典型意义,在于他"从清流健将到洋务殿军"的过程中"基本立足点是中国传统文化",而面对中西文化激烈碰撞的大势,又能顺应时局,抛开清流的卫道立场,在"中学为体、西学为用"的大旗下,接纳西方文化中的部分内容。他的以"中体西用"为核心的"洋务"和"新政"是当时复杂的文化转型历史面貌的集中体现;最终由接纳西方文化中的器物层面到制度层面再到精神层面。——以张之洞督鄂前后思想的变化为视角,可以透视出近代中国文化身份认同的转变;以武汉的早期现代化为视角,可以透视出中国文化转型之路——而这种文化认同的转变和文化转型正是武汉文化遗产无形文化线路的基础。

3.2 武汉无形文化线路的提出

以无形文化线路的理论观照武汉,可以看出:武汉城市的形成是在中国早期近代化的过程中,武汉三镇随着频繁交往而相互依靠,逐渐形成地区认同,又进而形成一个城市;武汉的早期现代化进程同步于中国近代文化变迁;武汉崛起中历史性的"开埠、开厂、开战"三部曲都对中国传统社会和文化具有深远的影响。由此可见,武汉文化遗产具有"文化显著性",而它在近代中国文化转型上的"纪念性完整"也十分清晰。

由此,可以把反映中国近代文化转型典型层面的"汉口租界区、汉阳工业遗产和武昌首义遗产"看成一体的文化遗产,定义为武汉的"中国近代文化转型遗产无形文化线路",简称武汉无形文化线路。

3.3 武汉无形文化线路的特点

武汉无形文化线路具有下面几个特点:

第一,武汉的无形文化线路所包含的文化遗产分散于武汉三镇,没有明确的实体线路为绝对依托,但它们在中国近代文化变迁的变化发展中产生、发展,并集中反映这种变迁。汉口租界、汉阳工业遗产和武昌首义遗产都是在中西文化交流碰撞的过程中,依托于中国文化自身的濡化力量,典型地呈现了一条文化认同的发展变化的线索。

第二,武汉无形文化线路也是中国近代文化整合的体现。文化变迁是一个永恒的过程,但无形文化线路只是其中的一段,在这一段中,文化的发展要达到相对的完整和稳定。武汉无形文化线路展现了中国近代文化中文化认同从不稳定(租界的进入)到相对稳定(进入共和)的过程,具有全国性的突出价值。

第三,武汉无形文化线路在一定的空间(武汉地区)和时间(1861—1927)内,呈现出不同文化层面的影响,并反映在其有形和无形的遗产上。无形文化线路在历时态的维度中会有不同的文化层的"多元一体",事实上,无论是汉口租界、汉阳工业遗产,还是武昌首义遗产,都是由一个"遗存聚落"组成,而这个聚落的文化层特点明显,彼此分散又依托于文化濡化的展开,突出了武汉近代文化遗产精神和价值上的统一。

特别值得提到的是,中国文化是世界上唯一的保持连续的古老文化,虽朝代更迭但不存在"时代"的变换,文化的本源从未被切断。所以,中国近代文化变迁的意义不仅仅是中国的,更是世界性的。武汉的中国近代文化转型遗产无形文化线路中隐含了中国近代文化认同的变化,见证了中国近代文化转型的历程。其不仅正是文化线路要反映的不同文化因交流而产生发展变化的实质的反映,更具有世界性的杰出的普泛价值。

4 历史文化名城武汉的无形文化线路解读

作为历史文化名城的武汉，其文化遗产集中于1861年以后的中国近代历史时期，并包含了中国近代文化转型的典型文化层面，即"租界殖民遗产—洋务运动遗产—共和革命遗产"。武汉的文化遗产历时性清晰、特点显著。破解武汉历史文化遗产的密码，关键是要彰显出城市文化遗产背后的无形文化线路，从狭义的武汉无形文化线路扩展开，以"三点连一线"，即把"中国近代文化转型遗产"无形文化线路中的三个武汉文化遗产层面作为三个"节点"，延伸为一条无形的轴线，连缀武汉其他的文化遗产，形成广义的武汉无形文化线路的概念。利用广义的武汉无形文化线路的观点，我们可以重新审视一些自20世纪80年代以来，对武汉文化遗产的解读上的误区。

4.1 武汉的历史文化名城定性

长期以来，武汉历史文化名城的类型划分比较含糊，摇摆于近现代史迹型和一般史迹型。由于目前历史文化名城定性的不明确，武汉出现了具有国家级和省市级别历史价值的且多数为近现代类型的历史建筑、历史街区被相对传统的"两菜一汤"式（即黄鹤楼、归元寺、东湖）的武汉文化遗产认知模式所淹没的情况。从调查的具体情况来看：

国务院公布的第一批全国重点文物保护单位武昌起义军政府旧址（红楼），距离20世纪80年代重建的黄鹤楼不过百米，但观者寥寥；

国务院公布为第六批全国重点文物保护单位的汉口近代建筑群的五个近代建筑及第七批全国重点文物保护单位古德寺，知者寥寥；

国务院公布为第六批全国重点文物保护单位有黄石汉冶萍煤铁厂矿旧址，但汉冶萍公司的汉阳旧址却早已不复存在；

武汉大量的优秀近代建筑被拆毁，一批优秀近代建筑被忽视，不属于任何保护名单。——经武汉市人民政府公布的历史保护建筑名单中，一级的33个，二级69个；而与武汉情况类似的天津，天津市政府颁布的历史风貌建筑有528个。

根据调研，目前武汉仅有的近代以前的建筑遗存只有4座古塔、2座古桥和1个牌坊。而从无形文化线路的角度看，武汉这座城市崛起于近代，是中国近代化的产物，所以，武汉市的历史文化名城类型应该属于近代史迹型。

4.2 对汉口租界影响的认识

有学者认为，武汉租界对武汉城市历史发展的影响不大，认为租界是"嵌入"汉口的，或者说"租界是租界，武汉是武汉"，所以"汉口租界不像上海租界对城市产生如此大的影响，……租界留给汉口的只是几栋建筑物"。

其实，这种看法不仅窄化了租界在武汉城市形成过程中的重要意义、降低了汉口租界的遗产价值，也是对武汉作为历史文化名城类型的认识模糊的具体反映。汉口租界绝不仅仅"留给汉口的只是几栋建筑物"，它的城市规划思想观念将原汉口沿汉水的布局转变为沿长江布局；建筑风格、基础设施、西方生活方式的展示等对武汉地区的冲击、对中国近代化的冲击，都直接影响了1911年的辛亥革命、1927年的正式合三镇为一城，以及中国文化的发展。所以，正如前面部分论述的，汉口租界的意义不仅仅在汉口一域，它更在于近代中国文化的变迁。

4.3 对工业遗产价值的认识

武汉三镇中的汉阳曾是洋务运动的中心之一、中国工业最主要的基地。特别是张之洞督鄂18年，工业化思想进一步成熟，确立了"以工立国"思想，主张中国要富民强国，必须"以工立国"，一心一意地"讲求工政"，发展近代工业，这才是"养民之大经，富国之妙术"。在张之洞的努力下，武汉形成了较为完整的近代产业结构，先后创办汉阳铁厂（1890年）、湖北枪炮厂（1890年）、大冶铁矿（1890年）、湖北织布局（1890年）、汉阳铁厂机器厂（1892年）、汉阳铁厂钢轨厂（1893年）、湖北缫丝局（1894年）、湖北纺纱局（1894年）、湖北制麻局（1898年）等近代企业，占同期全国新建官办与官商合办企业的24%，发展速度为全国之冠。所有这些，都使得当年湖北在"中部崛起"，以"一隅之地，足以耸中外之视听"，为武汉，特别是汉阳，留下了宝贵的工业遗产。

但令人遗憾的是，在近代中国大名鼎鼎的汉阳铁厂、"汉阳造"等汉阳的工业遗产，目前面目全非、所剩无几。究其原因，还是在于过去对工业遗产认识的不足。

工业遗产具有很高的价值，包含文化价值、历史价值、科技价值等，其中文化价值是工业遗产的核心价值，代表了近代一段时间内的文化认同。目前，加强对武汉的工业遗产，特别是中国最早的洋务运动的工业遗产的普查和保护，是一项急迫而有意义的工作。

4.4 对首义之都的认识

武汉被称为"首义之都"，意指在辛亥革命中，武汉扮演了首先发难的突出的角色。有此美誉，当然是武汉的骄傲，但从无形文化线路的视点看，称武汉为"首义之都"仍然是对武汉城市定位的窄化。

对辛亥首义在武昌爆发的原因，学术界有种种不同的观点，但它与中国近代化的发展及革命力量的聚集密切相关，这一点却是大家的共识。武汉1861年开埠，开放时间较早，得风气之先，城市规划、生活方式为之一变；近代工商业发展较快，形成了以商业资本家和金融资本家为主的武汉民族资产阶级，建立了商会、商团等组织；张之洞督鄂进一步促进了洋务运动在中国甲午战败后的继续发展；武汉近代新式教育发展较充分，聚集了一批新式知识分子，新思想传播较快，报刊等现代传播手段较发达；武汉军事近代化改革也进行得较彻底，武汉新军具备了完整的建制和相当的规模，而革命党人把武汉作为根据地，大批知识分子和新军官兵加入同盟会、共进会、文学社等革命组织，革命派在武汉形成一股强大的政治力量，并掌握了大约5 000人的新军武装。所有这些，再加上其他一些因素，武汉地区最终于1911年10月10日爆发了震惊中外的武昌首义，并逐渐成为革命力量的中心。

作为一个单纯的历史事件的发生地，说武汉是首义之都、首义之城，那么其范围应该是首义发生的武昌城，而根据有关资料和笔者的调研，武汉市目前与辛亥革命直接有关的历史遗址共30处，这些遗址遍布武汉三镇。进一步讲，武昌能成功起事，得益于武汉的崛起，而武汉城市的崛起则是中国近代文化发展的结果。所以，武汉更应该被定位在中国文化近代化这条主线上，更应该被定义为中国近代"文化转型之都"。

4.5 对无形遗产的认识

长期以来，无形文化遗产没有得到足够的重视；武汉无形文化遗产的凋零令人痛心。

在调查中发现，现在的武汉市民一般都不太了解武汉的历史，对武汉历史名人，可以视为文化遗产的各种实践、表演、表现形式、老字号、知识和技能及有关的工具、实物、工艺品和文化场所等，不仅知者不多，且大多漠不关心。而无形文化遗产与有形文化遗产紧密联系，所以武汉市在1980年以后被拆毁的历史建筑不下百座，不少名人故居、名人坟茔现状堪忧：湖北省林业勘察设计院内的黎元洪墓，不少近在50米内的居民不知道；2007年2月12日冯玉祥故居的拆毁事件在中央电视台的《今日说法》栏目被曝光。

地区无形文化遗产保护不得力的部分原因在于武汉对无形文化遗产的认识不足，部分原因在于过去缺乏对无形文化遗产普查的意识，以及过分强调社会的意识形态问题。无形文化遗产和有形文化遗产作为一个硬币的两面，它们共同见证历史、共同记录地区发展的文脉。如果我们过分强调了历史文化名城中的"革命历史价值"的意义，而给文化遗产打上了意识形态的印记，则有一部分无形文化遗产的价值和意义会被彰显，如毛泽东和武汉的毛主席故居、农讲所等，而另外一部分则会被忽略，如与张之洞、黎元洪相关的文化遗产。

5　总结

"无形文化线路"是在传统的有形文化线路的基础上产生的概念,它是对"文化线路"概念的补充和修正。

"无形文化线路"的概念以文化濡化线路为依托,强调了在特定的文化发展过程中,基于"文化显著性"上的"纪念性完整"的维护。

以无形文化线路的理论观照武汉的文化遗产,可以把武汉反映中国近代文化转型典型层面的"汉口租界区、汉阳工业遗产和武昌首义遗产"看成一体的文化遗产,定义为武汉的"中国近代文化转型遗产无形文化线路",简称武汉无形文化线路。

武汉无形文化线路可以被看作一种新的文化遗产类型,也可以被看作一种武汉文化遗产的解读方法和视角。从这个视角出发,可以澄清以往对历史文化名城武汉的解读误区,为今后武汉文化遗产保护的思路提出依据。

参考文献

·中文著作类:

[1] 李晓峰. 乡土建筑:跨学科研究理论和方法[M]. 北京:中国建筑工业出版社,2005.
[2] 冯天瑜,陈锋. 武汉现代化进程研究[M]. 武汉:武汉大学出版社,2002.
[3] 冯天瑜,何晓明. 张之洞评传[M]. 南京:南京大学出版社,1991.
[4] 阮仪三. 护城纪实[M]. 北京:中国建筑工业出版社,2003.
[5] 阮仪三. 中国江南水乡古镇[M]. 杭州:浙江摄影出版社,2004.
[6] 王景慧,阮仪三,王林. 历史文化名城保护理论与规划[M]. 上海:同济大学出版社,1999.
[7] 威廉·A. 哈维兰. 文化人类学[M]. 瞿铁鹏,张钰,译. 上海:上海社会科学院出版社,2002.

·期刊类:

[1] 吕舟. 文化线路:世界遗产的新类型[J]. 中华遗产,2006(1):11-13.
[2] 王志芳,孙鹏. 遗产廊道:一种较新的遗产保护方法[J]. 中国园林,2001(5):85-88.
[3] 孙华. 文化线路成为年度关键词[J]. 中华遗产,2007(1):32-35.

·外文类:

[1] UNESCO Convention Concerning the Protection of the World Cultural and Natural Heritage[C]. [S. l.]November, UNESCO, 1972.
[2] UNESCO Operational Guidelines for the Implementation of the World Heritage Convention[C], [S. l.]1 February 2005, WHC/05/2, UNESCO, 2005.
[3] Organizational Office of ICOMOS 15th General Assembly. Monuments and Sites in Their Setting: Conserving Cultural Heritage in Changing Townscapes and Landscapes: Vol I & Vol II[M] [S. l.]: World Publishing Corporation, 2005.
[4] Marie-Theres Albert. Global Society and Local Identity (2001).

网址:

Http:/www/icomos-ciic. org/CIIC/CIIC. htm

关于武汉申遗的珞珈山对话

THE Luojiashan Dialogue on World Heritage Application of Wuhan

对话人:冯天瑜教授、西格弗里德·安德斯教授
Prof. Feng Tianyu and Prof. Siegfried Enders

2014年10月5日,ICOMOS共享遗产委员会主席安德斯博士专程来武汉拜访冯天瑜教授,两位专家就武汉申报世界遗产的问题进行了深入而愉快的交流。在开始正式交谈之前,冯天瑜教授带领安德斯博士眺望了武汉大学早期历史建筑群,并共同回忆了他们在日本京都大学工作和生活的情况。谈及了日本的榻榻米以及中国的"席地而坐",又延伸至18世纪中国与英国使者马格尔尼著名的礼仪之争。冯天瑜教授还专门画了一幅安德斯主席的速写,并邀请安德斯主席题词。对话由此正式开始。

冯天瑜和安德斯

ICOMOS与世界遗产申请

安:我专程来拜访您,主要是因为我曾经和一些专家讨论过您的中国文化转型研究和武汉大学的历史价值。希望当面和您探讨。

ICOMOS是联合国教科文组织的咨询机构,主要是负责世界遗产的评选。我两年前被武汉市政府邀请到武汉进行考察,去年从政府方面获悉武汉市希望申报世界遗产,我在做这个武汉申报世界遗产报告之前想跟您了解一下,听听您的意见,包括武汉乃至中国的文化转型、武汉大学这些方面,以及它们的历史价值。我们委员会这次来了六个人,但是我作为委员会主席,我想先听听您的意见。从组织形式上来说,ICOMOS是联合国教科文组织官方的咨询机构及评审机构,虽然不能够成为申请世界遗产项目的主体,但是科学委员会的专家委员是可以帮助世界遗产项目申请做工作的,这也是个惯例。这也是我此行拜访您的主要目的。

申请世界遗产需要"关键人物"

冯:关于申遗的大概情况,能不能先请安德斯主席介绍一下?

安:好的。我参与过世界遗产的申请很多年,审查过很多世界遗产的评审工作。就我的经验来看,每一个世界遗产项目后面都有一个或者几个关键人物。这个关键人物对世界遗产申报的积极推动和对申遗其他力量的努力整合,会促使世界遗产申报成功。

申请世界遗产是国际"公共关系"

安:我注意到,你们所说的"茶叶之路",在国际上,一般人的理解是你们所说的"茶马古道";武汉这个

城市在国际上知道的人不太多。这些对于申遗是很不利的。一般来说,世界遗产申报之前需要有很多的出版物,并产生影响,比如说书籍、视频等,如果没有广泛的宣传,那么世界遗产申报是不可能成功的。进一步说,世界遗产的申请不再是私人的研究,而是演变成一个公共关系。要制造舆论,发出声音。这个非常重要。

申遗的几个步骤

安:其实,我也一直在思考这一问题,怎么把武汉申遗的可行性做成一个研究报告。我们需要知道我们有什么,哪些是确实存在的。然后,我们需要依据联合国教科文组织的世界遗产评选的六个条件,看我们的遗产符合哪一条,再逐一进行说明。我们需要明确我们的遗产特点,即 OUV(Outstanding Universal Value,杰出普泛性价值)。再经过分析研究、比较研究、申报材料、规划编制、专项整治、专家评议等大量的、程序性的步骤,然后我们的申请项目可以列入《世界遗产预备名录》。然后是正式向联合国教科文组织申请。

武汉"有极大的典型性"

冯:那我先谈谈我的一些想法。

武汉这个城市的历史有3 000多年(安:武汉的这个历史国际上很少有),——武汉不仅是一个有着悠久历史的城市,同时也是一个新兴的、很现代的城市。应该说,武汉在中国的城市转型,尤其是在中国古典的中世纪城市转型为近现代城市方面有极大的典型性。

安:是的,您说的这个可以是评估武汉作为世界遗产杰出普泛价值的评估点,同时也是评选世界遗产的关键点——OUV(杰出普泛性价值)

冯:关于这一点,西方的学者、日本的学者做了很多这方面的研究,当时有一个学者叫作水野幸吉,写过一本叫作《汉口》的著作,另外德国人、英国人都写过这方面的著作。

安:这是一个研究中国的日本学者?

冯:这个日本学者当年是日本驻汉口的总领事,19世纪末20世纪初就去世了。

我还是要从这里开始说:武汉由三镇——武昌、汉阳、汉口三部分组成。武汉有长江(亚洲最大的河流)横贯东西,汉水(长江最大的支流)与长江相交汇,所以形成了三部分。长江以南,也就是我们现在所在地方是武昌;在长江与汉水交汇的西边,是汉阳;在长江与汉水交汇的东北面,是汉口。武汉古老的城市建设在武昌和汉阳,这已经有两三千年的历史了,汉口是一个新兴的都会,大概从明朝中期才开始出现的,到现在大概有500年的历史。

近代典型性与申遗

安:您刚刚的这段介绍,我觉得可能近代是武汉申遗过程中最有意思,也是最值得大书特书的地方,因为在目前中国的遗产地之中,许多城市都有相当悠久的历史,如果我们要选择填补空白,发现我们武汉作为世界遗产的价值,我们可能要聚焦在19世纪这样一个较新的阶段。

冯:这也是我要接着想要讲的。武汉转化成一个现代化的大都会是从19世纪60年代开始的,那就是在第二次鸦片战争以后,《天津条约》规定了一些内地的沿江城市开放,汉口就是其中的一座城市。武汉在19世纪60年代开始对外开放,一些西方的主要的国家,英、法、德以及后来的日本、俄国都进入武汉,在这里建设近代工厂、银行、医院,后来建设租界,这样汉口就出现了五国租界——英、法、俄、德、日。租界的数量之多在国内的主要城市中名列前茅,比上海、广州、青岛都要多;保存之完整,也在国内的主要城市中是比较好的。

安：武汉的这些情况，我觉得在世界范围内知道的人不多。我想再次说的是，就我这么多年的审查评选世界遗产的经验来看，世界遗产的申报过程应当注重公共关系的处理。让世界上更多的人知道这个申报世界遗产对象的存在，这样一来这些世界遗产就变成了现在的当选了的世界遗产，变成了《世界遗产名录》上的世界遗产。比如，您可以参考日本广播协会NHK关于世界遗产的宣传片，以及中国中央电视台拍的历史纪录片，或者是英国广播公司BBC做的一些宣传片。包括一些欧洲重要电视台的节目都应该播出关于武汉的一些历史片、宣传片。

冯：关于公共宣传方面，您刚刚讲的非常重要。

我觉得武汉作为申报世界遗产有几点非常重要：首先是租界，租界是展现西方近代文明进入中国内地的一个物化的过程。再就是武汉成为现代化都会的一个非常重要的人物——从19世纪90年代开始做湖广总督的张之洞。他所主持的湖北新政是一系列近代工业、近代商业、近代文化教育包括近代军事的建设的源头，这一方面也留下了十分丰富的遗存。近代工业方面，比如说他建立汉阳铁厂、汉阳兵工厂都是当时中国乃至于亚洲最大的近代化工业，比日本明治维新时期的近代工业都要大。再一个就是近代教育，当时张之洞在湖北建立了一系列现代学校，武汉大学、华中农业大学、武汉科技大学的前身都可以追溯到当时张之洞创办的一些近代学校。

武汉大学的价值评估和历史主义风格

冯：我再说一下武汉大学，武汉大学的建筑风格应该说是中西方建筑风格非常完美的一个结合。另外武汉还有一系列的物质遗存，其中跟辛亥革命有关的物质遗存也很多，比如说红楼和辛亥革命纪念馆，这批建筑应该说是非常典型的中方和西方建筑文化结合的产物。武汉大学建筑的设计师是美国建筑师——凯尔斯，他设计时就把西方的建筑和中国的宫廷建筑结合起来，并且也运用得非常成功。

安：在我们介绍武汉大学这些中西合璧的建筑的时候，是不是已经从事了一些研究？在这些研究的过程中我们的学者是否把其中的中式的元素和西式的元素一起拿出来做了对照，然后详细地做了解释和说明？

冯：是的，有相当一批很有水平的研究成果，也有专著介绍，很深入地从文化学和建筑学专业来解读这些建筑。

安：像我们的这样一些对比和中国其他地方的对比，比如说跟武汉相似的南京等一些其他地方，是不是有区别，这些在OUV里面都是非常重要的……

冯：我们有一本很简单的宣传册，类似于宣传册的出版物也有很多，还有一些专业化的书，以后我们可以准备一套包括我自己编著的，一些从建筑、文化方面研究的关于武汉大学、昙华林的建筑的书籍。昙华林也很重要，那里有很多中西合璧的建筑，包括教堂、学校等等。要把那些保存得还比较好的建筑统统整理起来，展示武汉从中古形态城市转化成近代城市的物质遗存和文化传统，存量还是相当丰富的。

安：在欧洲也有一个始于1810—1820年代，主要在19世纪兴盛的历史主义建筑风格，是把之前的包括古罗马、古希腊一直到文艺复兴这一路下来的建筑风格糅杂在一起，呈现给大家的一些建筑方式。我们在这里看到的一些新的建筑艺术风格其实就很像是那个时期的建筑风格。这个历史主义建筑风格凸显的是对旧的建筑设计式样的回归，但是采用的建筑结构和材料又是当时新式的，比如我们在武汉大学看到的建筑是使用钢筋混凝土结构制作的，带有古典的中式色彩的建筑。

冯：我们现在将这个时期的建筑风格称之为民国风格。当时民国试图采用中西合璧建筑，在新中国刚刚成立的时候，中国著名建筑家梁思成也是试图接续中西合璧的建筑风格，这些探索都类似于刚刚您说的19世纪德国采用的历史主义建筑风格。

安：在日本也有一段时间，比如说一战之前的建筑也是采用了这种历史主义建筑风格。

冯：日本现在也有很多建筑，比如说其政府建筑包括议会的建筑都是这种风格，比如像日本的名古屋市政大厅都带有这种风格。

安：在专业的建筑家看来，这种结合式样的产生会带来一个问题，就是我们很多的传统式样在现代化的潮流中在美学比例上可能会显得有一点突兀，比如说原始的中式建筑可能在规模上不会像我们现在看到的一些结合了西式传统的式样有突然变大的一些比例。

冯：您也可以看一下19世纪30年代与武汉大学同时期建造的湖北省图书馆，位于蛇山下，是一个典型的中西合璧的建筑，它保持了中国传统的大屋顶，构建得非常完美。还有一个奇特的建筑是古德寺。我曾经在澳门讲过一段时间学，澳门现在申遗成功了，但就我个人看来，其实我们武汉的这些建筑要比澳门的建筑水准要高。

澳门世界遗产与武汉的申遗

安：我没有仔细看过澳门成功申报所符合的几个条件以及杰出普泛性价值，如果我们要在武汉和澳门这些世界遗产做对比的话，那么我们还是要回到刚刚我们说的那几个重要条件上，这样我们才能理解为什么我们有时候在澳门第一眼看到的，我们认为潜在的世界遗产建筑最终成为世界遗产。其实这些建筑背后是有杰出普泛价值做支撑的，我们在做武汉和澳门的比较中是需要研究这些普泛价值，这个普泛价值是需要进行阐释的。澳门是不是中国目前唯一的一个殖民统治时期的世界遗产？

冯：应该是的，因为澳门有15、16世纪葡萄牙人在那里做的一些碉堡、炮塔等一些建筑，还是比较有特色的。

安：我们刚谈到的澳门的情况，我们可能要使用我们的研究网络，因为我们的共享遗产委员会里有一个是澳门委员，这个委员是非常有帮助的，在澳门的地位也很高。我们还有一个委员是葡萄牙人，他曾经在澳门的文化遗产处做领导，这些关系都需要武汉来使用，如果需要，我们可以到那里去拜访他们。

城市的可持续发展、老租界与建筑的模仿

冯：2013年在杭州举办的一个联合国教科文组织的学术会议，是关于城市的可持续发展问题的。我作为中方代表做了发言。

安：您当时的主题发言是关于武汉的吗？

冯：不是，我当时讲的是中国文化，中国文化所提供的一些元素对于人类可持续发展的一些作用。

安：武汉需要邀请一些国际专家对武汉租界进行一些研究。

冯：当年德国在武汉的领事馆现在就是武汉市人民政府的所在地，这个建筑基本保存完好，只是将屋顶的鹰去掉了。中国内地的谘议局都是日式建筑，但是这个日式建筑也是日本从英国学来的，改造了一下。

安：日本的一个建筑师曾经设计了东京火车站，但是这个火车站是仿照荷兰的一个火车站建造的，这个建筑师曾经是在英国学习的，之后韩国的建筑师又仿造日本的东京火车站在韩国建造了一个火车站。

申遗过程中的文化遗产价值的增长

冯：武汉的发展是非常迅速的，尤其是在近20年内。上个世纪50年代只有一座桥梁跨江而过，但是现在已经有十座桥梁了，还有一条过江隧道，因此现在武汉不仅仅称为江城了——之前由于唐代诗人李白的一首诗，武汉也称为江城，现在武汉也可以称为"桥城"。有的专家也指出了未来武汉是世界上发展最具潜力的城市。

安：是的。我还想说一点：对于世界遗产的申请过程中，申请的这种阐释是会发生变化的，这种变化也会影响到最后的评估。

比如说在我自己的家乡，达姆施塔特（Darmstadt），那里的关于新艺术运动的建筑遗存并不是最好的，

尤其是跟法国或者欧洲其他国家新艺术时代的文化遗存相比，这些建筑的原真性并不是最好的——但是随着时代的变革，欧洲一体化的推进，在最近25年之内的，可能一些原始遗存的物质性的层面评估慢慢转变成了非物质性的评估。比如说跟当地的经济的一些融合，包括跟我们的设计等工业方面的一些变化，使得这些新艺术的评估发生一些变化。达姆施塔特一直在持续研究和发展"新艺术运动"这个主题，我想它是可望在今后成为世界遗产的。

武汉申遗要注重其内陆港口的特点

安：武汉申遗的另外一个点，可能就是武汉作为一个在江上的租界和一个由江上的码头组成的独特景观，我们可以做一个比较研究，比如说我们可以跟其他著名的河流上的城市做一个比较。

冯：这个对比我们正在做，比如说长江文明馆，这个是我们现在做的一个很重要的工作。

安：我不知道你们是不是跟重庆、天津做过这样的一些比较呢？

冯：这方面我可以画一张示意图。武汉在内河、内陆方面的独特性是显著的。

安：今天和你谈过之后我会尽快写一份武汉申遗的可行性研究，而不是叫武汉报告了。

冯：谢谢您的访问。我们在无界论坛上再见。

文化遗产作为城市发展指导原则的重要意义
The Significance of Cultural Heritage as a Guiding Principle for Urban Development

敏佳杨
比利时鲁汶大学雷蒙德·勒迈尔国际保护中心主任
联合国教科文组织世界遗产中心原副主任
Minja Yang
President, Raymond Lemaire International Conservation Center, Leuven University
Former Deputy Director, UNESCO World Heritage Center

How to integrate the old architecture into the new architecture is a question worth discussing. Urban preservation is diversified, including architectural preservation. The destruction caused by the development of tourism is usually regarded as the focus of concern affecting the preservation of urban heritage, but tourism should not be the only concern. In addition to the awareness of the common culture and the continuous memory, the urban conservation work also needs to pay attention to the heritage and regional development. Improving the quality of life in historical areas and increasing people's feelings towards the place of residence are conducive to the protection of local history and culture. Efforts should be made to extend the heritage, to preserve as many historical sites as possible and to allow cities to coexist with the past.

今天我们谈到了很多不同领域和专业,有可持续发展的建筑,还有阮仪三教授关于古民居的保护。我认为,这些古老的建筑如何融入新的建筑中,是值得探讨的问题。在城市中,不管是商业区,还是曾经的殖民区,都是我们未来需要的。当我听到有些地方对20世纪末建筑进行改造把整个地区完全拆除的做法时,我感到非常震惊。

城市保护是多样的,不是单一的建筑保护

今天,我们所关注的城市保护,是多样的,而非单一的建筑保护,尤其是在面积大人口多的国家,比如说中国和印度。在欧洲,很多城市的历史区可能占整个城市10%之多,在中国可能不到1%。我们的城市快速发展快速扩大,今天看到很多的案例,有做得很好的,比如扬州,但也有很多由于政策决定者等诸多原因,保护工作做得不是很好。

人们通常会将旅游业的发展带来的破坏作为影响城市遗产保护的关注重点,但旅游业不应是唯一的担忧。在大多数国家包括欧洲国家,这些遗产都是旅游最大的吸引力之一,这是一个我们要经历的过程。城市保护工作在让人们了解到共同的文化、持续性的回忆的同时,还需注意遗产保护与地区的发展之间的关系。为什么联合国教科文组织要参与到城市保护中?作为特殊的机构,它需要减少贫困、关注可持续发展、促进文化的交流,这就是它参与到这其中的原则。文化是城市重要的支柱,它可以被看作是一种工具、是一个过程。我们尝试让遗产与地区的发展相关,从20世纪60年代我们就开始这样做了。但是直到现在,在世界遗产大会上仍然可以看到,在很多的城市里仍然有很多的建筑被忽视了。很多的建筑是作为单

体而不是一个整体的来看,我们需要一个新的意识,告诉我们城市是怎么样的。不仅是怎样看建筑本身,还有如何理解建筑区域,尤其是怎样促进城市交通的发展。很多街道为了这样的发展被拆了,大家是规划专业的专家,对这些应该都很熟悉。

改善历史地区的生活质量,增加人们对居住地的感情

随着时间的推移,一个城市如何演变,既是指整个城市的变化,也指街道的功能及意义的转变。在1996年,联合国教科文组织遗产中心启动了一个项目,目的是改善历史地区居住者的生活质量。我想让大家注意我们这样的一个尝试,我要讲的这个案例是土耳其的一个城市区域保护,那里有非常多的难民,当年发生了洪水,很多的难民来到伊斯坦布尔地区,居住在这里,也有犹太人、希腊人居住,但是这些难民对于这个地区没有情感,他们只是找一个避难的地方。那时候我们建造了一个多功能的混合社区,来保证人留在这里而不是离开。所以我们改善了街道的交通情况,修缮了洗手间以及房间,让大家的生活质量提高一些、更加舒适一些。增加人们对居住地的感情,有利于当地历史文化的保护。土耳其政府为此提供了支持,我想中国也可以用这样的办法。

扩大遗产的内涵与过去共存

谈到遗产,有不少人只看到建筑本身,我们要看到所有的内涵。扩大遗产的内涵,与过去共存,也是我们提出的重要的概念,是2011年联合国教科文组织出台的建议。

接下来我要举三个例子,值得注意的是,这三个案例一个是发展中国家,一个是新兴国家,一个是发达国家。我们的目的就是要看到我们是否能有一个全球的价值观,这既关系到历史的建筑,也关系到文化的重要性,以及我们未来发展的指引,即以什么方式实现城市的目标,改善交通住房,加强经济,并且加强城乡之间的联系。

第一个例子是来自一个发展中国家——老挝。这是亚洲最贫穷的国家之一。由于战争的关系,只有30%受教育的人留在了这个国家。因为战争,很多地区都被人民忽视了,但这个区域对于自己的历史文化遗产是非常骄傲的。遗产保护工作者们推崇的是文化和区域的联系,还有不同的建筑间的融合,包括了传统的、欧式的、殖民的建筑,对于这三种建筑,我们进行了非常详尽的分析,包括对地形、地质等等。我们当时出台了管理的计划,有好几卷,包括各个方面。欧盟赞助了一个小的城市,也是在两条河之中,该项目现在有3 000万的资金注入,除了我们的项目,还有其他的项目。如果这样的发展,尤其是基础设施,包括道路、电力做得更好的话,实际上可以加强我们的保护模式,因为我们可以关注到这些我们该关注的层面,比如说建一个机场作为一个缓解区,这样很多部分都把整个城市规划纳入其中了,不仅是旅游,还有发展,在核心的区域。

第二个例子是来自于一个新兴国家——印度。这个城市有山有水,我们需要了解当地的魅力,包括什么地方可以进行合作、进行深化,甚至一个相关楼层的高度也需要限制,在山上建一个很高的楼,就会挡住山上的景色。现在有一些优势,特别是政府间的合作,有些问题可以从两国合作的角度加以解决。

最后的一个例子是我们在欧洲的一个项目。我们在做这个项目时发现,法国有很多这样的遗址,有的最黄金的位置做了赌场,但这个地方本身是一个遗产地区。与此同时,我们要尝试将核心位置进行扩展,扩大三倍,当然他们不希望将整个城市都注入这个之内,还希望接受我们的帮助,帮助他们进行这样的核心地区的扩展。我们做了一些新城市的拓展计划,包括相关的运河、山峰、基础设施等等,希望能够让这些地区更具流动性,让这个城市的交通尤其是公共交通升级,让它变成可再生的城市。每年有3 000栋新楼修整出来,七年之后,这个数字非常大。

再说遗址的延伸。很多人并不希望成为这个延伸的一部分,他们认为发展会受到限制,比如政府希望能够拿一些基金,大概占1%财政的预算,希望通过这些基金搭建一些新的设施,而我们则希望所有地区

的城市中心都是绿色的、可持续发展的。所以说如何能够将这些楼房塞入城市中心,就变成了非常难的问题,对于工作人员来说就要有责任,他们也需要具备多样性的观念。

我认为对历史的遗址保护是非常重要的,我们不能淘汰这些遗址,而要看我们能够为他们做些什么。有的时候一些遗址本身被破坏了,但是我们需要尝试,尽可能把这些遗址保留下来,让城市与过去共存。

系统认识名城价值，保护城市遗产网络
SYSTEMATIC APPRECIATION OF HISTORIC CITIES' VALUE AND PROTECTION OF THEIR HERITAGE NETWORKS

张杰　教授
清华大学建筑学院
Prof. Zhang Jie
School of Architecture, Tsinghua University

Resorting to the cases of Guangzhou, Beijing, Jingdezhen and Wuhan, this speech emphasizes the value of historic cities and the formation of "heritage network" under the circumstance of modern urban development.

一、广州的案例

"五岭北来峰在地，九州南尽水浮天""白云越秀翠城邑，三塔三关锁珠江""青山半入城，六脉皆通海"的诗句描述了广州三个层次的山水格局。

当广州提出把北京路和历史文化名城最核心的古城作为战略发展地区时，如何挖掘文化、保护遗产就成了人们必须关注的问题。我们在广州的工作中，通过与政府、地方的专家沟通，以及市民参与等方式，基本上形成了广州古城越秀区以文化、三产服务业为主的发展策略，归纳提炼出了古城遗产资源保护利用的框架。在这个结构下，还结合发展策略提出了一些具体的可以实施的项目。这一工作的重点就是，把历史要素重新梳理清楚，使这些内容在未来能得到彰显，同时融入城市和社会的发展过程中。另外，我们在规划上跟相关部门做了很多工作，比如推出更新单元的方式、人口的疏解以及进入政策等等。

2014年，《广州历史文化名城保护规划》得到省政府批复后，地方政府还做了大量的社会宣传工作。同时，广州规划部门非常及时地推出了老城和新区不同的规划标准，这个精神是非常重要的。

二、北京的案例

北京市政府也准备召开落实中央城市工作会议精神的政府会议，要出台一些文件，探讨北京的老城和周边山水之间的城市特色彰显及如何推进城市整体保护的问题。

清代北京城在畿辅地区形成了一个完整的都城地区。直隶布政使司共辖10府、23州、120县，整个疆域西达今山西东部，南至河北南部，东至山海关，北至承德等。畿辅的中心区域京师顺天府也包括了京郊周围的20多个县。

京城自身也不是孤立的，其周边还有很多与之相关、为皇家服务的重要场所环境，如日、月、地三坛一起构成皇家祭祀天地的场所。近郊以玉泉山为标志的三山五园是皇家重要的夏宫园林区。此外，永定河上的卢沟桥和拱极城（今宛平城）构成古城西南的重要防御节点。最后，作为漕运的重要河道，通惠河将京城与京杭大运河的重要港口——通州联系在一起。此外，天宁寺作为京城外的重要寺庙及天宁寺塔形成的地标,也是京城不可分割的组成部分。所有这些都在清代《大清一统志》的《京城图》中清晰地标绘出来了。

北京历史城区现在面临的主要问题是人口疏解,使之有一个合理的人口密度,使居住条件和功能有一个合理安排。人口高密度是北京旧城的顽疾,最近一个重要抓手就是北京要进行老城里的文物腾退。这就将带来一系列问题:人怎么迁?腾退后的房子应该装什么样的内容?最近北京探索了很多方案来应对这些问题。在探讨历史城市的功能变化和更新问题时,对实施模式的探索迫在眉睫。在北京大栅栏、杨竹梅斜街等地段,人们正在摸索着不同的模式,如院落人口的平移,力求对街区实施休克式疗法,逐步实现产业的替换,但这往往需要大量的资金为后盾,是否可持续,有待观察。

三、景德镇的案例

景德镇各级文物点共792处。可以分为六类:生产型遗产(矿冶遗产、碓房、窑址、作坊、工厂);生活型遗产(民居、府邸、井泉)、文化型遗产(祠堂、坛庙、会馆、戏台、碑刻);商业型遗产(店铺、商道);交通型遗产(桥涵、码头、栅门);其他遗产(城垣、洞穴、门楼、名人墓、牌坊、革命遗产)。

这些遗产具有网络特征,它们在每一个历史横剖面都是一个生产、生活、贸易、交通等的完整体系、在历史纵剖面,则展示了各个子体系的完整演进的构成。

景德镇是一个因传统陶瓷产业而繁荣的历史城市,也是一个现代陶瓷业城市。到1990年代随着国企改革,老工业区开始衰落,很多人下岗,在老城中剩下了大量的旧厂区和地段,导致城市中出现很多功能黑洞。在这样的背景下,城市如何利用原来的空间、资产等使整个城市再上一个台阶?显然,遗产保护、文化继承等就成为极为重要的契机。

我们在这里的工作是针对14个老厂区进行系统的研究,将老厂区的更新、改造及保护纳入整个城市的发展。其核心就是我很多年前提出的、现已被业内广泛接受的"织补城市"概念,最近在国家文件中称之为"修补"。"织补"不光是空间环境的织补,还是综合的社会各方面的织补,比如城市功能、社区设施的织补等。

四、武汉的案例

武昌古城区在过去一二十年武汉整体城市的发展过程中实际上是被遗忘的地区,也是持续衰退的地区。外围的发展使原有的城市中心从大的经济格局中脱离出来,给古城带来很多发展的压力,而保护面临的挑战也显而易见。今天社会认识到,古城不应该再衰退下去,它应在新的经济格局中起到应有的作用。我们结合城市发展的总体框架定位武昌古城未来的功能,对武昌区的历史、人文资源进行结构梳理。武昌古城的一个重要的特点是,它除了具有丰富的历史资源,还有多个艺术院校,教育资源很丰富。所以,将艺术与文化旅游结合,带动创新经济发展,改善民生,将成为武昌古城今后的重要发展战略。

黄鹤楼下的片区有很多私搭乱建和违章建筑,本来被列为类似棚改的改造项目。我们介入之后,跟地方政府多次沟通,对这个地区提出了整治和改造的设想。在方案中,能不拆的房子尽量不拆,赋予它新的功能。

五、结论

《中华人民共和国文物保护法》《历史文化名城名镇名村保护条例》,对历史文化名城和历史文化街区、村镇、文物、历史建筑的保护提出了明确要求,但这些内容应该理解为遗产保护的底线。随着实践和理论的深入,很多新的遗产类型将不断出现,各地方应根据自己的情况不断挖掘和确立新的类型。

《中华人民共和国城乡规划法》(2008年)第四条规定"……保护耕地等自然资源和历史文化遗产,保持地方特色、民族特色和传统风貌";第十七条将"环境保护、自然与历史文化遗产保护以及防灾减灾等内容"列为总体规划的强制性内容。据此《历史文化名城保护规划》作为法定规划,可以以更开放的形式容纳更多的遗产类型,经过社会参与、专家论证和行政程序,将需要保护的所有类型的遗产确定下来。这一做法符合中国的国情,同时也是推进新型城镇化的迫切需要。

澳大利亚 ICOMOS《巴拉宪章》及其在"环境"与"背景"中的应用

Australia ICOMOS *Burra Charter* and Its Application for "Setting" and "Context"

苏珊·杰克森-斯塔波夫斯基
澳大利亚 ICOMOS 前秘书长
ICOMOS 共享遗产委员会副主席
ICOMOS 历史村镇委员会专家
Susan Jackson-Stepowski
Former Secretary-General ICOMOS Australia
Vice President and Expert Member, ICOMOS International Scientific Committee for Shared Built Heritage
International Expert, ICOMOS International Scientific Committee for Historic Towns & Villages

本文介绍了澳大利亚 ICOMOS 的《巴拉宪章》及其在不同规模与类型的遗产点(包括乡土建筑、以及从市级到国家级历史建筑,乃至世界遗产地)中的应用。文章列举了悉尼歌剧院在保护与管理规划的制定过程中如何针对特别用途评估"环境"与"背景"的要素。

Why is the short title the "*Burra Charter*"? The Charter was adopted at the 1979 Australia ICOMOS annual meeting, held in the historic mining town of Burra in South Australia. Burra is a small rural town that has "shared built heritage". The mine infrastructure and many of the stone cottages were built by English Cornish miners in the 19th century. Burra is now a member of a world-wide series of Cornish mining sites around the world.

Why did Australia ICOMOS create the "*Burra Charter*"? *The Burra Charter* is a practical application of the *Venice Charter*.

Thirteen years after the UNESCO *Venice Charter* was adopted, Australia ICOMOS sought to review how to apply the *Venice Charter* to Australian situations. The *Burra Charter* adopted the general philosophy of the *Venice Charter* in a format that is practical and useful in Australia, aided by knowledge and experience of Australia ICOMOS members.

图 1 澳大利亚《巴拉宪章》封面(2013 年版)

It is a dynamic document. Since it was first adopted in 1979, the Charter has been periodically updated to reflect understanding of the theory and practice of cultural heritage management.

The *Burra Charter* has been translated into several other languages. It has assisted many individual national ICOMOS committees through being a basis for their national heritage practice documents. For example, the *Burra Charter* has been a particularly useful tool for our neighbours in Asia. It assisted in formulating the first edition of the *China Principle*, which since has been recently revised and presented to the 2016 ICOMOS annual meeting held in Fukuoka, Japan.

The *Burra Charter* approach has been incorporated into Australian heritage legislation at all levels of government to define cultural significance, for heritage assessments and for the management of heritage "places".

The *Burra Charter* format. The Charter is a short 8 pages, plus a preamble page and a flow chart showing the "3 step" process (see below).

The *Burra Charter* contains 34 articles arranged in 4 sections:

—Article 1 is about 15 definitions.

—Articles 2 to 13 deal with conservation principles.

—Articles 14 to 25 deal with conservation processes.

—Articles 26 to 34 deal with conservation practice.

The *Burra Charter* should be read and used as a whole document. That is, all Articles are of equal importance, and users of the Charter should not use one Article to the detriment of another Article.

Article 1 provides the definitions which are common language to help people to understand places of cultural significance and their conservation. There are 175 definitions. The first terms defined are "place", "cultural significance", "fabric", "conservation" and "maintenance".

In Australia, the word "conservation" has a particular meaning and should not be confused with the word "preservation". In Article 1.4 "conservation" means all the process of looking after a "place" so as to retain its "cultural significance".

Article 3 says to take a cautious "approach... required for changing as much as necessary but as little as possible", for example to keep patina of age, evidence of layers and past histories.

Article 5 is about values, which is a values-approach method.

"'Conservation' of a 'place' should identify and take into consideration all aspects of cultural and natural significance..."

In Australia, the following value criteria are used to identify and assess heritage significance.

—Historic

—Historic associations

—Aesthetic (all the senses not just visual)

—Technical (how it was built and what it can teach future generations)

—Social and spiritual associations (what it means to communities today)

—Integrity and intactness

—Rarity

Burra Charter and understanding "Shared Built Heritage". The heritage principal in Article 13 is about the "co-existence of cultural values should always be recognised, respected and encouraged...", while the heritage process in Article 24 says "significant 'associations' between peoples and a 'place' should be respected, retained and not obscured. Significant 'meanings' of a 'place' should be respected."

The *Burra Charter* supports the retaining of layers of fabric and of differing values that may reside in a "place". By doing so, the philosophy is to retain "evidence" that is represented in the physical fabric, the history, and/or the consciousness of people. Retaining layers of evidence also enables the understanding as to why that "place" is important and provides the evidence for future generations. The "fabric" (such as the buildings, spatial relationships, etc) may have potential for research, interpretation and to continue "telling the story" as to why that "place" came into being, and provide experience for both inhabitants and visitors.

The *Burra Charter* approach therefore is to recognise and respect layers of different cultural values to more than one cultural group or an era in the history, and to ensure management policies conserve all values and promote co-existence of these "shared values". Consequently a "place" maybe valued to a broader population than solely a local or regional community. Thus the *Burra Charter* approach is used by all levels of significance from local, municipal, provincial, through to national and world heritage places.

Without first understanding what the "shared" heritage values are, and to what communities hold such values, this is a prerequisite that must be undertaken before drafting policies and any subsequent management decisions made.

Burra Charter uses a 3-step process. Article 6 is summarised in the flow charter on the last page of The Charter. The Charter states that everything should be done in a logical order using three consecutive steps. Step 1 is to understand significance by gathering the evidence about a "place" and assessing that evidence. Step 2 is to devise policies that retain the significance of that "place" based on the evidence of Step 1. Step 3 is to implement policies that will retain significance.

These 3 steps should be done before any decisions are made about the future of a 'place', or works commence.

Brief background about the Sydney Opera House(SOH). The SOH is a multi-functional, active performing arts centre and this is its primary purpose. It is one of the busiest arts centres in the world. There are 8.2 m visitors per year, 2,400 events per year, plus ancillary activities, e.g. day guided tours, as well as managing and servicing various on-site concessions (restaurants, bars, food and beverage outlet).

The building complex itself contains 7 halls, practice spaces, recording studio, back-of-stage functions, offices, a storage, as well as rooms for various temporary uses. Frequently the SOH is involved innational and international commemorations, most recently for "Earth Day" which had all major sites world-wide illuminated in blue.

At a city level the SOH attracts persons from all parts of society—local school groups, pop concerts, opera, ballet, cabaret, drama, lecture series, to host ad hoc events. Annually it is the location of the Australia ICOMOS memorial—James Kerr's lecture. Overlying how the locals use the venue, the SOH is now a major tourist attraction as well as being located within the historic heart of the first European settlement in Australia.

And so the SOH has three concurrent functions: as a World Heritage site, for tourism and for performance. Further, the "brand" of the SOH is very important: it has become a symbol of the City of Sydney, and for the people of Australia as one of its national monuments.

How to value such an asset is difficult. A current estimate says the SOH generates 4.6 m Australian Dollars to State and Australia in tourism alone.

In terms of heritage legislation protection, in 2003 the SOH was listed on the New South Wales State Heritage Register, in 2005 on the Australian National List and in 2007 inscribed as World Heritage for its creative genius.

Below are five examples of applications of the *Burra Charter* from the SOH CMP:

The Sydney Opera House as an example of the application of the *Burra Charter*.
To illustrate some of the *Burra Charter* Articles, Step 1 (understand significance) and Step 2 (policies that retain significance), including a few examples, are drawn from the recently exhibited *Sydney Opera House Draft Conservation Management Plan (fourth edition)* (SON CMP).

my thanks to Alan Croker, heritage architect advisor to the Sydney Opera House Trust, and The SOH management for providing Aus. ICOMOS with a special briefing on the draft SOH CMP. Acknowledgment for use of extracts from the draft SOH CMP in this presentation. The draft SOH CMP can be down-loaded from the SOH web site. (http://d16outft0soac8.cloudfront.net/uploadedFiles/SOH_CMP_JUNE_2015.pdf)

The format and page layout of the SOH CMP is also deliberately designed to be very practical and user friendly to all staff and contractors involved—from cleaners, plumbers through to managers. This applied thinking behind the CMP format and its print version layout alone is a topic for a future presentation.

For the SOH, the key evidence is the original design objective by its architect, Utzon, plus design solutions by those who actually realised its construction, such as Peter Hall and Ove Arup Engineers.

This is known as the Utzon Design Principles. Each page of the SOH CMP incorporates the *Utzon Design Principles*, with explanations, such as why an individual element is significant, and the policy to guide that particular element's future management.

Burra Charter example: Article 1.1 definition of "place". The SOH is more than just a concrete building. The SOH "place" includes the surrounding promenade, seawall and the cliff face to the adjoining nationally significant Botanical Gardens. The World Heritage buffer zone includes the harbour setting and the Sydney Harbour Bridge, another Australian icon. Therefore crucial consideration must be given to its "expanded curtilage", and visual relationships of the SOH to the surrounding land and water stapes, including any approach from the city out onto this small peninsular.

"…a building in which functional, festive and inspiring manner will shelter the activities and the life within, and in so doing so enhance the face of Sydney". Jorn Utzon 1958

"…going to the Opera House is a succession of visual and audio stimuli, which increase inintensity as you approach the building, as you enter and finally sit down in the halls, culminating with the performance". Jorn Utzon 1965

Burra Charter example: Step 1 Understand what is significant by gathering the evidence about that "place".

For the SOH, "setting" and "context" are fundamental for its building's design principles and for all the values attached to it.

Evidence of Outstanding Universal Value (OUV) is about the SOH in its harbour setting. It is a "sculpture in the round" viewed from many sides, across water and land, from within the core and the buffer zones, and views are reciprocal, where are both to the SOH and from the SOH.

Article 1.12 defines "setting" as means the immediate and extended environment of a "place" that is part of or contributes to its "cultural significance" and distinctive character.

"Conservation" required the retention of an appropriate "setting". This includes retention of visual and sensory setting, as well as the retention of spiritual and other cultural relationships that contribute to the "cultural significance" of the "place".

The Xi'an Declaration on the conservation of setting of heritage structures, sites and areas adopted by ICOMOS General Assembly in Xi'an, China in October 2006 defines "setting" as: *"the immediate and extended environment that is part of, or contributes to its significance and distinctive character."*

The Xi'an Declaration further notes that "setting" includes not only the physical and visual aspects but also the intangible aspects, the "character of arrival experience" and "meaningful relationship with their physical, visual, and other cultural context and settings".

The "setting" and "context" of the SOH impact all aspects of its significance. Both are so important for the SOH, the terms 'setting' and 'context' are specifically noted in the SOH Statement of Significance and are the fourth most important policy for the management of the site.

Below is an extract from the SOH CMP about "context" and "setting".

5.4 CONTEXT AND SETTING

"The position on a peninsular, which is overlooked from all angles makes it important to maintain an all-round elevation. There can be no backsides to the building and nothing can be hidden from the view, not even from the air, - the building must form a free-standing sculpture in contrast to the square buildings surrounding it." [1]

The setting of the Sydney Opera House must be considered in its broadest meaning. The *Xi'an Declaration on the Conservation of the Setting of Heritage Structures, Sites and Areas*, adopted by ICOMOS in Xi'an, China, in October 2005,[2] defines *setting* in article 1 as:

"the immediate and extended environment that is part of, or contributes to, its significance and distinctive character."

It further notes that this includes not only the physical and visual aspects of the place, but also intangible aspects including *"the current and dynamic cultural, social and economic context"*, *"the character of the arrival experience"*, and *"meaningful relationships with their physical, visual, spiritual and other cultural context and settings"*.[3] The setting and context of the Sydney Opera House impact all aspects of its significance.

Policy 4.1 – Context and setting

The significant tangible and intangible aspects of the physical, visual, social, spiritual and historic setting and context of the Sydney Opera House should be retained, protected and conserved for present and future generations, in accordance with the Utzon Design Principles and this CMP. These are described in the Statement of Significance in this CMP and include:

- physical and visual relationship with the city and Sydney Harbour
- quality as a monumental sculpture in the round
- approach and arrival sequence of spaces, both beyond and within the site, providing an exceptional experience for patrons, performers and visitors.
- international recognition as a masterpiece of 20th century architecture and as an architectural icon
- function as Australia's pre-eminent performing arts venue
- place in the Australian psyche as a cultural icon and as a focus for national celebrations and events.

图 2

Regardless of being a tourist, a city office worker or a heritage professional, one is constantly aware of the position of the SOH in the city scape and in relation to Sydney Harbour—whether in the building itself, anywhere on the site, and equally on the approaches to the site or as seen from afar. The approach sequence itself—the "journey" to the site—has great importance, commencing from the central business district, followed by a sequence of arrival onto the site, into the building, and lastly circulation within the building itself. The SOH is the only performing arts centre in the world with a wrap—around foyer—where one can walk around the halls and where the orientation of all public spaces is towards the water.

SON CMP Policy 5.4 specifically states the importance of "setting" and that this must be retained and conserved, such as via:

—Tangible and intangible aspects of the physical, visible, social, spiritual and historic setting and context to be retained, protected and conserved for present and future generations;

—Protection of views into the SOH & out from the SOH;

—Guide development in the vicinity;

—Retaining an open and unclutteredness (down to management of food and beverage concessions, detailed design quality of structures, commercial leases);

—The maintained open unobstructed relationships with surrounding uses and development.

***Burra Charter* example**: **Step 2**—Devise conservation policies to retain significances.

The SOH CMP deals with matters from the macro to micro level of detail. Some examples of mico-management of significance are:

—shape of beams and way these fit together (Op Arab engineers) which were at the edge of the possibilty in technology of the time;

—prefab roof segments;

—structural glass (Peter Hall) (such use of glass at that time in Australia gained the name "glass panels");

—the SOH was the first use of computers in building design and on a large scale.

In devising policies for the SOH, the SOH CMP uses a "sensitivity-to-change tool" to assist managers in determining how in manage changes.

2014 marked the 40th birthday of the SOH. 2015 marked the beginning of a "decade of renewal programme" wherein 20.1 m Australian Dollars will be spent over the next 10 years as an active performing arts centre. Proposed changes and upgrades include:

—underground loading dock,

—removing kerbs and trip hazards,

—inserting a welcome centre especially to guide the growing volume of tourists,

—renewal of opera hall machinery.

Another example of Step 2 Policy concerns the SOH roof shells. This incorporates *Burra Charter* Article 3 "cautious approach" and Article 16 Maintenances.

In summary, the *Burra Charter* is a practical application of the UNESCO *Venice Charter* for situations in Australia. It can be used for any level of significance. The SOH CMP was given to illustrate that application of a few Articles of the Charter, and especially that of setting and context. The same should apply for protecting the setting and context of Wuhan's historic quarters, and even more to those having "Shared Built Heritage" international significance in the Hankow concessions.

澳门城市规划发展历程研究
A Chronicle Study on Urban Planning Development in Macao

童乔慧 教授
武汉大学城市设计学院
Prof. Tong Qiaohui
School of Urban Design, Wuhan University

The development process of the city planning of Macao from the year of 1557 opening port to the year of 1999 returning to motherland was considered to be a research object. Methods of history, investigation and cut-era history were used. Four periods were marked off in the development process. The action and characteristic of every period of city planning were elaborately analyzed and discussed. Evolvement and content of city planning were systematically and thoroughly investigated and researched. The discipline and characteristic of city planning of Macao were revealed.

澳门作为中国一个非常特殊的地理单元,其400多年来的城市发展向我们展示了中西文明和文化交流的浩瀚历史场景,这无论对于认识中国对外开放史、东西方贸易史、中西文化交流史,或者了解澳门参与国际市场而促进自身发展的规律性,都有重要的意义和价值。澳门城市规划发展历程研究因其城市特殊的历史背景而具有相当重要的价值。它不仅有助于我们了解澳门城市建筑的形成机制,也有助于补充和完善中国城市规划史研究。

澳门街景

澳门经过400多年的历史变迁,由一个普通的半岛渔村发展成为国际贸易港口的自治城市。本文所论述的城市规划历程从1557年开埠至1999年回归。从历史学的角度来看,澳门历史发展过程存在着双轨——华人社会一条线,葡人社会另一条线,双轨基本保持平行。从建筑学的角度来看,澳门是一个"中国建筑""葡萄牙建筑""果阿建筑"等多元文化整合并存的城市。从城市规划的角度来看,澳门是由葡萄牙人的城市规划体制占主导地位的城市。

澳门是中国最早开始受到西方的影响并逐步走向现代都市化道路的城市,"禁、驰之争"、"禁海"、"迁界"、鸦片战争、两次世界大战等国内外重大事件对于澳门城市发展的影响并不及内陆城市巨大,城市建设始终稳步向前发展。这正是澳门城市规划在时间上断代的特殊性、在性质和内涵上的连续性。同时澳门城市规划的发展不同于中国大部分受过殖民统治的城市,其在原有城市发展基础上被导入西方城市规划思想,规划章程也是葡萄牙的翻版,这是澳门城市规划在规划主体和类型上的特殊性。

1 澳门近现代城市规划的历史分期

从葡萄牙人入居澳门至今,已经过去近450年的历史。澳门的城市规划演变分期着重于葡萄牙人对澳门主权的掠夺进程以及葡人的城市规划思想及实践在澳门的延续。根据澳门城市发展的具体情况，将澳门近现代城市规划史时间段限定为1557年，标志性历史事件是澳门开埠，此后葡萄牙殖民者在澳门开始有城市规划的萌芽，成为澳门城市规划的起点。1949年前后的澳门城市规划从现象到本质都具有连续性和整体性。根据澳门近现代城市规划活动及其历史发展特点，澳门近现代城市规划历程划分为以下四个时期：

第一期：天主教城，城市规划的萌芽期（1557—1840），明朝廷官方同意葡人入居澳门，开始了葡萄牙人在澳门进行城市规划的萌芽期。

第二期：殖民开发，城市改造与扩张规划时期（1840—1911），通过填海造地以及入侵华人村落，葡萄牙人逐步对澳门行使主权并进行整体规划。

第三期：制定法规，城市规划制度完善时期（1911—1974），澳门政府制定了都市建设规章等一系列法令制度。

第四期：自治规划，城市规划的本地化发展时期（1974—1999），政府机构逐步独立与自治，制定系列澳门城市规划。

第一期与第二期的分界，是1840年鸦片战争爆发，关闸之战使得清政府首次失却对澳门的军事控制权。第二期与第三期的分界，是1911年澳葡当局完全占据路环岛，至此葡萄牙人已经完全占据了一直延续至回归前的澳门市全部属地。第三期与第四期的分界，是1974年葡萄牙"四二五革命"，葡萄牙在澳门的殖民政策逐渐走向消亡。

2 澳门城市规划过程及其内容

2.1 天主教城，城市规划的萌芽期（1557—1840）

澳门具体开埠的年代一直受历史学家争议。1557年澳门正式开通为商埠这一观点现在普遍被接受，这一年葡萄牙与广东海道达成协议。此后葡萄牙人将澳门作为其对远东贸易的据点，大批葡人涌入澳门。1586年，印度总督达罗卡伯爵在信中正式赐名为"上帝圣名之城"，澳门被升格为拥有和其他受殖民统治城市同等自由、荣誉和显著地位的城市，由市民选举产生统治者。葡萄牙人带来了西方中世纪的城市规划与建设技术，产生了澳门近现代城市规划的萌芽。由于澳门是葡萄牙人在中国的居留地，中葡双方各设行政机构，澳门城市在已经形成的以西方中世纪模式为主体的城市骨架上又生成了受中国影响的城市组织。

从澳门的历史地图中我们可以看出，澳门的城市空间结构主要是延续了葡萄牙城市空间结构特点。其表现为特有的一条主要的"直街"的线性与不规则的结构，而且有一连串的由教堂来画龙点睛的"前地"，这恰恰是葡萄牙中世纪——文艺复兴时期城市的标志。这种模式延续了葡萄牙人的筑城传统。教堂和前地有助于规划城市的布局，葡人进行城市建设主要由澳门议事局完成。

这段时期尽管葡萄牙人对澳门没有实施具体的城市规划，但澳门仍承袭了葡萄牙中世纪城市模式，城市已经基本形成以花地玛堂、花王堂、望德堂、大堂和圣老楞佐堂为中心的五个堂区，以堂区为中心不断发展居民区，至今澳门城市行政分区仍沿用这五个堂区。同时形成了以圣玫瑰堂和水坑尾城门为主的商业中心。[①]

2.2 殖民开发，城市改造与扩张规划期（1840—1911）

1840年鸦片战争以后，中国开始沦为半封建半殖民地国家。葡萄牙人通过强制性的军事占领，扩大其在华的殖民利益空间，逐步占领一直延续至回归前的澳门市全部属地，也就是今天的澳门半岛、氹仔和路环。同时澳门作为中国南海商贸中心的港口地位被迅速崛起的香港取而代之。

---

① 黄就顺，邓汉增，黄均燊，等．澳门地理[M]．澳门：澳门基金会出版，1993．

2.2.1 城市环境改造

1867年葡萄牙在海外领地建立工务司。1883年,由当时的工务局局长 Constantino Jose de Brito 担任主席的"澳门城市改善研究委员会"提交了一份报告,以文字的形式对澳门城市进行了总体规划。该报告中包含城市建设12个方面的指导性纲要,制定了许多与澳门居民生活息息相关的措施,其中包括:改善街道宽度和建筑物高度、制定未来道路线路、清除粪便、铺设管道、净化水源、改善居民内部卫生条件、外墙粉刷、道路绿化、花园整治等。

市政当局遵从城市改造原则,完善道路、广场、花园及现有建筑物,并建设新的道路、广场和花园,使得整个城市卫生、美观、舒适,同时还对新桥、龙田、沙梨头、塔石、美基、和隆及望德堂区实施了总体改善和更新计划。葡人称这些法令和措施为"改良风景"。

2.2.2 南北拓展、填海造地的水陆并进式城市扩张

鸦片战争以后澳葡当局以向南北拓展的方式入侵中国村庄,为下一阶段的城建开发奠定了基础,同时有意识地进行土地征用计划,以为新区的城建开发创造条件。被征地段交予议事会及工务局进行城建开发,制订在该区域的治理计划。随着殖民扩张的成功,市政府将澳门、青洲、氹仔、路环四岛结合起来统一规划,澳门城市建设开始在有统一性、整体性原则的指导下全面展开。

2.2.3 殖民色彩的土地利用模式

澳门土地利用模式反映了受殖民统治的城市特点。半岛核心地带是殖民统治的行政中心。商业区位于葡人居住区和华人居住区之间,可以充分发挥商业区的功能作用。北部是华人居住区和工业用地。氹仔和路环二岛以郊区农村为主。

可以看出,澳门城市从19世纪中叶开始,经过一系列城市规划政策的实施,结束了自发成市的局面。城市在原有的基础上,进行了开发新道路、完善旧城区交通、颁布建筑管理规章、新区规划、铺设下水道、设置街灯、整治海岸线、重新规划瘟疫区等工程,使得澳门城市形成了商业区、住宅区、工业区、行政机关的近代都市格局。

2.3 制定法规,城市规划制度完善时期(1911—1974)

2.3.1 城市建设制度的确立

"二战"以后澳门经济发展疲弱,只是进行一些局部性规划。1963年7月31日,经过不断修订、废止、重编,审议通过了《都市建设总规章》,这是从1912年《澳门私人工程服务暨都市建筑物之卫生服务规章》演进而来,因此可以说是葡萄牙建筑规章的本地化产物,它使得建筑质量立法化,这部法规一直到今天仍具有法律效用。

2.3.2 港口规划

在夺取澳门的管制权后,葡萄牙人开始寻求对澳门的发展,此时的葡人已经意识到英占的香港经过40多年的发展,已经逐步取代了澳门昔日的地位,因此对澳门城市环境及港口的改善与规划刻不容缓。于是在19世纪末20世纪初,围绕着港口及城市规划的设计报告接连不断地产生,这奠定了20世纪上半叶澳门城市的规模。1918年澳门港口改良委员会成立,并于1920年制定了澳门港工程总规划,此后它不断地对澳门港口以及新的填海区进行规划。

2.4 自治规划,城市规划的本地化发展时期(1974—1999)

1974年葡萄牙"四二五"革命之后,宣布实施非殖民地政策,两年后葡萄牙颁布了赋予澳门地区自治权的《澳门组织章程》,承认澳门是葡萄牙管治下的中国领土。[①] 澳门主权问题逐步得到解决,城市规划走向本地化的发展时期。

---

① 黄汉强,吴志良. 澳门总览[M]. 北京:中国友谊出版公司,1994.

2.4.1 城市规划法律的本地化

随着澳门城市规划法令本地化的展开,1976年澳门政府通过了第一部历史建筑保护法,并创立了澳门遗产保护委员会,1980年澳门自行制定了《土地法》,相关领域法律的本地化逐渐展开。1981年建立路环完全保护区,1984年通过了《保护建筑、风景和文化遗产的法律规定》。1986年,澳门政府完成了《澳门地区指导性规划》,但这是政府发出的传阅式文件,不具有法律约束力。

2.4.2 土地利用的分区规划及港口规划

根据规划需要将澳门半岛分成8个分区,氹仔分成6个分区,针对不同分区制定相应的土地规划。澳门西北区土地主要为政府地,用途是工业用地。澳门东北区主要为填海新区,规划条例和西北区一样。外港区发展和用途根据外港新填海区规章发展。南湾区主要作为商业和旅游用地。新马路、松山、西望洋山区主要是以往的商业贸易活动区,保留着许多20世纪初的建筑物,因此大部分区已作为文物保护区。氹仔分为市中心区、西北区、旧城区、圣母湾区和东北区。其中旧城区保留原有村落的结构形式,尽量保留历史风貌。路环主要是作为澳门休闲旅游开发区,设置了保护区加以控制规划。这些分区规划可供澳门今后20年发展使用。

大型计划协调司1989年解散后,由城市规划厅制定了一系列港口分区规划,对澳门城市的边缘进行了规定。填海造地的计划仍在进行,20世纪90年代还制订了氹仔北部城市化计划、氹仔北安湾填海计划及氹仔圣母湾填海计划,澳门城市形状和面积日益变化。

2.4.3 城市对外交通的发展

1988年澳门政府进行市政架构改革,彻底结束了带有殖民色彩的市政制度,澳门城市规划体制完全本地化。城市空间如何拓展一直是个不断被探讨的课题。1968年落成了路氹连贯公路;1974年建成的嘉乐庇大桥将澳门半岛和氹仔联系起来,促使城市人口向氹仔流动;1994年建成第二座澳氹大桥——友谊大桥;1995年启用澳门国际机场;1997年完成《香港大屿山至澳门、珠海跨海大桥初步规划》;1999年与2000年连接澳门与珠海的横琴、莲花大桥相继启用。这些重大对外交通设施的建立以及对外交通规划的制定,为澳门城市空间发展带来了新的契机,逐步改变了澳门寸土寸金、地狭人稠的局面。

3 澳门城市规划的特征分析

3.1 澳门城市规划发展历程的整体性

若以西方、外来殖民思想的引入作为中国近现代城市规划的开始,那么澳门的"近现代"足足比中国其他受殖民统治的城市提前了近300年。由于葡萄牙的国际地位和影响,澳门城市没有受到两次世界大战和外国侵略战争的冲击,城市规划发展不像内陆大多数城市那样具有跳跃式发展特性,其城市规划发展历程具有连续性和整体性特征。虽然澳门从主权上已经归属于中国,但其城市发展历程的特殊性使得它从属于世界城市史的范畴。

3.2 承袭葡萄牙城市规划思想

由于澳门曾受葡萄牙的殖民统治,所以一直到20世纪后半叶都承袭葡萄牙的规划法规和政策,其规划发展深受葡萄牙规划制度的影响。从历史上看,虽然是从1887年中葡签订《中葡和好通商条约》以后葡国才在澳门完全夺取管制权,但是这400多年来城市规划及发展方面一直都是葡萄牙城建规划体制起着决定性作用。这和香港、台湾等地有着本质的不同,日本占据台湾时其城市已经形成规模。[①] 值得一提的是,尽管澳门的规划思想是葡式的,但是在建筑单体、装饰构造等方面却带有中式特点,多元文化经过历史的沉淀与堆积,形成了今天的澳门。

---

① 董鉴泓.城市规划历史与理论研究[M].上海:同济大学出版社,1999.

3.3 详尽系统的城市规划观念

学术界一直有这样的观点,认为澳门完全是自发而建的城市。然而分析澳门城市规划历程,我们可以看出澳门城市规划总体上来说是沿着系统和完善的道路发展的,不同的历史时期有着因时因地制宜的城市规划大纲,并针对不同时期的城市建设有相应的部门进行规划指导和制定。这些规划工作对澳门城市化进程起到了至关重要的作用,而且为维持澳门本地区独有特色奠定了一定的基础。

3.4 缺乏具有法律效应的城市规划法

虽然澳门不断地制定城市规划,但迄今为止,澳门仍未公布一个囊括整个澳门半岛及路氹的总体规划来明确和规范城市发展的模式和方向。负责澳门规划事务的土地工务运输司对澳门有整体规划考虑,但没有对外公开,他们认为这样便于开发政策的调整和规划方案的修改。澳门的城市规划总是以分区规划的形式出现,而且还没有制定澳门本地化专门性的城市规划法,这样难免带来各个区域发展的不平衡与不协调。现有的城市建设仅仅按照1963年的《都市建设总规章》来进行,而这个规章大体上是葡萄牙城市建设规章的翻版,和当今城市化进程大大脱节,急需重新修订。

3.5 规划—先期规划—规划的无穷循环

由于缺乏一部具有法律效应的城市规划法,澳门城市规划的约束力有限。往往会发生这样的情况:关于一个城市总体规划的研究由草图变成了待修订的先期规划,由先期规划的修订图再到待重审的、已做过修订的先期规划;再由对已被修订的先期规划的重审图样,到对已被修订的规划,如此往复,形成一个规划—先期规划—规划的无穷循环。这样的规划与现实脱节且无任何法律效力,甚至对于同一地点同时存在多个研究、草图与先期规划。内港区就于1990年、1995年先后制定过重整规划。由于一些政策利益上的关系,城市规划有时陷入规划—先期规划—规划的无穷循环中。

4 结语

回顾澳门的城市发展历程,20世纪上半叶是澳门城市建设的繁荣时期,也是澳门今天城市发展的基础。由于葡萄牙在"二战"期间是中立国,澳门在两次世界大战期间没有遭到太多战争的破坏,城市建设稳步发展。在政治、经济和文化等多重因素的影响下,它由16世纪西欧中世纪式城建格局完成了向近代大都市化的城市结构的转变;从一个东方的欧洲城市逐步演变成一个东西方文化融合的城市。总的说来,澳门城市规划理论还是比较系统和全面的。虽然它也有不足之处,但还是对澳门城市化进程起到了很好的促进和引导作用。在以后的城市发展中,城市规划工作仍需不断完善和加强,以期从根本上维持澳门独特的城市形象和城市质量。

共享建筑遗产:委员会、城市及案例

Shared Built Heritage: the Committee, Cities, and Urban Redevelopment Case

西格弗里德·安德斯 教授
ICOMOS 共享遗产委员会主席
Prof. Siegfried Enders
President of ICOMOS International Scientific Committee on Shared Built Heritage

The Initiative of the ICOMOS-ISC

The initiative for the foundation of an ICOMOS International Scientific Committee on this issue came for the predominant part from the colleagues of ICOMOS Netherlands.

The colonial time figures prominently the history of the Netherlands and founded the prosperity and development of the country today in all aspects but mainly economic, social and cultural. The dealings with this heritage and its relics in all aspects of public and private life in the Netherlands affects to a great extent social life, politics and also science of history. The raising globalization might have been a motivation for the colleagues in the Netherlands to try to share their experience and practice with others, who are dealing with the same issue, mainly of former colonial powers and colonies in the world. The first activities of the Netherlands had been carried out by a (governmental) institution for the improvement of building and planning in developing countries.

In this regard and against this background this institution was constantly looking for new action fields, activities and jobs. It turned out that a research and training course on "Integrated Urban Revitalization and Heritage in Sri Lanka" was organized in cooperation with the State Conservation Authority (Netherlands Department for Conservation, NDC) and various Building, Planning and Heritage Authorities in Sri Lanka (1995).

Paralleling a technical assistance project, "Galle Heritage Project" was started by the Government of the Netherlands and an International Seminar "European Architecture and Town Planning outside Europe (Dutch Period)" took place in Colombo (Feb. 24-28, 1995). As an outcome of this seminar the "Declaration of Colombo on safeguarding of physical heritage deriving from Dutch contact with Asia" was given. As a part of it one will find the "Recommendation for ICOMOS to form an International Committee on Colonial Settlements/ Buildings of Dual Parentage/Mutual Heritage under ICOMOS Scientific Committees".

Development policy and economic interest issues met interest of science of history and together were looking for an international scientific awareness. ICOMOS Netherlands and ICOMOS Sri Lanka(at that time incumbent of ICOMOS world presidency) worked together under the leadership of the colleagues of the Netherlands and initiated the founding of a new ICOMOS International Scientific Committee in 1998. In its first statutes, the committee formulated the objectives and tasks.

1998—2001

The committee grew quickly and for the next meeting in Cape Town, South Africa Jan. 15-17, 1999 14 participants could be welcome. One of the main issue for this meeting was the discussion of the research on a development plan for the oldest mission station and settlement of the Moravian Society in the Cape, Genadendal. This project turned out to be one of the most important development projects of the Netherlands for the next 20 years. In 2011 the members of ISC SBH could visit Genadendal again and discuss the success of an outstanding urban conservation project.

In 1999 (Oct. 16 - 23), during the ICOMOS General Assembly in Mexico (Mexico City and Guadalaraja) the committee met again and decided besides other organizational issues to "start a new series of biennial publication (a journal) on mutual heritage". The scientific approach to the issue was already formulated in the first statutes.

In 2000, an international workshop in Galle, Sri Lanka (4 May-7 May) was a first attempt to find a proper balance between lectures and advisory work. The workshop focused on the discussion of the treatment of a protected site of Galle which became later a UNESCO World Heritage site, the Fort and Harbor. It was very well described and analyzed but the local government seemed to need other means for the implementation of conservation schemes. Main items of the agenda of the meeting were therefore the drafting of a master plan and the discussion about how to organize political commitments, identification of pilot projects, public awareness and economic feasibility.

In 2000 ICOMOS Argentina and the University of Buenos Aires have taken the initiative to introduce the activities of the Scientific Committee to students and scholars in South America. On September 1st 2,000 lectures were given for graduate and post-graduate students in the Faculty of Architecture.

The *Report of the Chair of SCAT* indicate in 2000 53 members, 10 from Asia and Australia, 16 from Europe, 11 from Africa and 15 from America and the Caribbean's.

The destiny of a scientific committee is very often much linked with the engagement of a single person. In the case of the International Scientific Committee on Shared Colonial Architecture and Town Planning this was Prof. Frits van Voorden, a professor of the Faculty of Architecture, TU Delft, the late President of the Netherlands National Committee of ICOMOS and the President of the Cultural Department of the Dutch National UNESCO Commission. Unfortunately, and very sadly Prof. Frits van Voorden passed away unexpectedly on November 27th, 2001 and all the activities of the committee came to a stop.

2002—2005

It took nearly one year to find and elect a new President which happened at the annual meeting December 4th, 2002 at the ICOMOS General Assembly in Madrid. 10 members attended the meeting and discussed the future of the scientific committee. The name of the committee was changed to "International Scientific Committee on SHARED COLONIAL Architecture". At that time there was already some resistance against the word "colonial", especially from the members of Indonesia and South Africa. The new chairman proposed for the action plan of the committee a so-called "Round Table Professional Forum" in order to use the expertise of the ICOMOS members to discuss the treatment of shared colonial heritage with the local representatives, decision-makers and stake holders.

In 2003, the board changed the name of the committee from SHARED COLONIAL to SHARED BUILT HERITAGE without consulting the members. The main reason was an application of the board of the committee for subsidy from the Dutch government who required to delete the word COLONIAL in the name of the committee as a condition for any subsidy.

The first Round Table Forum, which was planned to take place in Elmina, Ghana October 22-24, 2003 had to be cancelled (postponed) due to the lack of funds. Instead the board was able to initiate and organize one in Melaka (Malacca), Malaysia February 12-19, 2004. Melaka, a town in Malaysia with very interesting shared built heritage is a melting pot of culture, architecture and cuisine. It has Malay, Chinese, Portuguese, Dutch and British built heritage. In 2008 Melaka was inscribed together with George Town, Penang in the UNESCO World Heritage List. The SHARED aspect in the "living multicultural heritage and tradition of Asia" is a main issue of the OUV. In 2014, ten years after the Forum, members of a study tour of ICOMOS ISC SBH could allow themselves to be convinced of the success of the urban conservation process in Melaka. The impression of the historic part of the city was excellent. Most of the heritage buildings had been renovated and restored and had got an adapted new use. The infrastructure seemed to work well. However, ten-year urban development also led to the well-known problems tourism could create.

图1 马六甲世界遗产地的核心区与缓冲区

In 2005, the next Shared Built Heritage Forum was proposed to be held in Qingdao, China. Unfortunately, this couldn't be officially organized, however, about 10 members of the SBH committee managed to visit the place on their way to the General Assembly in Xi'an and made a study tour to the shared built heritage in Qingdao with the help of the guidance of some Chinese ICOMOS members.

2006—2009

In the years between 2006 and 2009 the activities of the committee focused more on the theoretical part and the discussion for the future of the committee. Many members lost interest in the committee including the chairman, who disappeared to other commitments. A new chairman from the Netherlands was appointed and encouraged the members to continue in their work. On two (annual) meetings during the General Assemblies (Xi'an 2005, Quebec 2008) and several Bureau, strategical meetings and workshops (in Amsterdam, Darmstadt, Wiesbaden and Amsterdam) the main issue of the discussion was the definition of the name of the committee in context with the "mission", the task and its formulation in the statutes.

This discussion about the mission and the task of the committee began with the "definition" in the first statutes of the committee in 1998, and could be found in the formulation of the "Objectives" ... to "identify and value/revalue monuments, sites, and landscapes of mutual heritage". "Colonial Architecture and Town Planning" was considered to be mutual heritage. The statutes were not changed and reviewed until 2006. In 2002, when the name of the committee was changed first to "Shared Colonial Heritage" Committee and later to "Shared Built Heritage" the definition was added in formulations like "it focuses on the shared or mutual colonial heritage around the world" or in the Mission. The committee "wishes to assist…in safeguarding, management and documentation of (shared) heritage to promote the integration of the (shared) heritage in today's social and economic life".

In the meantime, the idea of "shared" (built) "heritage" appeared in the scientific as well as in the political world. In 2005, the Council of Europe formulated the Faro Convention (a Framework Convention on the Value of Cultural Heritage for Society). It involved many "shared" aspects and how to deal with heritage inherited from other countries, e.g. by shifting the borders.

In 2006, the statutes of ISC SBH had to be reviewed according to the Eger-Xi-an Principles of ICOMOS and a given context that all scientific committees had to be followed. A draft of the statutes was circulated among the members. The first point of all statutes for the ICOMOS scientific committees was the "definition" of their issue, in the case of ISC SBH: "Shared Built Heritage includes historic urban and rural structures or elements, resulting from multi-cultural influence". On a Workshop in Wiesbaden 2008 the draft of the statutes was final discussed and adopted.

In 2009, ISC SBH returned to organize conferences and study tours and to build up an international network of experts working onor with shared built heritage.

2010—2017

In 2010, International Conference of ICOMOS SBH on Shared Heritage in Historic Cultural Landscapes was held in Surinam, theming in "A new life for historic cultural landscapes: examples of creative policy plans". The conference focused on the treatment of shared built heritage in a historic cultural landscape and their possible integration in the planning process for the regional and land-use planning, as well as outstanding conservation and restoration work on heritage buildings within the UNESCO World Heritage site of Paramaribo.

The issue of the treatment of historic cultural landscapes with a shared heritage aspect could be helpful to discuss the upcoming problem for the preservation of the elements of historic cultural landscapes of former plantations, which lost their function due to the change of economic development around the world. The comments and recommendation given by the conference and ISC SBH were quite helpful for the decision-makers and stakeholders.

In 2011, ISC Shared Built Heritage Conference (July 4-8, 2011) was held in Cape Town, South Africa. The conference addressed issues concerning the treatment of shared built heritage in theory and praxis on heritage buildings, urban and rural patterns and historic cultural landscape in Africa. A significant concern focused on intangible heritage, which turned out to be a very essential part of heritage in Africa. A Conclusion of the Meeting on Shared Built heritage in Africa was worked out by the participants in the symposium and published.

In 2011 there was also a mAAN Seoul Conference—Our Living Heritage: Modern Industrial Buildings and Sites of Asia. With regard to the mission of ISC SBH, i. e. "to support public and private organizations world-wide in raising awareness, safeguarding, management and documentation of shared built heritage". ISC SBH is to cooperate and participate in activities of other scientific committees of ICOMOS, Universities and Institutions for the preservation of shared built heritage. A declaration on Industrial Heritage in Asia was the first time announced in the mAAN Seoul 2011 International Conference.

In 2012 ISC SBH focused its activities on China. In the 2nd half of 19th century and the beginning of the 20th century there have been 38 foreign enclaves (Austria-Hungary 1, Belgium 1, France 6, Germany 3, Italy 1, Japan 8, Portugal 1, Russia 4, UK 11, US 2) and 3 international enclaves (Shanghai, Beijing, Gulangyu) in form of colonies and concessions in China. The last city under colonial rule, Macao, was handed over in 1999. Consequent to the history there is a lot of built heritage with a shared aspect in China, which is getting more and more attention of conservationists, architects, planners and developers. ISC SBH was invited by ICOMOS China and some local governments, NGO's and Universities to visit some of those former foreign enclaves and share its view with the local colleagues on the treatment of the shared built heritage.

In October, 2012, ISC-SBH was invited by the local government of Xiamen and ICOMOS China for a seminar and to pay a visit on this island next to Xiamen and discuss the preservation of the shared built heritage. This was also due to the application for listing Gulangyu on the UNESCO WH List. Gulangyu is a little island next to the island and city of Xiamen (Amoy) and has a lot of shared built heritage with a mixture of Western and traditional Chinese cultures.

Then ISC SBH was invited by ICOMOS China, Huazhong University of Science and Technology to participate in a workshop concerning the shared built heritage in the City of Wuhan. Wuhan at the Yangtze River, nearly in the geographical middle of China, is a city with a long history, consisting of three towns, i. e. Wuchang, Hankou and Hanyang, separated by the Changjiang River and Han River. During the Second Opium War(1856—1860), the government of the Qing dynasty was defeated by the western powers and signed the *Treaties of Tianjin* and the *Convention of Peking*, which stipulated eleven cities or regions as trading ports. Among them Hankou became an open trading port. In 1861 Britain was permitted to set up its British Concession with a consulate. France, Russia, Germany and Japan followed.

During the WW Ⅱ Wuhan was a key center along the Yangtze river and an important base for Japanese operations in China. Although Wuhan was heavily bombed by American bombers, most of the colonial architectures survived in the former concessions, except in the Japanese one. Besides the historic urban structure in its street pattern and infrastructure, many typical buildings in a quite outstanding architectural design have survived. Unfortunately high-rise buildings invaded because of the urban development the historic urban structure in some parts of the former concession areas.

In the rapid urban development of Wuhan to a 10-million-people modern metropolis since 1990, planners, architects, historians and decision-makers were looking for some significance and got aware of the former concessions. The Architectural Faculty of Huazhong University of Science and Technology

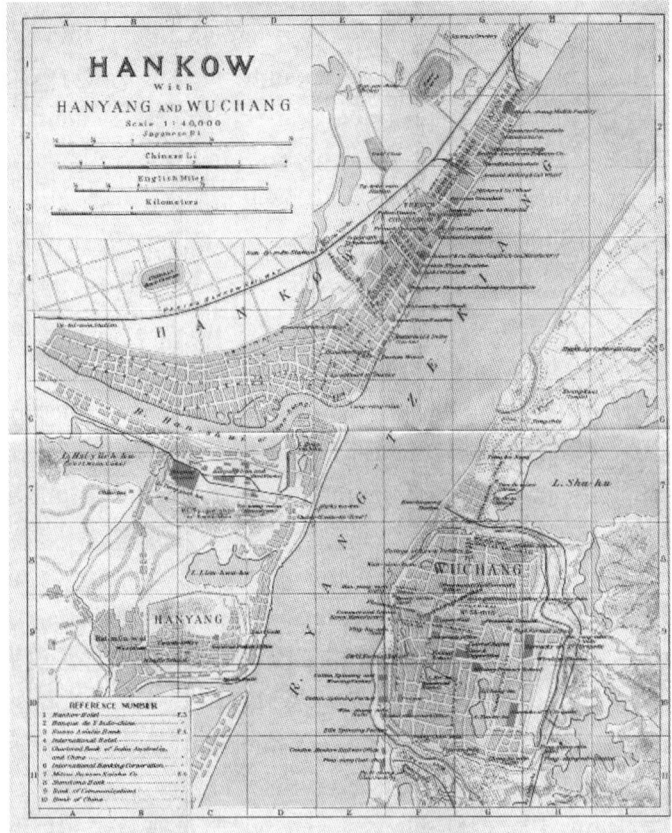

图 2 原汉口五国租界区域示意图

started to address the preservation of this shared built heritage and its integration into the urban planning process of the growing metropolis. In the Crossover Forums five symposiums were organized in which the preservation of heritage architectures, industrial heritage, historic cultural landscapes and the establishment of a cultural route were discussed on an international level. Since 2012, every year a Crossover Forum was organized with the help of ISC SBH and two more universities of Wuhan, i. e. The Central China Normal University and Wuhan University and the city administration.

To organize and manage these crossover forums, a Research Center for Shared Built Heritage—ICOMOS Wuhan Research Center on Shared Built Heritage was founded in 2013 by the help of ISC SBH, ICOMOS China, three Universities in Wuhan and the municipal government, under the auspices of ICOMOS International Scientific Committee on Shared Built Heritage (ICOMOS ISC-SBH). Besides the organizing of the crossover forums, international and Chinese colleagues have been involved in consulting the city government and other institutions in heritage issues. The restoration and conservation of James Jackson Gymnasium, designed by an American Missionary Architect, John van Wie Bergamini, an unique shared built heritage which combines Chinese and Western architecture as was demonstrated by the traditional curved roof, and Western architecture, which can be seen clearly in its interior design was supervised by the colleagues of the research center.

Also in 2012, a symposium was organized by ICOMOS China and ISC SBH in Beijing focusing on the heritage conservation management of the campus of Tsinghua University. After that, ICOMOS China kindly organized a day trip to Tianjin, a harbor city near Beijing.

In 2013, "Military Heritage in the Americas: Research, Preservation and valuing" was held in Cuba, organized by ICOMOS Cuba, Cuban National Council of Cultural Patrimony with the International Scientific Committees for Fortifications and Military Heritage (ICoFort) and ICOMOS ISC Shared Built Heritage (Feb. 11-15, 2013). The period between 1400 up to 1950 was an era of European empire expansion. Traders sailed around the globe and built trading posts, fortresses, administrative buildings, churches, new towns, etc. East Indian companies were the first multinationals in the world. They have left behind heritage, both tangible and intangible, of which we are witnesses today. Fortresses are one of the oldest evidence of this expansion. The castles, fortresses and fortified cities along the West Coast of Africa, in Asia and in Latin America are unique examples of mankind's heritage. They tell us the varied stories of the past. Forts, fortifications, walled and fortified urban structures with a "shared heritage" background are all over the world, mainly in the former colonies of North-Middle and South America, Africa, Middle East, Asia and Australia. These architecture and urban structure are characterized by diversity of European influence (Portuguese, Spanish, Dutch, British, French, German, Swedish,) and profited of the skills, techniques and design of the local and indigenous people when they were constructed.

In 2014, the Workshop: "Shared Built Heritage" was jointly held by ICOMOS ISC Shared Built Heritage, ICOMOS ISC Theory & Philosophy of Conservation and Preservation, and Chair of Global Art History, Heidelberg University in Institute of Art History, Max-Planck-Institute, Florence (Nov. 14-15, 2014). This two-day workshop aimed to discuss the challenges, approaches and methods, and the multilayered value structures involved which are grouped around term that has given the specific ICOMOS Scientific Committee (ISC) a name— Shared Built Heritage(SBH).

The discussion was structured by 4 headlines under which a theoretical discussion on shared built heritage was supposed to take place.

1. "Shared"-"Built"-"Heritage": Reflections of Difficult Terms

   This section re-evaluates the internal development of the Committee as regards terms, definitions, workshops, and meetings; investigates the general issue of heritage "participation" in (inter)national doctrines, charters, and conventions; and discusses the crucial terms "Shared" (inclusive, pluralistic vs colonial, hegemonic, top-down?), "Built" (tangible vs. intangible?), and "Heritage" (who inherits, who is excluded before/during and after the changes of regimes and their ideologies?).

2. Negotiating Periods of Significance(s)

   Not only on the national level, but also on the global level of UNESCO's World Heritage guidelines, strictly assigned determinations of a so-called period of significance create especially heavy conflicts within "Shared Built Heritage" configurations. Is it the original (colonial) monument as a historic source of architectural history or this monument's ongoing and dynamic increase in (various?) significance(s) through post-colonial appropriation and contemporary use values which should define protection and preservation guidelines?

3. Balancing Stakeholders' Interests

   Especially within "Shared Built Heritage" structures and ensembles after regime/ideology changes, the different interests of local stakeholders, of regional cultural traditions and peculiarities, of national administration and (economic, touristic) exploitation, and finally (short-term) international expertise following globalized heritage doctrines all create a multi-layered and often heavily contested complex. Balancing these different interests is an enormous challenge and requires long experience of cultural and political mediation, such as community hearings to workshops and conferences. Do we need other, more subtle instruments in this specific case?

4. Building Strategies-Structural Interventions-Short/Long-term Effects

Local knowledge, regional traditions of craftsmanship, the user's site-specific strategies of use and ongoing structural add-on interventions are increasingly acknowledged in internationalist "living heritage" policies, but in reality often clash with museological "embalming" strategies of historic monuments. Additionally, commercialization and "heritagization" processes (especially in declared National Protected Monuments up to the level of World Heritage Sites) often create social segregation on site. Do "Shared Built Heritage" monuments and sites need a specific sensibility and an open-process mentality with regard to structural interventions and long-term effects? The papers given under the four sections, mostly based on case studies of the treatment of shared built heritage around the globe, gave a lot of impulse and showed that the discussion has to go on.

In 2015, ISC SBH organized a Japan Study Tour to Shared Built Heritage. After the Meiji Restauration in 1868, Japan adopted a lot of foreign (Western) influences in almost all aspects of life, in science and industrialization and from clothes to food, entertainment to architecture. The fast growing industry, the new administration of the new government, the schools and universities, the army and the growing population needed many new buildings, which was impossible to be handled in the traditional Japanese way by traditional carpenters and craftsmen. The rebuilding phase in this social change created a very interesting architecture at the end of the 19th and the beginning of the 20th (Meiji, Taisho and Showa Period) century, which was designed by invited foreign architects or Japanese architects and engineers who returned to Japan after being sent to foreign countries to study. The buildings were carried out by Japanese craftsmen, who used their Japanese skills and construction/materials. A real Shared Built Heritage!

Among art and architecture historians, this kind of architecture was scientifically neglected until the 1990s. In 1996 an amendment to the cultural property act was added with a new category of built heritage—Registered Cultural Properties. The two-tier system of National Treasures and Important Cultural Properties was supplemented with a new class of Registered Cultural Properties, meant for items in great need of preservation and use, initially limited to buildings and acting as a waiting list for the list of designated Important Cultural Properties. A large number of mainly industrial and historic residential from the late Edo to the Shōwa period were registered and protected under this system.

The study tour helped us to learn about the Japanese way to protect and treat this built heritage which had a lot of shared aspects. We could meet those colleagues, who were in charge of the conservation jobs and discuss their concepts and work with them. A special concern was given to the churches around Nagasaki. There was an interesting discussion about their OUV for the application for UNESCO WHL as witnesses for a unique heritage issue: The hiding or survival of living Christianity in feudal Buddhist and Shintoist Japan for more than 200 years.

In 2016, ISC SBH organized the Study Tour: "2000 Year Shared Built Heritage in Central Europe-Border Region Germany-France-Luxemburg" in cooperation with the national committees of ICOMOS Germany, France and Luxemburg (Sept. 4-12, 2016). The study tour started in Trier, where besides the Roman relicts (Porta Nigra, Basilica, Roman bridge) the history of the restoration and conservation of the cathedral attracted the experts, went on to the late Baroque style palace and smelter Weilerbach, a relic of German, French, Luxembourg history and continued to the Vauban fortifications in Luxembourg. Shared Built Heritage of the 20th century was visited in Berus, at the French-German border: a former French Radio Station for Europe and in Saarbrucken, former French Administration Buildings (former French Embassy) relicts of the post 2nd WW history. In Metz and Strasburg, the focus of the study tour was on the German urban extension areas of the late 19th and early 20th century with outstanding architecture designed by French, German and other European architects. The German Empire was anxious to send the best architects of that time to the "new territories" after 1871, which explained the high quality of the architectural design. The European unification movement might be responsible for the growing acceptance of the shared aspect in this built heritage and it was very exciting for us to discuss the application dossier for UNESCO WHL with colleagues.

Also in 2016, ISC SBH organized a Study Tour to Nova Scotia, Canada (Sept. 15-24, 2016). Nova Scotia is an area in Canada where different immigrants from Europe, America and through the US also Africa settled. They created a built heritage consisted of elements which initially came from their countries they migrated from, adjusted to the climate here and mixed with the ones others brought with them. The 10-day study tour began in southern Nova Scotia's area, where Acadian and early British / loyalist / protestant German immigration started, then moved northwards to Cape Breton to visit the 19th-century Scottish and Irish communities and finished with a one-day visit to the Fortress of Louisburg National Historic Site, a French colonial early-mid 18th-century fortified port which had been partially reconstructed. Places which had been visited: Halifax, Annanopolis, Fort Edward, Uniacke Estate, Digby, Yarmouth, Shelburne, Lunenburg, Mahone Bay, Louisburg, Sydney.

In 2017, two big events took place for ISC SBH: a congress on shared built heritage at the University of Lisbon, Portugal, a study tour to Évora and the Annual Meeting and a study tour and seminar to shared built heritage in West Bengal, India.

Study tour to Évora and Annual Meeting 2017 (July 4, 2017) was associated with the congress on shared built heritage in Lisbon, Portugal (July 5-8, 2017). The committee was invited by the City of Évora and the Direção Regional da Cultura do Alentejo, to visit the UNESCO WH-site and the University City and held its Annual Meeting 2017 in the University. Congress on Shared Built Heritage, organized by ARTIS-Institute of History of Art, School of Arts and Humanities of the University of Lisbon, ICOMOS Portugal and ICOMOS-ISC-SBH: "Preserving Transcultural Heritage: Your Way or My Way?" (July 5-8, 2017). Questions on authenticity, identity and patrimonial proceedings in the safeguarding of architectural heritage are created in the meeting of cultures. In three days more than 85 papers on various treatment issues of shared built heritage have been given and discussed in 21 parallel sessions. 131 participants from 33 countries (Africa 3, America 4, Asia 5, Australia 1, Europe 15, Middle East 5). 20 members of ISC SBH attended the congress, and out of 124 speakers and lectures, 11 have been members of ISC SBH.

Issues concerned the various thematic areas of transcultural heritage. Three keynotes and a round table discussion complemented the congress. In addition to the papers and discussion results a book was published. All together the congress produced an enormous amount of excellent information which could be used as a founding for a curriculum to teach about shared built heritage. One of the Congress Tours was a visit to Sintra, the summer resort of the Portuguese royal family, which has outstanding heritage buildings with a shared aspect.

Study Tour and Symposium to Shared Built Heritage in West Bengal, India(Dec. 1-8, 2017) was organized by National Scientific Committee (NSC) for Shared Built Heritage & ICOMOS India East Zone.

The event demonstrated very significant the role of private engagement (NGOs) in heritage protection and management in a week legal and institutional (public) heritage management system. Amazing engagement and enthusiastic acting of people of all generations for heritage issues was overwhelming. In each place where we visited heritage buildings, urban quarters and cities we were welcomed by local and private people, groups and NGOs who showed and explained their conservation projects.

Cities with Shared Built Heritage

UNESCO began the task of listing historic cities on the WHL, since around the early 80s. And ofcourse in those cities—also in former colonies—the built heritage is and was the nucleus of many Urban Renewal Projects, mainly since it is required by UNESCO principals. Today one may identify about 24 historic cities on the WHL with SHARED BUILT HERITAGE, (mostly colonial heritage) around the world.

Share Built Heritage on the World Heritage List: (until 2015)
Africa:
Historic Town of Grand-Bassam (Côte d'Ivoire)
Lamu Old Town (Kenya)
Island of Saint/Louis Tanzania/Zanzibar Stone Town (Senegal)
Asia:
Historic Centre of Macao (China)
Town ofLuang Prabang (Laos)
Melaka & George Town, Historic Cities of the Straits of Malacca (Malaysia)
Historic Town of Vigan (Philippines)
Old Town of Galle and its Fortifications (Sri Lanka)
Hoi An Ancient Town (Vietnam)
Pacific:
Levuka Historical Port Town (Fiji)
Middle America and Caribbean:
Colonial City of Santo Domingo (Dominican Republic)
Historic Centre of Puebla/Historic Town of Guanajuato and Adjacent Mines (Mexico)
South America:
Historic City of Sucre (Bolivia)
Historic Centre of the Town of Olinda/Historic Centre of Salvador de Bahia/Historic Centre of SãoLuís (Brazil)
Historic Quarter of the Seaport City of Valparaíso (Chile)
Historic Centre of Santa Cruz deMompox (Colombia)
City of Quito/Historic Centre of Santa Ana de los Ríos de Cuenca (Ecuador)
Historic Inner City of Paramaribo (Suriname)

The case of the redevelopment in Singapore (Centre and China Town)

In former colonial cities—which are not listed in the WHL-, the treatment of built heritage does not always meet the expected requirement in urban renewal projects: important historic heritage buildings like churches, public buildings, office buildings, banks, department stores, markets, infrastructure (bridges) and sometimes also palaces, houses, apartment buildings might be protected, preserved and nicely renovated but the adapted reuse, a consequence of the urban renewal process, changes quite often completely the character of the place and in many cases the complete interior part of the built heritage and its urban setting. Lack of consideration of necessary buffer zones to high rise structures render the heritage buildings the appearance of being "out of place" that dwarf in comparison to the high-rise structures in the modern urban landscape.

The case of Singapore

Let me give you a quick approach to the history of the urban development by some historic plans of Singapore.

— Jackson Plan for Singapore 1828

— Captain James Franklin's Map 1829

— Thomsons map 1841—1855

— Map of Singapore J. T. Thomson 1848

— Moniot's map 1862

— Singapore 1924

— during the Japanese occupation in the 1940s

— Singapore 1945

— Singapore in the 1970s

The history of Singapore's urban renewal started already before WWII and had since then a continuous development in the last 70 years.

Redevelopment is and was the key issue in urban planning policy in Singapore-the main Urban Planning authority is called since the early 70s "Urban Redevelopment authority"! The tremendous problems of Singapore's housing environment had to be solved in order to develop a functional city which was on its way to become a global business player and international business hub. The mission of urban policy and the Urban Redevelopment Authority was from the very beginning and is "to make Singapore a great city to live, work and play".

In the 1930s there was already a rapidly increasing of the population of Singapore and a bad housing condition. Between the 1940s to the 1950s the previous evil of housing conditions continued to happen. During the 1950s, due to a big movement of migrants from peninsular Malaysia and a baby boom 240,000 squatters were placed in the Singapore. In 1959 overcrowded slums lacked the existence of service sanitation facilities.

In 1958 a master plan had been designed to solve the city problems. However, due to the lack of urban planning experts caused by the deficiency of professional staff, criticism came from many urban practitioners.

In 1961 a professional team—recommended by the United Nations then—was asked by the government to cope with the urban renewal matters and its redevelopment plan.

In the end of 1964 two pilot developments—based on the UN assistance report—were initiated by the government.

August 9,1965, after the Singapore government had been in charge, urban renewal included in the part of the national improvement policy was urgently put in action.

The basic idea of the urban planning policy was to develop huge housing complex in new districts with a kind of independent infrastructure and industrial zones in order to relieve the city center of the overcrowded population and give way for the development of business and economical centers. At that time, it was predictable that the regional and urban planning in Singapore will face the problem of being short of land. In the last 30 years Singapore claimed more than 100,000 sq m new land.

The new PAP (People's Action Party) government—a centre-right party—which is ruling Singapore since 1959 continuously, established urban renewal programs, which were classic urban redevelopment projects—removing the residents to other places, some where outside the city, demolishing the building and giving planning access to developer. However some difficulties were experienced. The obstacles came from the resistance of people who used to live in the slums and squatters, since those people were reluctant to be replaced. This became the major problems of 1960s redevelopment schemes. Affordable land value also became one of its reasons. Another problem was that the government had to purchase the private land owned by the middle and upper society to make the land vacant and be used for redevelopment.

The Central Area redevelopment plan visualized a combination of development public accommodation and infrastructure and private development and business and residential districts were planned. In this concept there was only little space for the preservation of historic houses and structures. In 1964, redeveloping started, finishing in 1982 The government demolished the old buildings in this area and left only a famous Mosque as a national monument of historical conservation

The policy had to be changed. In the late 70s it was the time-due to the rising political pressure by the pushed out residents and rising public awareness for the lost built heritage, when redevelopment was slowly changed to rehabilitation. However most or more or less the entire Chinatown was cleared of the residents and most of the built heritage in the Centre was demolished to give way for the development of business and commercial buildings.

In the 80s Heritage Building came more and more in the focus of urban planning policy. Its value for the raising tourism industry but also as a significant historic part for the improving of a national identity was recognized by the planners, decision makers and stakeholders. The outstanding colonial buildings like the Raffles Hotel, the public buildings, Parliament house, Court House, Hospitals, Banks, Churches and Temple etc. became restored and also the left over and abandoned shop houses of the China Town have been noticed as an important impact into a new urban renewal planning process.

In China Town they stopped the destruction of the shop houses and started a conservation program of the quarter in the late 80s. The importance of the picturesque Chinese Shop houses for tourism but also as an extraordinary living quarter was recognized by developers and their wealthy clients. The main roads turned to the typical tourist attraction with shops, restaurants, pubs and bars while the residential roads became clean and beautiful designed Shop-House streets with historic flavor, but actually without shops. The interior of the houses was changed by modern architects into posh apartments, mostly neglecting entirely the historic structure. Only the facades survived and have been professional restored. Some architects even managed to insert little swimming pools in the air wells of the shop houses.

In the Central district a row of heritage shop houses along the Singapore River was turned into a Disney Land like entertainment quarter. Some other shop houses survived in this former residential district.

The urban renewal project in Singapore is passed by the Urban Redevelopment Authority off as an urban planning success and it seems that in many developing countries it is regarded as one. And many people are happy with it: the authority, the tourist, the developers, the business men and the tourist industry, the new owners of the posh apartments. The former residents however and the spirit of the place disappeared and the memories went into the history books. Some superficial minded person might argue that the built heritage at least from the outside and some of the historic urban structure is "preserved".

Questions raising whether we could share this view. Do all the principles and guidelines for the treatment (conservation and preservation) of built heritage, which were set up by the international heritage community still work?

Could or would shared built heritage (colonial built heritage) get an impact on urban renewal projects in former colonies?

大学与城市

UNIVERSITIES AND CITIES

大学与城市相互促进的武汉建议

2014年10月,第三届"无界论坛"在华中师范大学召开。本届论坛的主题为"大学与城市",来自欧洲、北美、澳洲、亚洲等地的国际著名专家与我国的大学校长、城市市长及专家学者共聚一堂,围绕"文化之道引领城市发展"这一主题展开充分讨论和深入交流,会议达成以下共识:

大学的发展和城市的繁荣应该相互促进、相互成就。城市建设需要文化引领,而大学作为重要的学术和教育机构,一直与城市的繁荣兴衰紧密相连,是城市物质与非物质环境的重要组成部分,是城市创造力和城市活力的重要来源。

我们十分欣喜地看到,这次研讨会集中探讨了以"同济大学与上海文化遗产保护"为代表的以强烈的文化意识引领城市高质量发展的案例,不仅仅对中国,而且对全世界的"大学与城市相互促进"同样有着示范和推动作用。本次论坛代表共同发出"武汉倡议":

1. 整合大学与城市的力量,充分认识到"文化作为生产力"和"文化遗产保护作为城市发展一部分"的重要性和紧迫性,以开放的心态、传承的责任、无界的情怀,通过科学的机制与管理手段,让大学与城市在发展的同时,保护好文化遗产,拥有良好、健康的文化环境、生态环境。

2. 实现研究与实践的相互促进,大学的管理人员和专家学者要更多地关注城市的建设,以促进城市文明发展为己任,以扩大城市影响为己任,以保护文化遗产为己任,在研究和教学中求真务实,为城市的繁荣与发展不遗余力。

3. 实现知识与管理的相互关联,城市的管理者,特别是各级政府,要做好"文化引领城市发展"的"顶层设计",协调好政府、学术团体、企业的力量,建立科学的决策机制,建立科研保障的长效机制,努力展示和挖掘城市文化的价值,让城市成为"显山露水看大学"的美丽城市、智慧城市。

4. 积极构建大学学者、政府官员、大众间的互动平台,积极鼓励城市文化和城市遗产的普及和推广工作,实现决策者与公众的相互了解,政策决策的民主性和科学性的和谐统一。鼓励公众与专家共同参与城市文化建设、遗产保护和利用的宣传,用文化提升地区形象,营造良好社会环境。

以上为论坛全体代表的心声,我们呼唤社会各界人士加入这一行列,共同努力,推动文化建设和遗产保护事业的可持续发展,实现人类文明的永续流传!

论坛组委会

Wuhan Proposal on the Mutual Promotion of Universities & Cities

Development of universities and prosperity of cities should be highly interrelated and mutually reinforced. Urban development needs cultural guidance, and universities, as important academic and educational institutions, have always been closely linked with the prosperity and decline of cities. They are important part of urban material and immaterial environment, and significant sources of urban creativity and vitality.

We notice that a series of culture-led high-quality conservation cases, represented mainly by those projects carried out either by Tongji University or in Shanghai, were discussed and studied in this forum. Their demonstrative and promotive significance could be both national and international.

We herewith declare the Wuhan Proposal on the Mutual Promotion of Universities & Cities:

1. Integrating forces from both universities and cities, we ought to fully understand the importance and urgency to take culture as a productive force, as well as to take heritage conservation as crutial part of urban development. With openness, responsibility and devotion, we are supposed to apply scientific mechanism and administrative approaches in order to safeguard cultural heritage as well as healthy cultural and ecological environment along with the synergic development of universities and cities.

2. We have to realize the mutual promotion of research and practice. Taking the duty to promote urban civilization development, to extend cities' influence and to safeguard urban heritage, administrators and scholars of universities are supposed to pay more attention to urban development and to contribute heart and soul to the prosperity of their cities through pragmatic research and teaching.

3. Correlating knowledge and administration, cities' administrators have to make good top-level designs with fully acknowledgement of culture's leading role in urban development. Scientific decision-making mechanism and long-term mechanism to ensure scientific research should be established with the better coordination among governments, academic institutions and enterprises. We should try our best to discover and present values of urban culture and to make cities beautiful and intelligent with their both natural and cultural landscapes including universities.

4. An interactive platform among scholars, governmental officials and the public ought to be created. With active dissemination and promotion of urban culture and heritage as well as mutual understanding between decision-makers and the public, the harmonious unity of both democratic and scientific policy making could be realized. Common participation in urban culture construction and heritage conservation/utilization promotion by both the public and experts should be encouraged in order to enhance visibility of local cultural and to create better community environment.

上海城市历史文化遗产保护制度概述

A General Review over the Urban Conservation System in Shanghai

伍江 教授
同济大学副校长
Prof. Wu Jiang
Vice President, Tongji University

Urban heritage conservation is a very important part of urban planning and urban development management in Shanghai. This speech gives a general introduction to a formal administrative system that has been made available during the past two decades in Shanghai.

上海长期以来十分重视历史建筑和历史地区的保护工作，建立并逐渐完善了严格的城市历史文化遗产保护管理制度，保护了城市历史风貌，提升了城市品位，弘扬了都市文化，塑造了城市精神，进一步凸显了上海历史文化名城与现代化国际大都市相互交融的独特魅力。

上海市现有13处全国重点文物保护单位、113处市级文物保护单位。并于1989、1994、1999、2005年先后分四批确定了663处，共2 154幢、总面积约400万 m^2 的建筑为"优秀历史建筑"（其中61处为文物保护单位）。

2003年，上海确定了中心城区12个历史文化风貌区，包括外滩、老城厢、人民广场、衡山路—复兴路、南京西路、愚园路、新华路、山阴路、提篮桥、江湾、龙华、虹桥路，总面积为27 km^2，占上海市老城区面积的1/3。2005年上海又确定了郊区及浦东新区的32个历史文化风貌区，总面积约14 km^2。上海的城市历史文化遗产保护工作已逐步形成了一整套行之有效的法律制度和管理机制。

1 上海历史文化遗产保护制度逐步完善的历程

1.1 学术研究为先导

早在20世纪50年代，上海就开始着手进行有关城市建筑历史的"三史"（古代史、近代史和现代史）调查工作，对上海建筑历史特别是近代建筑历史有了初步的归纳，为后来的历史建筑保护工作打下了初步的基础。改革开放后出版的《上海近代建筑史稿》（陈从周、章明主编）和《上海近代城市建筑》（王绍周编著）即为这一工作的记录。

自20世纪80年代起，学术界对上海近代城市和建筑的研究工作逐步展开并不断深入。1993年，罗小未教授指导博士研究生伍江完成博士论文《上海百年建筑史(1840—1949)》，并于1997年正式出版。1999年，郑时龄教授的专著《上海近代建筑风格》出版。这些成果使上海城市建筑文化遗产的基础研究工作走上一个新的台阶。还有阮仪三教授及其领导的国家历史文化名城研究中心，以及同济大学一批教师和研究生对上海外滩、老城厢、提篮桥等历史风貌地区和大量历史建筑所做的长期调查与研究，为上海城市建筑文化遗产的保护打下了重要的学术基础。与此同时，有关上海的社会、经济、历史、文化等方面的学术研究工作在20世纪90年代出现高潮，涌现出一大批学术研究成果，并在国内外掀起一场"上海热"。

"上海学"俨然成为一门显学。这些都有力地支持了上海历史遗产保护工作。

1.2 率先提出保护名单、颁布保护法规

上海历史文化遗产保护工作真正全面展开是20世纪80年代。1986年,上海被国务院批准为第二批国家历史文化名城。1989年,在国家建设部和国家文化局的推动下,上海在广泛征求专家意见的基础上首次提出了优秀近代建筑保护名单。1990年,上海市人民政府正式公布了上海市第一批共59处优秀近代建筑(后来又增补至61处)。由于当时没有相应的法律法规保障,这61处保护建筑只能被列为上海市文物保护单位并参照文物保护的有关规定进行保护与管理。1991年12月,上海市人民政府颁布《上海市优秀近代建筑保护管理办法》,上海初步形成了由规划局、房地资源局和文管委共同负责的管理机制。此后,按照《上海市优秀近代建筑保护管理办法》,1993年、1999年和2005年,上海又陆续公布了第二批175处、第三批162处、第四批230处优秀历史建筑,一批近代产业建筑和新中国成立以后建成的建筑也名列其中;并由规划局负责编制保护建筑的规划控制要求(技术规定)。

除单体建筑保护工作的有序推进之外,上海市还较早地开展了历史风貌特色区域成片保护工作。1991年,上海市规划局开始着手组织编制上海市历史文化名城保护规划,外滩等11片区域被列为历史文化风貌保护区。1999年,上海市规划管理局又组织编制了《上海市中心区历史风貌保护规划(历史建筑与街区)》,对1991年划定的历史文化风貌保护区明确了保护范围和要求,确定了234个街坊、440处历史建筑群共计1 000余万平方米的保护、保留建筑。

1.3 进一步健全法制,强化风貌区整体保护

2002年,上海又在原保护管理办法的基础上通过市人大立法,正式颁布了《上海市历史文化风貌区和优秀历史建筑保护条例》,进一步提高了历史建筑保护的法律地位,并正式在法律层面上明确了历史文化风貌区的保护,同时还将保护建筑的对象由1949年以前建成的近代建筑扩大到包括产业建筑在内的具有30年以上的历史建筑。根据这一条例,上海市人民政府于2003年正式公布了中心城区12片共27 km²的历史文化风貌区。上海市规划局随即组织编制历史文化风貌区保护规划。2004年,《上海市衡山路—复兴路历史文化风貌区保护规划》编制完成并得到市政府正式批准,为上海市历史文化风貌区保护规划的编制作了富有开创性的探索。2005年,上海市中心城区12片历史文化风貌区规划全部编制完成并得到市政府的批准。同年,上海市规划局又开始着手郊区历史文化风貌区的划定工作,32片共14 km²的郊区历史文化风貌区在经过专家反复讨论和公共媒体公示后正式划定。保护规划的编制工作也随即展开。

2003年10月,上海市召开城市规划工作会议,正式提出"建立最严格的历史文化风貌区和优秀历史建筑保护制度",将上海的城市历史文化遗产工作提到了前所未有的高度。2005年,上海市政府正式成立"上海市历史文化风貌区和优秀历史建筑保护委员会",并下设由规划局、房地资源局和文管会组成的办公室。上海城市历史文化遗产保护工作又迈入一个新时期。

2 上海历史文化遗产保护的制度与机制

1992年1月1日起开始施行的《上海市优秀近代建筑保护管理办法》是我国第一部有关近代建筑保护的地方性政府法令。在其颁布实施后的整整11年时间里,一直规范和指导着上海近代建筑的保护工作,对于上海历史建筑的保护起到了非常重要的作用。上海历史文化遗产保护工作的基本原则(其中最重要者如分类保护原则)、制度框架(其中最重要者如规划局、房地局、文管委三个政府部门共同管理、各司其职的管理模式)自此基本形成。

作为一部政府行政法令,其法律地位有一定的局限性。同时,该管理办法仅涉及近代建筑的保护,对于城市大规模改造中成片历史文化风貌的保护难以约束。经过两年多的酝酿和各方面专家的反复讨论,2002年初,上海市人大常委会第36次会议正式开始审议由市规划局等政府部门和有关专家起草的《上海

市历史文化风貌区和优秀历史建筑保护条例(草案)》。2002年7月,上海市人大常委会第41次会议通过该条例,并正式公布于2003年1月1日起施行。自此,上海的历史文化遗产保护工作有了一部真正法律意义上的地方性法规。这部条例在法律层面上确立了上海历史文化遗产保护工作的法律制度、管理体制与运作机制。

2.1 保护原则

该条例不仅是对原管理办法法律地位的提升,也更加完善了原有的管理内容与管理制度。条例明确了上海历史文化风貌区和优秀历史建筑保护工作中"统一规划、分类管理、有效保护、合理利用、利用服从保护"的原则。

2.2 保护对象

根据该条例,上海的保护工作由单体建筑的保护扩展到"历史文化风貌区"的保护,并明确要求规划管理部门应组织编制风貌区保护规划,在法律层面上明确了区域保护的要求。

该条例也扩展了保护对象,由原先对建于1949年以前的"优秀近代建筑"的保护扩展到对建成30年以上的"优秀历史建筑"的保护。条例所确定的保护对象为:(1)建筑样式、施工工艺和工程技术具有建筑艺术特色和科学研究价值;(2)反映上海地域建筑历史文化特点;(3)著名建筑师的代表作品;(4)在我国产业发展史上具有代表性的作坊、商铺、厂房和仓库;(5)其他具有历史文化意义的优秀历史建筑。值得注意的是,该条例在国内首次提出了产业建筑的保护。

2.3 分级保护

在历史建筑保护管理上延续并进一步强调了分类保护原则,即根据保护对象的价值及完好程度分为四个保护等级:第一类,建筑的立面、结构体系、平面布局和内部装饰均不得改变;第二类,建筑的立面、结构体系、基本平面布局和有特色的内部装饰不得改变,其他部分允许改变;第三类,建筑的立面和结构体系不得改变,建筑内部允许改变;第四类,建筑的主要立面不得改变,其他部分允许改变。

2.4 仍存在的问题

《上海市历史文化风貌区和优秀历史建筑保护条例》为上海历史文化遗产的保护设定了基本法律框架,为上海历史文化风貌区与优秀历史建筑保护工作提供了有力的法律保障,同时也留下了一些管理上难以处理的矛盾。目前上海市对历史文化遗产的保护管理是采用由规划、房地、文物三个部门分工、协同管理的体制。文物部门负责文物保护单位的保护管理,房地部门负责优秀历史建筑的保护管理,规划部门负责历史文化风貌区和上述保护建筑的规划管理。但由于文物管理执行的是《文物保护法》,《文物保护法》中的一些规定难以适用于还处在使用状态中的历史建筑,而该条例中的一些行之有效的规定又与《文物法》的个别条款不尽一致。这样对于那些已被确定为文物保护单位的保护建筑就面临着适用法律上的矛盾。为加强各有关行政管理部门的协调,上海市政府在原有三部门沟通协调机制的基础上专门设立了保护委员会办公室,使三个政府部门能够有一个常设的协调机构。

3 上海城市历史文化保护制度的实施与操作

3.1 规划管理

《上海市历史文化风貌区和优秀历史建筑保护条例》为上海的保护工作制度确立了一个总体框架,但在具体管理中还必须有细化的规定与要求。首先,是必须针对历史文化风貌区编制具有法律地位的保护规划,对各保护建筑制定明确的规划管理技术规定,对每一幢保护建筑提出明确的保护要求。

在规划管理上,上海逐步形成了历史文化名城保护规划(总体规划)、历史文化风貌区保护规划(详细规划)、单体保护建筑规划与建设管理及风貌区建筑项目管理等不同层面的规划管理内容。其中,控制性详细规划是最重要的一个环节。它既是对城市历史文化遗产保护总体要求的具体体现,又是具体建设项目规划管理的直接依据。

3.2 建筑管理

据《上海市历史文化风貌区和优秀历史建筑保护条例》,市房屋土地管理部门负责优秀历史建筑的保护管理。为此,市房地资源局组织制定了各保护建筑的具体保护要求,并负责将保护要求和保护义务书面告知房屋所有人、使用人和有关物业管理单位。保护建筑若发生转让、出租行为,转让人、出资人有义务将保护要求书面告知受让人、承租人,受让人、承租人应承担相应的保护义务。若需对保护建筑进行修缮或有任何改扩建等改变保护建筑现状的行为,必须得到有关部门审核批准。若仅涉及建筑内部使用性质和室内布局,由市房地部门负责审核批准,若涉及改变建设工程规划许可证核准内容(如改变建筑的平面布局、立面形式、主体结构、面积、层数、高度等)则必须得到市规划局的审核批准。对于擅自拆除、迁移或不符合保护要求进行修缮的行为,房地管理部门有权责令其限期改正,恢复原状,并可对擅自拆除者处以相当于被拆建筑重置价三到五倍的罚款;对擅自迁移者,处以相当于被迁移建筑重置价一到三倍的罚款;对违反保护要求修缮者,处以该建筑重置价30%以下的罚款。

由于该条例不涉及文物保护单位,因此保护建筑属文物保护单位的,其保护管理由市文物管理部门根据文物保护法并参照《上海市历史文化风貌区和优秀历史建筑保护条例》负责管理。对文物保护单位的修缮工程,若涉及改变建设工程规划许可证核准内容的也必须得到市规划局的审核批准。

4 上海市历史文化风貌区保护规划

根据《上海市历史文化风貌区和优秀历史建筑保护条例》,上海市城市规划管理局从2003年起开始着手组织编制并于2005年完成了各风貌保护区的保护规划。这一规划的编制完成,得到了市政府的及时批准,为上海城市历史文化遗产保护提供了严格、规范并具有很强操作性的依据。

4.1 创新编制模式,强调整体保护,细化控制指标

该规划属于控制性详细规划层面,但又希望超出一般的控制性详细规划深度。它不仅要包括一般控制性详细规划的内容(如用地性质与建设容量控制、道路交通、市政设施、绿化景观、公共设施配套等),同时更突出保护的要求(如保护要素的认定、保护对象的分类、风貌街道与空间的保护等)。建筑尺度适宜且密度适中是历史文化风貌区的一大特点,因此规划明确风貌区内严格控制建筑总量,核心保护区内坚持"原拆原建",即严格保持现有建筑总量,并严格控制风貌区内新建建筑的高度。

城市历史文化风貌的保护不等于最有保护价值的建筑单体的保护。真正意义的城市保护是整体意义的保护。它不仅包括那些重要建筑物的保护,也包括那些重要建筑物所在整体环境的保护,特别是完整历史街区的保护。除建筑物外,道路和街巷格局、街道尺度、街廊景观、城市空间肌理、地块尺度与形状、绿化环境、墙面装饰、地面铺砌、典型材料和色彩等等,都是保护的要素。在建设控制方面,规划首先将风貌区划分为核心保护区和建设控制范围。核心保护区内的建设行为受到更为严格的控制,一般不允许大规模建设,且坚持"原(面积、高度)拆原建"原则。在建设控制范围内,明确只有"允许建造的范围""需要整体规划的范围"和"一般历史建筑""其他建筑"拆除后的空地内才有可能允许新建、改建和扩建行为。在建筑高度控制方面,按"沿街建筑高度""非沿街建筑高度""相邻建筑高度"和"住宅建筑高度"来控制。在建筑密度方面,更多地考虑地块原有密度、周边地区平均密度等因素进行控制,且规划建筑密度不得超过本街坊现状建筑密度的10%,以确保原有城市肌理得到延续。为保证原有街道尺度和界面得到延续,允许在建筑退界、后退红线、绿化覆盖率等方面适当突破一般规划技术规定。

4.2 通过规划控制,保证整体风貌达到最大程度保护

该规划的一个重要特点是对风貌区内所有建筑进行分类,用历史的眼光细致地对规划区域内的每一座建筑进行分类,在认真的甄别与鉴定的基础上明确每一座建筑的留、改、拆性质。事实上,法定保护建筑只能保护非常有限的一部分优秀建筑,而仅有少量保护建筑是不可能真正保护和延续城市的整体历史文化环境的。因此必须在更大范围内保留那些有历史文化特色,构成风貌特征的大量"背景建筑",并通过规划审批程序确保其法律地位,同时使其具有极强的可操作性。这次规划除法定的保护建筑外,对其他所有建筑是保留还是允许拆除都予以明确,并充分考虑规划及房屋土地管理的操作性,将风貌区内所有的建筑划分为保护建筑、保留历史建筑、一般历史建筑、应当拆除的建筑和其他建筑五类。具体地说,就是所有的各级文物保护单位和上海市优秀历史建筑都属于"保护建筑";其他具有较高保护价值或风貌特征明显的历史建筑,在本规划中被列为"保留历史建筑",规划要求予以保留,一般不得拆除。其他历史建筑(主要指建于1949年以前,房屋质量较差,但却是整个区域历史风貌的重要组成部分)被称为"一般历史建筑",允许拆除重建,但重建建筑一般要求原面积、原高度,且必须与原有风貌相协调。第四类建筑为"应当拆除的建筑",即那些与历史文化风貌不协调的各类违章搭建、危棚简屋。第五类称之为"其他建筑",即各类合法建造的多、高层建筑,虽与历史文化风貌不协调,但暂时没有条件拆除或不可能拆除的。这种分类使得风貌区内每一幢建筑留、改、拆的整治措施都得到了明确的落实。

4.3 确立分街坊图则,确保规划落地

在规划文本上的最突出之处是分街坊图则。风貌区内所有街坊均设单页,规划的所有控制要求和控制指标都在每一幅街坊单页上明确标示。每一幢建筑、每一条街巷、每一个空间、每一片空地和每一处庭院的规划控制要求都在图上清楚标识。尤其是对建筑保护分类(留、改、拆性质)、可建设用地范围内的容量要求、具体的建筑高度控制等,图上都应有明确规定。这种图则表达方式非常便于日常规划管理,已在目前的规划管理中发挥了非常积极而有效的作用。

4.4 建立特别论证制度,杜绝擅自改变规划

制度好的城市规划从来都不是一成不变的,规划的实施是一个动态的实现过程。问题是如何保证规划变更的科学性、权威性和合法性。为保证规划的有效实施,同时也为能使规划随着外部条件的变化而具有一定的灵活性,规划中特别设计了"专家特别论证制度"。也就是说,任何一个需要改变规划的决定,都必须经过专家组的专门论证后方可做出;而对该专家组的组成成员有明确的规定,其一半以上的成员必须来自市政府批准的保护专家委员会。将规划变更纳入合法程序,这对于改变目前我国城市规划管理中随意更改规划的现象将是一个有效的探索。

随着社会经济和城市建设的发展,越来越多的人认识到,在历史文化遗产保护过程中完善政府管理机制,是做好城市文化遗产保护工作的重要保障。我们有理由相信,随着保护意识的不断增强,随着法律制度的不断健全,随着体制机制的不断完善,上海的城市遗产保护工作一定会越做越好。

反思当代中国城市建筑追高崇洋逐奇现象

Reflections on the Craze for Foreign Deigns, High-rises
& Strange Appearances in Modern Chinese Architecture

黄永林 教授
华中师范大学副校长
Prof. Huang Yonglin
Vice President, Central China Normal University

Analysing the phenomenon of the craze for foreign designs, high-rises and strange appearances in modern Chinese architecture, the author proposes the countermeasures including the enhancement of cultural consciousness, cultural pluralism, emphasis on local characteristics, etc.

一、追高崇洋逐奇的主要表现

（一）城市建筑高度摩天化

在当代中国,城市建筑"摩天情结"泛滥,盲目追求全市、全省、全国、亚洲乃至世界"第一高度"。摩天大楼的发展正在进行高度的较量,大有展示"欲与天公试比高"的气魄。据有关资料显示,全球目前在建的300米以上的超高层建筑有125座,其中78座在中国,占比达62.4%。据说,到2016年,全国不少二三线城市都将出现超高层建筑。超高建筑早已被异化了——高度比功能重要,名气比造价重要,形式比内容重要。超高的摩天大楼在其所处的环境中显得突兀而缺乏美感,逐渐失去与城市之间的联系,失去了社会性,成为某些人追求政绩和荣耀的象征。

（二）城市建筑形式西洋化

目前一些城市建筑盲目西化,充斥着西方色彩,盲目克隆国外经典建筑——从埃菲尔铁塔、伦敦塔桥、到凯旋门、悉尼歌剧院等世界著名建筑,都可以在中国找到"孪生兄弟"。从雅典式的装饰,到罗马式的雕塑,从拜占庭式屋顶,到哥特式框架;从豪华的巴洛克、洛可可风格,到英国式的风情,在中国城市建筑中比比皆是。这样的"山寨建筑",实际上只是粗陋的仿制品,原建筑的风格和美感荡然无存,以致形成一种不伦不类的城市风貌。西方山寨建筑在中国大量涌现的现象,折射出人们对当下中国社会文化自信与认同感的缺乏。

（三）城市建筑造型奇葩化

当下中国城市建筑设计盲目追求个性,力图通过标新立异的"突破",追逐奇葩路线,产生"一鸣惊人"的效果,因此,千奇百怪的建筑越来越多。从苏州东方之门"低腰秋裤"、杭州奥体博览城大楼"比基尼"到上海LV大厦"靴子楼"、重庆"方便面桶楼"等等,不胜枚举。

一个又一个竞相建造的奇葩地标建筑,一次又一次地冲击着城市景观空间,挑战人们的视觉极限。

二、追高崇洋逐奇的重要原因

当下,形成追高崇洋逐奇的原因很多,大致可归纳为以下几方面:

(一) 文化自信失落导致建筑方向盲目化

20世纪80年代初,国门打开后,许多人惊讶于西方丰裕的物质消费水平,进而发展到全盘自我否定,对中国的文化自信更是降到了谷底。表现在建筑规划领域,就是盲目跟风现象普遍,眼睛盯住国外的设计大师,本土建筑师的文化自觉和自信都受到了极大考验。一方面复制别人的建筑,另一方面让外国建筑师把中国变成自己设计理念的实验场。许多大型现代建筑都与中国设计师无缘,全是外国人的作品。

眼下的中国建筑创作不仅仅缺少地域文化的自信,而且在多元化和跨文化的大背景下,中国建筑在面对西方建筑思潮时也缺少文化自信,这导致本土建筑文化话语权的弱势,在全球化过程中面临被边缘化的危险。

(二) 社会经济发展导致建筑价值浮躁化

近年来,中国的改革开放促进了经济社会的迅速发展,增进了地域间的各种交流,也使地域文化的影响范围扩大。人们的生活观念、文化观念发生改变,在财富积累的同时,也滋长了拜金主义倾向和暴发户意识。在建筑上,就体现为建最豪华地标式建筑炫富,以彰显自己的经济实力。

事实上,我国很多城市兴起的地标热只是一种商业炒作手段,甚至是房地产开发商提高价格的策略,目的是吸引眼球以赚取更多的利润。商业性地标建筑建得越高,让城市产生的不是越多的亲切感,而是日益强烈的疏离感和陌生感。

(三) 经济利益驱动导致建筑取向功利化

城市建设和经济发展是目前政府工作考核的重要指标,而城市建设相对经济发展来说往往见效更快,因此,长期以来一直是很多地方政府工作的重点。

地方政府官员从政绩意识出发,过多考虑建筑物经济方面的因素,即如何让"这座建筑更吸引别人的眼球",引起更多游客和投资者的注意,最大可能地产生经济效益,而不重点考虑建筑物的艺术因素和对城市建设发展的真正益处。于是以"奇特"为美,以"标志性"为荣,提高建筑的知名度,成为某些领导"特殊"的审美需求。再加上"短平快"的建设节奏、领导长官意志,难免导致决策失误,出现一批"非正常建筑"——开工快、建设快,忽略美丑标准的奇葩建筑。

(四) 趋利盲从导致建筑设计品位低俗化

当建筑物被简单视作商品时,部分建筑设计师为了争取设计项目的经济利益,刻意迎合领导、投资方和业主,完全按照他们的要求进行设计。在经济利益和行政压力下,有些建筑师不管建筑风格,不管建筑传统文脉,只顾行政长官或者开发商的喜好,违背建筑学的基本原理和规则,迷失对建筑人文精神的表达,设计出品位不高的建筑物。事实上,建筑物并不能简单等同于商品,在未来很长一段时期,它都要矗立在公共空间上,供大家评判。

因此,在城市建筑设计和建造问题上,中国的建筑师应该具有独立的思考精神和创造精神,坚守职业操守,以科学的态度设计出有深度和有品质的建筑物。只有这样,中国的建筑低俗问题才会有较大改观。

三、对建筑审美异化的文化救赎

建筑集中表现了城市的价值取向和文化追求,而城市又是人类文明的象征和标志。面对中国建筑文化审美的严重异化,文化才是拯救的唯一良方。

提高文化自信自觉。培养高度的文化自信,就是要深刻认识中华文化的源远流长和博大精深。培养高度的文化自觉,就是要自觉传承和弘扬中华文化。中国的建筑文化是中国历史上最悠久、博大精深、保存最完整的文化之一。充分汲取中国传统建筑文化中的精髓,始终坚持与自然、与城市以及与人的和谐精神,是增强民族自尊心、自信心、自豪感,促进建筑文化大发展大繁荣的应有之义。只要我们做到不断继承和弘扬这些优良传统,古为今用、推陈出新,为传统文化注入现代元素,就能使中华建筑文化成为发展社会主义建筑文化的深厚基础,这是我们培养高度文化自信的深厚底气。

突显建筑文化个性。城市建筑要契合城市性格,城市魅力要通过鲜明的文化和个性来体现。城市文化和特色,在很大程度上要依赖城市建筑载体才能得以存在和发展。载体是它们外部功能的体现,也是城市景观的核心要素。新建筑应当既是时代的产物,也是对传统的延续。在保护建筑遗产、凝聚千百年审美观照的自然景观的同时,这些宝贵的文化积淀也是城市建筑个性传承与创作的起点。必须立足现实,勇于创新,打造城市建筑的个性风格,体现人对美的追求,体现人与自然的和谐。

寻求多元文化融合。在"多元化"和"全球化"趋势中,必须坚持建筑文化的多元包容性,把创造既现代又富有当地特色的新建筑文化作为城市建筑发展方向。有特色的现代城市,既要认知和保护具有历史文化传统的旧建筑,又要在新时代充分挖掘其价值进行有效的利用。在继承民族特色建筑的同时,还要汲取借鉴西方建筑文化的精粹,采用东西建筑相互渗透、相互结合的创作手法,把国外建筑流派的风格融入民族传统建筑之中,创造出中国特有的建筑样式。

当今,保护好历史文化名城,延续城市历史文脉,凸显城市个性和特色,满足人们物质和精神文化需求,正越来越受到重视。这是一种新的发展趋势,也是我们追求的目标。

领导者树立正确的政绩观。要防止城市建筑审美异化,杜绝建筑垃圾产生,城市领导者必须拥有高度的文化自觉和文化自信,树立正确的政绩观。只有认真学习和研究中国历史文化,具有正确的审美观、价值观、历史观和生态观,能正确区分建筑的"美"和"丑",不被世俗审美观左右,城市建设领导者才能为城市建设做出正确的决策。

设计师要强化敬业精神。建筑设计师应有为城市建设服务的敬业精神和对城市建筑高度负责的精神,不断提高自身的素养,包括艺术修养、文化修养,勤于创作,借鉴世界先进的建筑理念和科学技术,找到一种可以同时表达城市文化传统和现代性的设计手段,用现代手法把中国传统建筑意境和文化融入现代建筑空间,勇于打造建筑精品、提升建筑文化品位、凸显地域特征、民族特色和时代风貌,设计出蕴含中国文化、韵味十足、服务百姓生活的建筑精品。

城市居民积极参与决策。城市建设规划涉及千千万万居民,一项规划的确定与实施,会影响几代人。因此,在制定城市建设规划时,应给每位普通市民以知情权、参与权,让民众共同关心、建设和管理城市。城市规划编制、重要建设项目方案设计要广泛征求市民意见,集思广益。特别是大规模工程建设,应采取专家和民众共同参与机制,确保城市建筑符合民意。

城市历史环境的可持续保护

Sustainable Conservation For Urban Historic Environment

张松 教授
同济大学建筑与城市规划学院
Prof. Zhang Song
School of Architecture & Urban Planning, Tongji University

Based on the analysis of the dual-crisis problems existing in urban environment and the common problems in historic and cultural cities in China, this paper concentrates on the policy and experience in the urban conservation, and mainly introduces the mechanism and system of historic environment protection and heritage assets management in the UK. Under the guidance of the *Recommendation on the Historic Urban Landscape* of UNESCO, based on the sustainable development policy and the social values of heritage preservation, it focuses on realizing the sustainable conservation and planning management for historic urban environment through preserving, renovation and improving the liveability of historic urban areas.

一、陷入双重危机之中的城市环境

2010年上海世博会的主题"城市让生活更美好"反映出了人们对城市时代到来的美好期盼。而到2015年底中央召开城市工作会议以最高文件形式所指出的如下城市问题："城市规划前瞻性、严肃性、强制性和公开性不够,城市建筑贪大、媚洋、求怪等乱象丛生,特色缺失,文化传承堪忧;城市建设盲目追求规模扩张,节约集约程度不高;依法治理城市力度不够,违法建设、大拆大建问题突出,公共产品和服务供给不足,环境污染、交通拥堵等'城市病'蔓延加重。"由此可以看出短短几年间人们对城市的认识和认知似乎有了巨大的转变。其实这些城市问题并不是在短短5年时间内发生和加剧的,而是快速推进城市进程以来长期积累的病症的普遍凸显。近年来雾霾席卷全国,一些大城市的PM 2.5指数持续攀至新高。高速发展的代价已日趋沉重,众多城市的大气、水和土壤的污染程度不断加剧,生态指数持续走低,城市宜居性等问题再次引起社会的广泛关注。

在自然生态环境持续恶化的局面下,城市地方政府为GDP增长和追求土地的财政效益,不断对旧城进行大规模的改造,旧改对历史环境造成了空前破坏。而且,东部发达地区大城市规划建设用地已基本用光,进入了所谓"存量规划"时期,如此一来对旧城的大拆大建是否会更为迅猛呢?最近20余年,由于地价不断攀升和拆迁成本不断增加,为了推进城市改造,一些城市弃城市规划的基本法规规范于不顾,随意改变容积率等控规指标,提高开发强度,导致高强度高密度开发盛行。缺乏细致的规划设计,必要的技术手段也没有配备完善,只是进行形式上的"曼哈顿化"(Manhattanization),其结果必将破坏到城市环境所应具备的宜居形态和人性尺度。

正如美国学者莎伦·佐金(Sharon Zukin)在《裸城:原真性城市场所的生与死》(*Naked City: The Death and Life of Authentic Urban Places*)的导论"失去灵魂的城市"中所指出的"所有大城市都忙着抹

去它们粗陋不堪、瓦砾尘土漫天飞扬的过去,取而代之的是一个亮闪闪的未来图景。北京、上海和其他中国城市正忙着消除市中心破落的狭窄胡同弄堂,将生于斯、长于斯的居民撵到城郊地带,用昂贵的公寓和设计宏伟的摩天大楼取代矮小老旧的平房",这一包含"绅士化"(gentrification)在内的广泛的再城市化(re-urbanization)过程,"最终创造的不仅是贫富老少之间的经济区分,同时也是文化隔阂",而这就是城市失去灵魂之事发生的时刻。①

毫无疑问,全国各地的大中小城市,正在陷入自然环境严重污染和历史环境快速消失的双重危机之中。对历史城区进行"大拆大建"等过度开发的做法,不仅导致城市环境容量急速扩张,城市的宜居性和包容性也越来越差,而且还破坏了城市的历史环境、地区文脉和场所精神。② 伤筋动骨后的历史城区变成了面目全非的"伤城",失去灵魂的"裸城"。

从全球范围看,环境保护运动从自然环境到历史环境,从资源综合利用到可持续发展,一步一步走到今天。反观国内城市可持续发展的情形,发展起步晚于西方发达国家,追求经济效益和发展速度成为近30年来的主要目标,可持续发展的理念虽然并不陌生,但多数时候只是作为口号和概念存在于现实生活之中,并没有触及人们的灵魂,也极少影响到地方政府的宏伟规划和实际行动。

同自然环境保护一样,历史环境保护作为城市发展的重要内容应当引起更加广泛的关注。历史环境的可持续保护,既包括物质环境的整治改善、风貌保护和文脉传承,还包含资源整合利用、社区复兴和可持续发展等目标。历史环境保护有利于城市社会结构和物质肌理(physical fabric)多样性的维持,关系到文化多样性和地域文化特色;而维护文化多样性如同保护生物多样性和维持生态平衡一样重要,关系到人类社会的全面健康和可持续发展。

二、名城保护中出现的普遍性问题

历史环境是指由与土地密切相关的文化遗产、场所环境及社区生活所构成一定范围的整体的肌理及其氛围,文物古迹、历史建筑是其中的重要元素,历史城区、历史文化街区可以作为历史环境中的典型代表或重点保护对象。历史文化街区是历史文化名城保护的重点内容,也是由真实的历史文化遗存所构成的整体历史环境景观。近年来,"建设性破坏"一直是我国城市遗产保护面临的主要威胁。一些违反法规、规范或管理程序的开发建设项目,直接对文物古迹和历史环境造成了无法挽回的损失。而在各种"建设性破坏"中,首先遭到破坏的就是那些保护地位不高的"不可移动文物"和保护身份不够明确的历史建筑和历史文化街区。

相对于大拆大建对文化遗产造成的"建设性破坏",近年来兴起的文化复古热潮又给历史文化名城带来了"保护性破坏"。在城市遗产保护依然举步维艰的情况下,从聊城、大同、开封,再到台儿庄、凤凰,一个个历史名城名镇加入古城复兴的行列中。拆真造假、拆旧建新,在制造"假古董"这类人造景观,对视觉环境造成虚假甚至负面影响的同时,也对真实的历史环境与文化生态多样性直接造成破坏或是不当的干预。短期内打造形成的仿古建筑群能产生多大的吸引力?这种新的同质化的古城风貌是否能够维持旅游的热度?恐怕都还是未知数,但是为了建造此类宏伟的复兴工程所遗留的、在短期内难以消化的巨大债务,却已经成为这些城市政府实实在在的财政难题。

2012年底,聊城、邯郸等8个历史文化名城因保护工作不力,致使名城历史文化价值遭到严重破坏,被住建部、国家文物局正式发文点名批评。虽说以大拆大建和推倒重来方式进行保护的聊城等名城已成为保护实践中的负面典型,但以风貌再造、重新辉煌的方式进行的古城文化复兴等项目却从未停止。此外,还有一些历史文化街区的保护整治,以旅游等商业开发为导向,以大量原住居民的搬迁为前提,虽然在基础设施和物质环境方面得到极大的改善,然而这种过度的商业化开发与运作模式,导致"绅士化"现象的

---

① [美]莎伦·佐金.裸城:原真性城市场所的生与死[M].丘兆达,刘蔚,译.上海:上海人民出版社,2015.
② 张松.历史城市保护学导论:文化遗产和历史环境保护的一种整体性方法[M].2版:上海:同济大学出版社,2008.

蔓延,历史环境中真实的生活景观(lifescape)被彻底"净化",最终引发城市社区的分化和社会结构的改变。

历史环境代表这地域的人文特色,其组成部分应包括建筑、街巷、场所、业态、活动以及独特氛围。保护地域特色、文化生态和场所精神直接涉及居民的生活状态(life condition)等实际问题。保护并不是要把历史环境现状固化下来,而是为了保持自然环境和历史环境的品质的动态维护与管理。对环境品质下降或已衰败的历史地区,则应当采取有效的整治改善措施进行抢救性保护。在历史进程中,历史城区和传统村落都在逐渐衰退,传统建筑由于常年得不到应有的维护维修,建筑破损较为严重,院落空间内搭建过多,一些历史地段甚至变成了建筑质量低劣的地区,这些都是客观存在的问题。但是,处理这种衰退地区的问题应当谨慎,应当基于社会公正的原则,而不是让贫困居民全部搬离。对于城市文化而言,任何死的东西都是没有特别重要意义的。历史环境一旦失去了长期生活在其中的居民,也就失去了真实的"生活世界"。

不少历史文化街区保护整治后的结果是城市历史景观的碎片化现象明显。正如格拉茨(Gratz)所言:"历史街区保护常常掩盖了一个事实,那就是往往所修复的东西对城市整体文脉来说微不足道,而且因所涉及的范围太小,以至于难以保留或再次成为更大城市结构中的重要历史文脉发源地……数不清的城市在炫耀其市中心那几个被修复的街区时,市中心的其他部分却陷入被推平与重建的梦魇之中。"[1]历史文化名城保护中出现这样一些普遍性问题的原因比较复杂,主要包括历史保护理念偏差过大,保护工程前期研究不足及缺乏科学的评估,在历史保护工程中也很少采取居民参与的自下而上的保护方式等。众所周知,历史文化街区保护的基本原则要从维护历史遗存的原真性(authenticity)、传统风貌的完整性(integrity)和街区生活的延续性出发,采取适当的整治改善措施和适度调整街区业态的方式。那些过度改造的商业化开发模式,事实上已经严重违背了文化遗产保护的原真性和完整性原则。拆真造假、再现历史辉煌的做法,事实上也是一种中断城市历史文脉和集体记忆的极端行为,而不是真正的历史环境保护。

三、可借鉴的英国历史环境保护政策

从表面上看,我国历史文化名城保护制度的制定已经 30 余年,起步不算晚,保护工作开展的时间也不算太短。然而,与西方城市保护的先进国家相比,就会发现在保护法规、公共政策等方面依然存在较大的差距,有效的可操作的保护措施相当有限,往往还是消极保存和被动应对。而且,曾经与历史文化名城和历史文化街区保护关系密切的城乡规划管理工具,伴随保护工作的开展似乎也有渐行渐远的倾向。作为公共政策手段的城市规划,几乎演变成了单一的"为增长而规划"工具。因此,学习和借鉴西方国家特别是欧洲城市保护的政策与经验就显得很有必要。

英国的历史环境保护有其自身的特色,其中历史环境保护与城乡规划的关系密切,通过城乡规划管理对历史环境实施有效保护,在可持续发展战略框架下有效推进等方面,尤其值得我们学习与借鉴。英国古迹保护的国家立法始于 1882 年的《古迹保护法》(Ancient Monuments Protection Act)。1913 年颁布了《古迹保护合并与修正法》(Ancient Monuments Consolidation and Amendment Act),合并 1882 年、1900 年和 1910 年的三项古迹保护法律。依据 1913 年法的相关规定,英国建立了古迹委员会以监督全国的古迹保护工作,保护范围也扩展到古迹周边土地。1913 年法还赋予了古迹保护工作的强制性,掐断了土地所有者为所欲为的念头。1931 年,对《古迹保护法》的修订中第一次提出应对古迹周边用地的建设活动采取控制措施,既实施"开发控制",这也是第一次将古迹保护置于规划体系之中。[2]

1953 年颁布《历史建筑和古迹法》(Historic Buildings and Ancient Monuments Act)强化了历史建筑保护法规内容,1967 年的《城市宜人环境法》(Civic Amenities Act)第一次明确规定在城乡规划中划定保

---

[1] [英]史蒂文·蒂耶斯德尔,蒂姆·希思,[土]塔内尔·厄奇,著. 城市历史街区的复兴[M]. 张玫英,董卫,译. 北京:中国建筑工业出版社,2006.

[2] Charles Mynors. Listed Buildings, Conservation Areas and Monuments [M]. 4th ed. London:Sweet & Maxwell Limited, 2006.

护区,对具有历史风貌特征的地区实施成片保护,1967年在英格兰划定了第一批4片保护区。1968年修订《城乡规划法》(*Town and Country Planning Act*)确立了建筑登录保护制度。

在英国,《城乡规划法》和《登录建筑与保护区规划法》(*Planning [Listed Buildings and Conservation Area) Act 1990]*属于议会法,而针对城乡规划管理的政策性法规《规划政策指引》(*Planning Policy Guidance PPG*)和现行的《规划政策声明》(PPS)属于授权法。随着2004年《规划和强制收购法》(*The Planning and Compulsory Purchase Act*)的出台《规划政策声明5:历史环境规划》(*PPS 5: Planning for Historic Environment*)取代了过去的《规划政策指引15:规划与历史环境》(1994)和《规划政策指引16:考古与规划》(1990),成为国家层面历史环境保护的重要法规。1990年的《登录建筑和保护区规划法》和2004年的《规划政策声明5:历史环境规划》是指导地方规划机构开展具体保护管理的重要法律依据。

《登录建筑和保护区规划法》中对保护区的定义为:"具有特别的建筑或历史意义,其特征或风貌值得保持或提升的地区。"[①]早期划定的保护区多为像巴斯古城(Bath)这样特征明显的历史城镇或历史中心区,现在的保护区包括了以渔业和矿业为主的村镇、乡村聚落、现代居住小区等,英国保护区的类型呈现出多样化与包容性。

按照英国政府2010年3月颁布的《规划政策声明5:历史环境规划》中的定义,历史环境(historic environment)是一定时期内人与场所(places)相互作用后遗留于环境的全部样态,包括人类过去活动所有的物质遗存,无论是可见的、地下的或水下的,还是景观、种植或人工管理的植物群。而那些可以体现历史环境重要性的元素被称为遗产资源(heritage assets)。遗产资源包括:确认其具有一定程度的重要性并值得在规划决策中考虑的任何一处建筑物、纪念物遗迹、场所、地区或景观。遗产资源是历史环境的重要组成部分,包括已指定的遗产资源,以及地方规划机构在规划决策或规划编制中确认的其他资源(含地方保护名录)。其中指定的遗产资源(designated heritage assets)包括世界遗产地、在册古迹、登录建筑、保护区、考古地区、注册历史公园和园林、注册古战场遗迹和沉船等历史遗迹。截至2006年7月,英国法定保护对象包括36 000座古迹、超过50万处历史建筑以及划定的10 500处保护区。[②]

英国历史环境保护体系相当严谨,国家和地方既对重要文化遗产和保护区进行保护,又针对遗产资源和历史环境实施细致的维护管理,并通过城乡规划实施全面有效的管理。英国政府希望通过保护历史环境和遗产资源,提升当代人和后代人的生活质量,让人认识到遗产资源是不可再生的资源,遗产保护具有社会、文化、经济和环境价值,遗产资源对地方特色塑造和场所感知具有积极作用。为实现可持续发展的目标,在任何规划政策制定和决策之前,都需要确保充分考虑到历史环境的保护,并且在遗产资源保护中应尽可能采用合理的措施,为其选择符合保护要求且合理可行的用途,与此同时,需要智慧地管理城乡历史环境的变化。

四、历史性城市景观与可持续城市

伴随着经济全球化和快速城市化,城市保护面临的局面日益复杂,包括快速城市化和再城市化带来的对场所感和社区认同的威胁、超强度开发或乱开发、全球变暖等气候变化、不可持续的资源消耗,等等。与此同时,受可持续发展理念的影响,人们对城市的认识也逐渐深刻——城市既是人类文明的成就,也是重要的人居环境形式。历史环境是人类的共享资源,也是社会和经济的财富,学习和娱乐的资源;作为地区文化、旅游和经济发展的催化剂,历史环境应当发挥其在塑造地区特色中的积极作用;历史环境还可以为地区带来高品质和富有想象力的设计。

---

① English Heritage. Conservation Principles: Policy and Guidance for the Sustainable Management of the Historic Environment[R]. London: English Heritage, 2008.

② UK Department for Culture, Media and Sport. Planning Policy Statements: Planning for the historic environments[R]. London: English Heritage, 2010.

2005年以来,国际遗产保护领域围绕"历史性城市景观"(Historic Urban Landscape HUL)理念展开了广泛的讨论,联合国教科文组织(UNESCO)于2011年11月在第36届大会上通过了一份新的有关城市保护的国际文件《关于历史性城市景观的建议》(以下简称《国际建议》)。《国际建议》引言中指出:"历史城区是我们共同的文化遗产中最为丰富和多样的表现,它历经世代所形成,并成为人类的努力与愿望透过时空所留存下来的重要见证;城市遗产是人类的社会、文化和经济资产,由持续存在的文化、累积的传统和经验所创造的历史层积性(historic layering)价值所定义,并作为它们的多样性被识别。"正因为如此,"城市保护不局限于建筑单体的保护,而是将建筑作为整体城市环境的组成要素看待,使得城市保护成为一个复杂的、多学科的领域,因而城市保护应位于城市规划中的核心位置。"①

在《国际建议》中提出的历史性城市景观(HUL)这一全新概念,是将城市建成区理解为一种具有文化的和自然的价值与特性的历史层积的结果,包括更广阔的城市文脉及其地理环境,超越了"历史中心区"或"综合体"等既有概念。《国际建议》所提倡的城市保护的景观方法(landscape approach)意味着在涉及城市以及更大区域的智慧规划中,应当基于对历史性城市景观这一大尺度演变的全面理解,认识到现时的城市是经过岁月累积在环境中形成的多重层积(multi-layers)。随着时间的推移,如何能够保持物质肌理的连续性和活力,以及伴随更广泛的演化和变革还能够维护并传承这种连续性,是城市保护面临的挑战和课题。历史需要让人感知,城市的多重积淀需要呈现与弘扬。对遗产资源变化的管理(managing change),需要有效的控制引导。反思近年来国内历史名城保护过程中的角色变化,紧密结合社会经济发展的城市保护策略十分必要,需要以可持续的方式维护城市历史环境的生命力。

城市规划可以塑造我们工作和生活的场所,在支撑国家广泛的经济、生态和社会目标和可持续发展社区中扮演着越来越重要的角色。因此,《国际建议》要求世界各国将城市保护战略纳入国家发展政策和行动规划之中,在该框架下地方当局制定的发展规划应以周全考虑到城市历史形态和传统城市的智慧思想为基础。历史城市的未来很大程度上取决于它与人们日常生活环境的整合状况,取决于其在区域和城乡规划中受重视的程度,因此,历史环境保护必须作为城乡规划中的重要目标,而不是可有可无的事务。遗产资源具有重要的社会、经济价值,不能只是要求避免拆毁历史建筑,还需要在当代积极发挥它们的社会作用。尽可能地延续使用或再利用老旧建筑和历史环境,是节约资源能源和环境友好的建设行为。这是因为在大规模开发和再开发过程中,伴随着建设量递增的是建筑垃圾和建筑能耗的不断上升。国外早期的保护政策更多地关注维护遗产本身的历史特性(pastness of the past),而以后的保护与振兴政策则更关注遗产的未来。保护工作的重点逐步转向促进投资和推动地方经济的发展方面,以便能够为历史环境保护和改善提供所需的经济支持。如何制定更有针对性的、适合各地的保护政策,更加注重提高管理水平,以振兴历史城市和历史文化街区,成为今天城市政府的努力方向。②

美国规划师艾本·佛多(Eben Fodor)认为:"评估一个物体使用的可持续性的时限最好是永久性。通过无限延长利用物体的时限,来简化可持续发展的定义是可能的。可持续发展是一种可持续的行动、政策或程序,它在不断降低自然环境的生态完整性和生命维持能力的情况下,无限期延续它们。"③可持续发展战略要求保护现有资源,所以积极保护和可持续保护管理城市遗产是可持续发展的必要条件。将保护对象看作是一种有限资源的观点,与生态和经济意义上的可持续性非常接近了。保护文化遗产"将尽可能多的意义传承给后人"的目标,与可持续发展的理念不谋而合。④ 在历史保护中如果没有可持续的概念,只是考虑当下使用者的利益,那么随心所欲地改变对象也就天经地义了。

城市文化本身即为一个完整的生态系统,与自然地理、社会经济、历史文化、科学技术等有着密切的关系。文化多样性不仅体现在人类文化遗产通过丰富多彩的文化表现形式来表达、弘扬和传承的多种方式,

---

① UNESCO. Recommendation on the Historic Urban Landscape[R]. Paris: UNESCO General Conference, 2001.
② [英]史蒂文·蒂耶斯德尔,蒂姆·希思,[土]塔内尔·厄奇,著. 城市历史街区的复兴[M]. 张玫英,董卫,译. 北京:中国建筑工业出版社,2006.
③ [美]艾本·佛多. 更好,不是更大:城市发展控制和社区环境改善[M]. 吴唯佳,译. 北京:清华大学出版社,2012.
④ [西]萨尔瓦多·穆里奥斯·比尼亚斯,著. 当代保护理论[M]. 张鹏,张怡欣,吴霄婧,译. 上海:同济大学出版社,2012.

也体现在借助各种方式和技术进行的艺术创造、生产、传播和消费等多种方式之中。《国际建议》再次强调了历史城镇整体性保护的重要性,指出"必须重视将历史城区的保护、管理和规划策略整合到地方的发展进程和城市规划之中"。①

可持续发展的原则要求我们认识到遗产保护的长期性和连续性,随着对文化遗产保护意识的提升,文化遗产已被视为社会可持续发展不可再生的战略资源。从这层意义上来讲,保护是对历史建筑、传统民居和历史街区等文化遗产及其景观环境的改善、修复和控制行为,为降低历史建筑和历史环境衰败的速度而对变化实行动态管理的全过程。正如《国际建议》中所指出的:"可持续发展原则要求保护现有资源,因而积极保护和可持续地管理城市遗产是可持续发展的必要条件。"②因而,在全球环境变化中,有形和无形的文化遗产是提升城市地区宜居性、促进经济发展、增强社会凝聚力的重要资源。人类的未来取决于对资源的有效规划和管理,因而保护就成为一种战略,旨在以可持续发展为基础实现城市发展与生活质量之间的平衡。

总之,只有基于对有形和无形的文化遗产和生物多样性的尊重,通过强化人与历史环境之间的良性关系,确定可持续发展方向,"我们梦想的未来"才有可能实现。众所周知,循环利用的3R原则,即减量化(reduce)、再利用(reuse)和再循环(recycle),不仅是自然环境资源保护利用的原则,也应当是历史环境、遗产资源保护利用的基本原则。对于人居环境而言,一座城市可持续性的目标是减少其对于不可再生自然资源的使用和废弃物的产生,同时改善其宜居性。而积极保护历史环境,以及对现存物质肌理的再利用,有利于减少建成环境资源的浪费与损失。可持续的城市应当是形态紧凑、高密度和多功能的,"可持续城市将力图依照自然环境、建筑环境和文化环境来保存、提高和改善其资源和财产"。③

保护和延续城市历史风貌和文脉肌理,与改善和提升其中的居住环境不可分离。在保护实践中,城市遗产的社会价值不应被忽视。无论是历史街区的保护整治,还是历史建筑的再利用,都应当尊重财产所有权。因此,今后城市历史环境的可持续保护,应当更多地关注与普通市民日常生活相关的历史场所与集体记忆的维护,通过利益相关者之间的合作与关系协调,将历史城区环境的全面改善与居民日常生活环境的改善、提升有机整合,在可持续发展的框架下扎实推进。只有长期不懈地努力,才有可能实现真正的城市文化复兴。

---

① UNESCO. Recommendation on the Historic Urban Landscape[R]. Paris: UNESCO General Conference, 2001.
② UNESCO. Recommendation on the Historic Urban Landscape[R]. Paris: UNESCO General Conference, 2001.
③ [英]丹尼斯·罗德威尔. 历史城市的保护与可持续性[M]. 陈江宁, 译. 北京: 电子工业出版社, 2015.

比利时鲁汶大学新大学城:向鲁汶历史文化遗产的城市空间创新致敬

The New University Town of Louvain(belgium): A Homage of Urban Spatial Innovation to Historic LOUVAIN/LEUVEN Urban Cultural Heritage

皮埃尔·拉孔特 博士
城市环境基金会主席
国际城市与区域规划师协会 ISOCARP 前主席
Dr. Pierre Laconte
President, Foundation for the Urban Environment
Former President, ISOCARP

鲁汶新大学城的案例告诉我们,如何在严苛的经济环境之下,充分利用生态智慧开发一座新的城市。本项目由鲁汶大学主导,涉及 1 000 公顷农业与林业用地的开发建设,其总规在 1970 年获得通过,并在 1972 年开始实施。经历 40 年的发展之后,这一案例在诸多方面的成功带来诸多启示,包括:全步行交通系统、节能建筑、生态林地的保护、面向生态多样性的景观设计、雨水收集系统等等。

Fig. 1　Pedestrian Spine

1. The location of the old City of Louvain/Leuven and the new Louvain

Central Belgium is a highly urbanised area, Brussels being the centre of a metropolitan region including the cities of Antwerp, Ghent Bruges and Louvain/Leuven to its north and the cities of Charleroi, Nivelles, Ottignies-Louvain-la-Neuve (as a result of its development) and Wavre to its south. Most of them are within commuting distance of each other and from Brussels (LACONTE, 2007).

2. Development of the City of Louvain/Leuven and its university

As most cities in the early Middle Ages the city of Louvain/Leuven developed at a river-road crossing used by the merchant's caravans. These merchant cities formed a maze some 30 km apart, corresponding to the distance caravans covered in one day. Within the Duchy of Brabant Louvain/Leuven and Brussels emerged as the most powerful cities. In 1312 Duke Jan II, under financial pressure, obtained consent from the people of Brabant to raise the level of taxes, in return for a charter. This charter guaranteed the rights of citizens, in line with the *English Magna Carta*, created a Council with dual representation (of cities and of citizens) and introduced the impeachement, i. e. the deposition of the Duke if he would not respect the charter. It was thus a forerunner of modern constitutions. The charter was signed in the abbey of Kortenberg, located between the rival cities of Brussels and Louvain/Leuven, and is known as the *Charter of Kortenberg*.

The prosperity of the city was mainly based on its textile industry. In the 15th century it went into decline because of international competition and reinvented itself by obtaining a papal decree authorising the creation of a university, in line with the papal creation of Bologna, Paris, Oxford, Heidelberg and Krakow, etc. The disused cloth market hall was adapted for reuse as the university headquarters.

The university became one of the greatest European universities. In 1516 Thomas More published his celebrated "Utopia" in Louvain/Leuven. The original teaching language in the university was Latin, later French and Dutch, in separate sections.

Louvain/Leuven was very heavily damaged in 1914 by German troops, when they forced their way through Belgium, notwithstanding its fierce resistance, and occupied the entire country (except for a small coastal area) until 1918.

After the war reconstruction took place, respecting most of the former street pattern. The style of the new buildings reflected the different styles of former centuries, but kept an overall coherence. This was criticised at the time as an imitation of the past rather than a bold step towards the future. Only at the end of the 20th century was the quality of this way of planning and building recognised internationally.

Fig. 2　The Birdview of New Louvain(2014)

Within old Louvain/Leuven the Groot Begijnhof/Grand Béguinage, located south of the town centre, is of particular interest.

It was a large enclosed neighbourhood occupied by a community of independent retired single ladies ("beguines"). Their rent was subsidised, making it a "social housing" estate before this term existed.

The majority of the houses date from the middle of the 17th century. They were constructed in the traditional local architectural style, enriched with some sober baroque elements. The facades are of red bricks with sandstone transoms and frames for windows and doors. As seen in the photo there are numerous dormers, often decorated with crow-stepped gables and round arched windows.

Some houses were replaced or constructed in the 19th century, but fewer than in other Flemish beguinages. Most of the beguines left in the 20th century because of the provision of more comfortable public housing. Although the area became dilapidated, it was perfectly fit for adaptive reuse.

This adaptive reuse was achieved by transforming the entire Beguinage into housing for university staff and students, equipped with modern appliances but totally respecting the dense urban character of the neighborhood. It was inscribed on the UNESCO World Heritage List in 1988.

This masterly neighborhood restauration was directed by historian Raymond Lemaire, who also became famous for other large-scale restorations, such as the temples of Borobudur in Indonesia, and for the creation in 1964, together with Piero Gazzola, of the International Council of Monuments and Sites (ICOMOS). He was teaching in both the Dutch-and French-speaking sections of the university. This was common practice in Louvain/Leuven, as in other bilingual cities such as Bolzano/Bosen in Italy, Neuchâtel or Biel/Bienne in Switzerland, or Turku/Åbo in Finland.

The gradual suppression of the French language in the Flemish region led to the banning of the French-speaking section of the university from Louvain/Leuven in 1968. This was the tipping point that led to the need to create a new French-speaking university.

Raymond Lemaire continued teaching in both universities and created the "Raymond Lemaire International Centre for Conservation" (RLICC) in 1976 within the Flemish-speaking Leuven University. This centre is located in the historic Arenberg Castle belonging to the university and has both research and training activities. Its president is Minja Yang (Japan), former Deputy Director of UNESCO World Heritage Centre and Director of UNESCO New Delhi Office.

3. Moving from the Flemish City of Leuven/Louvain to the City of Brussels or to the Walloon region? A difficult decision.

Within central Belgium, the historic town of Louvain/Leuven is the original seat of Louvain university. The languages used in teaching until 1968 were French and Dutch. In that year the French-speaking university (UCL) had to leave the City to find a new location in the French-speaking part, because it was located in the Dutch-speaking part of the country.

Facing this situation the French-speaking university had the option either to locate in the officially bilingual district of Brussels—the capital, where it owned land, or to locate in the French-only Walloon region.

The option taken by the board was the conclusion of a long rivalry between two mayors:

—on the one hand Baron Donald Fallon, Christian democrat Mayor of the Brussels large municipality of Woluwe-St-Lambert, who set aside 80 hectares, later reduced to 40, to locate his Alma Mater in Brussels; and

—on the other hand Count du Monceau de Bergendal, recently elected as Christian democrat Mayor of the small Walloon Ottignies, who realised the political opportunity for his Christian democrat party and his municipality of having the Catholic University of Louvain on his territory, as counterforce to the Socialist party, the largest in the Walloon region. The location proposed was an agricultural plateau, at some four km from central Ottignies and only accessible through the Brussels-Luxemburg National Road.

The Brussels location was supported by the Christian democrat Prime Minister of the time Paul Van den Boeynants and his coalition government colleagues. They offered the University to move all its faculties to Brussels except the Faculty of Literature ("Philosophie & lettres"). There was already a Catholic Faculty of Literature ("Faculté Saint-Louis") that wished to remain autonomous. The relocation in Brussels, emerging capital of Europe, would have reinforced its international character. Conversely it would have made Brussels a city of two large universities instead of one, benefiting both. Many academics and the university administration's general director Paul Walckiers also pleaded for a relocation in Brussels.

The relocation in the French-only Walloon region was supported by an active part of university board, including the Rector Edouard Massaux and the general administrator Michel Woitrin, who held a "regionalist" view and were eager to locate in a monolingual environment.

No referendum between the two options took place, as the national political debate was still going on.

Finally the board of the university decided in favor of the French-only Walloon region, notwithstanding the fact that its political majority was Socialist. It thus firmly refused the offer of the Christian democrat government to relocate in Brussels.

This unexpected decision of the Catholic university had the immediate side effect of provoking the fall of its most friendly government since WW II.

Now tied to the Walloon region the Catholic University chose to locate in the municipality of Ottignies and bought a tract of 920—ha farmland located 27 km south-east of Brussels, mostly owned by non-resident owners who are eager to sell.

Rather than building an isolated campus, following the US example, the University decided to build a new town, making use of the university's annual grants as equity. The central part of the site was set aside for high density-low rise development, and all forest land was to be preserved.

4. From the location in the municipality of Ottignies to the master plans of Victor Gruen Associates (1968) and the "Groupe Urbanisme Architecture" (1970)

Urban development on a wholly university-owned site met with strong opposition from the Belgian national education ministry, which preferred an isolated monofunctional campus such as the one adopted by Liège university (FRANKIGNOULLE 2012). It proposed and enacted a special law (24 July 1969) that forbade universities to sell land they had acquired with subsidies to non-university users.

Allegedly, it hoped in this way to avoid what was seen as an invasion of new non-socialist inhabitants onto its turf.

The university evaded this law by granting long term leases ("erfpacht") instead of selling land outright, making use of some 1824 legislation that never had been implemented. In addition, after a few years, the university administration began granting leases that could be sold with a right for the buyer to start the lease again.

In retrospect continuity of UCL ownership proved beneficial to the implementation of the master plan as it ensured the landowner's ability to preserve its initial planning objectives in the long term (LACONTE 2013).

The leases were initially granted to individuals and small developers and contractors. In later phases larger tracts were leased, e. g. for the shopping mall and for mixed used developments.

Having opted for building a new town in the fields, the university board decided—at the suggestion of its general administrator—to hire the established international planning firm Victor Gruen Associates (Los Angeles), a pioneer of American shopping malls, to draw up its master plan.

The Gruen Associates master plan, which was based on functional considerations, included a large central air-conditioned mall surmounted by high-rise buildings. All infrastructures had to be built before any part of the plan could be brought into use, entailing a large up-front investment cost.

The Gruen master plan was presented to the university board and the university community in September 1968 and rejected by a large majority.

At that point the university board decided—in October 1968—to entrust the master plan and architectural coordination of the new town to an interdisciplinary team recruited by the board itself. This team, called "Groupe Urbanisme-Architecture" (Groupe UA) was jointly headed by:

—R. Lemaire, professor of urban history, who achieved the restoration of Leuven Beguinage, where Groupe UA located its offices,

—J-P. Blondel, professor at the architecture institute of Brussels university, and

—P. Laconte, urban economist, former head of staff at the Brabant government for the Brussels—Capital structure plan and planning appeals.

Within the "Groupe Urbanisme-Architecture" (UA) R. Lemaire was in charge of the coordination between architects appointed by UA for the individual buildings, and also for reporting to the Academic Council. J-P. Blondel was in charge of the daily management of the staff, largely made up of his students. P. Laconte was in charge of institutional matters and relations with the political and administrative authorities (national and local) related to the project, including rail and road infrastructure, water management and the planning permits, as well as for reporting to the general administrator.

The Groupe UA master plan was adopted by the university on 15 October 1970 (GROUPE, 1970) and has been the guiding framework ever since. It embraces the model of traditional university towns, in particular Louvain/Leuven.

The Groupe UA took its inspiration not only from medieval universities but also from the garden cities developed in the UK in the early 20th century (primarily Letchworth). It relied on the millenial experience of successful multifunctional cities and neighbourhoods, rather than on a few decades of functionalism and the spatial separation of functions which required motorised transportation to link them.

The expertise of the university faculties was of great help to UA in dealing with the legal issues and the engineering projects related to infrastructure, forest and water management, long-term leases and municipal finance.

The general administration department of development and management ("Service de promotion et de gestion urbaine") was in charge of the implementation of planning decisions, in particular the supervision of the investments on the slab. Its coordination was handled by Jean-Marie Lechat from 1974 till 1997. Property development and relations with developers were handled from 1972 by the institute for site development (INESU), headed by Philippe Barras since 2007.

A major feature of the new town is a central linear pedestrian spine, a concept pioneered among others by the university of Lancaster in England (EPSTEIN, 2009). It allowed a step-by-step development, with automobile access to buildings and parking space located outside the spine, with occasional underpasses. Each phase of development included a mix of urban functions, allowing it to be put into operation immediately, unhindered by works on extensions. The total length of the spine is around one and a half km, as illustrated by Jean Remy (REMY 2007, page 133).

This pedestrian linear option allowed huge savings to be made in land take and in the cost of initial road infrastructure investment—but, more importantly, it favoured informal contacts among people.

The concept of a main central pedestrian spine was translated into actual urban design as a string of public spaces, starting from the existing road to the east. It came into operation in 1972 on the eastern part of the site, and was later extended to the railway station opened in 1975, and from there to the future centre of the city, and to the western part of the site. These spaces have different shapes and their street access is either perpendicular or tangential (LACONTE 1980).

This string of spaces has been compared with old Florence's string of piazzas by Piet Lombaerde (LOMBAERDE, 1977 & 1978).

Car access to buildings and parking is located outside the spine, with an underpass for cars. Outdoor parking space was treated from the start as a public garden. All open air parking spaces are planted with different tree species in order to attract a variety of birds, as a tribute to biodiversity (landscape architect: J.-N. Capart). They have in fact become a bird reserve.

The centre of the first phase was the science library, an iconic concrete building seen as the cathedral of a university town, with its public square ("Place des sciences") built above an automobile underpass. For some 45 years it has been a place for informal gatherings, with university buildings, shops and restaurants, conceived by the architect A. Jacqmain of the Ateliers d'Architectes de Genval (JACQMAIN, 2009).

In 2015 the same team of architects was entrusted with a facelift of the string of public spaces west of the "Place des sciences", to be implemented by 2018. The science library will move to the general library of the university and the building is to be converted by 2017 into "Musée L", new museum of the Louvain University.

A new station was built by the national railway company SNCB/NMBS in 1975. The railway station provides a direct rail link to central Brussels in 35 minutes, and is to be expanded as part of Brussels' new S-Bahn fast commuter rail network (LACONTE, 2014). It is entirely below ground. Open air tracks are to be covered at a later stage. The full development of the spine included a central slab covering the lower part of the site. Besides the railway tracks it hosts access by car, underground public parking, delivery services and storage.

5. Property development along the pedestrian spine and the central slab

On each side of the long pedestrian spine and of the central slab, mixed-use neighborhoods had been built by a large range of individual investors, in accordance with the 1970 master plan. The Groupe UA favoured small plots (100 to 200 m^2, including terrace housing and small gardens) and low-rise apartment buildings. These were cheaper than large apartment blocks, as they could be built by small contractors. They have proved very popular (MASBOUNGI, 2012) and have quickly attracted a diverse population.

As a result, from an early stage the resident population has been composed of people attracted by the environmental quality and the cultural activities generated by the university, rather than mainly of university employees or resident students. Today the town's 12,000 permanent residents not connected to the university are in a large majority (UCL, 2014).

The new sub-surface railway station put into service in 1975 opened up the possibility of developing a network of pedestrian streets at ground level, while allowing car and parking access underneath. The diagram shows how the slab uses the lowest part of the dry valley (ca 10ha, i.e. ca 1 ‰ of the site).

The ground under the slab remains the property of the university, while the infrastructure and buildings are leased for up to 99 years.

Streets are narrow and mostly canopied to save street space, as well as to protect pedestrians from rain and sun. Plots are kept small whenever possible to allow architectural diversity and to facilitate access to the university's building market by small contractors.

Courtyards are open passages, whenever feasible, for easier access from buildings to open space.

High-density low-rise buildings with interlocking courts and piazzas replicate the gathering places and colleges of traditional university towns (LACONTE, 2009).

The slab hosts numerous public spaces, large and small, planted with trees. Shops, cafés and restaurants adjoin pedestrian spaces, while automobile access, deliveries and parking are exclusively located underground.

The contribution of developers to the cost of the slab and it extensions has led to increasing the size of the plots. On-going mixed-use developments at the edge of the slab and next to the railway station are proposed by large developers. Larger developments included a 200-room hotel (BARRAS, 2012 & 2016). However, in order to keep the human scale character of the town centre, only a few larger developments have been accepted by the university—landowner, on or next to the slab (BARRAS, 2013).

The latest neighboorhood, launched by the university in 2006 to the north-east of the area set aside for residential developments, will include all types of housing, including community projects inspired by the Abbeyville community of Colchester in England.

New Louvain's slab proved a successful magnet for private investment. This investment was linked to the new railway station and was supported both by a growing group of train users, i.e. the staff and students of the university, and by the inhabitants arriving on foot.

This approach was in strong contrast not only with the "campus in the fields" approach but also the post-World War II new towns. As an example, Cumbernauld in Scotland pioneered a slab, but that slab was built before the indispensable feeder population had materialised, as this central infrastructure had to be built before any part of the plan could be brought into use, entailing a large up-front investment cost that was never recouped.

A similar approach had been tried in other post-war new towns and university campuses all over Europe (such as Toulouse-le-Mirail, France and the University of Essex, England). It has been considered by many to be disappointing.

Cumbernauld has been described as follows in Wikipedia (WIKIPEDIA 2016): "The intended core of Cumbernauld remains the Town Centre buildings, all of which is essentially contained within one structure, segmented into "phases", the first of which was completed in 1967 …. Designed to be a commerce centre, an entertainment and business venue and a luxury accommodation site, it was widely accepted …. Unfortunately, the town never developed to its planned size, and the town centre has never had the life envisaged. Wealthy occupiers for the centre's penthouses never materialised and some now lie empty and derelict".

The University of Essex campus inspired this comment on its 50th anniversary: "(The) expansion of universities has not led to much enlightened architectural patronage. Rather the opposite, in fact. The (Essex) University visual trope remains those dogged dreaming spires" (BAILEY, 2014).

The Louvain master plan, on the contrary, allowed changing land-use as long as it respected the high density-low rise linear pedestrian main concept.

A major land-use change occurred in 2005 when a 35,000 m^2 shopping mall ("L'Esplanade") and a new residential street ("Charlemagne"), directly linked to the railway station and the slab, came into use. This private shopping and leisure mall now has a patronage of 8 million visitors (2014) per year and is preparing to add another 20,000 m^2 by using the airspace above the rail tracks.

It has been a major windfall for the new town.

New neighbourhoods were developed in line with the university's and town's growth, attracting cultural investments (entertainment) and a private museum devoted to Hergé, the creator of the character Tintin, which is also located along the spine, close to the railway station (Arch. Atelier de Portzamparc, Paris).

The university's science faculties have attracted a science park of 230 ha located in the periphery of the town centre.

Meanwhile the railway station has been chosen by the Belgian national railways as the south-eastern route terminus of the new Brussels S commuter rail system ("S" for "S-Bahn", or "RER" for "Réseau express régional"), including a new parking complex. This evolution towards commuter traffic will be challenging, as it will generate a daily influx of rail commuters coming by car from surrounding municipalities who are not related to the population of the new university town. A residential complex ("Courbevoie") was, however, to be built above the new parking structure provided for the railway users (BARRAS, 2013).

The Ottignies municipality (4,000 inhabitants in the 1960s) has now become the city of Ottignies-Louvain-la-Neuve. It has a permanent resident population of 31,000. Within this total population the new town has 12,000 permanent residents, as well as 45,000 daytime occupants. Citizen participation in the new town has been ensured since 1972 by the association of Louvain-la-neuve inhabitants, which actively advises on all projects on the university site. It has been a key participant in the adaptation process to larger scale projects, critically advising among others on "L'Esplanade" shopping mall and the "Charlemagne" residential street, opened in 2005, and on the new "Courbevoie" housing project linked to the future enlargement of the railway station and the construction of a new parking structure.

Its former president, Jean-Luc Roland, was elected mayor in 2000 and during three terms of office has uninterruptedly pursued a policy of participatory development.

This has been another major windfall for the new university town.

6. Water management

A key feature of the new Louvain is the conservation of the Ottignies plateau's water resources. A dual water collection system has been installed in all buildings. Only waste water goes to the treatment plant. All storm water is collected at the lowest point of the site into an artificial lake that serves both as a reservoir and an amenity. The water level varies according to the amount of rain. The water collection of the whole new town was financed as part of the infrastructure subsidies for the industrial park, located by Groupe UA at the highest point of the site.

Pre-monitoring of water entering the lake and oxygen provision allows the fishing water quality to be checked (De BACKER, 2009). This water saving policy has become more pertinent than ever, at a time of increased resource awareness.

The collection of storm water into reservoirs treated as lakes with a variable water level has been adopted in some cities in neighbouring countries, e.g. at Billancourt, near Paris. Its large linear park (Trapeze) is inundated in the rainy season and becomes a lake (BAVA, 2014).

In monsoon areas this land-water interface has been successfully applied as a natural way to absorb heavy rain and avoid floods, e.g. in Bishan-Ang Mo Kio Park in Singapore (HAUSER, 2014). The celebrated Dujiangyan ecological anti-flood scheme in Sichuan (256 BC) draws upon the same water management philosophy (WEI-NING, 2014).

The lake has acted as a magnet to residential development close to both the central slab and to the park land surrounding the lake.

7. Conclusion: achievements, challenges and perspectives

Achievements

The achievements resulting from 45 years of urban development might be summarised as follows:

— The 1970 Louvain new university town master plan, largely thanks to Raymond Lemaire and Groupe Urbanisme Architecture, was an unspoken homage to the historic city of Leuven and its quality of life, while adopting innovative eco-development features, including a complete pedestrianisation of the town.

— From its first phase of operation (1972) it achieved a mix of land uses. Each phase could operate on its own but was linked to the following ones, all along a pedestrian spine that started in the east from the existing main road and extended for more than 1.5 km through the whole site, saving road infrastructure costs and generating a maximum of places for informal meeting between people. This feature proved the main attraction to both residential and commercial development. The preference for small plots generated in-built architectural diversity.

—The central part of the spine was developed above a new sub-surface railway station built in 1975 by the national railways, and directly connected to Brussels. This feature allowed "reverse commuting". The underground space hosted access roads, parking and room for storage, while the surface was reserved for pedestrian spaces, shops and cultural investments, attracting more residents.

—All storm water was directed towards the lowest part of the site and collected in a reservoir treated as a lake, which became another attraction to residential development unconnected with the university.

—Also linked to the railway station, a 35,000 m^2 shopping mall, mixed with residential development, started operation in 2005. By 2014 it had 8 million visitors per year and it is due to expand by another 20,000 m^2. The station itself will become the terminus of one of the new Brussels commuter lines, generating another boost to the town. Close to the station the Hergé museum is attracting young and less young visitors.

—From the start the new inhabitants and temporary residents, mainly students, organised themselves into a strong association of inhabitants, a contervailing power to that of the university landowner and private investors, as well as to the municipality of Ottignies, which meanwhile has become the city of Ottignies-Louvain-la-Neuve, led by Mayor J-L. Roland since the year 2000.

What in the late 1960s looked like a utopian project has turned into the fastest growing urban service centre in Belgium, boosting the whole area around it. The start-ups generated by university research now extend to the periphery of the university site and beyond. Some have become large international technology-based firms, such as the IBA group.

The originality of the Louvain new university town was recognised in 1978 by its being awarded the Sir Patrick Abercrombie Prize for town-planning by the International Union of Architects (UIA).

Challenges

Challenges are looming and will be met during the coming years:

—The demand for residential development and the status symbol of the place have led to larger projects, higher prices and higher developer profits. This may affect the social balance of the new town, made up of both the university community and a growing non-university population attracted by cultural and leisure activities.

—The planned transformation of the railway station into a large commuter terminal with park-and-ride and large parking spaces (Transit Oriented Development principle), will create a conflict of interest between the needs of future commuters and the aspirations of the association of inhabitants, which represents all segments of the present inclusive community.

—As a response the construction of a new neighbourhood above the new railway station, parking spaces are being provided to attract more higher-income residents. However, the present status of the existing lower-income "La Baraque" neighbourhood is being protected, and a new 30-ha neighbourhood planned by the university within the pedestrian town (What is a pedestrian town perimeter?) will use the "Abbeyfield Community Land Trust" system to allow ample affordable housing (BARRAS, 2016).

A tale of two sustainable cities.

The new university's town planning perspective remains focused on the full preservation of the pedestrian environment created by the 1970 master plan, which is considered by the residents as the key to its national success. No high-rise development is contemplated.

The old city of Louvain/Leuven has gradually become more pedestrian, green and blue (improving its Dyle canal and river front). The two cities have become "twin cities" and have jointly celebrated the 500th anniversary of UTOPIA's publication in Louvain/Leuven.

The university's relations with Brussels have taken a new turn. The Catholic faculty of literature ("Faculté Saint-Louis") that wished to remain autonomous has meanwhile developed as the "Université Saint-Louis". In early 2007, at the proposal of Rectors Pierre Jadoul and Vincent Blondel, the boards of Université Saint-Louis and of the Catholic university of Louvain decided to amalgamate, resulting in the prospect of a stronger urban university development in Brussels.

References

(BARRAS 2012), Barras Ph. "Les projets immobiliers en cours ou envisagé à Louvain-la-Neuve" (Ongoing or intended urban developments in Louvain-la-Neuve), Séminaire Grands Projets Urbains en Brabant Walloon (Seminar Large Developments in Walloon Brabant Province), 19 September 2012.

(BARRAS 2013), Barras Ph. 《On doit repousser les avances des promoteurs》 (developers should be contained), interview in Espace-Vie, September 2013.

(BARRAS, 2016), Barras Ph. "Projet Athena-Ferme de Lauzelle", Editions et Séminaires, 16 September 2016.

(BAVA 2013), Bava, H. Presentation in Brussels' Cercle Royal Gaulois 《JARDINS INONDABLES》 (Gardens occasionally flooded), http://www.ffue.org/wp-content/uploads/2013/06/CERCLE_G_130905_H-Bava-TER-cl.pdf (last read on 29 March 2016).

(BAILEY 2014), Bailey S. 《The only way is Essex》, The Spectator, 1 November 2014.

(DE BACKER 2009), De Backer, L. 《Le cycle de l'eau et l'environnement urbain》 (The water cycle and the urban environment), in: Laconte, P. (Ed.), 《La recherche de la qualité environnementale et urbaine-Le cas de Louvain-la-Neuve-Belgique》 (Searching for environmental and urban quality—The case of the new Louvain University—Belgium), Lyon: Editions du CERTU, 2009.

(EPSTEIN 2009), Epstein, G., "Les nouvelles universités et le cas de Lancaster" (The new universities and the Lancaster case), in: Laconte, P. (Ed.), 《La recherche de la qualité environnementale et urbaine-Le cas de Louvain-la-Neuve-Belgique》 (Searching for environmental and urban quality-The case of the new Louvain University-Belgium), Lyon: Editions du CERTU, 2009.

(FRANKIGNOULLE 2012), Frankignoulle P. "Le Sart-Tilmant et Louvain-la-Neuve: deux visions de l'urbanisme universitaire" (Sart-Timant and Louvain-la-Neuve: Two visions of University Planning"), Nouveaux Cahiers du développement terrritorial, N° 83, pp. 93-96.

(GROUPE 1970), Groupe Urbanisme-Architecture, Plan directeur Louvain-la-Neuve, 15 Octobre 1970, Document available at the UCL.

(HAUSER, 2014), Hauser, G., "It Takes A City To Raise A River Park—Bishan-Ang Mo Kio Park, Singapore", MyLiveableCity The Art and Science of it, Ironman Media and Advisory Services Pvt Ltd., October 2014.

(JACQMAIN 2009), Jacqmain, A., "La Place des Sciences (Louvain-la-Neuve): Circonstances, démarches, scénario à l'Atelier de Genval》 (The new Louvain Science Square: Circumstances, steps and design alternatives by Atelier de Genval), in: Laconte, P. (Ed.), 《La recherche de la qualité environnementale et urbaine-Le cas de Louvain-la-Neuve-Belgique》 (Searching for environmental and urban quality-The case of the new Louvain University-Belgium), Lyon: Editions du CERTU, 2009.

(LACONTE, 1980), Laconte, P., "Toward an Integrated Approach of Urban Development and Resources Conservation: The Case of Louvain-la-Neuve", in: Laconte, P. (Ed.), "Changing Cities: A Challenge to Planning", The Annals of the American Academy of Political and Social Sciences, Philadelphia 1980, pp. 43-158.

(LACONTE 2007), Laconte, P. and Hein, C (Eds.), "Brussels: Perspectives on a European Capital", Brussels: Editions Aliter, 2007.

(LACONTE, 2009), Laconte, P. (Ed.), 《La recherche de la qualité environnementale et urbaine-Le cas de Louvain-la-Neuve-Belgique》 (Searching for environmental and urban quality—The case of the new Louvain University—Belgium),

Lyon: Editions du CERTU, 2009.

(LACONTE, 2013), Laconte, P., 《Le démembrement du droit de propriété-évaluation d'expériences d'intérêt pour le développement territorial bruxellois et wallon》 (Long term lease experiences of interest for Brussels and Wallonia-urban developments), Nouveaux Cahiers du développement territorial N°84 (2013), pp. 58-60.

(LACONTE 2014), Laconte, P. (Ed.) "Accéder à Bruxelles" (Accessing Brussels), Brussels: Editions Aliter 2014.

(LOMBAERDE 1977), Lombaerde, P., "Louvain-la-Neuve, de eerste new-town in België sinds 1666" (The First new town in Belgium since 1666), in: Stedebouw en Volkshuisvesting, 2, 1977, pp. 67-83.

(LOMBAERDE 1978), Lombaerde, P., "Beeld en anti-beeld van een stad: Louvain-la-Neuve" (Image and anti-image of a city), in: A+, 45, 1978, pp. 27-56. (also published in French in the A+ French edition).

(MASBOUNGI, 2008), Masboungi, A. 《Faire la ville avec des lotissements》 (Neighbourhood made cities), Paris: Le Moniteur, 2008.

(REMY 2007), Remy, J. "Louvain-la-Neuve. Une manière de concevoir la ville. Genèse et développement" (Louvain-la-Neuve. A way to conceive the city. Origin and development), Louvain-la-Neuve: Presses universitaires de Louvain, 2007, p. 133.

(UCL, 2014). "Louvain-la-Neuve-Faits et chiffres" (facts and figures), Office de tourisme Inforville, updated 2014.

(WEI-NING 2014), Wei-Ning Xiang "Doing real and permanent good in landscape and urban planning: Ecological wisdom for urban sustainability", in Landscape and Urban Planning 121 (2014) pp. 65-69 (Elsevier).

(WIKIPEDIA, 2016), http://en.wikipedia.org/wiki/Cumbernauld_Town_Centre (last read 28 March 2016) and Leuven Groot Begijnhof (last read 28 October 2016).

Other readings

Amanti, Lund I, et al. Baucher-Blondel-Filippone. Trois architectes modernistes (Bruxelles: Fédération Wallonie-Bruxelles / Cellule architecture, Faculté d'Architecture La Cambre /Horta de l'Université Libre de Bruxelles, 2012).

Guisset, E. Les néo-louvanistes, combien sont-ils? Qui sont-ils? (Louvain-la-Neuve: Presses universitaires de Louvain, 2007).

Hiraux, F. L'avènement d'une ville universitaire. La création de Louvain-la-Neuve. Hommage à Michel Woitrin (Louvain-la-Neuve: Academia, 2009).

Houbart, C, Raymond Lemaire (1921—1997) et la conservation de la ville ancienne: approche critique et historique de ses projets belges dans une perspective internationale》 (KULeuven-Thèse de doctorat, 2015).

Laporte, Chr., Yves du Monceau (Bruxelles: Racine, 2012).

Lechat, J-M, Louvain-la Neuve. Trente années d'histoires (Louvain-la-Neuve: Academia, 2011).

Ringlet, G, Une aventure universitaire (Bruxelles: Racine, 2000).

Roegiers, J and Vandevivere, I (eds), Leuven-Louvain-la-Neuve. Aller Retour (Leuven: Leuven University Press/ Louvain-la-Neuve: Presses universitaires de Louvain, 2001).

Roland, J-L, Un bourgmestre vert à Louvain-la-Neuve (Bruxelles: Luc Pire, 2006).

Roland, J-L, Ottignies-Louvain-la-Neuve: paradoxes, réussites et perspectives d'une ville atypique (Louvain-la-Neuve: Academia 2011).

Thielen, P, Louvain-la-Neuve du temps des pionniers. Nos utopies réalisables des années 70 (Louvain-la-Neuve: Academia 2011).

Woitrin, M, Louvain-la-Neuve. Louvain-en-Woluwe. Le grand dessein (Gembloux: Duculot, 1987).

遗产研究:为新一代学者创建的一个研究领域

Heritage Studies: Constructing a Field of Research for a New Generation of Scholars

[德]玛丽-塞莱斯·阿尔伯特　教授
联合国教科文组织世界遗产研究教席前持有人
Prof. Marie-Theres Albert
Former Chair Holder, UNESCO Chair in Heritage Studies

在文化遗产研究在世界范围内日益成为一门显学的时候,文化遗产研究这门学科本身也应该根据不断变化的时代与要求调整自身的学科视角。在现有的科学与政治话语之外,它应该促发对"文化遗产"的重新认识与思考。通过对"理论与方法""范式""历史与档案"以及"案例"等诸方面探讨,"遗产研究"丛书系列能够帮助新一代学者在文化遗产研究的广阔领域中搭建起一个具有系统性的研究框架。

World Heritage Studies as it has been created in Cottbus as a Master's Programme has existed now for nearly 20 years. Heritage Studies as a PhD programme was established in 2010. The intention was and still is to develop research based on a holistic understanding of heritage and on the paradigm of heritage as promoter for sustainable human development. Meanwhile, this concept of Heritage Studies has been accepted worldwide.

In the scientific discourse, it is of equal importance as the concept of "Critical Heritage Studies" based on a postcolonial approach, or the concept of "Material Heritage Studies" based mainly on material sciences such as architecture, urban planning or conservation and preservation. The Heritage Studies discourse understood as Heritage Transformation Processes and Human Development is the research focus of the "Institut Heritage Studies" at the "Internationale Akademie Berlin" and has been published via the Heritage Studies series with de Gruyter from 2012—2015.

I believe that with this new paradigm we will be able to contribute to further establishing Heritage Studies, because with this concept we are able to scientifically identify the challenges of modernity for our heritage and to develop strategies to sustainably deal with them. This means that we will be able to give answers to the questions raised by the high number of alumni of the Cottbus World Heritage Studies programme, who are now confronted with current and future challenges for heritage protection and use. Today, more than ever, our heritage is affected by many features of the globalization and we have therefore to go further in finding answers to the most striking challenges for protecting and using our heritage worldwide.

Heritage protection and use, within the processes of globalization and modernization and with all the implications, such as climate change or mass tourism, commodification of our heritage or migration processes of millions of people, can no longer be managed through political declarations exclusively, but have to be analyzed, interpreted and handled based on corresponding scientific research. I'm convinced that the "Institute Heritage Studies", with our concept of Heritage Studies and with our series of publications, contributes to identifying those most striking developments and their causes, as well as developing sustainable strategies to deal with the challenges.

Our epistemological understanding of Heritage Studies is comparable to Cultural Studies. It includes different paradigms, scientific concepts, constructions and approaches in a systematic form. I think that we will meet at least some of the challenges by encompassing and working on the manifold expressions of heritage which are shaped by the modern world in a variety of ways.

Heritage and the City

This Crossover Forum 2017 deals with challenges, mainly those arising from modernization and urbanization. Therefore, also in this specific field of heritage protection under processes of urbanization, the phenomena have to be seen, interpreted and understood by analyzing their formations, conditions, appearances and effects. Also, processes of urbanization need research measures for sustainable treatment and conflict solving strategies.

Therefore, also for this Forum, I think we shall include the paradigm of heritage as an approach for sustainable human development. I would like to give some examples of current developments which are affecting our heritage: The first one is mass tourism. And even though many experts in the tourism business are aware of the threats that worldwide tourism poses to the material substance, the authenticity and the values of world heritage sites, the commercialization of World Heritage proceeds. As long as the commodification of heritage dominates the discourse, no alternatives of sustainable use of heritage are investigated.

Analysing this phenomenon, it has to be stated that a paradigm change has occurred. World heritage is understood less and less as a universal good, which according to the convention must be protected as such. In the course of time and through the processes of commodification, world heritage has transformed from being a good to a product. This product is merchandised and becomes therefore subject to the rules of the market. The consequences that this change of value has brought forth in the construction of world heritage, are fundamental and also have to be researched.

For example, demands for sustainability in tourism development, which deals solely with visitor numbers, have not been very far reaching. On the other hand, it has to be stated, that the more people who know what a world heritage site means, why it exists and what its function for future development could be, the more the values of world heritage can be promoted. But sustainable tourism will only become possible if the tourists themselves learn and accept the need for sustainable development for the specific sites they visit. If you look at this picture, I think, a lot of changes have to be initiated.

Another reality which affects our heritage is refugee movements and migration due to many reasons. Contrary to the phenomenon of mass tourism, the effects of those movements of the people affect the people themselves and their heritage in many ways. They relate to the tangible and intangible assets of people and their monopolization led by different interests. They characterize the various constructions of human heritage and adapt them to the dynamically changing cultural and social processes.

The different current migration processes, which can be observed worldwide, have changed the understanding of heritage to be protected already. However, there are insufficient analyses of the causes, and effective measures to deal with the phenomena have not been taken. What happens with the heritage of humankind if war and terrorism, impoverishment of people due to socioeconomic changes or obliteration of cultural and natural landscapes become constituent elements of whole regions, has not at all been reflected upon. These developments are related both to the heritage of immigrants and to that of emigrants, though in different ways. While people as emigrants often leave formerly occupied spaces or cities such as rural or urban wastelands, as immigrants they create new structures where they have to share places with the locals.

The currently observed problems with racism and discrimination against refugees, for example, which are based not only on real racism in the world but also on incompetence of societies for integration, are also not new. They were already analyzed and explained by Norbert Elias in his book *The Established and the Outsiders* published in 1965.

As I have already mentioned at the beginning, Heritage Studies has to go beyond the current scientific and political discourse; however, it has to include the stated reasons and interests in protecting heritage in accordance with the conventions and its operational guidelines.

The community, consisting of responsible citizens, bears responsibility for the commons. In the area of cultural heritage, sustainability concerns the cultural and natural goods of mankind, and responsible citizens who want to preserve them as they are granting a sense of identity. It has been proven in many projects that people are able to engage in a responsible way, and they do so especially when it comes to their heritage.

But it has also to create a new understanding of heritage, of inheriting but much more of adapting the original perception and goals of heritage protection defined in the World Heritage convention to current developments. This is necessary because we need to create new responsibilities. One striking example is currently the discussion on the "Commons".

This concerns, in particular, the idea and the concept of the commons that was also developed and promoted in the 1990s by the late Nobel Prize winner Elinor Ostrom. The idea of the commons, as it has been developed by Elinor Ostrom, is that scarce resources such as air, water and—this is my proposal-the heritage of mankind are not to be regarded as private or public goods, but that they are common goods and must be treated as such.

Based on the former proposals our institute has begun to develop our constructions of Heritage Studies in a multistage process and with four focus areas. For example, we ask questions about, how, if at all and if so, heritage in the context of the 1972 Convention is constructed in the sense of human ecology, law, architectural history, art history, planning or ecology. We deal with the anthropological, ethnological, historical or museological approaches in the heritage constructions of the 2003 and 2005 conventions.

We ask whether and in which manner we can speak of inter-and transdisciplinary research interests in these constructions and how they are aligned. Furthermore, we are not concerned about the scientific discourse as such. Our aim is to capture the diversity of heritage, to process it holistically, to open up yet unidentified opportunities of knowledge and practice.

In other words, our concern is to complement the politico-practical discourse, which is expressed in the conventions and their implementations, by an academic discourse, that is, a disciplinary and interdisciplinary, thematic and systematic discourse. Not least we want to initiate a discourse which no longer merely demands sustainability in the implementation of the conventions in a populistic sense—which is unfortunately currently a problem—but analyzes it scientifically and embeds it within the discipline to be constituted, Heritage Studies.

This means, that the concepts of development and participation have not only to be determined under the wording of sustainability and sustainable development but under the reality of social, cultural or economic backgrounds. I furthermore think that it is not enough to adopt new declarations. It is much more important to look precisely what sustainability or sustainable development mean for or within a specific situation, concept or measure.

In other words, we all know that sustainability depends on participation of stakeholders in all development processes. This has been propagated within the political discourse since the *Brundtland Report* in 1987. However, the results of and the reasons for, the lack of successful implementation have not been evaluated sufficiently.

The research which has to be addressed is to find out why the strategies that have been employed up until now, have not been effective, neither the sustainability nor participation strategies. After all, for more than 40 years now, different participation concepts have been developed and tested. I remember when I started with my studies at the TU Berlin in sociology in the late 1960s, besides theories of science we learnt about concepts of participation for improving the "third world" development policy. We will have to further analyse if political ambitions and their expressions—locally through the regional communities, nationally through political representatives or internationally through organisations in the UN system—will be able to set processes in motion. If they are not able to do so, we will have to look for alternative mediators and supporting measures.

Heritage Studies

How should we construct Heritage Studies so that they can be positioned in the scientific discourse and paradigmatically? How are they to be conceived so that they can do justice to the breadth of heritage phenomena? Which disciplinary, interdisciplinary and/or transdisciplinary discourses are to be integrated into the Heritage Studies and, last but not least, what epistemological and methodological preferences are attributed to them?

If you look at the structure, you will realize that heritage is conceptualized for its potential for human development and sustainability and to be orientated accordingly. Only against this backdrop, do goals such as identity development attain their meanings. This also applies to its potential for peace building and conflict resolution. Conservation and usage of heritage require an extensive individual and social responsibility of all stakeholders. Only in this way is sustainability achievable. This, in turn, requires the involvement and participation of all stakeholders in the process of the responsible appropriation of their heritage.

In the presented layout, Heritage Studies positions itself also epistemologically through the outlined transformation processes. It is seen as a critical discipline which works on its research questions and issues inter-and/or transdisciplinarily, but which explicitly derives them from the demands of realities which evolve daily and differently for the peoples of the world.

This includes the positioning of the cognitive interest in the context of the diversity of our world. It means reflecting the cultural diversity of the world in the approaches and methods of Heritage Studies without becoming arbitrary. Not least, it means developing strategies for the future, for example, for a sustainable approach to heritage. In other words, it is not about gaining abstract knowledge, but explicitly about conceptualizing Heritage Studies paradigmatically for human development.

As mentioned above, we have designed a series of scientific publications, *Heritage Studies*, for the implementation of the formulated goals. This series shall encourage experienced and young scholars to conduct systematical research in the broad field of Heritage Studies and make the results available to the national and international, theoretically and practically oriented, disciplinarily and interdisciplinarily established heritage community. This series aims to initiate discourses that reflect the facets of heritage essentially in four dimensions.

Theory and Methods

In this section, research will be published that captures the diversity of heritage including its different paradigmatic approaches with the aim of sustainability in mind. Essentially, this section will be about new insights to be gained disciplinarily and interdisciplinarily on the understanding of heritage and appropriate epistemological and/or methodological approaches. The Theory and Methods section will also include new areas of application for sustainable uses of heritage.

Paradigms

In this section, publications will appear that deal with the normative aspects of heritage. At the centre of this section are intentions and constructions associated with the heritage conventions and the concomitant perceptions. The main cognitive interest in this section is essentially to initiate publications that confront the future viability of heritage with the transformation processes brought about by globalization and to do research on them in the interest of human development.

History and Documents

The research in this section focuses on the understanding of heritage in the context of the UNESCO Conventions listed above and UNESCO's Memory of the World Programme. Rationalizations for and adaptations of the understanding of heritage, which changes in the course of historical developments, as well as their concrete application at different stages of the implementation of the conventions will be researched and published. The interpretations of the heritage laws which are flowing from these conventions in the historical context are also to be researched and published in this dimension.

Case Studies

The basic research interest in this section is aimed at the analysis and systematization of the many different forms of practice and the experiences derived from the diversity of case studies. This applies not only to the cultures of the world and their heritage itself, but also to the different conventions, their uses and valuations. This section thrives on the diversity of heritage and contributes in this way to a lasting understanding of heritage.

武汉大学早期优秀建筑保护与校园规划
Preservation of Historic Buildings and Campus Planning of Wuhan University

王国恩　教授
武汉大学
Prof. Wang Guoen
Wuhan University

This speech presents the historical information and current status of heritage buildings in Wuhan University, along with the renovation and environment enhancement project as well as campus planning that correlates these historic buildings with new ones in a holistic approach.

一、武汉大学早期建筑群

江城多山，珞珈独秀；山上有黉，武汉大学。

武汉大学环绕东湖水，坐拥珞珈山，校园环境优美，风景如画，被誉为"中国最美丽的大学"。学校占地面积5 195亩，建筑面积272万平方米。中西合璧的宫殿式建筑群古朴典雅、巍峨壮观，26栋早期建筑被列为"全国重点文物保护单位"。

图1　1931年的武大老牌楼

1928年夏，国民政府聘任李四光、叶雅各等名士筹建武汉大学。李四光骑着毛驴实地勘察，相中了东湖之滨、远离闹市、山丘起伏的珞珈山一带，并聘请美国建筑师开尔斯（F. H. Kales）为武大校园总设计。1929年新校址因为需要修路迁坟，触犯了一些坟主，百余名坟主以新校舍破坏风水为由而阻碍新校址的圈定和校舍建设，甚至要纠集乡民跑到王世杰老家挖其祖坟，省教育厅厅长甚至唆使人在工地闹事。国立武汉大学筹备委员会曾昭安按王世杰的示意，组织教授会向教育部力争"像珞珈山这样的好地方，应该建校，无论哪个总统、主席也阻止不了"，结果获准。石瑛也积极支持王世杰，以"建校乃千年大计，不要迷信风水"严厉地驳复了反对迁坟者。

武大校舍建筑于1930年动工。从建筑到竣工一气呵成。包括武大牌楼，文、法、理、工四个学院大楼，宋卿体育馆、老图书馆及广场，男生寄宿舍（樱园学生宿舍），学生饭厅及俱乐部、半山庐、十八栋别墅、华中水工试验所等一系列建筑群，共68栋，7.8万平方米。这是中国近代史上惟一完整规划和统筹设计，并在较短时间内一气呵成的大学校园，代表了当时一流校园的理想模式。建筑群整体上遵循"轴线对称、主从有序、中央殿堂、四隅崇楼"的中国传统原则，形成以图书馆、理学院、工学院为主体的三个建筑团组，又引入西方古典式样，融合了中西建筑之长。

国立武汉大学牌楼

原位于街道口大学路起点一侧的象征学校大门的老牌楼，历史上曾两次修建。第一次是四柱琉璃飞檐木结构，结构古朴、描金彩绘，漆彩画甚是别致，目前尚未见到有确切记载的建造年代（可能是1931年）。木牌楼应该在1934年6月前竣工。可惜次年毁于龙卷风。因此难以弄清牌楼上的字系谁人所书（可能是王世杰）。

六一纪念亭

该亭为纪念"六一惨案"死难烈士而建于1947年11月，1948年4月竣工。六角飞檐，碧瓦熠熠，六根朱红圆柱支撑，都蕴含六月之意，亭四周植有冬青和绿草。

宋卿体育馆

1936年7月竣工，馆长约35.05米，宽约21.34米。黎元洪（字宋卿）病逝于天津后，原想迁葬于珞珈山南麓（当年的珞珈山尚无茂林，天气晴好时，放眼望去，可以在山体上清晰地看见九条龙脊，被誉为九龙戏珠的风水宝地），校方没有答应。后来黎元洪的两个儿子黎绍基和黎绍业将黎元洪筹建江汉大学的基金十万大洋（中兴煤矿股票）转捐给武大，建造了宋卿体育馆。

体育馆四周绕有回廊，采用钢筋混凝土梁、柱，屋顶采用跨度三十多米的三铰拱承重，这是当时西方非常先进的建筑工艺，正面看台又有中式的重檐——三檐滴水，馆里还

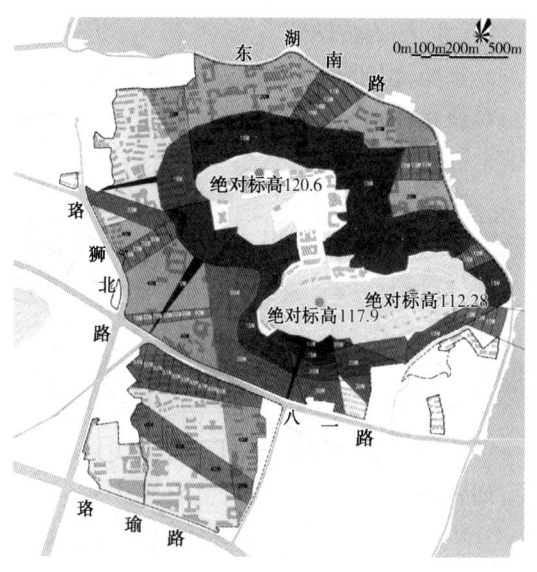

图2 校园规划中的建筑高度控制

做了只有宫廷或者高规格庙宇才采用的斗拱。里面有看台，外有观景台，开尔斯原本想要在馆前建一个游泳池，未被采用。同时拟在馆内建辛亥革命首义纪念馆，由于抗战爆发而未果。屋顶覆绿色琉璃瓦，利用密檐高差采光通风，侧墙框架结构，山墙取巴洛克式，是典型的中西合璧建筑。

1938年3月，国民党临时全国代表大会在这里召开，推举蒋介石为国民党总裁。会后，蒋介石在此发表抗战演说，号召全国军民团结抗战。1947年，武大"六一惨案"追悼会在这里举行。

老图书馆

图书馆工程施工中，由于墙体砌砖方法不对，承重力达不到设计要求，缪恩钊要求施工方采取补强措施，在大阅览室四角增加四对钢筋混凝土柱子才达到承重要求，这一补强措施使施工单位增加造价2万元。又因为施工方将屋角做成了南方式的上挑形而非北方式的平缓形而被要求返工重建。外部装饰极具中国传统特色，顶部塔楼是八角垂檐、单檐双歇山式，上立七环宝鼎，兼有排气之功用。屋顶上有采暖烟囱，南屋角立有粗大的隅石，北屋角立有小塔，其间护栏以左右的勾阑和中央的双龙吻背，造成"围脊"的效果。两副楼屋脊与大阅览室相连，叫"歇山连脊"。在大门上方镶有老子的全身镂空铁画像。正面5楹（间），中间3楹（间）为大阅览室，两边副楼，后两角处各有一书库楼。

功能性：图书馆平面呈"工"字形，由目录厅、检索厅、阅览厅、书库和辅助服务厅五部分组成，其中书库使用面积约1 186平方米，能藏书近200万册。

形式创新：该馆的设计在平面布局和空间组织上突破了中国古典建筑"相沿"的陈式，内廊的四隅切角处设有半圆弧形楼梯。南面的主入口为三开间单洞门，既用了西式双联廊柱，又用了中国古典建筑中的雀替、额枋；瓦作、施斗拱，皆参照清代建筑样式，中央主体顶层为八边形，北面的书库地下层外墙有收分，上立勾阑，形成高大的台座。两库间的联接体作如下处理：地下层外墙有以方窗为单元组合的大片玻璃窗，第二层的"围脊"上方中央有以五窗突起的阁楼。

建筑价值：该馆是中西建筑设计理论、技艺、手法相互渗透、融会贯通的佳作，为中国近代建筑史上率先采用新结构、新材料、新技术（钢筋混凝土框架和钢桁架混合结构）仿中国古典建筑的成功之作，体现了当时的文化潮流、科学技术和时代精神。

文学院（1931年竣工）、法学院（1936年竣工）

形式与寓意：文学院的屋顶采用翘角，意为文采飞扬；法学院的屋顶则是平角，意为法力严肃。屋檐上有"仙人骑鸡"，后立七个脊兽，有镇火灭奸人之意。

老文学院目前为数学院使用，其中一楼大教室为全校使用。老法学院一楼作为教室使用，二楼为质量

院,三、四楼为数学院。

布局:位于图书馆的左右两翼,是中国传统文化中"文左武右"的体现,意为文武相谐、文华武英。两院相对矗立,是一对姊妹楼,平面为方形四合院,立面有4层,宫殿式屋顶。文学院竣工于1931年9月,这里曾是国立武汉大学历任校长办公的地方;法学院竣工于1936年8月。

男生寄宿舍(1931年竣工)

格局:又名老斋舍,亦因紧靠樱花而得名"樱花城堡",是一座仿布达拉宫琉璃瓦建筑。1931年9月竣工。当时的造价为55万元。宿舍依狮子山南坡顺山势而建,具有良好的日照条件。建筑主体以花岗岩的灰色为主色调,显得朴素大方,厚重沉稳。入口处平面修建多层阶梯,外形统一,气势宏伟,为了突出其导向性,又在此基础上,将拱门上部垫起一层,作成顶部单檐歇山式亭楼。

文化内涵:中间的城楼与图书馆位于一条轴线上。斋舍分为四个单元,共设十六个出入口,四栋宿舍一字排开,加上三个圆形拱门配以门楼,各层宿舍分别以《千字文》中的"天地玄黄,宇宙洪荒,日月盈昃,辰宿列张"命名。

单个房间尺寸为3.3米宽、4.5米长,使用面积为13平方米,内有壁柜,共有300多间房。建筑平面采用不同层次的依山组合,巧妙地顺应了自然地势的变化,同时借助山势构成气势磅礴的立面效果。在不同标高处,沿等高线建成不同层次的房屋,各排房屋底层地面在不同高度上,而屋面则在同一平面上,形成"天平地不平"的格局,有曲径通幽之感。钢筋混凝土平屋顶与图书馆前区连成一片,形成一个大广场。两单元宿舍依山设有95级阶梯(原为108级,但底层已被提升的路基淹没)作为自校前路上图书馆的径道,又是宿舍的主要楼梯。"中华民国十九年国立武汉大学建"碑传为燕树棠书。

学生饭厅及俱乐部(1931年竣工)

下层是饭厅,在饭厅锅炉房的背后,还供奉着一尊灶神,专门设有神龛。上层为俱乐部(临时礼堂),内部装饰极富民俗特色,房梁上有三层画着戟的图案,称为"连升三戟",即祝福学子连升三级。

蔡元培、胡适、张伯苓、张君劢、周恩来、董必武、陈独秀、蒋介石、汪精卫、陈立夫、李宗仁、陶德曼、司徒雷登等中外要人曾在此演讲。

目前,学生俱乐部的饭厅为后勤集团学生食堂、俱乐部为校团委使用。

理学院(1931年竣工、1936年竣工)

位于男生寄宿舍东侧,整体建筑分两期建造。主楼和前排配楼为第一期工程,1931年11月竣工;后排配楼为第二期工程,于1936年6月竣工。主楼采用八角面墙体和拜占庭式的钢筋混凝土穹隆屋顶(直径20米),与南面的工学院方形墙体和玻璃方屋顶相呼应,体现出天圆(北)地方(南)的建筑理念。

同时,圆顶也是为了抗东湖边吹来的强风。中部主体为科学会堂,首层有三个阶梯教室(也是中国最早的阶梯教室),二层为理、工学院的教室,三层为生物系的标本室和数学系的模型室。两侧配楼为化学楼和物理楼(实验室),楼高4层,单檐歇山式,绿琉璃瓦。会堂与配楼有连廊相通构成整体。1948年10月10日,华中区科学团体联合会在此召开。

李四光先生曾经两次在理学院演讲,题目分别为《庐山冰川》和《东亚恐慌中中国煤铁供给问题》,当时正是日本侵略军占领东北向华北节节进犯之时,李四光先生大声呼吁:"幸国人早日醒悟,急早图之!"

目前,理学院中的教学楼为全校教室、东北楼中的三楼为测试中心使用、西北楼中的三楼为生科院和文学院使用。老理学院维修后拟全部调整给数学院使用。

工学院(1936年竣工)

功能:西方建筑很注重功能,在工院大楼首先体现在采光上。

公共空间:主楼为教学用房,平面呈正方形,楼内中部有5层共享大厅,四廊相通,亦为学生课间活动的公共空间——"玻璃中庭"。

形式:矩形平面,有内廊,单檐歇山式,绿琉璃瓦。主楼正方形墙体上带有明显的"侧角",这是因为中国传统的城墙墙面是斜面的,为了使建筑样式符合传统形式的要求,故采取了削斜墙面四角的方法,利用人们的视觉误差,造成墙体斜面的假象,使这一现代建筑亦带有中国传统建筑的神韵。同时,为了整体协调,斜角上方的石刻栏杆采用独特的圆角过渡。

攒尖式四角重檐玻璃屋顶,共享空间的玻璃中庭构造,是全世界最早采用空间共享这一建筑风潮的建筑之一。与外围的四座中国传统配楼和正前方的两座罗马式碉楼相组配,是典型的中西融合式建筑。四角的圆盘形水斗,既解决了大屋顶的排水问题,同时又成为美化建筑的装饰;中国传统建筑中罕见的狮面兽装饰,独具匠心。

格局:工学院两边的两个副楼做得也很西式。很明显就可以看出,它们都有两个大穹顶。这个在西方很常见,比如说俄罗斯索菲亚大教堂、梵蒂冈西斯廷大教堂、美国白宫等。有建筑学家指出,西方高大拱形穹顶体现着宗教寓意。

细节:工学院主楼的细部处理极为讲究,集美观性与实用性于一体。例如墙面上方配有多个中国传统建筑中罕见的狮面兽装饰,独具匠心;而在屋顶的四角飞檐下,还装有4个圆盘形水斗,称为"盛露盘",形似吊灯,实则是屋面的排水口,既承接双层大屋面雨水的集中排放,不致损害墙脚,同时又美化了飞檐翼角。并覆有孔雀绿琉璃瓦。主楼高大的墙体被宽大的落地玻璃窗和削斜式侧角所美化,四角由绿色琉璃瓦歇山顶的中式配楼护持,更显雍容华贵、典雅大方、壮丽多彩。

半山庐(1933年竣工)

位于珞珈山腰西北,高达7米,由两个阳台将三栋两层的楼房连缀而成,中间一楼伸出一个装饰性屋檐为入口,八个飞檐毫无雕饰讲究,整栋楼用色简拙,皆青砖墨瓦,外表极显质朴无华之能事,与珞珈山的苍秀山势混为一体。据说半山庐的建筑与选址是武大一位研究易经的教授所设计。虽依山而建,但庭前却异常开阔平坦。本是单身教工宿舍,家眷不在武汉的教授大多住在这里。1937年至1938年,"武汉抗战"期间,蒋介石和宋美龄曾寓居与此。

周恩来故居(1931年竣工)、郭沫若故居(1931年竣工)

位于珞珈山腰东南的第一教职员住宅区,1931年9月首期建成18栋,1933年增建3栋,抗战期间被侵华日军拆毁了1栋,1947年又增建1栋,此后又陆续毁掉了2栋,目前实际一共为19栋。建筑风格整体采用英式乡间别墅风格,2～3层砖木结构,同时每一栋建筑都自有其特点,主要由石格斯和沈中清等设计、汉协盛营造厂建造。侵华日军侵占武汉后,将有些别墅的内构部造改成日式的。作为全国重点文物保护单位的周恩来故居与郭沫若故居即在其中(分别为一区19栋27号和12栋20号)。周恩来故居是一栋标准英式田园别墅,红瓦青砖,地基开阔,庭前屋后被参天大树环绕,通往山下的是几条石阶小径。别墅由两个哥特式风格的拱形门栋分开,楼栋之间有一精致花园,种有一棵大芭蕉树。武汉会战时期,因国共第二次合作,国民政府安置周恩来与邓颖超下榻于此,两人时常到东湖边散步。邓颖超在世时,有人建议把这里建成一个纪念馆,被她否定了。与周恩来故居相邻的是同为政治部副部长的黄琪翔旧居。

李达故居(1952年竣工)

位于珞珈山南麓西部,是一座由院墙围合的砖木结构平房,1952年建成。平面布局呈"干"字形,由李达自己绘制示意图后,工程人员再据此进行的设计。

二、武汉大学早期建筑群价值

1. 历史价值

她记载了近现代中国大学校园建设的艰辛足迹。武汉大学的建设过程无不饱浸着当时的教育者、仁人志士的爱国热情和对教育的热爱,体现了他们求真务实、尊重科学、艰苦奋斗等精神。

她是近代中西文化交流的重要史证。

珞珈校园的建设时期,正是欧风美雨向中国内陆逐步渗透的时期。建筑既没有完全西化,也没有完全的中国化,体现了中西合璧的风格。

1950年,湖南大学水利系划归武汉大学,与土木系水利组合并,成立武汉大学水利系;医学院分出,与同济大学医学院合并成中南同济医学院(即后来之同济医科大学、华中科技大学同济医学院)。1952年,河南大学等校的水利系划归武汉大学,与水利系合并成武汉大学水利学院;农学院分出,与湖北农学院合并成华中农学院(即后来之华中农业大学)。1953年,工学院从武汉大学分出,成立华中工学院(即后来之华中理工大学、华中科技大学)。1954年,水利学院分出,成立武汉水利学院(即后来之武汉水利电力大学)。

国立武汉大学的新校舍为培养高级人才和科学研究提供了良好的条件。武汉大学的学术地位和教学水平令世人瞩目,为教育、科研事业作出了积极的贡献,是活化文物。

这里也是弘扬爱国思想的圣地。抗日战争时间,蒋介石和周恩来因国共合作一起在这里居住工作过。

2. 科学价值

校园选址科学,有山有水,自然风光优美。

建筑规划布局科学合理,设计师面对山水,没有一开始就大动干戈,而是尊重自然、依山就势,运用中国园林、殿堂建设的惯用布局方式,在散点、放射状的自由式总体布局的基础上,利用山体山势、地形地貌,精心布置建筑群。

建筑设计思路上,建筑风格独树一帜、中西融合,科学地将装饰性与实际性巧妙地结合。

3. 艺术价值

尊重自然,建筑人文景观与自然景观有机结合。

建筑丰富多样,富于变化,规整的格局中渗透着自由的布局,自由的布局中存在着严整的片段。

运用西方建筑手法,单体建筑造型宏伟高大,多姿多彩。把西方的水泥、钢结构、西式的双立柱与中国的歇山顶屋檐结合,使单体建筑有了西式的宏伟,群体建筑有着中式的宫廷楼阁。建筑的装饰考究,把丰富的文化内涵和审美情趣相结合,重复体现了建筑的艺术抽象性、象征性的特征。

三、武汉大学早期建筑修缮

1933年10月位于狮子山顶的老图书馆整体开工。1935年9月老图书馆竣工。它由一座主楼和前后两翼的四座附楼联结而成,占地呈"工"字形,体现了中国宫殿式建筑的威武和庄严。整体外观为中国传统殿堂式风格,内部则采用了西式的回廊、吊脚楼、石拱门、落地玻璃等,将"中西合璧"的建筑风格发挥得完美而极致。建成后的老图书馆是武汉大学的标志性建筑和精神象征。

历经80多年风雨,老图书馆一直在持续使用中,病害与破损情况也在不断蔓延,如:琉璃瓦屋面破损、屋面及墙体的渗漏雨现象严重,门窗锈蚀,墙、顶面抹灰粉化、霉变,潮湿的环境加剧了钢筋的锈蚀等。

在确定保护设计方案的前期,文物保护管理部门除了重视对老图书馆等早期建筑进行病害分析外,还强调对建筑物的结构进行勘察与检测,通过这些认真细致的工作,认真贯彻各项技术管理制度,使得接下来的方案设计工作能够顺利进行,并为后期的施工环节打下良好的基础。

施工前充分组织图纸会审,进行设计交底工作,使施工人员尽可能充分了解设计意图、理解设计图纸内容。在施工中认真检查执行情况,全面开展管理活动,做好隐蔽工程、技术复校记录,认真做好工程质量检验和评定工作。

完成修缮工程之后的老图书馆,不仅外观上遵循了"修旧如旧"的原则,而且有效地修复了病害与破损,并根据不同的功能需求,合理、充分、有效地利用了现有空间。时间仿佛没有走过这座宏伟、庄重、艺术感极强的建筑佳作。

行政楼前身为工学院大楼,1934年11月开工,1936年竣工。主楼为五层高、四角重檐尖顶的内回廊式方形建筑,与外围的四座歇山顶附楼和正前方的两座罗马式碉楼相组配,典型的"中西合璧"。主楼内部回廊里面是通高五层的"共享空间",采用钢梁屋架、透光玻璃做屋顶,形成明亮的"玻璃中庭"。在大型公共建筑中,这种设计艺术在国外是20世纪60年代后才逐渐流行的。

修缮前对行政楼做了全面深入的研究,包括其现存的原始图纸、文档、资料照片以及媒体报道等,全面地把握文物完整的面貌和完整的历史信息,并力求在保护修缮中做到完整统一。通过本次修缮建设,保留文物建筑所具有的物质和非物质的历史文化元素。

修缮工作受到了高度评价。特别是国际古迹遗址理事会（ICOMOS）专家在参观后，一致认为武汉大学的历史建筑保护与修复工作具有非常高的专业水平，合乎《威尼斯宪章》所订立的标准。这些修复工程体现了《中国文物古迹保护准则》所订立的方法准则。

未来发展：

（1）按照"十三五"期间的文物保护修缮计划，继续做好修缮工作。

（2）与文化部、国家文物局等加强合作，组建相关科研机构，进一步推进文化遗产保护方面的科学研究，使其成为学科建设新的增长点。

（3）深入发掘早期建筑的各项价值，充分发挥其历史文物功能。

四、武汉大学校园规划

1. 早期建筑及珞珈山历史文化风貌街区划定

国家级文物保护单位"武汉大学早期建筑"保护范围和建设控制地带，2000年由武汉市文新广局划定，2008年纳入武汉市紫线专项规划。

珞珈山片历史文化风貌街区的保护范围和建设控制地带，2006年由《武汉历史文化名城保护规划》确定，2008年纳入武汉市紫线专项规划。

2. 建筑高度控制

武汉大学主校区珞珈山和狮子山为校园现存主要山峰，珞珈山上主要分布有十八栋教师宿舍（含周恩来故居、郭沫若故居），山峰最高处绝对标高117.9米，狮子山主要分布了图书馆、老斋舍等主要早期建筑群，山顶最高处绝对标高120.6米，为校内地势制高点。在校园总体规划中，以山体及其上优秀早期建筑为视觉焦点，对校内建筑高度进行分级控制，保证珞珈山、狮子山优美的山体天际线轮廓和良好的景观效果。研究生教学科研大楼等四个项目在建筑高度上均严格按照校园总体规划进行控制，符合早期文物建筑保护和校园总体规划控制要求。

3. 部分新建筑与早期建筑及珞珈山的空间关系

根据武汉大学校园总体建设规划，通过对校园建筑高度、视线廊道、校园界面等实施良好的控制，达到保护校园早期建筑与珞珈山自然天际轮廓线，凸显珞珈山、狮子山早期建筑群优美景致，与东湖风景名胜区保持良好对话之目的。

4. 新建筑风格与早期建筑的协调

研究生教学科研大楼项目位于武汉大学主校门东侧，紧邻八一路汉林绿道，总用地面积12 537平方米，总建筑面积约21 190平方米，5层，建筑总高度23.6米，项目使用功能为研究生教学活动中心及杂交水稻国家重点实验室。建筑外墙采用灰色、屋面采用孔雀蓝琉璃瓦，建筑色彩及风格吸取了早期建筑——图书馆及老斋舍的建筑元素。

5. 文科综合楼

项目位于武汉大学主校门北侧，北邻化学学院，总用地面积18 986平方米，总建筑面积约21 200平方米，共6层，建筑总高度23.6米，项目使用功能为文学院、历史学院、哲学院教学及办公。建筑外墙采用水泥灰色，屋面采用孔雀蓝，建筑色彩和风格吸取了早期建筑——工学院（现行政楼）的建筑元素。

6. 大学生体育活动中心

建筑高度30米，项目使用功能为大学生体育教学及活动。建筑外墙以水泥灰色为主，屋顶色彩为孔雀蓝，建筑色彩与风格与早期建筑——宋卿体育馆相呼应。

乡村遗产与乡村旅游

Rural Heritage and Rural Tourism

周俭 教授
同济大学建筑与城市规划学院
Prof. Zhou Jian
School of Architecture & Urban Planning, Tongji University

Rural heritage is a resource for rural developments. As a cultural landscape, rural heritage embodies unique economic and aesthetic values. It is insufficient to simply "protect" the rural heritage. Since it is inseparable from the rural community that it connects to, conservation of rural heritage should be integrated with the development of the community in a composite resource management system, so as to achieve sustainability in both heritage protection and community development via rural tourism.

一、乡村遗产与乡村发展

乡村遗产是乡村发展的资源。乡村遗产作为一种文化景观,具有独特的经济和美学价值。乡村遗产由于其与乡村社区有着不可分割的关系,因此,不能简单地冠以"保护"的意义。乡村遗产的保护必须与乡村社区的发展一起考虑,应该纳入乡村发展的整体资源体系中,从而实现可持续的保护和社区发展的双重目标。

乡村发展最基本的含义可以从三个方面去理解。首先是村民收入的提高。这对每个村民而言是切切实实的利益,也是衡量乡村发展最基本的指标。其次是村民就业能力与适应能力的提高,即乡村社区能力的提高。村民和村集体通过自身知识、技能的拓展和提升,能够更多、更好地适应市场的变化和季节的变化,具备把握各种机会的可能性。最后是村落自身价值的提高。这是指在发展中不损害自身具有的各种价值,包括文化、遗产、传统、社区、自然以及产业,并通过发展使自身的价值持续得到提高。

发展旅游是具备遗产价值的村落发展的有效途径之一,但我们现在往往将乡村的遗产旅游异化成旅游景区的建设活动。我们需要认识到,旅游村落(景区)是一种功能定义,因此极易演变为物质性和功能性的建设活动和政策导向,为此我们应该反思如何将乡村遗产旅游从大规模的功能性建设转变为关注村民和乡村社区本身,关注创造文化景观遗产的人及其社会结构。

二、社区旅游与参与发展

20世纪80年代,世界范围内的旅游业迅猛发展,过度开发所引发的一系列资源破坏和环境污染问题愈发严重,旅游规划学者Murphy面对旅游开发和社区发展脱节、社区村民对旅游开发不满等问题,于1980年提出"社区旅游"这一概念。在研究中,他强调社区旅游是作为一种规划理念和方法,通过社区村民的参与影响旅游规划的决策,以减少社区村民对旅游的反感情绪和冲突。①

唐顺铁在1998年提出了我国最早关于社区旅游的定义:从社区的角度考虑旅游目的地建设,以社区的互动理论指导旅游区的总体规划和布局,通过优化旅游社区的结构提高旅游流的效率,谋求旅游业及旅游目的地经济效益、环境效益和社会效益的协调统一和最优化。社区旅游为寻求实现旅游业可持续发展提供了一个新途径,并将其与传统旅游进行了比较(见表1②)。

表1 传统旅游与社区旅游的比较

	传统旅游	社区旅游
对象	景观	景观、环境、社区
目标	最大经济效益	经济效益、环境效益和社会效益的协调统一和优化
开发原则	发掘景观吸引力	从社区互动、社区进化和社区结构优化的角度指导旅游开发
当地村民与旅游开发的关系	无关或被动参与	当地村民是旅游开发的重要力量

参与式发展理论是20世纪70年代出现的概念,时至20世纪90年代初期,世界银行等一些主要的援助机构开始将其重心转向促进社区的参与式发展,也正因此,参与式发展开始了世界范围的传播。③

参与式发展是让社区自主参与旅游项目的决策、实施、经营、利益分配及监督和评估。④ 其实质是在以社区村民为主体的多方参与下,发现、确认社区发展的机遇,并通过合理有效的发展机制的建立,来实现资源的公平和合理的配置与管理,以实现社区的可持续发展,⑤其重点是以社区中人的发展带动社区的发展。"参与式发展"主要依靠社区的内在力量来推动其自身发展,同时也借助政府和第三方机构的外力,以自身为主体把优势资源进行最优化整合。

与传统的旅游只注重发掘旅游目的地的景观吸引力的开发原则相比,社区旅游更注重从社区互动(社区和各利益相关者的相互作用)、社区进化(社区能力提升)和社区结构优化(空间、经济、社会结构)的角度指导旅游开发,突出了社区的主体地位。

三、路径选择

为实现作为传统村落中社区村民对于旅游的参与式发展的目标,政府、社区和企业这三种旅游发展中的主要利益主体需要重新选择各自的路径,即"社区自觉能力建设""政府有限干预"和"企业合同制约与法制规范",同时为弥补我国相对弱势的社区在强势政府和企业面前的力量不足,建议第三方力量介入社区旅游发展过程,完善社区参与旅游发展的体系。

(一) 社区自觉性的能力建设

1. 传统文化价值教育

许多旅游者在乡村所追求的价值往往被当地村民所忽视,村民司空见惯的生产、生活方式正是广大旅游人群所追求的自然属性的怀旧之精髓所在。只有让当地村民明白自身资源的旅游价值和文化价值,才能激发他们对自身文化的筛选、保护和再诠释,从而给社区发展的可持续性提供根本保障。

2. 旅游影响教育

社区村民对于旅游发展的热情高涨很大程度上是因为他们对于旅游开发只有正面效应的认识,对于

---

① Murphy P E. Tourism: A Community Approach[M]. New York: Methuen, 1985.
② 唐顺铁. 旅游目的地的社区化及社区旅游研究[J]. 地理研究,1998(2):145-149.
③ 周大鸣,刘志扬,秦红增. 寻求内源发展:中国西部的民族与文化[M]. 广州:中山大学出版社,2006.
④ 刘金龙. 参与式发展在中国实践的回顾与展望[C]//李小云. 谁是农村发展的主体. 北京:中国农业出版社,1999.
⑤ 林志斌. 参与式社区发展[C]//李小云. 谁是农村发展的主体. 北京:中国农业出版社,1999.

旅游的负面效应如社会文化变迁、自然环境破坏、社会秩序失衡、文化传统失落和道德伦理沦落等无所预知。如果村民能够认识到旅游的各方面影响，就能对其参与行为进行理性调整，从而使其易波动的"原始淳朴"转变为相对稳定的"理性淳朴"。

通过对村民的此类"预警"式教育，也能一定程度上抑制社区对于旅游的过度参与。如果能够让社区村民意识到发展旅游可能带来的正面和负面效应，有的时候"不参与就是最大的参与"，对于传统文化和传统生产、生活方式的保育就能从内源上找到实现的可能。

3. 旅游从业人员培训

传统的旅游培训主要针对社区村民旅游技能的提高，忽视对于观念的培养，而后者往往比前者更重要。许多旅游从业者在经营过程中商品意识开始觉醒，却容易对自身资源的认识产生偏差。比如若对社区旅游从业者家庭旅馆的改建观念进行教育，就能很大程度上避免传统建筑风貌的破坏。

（二）政府有限性的干预

地方政府在参与村落旅游发展中的角色定位应当是：做好社区参与旅游的规范制定者，脱去经营者的角色，充当与旅游相关的各方利益群体的协调者。

对于社区参与旅游，政府可以采用一系列积极的政策工具，比如鼓励企业在旅游开发过程中承担一定的社会责任、鼓励可持续的旅游行为、鼓励企业合理分享一部分通过社区资源获得的收益，以及宣传并敦促旅游行为规范等。

在乡村旅游开发中村落社区的制衡力量相对微弱，因而政府合理的公共政策的制定显得尤为重要。政府作为旅游开发的管理者和开发主体之一，应该保证政策制定和实行的法制化和规范化，为社区旅游的发展提供良好的政策、制度基础和优质的投资环境。

（三）旅游企业合同制约与法制规范

旅游公司在村落社区参与旅游发展的过程中是主要的直接管理者、资金的投入方和旅游收益分配的决策者。随着法制观念的觉醒和进步，村民也渐渐从原有的乡规民约中走出来，渐渐接受并合理利用这一事实谋取利益或限制自身的行为。因而公平合理的合同制定就成了旅游企业在乡村旅游发展中保障村落社区参与旅游发展和收益分配的核心。合同更是可以作为社区村民这一相对弱势群体保障自身利益的有效手段。

村民是社区旅游的参与主体和重要资源，如果不取得他们的配合，一切旅游发展都是纸上谈兵，关键是合同的公平性和公开性需要得到保障。如果由于合同的缺乏公平性、透明性，导致很多村民失去了表达的机会，产生了反感情绪，矛盾和冲突也随之而来。因此应该在法制上、内容上保证公平，以消除潜在的冲突和矛盾。旅游企业不能忽视村民在合同中的合理权益，只有相互尊重、平等以待，才能保证乡村的可持续发展。

四、对世界文化遗产地红河哈尼梯田保护的思考

一方面，乡村社会是构成乡村文化景观的重要组成部分。根据联合国教科文组织关于"文化景观"的分类和定义，乡村遗产被归为"有机进化景观"（Evolving Landscape）中的"持续性景观"（Continuing Landscape），它是指"在当地与传统生活方式相联系的社会中，保持着一种积极的社会作用，而且其自身演变过程仍在进行之中，同时又展示了历史上其演变发展的物证"。从乡村文化景观的定义可以看到，乡村遗产依托于乡村社会，乡村社会的发展演变必然给乡村遗产的表象和内涵带来变化。另一方面是，如果乡村遗产离开了乡村社会，乡村遗产也就不可能对当地产生积极的社会作用，其自身的演变要么被停止，要么被异化。

乡村遗产旅游必须与乡村发展的目标相结合，而社区参与是达成目标的重要途径。发展乡村遗产旅

游是为了保护乡村遗产,而保护乡村遗产的目的归根到底是乡村的发展。因此,对世界文化遗产地红河哈尼梯田的保护,需要与从事遗产地梯田耕作的村民及其社区的发展一起考虑。

哈尼梯田遗产价值的根本在"民",如果现在耕作梯田的这些村民不再耕作了,那梯田就可能荒废或者转为它用,梯田的文化景观价值也将不复存在。梯田旅游的发展会不会带来这种负面影响?虽然现在下结论还为时尚早,但这种潜在的风险是存在的。辛苦、劳累、产量不高,都可能成为旅游发展起来之后村民放弃(或部分放弃)继续从事梯田耕作的理由。

哈尼梯田保护的关键因素包括气候、水系和民众,其中最复杂、最困难的因素还是村民。乡村社会的发展是必然的,由此带来的社会关系、生产关系的变化也必然引起表象景观的变化。要保护梯田景观,需要考虑其背后营造景观的村民及其社区的发展诉求,因此,应该让遗产地的社区积极地参与到遗产保护和旅游发展中,让社区对自己的发展方向表达充分的想法。"参与式发展"强调参与范围的不断扩大、参与事项的具体化和个体化,内容则相比传统的"社区参与"拓展为9个方面:(1)决策及选择过程的介入;(2)发展过程中全部项目循环中的介入;(3)对社区乡土知识的信任;(4)资源的利用及控制;(5)发展对象的能力建设;(6)发展成果的利益分享;(7)社区自我组织及自立;(8)权力和民主的再分配;(9)促进机制的建立。

哈尼梯田遗产地的旅游业尚处于发展的前期,以下一些问题需要我们去研究和思考。首先,遗产地的梯田在未来究竟需要多少从事耕作的人口?这一耕作人口的底线需要政策在一定时期内予以一定程度的扶植。其次,社区参与旅游发展的机制设计需要结合当地社会的特征,尊重当地的社会价值观和社会结构,以保障社区和村民的利益与发展权利。最后,社区参与旅游发展的机制设计应该将社区能力建设放在突出的位置,使遗产地的保护机制成为遗产地可持续发展机制的重要组成部分。

基于历史地图的城市历史环境保护研究
——以当涂老城为例

Study on the Conservation of City Historic Environment Based on Historical Maps: in the Case of Old Town of Dangtu

董卫 教授
东南大学建筑学院
Prof. Dong Wei
School of Architecture, Southeast University

Using the Historic City of Dangtu for a case study, this speech asserts the importance of information retrieved from historical maps in guiding heritage-related urban planning. Overall historic environment, instead of mere historic buildings should be given more emphasis during this process.

一、研究背景

我国遗产保护工作较西方国家起步晚,尤其是城市遗产保护工作,是从早期的对文物古迹、历史建筑的保护逐步演变而来。我国对历史名城的保护工作最早可追溯到1950年代梁思成先生对古都北京保护的研究;1982年,国家基本建设委员会等部门颁布《关于保护我国历史文化名城的请示》,自此,兴起了名城保护的研究。尽管三十余年的时间中,我国历史名城保护的理论与实践取得了不小的成绩,但是由于我国地域宽广,历史文化遗产星罗棋布,遗产的保存状况、城镇的经济发展、人们的生活形态都存在较大的差异,因此在实践过程中,不应套用周庄、丽江等历史文化名城的保护模式,需避免在规划中出现"公式化"的趋势。

对于城市的保护不仅是对文物古迹、历史街区的保护,还应该尊重本地的历史和现实交织而成的社会和经济网络结构。尤其对于留存遗迹较少、历史信息价值较低,但是历史地位较高的城市,应该着眼于城市的未来发展,对影响城市的自然环境、人工环境、人文环境等众多方面进行综合性的分析。基于此,本文选择安徽省当涂县为研究对象,试图用古代地图转译的方法,从城市历史空间生成与变迁的现象中,找出城市历史环境的变迁,进而探讨与之相应的保护方法。这是研究城市遗产保护的一种新的趋势,并对认识城市、指导城市建设以及规划设计有所帮助,同时还是未来要实现历史文化与自然生态等综合性规划目标的前提。

二、当涂老城简介及价值认同

当涂县隶属安徽省马鞍山市,位于安徽省东南部,长江安徽段东岸,南京与芜湖之间,地处长三角城市群顶端,与江苏边界线总长达126.9千米,坐拥20千米长江岸线,是安徽省重要的沿江、沿边县。县辖区面积1 346平方千米,当涂老城辖区面积为2.8平方千米。老城地处长江下游河、湖交汇区,境内多河流、湖泊,水网密集,沟渠纵横,水陆交通非常发达,是附近城镇的服务中心。

从现存的记载来看，当涂历史久远，它的历史文化价值主要体现在：

(一) 当涂县在中国城建史上有着重要的地位

当涂是全国最早的建置县，秦以来已有2 200多年置县史，秦代称丹阳，隋初易称"当涂"。当涂县不仅是南朝南豫州、宋代太平州、元代太平路、明代太平府治所，清代长江水师提署和安徽学政驻地，而且长期以来占据这一区域政治、经济、文化、交通的中心。

(二) 当涂是典型的因"沿江沿河"而兴的城市

古代当涂地区西濒长江，南临芜湖，东枕丹阳湖，北靠慈湖，水网密布，纵横交错，向西可至江淮，向东可达江浙，临江近水，水运交通便利。当时的古河道一条是源于十里长山经姑溪河，上接水阳江及丹阳、石臼两湖，下泻经乙字河由牛渚矶头入江；一条源于向山经慈姥山流进长江。古河道和古丹阳湖是当涂地区人类发祥的摇篮。后随着中原百姓的南迁，沿河择居于水系两岸的人数增多，到唐代，当涂老城发展已颇具规模。早在置县之先，秦统一中国时，今当涂地区的丹阳县已是一座颇具规模的贸易城镇，姑溪河是丹阳与外界联系的水道之一，在该地区的航运中发挥重要的作用。随着聚居人数的增多，姑溪河两岸逐渐成为当涂港的雏形，河南岸的"马驿街"是当涂的古驿站，当涂老城北通采石水驿，南通皖南宣歙，商贸繁荣，是连接长江上下游的重要水上要道。随着长江岸线的变迁，南北向的长江岛链将南京、合肥、马鞍山、当涂、芜湖等地联系起来，内河水系石臼湖、丹阳湖、圩田水网、姑溪河、青山河、巢湖等形成东西向的水道，当涂恰好就位于黄金水道交汇处，未来可成为该区域经济、旅游、文化发展的服务中心。由此，古代当涂因江河而立而兴，并且这种影响将延续至未来。

(三) 当涂地居襟要，自古便是军事要地

当涂曾是长江下游的重要渡口，控制长江之要津，扼金陵之咽喉，雄关屏立，险要甲于东南，历史上曾发生过多次重要战役。春秋时吴楚之战、东晋及南朝的多次战乱、隋伐陈、宋伐南唐，南宋虞允文大败金完颜亮，明将花云战陈友谅等均发生于当涂境内。清末太平军东进过江之战、北伐之战第二阶段的会战南京、抗日战争均在当涂发生多次激战。地理位置的重要性使当涂自古便成为兵家必争之地。

(四) 当涂是典型的山水文化之城

当涂北拱群山，东抱石臼湖、固城湖、南湖，西濒长江，南怀万亩公圩。在城市整体格局上环水面山，体现了江南城市特有的"山—江—湖—圩—城"的环境格局，展现了"山水都"的古代城市规划建设思想。自然景色秀丽，自古有"当涂虽小，三塔两浮桥"之美誉。当涂曾吸引历代骚人墨客钟情吟游：南朝大诗人谢朓称誉当涂为"山水都"，"唐宋八大家"之一曾巩誉当涂为"江山之胜，天下之奇处"，唐朝大诗人李白晚年定居当涂，留下了许多千古绝唱。秀丽奇险的自然风光，孕育出丰富多元的当涂文化，历史上姑孰画派、当涂艺文、当涂民歌等名闻遐迩。县域内除分布着10多处省市级重点文物保护单位外，还拥有许多非物质文化遗产资源。

由此可见，当涂具有丰富的历史文化价值。古河道和古丹阳湖是当涂地区人类发祥的摇篮。重要的地理位置、山水格局使其成为历代侨置之地及兵家必争之要津。明太平府时更是府治所在地，一度成为政治、经济、文化中心。今当涂县位于合肥—上海—南京—皖南的交汇中心，通达性较好，旅游文化资源丰富，未来有条件成为休闲型城郊及周围城市的文化旅游服务中心。

三、基于历史地图转译的当涂老城历史空间变迁

(一) 城市历史地图转译技术路线

首先，将与城市历史空间相关的信息提取出来。通过对当涂清乾隆十五年(1750年)城郭图、太平府

当涂县山川图、当涂县江汛图、当涂县1984年地形图以及《当涂县志》(民国)等当涂古代地图及志书解读,将与城市空间信息相关的要素,如山水系统、城垣城池位置、街巷系统、府衙学宫、城市用地等要素提取出来,加以整理。接着,将从历史地图中提取出来的空间信息按朝代,按城垣、城池、水系、街巷、城市用地等要素进行分类,这种分类便于将繁杂无序、不准确的信息抽离出来,形成具体的空间实体要素,然后加载在现代城市空间系统中,在现代的城市空间结构上进行重组,将历史信息要素在现代城市空间进行坐标定位,使各个不同时期的信息在现代地图上具有关联性,同时具有可量化的空间特征。对空间要素进行横向、纵向分析,可以发现和总结城市演变过程与发展规律,明晰历史空间要素在现代城市空间格局中所起到的作用。

(二) 明之前的城市格局

据《嘉庆一统志》记载,今当涂县(即姑孰城)最早有城之奠基的记载为孙吴黄武年间(222—228),东晋咸安七年(372年),杰出军事家、权臣桓温重新建筑当涂城墙,并修筑了子城于城内。唐时,南部城墙跨姑溪河而筑。宋代,当涂老城城郭格局已基本形成今制,为了防止水贼侵略,南城墙移筑于姑溪河之北,将姑溪河置于城外,城郭修筑了行春、澄江、南津、湖熟、清源五座城楼,并且修筑城内市河,至今在当涂老城内仍有局部市河。

(三) 明末清初的城市格局

明末清初当涂老城的城池系统在宋代的基础上多次改建加固,城市格局已经基本形成,是一座具有江南水乡特点的老城镇。老城街巷基本形成"九街十八巷"的格局,街与巷坊形成棋盘格式的道路系统,城中权力空间、经济空间、教育空间、军事空间、居住空间均完善,民居主要集中在东、西街及马军寨之间,街巷密度较大,多为青砖瓦房。商业用地主要集中在城南沿河南寺巷一带及姑溪河上下浮桥两岸埠头。随着朝代更迭,当涂的发展尽管跌宕起伏,但是作为明清两代太平府治,当涂一直保持着周边地区中心城镇的地位。

根据城市历史地图资料以及相关方志文献,对这一时期当涂老城城垣、城壕、市河、街巷、功能空间分布等历史信息内容进行空间定位,由于这一时期历史信息较模糊,空间定位准确率较低,因此对这一时期城市格局的再现也仅能做到相对准确。

(四) 清末民初的城市格局

清末太平军在当涂进行了10年的攻守战,对当涂整个老城的城市格局造成很大的破坏,整个城市发展相对停滞衰败。城垣系统遭到彻底破坏,街巷和市河的格局破坏不大,主要是用地的功能发生了较大置换,这一变化的主要原因是当涂县屡次成为驻军地。城市建筑遭到大规模毁坏,至民国22年(1933年)老城内仅5 000余户,较大的商店449家,建设基本停滞。对这时期的城市格局研究除了继续关注城垣、城壕、街巷、市河、桥梁、功能等空间要素外,还要关注城市空间变迁的动因。这一时期历史信息的空间定位的准确率有所增强。

(五) 民国末期至20世纪80年代的城市格局

抗日战争前,旧城墙尚存两座残破的城门。当涂沦陷前,为防止日军盘踞,将其全部拆除。当涂老城巍巍壮观的城垣虽已不复存在,但是城东、西、北三面,长约4千米宽近百米的护城河遗存至今,其保存完好程度,在全国已不多见。民国二十六年(1937年),当涂沦陷时,日军入城大肆洗劫,城内房屋被炸毁近三分之一,东十字街、马军寨一带几乎成为废墟。抗战胜利后,虽修复了部分街道和房屋,但老城内仍残墙断瓦,街巷狭窄,土路坑洼不平。至20世纪80年代,街巷格局基本保持"九街十八巷"格局,仅某些街巷名称改变,如秦陆巷更名为王宫巷,顶城街更名为当铺巷,裴家巷更名为花园巷。市淮河南段填后建"新菜市",官沟南段填满,南城壕剩局部水系肌理。

新中国成立后当涂老城城市空间在其原有格局上向东、西两个方向拓展，主要用于工业用地。提署街以北为八六医院用地，政府机关用地分布于城南南寺街附近，东西街及提署街之间仍为民居，教育用地延续了清代及民国时期的教育中心，位于老城的东南隅，商业用地仍然以清代、民国的南寺街一带为主。此时，城市的街巷分级很明晰，这一时期可以参考大量的城市建设资料及规划图纸，城市空间定位很准确。

（六）改革开放后的城市格局

改革开放以后，在市场经济条件下，新中国成立初期的一批小型工业逐渐解体，老城内工业仅剩西北角当涂铁厂、西南角的粮油购销有限责任公司以及东南角的姑溪酿酒厂及家属院、当涂树脂厂（原纽扣厂）等。新的资本和产业远离老城，向护城河外的西北角以及姑溪河南岸发展及聚集，权力空间也移出老城，聚集于城外东北角。在当涂最新一轮城市规划中《当涂县城总体规划（2011—2030）》，当涂老城也已经失去了中心的地位。当涂老城虽处于主城内，却得不到政策支持，无法形成龙头产业，其政治和经济地位不断下降。在这一情况下，老城只能通过土地经济来实现地区的发展，而这又反过来破坏了古城的形态。

自2000年以来，老城十字街以南经过多轮城市更新，目前形成了大面积的现代住区，传统的街巷肌理消失殆尽。如今的当涂城难见当年传统的城市格局，由于对城市历史空间的破坏，老城已经逐步淹没在拔地而起的高层住宅中。

（七）城市用地的延续性

此前，有不少研究利用此法在重要历史城市层面上做过尝试，但是我国一般的小城镇很难有系列的地方志及历史地图、照片，即使有些城市在某段历史时期有十分重要的历史价值，由于战争、地理位置、城市规模、政策倾向以及经济发展所造成的"建设性"破坏，早期偏门的保护思想所造成的"消极静态""片面单一"的保护等诸类原因，因此，对今天城市功能空间历史的查阅和解读在研究中显得尤为重要。

本案当涂的保护所面临的实际困难是当涂老城的历史价值十分重要，今当涂县与之相去甚远，大规模的城市建设使得老城区遭到毁灭性瓦解，几乎无遗存的历史信息可寻。政府、专家学者及市民将精力投入到大型历史城市或者保存较好的古村落，往往忽视了此类小城镇的存在。无论是出于经济效益还是人文情怀，当需要对其进行保护性建设的时候，可以根据城市空间功能延续的特征进行分析。

在对当涂城市历史地图转译的过程中，对用地要素进行纵向的垂直比较，会发现某些用地在历史的变迁过程中会被重复使用，后一朝代延续前一朝代的城市空间，用地的功能性质完全继承前朝。这类用地主要是非居住类的公共用地，多为府署、学院、寺庙等用地功能之间的转换使用。当涂老城重复用地约占老城总面积的20%。通过对用地性质纵向的梳理，不但能够发现城市空间形态与结构的变化方式，而且能够揭示其变化的机制。城市用地是存在历史痕迹的，往往今天的学校、政府、工业等用地在古代就是学宫、府衙、寺庙。这对于我们认知今天的城市、寻找城市历史空间有很大启发和帮助。

四、历史地理与老城格局变迁的形态分析

从上文老城历史空间变迁的分析中不难看出，水系改变、连年战争、人口迁徙等均是老城形态变迁的动力机制，其中历史地理要素最为重要。下文通过城墙、水系的变化来实证老城格局的变迁。

（一）城墙要素实证分析

据县志载，唐代城墙"高三丈三尺，周十五里，跨姑溪河，东西置水门，为上下栅"，可见唐代南部城墙跨姑溪河而筑，长约为今8 100米，老城内面积约为253公顷；宋代城墙"减旧制三之一"，长度约为今5 600米，老城内面积约为197.6公顷；明代当涂县城墙在宋代基础上又做了进一步的调整，由于"城西南隅濒溪"，于是南城墙"北移去溪岸二十余步"，"周城减至九里十八步"，城墙长度约为今5 573米，老城内面积约为195.3公顷；清代城墙格局不变，只是逐渐衰败，至民国已不复存在；1980年的当涂约有长2 277米的城墙遗址存

在,其上搭建房屋,此时老城面积以护城河内为准,约为238公顷,如今老城外县域面积已达1500公顷。

从数据可以看出老城空间范围成呈"U形曲线"变化,早年随着姑溪河水拓宽、城防系统加固,老城向内收缩。民国时期虽然城墙被拆除,由于护城河的宽广,城市并未向外快速扩张,大量工厂、居住建筑在城内择地而建,因此老城内部空间遭到严重破坏。对当涂而言,城墙要素对界定城内外的空间意义不及护城河和姑溪河重要。近年随着提署路、姑孰路与城外的联结,现老城已逐步向城外发展。

(二) 水系要素实证分析

唐代当涂无南护城河,城墙周围有水系,据史料载,并未进行人工浚壕,此时姑溪河穿城而过;宋代"沿城浚壕",引姑溪河水入城壕,城池已形成;明代由于南护城河较窄,连年受灾,因此崇祯年间拆除广安坊、源清坊沿城壕的民宅,扩大南濠,"虽增旧壕之半,犹不及东西北三分之一焉"。当涂县于宋代就有市河;明万历年巡按浚壕建闸,外河入濠河,濠河入市河,市河主要由三条水系组成——治河、官沟和市淮河、玉带河,据县志明万历年巡按浚壕建闸,外河入濠河,濠河入市河,市河主要由三条水系组成——治河、官沟和市淮河、玉带河,明代老城水系格局形成,至20世纪80年代,基本保持整体骨架的完整性和连续性。

从明代开始南护城河的修筑使得老城空间逐渐向北,姑溪河的逐渐拓宽压缩了河南城市用地。明清时期城市有很多水荡,随着城市发展,城市中的大量水塘和水系被填埋,尤其是城南一段,从20世纪80年代到今天,水系迅速减少,街巷系统也被彻底摧毁。

五、历史环境保护对于城市保护及发展的意义

从20世纪60年代开始,ICOMOS陆续发表一系列关于历史环境保护的法律文件。近年来,历史环境保护作为城市建设的一项重要内容,受到越来越多的重视。历史环境是一个复杂庞大的体系,从城市的角度而言,包括物质环境与非物质环境、建成环境与人文环境,因此既要重视历史环境保护的物质价值,也要重视对历史文化价值的理解。历史环境保护是保护历史建筑、传统街巷、历史街区及其周边自然环境和场所特征的整体性保护,不能像文保单位那么简单,不是要保存(preservation)某个建筑物或建筑群,而是从整体上保护(conservation)城镇的建设特色,对于有损历史环境空间品质和景观的特色的部分,可适当地整治(rehabilitation)。

城市是复杂的综合体,一直是在保护、更新、再开发三部分不断变化、交替进行的,它的发展演变过程是延续性的、动态叠加的。历史环境保护,就是要保持历史发展的延续性,不仅侧重于历史古迹的保护,还要保护城市过去发展的历程,以动态的角度对城市进行保护和更新。城市保护不是要重现逝去的物质形态,而是要保留现在美好的、着眼于城市未来的发展,避免具有经济吸引力的并且能够继续使用的生活场所遭到不恰当的改变,保持当地居民生活的稳定性,使城市能够在同一时代,具有历史多样性、和谐性的均衡发展。这是城市保护的真正意义所在。

对于一些遗产留存较少、历史信息破坏严重的而具有历史价值的城市,在谈到保护时应更多地侧重于历史环境的保护。按照历史文化名城的概念和《文物保护法》评定标准,此类城市没有任何保护实施的可行性,若非要进行保护,很可能出现"仿古一条街""假古董"等建设性的破坏,这就严重违背了原真性原则。城市历史环境的原真性包括一座城市它形成的人文、自然因素,它所继承的所有东西,以及它曾经存在过的历史证据,这意味着一定程度上的缺陷和不完美状态(历史信息)的存在。这种情况下,历史环境的保护更具意义。历史环境在不同层次的文化遗产保护过程中扮演着极为重要的角色,使不同层次的文化遗产融为一个整体,形成一种历史的氛围。在现实中有活力的城市必须为经济发展提供机会,文化遗产作为一种资源成为城市发展的新经济动力是无可厚非的。关键是在实施的过程中采取合理健康、可持续的方式,杜绝大拆大建的政绩工程。

六、当涂所面临的保护问题和策略

如上文所述,城市遗产的保护并不是静态的保存物质形态,而是保护城市生长的过程,是一种对现在和未来的尊重。在当涂的案例中,首先明确保护不是孤立的,它是城市规划的重要组成部分,涉及城市设计、城市更新以及城市未来发展等问题,保护是为了增加城市动力,激发城市活力,以保护更新带动城市发展,以此为指导思想,来分析当涂所面临的问题,并提出相应的策略。

当涂历史信息缺失严重,通过上文对历史信息空间的转译,绘制可与今天当涂县城市地理空间相叠加的、可度量的数字化历史地图,将具有价值的信息准确定位,采用物质文化与非物质文化相结合、景观保护与环境保护相结合等方法使当涂老城历史遗产得以保护,空间文脉得以延续。

七、结论

我国城市化的浪潮已经从东部沿海地区逐渐向中西部地区转移,我们不去谈市场化后给城市遗产保护带来的冲击,也不回避我国的保护规划的功利性。事实上,社会效益和经济效益确实是城市发展的动力,也是城市文化遗产保护的动力之一,尤其对于当涂这类历史信息缺失严重且具有一定历史文化价值的城市,既要承担继承历史文脉的责任,又要担当促进地区经济发展、社会进步的使命。基于这样的认识,在保护过程中需逐步调整保护的态度和观念,用历史环境观的整体性思维去操作,将保护看作城市发展的契机之一,以城市发展为目标,通过历史文化的复兴来激发城市的新活力。

参考文献

[1] 董卫.城市历史环境保护与整治的梯度方法[J].北京规划建设,2012(6):34-37.
[2] 刘奔腾,董卫.基于空间发展的历史村镇保护方法研究:以浙江省义乌市赤岸镇为例[J].《规划师》论丛,2010(00):18-22.
[3] 李建,董卫.古代城市地图转译的历史空间整合方法:以杭州市古代城市地图为例[J].城市规划学刊,2008(2):93-98.
[4] 薛春霖,仲德崑.从廿八都谈欠发达地区历史文化村镇的保护[J].新建筑,2007(4):12-16.
[5] 张松.历史城市保护学导论:文化遗产和历史环境保护的一种整体性方法[M].2版.上海:同济大学出版社,2008.

大学与城市:校长们的话
Universities & Cities: According to University Presidents

大学与城市:共生共荣、砥砺同行、相互牵引
李晓红(时任武汉大学校长/中国工程院院士)

武汉大学和大武汉因武汉这个同样的名字共生共荣地联系在一起。这就是一部大学与城市共生共荣的成长史,一代代武大人用思想与智慧在武汉这座城市留下了深深的"武大印记"。

立足地方经济社会发展、服务城市的文明建设,是大学承载的光荣使命。武汉大学在复兴大武汉的宏观格局中,成功扮演了三个角色:出色的预言家、可靠的加油站、默契的合伙人。

大学与城市应该具备以下关系:大学发展与城市发展"共生共荣"、大学精神与城市精神"砥砺同行"、大学创新与城市创新"相互牵引"。

武汉大学与武汉这座城市之间到底应该构建怎样的互动关系?唐良智市长在武汉大学120周年校庆典礼上讲道:"有什么品质的大学,才有什么品位的城市";"武汉大学需要做的事我们一定做好,武汉大学不希望做的事我们坚决不做"。

最后,我想引用一句话作为对唐良智市长在武汉大学120周年讲话的回应:只要大武汉有召唤,武大人就必然有行动;只要武汉市人民有期待,武汉大学就必将努力有作为。

文化传承与创新是大学的重要功能
马敏(时任华中师范大学党委书记)

纵观人类历史的发展,每一次社会转型都伴随着巨大的文化变革,而每一次文化变革,大学都发挥了巨大的推动作用。文化传承与创新成为大学的第四大功能。

历史文化遗产保护中,大学与社区的互动尤为重要。高校是历史文化遗产保护的文化、科研、信息资源的宝库,对社区有"三个提升"作用:提升社区居民保护历史文化遗产的积极性,提升社区居民完善自我的意识,提升社区及居民的文化品位。反过来,社区的历史文化遗产为高校提供了"三个平台":优质的教育平台、社会化平台、思想道德教育平台。要高度重视高校与社区的协同共治,比如:位于华中师范大学校内的黎元洪墓,学校与周边单位和社区共同予以保护并对公众开放。

政府应主动担当起高校与社区融合的推动者,高校则要加强与社区的对接及互动。建立高校与社区协同融合及共享机制,比如加强沟通,建立联席会议制度;加强研判,了解发展需求,确保实现双赢;加强宣传,激发双方参与积极性等。

打造世界级名校与名城
邵新宇(时任华中科技大学常务副校长)

现代大学往往坐落于城市之中,它同时是城市的大学和市民的大学。大学与城市在空间上融为一体,在功能上相互依存,在文化上和谐共享。思想与文化是城市的灵魂,而大学是思想与文化的策源地。

创新能力是城市发展的关键，而大学是科技和知识的创新地；人才是城市的活力之源，而大学是人才聚集的高地。

纵观世界各国，名城与名校交相辉映，此兴彼起，共赢发展。名城是孕育名校的摇篮，名校是成就名城的希望。大武汉给创造了华中科大"天时""地利""人和"；华中科大支持了大武汉，它是创新人才的摇篮，是科技创新的引擎，是社会服务的典范及文化传承的高地。

《武汉2049远景发展战略规划》的目标是迈向世界级城市的位列，华中科大提出的"三步走"战略设想，其目标是跻身世界一流大学行列。发展目标的交会为校、市加强合作、实现互利共赢提供了历史性机遇。华中科大作为国家985高校之一，将与武汉市携手奋进，共同成为世界级名校与名城。

（特别鸣谢：蒋太旭）

"80后"对话"90后":阮仪三教授与张良皋教授的民族建筑世纪对话

One in His 80s vs One In His 90s: A Millennium Dialogue on National Architecture between Prof. Ruan Yisan and Prof. Zhang Lianggao

对话人：阮仪三教授、张良皋教授
Prof. Ruan Yisan and Prof. Zhang Lianggao
主持人：何依教授
Host：Prof. He Yi

2014年10月，无界论坛首次推出了"无界对话"系列，因为参与首场对话的是当时八十岁高龄的阮仪三先生和当时九十一岁高龄的张良皋先生，组织者为这场对话取了一个诙谐而富有时代感的标题——"80后"对话"90后"。在这场"无界对话"中，同为"民族建筑杰出成就奖"获得者的两位建筑遗产保护界泰斗人物进行了一次历史性的对谈。两位老先生与民族建筑遗产结下不解之缘的人生在"无界对话"这个特殊的时空中碰撞、交织，熠熠生辉。"对话"结束后仅3个月，九十二岁高龄的张良皋先生于2015年1月仙逝，这场对话也就成了张良皋老先生的最后绝唱。

"80后"对话"90后"

一个是1947年中央大学建筑系（今东南大学建筑学院）毕业，一个是1961年同济大学建筑系毕业留校，两个人与建筑专业结缘都有一段不平凡的故事……

张良皋：阴差阳错，"水利人"变"建筑人"

那时湖北省政府在抗战后方恩施开办了一个联合中学，我在那里取得了保送中央大学的资格。我一开始填的志愿是水利系，但是因为我们到重庆的时间晚了，中央大学不肯收，后来还是经过多方交涉才收下了我们。虽然进了中央大学，但是因为开课已经过了一个月了，工学院的老学长们告诉我，"你现在就是进了中央大学，你这个读工学院的课，差一个小时都不行，你这差一个月，你再有本事那也没办法赶上大家呀！"于是我准备按照他的建议，来年再考进来。不过一听我说还要考水利系，这位学长就说："哎！别别，我引你去看建筑系，好像比较适合你，跟你喜欢的文学、艺术、历史关系比较密切一点。"于是他真把我带到建筑系。我一看建筑系的课表："呦喂，真是一见钟情！"我说："算了吧，水利系不要了，明年来考这个建筑系！"

当然，在此期间让我更坚定不移地报考建筑系的原因还有一次全国美术展览。这次全国美术展览里面有一个建筑画展，我在展览上看到了一张仿罗马式教堂的水墨画，画得真好，真美！我说天下还有这样的画吗？这张画让我顿时决定了，我一定要报考建筑系！那张画是谁的作品呢？是我们的启蒙老师，后来当了建工部副部长的戴念慈先生的画。我就这样进了中央大学建筑系的大门。

阮仪三：被迫中断的军旅生涯，开启另一种人生

我在1950年响应毛主席的号召，投笔从戎，参加了抗美援朝。我当时所在的初高中有80个优秀共青团员参加了中国人民海军，我从联合海军学校出来以后就上了军舰，当时叫华东海军，也就是现在的东海舰队。后来我参加过战斗，也立过战功，得过军功章，也得到过全国共青团的通报表扬。后来又怎么会学了建筑的呢？因为后来我父亲被打成了右派，我就成了四类分子，不能再当兵了。从部队退回来以后，我回到中学里继续念书，临到要考大学了，我就去找我原来部队里的同志，请教到底考什么好。我们古田舰的舰长、政委就告诉我说："你要念书，不要去考复旦，复旦大学全是搞文啊史啊哲啊政治啊，你这个家庭出身不好，祖父是大官僚，父亲又是右派，读这些将来不会有出息的！也不要去考交大，交大都是电子啊军事啊，没你的份，不会让你去的咧！你考土木吧，土木没问题，考同济！"然后我也就像张老师一样，去了解了一下建筑系。考建筑系先要加试美术，这个正中我下怀，我画画画得蛮好的，小学毕业的时候，全苏州市小学生绘画比赛，我拿了第一名，后来在部队里也经常画宣传画，搞墙报啊什么的，所以画画没问题，高分录取。

阮仪三的护城"三招"

上个世纪50年代末，同济大学邀请了一个民主德国的威德尔教授来上课，他看到中国的情况以后，专门给我们开了一门课，叫"欧洲城市史"。他在课上就提出来，欧洲现在正在执行着古城复兴运动，同时也有新城建设运动。你们中国只有新城运动而没有古城运动，你们中国也要研究城市的历史，因为历史是一面镜子。于是我们同济大学就以我老师董教授为首编写《中国城市发展史》，我当时是他的助教。1961年毕业后，我就从大同沿线一路看下来，当时整个山西、陕西省的古城基本上都保持唐宋以来的风光。但是到了80年代的时候，我又到山西去搞城市规划的时候，看到包括平遥在内的各地都在拆。当时全国上下有很多口号，什么"汽车一响，黄金万两""想要富，先开路""拆了旧城建新城"等等，我们上海也提出"一年一个样，三年大变样"。当时所有的城市都是要求政绩，拆了城墙修马路。当时我到平遥去一看，平遥正在拆，拆了180栋清代建筑，拆了90栋明代建筑。90和180加在一起，差不多有快300栋建筑了，一条大街也都被拆掉了。其他城市，在它旁边的太谷、介休、沁县、祁县等等，都在拆，全在拆，全国都在拆。

当时因为平遥最穷，拆得慢了一点，同时也因为平遥的两个文物队长也来找过我，我们想办法找了省建委的同志，我说："不要拆了，我来帮你做规划吧！你们的规划做得不对！"当时所有的城市，大家的思想就是把城拆了修个大马路，社会主义建设就完成了！在这个情况之下，我们叫他停下。这个省建委主任就要求我一个月之内把规划做出来给县政府。我担心后面还会有很多纠缠，于是想到了一招。我就到了北京，直接找到罗哲文和郑孝燮两位大学者，他们两个都是全国政协的常委，郑孝燮是建设部总顾问，罗哲文是国家文化部文物处处长，那个时候还没有文物局，所有修文物的资金全在他手上批。看了我做的规划，他们都说很不错。我就请他们把这些话说给省长书记们听。于是我把两位常委请到了山西。一到了山西，省长、书记就都出来了。他们两位老先生就给省长讲，阮仪三做的规划如何好，我就在旁边叫秘书都记下来，这样好叫省长发红头文件。后来省里的红头文件发下来，指示平遥按照阮仪三做的规划实施，平遥古城这才被保了下来。

所以说这是我的第一招。保下来再干什么呢？还要修！于是我就请罗处长拨钱。那时候他手上只剩下八万修长城的钱，说修长城的钱不好修平遥。我说不对啊，你不是说过所有城墙都是长城的一部分，因为我国所有城市的城墙都是从洪武三年开始修的，是一个体系的！他说对对对，你说得很对！于是，这八万块钱就成了平遥的文物维修资金。1980年，这八万块钱到了平遥，我又担心这钱拨不到文物上，于是就派我的研究生盯着，看钱是不是到了，到了以后要建立专门的古城修缮委员会，专款专用，免得被地方干部拿来干别的事情了！

这是我的第二招,还有最后一招就是把他们所有管城市建设的领导干部、建委正副主任和规划处长都弄到同济大学来学习。他们说没钱,我就说没钱我来出!这个培训,每年上学期一班,下学期一班。一共来了六批12个人,这12个人就成了保护平遥的骨干力量。后来在保护江南的周庄、同里、乌镇这些古镇的时候,我也是出钱请地方干部们一起到法国去学习,请联合国教科文组织培训他们。我们搞设计的有一点钱,我们的钱不拿去造房子,不拿去买汽车,就可以派上用场了。这些人一到欧洲学习回来以后观念就变了。所以说学习很重要,有了学习以后他才能晓得什么是好的,什么是错的,什么叫破坏,什么叫建设。

阮仪三：留住乡愁，留住"记忆"

谈到留住乡愁,就让我们想到古村落。现在我们一共还有多少?据统计,一共可能是110万个,已经消失了70万个,剩下的还有40万个。我们说要留住乡愁,乡愁是什么?乡愁就是你童年的或者过去的对自己故乡的留恋,而这种愁是什么?是一种痛苦的、无奈的心情的流露。那么我们要留住乡愁,就要把这些历史和记忆保留下来。除了这个"记忆",我们还需要保留的就是"技艺"。我们有很多的技术和艺术都扔掉了。所以说,我们有职责传这个代!我们编书、做调查,意思就是要把"技艺"传给我们年轻一代,让他们能够继承我们这些老头们的事业。他们再留给他们的儿子和孙子,这样中国才有希望。不然到了下一代,什么都没有了,全是水泥森林,全是排排房,全是干巴巴的高楼大厦,我们叫作"千城一面,万户一貌"。这种城市是没有象征力的,这种城市留下来是没有记忆的。

张良皋：发扬国故，回望中国的"文艺复兴"

我刚才听到阮先生提"留住乡愁"。乡愁,是一种很高尚的情操,我也补充一个——"发扬国故"。有人说中国人建筑不用石头,是输在了起跑线上。我却认为这跟中国与西方的"永恒观"有关联。中国人我们认为有风有树,有风土上面长树,生生不息,这表示永恒。我们鼓励六材并用,土、木、金、石、皮革、草,皮革和草都是百工用的材料。所以我认为我们并没有输在起跑线上,而是做了正当的选择,从一开我们的包容性就很大。即使在中间黑暗时代,我们河南登封的嵩岳寺,造型和砖工都很出色,不亚于西方的圣苏菲亚教堂。因此即使在中间的发展上我们和西洋也是同步的。而我认为我们湖北的武当山,是中国文艺复兴的标志性建筑,这就表示中国的文艺文化在明朝初年,就已经发展到了顶峰状态。明朝是一个光辉灿烂的朝代,从洪武皇帝朱元璋登基到崇祯皇帝朱由检在煤山上吊这两百多年,明朝一直是全世界的第一大国。我们的武当山建成于1418年,佛罗伦萨主教堂开工时间不知道,完工时间为1419年。也就是说,我们的文艺复兴跟欧洲的文艺复兴分秒不差,你如果真正要计较的话,我们比它还早。所以我极力主张我们中国也有文艺复兴,而明朝就是文艺复兴的辉煌朝代。武当山整个建筑群比起佛罗伦萨主教堂,大家看看谁的规模大、谁的气势雄,谁的建筑美。哪一条都可以跟人家相比,我们并不落后。所以我就要为我们中国从来没有落后于欧洲这个命题大声疾呼。

佛罗伦萨一定会在2019年举行庆祝文艺复兴600周年。那我们为什么不在2018年庆祝武当山这一个文艺复兴标志建成600周年呢?我们应该组织一次庆典,邀请佛罗伦萨的客人到我们湖北武当山来做客。我们明年(2019年)再组团回访。我们的确是平起平坐的,必须提高我们中国的文化自信,提高我们中国文化在世界的地位。我希望我能够有幸活到武当山能够作为中国文艺复兴标志的庆典之日。我就是祈祷上帝再给我三年时间。我想这不算奢望吧!到2018年,我95岁,我们来庆祝武当山,至于到不到佛罗伦萨去,关系也不大,能够让我跑一趟佛罗伦萨,那有什么不好呢,我就是拼老命也去啊!

2015年1月,张良皋先生在武汉病逝,终没能如愿向上帝借到这三年时间。无论张良皋先生关于"中国文艺复兴600周年"的倡议是否会在他老人家身后得到所有人的支持,他和阮仪三先生在那场世纪对话中所传达的"留住乡愁、发扬国故"的精神都将通过这场对话的听众以及他们多年培养的一代又一代学生散播出去。

创意城市与文化遗产

CREATIVE CITIES AND CULTURAL HERITAGE

为什么是创意？为什么是城市？
（节选）

如今，新的战略、政策和举措都集中于促进发展，激励创新，提高社会凝聚力，提升公民幸福感，促进跨城市交流，以此推动文化和创新在可持续发展和城市升级中的动力作用，而城市正是这一系列新战略、政策和举措的发展根基。也正因为如此，城市才能有效应对诸多重大挑战，如经济危机、环境破坏、人口增长和社会紧张局势等等。

除此之外，城市还是当今世界过半人口及世界四分之三的经济活动的家园，这其中也包含了很大比重的创意经济。

城市在促进可持续发展方面的关键作用体现在人和人权两大方面，这也是2015年后发展议程一大显著共识。2015年后发展议程共涵盖了17大目标，而这17大目标紧紧围绕着一大中心点，即"让城市和人类居住区更具有包容性、安全性、弹性及可持续性"，并以此为出发点，将文化和创新确立为主要推动力之一。

首先，从区域角度而言，文化和创意存在于我们日常的生活和实践之中。因此刺激文化产业的发展，鼓励创新，促进公民以全新的视角参与文化活动以及推动公共权力机关与私营部门和民间组织的合作意义重大，能进一步推动更符合地区实际的可持续发展。

在此背景下，成员城市之间相互合作及分享经验和知识能够有效推动创意成为城市发展的杠杆，促进新的解决方案的形成以应对共同的挑战。在这方面，联合国教科文组织创意城市网络为各城市提供了无与伦比的机会，让它们通过借鉴同行学习过程和协作项目，充分利用他们的创意资产，并以此为基础推动经济、文化、环境和社会各方面的可持续、包容性和均衡发展。

联合国教科文组织

WHY CREATIVITY? WHY CITIES?
(Excerpt)

  Urban areas are today's principal breeding grounds for the development of new strategies, policies and initiatives aimed at making culture and creativity a driving force for sustainable development and urban regeneration through the stimulation of growth and innovation and the promotion of social cohesion, citizen well-being and inter-cultural dialogue. In this way cities respond to the major challenges with which they are confronted, such as the economic crisis, environmental impacts, demographic growth and social tensions. Not to mention that cities are today home to more than half the world's population and three quarters of its economic activity, including a large share of the creative economy.

  The crucial role of cities in promoting sustainable development focused on people and the respect of human rights is notably recognised in the 2030 Agenda for Sustainable Development which includes among its 17 goals a specific objective to "make cities and human settlements inclusive, safe, resilient and sustainable" and identifies culture and creativity as one of the essential levers for action in this context.

  It is first and foremost at local level that culture and creativity are lived and practised on a daily basis. It is therefore by stimulating cultural industries, supporting creation, promoting citizen and cultural participation and approaching the public sphere with a new perspective that public authorities, in cooperation with the private sector and civil society, can make the difference and support a more sustainable urban development suited to the practical needs of the local population.

  In this context, cooperation and the sharing of experience and knowledge is crucial for making creativity a lever for urban development and conceiving of new solutions to tackle common challenges. In this regard, UNESCO's Creative Cities Network offers unparalleled opportunities for cities to draw on peer learning processes and collaborative projects in order to fully capitalize on their creative assets and use this as a basis for building sustainable, inclusive and balanced development in economic, cultural, environmental and social terms.

UNESCO

城市与遗产管理的工具：IBA
——一个德国的城市发展项目与政策

Tools for Urban and Heritage Management: IBA
—An Urban Development Program and Policy in Germany

西格弗里德·安德斯 教授

ICOMOS 共享遗产委员会主席

Prof. Siegfried Enders

President of ICOMOS International Scientific Committee on Shared Built Heritage

IBA 国际建筑展具有多重面相，它既是一个地区性规划与发展的项目，也是一个机构、一种哲学理念、一套规划工具，以及一种行政、管理和融资手段。它在德国及欧洲，尤其是在那些地方工业与经济衰落的地区获得了巨大的成功。这种发展超过百年的管理策略为世界其他地方应对类似困境提供了启示，促进区域规划以及遗产管理领域的视野扩展与品质提升。

What is an IBA (International Building Exhibition)?

The name or expression "International Building Exhibition" is somehow confusing since it doesn't describe at the first moment the whole meaning of this event.

Since the Romans and Medieval Times, trading fairs can be found all over Europe. The main purpose of a fair was to sell and buy goods, however, there was also an intention to exhibit something like a product or a service and to entertain.

Since the early 19th century, with the beginning of industrialization and the start of globalization, international exhibitions have been invented as an international event. They were used to present new products, new inventions, design, technology, architecture, fashion, food and drinks in a kind of competition among the leading industrialized countries. The most famous one was The Exposition Universelle of 1900, a world's fair which was held in Paris, France, from 15 April to 12 November 1900, to celebrate the achievements of the past century and to accelerate development into the next. The style that was universally present in the Exposition was Art Nouveau. The fair, visited by nearly 50 million, displayed many machines, inventions, and architecture that are now nearly universally known, including the Grande Roue de Paris Ferris wheel, Russian nesting dolls, diesel engines, talking films, escalators, and the telegraphone (the first magnetic audio recorder).

In the world of art, exhibitions were the essential tools and events for presentation, discussing and developing fine arts.

No wonder that artists and architects developed the idea to create and develop a similar event that

"柔性房屋"

(图片来自 IBA Hamburg GmbH 斜杠 Bernadette Grimmstein)

would deal with architecture and everything associated with it, like design, construction, building material, technology, arts and crafts and urban planning. The realization of this dream became true when this idea met the economic and political interest of decision-makers to promote the upcoming manufacturing and industrialization in their city, state or region. Because this was the key to urban development to hosting an increasing population, economic growth and political power.

Since 1900 until today there have been around 13 building exhibitions of international importance in Germany, Switzerland and the Netherlands.

International Building Exhibition (IBA) has been the most influential tools for urban development policy over the past 100 years in Germany. IBA has always been synonymous with innovation and creativity in design, manufacturing, architecture and urban planning.

Cities, regions and states with exceptional development ambitions opt for an IBA as a planning instrument when they are looking for future-oriented and sustainable solutions for complex urban and regional spaces. An IBA always serves a dual purpose: It drives urban development and is a laboratory for a limited period. An entire city district functions as a lab.

Many leading international architects have been invited to participate in the planning process.

After cultural heritage became an issue in the sociopolitical discussion in the 70th, heritage management became an essential part of the urban development goals of an IBA.

The initiation, intention, architectural, urban and social results of the 13 building exhibitions in Germany could and should be analyzed in order to find out how the policy and strategy of an IBA could be useful to be implemented in other international urban and regional planning processes and in urban heritage management.

In the first step, the exhibitions are going to be introduced:

1-4. Building Exhibition in Darmstadt 1901, 1904, 1908, 1914

5. First General Exhibition for Urban Planning, Berlin 1910

6. Exhibition of the "Deutscher Werkbund" (German Association of Craftsmen),

Weissenhof Estate (Weißenhofsiedlung) Stuttgart 1927

7. German Building Exhibition: "The dwelling of today", Berlin 1931

8. International Building Exhibition (Interbau) Berlin 1952/1957

9. IBA-Berlin 1984/1987

10. IBA-Emscher Park, Regional and Urban Redevelopment of the "Ruhr"-District, North Rhine-Westphalia 1989—1999

11. IBA-Fürst-Pückler-Land, Regional and Urban Redevelopment of the industrial region of 2000—2010

12. IBA-Stadtumbau 2003—2010

13. IBA-Hamburg 2006—2013

14. IBA-Basel 2010—2020

1-4. Building Exhibition in Darmstadt 1901, 1904, 1908, 1914

The artists' colony was founded in 1899 by Ernest Ludwig, Grand Duke of Hesse. It was initiated by him and the Vienna Architect Joseph Maria Olbrich. Olbrich's intention was the challenge to create Art Nouveau Architecture by combining art and architecture and the Grand Duke expected the combination of art and trade to provide economic impulses for his country.

The Darmstadt Artists' Colony refers to a group of Art Nouveau (Jugendstil) artists as well as the buildings in Mathildenhöhe in Darmstadt in which these artists lived and worked. The artists were largely sponsored by patrons and worked together with other members of the colony who ideally had concordant artistic tastes. The artists' goal was the development of modern and forward-looking forms of construction (architecture) and living.

The results of this cooperation of artists, architects and craftsmen were presented in 4 exhibitions, 1901, 1904, 1908 and 1914.

First Exhibition 1901

The first exhibition of the artists' colony took place in 1901 with the title "A Document of German Art". The focus of this exhibition was on eight residential houses, each conceived as an integrated whole, fully decorated and furnished, and arranged in a clear urban setting surrounding the central studio building, the Ernst Ludwig-House. The exhibits were the colony's individual houses, the atelier and various temporary constructions.

Second Exhibition 1904

The second exhibition featured almost only temporary constructions after the large financial losses of the first exhibition. Olbrich created ephemeral pavilions, the "Dreihäusergruppe", an arrangement of three artist-designed middle-class residences serving as model homes. The idea was to present an example and set a standard for a well designed and economical middle-class house.

Third Exhibition 1908

"Hessian State Exhibition of Fine and Applied Arts"

It was designed to attract the public of the whole State of Hesse and demonstrate on the national and international level the quality of architecture within an urban setting and living goods of Darmstadt and the region. Mathildenhöhe's most striking structure by far is Olbrich's Hochzeitsturm ("Wedding Tower") with the Exhibition Hall. The ensemble was built for the third exhibition. After the demise of Joseph Maria Olbrich, Albin Müller was in charge of the exposition, which featured, among other exhibits, a model estate of six fully furnished workers' homes, three of which were rebuilt on a site nearby after the exhibition ended. The third exhibition, which was open to artists and craftsmen from Hesse, was centred on a colony of small residences, in order to show that modern forms of living were attainable with limited financial means.

Fourth and Last Exhibition 1914

Under the guidance of Albin Müller, this building exhibition intended to give an answer to the increasing demand for social houses in a good artistic and architectural quality. The focus has been the planning of social apartment houses and the artistic elaboration of a grove of platanes. An entrance gate with lions and the arrangement of an artistic water basin in front of the Russian Chapel were other highlights of the exhibition.

5. First General Exhibition for Urban Planning, Berlin 1910

The exhibition was a result of the first fundamental scientific discussion on urban planning and development in Germany and central Europe. The chaotic rapid growth of the big cities shaped by private developers created enormous social and economic problems. Since 1903, a scientific discipline for urban planning was founded and crowing at the Berlin University. Series of lectures led to the awareness among the decision-makers in the city to look for the solution to structuring the urban and regional space around Berlin. A number of cities and towns had to be linked and coordinated in their urban development and the living circumstances needed improvement.

An urban planning competition was started in 1908 and the result was presented and discussed in conferences and other events linked with the exhibition.

3 main topics have been dominated in the tasks for the competition and the discussion:

——How to strengthen and design a monumental center for the upcoming metropole

——Find a human solution for the mass-social-housing for the workers

——Create new suburbs, settlements, garden cities at the outskirts

The Berlin town planning exhibition was a fundamental scientific contention in urban planning in Germany and had an enormous impact on the development of urban planning in Europe and the World.

6. Exhibition of the "Deutscher Werkbund" (German Association of Craftsmen), Weissenhof Estate (Weißenhofsiedlung) Stuttgart 1927

Motto: "Housing for modern city dwellers"

The estate was built for the Deutscher Werkbund exhibition of 1927, and included twenty-one buildings comprising sixty dwellings, designed by seventeen European architects, most of them German-speaking. The German architect Mies van der Rohe was in charge of the project on behalf of the city, and it was him who selected the architects, budgeted and coordinated their entries, prepared the site, and oversaw construction. Le Corbusier was awarded the two prime sites, facing the city, and by far the largest budget.

The twenty-one buildings vary slightly in form, consisting of terraced and detached houses and apartment buildings, and display a strong consistency of design. What they have in common are their simplified facades, flat roofs used as terraces, window bands, open-plan interiors, and the high level of prefabrication which permitted their erection in just five months. All but two of the entries were white. Bruno Taut had his entry, the smallest, painted in various colors.

Advertised as a prototype of future workers' housing, in fact, each of these houses was customized and furnished on a budget far out of a normal worker's reach and with little direct relevance to the technical challenges of standardized mass construction. The exhibition opened to the public on 23 July 1927, a year later, and drew large crowds.

The Weissenhof-Settlement is considered one of the most important monuments of the "Neues Bauen" movement. None of the subsequent expositions by Deutsche Werkbund achieved a comparable international charisma. In some special way, Weissenhof-Settlement represents the social, aesthetic and technological changes following the end of World War I. Using the programmatic title "Die Wohnung" (The Housing), this Werkbund exposition demonstrated the renunciation from habitats characterized by pre-industrial periods. In these 33 houses with 63 apartments, a total of 17 architects from Germany, France, Holland, Belgium and Austria formulated their solutions for the living arrangements of the modern big city dwellers, coupled with the use and implementation of new building materials and effective construction methods. As part of this novel and overall urban concept, typical buildings for cost-effective mass production were created as well as buildings of great architectural variety.

The estate rightfully derives its place in architectural history from the participation of architects who were then known only among the avant-garde but who are considered today among the great masters of the 20th century: Ludwig Mies van der Rohe, Walter Gropius, Le Corbusier, Hans Scharoun and others. Nearly all of the participating architects were then under the age of 45, the youngest of them, Mart Stam, was only 28. Only Hans Poeltzig and Peter Behrens were considered the exception as senior statesmen and pioneers of modern movement architecture.

Approximately 500,000 visitors came to see the Werkbund Exhibition, and publications worldwide would highlight its ideas. As a result, contacts were made and maintained, which in June 1928 led to the foundation of CIAM (Congrès Internationaux d'Architecture).

Intentions of the Exhibition

"Efficiency measures in all areas of our lives do not stop where housing is at issue. The economic conditions of today prohibit any kind of waste and demand the maximum effect with minimum amount of means, requiring the implementation of such materials and technological appliances which will lead to lower building and operational costs, and will lead to a simplification of households, and to improvements of living itself."

As part of continued preparations, the goal of housing standardization was moved to the background, partly because of the hillside exposure of the property, and partly because the overall leader, Mies van der Rohe, granted a great degree of design freedom to the architects. The target group of the "modern city dweller", envisioned by Gustaf Stotz, the President of the Württemberg Working Group of Deutscher Werkbund and founding father of Weissenhofsiedlung, made it possible to create somewhat larger living quarters, by the standards, for the educated middle class which would also include a maid's room.

Weissenhofsiedlung represented a new type of building exhibition. For the first time, fully functional experimental buildings were erected that would later on serve as "regular" lease apartments. At the time of the exhibition, they were furnished in accordance with ideas of "Neues Bauen" (Functionalism). In addition, there was an experimental area where different building techniques and materials were shown, complemented by an indoor exhibition with the latest technological devices, furnishings, furniture and household equipment.

An important supplement to the presentation of avant-garde architecture was the plan and model exhibition "International Functionalism Design" where more than 60 national and international architects introduced their buildings and designs, including all architects involved at Weissenhofsiedlung as well as Hugo Häring, El Lissitzky, Ernst May, Erich Mendelsohn, van der Vlugt, and Frank Lloyd Wright.

The role of the City of Stuttgart in 1927

The building exhibition of Deutsche Werkbund was funded by the City of Stuttgart.

Weissenhofsiedlung was created as part of the municipal housing building program in which the City of Stuttgart attempted to battle housing shortages following World War I and subsequent major inflation. With its decision in favor of Weissenhofsiedlung, the City of Stuttgart underlined its willingness to remain open for new ideas in architecture which were concurrently demonstrated in other estates and buildings within the city. Despite its rejection by prominent traditionalists, the Municipal Council approved the project in 1926 with a clear majority. The city provided the property and assumed costs for development and construction, as well as professional fees for the architects.

7. German Building Exhibition: "The dwelling of today", Berlin 1931

In the middle of the world economic crisis, Mies van der Rohe and his colleagues Walter Gropius and Hugo Häring organized an international building exhibition in Hall No 2 of the Berlin Trade Fair Campus. In 23 dwelling units, the exhibition shows examples and vision for dwellings of the time and the future. Considering the economic crises, the design should meet the living expectation of the middle class.

8. International Building Exhibition (Interbau), Berlin 1952/1957

Motto: *"Reconstruction in the line with the concept of a structured, yet widely-spaced city"*

By 1948, the political division of Berlin was confirmed. The urban planning in East and West started to pursue different paths. While East Berlin was announced the capital of the GDR, the isolated West Berlin became the object of "propaganda" demonstration of the West.

East Berlin started in 1952 an international building exhibition by the prestige project "Stalinallee" as the "first socialistic street" in Germany. The Stalin Avenue was conceived as the central spine of the GDR capital. Geared to Schinkel's formal repertoire, based on the "16 Principles of Urban Building in the GDR" and developed along Soviet models, monumental "residences for workers" were built here with historic style elements from 1953 on. With regard to urban planning, East Berlin continued the idea of the "beautiful compact city" along the basic principles of traditional architecture. In the context of the national development program, the Stalin Avenue was celebrated as "the cornerstone of the constitution of socialism in the capital of Germany" (W. Ulbricht)

In West-Berlin, funded by the Marshall Plan, the change from the basic repair of the city into a fundamental reconstruction took place in the 1950s. There was a dream of a structured but relaxed city—definitely closing the tradition of the city of tenements originated in the 19th century. This new approach came to evidence in the first international building exhibition after WW II—the Interbau Berlin 1957. The government of West Berlin reacted to the urban planning demonstration of the Stalin Avenue in East Berlin with an international urban planning competition. The results of this competition needed to be presented to the international community by an international building exhibition. The goal was not to reconstruct an urban quarter but a demonstration of urban planning of the "free and democratic West". After the deconstruction and the redevelopment of this heavily destroyed bourgeois quarter, the Hansa Quarter as an exemplary exhibition project was planned to be an example of "the City of Tomorrow".

Under the patronage of the Berlin Senate 53 internationally renowned architects were elected to develop single objects in a park-like landscape. The new Hansa Quarter wanted to bury the memory of the old quarter completely in oblivion. In place of the old block structure, a mixture of high rise and flat buildings appeared in the landscape.

Today the Hansa Quarter stands as a built document of planar rehabilitation in the period of modernism while functional buildings of the area are mostly weakly planned. In its pedagogical claim, the Interbau invited the post-war architects to enter the new models of international modernism. The Interbau was planned as the biggest building industrial and architectural show as well as a demonstration of the superiority of the West towards the East by this instrument of an international building exhibition.

9. IBA-Berlin 1984/1987

The International Building Exhibition Berlin (IBA Berlin) was an urban renewal project in West-Berlin, Germany. Initiated in 1979, it was completed in 1987, matching the 750th anniversary of the founding of Berlin.

Urban planning theory after WWⅡ in Germany, especially in West Germany, rejected historic urban structures, like condensed yards in block of buildings, which dated back to the Mediaeval Times.

Such dense urban structures in German cities created a lot of problems like insufficient natural lighting and ventilation, unhealthy living conditions, fire hazards and no space for the increasing individual transport.

As a result of this theoretical urban planning approach whole urban areas have been not rebuilt or reconstructed after the war destruction but completely demolished and new urban structures with a lot of open space and room for the immense growing amounts of cars have been constructed. In many inner-city areas, private investment was looking for high rise development, well preserved historic houses have been neglected and torn off as well.

Urban planning policy in the 1960s and 1970s in West Germany was shaped by ignorance for historic buildings and historic urban structures.

There was a growing civic resistance at the end of the 1960s, first by the former inhabitants of the demolished housing and later by the students at the universities (1968) who were sent to these areas to study the situation. This led finally to a change of urban planning policy, after acknowledging that a dense block of houses structure could provide good quality for urban life as well, especially at the social level. The total destruction of historic urban structures was banned and it was necessary to develop concepts for the future inner-city urban structure and the urban life of their inhabitants. This should have been the goal of the IBA 1977—1987.

The IBA followed two distinct strategies: "careful urban renewal" and "critical reconstruction".

In 1979, Josef Paul Kleihues was appointed director of the IBA Neubau (New) section by the Berlin Senate; Hardt Waltherr Hämer was director of the less-publicised IBA Altbau (Old). He organized the exhibition along two distinct themes: IBA Alt aimed to explore methods of "careful urban renewal" and IBA Neu for experimenting "critical reconstruction". He invited many international architects including Peter Eisenman, Vittorio Gregotti, Herman Hertzberger, Hans Hollein, Arata Isozaki, Rob Krier, Aldo Rossi and James Stirling. Consequently, the IBA was called by *Time* magazine "the most ambitious showcase of world architecture in this generation".

10. IBA-Emscher Park, Regional and Urban Redevelopment of the "Ruhr" District, Emscher Park: from Dereliction to Scenic Landscapes

Once one of the most polluted and environmentally devastated regions of the world, the Ruhr district has been reborn. With the "International Building Exhibition (IBA) at Emscher Park" initiated in 1989, the run-down industrial landmarks of the region have been transformed to serve new recreational uses while still preserving the area's rich history. The redevelopment has given the region a greener image, created a more cohesive community and maintained the area's identity.

The Ruhr district of Germany was once the heartland of Europe's steel and coal industries. Over the past 30 years, these heavy industries have been massively restructured, causing the abandonment and dereliction of many steelworks and coal mining operations throughout the region. Consequently, Ruhr has been left with a legacy of high unemployment and the scars of environmental contamination as the old industrial work yards have slowly become brownfield sites in need of restoration.

In the face of this abandonment and decay, the State Government of North Rhine-Westphalia created a regional redevelopment plan entitled the "International Building Exhibition (IBA) at Emscher Park" in 1989. Over the course of a ten year period, IBA Emscher Park was to encourage the ecological, economic, and urban revitalization of the Ruhr Valley and the Emscher River through several collaborative partnerships with various agencies and, notably, 17 local authorities of the Ruhr district. Specifically, the two primary objectives of the IBA were to give the region a greener image and breathe life into the old industrial plants. After the IBA expired in 1999, a successor plan to promote redevelopment called "Project Ruhr" took over the task of management and, presently, the entire project series is in its final phase, which focuses on cleaning up the Emscher River. If all goes according to plan, this series will be completed in 2014.

A crucial vision for the redevelopment under the IBA was an Emscher Landscape Park that would act as a "green connector" between the settlements of the Rhur valley, following the path of the Emscher River and using the abandoned industrial areas along it as a unique form of greenspace. In addition to connecting the 17 towns located along the river valley, this new east-west oriented green corridor joins seven existing but expanded north-south greenbelts.

The park is composed of regenerated brownfields, reclaimed forests, and existing recreational areas that together provide a cohesive set of green infrastructure for the entire region. The specific projects that created the park system ranged from the development of large fallow land areas to small scale construction schemes to installations of biotopes to the simple planting of trees. Today, the Ruhr-Emscher district is enveloped by a beautiful green curtain that occasionally includes a historic industrial landmark standing just over the trees.

The masterplan for the region specifically targeted abandoned industrial sites so as to improve the quality of the undeveloped areas surrounding them and to save money by making use of the existing infrastructure. Once active collieries, Coca-Cola plants and steelworks, the region's massive and muscular structures are now filled with art, culture, housing, commerce and offices. Concerts are staged in the aging steel frames of former factories. Grassy recreational areas, completed with hiking trails and climbing walls, have been sculpted from the old hills of coal pilings. Paths through glades of trees linking the many different components of the park follow the former industrial roads and rail lines.

After 20 years of planning and implementation, the Emscher Landscape Park has gone from a purely fantastical vision to a reality that has inspired new urban development. The project has achieved lasting improvements in the living and working environment of the involved towns by upgrading the ecological and aesthetic quality of their nearby countryside. Furthermore, by reusing and preserving the impressive relics of the industrial era, the Ruhr region has been able to keep its unique identity and has branded itself as an ancient monument of industrial society.

Regeneration of the Emscher river system

A central goal of the Emscher Park project was to clean up the Emscher River, which runs through the very middle of the green plan and stretches a distance of 70 kilometers from east to west through the region. For decades, the river had a reputation of being a biologically dead "open sewer", acting as a wastewater canal since the end of late 19th century.

Now that much of the mining in the region has ceased, underground sewers have been installed to carry waste away from the river and promote its re-naturalization. Additionally, the river has been re-profiled to allow for better flooding management, and to slow the speed of the currents, part of the river's course has been changed from a straight narrow concrete channel back to a wide curved pool. Trees and native plants have been introduced along the bank, which have improved the water quality as well as the ecosystems in the area.

Altogether, the process of river regeneration has required an investment of 4.4 billion Euros and will take until 2014. However, it has provided a highly visible symbol of positive change that should have lasting benefits for the Rhur valley.

Financing

Funding for Emscher Park was derived from a variety of sources. The State Government of North Rhine-Westphalia allocated 17.9 million EUR for IBA but much of the invested money in fact came from developers, private companies, non-profit groups and local town governments that worked specifically on individual projects connected to the park. By the summer of 1993, a total of EURO 2.5 billion had been invested in the redevelopment, of which about two thirds came from public funds and one third from private investments.

After finishing the IBA, Project Ruhr—a neworganization that will promote projects in the Ruhr area—took over the task of project management.

11. IBA-Fürst-Pückler-Land, Regional and Urban Redevelopment of the Industrial Region of 2000—2010

The IBA Lausitz—A Laboratory for New Landscapes

IBA Fürst-Pückler-Land has been guiding the reshaping of the Lausitz region after the end of the mining economy and promoting new uses for old monuments of the industrial age.

The Lausitz region (Lusatia) was the coal and energy centre of the German Democratic Republic. Millions of tons of brown coal were mined and processed in this area of East Germany. When 17 strip mines were closed at the beginning of the nineties, the jobs disappeared, too. What remained were gigantic crater landscapes and unused industrial buildings. With the IBA Finale 2010, the process that has been set in motion will by no means be over. The reinvention of the Lausitz is taking place under the banner of tourism and cultural development and marketing.

The flooding of the former brown coal pits on the state boundary between Saxony and Brandenburg is giving rise to a landscape of lakes and ponds, which, with its total of 14,000 hectares of water surface is larger than Lake Starnberg and Lake Chiem together. Of this, 7000 hectares are connected by navigable canals. The process of flooding with river water is being carried out by the federally-owned redevelopment company Lausitz and Central-German Mining Administration Company (Lausitzer und Mitteldeutsche Bergbau-Verwaltungsgesellschaft-LMBV), and is to be completed by 2015 (no later than 2020). Then, 23 new lakes will draw visitors. Or new residents, for that matter, since the IBA, together with the LMBV and the Lausitz University of Applied Sciences (Fachhochschule Lausitz), has also made a name for itself as a "Competence Centre for Floating Architecture." (Fachhochschule Lausitz)

Floating Architecture

This initiative, started in 2006, has set itself an ambitious goal: in the coming years, the region is to position itself as a centre for the development and export of floating architecture. It all sounds very visionary, making floating houses the hallmark of the Lausitz lakescape. But start-ups are already in progress. In summer 2006, the first floating holiday home was opened on Lake Partwitz together with a floating diving school on Lake Gräbendorf. In July 2009, a model house by the company Steeltec 37 was opened to visitors on lake Geierswald—the investor Thomas Wilde is planning a floating residential harbour with 20 houses at this location, to be completed in 2011. The new is still emerging and the old is gone forever. On Europe's largest landscaping construction site, visitors can directly experience how the canyons of the decommissioned coal mines are changing into a lakescape, centimetre by centimetre.

Coal mining in the Lausitz has a tradition going back 150 years. Many historic monuments of steel and stone have disappeared in the meantime. A few giant industrial buildings could nonetheless be saved with the aid of the IBA and its project partners, among them Europe's oldest brown coal power plant in Plessa, the Biotürme, a decommissioned organic treatment plant for phenolic wastewater produced by the large coal-firing plant in Lauchhammer, and the overburden conveyor bridge F60 in Lichterfeld, to the west of Großraschen. A prime example of a successful IBA project, the F60 demonstrates that industrial monuments of times past can also serve as guideposts for the region's future.

Guideposts for the future

The F60, one of the world's largest movable machines, was used in the Klettwitz-Nord strip mine and—as the "miners' gofer"—transported mining waste directly into the open coal seam. After the closing of the colliery in 1992, this 11,000-tonne, 500-metre long steel giant was now superfluous, and like so many other strip-mining machines, was slated for detonation. But then, the township of Lichterfeld-Schacksdorf envisioned transforming the F60 into a public exhibit mine, and with support from the IBA, their dream has become a reality. This masterpiece of engineering, which looks as though someone has transplanted the Eiffel Tower from Paris to the Lausitz, is now a regional landmark and tourist attraction. About 70,000 visitors a year climb the monument on foot, to explore the dimensions of this steel giant and the expanse of the landscape. The F60 is a venue for concerts and other events, and even turns into a work of art at night. A light-and-sound installation by Hans Peter Kuhn enhances the contours of the overburden conveyor bridge with a "cross-hatching" of light, and enlivens the colossal structure with the sound of various kinds of work-related noise through loudspeakers.

Today if you look at the landscape of Lusatian Lakeland, you can hardly imagine that you are standing at the edge of a former open cast coal mining region. The ENERGY Route, a premium product under the umbrella brand Lusatian Industrial Culture, presents at ten impressive original settings a large-scale view of what people have achieved in energy production. At the same time you can also experience why the Lusatian Lakeland-Europe's largest artificially created water landscape—was developed.

What's special? —Visitors can walk through sites, see and touch (almost) everything that was formerly closed to the general public, or visit sites of ongoing active production, as in the open cast mine, Welzow-Süd.

You can experience close up the Conveyor Bridge F60 [Besucherbergwerk F60], a visitor mine. Or for a great view climb up to the Lauchhammer Biotowers [Biotürme Lauchhammer], all that now remains of a huge coke oven plant. Also, visit the fascinating control room of the Plessa Adventure Power

Station [Erlebnis-Kraftwerk Plessa] and take a stroll through Marga, Germany's first "garden city" [Gartenstadt Marga]. In the Briquette Factory LOUISE [Brikettfabrik LOUISE] the functional technology of the 19th century production era comes alive again, and the Art Museum Diesel Power Station Cottbus [Kunstmuseum Dieselkraftwerk Cottbus] presents varying exhibits in a technological setting. If you wish, you can experience a "Shift Start" three times daily in the Knappenrode Energy Factory [Energiefabrik Knappenrode] on the Factory Adventure Tour, or also take a look at the modern Schwarze Pumpe Power Station [Kraftwerk Schwarze Pumpe]. Tours in the active Mines of Welzow-Süd [Tagebau Welzow-Süd] promise you an unforgettable experience, along with a visit to the excursio Visitor Centre [excursio-Besucherzentrum]. The starting point for your explorations of this landscape in transition is the IBA Terrasses [Besucherzentrum IBA-Terrassen] in Großräschen, and the Visitor Centre of the Lusatian Lakeland directly at the edge of the mine—the future Grossräschen Lake.

12. IBA-Urban Redevelopment Saxony-Anhalt 2003—2010

The IBA Urban Redevelopment Saxony-Anhalt 2010 embraces the federal state of Saxony-Anhalt as a laboratory for the city of tomorrow. Exemplary and innovative urban redevelopment tools are put to the test in 19 cities, which are affected by demographic change.

Discourses and topics: City types

Cities with ever-decreasing populations must adapt existing structures to ensure their continued ability to function. Shrinkage is accompanied by harsh economic conditions. Planners can often merely intervene on a small scale, rather than taking sweeping measures to improve standards.

Councils must also cooperate with residents, local political agents, and the business community. This requires an attractive common vision. If the increasing amount of available space and vacant property can be successfully transformed, quantitative shrinkage can yield qualitative growth. There will not be an ideal city of the future. Every place will have to devise its own development solutions. Aschersleben, for instance, engages in functional and structural concentration at the centre, Bitterfeld-Wolfen is becoming a polycentric urban network, whilst Sangerhausen is fostering specific profiles of each individual area. Stendal is cooperating in a city triangle with Tangermuende and Arneburg. Halberstadt is building on its disused inner-city properties, and Strassfurt's central area is being landscaped.

Landscape

Under shrinkage conditions, the ratio of city to landscape must be re-negotiated. In the densely populated city, the green spaces primarily compensated for the built-up areas. In the less densely populated city, however, a more balanced coexistence can develop.

In view of a large amount of development land becoming available, the question arises of how to develop and maintain attractive and diverse landscapes, despite limited funding. Can the notion of an urban landscape give rise to new urban concepts? How much landscape can the city tolerate? Ideas about how city and landscape can collectively generate new forms of urbanity are still being sought. Often, a landscape design is perceived as temporary, until the urban sites are again turned over to development. However, is it not possible to view the landscape itself as an urban quality? Dessau-Roßlau, for instance, describes its cityscape as urban islands in a green corridor; Magdeburg is developing diverse landscapes along the river Elbe, while Schönebeck is focusing on renaturation strategies that relate to the historic cityscape. In Weißenfels, a central green zone that connects the city's historic layers is forming on derelict industrial sites.

Education

Regeneration cannot depend entirely on construction. Soft factors are increasingly gaining importance, especially in Sachsen-Anhalt's shrinking cities. Education is vital: declining birth rates mean fewer students at all levels, with adverse effects for local communities and businesses.

Providing educational and cultural opportunities can help to stem the tide and retain young families as well as attract new families, students, research-based industries, and cultural tourists from the outside. Further educational facilities are needed to cater for the rising number of an increasingly older work force and older jobless people. Evidently, a sound education is also a vital prerequisite for public participation in the regeneration process. Educational programmes on building culture can raise identification levels as well as create an active awareness of questions of municipal organization and urban regeneration. Naumburg is already developing new programmes for all ages, whilst Bernburg and Wittenberg are betting on closer cooperation and the improvement of existing facilities; Wanzleben has forged a family-friendly reputation with excellent provisions for youngsters and children.

Structural legacy

Saxony-Anhalt has a wealth of listed buildings and historic towns of great merit. While the cities increasingly draw on their historic periods of prosperity to shape their urban identities, population decline presents an acute threat to their structural legacy. There is a lack of funding for often complex renovation or conservation projects, and a shortage of users. Inner-city disuse and neglect therefore often affect those historic buildings which collectively characterise the overall historic picture of the city.

The cities must attract new interested parties as protagonists, and stimulate or foster their citizens' interest. In order to renovate old towns cooperatively in a manner befitting their historic (and protected) status, the redevelopment process must be moderated in a focused way, with the inclusion of all the participants. The whole of Quedlinburg's historic town has been a UNESCO World Cultural Heritage site since 1994, yet it is still under-populated. Unconventional methods are now being deployed to protect the listed historic buildings from further deterioration until a new interested party is found. Halle on the other hand consists of two contradictory towns: a historic old town (Altstadt) and a modern new town (Neustadt). This raises a more basic question: Which building stock is so important for the city's identity that it must be preserved as a structural legacy, even when demolition prevails?

Identity

The radical change in the cities of Saxony-Anhalt also leads to the creation of new urban identities and profiles. Particularly affected are the cities which during the GDR era derived their profiles largely from their industries. Here, the closure of factories destroyed both the job market and the communal identity. While the regional histories seldom played an official role as a point of reference in the GDR, since 1990 many cities and regions have again been drawing strongly on the identity-forming and aspects of their urban history.

These historic references are publicised in the cities through events, through architecture or in the form of educational provisions. The updated historic urban identity is meant to strengthen the inhabitants' sense of identification and engagement, and also to attract people and businesses from elsewhere.

Köthen takes up the tradition of homeopathy in the town, making the health-care industry the driving force of its economic, cultural and scientific development. Lutherstadt Eisleben structures its innercity development with the new Luther Trail, and Merseburg aims to attract new residents by raising its profile as a cathedral and university town rich in tradition.

Climate Change

Whilst the actual impact of climate change will probably be comparatively mild in Saxony-Anhalt, climate protection and the transition into the post-fossil era requires radical steps. Standard settlement models and everyday patterns of how we live, currently based on the premise of abundant supplies of fossil fuels, will have to alter radically as these resources become scarce and expensive. Energy-intensive activities will be restructured, reduced or altogether replaced.

Apart from massive cuts in energy consumption, the generation of renewables from solar, wind, water, geothermal and biofuel sources will gain vital importance. Conditions for Saxony-Anhalt's taking a lead in the transition towards a post-fossil world are good. Renewable energy already makes up 35 percent of the State's net electric power generation. Furthermore, numerous important manufacturers and research institutions from the renewable energy sector are already established here.

Debate on shrinkage

Where cities shrink, the era of growth has come to an end. It is evident that shrinking cities shed populations and economic activity in equal measure, yet the reasons for the phenomenon of shrinkage and its impacts are many and diverse.

The phenomenon of shrinking cities is nothing new. Throughout history, phases of growth have been followed by periods of population decline. Wars, catastrophes and epidemics decimated populations in cities and across the country; technological, economic or political shifts robbed even erstwhile capital cities of their relevance.

Since the outset of industrialisation some two centuries ago and the evolution of the modern metropolis, growth has been accepted as the universal indicator of urban development. In industrial countries, populations and economic power grew almost continuously and usually rapidly. This was accompanied by greater prosperity, and the cities grew. The global urban population increased from three per cent in 1800 to 14 per cent in 1900. By 2000, this figure had grown to 47 per cent; approximately half the global population now lives in steadily growing cities. Up to the present day, this growth paradigm has influenced our thinking about urban development: growth has become a matter of course. However, the developments of recent years show that this historic era is drawing to a close. The populations of industrialised countries are beginning to wane, the urbanisation process is on the decrease and although the economy (measured according to the gross domestic product) is still showing limited growth, rates of employment have been steadily falling for some time.

Urban shrinkage in the 20th century differs significantly from its historic antecedents. No longer the consequence of fateful catastrophes, it is increasingly becoming the norm in urban development. Some sixty years ago, large cities in the Western world had already begun to shrink, but what was initially perceived as a localised maldevelopment has meanwhile become the rule in many regions of the world.

Nevertheless, to the present day, every attempt has been made to give these new challenges a wide berth. A veritable arsenal of censorship vocabulary is in circulation, which obscures the heart of the problem. For a long time, the notion of "shrinking cities" was frowned upon, and it is only now beginning to establish itself in the public debate. However, shrinkage does not exclusively have to be perceived in a negative light, just as growth is not always experienced as a positive process. Even shrinkage harbours potentials—potentials, which are revealed wherever the guiding principles change in fundamental ways, and modes of action and practice are reorganised. The result is widespread social reform. The open exploration of the phenomenon of shrinkage is an incisive step on the path to this end—a confrontation, which the federal state of Saxony-Anhalt boldly faced in 2002 with the IBA Urban Redevelopment 2010 Saxony-Anhalt.

IBA-Städte im Überblick

1. Aschersleben: From the Outside to the Inside—Focussing on the Centre
2. Bernburg (Saale): Generating a Future in Education—Learning at the Centre
3. Bitterfeld-Wolfen: Network Town
4. Dessau-Roßlau: Urban cores—Landscape Zones
5. Halberstadt: Cultivating Empty Space
6. Halle (Saale): Balancing Act: Dual City
7. Hansestadt Stendal: Central Town in a Rural Region
8. Köthen (Anhalt): Homoeopathy as a Development Force
9. Lutherstadt Eisleben: CommonResponsibility—Redeveloping Luther's Town
10. Lutherstadt Wittenberg: Campus Wittenberg
11. Magdeburg: Living alongside and with the Elbe
12. Merseburg: New Milieus—New Opportunities
13. Naumburg (Saale): City Formation—Citizenry and Building Culture
14. Quedlinburg: Perspective: World Cultural Heritage
15. Sangerhausen: Rating—Livable Neighbourhoods
16. Schönebeck (Elbe): Seventeen Seventy-Four
17. Staßfurt: Relinquishing the Old Centre
18. Wanzleben: Family Town
19. Weißenfels: A Time for Founders

13. IBA-Hamburg 2006—2013

Hamburg is looking to grow its inner city and make the "Leap across the Elbe". Between the northern and southern branches of the river, the St Pauli landing stages and Harburg, lies a 35 square kilometre area of the city that had become something of a backwater following the storm surge of 1962.

Europe's largest river island, Wilhelmsburg, is home to docks, industry, green oases, and over 50,000 people. Together with the small neighbouring island of Veddel and the "Harburg Upriver Port", from 2006 to 2013 Wilhelmsburg formed the project area for the Internationale Bauausstellung IBA Hamburg (International Building Exhibition).

Together with its many committed partners, the IBA Hamburg has devised and implemented seventy projects here, creating an impetus for sustainable, environmentally friendly, and socially balanced urban development.

Under the key theme of COSMOPOLIS, the IBA Hamburg has demonstrated how cooperation might be nurtured within major cities in the future. METROZONES offer space for growth within the city, providing easy routes between living and work. CITIES AND CLIMATE CHANGE demonstrates how major cities can grow in an environmentally friendly way by generating decentralised renewable energy and using their own resources efficiently.

Here you can learn all about the IBA Hamburg: its projects, stakeholders, and the results of seven years of research within the living city in Wilhelmsburg.

The IBA-Competence

An international building exhibition is much more than an exhibition in its classical sense: just like a laboratory, it embraces research and development. The built results of the research can be explored on site of the international building exhibition. Reflexions on various topics and themes, which the IBA Hamburg and its partners dealt with, are located here.

14. IBA-Basel 2010—2020

The Structure of the IBA Basel 2020 is based on the trinational Eurodistrict Basel (Switzerland, Germany, France).

The IBA Basel was developed in a 10-year planning process of regional and city planning visions. In this time various projects of architectural, city and landscape planning and cultural scope should be realized.

If there is any town that can surprise you, then Lörrach. 49,000 inhabitants live in the district town that is the cultural and economic center in the tri-border region of Germany, France and Switzerland. Lörrach is well-known for its picturesque market places, the excellent cuisine and the STIMMEN (VOICES) festival. The beautiful historical center with a large pedestrian zone and street cafes with southern atmosphere invites to stroll around at leisure.

The groundbreaking development of Lörrach to a center of service industries is continuing to create interesting jobs. Since Lörrach offers a manifold of educational offers and leisure activities, it is a sought-after location.

Conclusion

IBA as an institution, political program for regional planning and development, philosophy, planning tool, political and administrative funding instrument, was very successful to develop many cities and regions in Germany and Europe, special those which suffered of an industrial and economical demise by what so ever reason. The management skills, which were developed in more than 100 years could be used for similar tasks elsewhere in the world.

IBA1989—1999：德国埃姆舍公园国际建筑展的实践与影响

IBA1989—1999：Practice & Influence of Internationale Bauausstellung（IBA）in Emscher Park in Germany

克劳斯-皮特·艾希特 博士
ICOMOS 历史村镇委员会秘书长
Dr. Claus-Peter Echter
Secretary General of ICOMOS-CIVVIH

从20世纪80年代的柏林到90年代的埃姆舍公园，国际建筑展（IBA）项目都在基于历史遗产的城市修复与再生实践中产生了重大影响，其在管理、组织、融资等项目实践中获得的经验都值得探讨。埃姆舍公园项目由德国北莱茵威斯特伐利亚州于1990至1999年期间组织实施，推动了传统工业区鲁尔区的生态、经济及社会更新。

1. Some aspects of the historical development of the International Building Exhibition

An Internationale Bauausstellung (IBA) or International Building Exhibition is a German tool for urban engineering and architecture, in order to show new concepts in terms of social, cultural and ecologic ideas that are considered necessary for an urban and landscape change in a city or a region. By the desired participation of urban planners, architects, landscape architects and companies across borders the international competition in the projects shall be stimulated.

In Berlin, the Interbau took place in 1957 with a focus on "rebuilding the Hansaviertel". IBA Berlin (1979—1987) was an urban renewal project which followed the strategies of "careful urban renewal" and "critical reconstruction".

位于埃森的关税同盟12号煤矿

A worldwide outstanding example was the International Building Exhibition Emscher Park (IBA Emscher Park) from 1989 to 1999 that was installed as a program for the future of North Rhine-Westphalia. The entire region of heavy industry between Duisburg and Dortmund, with many, often with toxins, contaminated brownfields has been transformed into a modern residential, cultural and recreational landscape with ecological standards. Thus the IBA Emscher Park aimed at restructuring a former industrial region, the Ruhr, by sparking urbanistic, architectural, cultural, and economic incentives.

With the IBA Basel 2020 (2010—2020), the tri-national region Basel, which lies in Germany, France, Switzerland, faces the task of actively shaping the common development of the region through cross-border projects.

The IBA Parkstadt (2012—2020) is the first IBA to be held completely outside of Germany, in the former mining region of Parkstad Limburg in the Netherlands. Currently, at least 39 projects have been chosen to develop further.

2. The purpose of the IBA Emscher Park

As a project organized by the state of North Rhine-Westphalia, the German Federal Government and local authorities, between 1990 and 1999 the IBA Emscher Park developed and implemented concepts for the ecological, economic and social renewal of the Ruhr district. It concerns an area between Duisburg and Dortmund of around 40 km in east-west direction and 20 km in north-south direction with about two million inhabitants.[①] The region is characterized by a mixture of industrial wastelands, slag heaps, still functioning industrial areas, workers' housing estates, canals, railroads, and highways, as well as major scenic open space and important cultural institutions. The renewal of the industrial landscape Ruhr area was a central and important challenge for the Federal Republic of Germany and Europe.

The Ruhr region had solid conditions in order to cope with this task: qualified and industry experienced workers, a tight network of efficient roads, railways and utilities, the dense and diverse range of cultural, sports and recreational facilities and its central location in the European internal market. A major disadvantage for the Ruhr region lay in the lack of free space, landscape and urban quality associated with major environmental impacts as a result of rapid and largely uncontrolled industrialization. The forward-looking conversion of a densely populated industrial landscape requires as much planning preparation and public control as the expansion of urban areas at the expense of uninhabited premises in the past.

3. Instruments, stakeholders, management, organization structure

The IBA Emscher Park was an offer from the state of North Rhine-Westphalia to the Emscher Region. The state government had provided an appropriate form of organization with the IBA Emscher Park Limited Liability Company[②] and given priority in funding from existing programs for IBA projects.

The Emscher Park exhibition has worked with many partners on a wide base—municipalities, companies, associations, initiatives and citizens. The 17 townships have joined the Building Exhibition when it was founded by decision of their councils: Dortmund, Duisburg, Essen, Gelsenkirchen and others. The Building Exhibition was a process with many stakeholders.

Responsibility for individual projects was the organising institutions, which were usually the municipalities, as well as companies or initiatives. The figure illustrates the instruments, the stakeholders and the organizational structure of the IBA. The International Building Exhibition was a 100% subsidiary of the state North Rhine-Westfalia and organised as a Limited Liability Company under private law, managed by the executive director Prof. Karl Ganser. For scientific advice and support of the work of the In-

---

① Thomas Sieverts, Neue Aufgaben für den Städebau im alten Europa-Voraussetzungen, Prinzipen, Beispiele. pp. 1-34, here pp. 12-14.
② GmbH.

ternational Building Exhibition, a board of five university professors was installed. A Steering Committee decided the acceptance of projects chaired by the minister for urban development of the state.

To finance the projects, no additional means have been provided. The project financing has been assured by the existing programs of the state combined with structural support of the Federal Republic and the European Community (a total of 36 government subsidy programs), including traditional programs such as urban renewal and economic and housing subsidies and funding for training programs and the framework for coal areas. A total of 2.5 billion euros have been invested in the projects, thereof two-thirds of public funds and one-third private investment. ①

The IBA had six main fields of activity also referred to as "pilot projects" with allocated sub projects. These six approaches were identified as the most important principles of operation. ②

3.1 The Emscher Landscape Park was an important pilot project and the unifying theme of the International Building Exhibition Emscher Park . This should be the core of a new future-oriented regional infrastructure. The projects were ranging from the large-scale development areas that have declined up to small measures such as the installation of habitats and tree plantings.

3.2 The ecological reconstruction of the Emscher river system means that the wastewater is led to underground channels and clarified decentralized and the streams are transformed in harmony with nature or as urban waters. The Emscher and its tributaries are gaining importance—as formative structures in the landscape and as recreational and adventurous spaces for the people in the cities.

3.3 At 19 locations in the region vacant spaces have been developed to modern commercial-, service-and science parks developed under the guideline "Working in the ark".

3.4 Conservation of industrial monuments and industrial culture-Monuments like gigantic mines, blast furnaces and winding towers are architectural testimonies and explain the history of the region. They are widely visible and form landmarks, view points for the people in the region and thus structures for identification. The IBA focused on the preservation of heritage testimonies of the industrial culture. The industrial buildings of the 20th century assigned new tasks for the preservation, conservation and restoration because of their magnitude respectively dimensions and their inherent steel and iron aesthetics. Furthermore, the economic preservation or maintenance for large industrial plants was more difficult to calculate. A selection of really typical, historically significant industrial plants was thus inevitable.

3.5 New residential and urban development

Village life in the Ruhr area: Since the 1990s, many garden cities and traditional worker's housing estates in the region are highly estimated by its population. In the 1960s and 1980s many of these estates were neglected or heavily and badly transformed. In the 1990s most working—class quarters and garden cities were renewed and saved with a focus on the tenant participation. 3,000 already existing dwellings were modernized and renovated.

3.6 Social initiatives and employment: Many citizens from the Ruhr region contributed to and worked on projects with the IBA. They helped to make new settlements worth living, they developed ideas for the use of old buildings, they assisted to understand the history of the coal mines Baltic mines and smelters, they worked actively in shaping their local recreation areas, or they took initiatives in the sociocultural, social or ecological sector. Such projects made a significant contribution to the improve-

---

① Karl Jasper, Strategies, Methods, Werkzeuge, in: Christa Reichert, Lars Niemann, Angela Utke (eds), Internatinale Bauausstellung Emscher Park: Impulse Lokal, regional, national, international, Essen 2011, pp. 42-52, here p. 46.
② Ibid. pp. 46-51.

ment of infrastructure services, to local networking of community-oriented activities and for (re-) use of derelict areas and buildings.

4. The projects of the IBA Emscher Park

The IBA Emscher Park recognised the decentrally organised agglomeration of the Ruhr area as a cohesive region, placing it in the context of an International Building Exhibition.[①] For the first time, the ecological and urban renewal of an industrial region became the central subject of a program for structural change. The new development model of the IBA "change without growth" was designed to be strongly oriented towards the values of sustainability, the recycling economy, and structural and spatial quality.

Industrial heritage was to be treated with respect and strengthened through cultural uses with an openness to contemporary trends. Discussing the Emscher area in terms of a landscape park was a novelty for International Buildings Exhibitions. The IBA projects have ensured that "industrial culture" is now regarded as the central root of the entire region's cultural identity. This sustainable contribution to regional identity is of inestimable value for the Ruhr area's further development. The IBA attempted to utilise existing resources, promote networks and secure the quality of results. The projects shaped through many small, acupuncture-like interventions the IBA's structural program in the Ruhr area. Some projects, such as huge former Zollverein coal mine site, "the Zeche Zollverein" in Essen is still not complete.[②] In 1999, 19 cities and municipalities and a series of initiatives and companies had planned and executed more than 100 projects like the following ones:

4.1　Welheim Historic Garden City, Bottrop

Built from 1913 to 1923, its winding streets and avenues still defines the appearance of the entire Bottrop-Welheim district. The estate's exemplary renovation included a socially acceptable modernisation of its in keeping with conservation practices, improving the residential environment in public spaces, supplementing communal facilities, and improving the area with regional green space.[③]

4.2　Schüngelberg Garden City Renovation, Gelsenkirchen

The Schüngelberg workers housing estate was erected from 1897 to 1919 for miners from the neighbouring Zeche Hugo coal mine. The estate's historic buildings were renovated and extended according to conservation practice from 1988 to 1998. The overall concept for Schüngelberg included also urban planning and landscape improvements to the surrounding area with the design of the neighbouring Rungenberg slag heap as a recreational and leisure area and the regeneration of the Lanferbach stream.[④]

4.3　Teutoburgia Estate, Herne

The Teutoburgia Garden city was built between 1909 and 1923 as a worker's housing estate for Zeche Teutoburgia coal mine. The estate's centre is the "Teutoburgiahof" built in 1918, which was planned as cohesive housing estate. From 1988 to 1998 a fundamental modernisation was carried out to the residential environment. Despite its costly and complex modernisation, the estate's typical garden city appearance was conserved.[⑤]

---

① Introduction, in: Fachgebiet Städtebau, Stadtgestaltung und Bauleitplanung, Fakultät Raumplanung, TU Dortmund (eds), International Building Exhibition Emscher Park. The projects 10 years later, Essen 2008, pp. 8-10.
② Foreword, in ibid. p. 6
③ Ibid, pp. 220f
④ Ibid, pp. 230f.
⑤ Ibid, pp. 234f.

4.4 Zollverein Shaft XII Coal Mine, Essen

Zollverein coal mine and coking plant, built from 1928 to 1932, has an industrial history as the world's "biggest and most productive" coal mine in the first half of the 20th century. The conservation of the Zollverein as a cultural monument preserves an accessible icon and milestone of the industrial era and of industrial architecture in the Ruhr area.[①]

4.5 Zollverein Coking Plant, Essen

Like Shaft XII of the Zollverein coal mine, the coking plant was built in Modernistic style by industrial architect Fritz Schupp from 1957 to 1961. It closed in 1993. In conjunction with its neighbouring Shaft XII, it forms a cohesive ensemble embodying an excellent example of industrial history and was listed in 2001 as a UNESCO World Heritage Site. The coking plant opened with the "Sun, Moon and Stars" exhibition, and the solar power plant started operation together with the light installation at the coking oven batteries, all in 1999.[②]

4.6 Industrial Heritage Trail, Ruhr Area

The Industrial Heritage Trail is a thematic route linking the major historical witnesses of all eras of the Ruhr region's industrial development, including industrial plants, the housing estates of the workers, significant technical and social historic museums, and lookout points with panoramic views across the industrial landscape and selected sites of nature resulting from industrialisation. The sites are connected via a 400km-long circuit featuring information signs.

5. Impact, influence and impulses of the IBA Emscher Park

Many people, experts, scientists and politicians from all parts of Germany and other countries have asked constantly and are still asking: Why has the IBA Emscher Park been able to activate so many change processes in the region since its beginnings?[③] In what ways have the IBA projects exerted an influence on the whole region? They are interested in the IBA's mode of action, its form of organization, its individual projects and the impulses it has given.

With the IBA the image of the Ruhr district in its entirety has changed. By visitors and experts at both national and international level, the IBA scheme as a whole, and the individual projects carried out under it, are seen as a model approach to dealing with the physical realities of the region and its economic framework conditions since the 1980s.

Many projects and activities were still incomplete in the presentation year of 1999. Up to this date 19 towns and cities and a large number of initiatives and business enterprises conceived and realized over a hundred projects. All of them can be regarded as successful.

"The IBA Emscher Park has had a sustained influence on the region bounded by the rivers Ruhr and Lippe beyond the actual duration of the event. In many individual projects, in ways of thinking and seeing, in political decisions and attitudes to regional planning, its affect can still be felt today".[④]

5.1 IBA Emscher Park—A source of inspiration for regional thinking

This event initiated regional projects and was a source of inspiration for ideas and development processes in many different ways. The Emscher Landschaftspark and the ecological regeneration of the

---

① Ibid. pp. 276-299.
② Ibid. pp. 280f.
③ Christa Reicher, Lars Niemann, Angela Uttke (eds), Internationale Bauausstellung Emscher Park: Impulse, Essen 2011, p. 16
④ Ibid.

river, which had become nothing more than open drain "are emblematic for the regional project dimension". ①Other regional activities such as the 2030 Guideline process or the application as European Capital of Culture Essen ("Ruhr 2010") would not have been possible without the IBA. Therefore necessary regional cooperation and communication structures were initially evolved during the IBA and then developed further through the subsequent activities.

5.2 IBA Emscher Park—A source of impulses for a new building and planning structure

Prior to the IBA Emscher Park there was no building and planning culture debate over the Ruhr district. A special focus can be seen in the encouragement of new planning approaches through the IBA. The IBA strengthened the use of qualifications procedures and instruments as well as the involvement of local actors and groups. Urban planning competitions, investor competitions—in some cases with international participation—and design workshops were generally implemented. The establishment of an art and design advisory board, the planning in alternatives, or the involvement of external expert opinions can be regarded as innovations resulting from the IBA.

5.3 IBA Emscher Park—Promoting administrative reforms

In contrast to previous IBAs, like that in Berlin, the IBA Emscher Park projects were not completely separated from the local administration. There were parallel structures that were not organized independently of the existing administrative structure. A form of inter-departmental and inter-authority project work was established in which responsibility was delegated to the respective project managers, who were involved throughout the entire process, from the preliminary planning deliberations right through to realization. Characteristic was a holistic view being taken of planning processes. The IBA has strengthened the cooperation between local authorities.

Other innovations were: to guarantee the acceptance of projects and ensure subsequent use, the involvement of users and local residents in the planning process and the setting up of specific projects offices as part of the everyday local authority planning. The processes were also accompanied by meetings and conferences and inter-communal exchange and collaboration with international experts.

5.4 IBA Emscher Park—Ecological and economic valorization

The IBA was primarily a structural development process, not an economic program. But under the vision of ecological, cultural and social renewal of an old industrial region it caused a change of direction towards a sustainable economy. The project of regeneration of the Emscher shows that ecological renewal can generate jobs through new technologies and generates an economic valorization.

5.5 IBA Emscher Park Impulses

With the IBA, the image of the entire Ruhr district has undergone a fundamental change. Its projects can be seen as a model approach to dealing with the physical realities of the region and its economic framework conditions. The IBA is highly reputed in Europe and worldwide and viewed as an example to be followed in tackling restructuring processes. The methods and projects of the IBA and their further developments can serve as a local, regional, national and international laboratory for the transformation of industrial regions.

"In its outcome, the IBA Emscher Park has been far more than a finitely defined structural programme on a regional scale. Impulses from it can be seen at local, regional, national and international level which, especially in terms of managing structural change, set planning activities on a new course not only within the region but also far beyond, and continue to do so today."②

---

① Ibd, pp. 17
② Christa Reicher, Lars Niemann, Angela Uttke (eds), Internationale Bauausstellung Emscher Park: Impulse, Essen 2011, p. 15.

IBA2006—2013：德国汉堡国际建筑展的实践与影响
IBA2006—2013：Practice & Influence of Internationale Bauausstellung in Hamburg, Germany

皮埃尔·拉孔特 博士
城市环境基金会主席
国际城市与区域规划师协会 ISOCARP 前主席
Dr. Pierre Laconte
President, Foundation for the Urban Environment
Former President, ISOCARP

汉堡是德国第八个国际建筑展项目所在地。在超过一个世纪的发展过程中，IBA 的目标就是通过创意来形塑城市生活。每个 IBA 展都有自己独特的主题，汉堡 IBA 展的主题为"城市与气候变化"，以求顺应当地在能源上实现自给自足的发展目标。

1. Introduction

IBA Hamburg focuses on the section on the city (55,000 inhabitants) where the north and south arms of the River Elbe wrap around the largest river island in Europe.

Dykes surround the island to protect it from flooding from the North Sea or when the River Elbe is running high. However, in 1962 the water of a storm tide breached the dykes, with disastrous consequences for many residents—more than 200 people drowned in the chilly water.

After that many people left Wilhelmsburg, the main Elbe island, and new residents arrived in their place—most of them from less wealthy sections of society and/or with an immigrant background.

Although in the 1980s a lot of public money was invested in bricks and mortar, the social conditions barely changed.

In 2005 the Senate of the city of Hamburg decided to stage an International Building Exhibition (IBA) on the theme "Cities and Climate Change".

International building exhibitions are led by a task force with a time limit. It is structurally separate from "normal" administrative units, being usually incorporated as a German GmbH (Gesellschaft mit beschränkter Haftung), or limited liability company. It thus has a certain amount of independence from classic administrative hierarchies and can act more like a private enterprise.

Although an IBA has no sovereign rights and administrative tasks, it does have a remit defined by the parliament (called Bürgerschaft in Hamburg) and it is thus legitimated by a democratic process.

IBA's GmbH has initiated 70 building projects and 14 demonstration social and cultural projects to illustrate the possibility of remodelling an entire city district according to social and environmental considerations.

A key message is that a hitherto somewhat neglected district of Hamburg with a negative image can reinvent itself as the pioneer of energy-efficiency in the city. Therefore IBA Hamburg is concerned with both planning and social issues.

2. Future concept for energy efficiency in the city

The foundation for making the city a more energy-efficient environment is the "Future Concept Renewable Wilhelmsburg" (Zukunftskonzept Erneuerbares Wilhelmsburg), which was developed between 2008 and 2010 by an international committee of experts in collaboration with IBA.

This idea included the setting up of an "Energy Atlas".

The various types of building on the Elbe islands were assessed from an energy perspective (for example, their suitability for solar thermal, photovoltaic, or shallow geothermal systems).

The conclusion reached was that a smart combination of measures to improve the energy efficiency of existing structures and building services, plus a supply of renewable energy that would enable Hamburg's Elbe islands to produce enough power to meet all demands from the islands' residential areas for electricity by 2025 and for heating by 2050. Currently, there are some 21,500 dwellings in total, housing around 55,000 people.

IBA has planned three local district heating networks to supply buildings, of which two have already been realized and one is still in the planning stage.

The first local district heating network is located in a disused WW II flak bunker that was converted into an energy bunker.

A buffer storage tank holding 2,000 m^3 of water was installed in the bunker to store surplus heat from solar thermal units biomethane coming from a Hamburg based-composting plant. Back up the capacity of 15% to cover peak hours is available from natural gas. When completed, the energy bunker will supply heating to about 3,000 households.

Currently, the first stage of the project in the "Weltquartier (Global Neighbourhood)" is being connected to the energy bunker.

The second network, not yet realised but in the final planning phase, will utilize the deep geothermal energy potential of the island.

Hot water at 130℃ is believed to be present at a depth of 3,200 m that can be exploited for heating.

The third heating network takes a unique approach, connecting a total of some 115,000 m^2 gross floor area of buildings, including dwellings and business users. The network supplies heating as well as allows decentralized consumers to feed heat into the grid. This extends the feed-in principles in respect of electricity to the provision and "export" of heating to IBA new buildings in central Wilhelmsburg.

Displaying a variety of innovative designs these 'model houses' serve to demonstrate what the future of energy-efficient building might be.

Three of these buildings are equipped with heat pumps and not only provide heating to consumers but also feed into the system any excess heat produced.

The grid operator pays them a fixed fee for every kWh of heat that they export if generated solely from renewable sources.

The first building, the "Smart Material House" (Smart ist grün) to be integrated with the heating grid is a 15-unit residential building by Zillerplus architects, Munich.

The overproduction in summertime will be first stored in a phase change material (PCM) system and fed into the grid later.

Another example is the BIQ by Splitterwerk architects, Graz from Austria. The energy concept combines heating through geothermal sources with the production of biomass by algae within the façade. The biomass generated through the photosynthesis and growth of the algae can be re-used in a biogas plant to generate energy or used for research purposes.

Equally the four Water Houses feed into the grid. The Water Tower and the triplex town houses by Schenk Waiblinger architects offer 34 units. Heating for the buildings will be supplied by shallow geothermal sources (through the medium of heat pumps), solar thermal and the district heating network. Any excess solar thermal energy will be fed into the grid.

Kennedy & Violich Architecture (Boston) present "soft houses" which demonstrate that residential buildings can be climate neutral not only with regard to their energy consumption, but also in terms of their entire life cycle. Overall, the energy association in central Wilhelmsburg will reduce CO_2 emissions to nearly zero, if electricity generation in the CHP plant is taken into account.

3. Decentralisation of energy supplies

IBA Hamburg is a determined advocate of energy supplies that are "preferably decentralized".

Decentralized utilities, secure jobs and income for local communities. Moreover, decentralized systems are considerably more resilient in the face of natural disasters than new, industrial-scale mega systems.

4. Energy self-sufficiency

Despite the forecast population growth of more than 40%, the goal is to reduce the demand for heating and increase demand for electricity.

It should be possible to reach self-sufficiency in electrical power by 2025 and in heat towards the end of the 2040s.

Since the buildings on the Elbe islands date from different periods of history, including many that are listed as protected monuments or are iconic elements of the cityscape, the Renewable Wilhelmsburg Climate Protection Concept defines a number of different standards.

In order to achieve the target, IBA Hamburg and several project partners have supported the issue of energy certificates providing quality assurance, and three-yearly monitoring to check that energy saving renovation work remains effective.

5. Building exhibitions—laboratories for urban development

In December 2013 the Senate of the Free and Hanseatic City of Hamburg decided to transform IBA Hamburg into an urban development company with additional tasks in planning and implementation. Hence IBA Hamburg is charged with developing some 7,000 housing units in the next few years. Alongside that, IBA intends to pursue the concept "Renewable Wilhelmsburg 2.0".

This includes further studies on the islands' power supplies, including load-balancing strategies using smart grids, integrating decentralized generators into the grid, the integration of storage facilities and linking local heating networks with Hamburg's central heating supply grid.

Both the residents of the new houses and visitors will be able to access the district via a new footbridge from the revamped Wilhelmsburg Urban Railway Station.

IBA、HUL 与武汉的老城新生

IBA，HUL，and WUHAN：The New Life of an Old City

郭粤梅　教授
联合国教科文组织工业遗产教席持有人
Prof. Guo Yuemei
Holder，UNESCO Chair on Industial Heritage

Resorting to a profound understanding of the cultural essences of the historic city as well as international practices such as IBA and HUL, this paper tries to analyse Wuhan's orientation in its application for the membership in the UNESCO Network of Creative Cities as a City of Design, hence making suggestions on its urban development after the designation.

2017年，武汉向联合国教科文组织成功申报"设计之都"，其申报的主题为"老城新生"。本文从"设计之都"的阐释、武汉"老城"的理解、"IBA"计划和"HUL"的解读等几个方面对联合国教科文组织"设计"理念进行阐释，并对武汉市成为"设计之都"之后的城市发展提出思考与建议。

对"设计之都"的阐释

联合国教科文组织是负责教育、科技与文化的政府间组织，它存在于联合国体系之下，目前拥有195个成员国。区别于一般的政府组织，联合国教科文组织着重于推动"世界遗产""世界地质公园网络""学习型城市"和"历史性城镇景观"等重点项目。这些重点项目背后的理念是一致的，而其中最著名的就是"世界遗产"。它处于法定的框架中，从国际法到国家法，再到地方法。其他几个项目的影响力相对较弱，但是它们也套用了"世界遗产"的体系，尽可能地将其内容融入法律法规的层面。

"创意城市网络"是联合国教科文组织于2004年创立的项目，分为七个类别："文学之都""电影之都""音乐之都""设计之都""媒体艺术之都""民间艺术之都"以及"烹饪美食之都"，武汉申报的"设计之都"就是其中之一。

从2009年武汉提出申报"设计之都"的设想，到2017年正式申报，历经多年，不少专家学者对"设计之都"都有自己的理解。但是这些理解中，存在着对"设计之都"的误读。例如有的专家认为"设计之都"入选的标准，应该是具有相当规模的设计业、以现代设计为主要元素的文化景观、拥有大批的设计人员、办设计博览会和设计展的传统。这种解读看似符合中国人对"领头城市"的预判，但这其实也是一种误读。

"创意城市网络"致力于发挥全球创意产业对经济和社会的推动作用，促进世界各城市之间在创意产业发展专业知识培训、知识共享和建立创意产品、国际销售渠道等方面的交流合作。联合国教科文组织官方只有"创意城市网络"的评选标准，从未单独设定过"设计之都"的入选标准。

武汉申报"设计之都"一直以市建委为依托，以"工程设计之都"为主题，我们曾对此提出建议，并借助2013年第二届"无界论坛"，探讨了一批作为典型向社会推广的大型工程跟文化遗产遭遇的案例，提出了工程和文化相互促进的倡议。如葛修润院士做的"白鹤梁"作为三峡的重点工程，在保护文化遗产的同时，也和水利工程相协调；铁四院做的"京沪高铁穿越明皇陵"，避开了缓冲区。这次论坛我们明确提出：武汉市要申报"设计之都",一定要注重文化,注重文化遗产保护。

武汉"申都"主题的最终确定是2016年6月,武汉市政府代表团和联合国教科文组织文化助理总干事班德林进行了交流。班德林先生说:"每个设计之都的主题都是不一样的,设计不是从天而降的,武汉'设计之都'的申报可以以文化遗产保护为主题。"基于这位联合国教科文组织高级官员明确的建议,武汉将保护和发展进行协调,推出的主题为"老城新生"。

对武汉"老城"的理解

2014年武汉与同济大学交流会上,同济大学副校长伍江教授语出惊人,他说:"邓小平在1992年南行时讲到改革开放政策应先在上海实施,他说的话是戏言,不能当真。改革开放之初,深圳是一个渔村,可以做试验,上海是一个国家重镇,不能做试验。150年前,第一次鸦片战争的时候,上海和武汉的地位类似于改革开放之初的深圳和上海的地位。当时武汉是一个成熟的大城市,而上海则属于苏州道下面的三级单位,所以拿上海做试验,不会拿武汉做试验。就像改革开放之初,拿深圳做试验,失败了也不会影响,不会将上海拿出来做试验。"

推而言之,武汉在近代其实遭遇了四次重要的"中央决策"。除去1840年鸦片战争时开放沿海保内地外,第一次是1858年第二次鸦片战争中国战败,列强明确地提出要到内陆做生意,中国政府开放汉口,留住武昌和汉阳。第二次,1911年的辛亥首义,中央政府做了一个重要决策:放弃政权,走向共和。第三次是1938年,正值抗日战争激烈时期,武汉炸掉、拆掉了国家重点投入的国有厂矿,对武汉的经济造成巨大损失。第四次1953年至1954年"一五"期间,大量重点工程投入武汉,国家的几次投资奠定了武汉的城市面貌。

冯天瑜老师认为,武汉的城市发展史有四个阶段:第一个是城垣的建制阶段——盘龙城;第二个是行政制度建立——汉朝时期金口建立;第三个是商业——明清时汉水改道;第四个是近代都会时期——武汉近代面貌产生。

2007年德国《明镜周刊》某一期主打封面的标题是"德国是德国人的创造"。美因河和莱茵河相交处,格局类似于武汉,两河相交将周边分成了三个城市,分别为威斯巴登、美因茨以及格罗斯-格劳县。纵观武汉的历史,如果说德国是德国人的创造,那么武汉就是武汉人的创造。因为近代150年左右的时间内,武汉开埠、开厂,又开战,伴随着交流的增多,也形成了地区的认同。

对于武汉"老城"的理解,武汉可以提出一个比较鲜明"一级概念"。例如我们曾给国外专家做过一张介绍武汉的海报,题目是"武汉:隐藏的形态,潜在的结构"。这张海报做出了武汉的文化层:租界一层,洋务运动一层,辛亥首义一层,洋务运动一层,20世纪二三十年代碰撞为一层。从这张图中可以看出,武汉不但经历了文化转型的全过程,还是中国文化转型的塑造者。武汉可以定义为"中国文化转型之都",这是武汉的特殊价值。

对"IBA"计划的解读

对于武汉城市"新生"的理解,要以申报"设计之都"为契机,以城市未来的发展为基础。可以借鉴的"他山之石",是德国的"IBA"计划。

东、西德合并前后,德国面临东德的很多问题,例如煤炭和钢铁行业的没落。德国在城市发展过程中的社会问题值得关注和借鉴:从国家层面看,对城市的相关政策比较少;从财政体系看,地方财政削弱,税收需要改进;从公私合营方面看,合理利用私人财产尤为重要。从发展阶段来看,德国正是从大拆大建到存量更新,从城市快速扩张到内涵增长。

"IBA",Internationale Bauausstellung,指的是国际建筑展,是德国的一个"品牌活动"。德国利用"国际建筑展(IBA)"这一品牌做了"城市再生"的计划,通过建筑、设计、艺术、教育和文化跨领域的多方合作来解决这些问题。通过德国政府的政策,"IBA"计划用10年时间,在柏林等城市通过新建项目和旧区改造,实现"批判城市重构"和"仅剩的城市更新"。它以保护工业遗产,恢复生态环境,改善居住条件,复兴老城活力,提升城市形象,促进新产业发展为目标,通过17个城市政府的参与,实施了120个项目,达到了提升城市形象的成效。例如,鲁尔工业区的旅游计划项目,就是从国家计划延伸出的城市计划。鲁尔区当时非常衰落,环境也很糟糕。它通过走设计和工业遗产旅游之路,逐渐拥有了19个工业遗产景点、6个国家级的工业技术博物馆、12个典型的工业聚落,并且申报成为世界遗产,振兴了当地经济。

对"HUL"的解读

联合国教科文组织文化助理总干事班德林先生曾建议,武汉要成为"设计之都",可以使用"HUL"这种方法。

"HUL",Historic Urban Landscape,指的是"历史性城镇景观",是联合国教科文组织推广的一种既保护文化遗产又尊重其发展的设计方法。它的推出是通过联合国教科文组织2005年的国际文件《维也纳保护具有历史意义的城市景观备忘录》以及2011年的《关于历史性城镇景观的建议书》。2015年,"HUL"的方法就进入了世界遗产的评选操作指南。

目前,"HUL"有6条具体的操作方法。第一是对城市的自然、文化和人类资源的全面调查与图录;第二是在利益相关方之间,就遗产价值达成共识;第三是评估遗产面对社会经济和气候变化的脆弱性;第四是从城市发展框架来看待遗产的价值特征及脆弱性;第五是遗产保护和发展行动成为优先事项;第六是构建多方合作和当地管理的框架。

"HUL"在全球有多个试点,例如澳大利亚的试点,是以联合社会各方力量和市民参与为特点;京都的试点则着重于延续历史文脉、城市肌理,以"让京都一直都是京都"为口号。美国的"911"的纪念地也是试点之一。中国的上海也是联合国教科文组织希望重点推广"HUL"的基地。

关于武汉的"老城新生"的思考和建议

关于武汉的"老城新生"的思考,大学与城市的融合很重要。2014年在华中师范大学举办的第三届"无界论坛"的主题是"大学与城市",会议上提出了武汉的大学与城市的融合不够,还有很大的挖掘空间。2015年,在武汉市政府的文化政策里面,第一条写的是大学与城市的融合,接下来又提出大学的高度就是城市的高度。武昌作为大学之城,要树立榜样,不然会留下很多遗憾。

借用一下何依老师的《四维城市》中的理念:一个好的城市,一个非常让人喜欢的城市,是一个四维城市。一维城市的功能是由一个点到另一个点,能够进行简单的生活,是一个生存性的城市;二维城市要有城市的肌理,能够留住街巷的肌理;三维城市指的是一个城市的空间组织,能够将城市的建筑留下来,即使这个建筑不能全部保留,但是留下来部分东西,也是很好的;四维城市是有现代和历史的文明间的对话,这样的城市,才是让人觉得很丰富的城市。现在人越来越有钱,科技和医疗的水平越来越多高,大家很愿意花钱来延长生命。除此之外,在有限的生命时间里,提高生命的质量、宽度和厚度是很有意义的一件事。如果生活的城市是一个四维城市,是很让人享受的,这种城市是很美好的。这是武汉进行"城市更新"和"老城新生"的一个方向。

2017年上海提出的"创意城市""人文城市"和"生态城市"三大城市目标,值得武汉参考。所谓"项目跟随人走,人跟随环境走",如果当地没有很好的人文和自然环境,是没有人才跟随的。2017年,"从拆改留到留改拆"是上海时任书记韩正一直在做的一件事,就是在城市更新之中,将能留的先保留下来,不能留的再进行改动,实在不行的将其拆除。现在,按照上海的刚性要求,存在50年以上的建筑必须留下来,而武汉还是有点大拆大建,很让人担忧。例如说今年比较有名的上海"巨鹿路"事件,巨鹿路888号被拆毁了,业主被罚了3 050万,处理了相关人员10个,从负责它的领导,到设计师,再到施工队,全部都处理了。

武汉处理拆毁历史建筑,罚款从来不超过50万,这是两者的区别。

武汉现在在申报"设计之都"不仅仅是一个名头,也是一个与国际对标的好机会。武汉申请"设计之都"需要与联合国教科文组织的"创意城市网络"进行三个对标,第一是基本要求上要对标,比如说联合国教科文组织列的一二十项必答题,武汉需要进行填写,这就是需要进行对标;第二是组织架构上要对标;第三是价值观上要对标。武汉现在提倡"每天不一样",但其实每天都不一样的城市更需要一个稳定的价值观,这就是武汉申请"设计之都"的意义所在。

20世纪末期旧有建筑改造的探索与实践

Exploration and Practice of Renovation and Transformation
of Old Urban Buildings Contructed in 1990s

高安亭
中信建筑设计研究总院有限公司副总建筑师
刘琛
中信建筑设计研究总院有限公司第四设计院院长助理
Gao Anting
Deputy General Designer, CITIC General Institute of Architectural Design and Research Co., Ltd.
Liu Chen
Director Assistant, No. 4 Design Institute, CITIC General Institute of Architectural Design and Research Co., Ltd.

With the case study of the unimplemented dwarfing design of one teaching building in Wuhan University as well as transformation design of a hotel, this speech elaborates on the issue of renovation and transformation of old urban buildings constructed in 1990s.

一、逆生长——武汉大学某教学楼的拆除

大家都知道武汉大学有一栋机器人楼,2016年教师节那天被炸掉了。它位于东湖边,而东湖是武汉一个重要的景观绿道和市民共享的绿化空间,这栋楼就位于东湖绿道的一个节点。这栋楼本不属于武汉大学校内的建筑,建成于1998年,2000年投入使用,和武大百年校园在结构上存在冲突,当时称它为"变形金刚楼"。设计的时候,屋顶瓦片的颜色和武汉老教学楼有一定的呼应,建筑高80米,最高点稍微超过了武汉老的山顶图书馆。这样的楼,并入武汉大学校园之后,成

武汉大学"变形金刚"的逆生长设想

了武汉大学典型的"负资产"。它所在的区位非常关键,周边教学楼非常多,位于中枢的位置。南侧面向东湖的广场,其中有两个回廊,北侧是绿化的广场,中间有一个喷泉。我们想炸掉这栋楼之后,修建一个低矮的楼,既能体现新的风貌,又能和东湖岸线联系。我们搜索了很多国际、国内的案例,如东京赤坂王子大饭店,高140米,周边有一个寺庙和河道,他们用"逆生长"的方式,让这栋楼整体"下降",实现闭锁拆除。我们能否也用这样的方式让这栋楼的特征保留下来呢?

这栋楼在往下"生长"的过程中,拆多少,还多少?设计保留最顶部的特征,由上而下地到地面,下降之后,背后形成峡谷式,前面形成广场,这样就更加和谐。我们希望整个扩建部分和前面广场形成有机串联,形成综合的整体。我们希望整个建筑安静地坐下来,以谦虚的姿态面对东湖的景色,将历史的记忆和现代的教学功能和方式结合起来。

二、存量激活——鄂钢大酒店改造

鄂钢大酒店，建于1985年，现在改造成了2049大厦。

20世纪五六十年代，武汉的建筑以苏联风格为主，如中苏友好宫；改革开放以后，八九十年代，国际风格进入武汉，出现了一些涉外的酒店，如长海大酒店、中南大酒店；现如今，我们逐步有了新的风格，有了像绿地中心、旋风球场、琴台剧院。

该项目原来作为企业酒店，建设不是很精细，但区位非常重要，周边都是很古老的里分，建筑非常的低矮，而它以50米高度矗立在这里，有点"鹤立鸡群"。

整个区域由13层的酒店、客房、锅炉房、设备间组成，建筑经过转手之后，很多商家对其进行了改造，形成了很杂乱的情况，显得非常破败，成了一个快递的停车场。我们对既有的现状产生一定的干预，对拆除部分进行控制，尽量保留它良好的结构体系，同时通过加建，把锅炉房改建成一个立体机械停车库，解决停车配比严重不足的问题。这就是A区，2049大厦。在沿街部分做一个玻璃盒子，映照周边的城市场景，同时也可以吸引居民的注视。裙楼部分，采用印刷玻璃，从外面看到室内，可以看到周边的场景，而室内看外面，形成通而不透的效果暂时远离外面的纷扰。北侧和老的街区之间，以绿化的平台进行新旧对话，缓解了紧张的关系。在贯穿A、C中间共有部分，通过屋顶天窗凸显玻璃、木材、竹子之间的对比，作为主要门厅的引导要素，引到二楼。我们在二楼设计了一个复合空间，拥有各种空间使用的变换可能性——展览厅、报告厅、塔楼主题扩展。

材料部分，我们用的就是武汉钢铁厂出厂的圆钢结构，通过结构加固的支撑和原有的楼梯产生一个好的连接，体现出"鄂钢大酒店"的寓意。功能、结构、形式三者取得了较好的统一。拆除原锅炉房间，做立体车库的空间，我们做了一些创新。我们把以前从来没有做过的阳光板做成了机械车库的外围结构，这样有一种朦胧的美感，让车在里面运作的时候，外面的人可以感受到这种运动感。阳光板可以带来特殊的光感，产生轻盈的感觉，阳光板把夜间照明映在上边，我们希望将来内部的灯光能够把整个材质空间，无论是白天还是夜间充分体现出来。同时在玻璃幕墙的夜间表现时尚，将LED灯打到光板上，会非常美。

整个的介绍主要是两个不同的案例：一个是方案，没有完全实现；另一个是改造，已经完成。两者都是20世纪末的建筑，限于历史条件等原因，它们依然是有价值的，结构在生命周期之内，依然保留了好的施工调动和施工质量。我们更多地考虑将它进行适当的复兴。通过这种新的结构维护的方式，通过新的设备的改造，通过新的材料工艺手法，让它们在新的市场上来焕发新的活力。

武汉文化遗产保护中的西班牙理念启示
Ideas from Spain for Heritagf Preservation in Wuhan

洛伦佐·巴里奥努艾奥　教授
浙江大学客座教授
西班牙 ARQTEL BARCELONA 公司合作伙伴及联合创办人
Prof. Lorenzo Barrionuevo
Adjunct Prof. of Zhejiang University
Partner & Co-founder of ARQTEL BARCELONA

西班牙拥有不同历史时代留存下来的各类文化遗产,对于它们的保护和利用经验为武汉的文化遗产保护与利用提供了借鉴,并为未来的合作指出了方向。

Spain has a big patrimony of historical buildings since the Romans, Arabs, Middle Ages, Romanic, Gothic, renaissance, 18 and 19 century, until the beginning of 20 century. There are different kinds of public buildings like palaces, castles, theatres, factories or religious buildings like churches, monasteries, convents...

Our experience working in Spain allows us to give some interesting ideas and suggestions for the heritage preservation in Wuhan. The following are the proposals that we think are very appropriate to promote the recuperation, refurbishment and restoration of Heritage and Historic Buildings of Wuhan city.

巴塞罗那城市肌理

1. Developing the regulations for heritage preservation of the Wuhan city, establishing the definition of grades of preservation of the buildings taking into consideration its historical value, conservation state and the way of preservation. Establishing the criteria and objectives.

Barcelona Case:

——1st regulation October 30th, 1962. The first document in Spain for heritage preservation.

——Definitive January 18th, 1979 with all the historical buildings in the city.

——Year 2000 revision in order to coordinate the protection criteria of buildings with the urban planning criteria. "Special Plans for the Protection for Architectural Heritage".

——Classification in four grades of protection of buildings.

A level: National Cultural Heritage.

B level: Local Cultural Heritage.

C level: Sites of Urban Interest.

D level: Sites of Documentary Interest.

2. Defining the areas of the Wuhan city to preserve heritage buildings, establishing the preference order of preservation and reason for it.

3. Analysis of benefits for the city of Wuhan preserving all the aspects like economy, sustainability, attracting tourism from zoning, ... heritage buildings in China and outside.

4. Analysis of existing historical and heritage buildings to change its use as public/private facilities:

—Public buildings

Museums/Public offices/Cultural centers/Libraries/Social centers/Centers for elderly people or young people/Hospitals.

—Public/private buildings

Hospitality centers. (Example of Paradores of Tourism.)

—Private buildings

Boutique Hotels/Banks/University/Private foundations./Shopping Malls/Retail spaces/Gastronomic spaces/Offices of enterprising companies.

The mixture of heritage buildings and new buildings.

5. Asking for original photography to know the original state of heritage buildings to the population of Wuhan in order to imply the citizens in the recuperation of the heritage buildings of Wuhan.

—Original drawings of the buildings.

—Information about work made during the history of buildings.

—Information about the circumstances of construction of buildings.

—Historical photographs of the buildings.

—Newspapers and magazines of the city.

—References to make the recuperation and restoration of heritage and historic buildings.

6. "PPP projects" for recuperation, refurbishment and restoration of heritage and historic buildings of Wuhan allow in these buildings some private businesses like boutique hotels or offices of enterprising companies that show commitment to the city of Wuhan.

—Public owner of heritage and historic buildings and private companies helps to pay for the works of recuperation, refurbishment and restoration.

—Pay directly or get fiscal benefits.

—Foundations of banks.

—Foundation of construction companies.

7. Giving some funds to private owners as anincentive.

—Funds from the national or provincial government for public and private owners.

—Funds from the municipality for private owners.

—The amount depends on the situation of the heritage and historic buildings in the city, the state of preservation and the economical situation of the owner.

—Non Refundable Subsidies on part of the budget of the work for recuperation, refurbishment and restoration.

—Agreed loans.

—Reduce of local taxes for construction works.

—Information offices for the citizens and diffusion campaign about preservation of heritage and historic buildings.

—To get these funds, the works will make according to the local regulations for recuperation, refurbishment and restoration of heritage and historic buildings.

8. Promoting research about heritage preservation.
—Municipality/University cooperation research agreements.
—Municipality/Private foundations cooperation research agreements.
—National Heritage Conservation Research Plan from the government of Spain to unify the research action protocols.
—R & D projects in research about heritage.
—Research on new materials and techniques of study and analysis.
—Research about the pollution and humidity affecting the heritage and historic buildings.
—Giving financial support for research about Heritage.
—Creating Public Municipal Institution to coordinate all the research works in this subject.

9. Training courses for technicians and construction workers on the techniques and methodologies of recuperation, refurbishment and restoration of heritage and historic buildings of Wuhan city.
—Work in heritage and historical buildings is like a surgery.
—You need good knowledge of how to work in these buildings.
—Use of no common materials and techniques.
—You can make irreparable damages to buildings that have been preservd for centuries.
—Construction Institutes from the municipality, government or private initiative.

10. Finding ways of showing heritage and historic buildings

1) Free guided tours for Wuhan citizens to show them the patrimony of heritage buildings in Wuhan. The guides will be volunteers that live near the heritage buildings.

Use volunteers with the support of municipality for free guided tours to visit heritage and historic buildings. (Students of Architecture or Art History/Architects/Art experts/Retired people)

2) Open of Heritage and Historic buildings
—Open heritage and historic buildings doors that are close to the citizens of the city.
—Periodic celebrations, during weekends.
—Dissemination of the architectural heritage of the city.
—Main goals to promote architectural heritage, teaching to see it, discover it.

3) Route in the city
—Maps of the city with the route.
—Indication of buildings in the city.
—Smartphone app to learn all about heritage and historic buildings.
—Web page with information about the route.
—Discounts to access to emblematic buildings.

11. Creating community heritage organizations to promote and encourage recuperation, refurbishment and restoration of heritage and historic buildings of Wuhan.

12. Creating a prize to promote recuperation, refurbishment and restoration.
—City prizes to reward the creation, research and production of quality in the city.
—Periodical prize for heritage and historic buildings.
—Goal to promote the works of recuperation, refurbishment and restoration of the city in the country and worldwide.

13. Benefits of recuperation, refurbishment and restoration
—Know much more about the local heritage.
—Job creation.

—Reference of sustainable politics.
—Source of economic growth.
—Wealth creation.
—Stimulus for tourism(cultural tourism).
—Social appropriation for the citizens of the city.

创意城市、可持续发展与世界遗产：
一个观点与理念汇聚的时代

Creative Cities, Sustainable Development, and World Heritage: A Time for Convergence of Ideas and Concepts

詹姆斯·瑞普　教授

ICOMOS 法律、管理与财经问题委员会秘书长

美国佐治亚大学教授

Prof. James Reap

Secretary General, ICOMOS International Committee on Legal, Administrative & Fiancial Issues

Professor, University of Georgia

　　本文回溯了联合国教科文组织创意城市网络的创建背景与过程，同时指出了创造力与文化遗产之间的相互关系。同时，本文还通过研究联合国教科文组织《世界遗产公约》、《文化与可持续发展全球报告》、联合国"人居三"等文件与会议对相关议题的表述以及 ICOMOS 对其进行的回应，探讨了创意与文化遗产作为人类社会可持续发展核心动力的角色。

　　This is a time of change and challenge for the world of heritage conservation. Ideas and perceptions concerning cities, the environment, culture, and heritage have evolved and expanded rapidly in a globalizing world. Relationships and opportunities that were for the most part unseen when the World Heritage Convention was drafted now seem much clearer, and the time to take advantage of these synergies is now. Otherwise, we may lose an opportunity to see culture and heritage as key components of sustainable urban development.

　　In examining the relationship between creative cities, sustainable development and World Heritage, we have to first look at contemporary cities. The twenty-first century has been described as the urban century. Over 50 percent of the world's population live in cities and projections have that percentage rising to over 70% by 2050. While there is no universal definition of what constitutes a city, for our purposes we could say that it a physical location where the population is concentrated in order to satisfy their needs. This could be summarized as follows: "Certainly the city is a place of trade and manufacture, residence and recreation, education and welfare. But the quintessential and most elevated purpose of the city is as a crucible in which culture, creativity and consciousness continually evolve." (Buchanan, 2013).

　　The concepts of the creative city, creative economy, creative class, and creative industries began to be explored in the latter decades of the twentieth century and more fully elaborated in the first decade of the twenty-first. The literature in this area has been extensive, as has been the subject of extensive debate(Landry, 2008; Howkins, 2001, 2013; Florida, 2005, 2012). Beginning in the 1990s, the Department for Culture, Media and Sport in the United Kingdom developed a list of creative industries embracing a range of endeavors from advertising and architecture to fashion, film, software, games, and television. Howkins included the concepts of research and development in his list, but didn't include heritage, as it was apparently not deemed related to creativity. A similar restrictive view is the definition of the creative class which is characterized by highly-educated, well-paid, mobile professionals. It is a definition that would exclude some of the great innovators of history (Rodwell, 2013).

As it emerged, the creative city concept concentrated on a rather restricted group of creative industries and an elite creative class. The focus often tended to be on the fashionable and transient while ignoring the vital and unique local culture of the city, a culture which had grown naturally from the society's engagement with the natural and built environment. The UNESCO Creative Cities Network was created in 2004 to promote cooperation and sharing of ideas among cities that had the objective to place creativity and cultural industries at the center of their strategic development plans. (UNSECO Creative Cities Network). However, the Network has embraced just seven fields—crafts and folk art, media arts, film, design, gastronomy, literature, and music. Broadly speaking, these fields do represent expressions of intangible cultural heritage, but have little direct relationship to tangible heritage. While the literature of the Network does identify and celebrate the tangible heritage existing in these cities, it is not embraced in the core of the concept. Their literature does not explicitly establish a relationship to one of the most important programs in the UNESCO family, the World Heritage Program and World Heritage Cities in particular (UNESCO Creative Cities Network, 2015). Are these locations of outstanding universal cultural value not themselves exemplars of creativity? To be fair, a significant number of the cities within the network possess substantial elements of tangible cultural heritage and a number are also listed in the World Heritage List or contain significant World Heritage properties within them: Lyon, Graz, Beijing, Helsinki, Seoul, Buenos Aires, Sydney, just to name a few. It could be argued that the creativity that gave rise to the elements qualifying for World Heritage listing should surely also be considered as part of the criteria for a creative city.

At first glance, it would seem that advancing creativity and the conservation of historic cities might be diametrically opposed. When one thinks of creativity, it is generally of something that is entirely new, a break with the past. Conservation, on the other hand, focuses on the preservation of the tangible past and its transmission into the future. While conservation is necessary, the creation of new values and elements is also necessary to fulfil the current and future needs and aspirations of the community. This could involve additions to existing structures or new structures added to the existing fabric in a creative and innovative way.

This is actually necessary to ensure the continuing evolution and appropriate use of the existing heritage within its cultural context. Tamás Fejérdy suggests a comparison to the concept of "embodied energy" in existing buildings which must be taken into account in assessing their energy efficiency. The "embodied creativity" of past generations is still present today in the fabric of historic cities. This creativity has been recognized by the UNESCO World Heritage Committee in the designation of World Heritage Cities and cultural landscapes. These listed properties are, in fact, the result of a creative process through prior generations in response to the existing natural and social environment. There has historically been a continual creative interaction between new interventions and the existing fabric. The current (creative) historic city becomes, in fact, the setting for present and future creative expressions. (Fejérdy).

Of course, in addressing new challenges arising from the natural or social environment, it is often tempting to simply import "solutions" from elsewhere because they have been successful in other locations or are viewed as fashionable or trendy. An example would be the work of famous architects, "starchitects", which can be found all over the world. While it could be argued that their creators have adapted their creations to the local environment, these imported pieces may in fact be in conflict with the evolving creativity of the historic city. Nevertheless, they are often celebrated (and replicated) for their "creative" intervention. This is not to say that creating contrast is wrong. It can be quite useful in emphasizing in a positive way the existing cultural heritage. However, it must be done with great care, taking into account the evolved creativity of the place. Executed well, the effective contrast between old and new actually lends authenticity to the new. (Fejérdy)

Sustainable development is arguably the key agenda of our time. Beginning with the areas outlined in *The Bruntland Report* (World Commission...), the concept of sustainable development came to comprise environmental protection, economic development and social equity. Since 2000, cultural diversity has been seen as the forth "pilar". It is the cultural aspect that is seen as the factor that can catalyze a comprehensive integrated approach to sustainability. Culture can be said to be the distinguishing characteristics of what a society "has (material possessions and objects), thinks (ideas, traditions and beliefs), does (behavioural patterns including recreations), and how it relates to and interacts with its natural and man-made environment". It is dynamic and inclusive without assumption of superiority between expressions, forms of creativity, or groups. In this view, arts and literature are not distinguished from the sciences, nor are occupations or sectors that might popularly be considered "uncreative" excluded. This expansive definition of culture is not universally embraced even within the United Nations system. (Rodwell, 2013).

Heritage, like culture, can be viewed narrowly or broadly. In the broader context relevant to our discussion of creative cities and sustainable development, it is important to consider both tangible and intangible expressions as well as the societies that created and sustained them. The social importance of heritage can be found not only in high-style listed monuments, but in the unlisted buildings that "enshrine the human stories, the memories of the community. ... It is they that determine the sense of identity, of place, and of belonging. These are the places where the historic environment is at the heart of sustainable communities." (Felicity Goodey quoted in Rodwell). Andy Pratt and Jane Jacobs insist that creative cities cannot be "founded in the desert" or planned from scratch" (Pratt, 2005; Jacobs, 1969). It is therefore crucial to recognize and promote the unique evolved heritage and cultural environment of each city and utilize them as a driver for their successful development.

UNESCO documents have observed that heritage has been largely absent from the mainstream debate on sustainable development in spite of its contributions to social, economic and environmental goals. It has been widely suggested that to recognize these contributions heritage should be explicitly integrated into the UN post-2015 development agenda. While the contribution of heritage to human development is undeniably crucial, neither heritage nor culture was explicitly part of the Millennium Development Goals. World Heritage and heritage in general can make direct contributions toward alleviation of poverty and equality and contribute toward providing basic goods and services. While the *World Heritage Convention* makes no reference to sustainable development, World Heritage cities and sites have been developed through time as an adaption between communities and their environment, as mentioned above, and have a continuing role in development, exhibiting sustainable patterns of land use, consumption and production developed over time. Experience has also shown that the traditional knowledge and skills that have given rise to a well-conserved environment reduces risk from natural disaster and strengthens resilience.

Articles 4 and 5 of the *World Heritage Convention* recognize that States Parties have the duty "of ensuring the identification, protection, conservation, presentation and transmission to future generations of the cultural and natural heritage", and "to adopt a general policy which aims to give the cultural and natural heritage a function in the life of the community and to integrate the protection of that heritage into comprehensive planning programmes". In fact, the convention clearly goes beyond listed sites to embrace all national heritage policies for the perpetuation of the natural and cultural heritage. (World Heritage Convention, 1972). Both the *Operational Guidelines*, beginning in 1994, and the *Budapest Declaration* (Budapest), address sustainable use of cultural landscapes and a balance between conservation, sustainability and development so that World Heritage properties could contribute to the social and economic development of their communities. Additional statements regarding sustainability appeared in the 2005 edition of the *Operational Guidelines*, and more recently in the *Strategic Action Plan for the Implementation of the Convention*, 2012—2022 (*Strategic Action Plan*). In 2013, the International Congress "Culture: Key to Sustainable Development" held in Hangzhou, China, was the first UNESCO international congress specifically focusing on links between culture and sustainable development since Stockholm in 1998.

At its 39th session in Bonn in 2015 the World Heritage Committee endorsed the Policy Document for the integration of a sustainable development perspective into the processes of the *World Heritage Convention* and recommended its adoption by the *20th General Convention of UNESCO* later this year. The document states in part, "States Parties should recognise, by all appropriate means, that World Heritage conservation and management strategies that incorporate a sustainable development perspective embraces not only the protection of the OUV (Outstanding Universal Value), but also the wellbeing of present and future generations." The report further provides that such strategies should be based on three overarching principles—Human Rights, Equality, and Sustainability, through a long-term perspective. Elaborating on the latter principle, the report stated, "Sustainability, broadly defined, is inherent to the spirit of the *World Heritage Convention*. It should serve as a fundamental principle for all aspects of development and for all societies. In the context of the *World Heritage Convention*, this means applying a long-term perspective to all processes of decision-making within World Heritage properties, making within World Heritage properties, with a view to fostering intergenerational equity, justice, and a world fit for future generations" (UNESCO World Heritage Thirty-ninth, 2015).

In the context of the discussion of the Post-2015 Development Agenda, UNESCO is developing a Global Report on Culture and Sustainable Development that demonstrates the role of culture in sustainable development. This effort recognizes that cities are key actors in the promotion of sustainable development and that culture and heritage are primary tools. This will be a significant contribution to the third United Nations Conference on housing and urban development (Habitat III) in 2016. This conference is expected to review actions taken in the last 20 years on the basis of the dramatic and continuing increase in the world's urban population. UNESCO had been addressing human settlements for some time, but the Recommendation on the Historic Urban Landscape of 2011 reaffirmed the focus on human settlements and culture and their links with development (Historic Urban). The UNESCO Cultural Conventions are linked to the "urban context" and cities are, in fact, the most represented category on the World Heritage List and the subject of much conservation concern. In its report, heritage and creativity, both parts of UNESCO cultural policies, will be explicitly offered as an appropriate approach to urban regeneration and sustainable development—managing change in cities utilizing heritage as a driver of development (Concept Note: Global Report). The Habitat III Issue Paper on Urban Culture and Heritage provides another valuable contribution to this line of argument (Urban Culture).

However, in spite of the worldwide campaign led by UNESCO, culture has not been fully incorporated into the draft Sustainable Development Goals (SDGs). The Open Working Group (OWG) established by UN Conference on Sustainable Development in Rio de Janeiro, Brazil in June 2012, adopted the "Proposal of the Open Working Group for Sustainable Development Goals" at its session on 19 July 2014. The OWG's proposal on SDGs has been submitted to the UN General Assembly for consideration as part of the broader post-2015 development agenda to be adopted in late 2015. The document includes cultural elements in several targets: full and productive employment through creativity and innovation (8.3)… And the promotion of sustainable tourism, local cultures and products (8.9, 12b); education of all learners on cultural diversity and the contribution of culture to sustainable development (Target 4.7).

The most important reference is in Goal 11, which has been called the "Urban SDG": "Make cities and human settlements inclusive, safe, resilient and sustainable." Within this goal, target 11.4 calls for strengthening efforts to protect and safeguard the world's cultural and natural heritage. Intergovernmental negotiations are now focused on establishing metrics called "indicators". It is important to include heritage in these measures which will be used for monitoring, policy-making, communicating progress, and advocacy and form the basis of reporting. It has been suggested that one indicator might be the share of the national (or municipal) budget which is dedicated to preservation, protection and conservation of national cultural and natural heritage including World Heritage sites.

To advance this discussion, the International Council on Monuments and Sites (ICOMOS) developed a Concept Note on Cultural Heritage and Sustainable Development for the UN-Post 2015 Agenda and the Third United Nations Conference on Housing and Sustainable Urban Development (HABITAT III). In order to realize the potential of Target 11.4, ICOMOS advocates:

—Integrating cultural heritage into sustainable urban development.

—Adopting policies that recognize that local institutions and traditional knowledge systems play a key role as important resources essential for sustainable development.

—Integrating protection of heritage properties and their attendant values into efforts for inclusive social and economic development and poverty alleviation for the local communities so as to mutually benefit both communities and heritage properties.

—Legal frameworks for planning and development management that are transparent, participatory and incorporate the use of heritage and traditional settlement patterns and materials as a key component of livability and sustainability.

—Developing tools, instruments, and detailed guidelines for actions would help cities implement the goals and achieve their targets (Statement by ICOMOS).

In conclusion, this is an exciting time for cities—creative cities, sustainable cities, World Heritage cities. These all converge on cultural heritage and its key role preserving tangible and intangible heritage inherited from previous generations, employing it constructively and sustainably to ensure that cities develop in a way that is reflective of the continually evolving culture that created and sustained them. There is a lot to be done. This is an opportunity that the cultural heritage community must not miss.

References

Buchanan P. The Big Rethink: Urban Design[J]. The Architectural Review, 2013, pp. 83-93.
Budapest Declaration (2002) http://whc.unesco.org/en/decisions/1217/, accessed 20 September 2015.
Concept Note, Global Report on Culture and Sustainable Urban Development. (2015) http://www.unesco.org/new/filead-

min/MULTIMEDIA/HQ/CLT/images/Concept_Note_Report_CultureandCities. pdf accessed 12 September 2015.

Earth Negotiations Bulletin, Summary of the Thirteenth Session of the UN General Assembly Open Working Group on Sustainable Development, http://www.iisd.ca/vol32/enb3213e.html accessed 21 September 2015.

Florida, R. (2012) The Rise of the Creative Class Revisited.

Florida, R. (2005) Cities and the Creative Class.

Girard, L. (2013) Toward a Smart Sustainable Development of Port Cities/Areas: The Role of the "Historic Urban Landscape" Approach, http://www.mdpi.com/2071-1050/5/10/4329/htm, accessed 20 September 2015.

Hangzhou Congress (2013) http://www.unesco.org/new/en/culture/themes/culture-and-development/hangzhou-congress/, accessed 20 September 2015.

Historic Urban Landscape, Recommendation on (2011) http://whc.unesco.org/en/activities/638, accessed 18 September 2011.

Howkins, J. (2001; 2013) The Creative Economy.

Jacobs, J (1969). The Economy of Cities.

Landry, C. (2008). The Creative City: A Toolkit for Urban Innovators.

Pratt, A. (2005). Creative Cities? in Urban Design Journal, 105, p. 35.

Rodwell, D. (2013) Heritage as a Driver for Creative Cities, https://www.academia.edu/attachments/35799298/download_file?st=MTQ0NjA5ODEwMCw2MS4yMDYuMjAuMTYy&s=swp-splash-paper-cover, accessed 25 September 2015.

Statement by ICOMOS on the Adoption of the UN Sustainable Development Goals (2015) http://www.icomos.org/en/about-icomos/mission-and-vision/icomos-mission/documentation-centre/178-english-categories/news/4372-statement-by-icomos-on-the-adoption-of-the-un-sustainable-development-goals, accessed 25 October 2015.

Strategic Action Plan for the Implementation of the Convention, 2012—2011. http://whc.unesco.org/archive/2011/whc11-18ga-11-en.pdf, accessed 1 October 2015.

UN Open Working Group Proposal for Sustainable Development Goals, https://sustainabledevelopment.un.org/content/documents/1579SDGs%20Proposal.pdf, accessed 20 September 2015.

UNESCO Creative Cities Network, http://en.unesco.org/creative-cities/home, accessed 20 September 2015.

UNESCO WORLD HERITAGE COMMITTEE, Thirty-ninth session, Bonn, Germany 28 June-8 July 2015, http://whc.unesco.org/archive/2015/whc15-39com-18-en.pdf, accessed 25 September 2015.

Urban Culture and Heritage, UNESCO Issue Paper (2015) http://unhabitat.org/wp-content/uploads/2015/04/Habitat-III-Issue-Paper-4_Urban-Culture-and-Heritage-2.0.pdf, accessed 30 September 2015.

World Commission on Environment and Development (1987) Our Common Future (also known as the Brundtland Report) http://www.un-documents.net/our-common-future.pdf accessed 20 September 2015.

World Heritage Convention (1972) http://whc.unesco.org/en/conventiontext/, accessed 20 September 2015.

World Heritage Operational Guidelines (various dates) http://whc.unesco.org/en/guidelines/, accessed 20 September 2015.

来自过去与未来的灵感之源：
让生态性与包容性转型在当下成为可能

Sources of Inspiration from the Past & the Future: to Enable the Ecological & Inclusive Transition in the Present

弗雷德里克·奥克莱尔
法国国家首席建筑与规划师
法国遗产建筑师协会前主席

Frédéric Auclair
Chief Architect and Urbanist of the State, France
Former President, National Association of French Heritage Architects

在面对人类社会可持续发展的议题时，我们可以从过去与未来两个方向得到启示。在朝向建筑生态性与包容性的当下，遗产保护需要一种合作的工作模式。这种合作不仅意味着不同文化间传统与实践的联系，而且意味着原本看似相互冲突的二元之间的调和。在这样的语境下，遗产保护同样可以与现代性以及全球化共存。

Introduction: What are Sustainable Buildings?

Looking at the statistics of the world population increase, if we want a shelter for everyone on Earth, we will need to double the number of square meters being built by 2050. Most of those square meters will be created in the regions of Asia, Africa and Latin America, where future population growth will be the highest. The challenge is to create sustainable buildings in those areas.

But what do we understand by sustainable buildings?

In terms of the *Paris Agreement* objectives, this means fewer Green House Gas (GHG) emissions and less energy consumption, which requires a greater equilibrium in the use of resources.

Evidently, this is not the only possible definition. We cannot limit the question of sustainability to the question of possible pollution or energy efficiency. A building which is designed to be resilient for more than four centuries with natural materials and smart design inspired by the observation of nature and climate, as we learn from the research into biomimetism, is the best evidence of real sustainability. We have to be careful not to fall victim to trends which provide only one side of a global equation.

Sources of inspiration for their most appropriate design.

Regarding these challenges, we not only need to combine solutions inspired from the past but also need to imagine what the future can teach us.

Sources of inspiration from the past

When we speak of sources of inspiration from the past, we mean buildings or urban patterns that we can still experience at present. It represents an enormous amount of passive solutions that we can learn from history. This physical experience, more than the pleasure of examining archives or looking at images from yesterday, is made possible by the conservation of heritage.

In Europe, and especially in France since the Revolution, there is a strong tradition of conserving buildings, a tradition which is both philosophical and ideological in nature.

However, China has its own history and its scale is completely different. But we are still talking about a piece of real human history wherever the story takes place.

It is important not to be imprisoned by our beliefs. What has worked in France, as well as in the UK, Germany, Italy, Spain or Israel, for heritage management, may not necessarily be the same in the Chinese context.

The words of Professor Ruan Yisan while describing the treasures of invention in Chinese heritage, reiterate the importance of wise heritage management as a component of the incredible evolution of China, in order to maintain the real diversity of sustainability. By conserving examples of architecture designed with passive and resilient structures, we keep normal demonstration of building without need to plug into any source of energy to healthily live inside.

It is sometimes useful to seek other scientific approaches, not only in architecture but more globally in terms of how we position the spirit of our work in heritage, architecture, urban design and landscapes.

Sources of inspiration from the future

If we also look at the latest research on quantum physics, well see that there is an infinity of potential futures. For example, we are all too familiar with the debate on climate change, and aware that a terrible future could be in store for humanity, albeit not necessarily for Earth.

In quantum physics, you discover that the timeline is not exactly as you used to learn in school. In some novels of social science-fiction as well, we imagine hypotheses of beings who come from the future to modify the past and enable a change in the course of the present. Would it sound unorthodox to follow such an inspiration?

In some cases in our own lives we have something horrible in our past which has consequences on our behaviour or psychological patterns in the present. With different methods or technologies, we can change the memory of our past, and also the present, as a consequence.

Let us imagine that we are coming from the future to modify our way of looking at the situation today with the experience of tomorrow.

The conquest of space, for example, obliges us to develop solutions to cross long distances to travel as far as other planets such as Mars. To move your spaceship and to organise the resources to provide its crew with a comfortable habitat, you can use the sun for your energy, and an antigravity system. It is with this paradigm that we can today benefit from space research on solar energy to produce electricity on Earth. One thing is sure: you cannot travel using primary energy for such a journey because it is simply impossible to carry enough in the three-dimension reality.

In this foreseeable future, your habitat also needs to be the place to transform energy directly from an unlimited source like the sun, air, or water currents, or the heat from magma.

Some people try to create a tower of more than a kilometer high to speak of the tower of 2100. But probably in 2100, there won't be towers anymore because it is the perfect example of what is not sustainable at all. Today there are incredible towers in Dubai for example but let's come back in 30 years after the erosion of the sand and the wind of the desert. It will be very difficult to restore these buildings.

Quantum physics also insists on the spirit of the observer with the capacity to create and to change the reality of the phenomena.

We are the observers. We may live in illusion but we can create a better reality as well.

Enabling the ecological and inclusive transition in the present

After talking about the memory of the past and the different possible futures, we need to keep our minds open to harmonious solutions of development without forgetting our connection to mother Earth as the only guarantee to survive. A large part of our creativity should raise up energy of human awareness, and our capacity to remember Future and Past to bring from unconsciousness to consciousness a better reality of our world.

Today, inspiration is affected by globalization and we often question globalization.

For example, why should we only use one language to share ideas? It is good to remind ourselves that there are only six official languages in the United Nations and even in certain services it is forgotten that English is not the only one.

In the future, we will certainly no longer need to speak, because we will use direct telepathic communication, and it will be far easier to share ideas without erasing the memory of different cultures through their languages.

The same is true for architectural and urban design. There is currently a single shape to contemporary architecture irrespective of the needs or the "genius loci" as illustrated by the similar towers in the mega cities of each continent.

Conclusion: Combining sources of inspiration and relearning what we already knew

Today is the time of choice.

The question of energy, the question of the pleasure to live in a city, to breathe in the morning, to see the blue sky, the question of conservation of heritage... how can we combine all these notions?

I strongly believe that we have to create cooperation to have the physical experience of real conservation.

Do we have a more reasonable choice?

We should keep in mind that what we are doing in Wuhan has consequences for the rest of the world. It is the same in France, in Jerusalem, in Berlin, in Barcelona: the connection exists.

Nevertheless, unicity and being connected are not the same thing. What seems important is to work with the spirit of unity more than the concept of "working against" instead of "working with".

When we consider a heritage building, we often think about a form of conflict: we conserve heritage to avoid its demolition in favour of other buildings. We construct a flood barrier or a seawall to fight against the probability of a flood of a river or a tsunami from the ocean. We are "working against". We are not working in a spirit of unity. But when we work against the ocean or a river, we know that the fight is already lost.

The question of heritage should not be disconnected from the so-called modernity. It is a continuous flow of creativity. To restore a building is also an act of modernity to enable the coexistence of past and future.

留住乡愁：新常态下的文化遗产保护

Nostalgia: Heritage Conservation in the New Normal

阮仪三　教授
同济大学国家历史文化名城研究中心主任
同济大学建筑与城市规划学院教授、博导
Prof. Ruan Yisan
Director, Research Center on National Famous Historical & Cultural Cities
Doctoral Supervisor, School of Architecture & Urban Planning, Tongji University

Referring to the contemporary value of vernacular space in those historic water towns in the lower reaches of the Yangtze River, the author touches upon the role of nostalgia in heritage conservation in the developmental condition in China which is called "New Normal".

江南水乡城镇空间的当代价值

近20年来，江南小桥流水的古镇民居成为旅游热点，来自全国甚至全世界的游客都似乎在这里找到了一些家园的概念，其中既因为水乡市镇是中国传统居住文化的典型代表，也反映出现代中国城镇生活中某些价值要素的普遍缺失，才会令人更加珍视古镇中弥漫的亲情与温情。

从生活品质上，这些小城镇保留了比大都市更多的田园风光和熟人网络，更加亲切舒适，但又比传统村落拥有更优良的物质条件和交往的开放性。

水乡的主要街道大多布满店铺，卸掉排门板，便是熙熙攘攘的街市买卖；转进巷弄，顷刻就跨入了闲静的生活，粉墙黛瓦、小院门头，巷弄是街坊内部延伸的交通空间，更窄、更内向、更多变，在老街两边作鱼骨状散开，一头连缀着喧闹市声，一头连缀着日常生活。如南浔的花园弄、西塘的石皮弄、同里的穿心弄等，起到防火、通风、隔离与连通的多重功用。巷子伸到河边，必定设个埠头，是上下船的地方，大大的踏步，方便取水，埠头旁的一小块空地，斜向河面的老树，是一边洗涮、一边闲话的好地方。

如果说巷弄承载了相互守望的邻里生活，那长长的、蜿蜒的廊棚，则是充满包容性和公益精神的半公共空间——晴天不打伞，雨天不湿鞋，不仅是民居的前庭，也是店铺的扩展，更是风雨无惧的街道。室内与室外、路过与驻留、公共与私密，都在廊下融为一体，连接成一个情感上的"共同体"，人们在此处行走、相遇、纳凉、摆上小桌子吃饭，互相打招呼、闲话，处处反映出对生活便利和人际沟通的需要和尊重。"小空间的价值"体现得淋漓尽致。

反观当代功能型的城市空间，虽然科学性很强，间距、日照、通风考虑得很细致，但是缺乏人际网络，失掉了这种社会和谐的关系。人们为了寻求更好的工作和求学机会，涌向越来越拥挤的大城市，而在大规模工业化和恣意扩张中失去自我的中国城市却始终未能让人们安下"家"来。王安忆在《江南物事》中认为江南水乡特有的生活氛围和归属感让她难以忘怀："江南小镇的亦静亦闹，可以疗治虚无的病症，药方就是生活"。

江南水乡古镇雅致多变的城镇空间、悠闲轻松的生活节奏、亲切纯朴的邻里交往、家庭化生产的丰富多元，与现代社会快捷而单调的生活相比，显得弥足珍贵。更有序的关系网络、更友善的社区、更舒适的环境永远是人们对生存状态的共同追求。

珍惜乡愁,留住乡愁

乡愁不仅是个人的情思,还包括对国家、对民族的遭遇,在懊悔中寻觅丝丝残存的回甘余味;不仅仅是视觉的,更是潜移默化的身体感知和文脉传承;不仅仅是根植于某个场所的,更是一个时间概念,是对逝者如斯的那些记忆的叠加和再现。

珍惜乡愁,不是廉价的矫情,不是固守成规,更不是企图重现哪个过去时代的家园。乡愁不是专给外人观看的肤浅的风景,不是现代喧嚣的旅游产地,不是生造臆想的、仿古做作的粗俗街市、旧屋、楼台亭阁。

生搬硬造的假古董无法激发人们的共鸣,没有对历史、对先民生活的尊重,也就构不成乡愁。

珍惜乡愁,是对生活积累的思考,是珍惜家园本身所包含的历史意义和过程,是为了在回顾历史中寻找没有被抓紧实现的机遇。

当代中国正进入日益现代化的世界结构中,能否保持自身深厚的历史传统、走出一条有自身特色的城镇发展道路,在于其在发展理念上是否具有主体性,能否提出足以影响全球化的进程的理想图景。

要留住乡愁,首先要将家园尽可能地保护好。对那些历史文化名城、古镇、古村、古民居、古桥、古树的保护,不仅是为了发展旅游,为了经济利益,更是为了留存祖先留给我们的精神财富和生活哲学。只有能让人"身心两安"的地方才能称作是"家",按照科学的理念和正确的方法去保护,不要再做破坏性的保护和保护性的破坏。发扬其中饱含的传统中国城镇的优良文化,在这新一轮的发展浪潮中安放好我们的城镇、安放好我们的家园!

当东方遇见西方

When the East Meets the West

对话人：冯天瑜教授、皮埃尔·拉孔特博士
Prof. Feng Tianyu and Dr. Pierre Laconte
主持人：周婕教授
Host：Prof. Zhou Jie

2012年10月的第一届"无界论坛"，主题是"跨文化遗产保护与发展"，从那时起，"无界论坛"就一直在努力将自身打造成武汉与国际文化遗产保护界交流的平台。2015年11月，第四届无界论坛再次推出的"无界对话"也将主题聚焦到"东方"与"西方"这两个大的文化概念，邀请武汉大学著名的文化史学者冯天瑜教授与中国的老朋友、比利时的皮埃尔·拉孔特博士开启了一场"东方"与"西方"之间的对话。

一个是来自武汉大学的人文社科资深教授和中华文化史著名专家，一个是来自比利时的国际城市规划与环境可持续发展领域的杰出人物，不同的文化与学科背景令两位对话嘉宾对什么是"东方"，什么又是"西方"有着各自的认识，他们也尝试着通过对话对彼此有更多的理解。

当东方遇见西方

冯天瑜："东方"与"西方"，它们首先是一个地理概念

应该说，东方和西方，它首先是一个地理的概念，是一个空间的概念。同时，在空间和地理的这样的一个范围内，又分别生长出特定的以及非常丰富、非常复杂的文化的内涵。所以，东方和西方同时又是一个文化的概念。在我们所了解到的东西方，这个历史，关于东方和西方的概念，首先是受到古希腊人的一些说法的启示。古希腊人，他们把爱琴海以西的地区，称作是欧罗巴，以东的地区称作是亚细亚。这个大概就是做的一个东方和西方的地域的划分，以及随之而来的文化的划分，从古代到中世纪以至于近现代，沿着这样的一个概念的理路，又在不断地向前推演。

拉孔特："东方"与"西方"——差异的话语与矛盾的历史

对于东方和西方的划分，其实在西方史学界也有长期的研究传统，但"西方人"描述"东方"的方式与"东方人"描述"西方"的方式存在很大的不同，尤其是当我们研究"东方"的阿拉伯文化的时候，这种描述方式不对等的情况就更加明显。另外一个重要史实就是古罗马帝国在公元4世纪时的分裂。分裂之后的东罗马帝国有相当大的一部分在亚洲。有趣的是，当时西罗马帝国的皇帝对东罗马帝国的疆域没有太大的兴趣，但东罗马帝国的皇帝却觊觎西罗马帝国，希望能够实现统一。当然，还有一个值得一提的情况就是基督教与伊斯兰教之间的长期矛盾与战争。早在7世纪的时候，穆斯林就曾大举征服欧洲，包括伊比利亚半岛,最后止于法国。这种矛盾的关系从某种意义上说在今天又再次显现了出来。

冯天瑜:"东洋""西洋""远东""近东"……中国人对"东方"与"西方"认识的演变

就中国而言,在自古以来,对于东方跟西方的认识,是有一个演变过程的。一直到元明清的时候,中国关于东方和西方,或者叫作东洋和西洋,大概有这样一个划分,那就是从中国的广州向南画一条线,到婆罗洲,就是现在的印度尼西亚的北部,以及爪哇,这一条线,这条线以东被叫作东洋,这条线以西就叫作西洋。所以郑和,明代的著名的航海家,所谓的郑和下西洋就指的是他通过了马六甲海峡,进入了印度洋。这个印度洋,当时就是西洋,因为它在广州和北婆罗洲、爪哇这条线以西,这是从海洋上的划分。而在大陆上,我们中国的长安以西的地区一般就叫作西方,通过丝绸之路,就是河西走廊,以西的地方,在我们中国古代叫作西域。所以整个中亚、西亚以及南亚次大陆在我们中国的古代汉唐以来,都是称作西方、西天,所以玄奘到印度去求取佛经叫做到西天取经。因此,中国关于西方和西洋的概念在古代大概是这样的一个范围。当然欧洲肯定也是西方的一个重要的部分,在秦汉以后就把刚才拉孔特先生所谈到的罗马帝国叫作大秦了,它当然也是属于西方的一部分。在比较严格的意义上,我们今天所谈到的东方和西方这个概念,是欧洲人特别是西欧人,在进入了大航海时代以后,站在欧洲的立场上提出来的。他们以欧洲为基点,把现在的埃及、叙利亚这一带称作是中近东,就是比较接近于西欧的东方;然后把中国、日本叫作远东,就是离欧洲很远的东方。因为地球是圆的,也很难说绝对的哪个地方是东边,哪个地方是西边,所以这都是欧洲人站在自己的立场上得出的概念。

就东西方的概念界定,基本上是到了近代以后才有了这样一个明确的意识。而这一点,又是由于海道大通以后所确立起来的。所谓"海道大通"就是在古代和中世纪,人类各个民族当然也有海上的运输,但是是地域性的,比如中国,中国古代的海上运输就是在现在的西太平洋和印度洋,最远也就是到达了东非。那么欧洲人的航海主要是在大西洋,主要是在北大西洋,包括它的地中海这些地区。所以古代一直到中世纪的东西方的交通主要是通过陆地的运输进行的。特别著名的那就是我们中国人像张骞他们从汉代开始开辟陆上丝绸之路以及汉唐以后的海上丝绸之路。海上丝绸之路也没有真正地直接通过海路到达西欧,海上丝绸之路只能到印度洋、到波斯湾,然后又从陆上,通过阿拉伯半岛,通过现在的土耳其这样的一些地方,进入到地中海。所以这是古代和中世纪的东西方的交通。

冯天瑜:"东方"与"西方"的阻隔与大航海时代的来临

随着奥斯曼帝国的崛起,西方人通过陆上交通到远东来有困难,而西方人又非常需要远东的一些产品,譬如像茶叶,譬如像香料,大家都知道欧洲人是以肉食为主,这个肉食如果没有盐来腌制,没有香料来调制,那么放久了就会发臭,所以香料、茶叶对于欧洲人来说是生活必需品,奥斯曼帝国又中止了这个陆上的交通,所以欧洲人千方百计地想通过海路到达东方。从西方到达东方,这个过程是从13世纪马可·波罗以后到15、16世纪这样的一个突破性的旅行才得以实现,做出最重要的、创造性的贡献就是葡萄牙人达伽马。达伽马是那个大航海时代的三大航海家之一,他的贡献就在于他一直沿着非洲大陆向南航行。为什么这么说呢?因为欧洲人在古代和中世纪曾经多次做过这种航行,但是当时他们有一个错误的地理观念,以为大西洋和印度洋是分隔开来的,而下面的南极洲这些地方是把它封起来的。所以古代和中世纪欧洲人都曾经想挖过苏伊士运河,但是又不敢挖,因为他们误以为红海的水位比地中海要高几公尺,如果一挖那会把地中海沿岸甚至意大利都淹掉。这是一个错误的观念,以为大西洋、印度洋、太平洋是几个分隔独立的大海。最终打破这样一个错误观念的人正是葡萄牙的航海家达伽马。他沿着非洲大陆一直向南航行,到达了好望角,终于发现非洲大陆并不是无限向南延伸的。然后他就向东拐,于是在人类历史上第一次从大西洋进入了印度洋,最后就到达了印度半岛东部的果阿。这次航行对于东西方交通以及东西方文化的交流非常重要,之后追踪达伽马的航线进行航海探索的人就越来越多了。

冯天瑜:从"利玛窦规矩"到"西学东渐"——从"中学西渐"到交流失衡

这里特别值得提出来的就是在16世纪的西方传教士。我认为在人类交通事业的开辟以及文化的交流方面,有三种人做出了很重要的贡献。其中一种人是商人,一种是军人,而第三种人就是宗教职业者。因为宗教职业者他们有着非常顽强的献身精神。在16世纪,西欧的基督教系统里面有一个重要的派别,这就是耶稣会。耶稣会的一个重要的宗旨就是到世界各地来传播基督的福音。当时耶稣会确立了一个方针,叫作"学术传教"。这是耶稣会的一个特点,就是耶稣会多半都是一些学识渊博的学者,他们到欧洲以外的地区来传教,一个重要的手段就是通过学术来跟当地的人结交,来传播基督福音。最先在中国定居下来的耶稣会传教士也是意大利人,名叫利玛窦。他从广东边缘的澳门进入中国,澳门这个地方当时是西方人进入远东各国,包括中国、朝鲜和日本的一个重要的中介点。利玛窦他们到了澳门就开始学习中文以及中国文化。经过几年的准备,然后就从澳门进入当时广东的首府肇庆,然后到南昌和南京,最后到达北京。利玛窦是西方传教士中第一个比较长期地在中国定居,系统地在中国进行"学术传教"的人物。

说到利玛窦在"西学东渐"中的重要角色,还必须一提的是所谓的"利玛窦规矩"。"利玛窦规矩"的意思就是尊重当地的风俗习惯,尊重当地的文化传统。利玛窦并不反对他的教民去祭孔、继续信仰儒家的学说等等。所以这样一来,利玛窦的这样一套办法在中国得到推行;更重要的是,这也使利玛窦结交了当时明朝的一些杰出的中国知识分子,跟他们一起来翻译、介绍西方各领域的学术成就。除了包括《圣经》在内的宗教典籍以外,同时也翻译了西方的自然科学和社会科学的很多重要的著作。比如像几何学、地理学,包括当时五大洲四大洋的概念都是在利玛窦和徐光启的翻译当中介绍过来的。另外还有像天文历法和火炮技术等等。本来火药是中国人发明的,经过阿拉伯人的中介传播到了欧洲,欧洲在中世纪的后期就开始大量地制造火炮,进入热兵器时代,而在这个时候他们又把火炮技术翻译、介绍到了中国。因此我们说明末清初是中西文化沟通的一个非常重要的时间节点。

应该说那这个时候的东西方文化互动除了"西学东渐"以外,还有一项重要的工作,就是"中学西渐"。"中学西渐"的意思就是通过利玛窦以及后来的这些传教士,又把中国的学术、文化翻译、介绍到西方,这样给西方的文化也带来了很丰富的营养。应该说西方人在了解到了东方的学术文化以后,对于西方文化的发展也起了很重要的作用,这个作用尤其体现在18世纪的欧洲,西欧的启蒙运动当中,像伏尔泰这些人,都从中国文化当中吸收了很多东西。比如在哲学、伦理学、儒家、道家的学说都在那个时候传到了欧洲,对欧洲的启蒙运动产生了积极的影响。在"形而上谓之道"的层面,伏尔泰、狄德罗这些启蒙思想家都对中国的理性主义给予很高的评价;而在"形而下谓之器",即在器物的层面,对西方也有相当的影响。比如在建筑层面,中国的宫廷建筑、园林建筑,都通过传教士把它介绍到了西方。中国的文学对西欧那时期的文学影响也很大。比如说伏尔泰就把中国的一个著名的战国时候的故事,改编为一个戏剧,把中国战国时候的诸侯王改成了成吉思汗,因为欧洲人讲到中国的暴君只知道成吉思汗,因此他做了修改。这个故事成为欧洲非常有名的戏剧。这就说明当时17、18世纪,中国文化的方方面面对于欧洲都有相当的影响。应该说我很怀念明末清初这一轮中西文化的交往。这时候西方人还没有强大到能够用他的坚船利炮来侵略中国。所以这个时候中西之间的文化交流是比较平等的,而且是和平的,产生了相当好的双向的互动的作用。然而到了19世纪,情况就发生了变化。

从18世纪末期开始,尤其是进入19世纪以后,东西方的文明,出现了严重的不平衡。这不平衡的结果就是出现了西方的殖民扩张对东方文明的侵略。这是一个客观存在的历史事实。在这个意义上,19世纪的东方遭遇了什么样的西方呢?我认为是一个两重性的西方。一面是代表先进文明的西方,另一面是以侵略者形象出现的西方。所以这个时候,东方国家东方人面对西方,呈现出一种非常复杂的心态。有几种情况,有一些先进的东方人,一方面维护自己的民族独立、国家独立和文化传统,同时又竭力地主张要学习西方文明。中国这方面的代表就是戊戌变法时候的康有为、梁启超,以及革命派的孙中山、黄兴、宋教仁。另一方面则在东方国家、东方民族中激起了相当强烈的民族主义，产生了对西方文明的对抗或抵抗的一种倾向。我认为，从历史发展的大势来看，梁启超、孙中山他们所代表的这样的一种态度是最正确的。一方面，他们是爱国主义者，他们是维护民族独立，而且是坚守我们传统当中优良的东西。同时他们主张虚心学习西方的先进文明，要以西为思。只有这样东方才有可能强大起来，才能重新回到东西方平等交往的年代。

近代以来，随着"西风东渐"大潮而来，对中国社会产生影响的还有西方的建筑与城市规划理念。但是如何让拥有不同文化根基的中国古城在现代城市更新的大时代中找到自身的定位与合适的城市发展模式，拉孔特博士有自己的一番见解。

拉孔特："西方榜样"的甄别取舍与城市规划的欧洲经验

中国要向西方学习，但是学什么、怎么学仍然是今天的中国人必须思考的一个问题，例如在城市规划领域，中国的城市规划越来越受美国的影响，而不是欧洲，最像的就是拉斯维加斯。美国的方式是土地使用最大化，即使这个土地是保存古代遗迹的。美国修建了很多的高速公路，私家车大行其道。但是在欧洲，更注重发展公共交通，使得私家车和公共汽车的数量达到平衡。平遥和昆明，它们在环境保护和公共交通方面都非常好。在控制汽车数量方面，北京是最差的。相比之下，扬州就是个很有魅力、很舒服的城市，中国的其他城市要向扬州学习的就是要更适宜生活，人们去任何地方都可以步行。

另外，要想实现中国传统建筑文化与现代城市规划结合，关键就是要把可持续发展的理念带进去。北京的胡同不就又开始热起来了吗？胡同很好地利用了空间，密度很高。在上海，现在能保存下来的里弄已经像博物馆一样了，已经变成了购物中心，里面没有居民了。我更喜欢真的有人住的里弄。但是我并不是反对高楼，一些人喜欢住胡同，就可以保留，一些人喜欢住高楼，也可以住高楼。矮房子高房子都要有。在欧洲，我们就不会要这些人搬出来，而是政府出钱来改善他们的生活条件。政府可以在修缮期间，将这些人先安置到其他的地方暂时居住。

这些人是否能够在修缮完成后再搬回来居住还取决于政府，到底是想要改善这些人的居住条件，还是为了赢利而把人赶出来。社会问题归根到底还是在于是否尊重人们的权利，让他们住在他们想住的地方。现在越来越多的中国人已经意识到，他们的权利是应当被维护的。城市规划不仅仅是一个规划问题，而是法律和制度的问题，它要保证当居住权受到侵害的时候，能自由地发表言论和观点。这才是一个国家真正长治久安的关键。

因此我常说，一个好的规划师是需要规划与政策两者同时兼顾的。欧洲的规划师和中国碰到的问题是一样多的，特别是土地规划师。土地是规划的关键，我们有两种方法来控制土地，一是自己拥有土地，二是从规划的角度对土地的业主施加影响，让他接受建议。

已经来过中国 30 多次的拉孔特博士在五十多年前第一次来到北京的时候，做的第一件事就是花了 20 美元从旧书摊上买了一堆中国字画。数次来到中国的拉孔特博士是"中学西渐"的一个受益者，他从年轻时代就通过各种渠道接触到中国文化，尤其是中国艺术的博大精深的艺术。

拉孔特："中学西渐"与对东方文化的热爱

中国文化对世界的影响都是有目共睹的，早在我们说的"中学西渐"以前，中国文化的很多元素就以各种方式向世界各地输出。在建筑方面，我们可以清晰地辨别出中国建筑对日本建筑的影响。

中国的戏曲艺术在世界上也有它的地位。我本人从我很小开始就对京剧很感兴趣，说起这个主题，还有一段有趣经历。有一次在巴黎，我看到关于中国京剧和中国文化的展演，顿时就被深深地吸引了。记得那一次刚开始人比较少，但是当京剧表演进行的时候，越来越多的人开始涌进观众席，来领略这种不同于西方戏剧的东方剧种的魅力。我认为，京剧和中国的其他一些表演艺术一样，都十分博大精深，对它们了解越多,就会觉得越来越被它们吸引住,这些是为什么我能够连听20个小时的京剧仍然乐此不疲的原因。

当然,我们还不能不谈谈别具一格的中国画,它是世界美术大家庭中的一个重要组成部分。我对中国画很感兴趣。记得我当年曾经看过一个画展,被几位中国画家的作品深深震撼了。我以前从未接触过那样的画风,是那样的传神,似乎引领人们进入了一种无限与永恒的空间。中国画构图简洁,富含禅意,常常达到一种形散神不散的境界,看似平面其实有着清晰维度,总是让观者意犹未尽、回味无穷。也正是因为如此,我一接触到中国画就喜欢上这种绘画艺术形式了。当然,因为中国画非常写意,拥有大量值得探究的、含蓄的元素,所以它和西方绘画艺术出发的角度有所不同,一开始的时候容易让西方的观众产生误解,但当我们西方人进入它的世界后,就会慢慢产生兴趣。另外,在某些维度上,中国画对欧洲绘画艺术也产生了重要影响,它们之间也存在着一些相互联系的元素。

时间与空间：城市更新中的文化遗产

TIME & SPACE: CULTURAL HERITAGE
IN URBAN RENEWAL

《四维城市》序言节选

"城市空间作为社会历史活动的物质载体,是不同历史时期空间要素累积的结果,后一时段的城市空间必然包含前一时段的形态和要素。千百年来的时空更替,使城市空间在时间顺序上此消彼长、关联耦合,在整体上呈现出四维形态,构成了城市空间的复杂性和多样性。刘易斯·芒福德在《城市发展史》一书中将这样的城市空间比喻为'容器'。'城市从其起源时代开始便是一种特殊的构造,它专门用来贮存并流传人类文明的成果。!'其中,贮存是空间属性,是历史积累在三维概念中的'广延'性存在;流传是时间属性,是历史积累在四维概念中的'持续'性存在……"

"……在四维城市中,结构性要素转换成时间要素,功能性存在转化为纪念性存在,体层面转化为底层面,整体转化为碎片,由此来发现历史格局在时间中的形式转换和文化转译,揭示出城市空间中所蕴含的历史意义,并进一步将保护工作建立在四维城市的基础上,不仅要保护既有的历史要素,也要强化那些经过时间的蜕变后而转换的历史记忆。"

"……在四维城市中,原型进一步转化为类型,类肌理不仅指可见的建筑事实,还包含一种'建构',长期的集体建构,反映了社会成员对某种生活模式的认同和创造。城市作为一个不断生长的有机体,能够'长时段'保持自身的特色,并不是通过简单地复制历史,而是通过类推现象。"

"由于发展模式及保护意识所致,我国的历史城市与西方传统意义上的古城有着显著差别,尤其是经历了大规模的旧城改造后,很少有结构完整、空间均质的古城或旧城区,城市历史环境主要由一些散落在现代城市空间中的历史建筑、历史街区、历史景观等'碎片'组成……建立在空间关系上的'完整性'和要素更替上的'原真性',对突破目前静态和孤立的城市文化遗产保护模式具有一定探索意义。"

EXCERPT OF THE FOREWORD OF *FOUR-DIMENSIONAL CITY*

"... The urban space is the result of various periods' factors. The later urban space embraces the prior periods' form and factors. During thousands of years' transition, the urban space experiences reciprocal growth and death, correlation and coupling, makes the city have an integrated four-dimensional form, with great complexity and variety. Lewis Mumford in his book *The City in History* describes the city as a carrier: 'The city has been a special structure since it emerged, used to store the human civilization. The storing is the space's property, by which the history can be maintained in the three-dimensional concept in a wide way. The handing down is the time's property; the history can be maintained in four-dimensional concept in a continuing way...'"

"... In the four-dimensional city, the time factor can be seen as a structure factor, while the function being be viewed as monument being can, the main body can be looked as the background, while the entity is transformed into fragements. Hence, the historic pattern's transition can be studied, indicating the historic meaning hidden in the space. Furthermore, the conservation planning established on basis of the four-dimensional concept, the conservation not only refers to the factors, but also strengthens the historic memory transformed in the time..."

"... In the four-dimensional city, the prototype transforms into typology, hence the semi-texture not only refers to the real solid buildings, but also contains a kind of "rebuilding" theory. After long time collective construction, the social subjects have reached an identification with this life model. The city becomes a constant organic body keeping growing, by the analogy, rather than the copy, reflecting the various stages' features."

"Because of the development models and conservation awareness, there are remarkable differences between the Chinese historic cities and Western historic cities. Especially after experiencing large-scale regeneration of the historic cities and Western historic cities, there are few historic cities or areas with integrated structure and homogeneous space. The entire historic environment is mainly composed of some scattered historic buildings, districts, and landscapes in the modern urban cities pieces mainly... (A new perspective to the historic environment is) to establish an integrality based on spatial relations and authenticity based on the replacement of elements. Hence, it can break through the existing static and isolated preservation model of the historic heritage."

对建筑遗产基本问题的认知

Reflections on the Fundamental Category of Heritage Architecture

常青 教授
中国科学院院士
同济大学建筑与城市规划学院
Prof. Chang Qing
Academician of Chinese Academy of Sciences
School of Architecture & Urban Planning, Tongji University

Based on the author's reflection on the theory and practice of architectural preservation and restoration, this article systematically reviews the fundamental category of architectural heritage regarding its major themes, latest debates, and the different contexts between China and the Occident. In particular, it analyzes the disputable definitions of the basic concepts of architectural conservation, the multiple criteria of evaluation, the contradiction in preservation and restoration, and the characteristics of Chinese historical architecture and its tradition of building restoration. The article ends with a discussion of the transformation and rebirth of the historic city from a comparative perspective between China and the West.

引言

建筑遗产（heritage architecture）的保存与再生是一个跨越人文、社会科学和工程技术科学的新兴学科领域，具有很强的实践应用性和交叉综合性。但"建筑遗产"本身却是一个表示历史建筑身份属性的宽泛概念，而不是一个普适于本领域研究和应用的专业术语。鉴于核心概念对于新兴学科领域的基石作用，故有必要首先澄清"建筑遗产"和"历史建筑"的语义和语境。

在对该领域具有研究和应用的国际语境中，广泛使用的核心概念确实并非"建筑遗产"，而是"历史建筑"（monument，historic building）、"历史地段"（historic area）、"历史地"（historic place），以及"历史环境"（historic environment）等体现保护对象本体性的词汇。由于中国目前存在文物类建筑和非文物类建筑（"历史建筑"）之分，这两类建筑在概念上不能互涵，故权且用"建筑遗产"或"历史城市"看作"建筑遗产"或"历史建筑"概念的外延，并将其范畴限定于除建筑之外的街道、广场等建成物（artifacts）。

1 建筑遗产的核心概念及价值观

建筑遗产作为一个地方文化身份的重要载体，既是历史上留存下来的物质资产，也是未来发展所需的文化资源。保护建筑遗产，如今已不仅仅限于对其进行保存和修复，而是要在城乡建设中，探索各类历史建筑及其环境保存与再生的适应性方式，并将之纳入所在地社会和经济发展的整体格局。但是这一切都需建立在对建筑遗产深刻认知和系统研究的基础之上。

建筑遗产在当代国际语境中有广义和狭义之分,广义泛指历史上留存下来的"故旧建筑"(historical building),狭义特指依法登录保护的"历史建筑"(monument, historic building)。迄今为止,中国大陆和台湾地区的"历史建筑"概念,与西方语境中的"historic building"一直是有区别的。后者可概括所有具历史保护身份的建筑,而前者却在作为"文物"或"古迹"的身份认定之外。近年来,台湾地区制定的"文化资产保存规定",已将古迹、古物、历史建筑,以及非物质文化遗产等,整体纳入了文化遗产一体化管理系统。大陆地区目前除了已颁布的《文物保护法》和《历史文化名城名镇名村保护条例》等法律和法规文件外,也已制定了《非物质文化遗产保护法》,但由于管理体制和量大面广等原因,还没有整合出包括所有文化遗产的上位保护法。

建筑遗产研究的第一步是进行本体及其环境的调查与实录,包括现场勘察、详细测绘、文档检索和口述史辅证等,目的是为价值认定提供可靠依据。而价值认定的核心是辨析建筑遗产的"真实性"(authenticity),这一概念在本质上不同于绝对的文物断代,而是要相对地确定从初建到演变的某段时空范围内,建筑形成方式和其形态特征之间的有机关系是否保持完好或基本完好。其实质即形态特征与材料、工艺之间的对应关系是否真实存在。历次的使用变更,以及人物和自然破坏,使建筑遗产总是或多或少地处在不断的变动、损害、整修和重建之中,因而建筑遗产的"真实性"就与一般古董器物的真实性迥异,是各个时期变化叠加的结果,蕴含着历史空间变迁自身的逻辑和辩证法。

价值认定需要综合运用诸如人类学分析、考古学鉴定、文献学考辨、类型学和形态学比较等方法,并借助现代检测工具及技术手段方能完成。自启蒙时期以来,西方的价值认定经历了从"以美掩真"到"以真为美"的转变过程,逐渐形成了真、善、美主次分明的遗产价值观。而中国固有的建筑价值观则与之有别,历来"轻物重式",打桩拨正、移梁换柱、重修增制,甚至拆除重建习以为常,是故虽迁延渐变,却一脉相承。今天看来,对价值"真实性"的理解和认定,似应秉持既接受普世遗产价值准则,又尊重本土遗产价值传统的适应性态度和解析式方法。也就是具体问题具体分析,不同对象不同处置;以原则约束策略,以策略践行原则。

建筑遗产的价值属性是多维度的,大致可分为四种:其一,重要历史事件或特定生活形态的见证,并可引申到历史公共空间。如历史街区及广场,是集体记忆的空间载体,可以印证其本身及其所在地的"身份"(identity)由来,因而具有历史纪念价值(memory)。其二,某个时期艺术风格和技术特征的代表,作为具象的历史形态,使文明留下了空间实体的印记,因而具有"标本"(sample)的留存和研究价值。其三,某种情感、理念、信仰、境界等观念形态的载体,作为一种文化符号,被赋予了相对恒久的意义,因而具有文化象征(symbol)价值。其四,作为一种空间资源,建筑遗产还具有很高的适应性利用价值(adaptive reuse)。

以上这四种价值对于具体的建筑遗产来说可能所占比重不一,但都反映了其历史的内涵,提供了保护的缘由。就一个地方的历史身份、特色和行为主体而言,这些价值也是环境和文化的可识别性、多样性,以及认同感与归属感的重要源泉。这一认知,源于19世纪后半叶以来西方对建筑遗产价值判定的长期讨论和评判。颇具代表性的,例如价值学说的系统阐述者奥地利的李格尔(Alois Riegl,1858—1905),将建筑遗产的价值概括为两大部分四个方面,即:第一,"往昔价值"(commemorative value),由承载纪念性的"历史价值"(historic value)和留存岁月印痕的"年代价值"或"故旧价值"(age-value)构成;第二,"当代价值",由"艺术价值"和"使用价值"构成。①[1] 李格尔所说的"年代价值",是要强调历史建筑经由时间印痕所获得的"沧桑感"及作为"古董"的审美特征(即所谓"patina"——古色②)。这一点在19世纪的古迹修复运动中

---

① 当代学者阿兰·柯尔孔(Alan Colquhoun,1921—2012)如此解释李格尔的发现:"历史主义在古迹修复中从未关注保留岁月沧桑印记(oldness),而是追求焕然一新效果(newness),也即只把历史当作一种虚像(pastness)呈现,以适应当时的审美消费取向。"参见 Colquhoun A. Three Kinds of Historicism [M]. // Nesbitt. Theorizing a New Agenda for Architecture. New York:Princeton Architectural Press,1996:208(另参见江坦先生译的载于《新建筑》1985年第4期的《三种历史主义》)。

② 李格尔对岁月印痕——"古色"(patina)价值的发现,在意大利的《1972修复宪章》第6条中被再度强调。但李格尔所述对象主要指艺术品表面锈斑和瘢痕的年代价值及其对艺术品本体的保护作用,而历史建筑表面陈迹的形成过程复杂,需要对其成因、时间及价值做具体分析,故不宜不明就里地一概看作是"古色"。

被严重忽视了,所以他认为"年代价值"是一个全新概念。其实这也是以那场修复运动的饱受争议为背景的。

世纪之交以来,国际文化遗产保护界一直在尝试定义和推举具有"显著普世价值"(Outstanding Universal Value)的"世纪文化遗产"的通行标准,近年来又注重从各国、各地域文化遗产的类型及所属文明的时空特性和所承载的文化内涵等方面来对其进行检视和认知。[2]

若从朱启钤先生发起成立中国营造学社算起,中国的建筑遗产研究至少已有80多年的历史,为梁思成(1901—1972)和刘敦桢(1897—1968)两位学科巨擘所开创的中国建筑史研究体系所涵盖。长期以来,这一体系研究的目的,既是为了满足文献与实物史料的整理、鉴定、分类、编年等治史需要,更是为了满足表达民族国家理念及其建筑象征的政治诉求,因而官式建筑研究曾经是重中之重。所谓"中国固有式""宫殿式"的提出等,均是出于后一种目的。同时,中国在文物建筑的保护修缮方面长期以来也积累了极为丰富的经验,形成了自己的特色。而以当代的文化遗产价值认知理论、研究范式和保护方法,以及适应性利用实验等为工具,对各类建筑遗产进行更具有现实及未来意义的创造性探索,在中国只能说还处在早期阶段。

中国的建筑遗产大致可分为三大部分:其一为以官式建筑为代表的古典建筑遗产,其二为分布于各个地域的风土建筑遗产,其三为西方建筑影响下的近现代建筑遗产。随着时代的变迁,第一部分建筑遗产所由生的历史功用多已改变,因而大多已成为标本式的"死"遗产;而第二和第三部分建筑遗产,却因生活形态的存留或对现代功能的适应,大多仍是旧体新用的"活"遗产。

由于历史、国情和体制等原因,中国古代存留下来的建筑遗产(1840年以前)和一些具有特殊纪念意义的近现代建筑遗产,多数都被列为国家到省、市和区县的各级文物保护单位,受到了《文物保护法》的保护。除此之外,在大量从材料、工艺到式样延续地方传统匠作体系的城乡风土建筑遗产,以及年代、材料、技术及式样均属近现代的建筑遗产中,有不少已在30年来的城市化进程中消亡,仅有一部分受到地方保护法规的保护,其中一些保护对象还同时具备各级文物保护单位的双重身份。除此之外,仍有大量价值较高,应予保护的城乡建筑遗产尚未得到认定,在地方的旧区改造中面临着被毁弃的厄运。这些均为建筑遗产研究的重要方面,并亟须建立起切实可行的"抢救评估"和"先予保护"机制,使其免于遭到持续的破坏。

若将建筑遗产概念扩展到城市历史空间的层面上,可以认为,除了环境的适宜,管理的先进,设施和服务的齐全、便利,一座城市的个性魅力还来自其承载着历史底蕴与文化多样性的有形和无形的文化遗产,并在不同历史时期、不同形态构成的城市"文化层"中呈现出来。无论缓慢的渐变还是急剧的突变,历史城市总是处在进化状态中,有着自己的生命周期、文化积淀和演进方向,积淀愈厚,底蕴愈深,多样性亦愈丰富,城市集体记忆也就愈历久。同时也应看到,一座仅锁定在某一历史时期的城市是终结了"历史"的城市,或者说是一座巨大的城市博物馆,如威尼斯城和平遥城,是专供旅游观光的。那是一种标本,一种特例,实际上绝大多数历史城市既不可能也不应该维持原封不动的状态,有"延"有"续"才是健康的城市保护与再生观。问题是许多历史城市在短视的低水准"改造"中,只"续"不"延",还没来得及思考、判断和选址,就把有保存价值的东西匆匆毁掉了。从这个意义上说,真正有魅力和生命力持久的城市,就应是适应于文化与社会演进,既"延"又"续",不断获得再生的"拼贴"城市。而要实现历史城市的保护与再生,就要对其历史空间遗产进行系统地研究,特别是重点研究如何"延"和"续",有哪些可供选择的适应性方式,以为城市的可持续演进坚实的文化基础(详见本文第4节)。

从整体上看,中国传统建筑遗产所由生的宗法社会结构自"五四运动"以来早已崩解,而其空间结构则因城市化进程缓慢而得以延续,但随着近30年来的高速城市化正走向消亡,于今已凋敝零夷,幸存什一。虽然文明进程不可逆转,但一个社会在走向进步的同时,终须以历史遗产见证自己的身份和由来,回眸不见厚实的历史,很难自信地眺望未来。因而,建筑遗产作为稀有文化资源的价值不言而喻,其存续与活化之于社会存在和演进的重要性显而易见,需要花大力气对其历史标本价值、集体记忆价值、文化象征价值及保护和再利用方式进行综合的研究与实践。

2 保护的意义与局限

保护也有广义和狭义之分。狭义的"preservation"仅指维持历史建筑不继续损坏的"保存"。[3]而广义的"preservation"则和"conservation"一样,包括了:第一,对历史建筑的保存研究和价值判定;第二,干预程度较低的定期维护(maintenance)和修复(repair, minor restoration);第三,干预程序较高的整修(rehabilitation)、翻新(renovation)和复原(major restoration);第四,在特殊情况下的扩建、加建(addition)和重建(reconstruction)等。

这些概念的分类及其操作的实施,均应以历史建筑的法定身份、保护分级、保存状态和使用性质为依据,具体问题具体分析,不同案例不同对待,以原则约束策略,以策略活用原则。这是因为大多数建筑遗产都是以现代功能被持续地使用着,保护需要投入大量的经济和社会成本,牵扯所有的利益攸关方,不仅仅是坚持保护原则和价值观就可以实现的。因而价值判定后对保护操作的落实,就不应仅仅囿于专家领域和专业范围,也不是一种可以独立存在的事体,而是需要使用者、投资者、管理者、专家学者和公众的多方参与,取得保护前提下的社会共识和利益平衡。尽管做到这一步极其困难,但这却是推进建筑遗产保护事业的大方向。从某种意义上可以说,建筑遗产作为可持续发展的宝贵空间资源,一旦纳入保护和再生进程,就成为了关联到政治、经济和文化战略及其走向的社会工程。

回望20世纪以来的保护历程,还从来没有过像今天这样,在如此大的范围内,为那些故旧的,同时又在使用之中的空间遗存设定广义的保护约束,从而在社会上引发观念和利害的冲突,这是发人深思的。起码可以判定,现代文明对建筑遗产的态度是多元化、多维度的,包括了文化资源视角的、历史价值观的、怀旧情绪的、审美取向的、经济动因的,乃至政治考量的诸多复杂因素。

但归结为一点,建筑遗产保护的主要目的,在于保存体现其价值的历史信息的"真实性"与"完整性"。应尊重保护本体在不同历史时期、不同文化背景下的形态特征与变迁过程,采取辩证的历史观和价值观对其进行认定和保护。西方当代一种具有代表性的观点认为,保护本身是手段而非目的,不过是借以保持和强化某一保护对象的意义,甚至只是为了表达其所象征的东西。这一看似有些抽象的观点,实际上是要回返到常识的层面上来,面对两个更深层次的问题:到底为何保护? 为谁保护?[4]

历史长河中,保存古迹和纪念物这类智性的思想和行为并不鲜见,但现代意义上的"历史保护"概念,却是西方启蒙时期以来形成的,涉及价值判断、规则控制和具体的技术操作。从相关的领域看,现代考古学、博物馆学、艺术史理论和遗产保护的制度、法规等都围绕着一个主题,即对具有时代纪念意义的遗产物合情、合理、合法地保护。保护首先是国家层面的,将之作为政权合法性的空间象征。如美国独立战争尚未结束,就开始考虑保护未来新国家的历史象征物了。又如中国近代北伐战争完成不久,国民政府便立即颁布了古物保存条例和保存法,也是出于政权继承合法性的动机。保护也有社会层面的,将之作为地方和社会阶层存在价值的空间表述。在不少国家和地区,历史城镇、街区的居民和社会团体把拥有和保护历史遗产作为自己的天赋权利。还有个人和家族层面的。在产权私有的地方,历史建筑的主人在保护契约之外,也以守望这些家族遗产为己任,并引以为荣。也就是说,当历史建筑的使用者同时也是建筑遗产的所有者时,保护遗产和守卫资产具有同一性。在这些国家和地区,保护已是生活方式的组成部分。无论对城市还是对城市人而言,历史与我同在,同时也是城市多样性的体现,这种理念早已深入人心。包括普通百姓在内的社会各阶层,已不仅仅把建筑遗产看作物质层面的东西,而且也看成是他们的精神寓所。而不断调适的保护法规也维护了建筑遗产所有者的权益。对于大部分仍在作为社会生活空间被广泛使用着的历史建筑来说,在保护目标实施的过程中,其所有者和使用者显然也应拥有参与权或知情权,他们的权益诉求是不可回避的。建筑遗产同时也是一种资产,所有者和使用者维护权益的动机合情合理,因而保护政策和补偿措施就成为必不可少的考量因素。

中国近现代文化遗产保护法规产生的历史语境与欧洲有所不同,大多属于针对建设性破坏的抢救性举措。这类保护法始于1906年清政府拟定的《保存古物推广办法》。随后陆续出台的国家层面保护法律和行政法规主要有：国民政府1928年颁布的《名胜古迹古物保存条例》和1930年颁布的《古物保存法》；中华人民共和国政府1961年颁布的《文物保护管理暂行条例》，1982年颁布的《文物保护法》和2008年颁布的行政法规《历史文化名城名镇名村保护条例》等。

在中国国情条件下，一方面，建筑遗产的所有权和使用权往往是分离的，除了非利益攸关的部分社会精英，人们对其价值判断的标准和情感依恋的程度与西方相比有明显差异。另一方面，随着人们对历史建筑价值的认知水平提高，以及观光休闲业的推动，本来狭义的历史建筑保护，已经延展到了既存的、涉及人们日常生活的广义保护层面。对于中国的历史建筑保护而言，时下最紧迫的任务是保护观念的普及和保护法律法规的健全。

3 对"修复"的反顾

3.1 西方的修复矛盾

修复的历史贯穿于建筑存在和演变的始终，从技术层面上看，一部建筑史同时也是一部修复史。实际上，一切建筑遗产保护问题的核心都与"修复"有关。房子用久了要修，缺损了要补。本来天经地义，但到了近代，当古今分野的现代意识伴随启蒙产生后，至少对一些重要的古迹和历史建筑来说，修复成了一个歧义纷呈、充满争议的保护价值观问题。

正如人需要补充能量以维持和恢复肌体的活力，建筑也需要不断修复以维系和活化利用的价值，因此在西语的词汇中，"修复"与"进餐"同源。如英语中的"restoration"（修复）一词，源于法语的"restaurabo"，本是"餐馆"的意思，与另一个词"restore"（填饱）同源。与之相关，19世纪广泛使用的"restauration"一词也有两重含义：其一为日耳曼语系民族所称的"食堂"；其二为"规整"，牛津词典将之定义为"修补""重建""复原""复建"等等[5]13。"修复"一词用于历史建筑，与法国大革命后的古迹重修运动密不可分。

从18世纪德国温克尔曼（Johann Joachim Winckelmann，1717—1768）的《古代艺术史》开始，艺术史以"风格"进行分期，使"复活"某一历史时期的艺术风格有了基本学理和历史形态学的依据。与之相伴随，工业革命初期的影响、法国大革命的涤荡、中世纪延续下来的人文景观的颓萎，使人们既对新时代憧憬犹疑，又对旧时光难舍难分，从而导致各种各样的复古主义思潮此起彼伏。这也同时引发了18世纪末到19世纪以中世纪教堂为主体的古迹修复热潮，以致矫枉过正，混淆了"古迹存活"（survival）的"修复"与"古迹复活""复兴"（revival）的"重塑"（remodelling）的不同性质，即有根据的修复、复建，与臆测性的复原、改建之间的明确界限被模糊化甚至去除了。由此，"修复"一词在19世纪后期竟成了"彻头彻尾破坏"的婉辞。进而也可以了解，"哥特复兴"在当时的盛行，也连带了对中世纪哥特建筑的修复性破坏。

如在法国大革命以后的一段时期及英国的维多利亚时代，对大量哥特式教堂等建筑作了没有根据的形态美化和风格完形，即"风格性复原"，以"'哥特复兴'为基调，翻建了许多其从中获得了灵感的中世纪建筑，将之改头换面，弄得无比光鲜，简直当成了自己的作品，如果不考虑尊重原物，它们当然更加漂亮"[6]。与之相关的巴黎巨变由奥斯曼（George-Eugene Haussmann，1809—1891）的旧城改造计划所引发，这一计划拆除重建了60%的旧市区，连带拆除了1/3以上的城市故旧景物，其中以西堤岛的改变为最剧。然而，今日巴黎引以为傲的香榭里大道及其两旁的林荫、绿地和一些新古典建筑群，无疑也是奥斯曼时期留下的景点城市遗产，说明历史总是在成就与代价中演进着，留给后人的唯有智慧与谋略的经验和教训。

这一时期，法国古迹修复运动巨擘维奥莱-勒-杜克（Eugène-Emmanuel Viollet-le-Duc，1814—1879）以其非凡的学识和信念与中世纪的哥特建筑师神交。虽然他早在1860年以前就指出了不当修复的负面后果，但他从骨子里就是一位创新型建筑师，如法国夏约学校的本杰明·穆栋（Benjamin Mouton）教授所概括的："非为保存而保护，实为创造而修复。"① 由此，他负责的不少修复工程均遭到非议，这是建筑师的创

---

① 据本杰明·穆栋 Notre Dame Cathedral de Paris：History and Methodology of Conservation 原稿。

作冲动及过度修复作为，与考古学家及保护主义者的敬畏之心及现状维护原则的冲突，亦即是继承古代建造精神，使修复对象趋于勒-杜克们所理解的完美，还是竭力留存历史信息，使之保持住现状。今日看来，对此问题要依修复对象的性质和条件，对症下药，难以非此即彼，一概而论。

同时期英国古迹修复的代表性人物乔治·吉尔伯特·斯科特（George Gilbert Scott，1811—1878）也曾提醒道："激进修复的现代体系正在比狂热的蛮干更厉害地毁灭着古代艺术"，使之失去"全真"（truthfulness）。但他同时又推崇必要的"复原"，提出古迹"后加部分在修缮时应该去掉，并在确有把握时可以恢复原貌"。这里的"复原"，比之勒-杜克的创造性修复似乎还要严谨保守一些，虽然斯科特的许多修复也强调了继承中世纪匠作的精神，但他在风格式修复的工程案例中却被认为做过了头。就连当时著名的建筑师诺曼·肖（Richard Norman Shaw，1831—1912）也站在地方风土和贵族口味的立场，挪揄斯科特的哥特复兴是对哥特遗产的"作践"。[6]

18世纪末以降，这一抹去大量真实历史信息的古迹修复风潮招致了拜伦（George Byron，1788—1824）和拉斯金（John Ruskin，1819—1900）等考古界和文艺界反修复人士的严厉批评和强烈质疑。[5]这些保护主义者认为，对建筑遗产最大的尊重，就是放弃对其哪怕是最小的修复干预，即损坏再严重也不应去碰它，而是宁愿在缅怀中任其自生自灭，并认为任何的"修复"都是篡改历史真实的"谎言"，是建筑所能遭遇的"最惨境遇"，"修复就像唤醒死人一样徒劳"。[7]在对修复运动的声讨中，首当其冲的建筑学也被斥为"就像个幼稚缺教的顽童"。[6]这可以说是保护观念的另一种极端，若是特指当时的宗教建筑修复运动对古迹的过度干预及篡改，还是很有道理的，但若泛指所有使用中的建筑遗产，就显得偏激、非理性，甚至荒谬了。使用中的建筑破旧了怎能不修复？更有甚者，人们怎能待在废墟之中生活呢？所以说到底，拉斯金所指并非废墟之外所有的建筑遗产。

但无论如何，反改造、反修复的积极意义是在提醒人们，"真实"才是遗产价值的关键所在，由此也直接推动了后来欧洲各国现代古迹保护法的建立和完善。如法国在1840年和1887年，意大利在1872年，英国在1882年，分别有了现代意义上的相关历史建筑保护法。这些规则性的控制——专项的保护法，恰恰首先都是针对修复性破坏的，设置了实现保护目的、协调保存和修复矛盾的底线，即保存和修复中的"最小干预"（minimum intervention）原则，而这是无奈之下的一个不确定的概念，究竟"最小"的"度"如何拿捏，不同对象的"度"又有多大差异呢？事实上，当时的古迹保护法所指的对象是以不再使用的废墟为主，由此维修成为难题，因为实施中要冒违法的风险。1889年，当英国古迹保护委员会指责著名的中世纪废墟格拉斯顿伯利的修道院残迹维修不力时，责任人这样说道："拜托，它们现在是废墟，彻底坍塌后依然是废墟，那么你们到底还要怎样呢？"[6]

往事无可追，今世犹可鉴。今天如何看待19世纪那场留下了重要印记的修复运动呢？当代著名建筑理论家尼古劳斯·佩夫斯纳（Sir Nikolaus Pevsner，1902—1983）这样总结道："且不说斯科特对哥特教堂的修改是那样的精美而富于创造力，若要将维多利亚时代对教堂建筑的美化再复原到其以前的样子，就是重复了那个时代的错误。如果这样，我们的后代也将会像我们清算维多利亚学派那样清算我们。"[5]8这里，佩夫斯纳是在阐述一种历史的真实乃是变化叠加结果的遗产史观，即使今天已不宜再犯历史上那些失当叠加的错误。这样的评说及其史观，与法国主流舆论对奥斯曼计划的评价和反思如出一辙。

从历史建筑信息"真实性"保存的原则看，不当的修复行为无疑是对其进行折减甚至篡改的干预。但无可辩驳的常识却是，历史建筑如同老化多病的有机生命体一样，必须通过"诊治"手段延续生命甚至恢复活力，以实现再生活"活化"的目标。只保存不修复，对多数持续使用的历史建筑和一些有特殊复原意义的历史废墟来说，显然也是不切实际的清淡。因此，"诊治"作为保护与修复的系统工程是必要的，也是必需的。首先，要通过实测、检测、调查、建档等"诊断"手段，搜集和分析尽可能翔实的图文和样品信息资料，对其进行"病理诊断"。其次，运用维修、加固、整饬等特种技术，对其进行"治疗"。包括"皮肤"——面层的维修，"肌肉"——维护体的整修，"骨骼"——承重体的加固，"血管""神经"——管线设备的改造，"脏腑"——空间的整理和利用等。从修复技术看，现代的结构、材料及工艺仍处在不断研发之中，并在适应性运用中得到改良。而传统"低技术"的修复方法由于与历史建筑的相对兼容性，也需要发掘研究，并与现代技术综合应用于保存和修复的对象。在某些情况下,以不违反保护法规为底线,建筑遗产的周边也会进行加建或扩建(addition),或在内部遵循"可逆性原则",插入适应功能需求的新元素进行整饬设计。

"治疗"手段的选择,与所干预对象的性质和功用(如古迹观光或现代功能),所在环境的约束条件(如有关历史保护的法律法规)、文化传统(如修复方式及其文化意涵)和技术水平(如最小干预的适应性方法)等密切相关,并影响着最终的"治疗"效果。对此,19世纪中叶英国的弗里曼(Edword Augustus Freeman,1623—1892)提出,在追求美化的"破坏性修复"和只维修不复原的"保护性修复"之外,还可有在维修的同时,经实证恢复始建时原貌的"折中修复"(eclectic)的选择方式。即使做不到恢复原貌,也可以恢复到晚近的状貌。"折中修复"并可与"保守性修复"方式相结合。[5] 实际上,建筑师与保护主义者在价值观上最大的分歧,是在"美"与"真"之间如何进行权衡。比如1904年国际建筑师第六届大会上通过的《马德里会议建议》就曾指出,对于不再使用的纪念性古迹或废墟,其价值保留,就在于维持原状;而对于使用中的历史建筑,却应以美的准则进行修复,但后加部分如有价值且不妨碍美感,亦可予以保留。这是一种将"美"置于"真"之上的修复观,但已与依据对象区别处理的辩证修复观非常接近了。

上述辩证修复的理念与方法在意大利尤为典型。从19世纪末至"二战"前,意大利保护界逐渐修正了风格修复的路子,倡导实证主义的思路,对保护对象先后提出了侧重不同的修复方法,如以形态语言辨析为基础的"历史语言式修复法"(restauro filologico),以文献考释为基础的"史料佐证式修复法"(restauro storico),以及以综合评价为基础的"辩证评判式修复法"(restauro critico)等。其中,以著名古迹修复专家古斯塔夫·乔万诺尼(Gustavo Giovannoni,1873—1947)为代表,将已被广泛采用的加固(consolidation)——确保结构安全的技术措施;复位(anastylosis)——将散落构件回归原处;释放(liberation)——去芜存精,重现经典原貌;完形(completion)——修补缺损使历史形态完整;翻新(renovation)——翻修中的适应性改进等五种修复方式加以整合,并引入现代修复材料与技术,提出了涵盖现代保护工程主要范畴的系统理论与方法,即所谓"科学修复法"(restauro scientifico)[8],对1931年有关国际古迹保护与修复的《雅典宪章》制定有直接的影响,并与1964年诞生的《威尼斯宪章》不无关联。在国际古迹遗址理事会(ICOMOS)的前身历史古迹建筑师及技师国际会议的推动下,作为第一部具有深远影响的国际纲领性文件,《威尼斯宪章》总结和提升了19世纪以来历史建筑保存与修复的基本思想和原则,其精神可以用"修旧如旧,补新以新"八个字加以高度概括,目的就是把历史建筑真实、完整地传给后代。

总括看来,国际上现代的建筑遗产保存和修复趋势是,受到保护原则约束的操作策略需根据对象区别运用,承认真实与完整是各个时期变化的叠加,对这些叠加要根据其价值进行具体分析,以充分的断代修复理由和历史资料作支撑,进行合宜的取舍和选择,对新旧部分进行可识别的区分等,并在修复中适当地引入现代的材料和技术。

3.2 中国的修复传统

"形而上者谓之道,形而下者谓之器。"(《易·系辞上》)意即本体(源)及规律在物体及存在之上,"事"的价值在"物"的价值之上。今天讲的非物质遗产价值,正是"道"这个形而上的理念在遗产本体价值中的体现。比如,从中国古代界画的名楼中可以明显观察出,岳阳楼、滕王阁一类著名的建筑景观往往相互类似,它们的差异主要是从地点性及建筑所承载的不同人文意涵确定的。因此,中国古代虽把前朝遗留下来的典章、器物、建筑等均视作文物,但古人并不看重建筑原物的长存,认为其与永恒的时空相比微不足道,杜牧的"六朝文物草连空,天淡云闲今古同"(《题宣州开元寺水阁》)就形象地表达了这种感叹。李德裕的"譬诸日月,虽终古常见而光景常新,此所以为灵物也"(《文章论》),即"亘古弥新"的意思。司空图将古体四言诗对美景秀色的描述作了新的演绎,并在其中形象表达了类似的古今观:

采采流水,蓬蓬远春。

窈窈深谷,时见美人。

碧桃满树,风日水滨。

柳阴路曲,流莺比邻。

> 乘之愈往,识之愈真。
> 如将不尽,与古为新。
> ——《二十四诗品·纤秾》

后两句的意思是,如《诗经》描述一般的景致令人神往,感知真切,只要承上启下,存故续新,这些景致便会享受不尽。最引人关注的是最后一句——"如将不尽,与古为新",这在寓意上似乎做了因果倒装,强调只有新旧共生,方能永续不朽。

正是怀着这种通融古今的自然主义理念,中国古代对古迹修复秉持了"朽者新之,废者兴之,残者成之"(《西京大华严寺佛日圆照明公和尚碑铭并序》)的坦然态度。"修葺原物之风,远不及重建之盛;历代增修拆建,素不重原物之保存,唯珍其旧址及其创建年代而已。唯坟墓工程,则古来确甚意于巩固永保之观念……"[9]

尽管如此,中国传统的修复观还是以经济可行性和实用主义为主导的,修复抑或重建,全视具体情势和物质条件而定。特别是清朝入关后,修旧而非建新占了上风,对明代坛庙社稷以下的建筑遗产全盘修葺利用,不再重蹈历朝拆旧建新的旧辙。地方亦是如此,比如清代岳州知府吕恩湛在《重修岳阳楼记》中就明确提出了"因旧为新"的修复观。但这并不表示中国自古就有建筑遗产的存真意识,而是在建筑修复中重在"原式"的传承,而非"原物"的永恒。比如北京故宫的一些重要建筑,由于多次重修,清康乾与明永乐相比就有不少变化,从清末到当代也有过数次大规模的修缮和局部的改动。那么,假如今天再次修缮,应该修到什么时空状态呢?是维修和维持现状,还是恢复到某时期的原状?这必然面临中国古代修复传统与国际现代修复理念的博弈与选择。

20世纪后半叶以来,中国的历史建筑修复,更多地倾向于追求完形的风格复原,更多地倾向于追求完形的风格复原,这既与中国的传统有关,重"式"轻"代",也受到了西方近代风格性复原的影响。如山西五台山南禅寺大殿、福州华林寺大殿和上海真如寺大殿的外观,分别是根据唐、五代和元的木构歇山风格复原的,而非其初建时或某个特定时期的原初面貌。由于直接文献和图像证据的不足或缺失,那是根本不可能原真再现的。[10]

至于修复前后的识别性,即《威尼斯宪章》关于修复痕迹的保留原则,是否适合中国传统木构建筑的实际情况,这一点虽一直存在很大争议,但起码可以判定,修复痕迹应该兼顾整体协调和细察可辨的原则,而不应一概疤痕毕现或者相反——天衣无缝。1994年,联合国教科文组织世界文化遗产委员会《关于真实性的奈良文件》提出,文化遗产的"真实性"认定是相对的、多样的,不同文化传统的国家和地区在标准的把握上可有所不同。1996年的《圣·安东尼奥宣言》更提出,文化遗产的真实性与所在社会不同时空、不同族群背景下的文化身份直接相关,因而对价值真实性的认同是多样性的综合。

3.3 关于"复建"

当建筑遗产全部或大部损毁后,是保留废墟还是整体复建(major restoration),应视必要性和可能性而定。大部损毁就意味着"标本"价值已大大降低,其所含历史信息已大部消失。但设若内在的记忆价值或象征价值依然存在,经过缜密论证,如确有必要,又有充分的图像和文字材料佐证,对某些特殊对象而言,似可考虑原址原貌复建的可能性。实际上,当代关于建筑遗产损毁后的复建问题比较普遍,如"二战"后伦敦、柏林、华沙等欧洲城市的重要历史建筑,大都是在废墟中复原重建的,这与既无历史价值又无复原依据的"假古董"在性质上完全不同。但如果保留废墟更说明记忆与象征价值,就应对其现状进行保存维护,如圆明园遗址作为国耻纪念地及其象征,就不应当在遗址上进行整体复原。

诚然,古代已毁弃的建筑遗址,可以做复原设计研究,但却很难据此进行原址原物的复建,因其古代已是废墟,真实的历史信息大都荡然无存了,基本上不可能有非常可靠的复建依据。反过来,原物有完整保存,因为某种原因将其拆除后"复建",就应慎而又慎。虽然对木结构而言,"落架大修"(即拆解重装)是古来的传统做法,但对某些国宝级文物建筑,比如应县木塔,下部结构因长时期的超荷承压,构件榫卯已僵结刚化,根本无法拆解,彻底落架就意味着离断式拆毁,势将以丢失古代巨制中那些千载沧桑的特征构件及其真实历史信息为代价。在这种情况下,"卸荷存真"的方式就似乎更为合理,属于"标本式"保存的超前探索。而对于那些具有精美砖饰的建筑外观,拆除"复建"亦为下策,因为即使材料、工艺可以模仿,年代价值及历史真实感却将不复存在。故对重要的历史地标建筑而言,原址原貌固然是保护的底线,如原物犹存,竭力避免拆除"复建"就更为可贵了。至于为了历史意象呈现或商业观光目的,在遗址外择地"复建"古代名胜,其利弊得失与保护命题无关,就不属本文讨论的对象了。

这里仅就现代造成的历史建筑废墟复建问题简析几个特殊的例子。

第一个例子是柏林议会大厦废墟部分的创造性重建。这座新古典主义建筑中央的重建部分与周边的保存部分在材料和结构上反差强烈,反倒体现了新旧区分的可识别原则。中央的废墟重建为一个体现当代生态技术的屋顶平台和玻璃穹隆;周边则完全突出保存和修复的理念,甚至连二战炮火痕迹,特别是攻克柏林留下的记忆,如弹孔、苏联红军的题字等都作为历史信息保留着。

第二个例子是瑞士卢塞恩的卡佩尔廊桥,建于 1333 年,是欧洲现存最古的木构廊桥。1993 年遭大火焚烧,灾后照原样复建,但将过火后的残存桥体结构予以保留,连构件焦黑的表面也未作去除,为的是让原物部分与新补加部分清楚区分,并将火灾本身作为事件记忆下来。

第三个例子是德国的德累斯顿圣母大教堂(Frauenkirche)。"二战"后期被战火摧毁,只留下废墟中的几片残垣断壁,复建工程历时 7 载,这座伟大的纪念性建筑终于在战争结束 60 周年(2005 年)之际再现于世,废墟和残件与复原后的教堂整体完美地融合在了一起。这个例子不但重新诠释了废墟对城市和建筑的不同呈现方式和多元价值,而且也使战后欧洲民族国家间的和解以一座地标的复建获得了象征性意义。从这个角度看,再现这一类历史建筑,就不再仅仅是遗产本体能否复原的问题,而是涉及了城市历史身份及其对遗产空间存续诉求的满足。

笔者的亲身感受,来自数年前主持外滩 9 号轮船招商总局大楼修复和再生工程的经历。这一修复工程试图恢复一座百年建筑的原貌并改善其内部使用空间。这座建筑在修复前已历尽沧桑,坡屋顶被拆掉,外廊被封死,经典的红砖墙和砖雕线脚大都被水泥砂浆覆盖,已经看不出来历史原状了,但有历史图像和实测资料为依据,做比较逼近历史真实的保存和修复设计既是必须的,也是可能的。工程设计最终选择了严格按历史原状恢复外廊、红砖墙、坡屋顶和山花,对其室内进行了整饬设计(renovation),并利用恢复后的坡屋顶内部空间做了一个精致的阁楼会所。

笔者主持的西藏日喀则桑珠孜宗堡大部损毁后的复建工程是又一个典型例子。初建早于布达拉宫 330 年的桑珠孜宗堡,在 600 余年的历史长河中,一直都是日喀则古城天际线的制高点。这座雄伟的地标建筑不幸毁于"文革"初期。40 年后,在当地藏族各界的强烈呼吁下,作为上海市最大的一个援藏项目,桑珠孜宗宫堡台废墟保存与宫楼外观修复工程历时 6 载终于顺利完成。工程恢复了这座古城的历史天际线,内部建成了后藏地区第一座民俗博物馆。国内外出现了不少惊叹和质疑:这样的修复工程价值如何?依据何在? 我们认为,桑珠孜宗堡作为日喀则的城市天际线和当地藏民的心理地标,有充分理由和依据进行存遗和"完形"的尝试,即保存下部的堡台废墟,恢复上部的宫楼形态,以弥补城市历史天际线和藏民心理地标的缺失。其结果是既满足了社会各界对历史地景的观瞻诉求,同时也兼顾了保存部分和复原部分的可识别原则。[11]

4 城市更新与历史空间再生

如果把城市比作有机生命体,其便会有从诞生、发育和成熟,到老化、多恙和衰亡的生命周期。刘易斯·芒福德(Lewis Mumford,1895—1990)以社会达尔文主义的观点诠释了人类城市的进化过程。他认为,城市历史遗产所代表的不过是消失的过去,正因为其已死亡,才获得了纪念性和遗产身份;唯有更新和再生,才能延续历史城市的生命。但他同时也提醒,更新不是毁掉过去的所有痕迹,不能再延续 19 世纪那种大拆大建的城市改造方式[12]。与芒福德的历史观相类似,现代建筑的先驱们大都认为,历史城市要面向未来,就难逃改造和更新的宿命。那么,城市的更新还能给历史空间的保护和再生留下多大的余地?单就旧城改造而言,20世纪的西方建筑界又是如何思考和行动的呢？

早在1925年的《都市规划》(Urbanisme)一书中,勒·柯布西耶(Le Corbusier,1887—1965)就提出,相对于城市现代结构(新城区),其历史结构(历史空间的物质存在)只能是比例极小的片段。他认为应当大规模地拆旧建新,只要保留最具价值的历史中心(历史纪念地)就足够了,大有要启动新一轮"奥斯曼计划"的豪情。幸运的是,他的巴黎"伏瓦辛规划"(the Plan Voisin for Paris)并未付诸实施。随后《雅典宪章》对历史遗产的关注似乎也增加了。但柯布西耶绝对是现代性的激进思想者和实践者,而且并非特立独行。弗兰克·赖特(Frank Lloyd Wright,1867—1959)对历史城市更新的看法与柯氏如出一辙。在1939年出版的《有机建筑——民主的建筑》(An Organic Architecture: The Architecture of Democracy)一书中赖特就提出,伦敦改造应拆除大片的帝制旧城区,只需保存重要的历史地段[13]。两位大师思想上的共同点在于：第一,均不主张完全保留历史结构,而是要拆掉他们认为没有保存价值的旧城区,代之以大片绿化带,使历史中心与新城区隔离开来,成为被膜拜的墓园和圣地；第二,都不屑于历史与现实的混搭,而是主张将所保留的历史结构与现代结构二元化,并未考虑通过再生使前者融入现代城市生活的可能。与之相关,1950年梁思成与陈占祥(1916—2001)提出的北京旧城与新城东、西分开的"梁陈方案",正是西方这一新旧分立思想影响下的产物。但两者的结局却差异明显,西方后来的城市生长进程虽接受新旧分立,但否定了旧区激进改造,如巴黎和伦敦都完整保留了历史结构并进行适应式更新,前者的新城区集中于拉·德方斯(La Dèfense)等开发区,后者开辟了旧工业区改造性质的商贸城(London Docklands)。中国则相反,否定完整保留旧区的新旧分立,选择了旧区激进更新和新区开发并行的发展道路。如北京保留了历史中心(故宫),以多圈同心圆结构对周边进行改造和扩建,最终使新旧城区形成了交错共生的演化态势。并且,现代结构后来居上,膨胀式生长,导致历史结构被一点点地碎片化。从某种意义上说,这种同心圆扩张方式,不正是中国古都历史结构在特殊的社会变迁时空背景下,充满矛盾性和复杂性的现代演绎和变异吗？

中西这一城市演进差异的个中缘由是多方面的,从深层的观念根源看,它显然反映了现代性在不同国情和历史背景、不同演化阶段中的不同呈现方式及其所导致的不同结局。一个不应忽视的历史事实是,同为迈入现代的首次大规模旧城改造运动,中国的起步比西方晚了至少一个世纪。也就是说,西方在19世纪中后期,已拥有工业化改造后的现代城市,而中国直到20世纪后半叶,绝大多数城市才刚刚从农耕文明蹒跚走出。二者的"旧城区"完全不在同一个演化的时空层次上。对于中国的这些历史城市和风土建筑而言,保护与再生的难度大大超过西方是显而易见的。因此,中国的历史城市必然地要走不同于西方的道路,而这一切都应该以对城市遗产的基本认知为基础。相比而言,中国19世纪的开埠城市,近代化程度与西方城市接近,更有条件在旧城改造的同时留住尽可能多的历史馈赠。比如上海,自20世纪末开始旧城改造以来,规划保留了近27 km^{2}的近代历史文化风貌区,约占民国末期旧市区面积的1/3,并在其中引入了一些现代转换与活化的方式。[14]

如果说历史城市遗产本体的保存是决定性的,那么对其周边环境的更新便是相对性和选择性的,但目的都是为了延续城市的传统精髓并加以转化,而不是任意重建。对此,建筑类型学(Typology)提供了影响广泛的一种选择。阿尔多·罗西(Aldo Rossi,1931—1997)20世纪60年代中期在他的《城市建筑学》(The Architecture of the City)一书中认为,历史城市具有传承"集体记忆"(collective memory)的社会功能。而所谓"城市集体记忆",指的就是城市人对既往人为物象(artifacts,包括建筑物、街道、广场等城市要素)的各种类型在集体无意识中所认同和获得的类似经验的形式,反映在建筑上,就是不同类型表象内部所蕴含着的共同"原型"。根据这种类型学思考,在旧城更新中就存在着调和历史结构与现代结构矛盾对立的可能,其关键点在于能否析出新旧结构(类型)中所蕴含着的共同"原型"。美国式的思考和行动往往更加实用主义,比如哥伦比亚大学出版的《加法建筑学——设计与规则》(The Architecture of Additions: Design and Regulation)一书,以欧美近半个多世纪来的大量实例,评介了历史空间在新旧交融中生长的设计方法及规则,意图说明城市建筑总是在不断地叠加中进化的,但处理新旧关系需要加以约束和限定。[15]从该书所举实例的情况看,这些约束和限定,仍给设计创意留下了很大的发挥空间,相对性和选择性是极强的。

实际上，历史空间再生应当是在专业理想、业主欲求和公众利益三者间进行权衡与调适的创新性活动。再生的前提是适应性，可归纳为三个方面：一为社会的适应性。由于复杂的权益关系，历史空间再生是一项多方参与的社会工程，要解决的相关问题包括：参与的层面与范围如何确定；参与的社会机制和组织形态如何形成；如何通过策划与规划，将再生工程纳入所在区域经济与社会发展的系统，密切关联所在社区生活及其文化品质的提升等。二为经济的适应性。历史空间不但是文化遗产，也是文化资产，除了政府通过保护法规和税收政策进行调控外，还必须在各权益攸关方的成本—效益间寻求平衡，包括资金来源、容积率补偿、文化与商业项目的适度开发等，并要与所在区域的发展形成联动关系。三为环境的适应性。如何使历史建筑的再生与周边环境要素(包括地貌、景观、交通、建筑等)相适应，如何整合新旧空间肌理，使之更为宜居，是历史空间再生的艰巨挑战。

在中国此方面的尝试中，20世纪80年代末北京菊儿胡同改造工程颇具典型性。该工程以一个仅仅2 700 m^{2}的四合院建筑更新为样板，提出了一种探索的途径。这一工程延续了北京胡同原有的历史结构和肌理，在四合院原型基础上成倍拓展了居住空间，大幅改善了居住条件。[16]十载后的上海黄陂南路"新天地"项目，将占地30 000 m^{2}的石库门住宅及所在弄堂，以保护与更新的名义，改造成了休闲观光的酒吧街坊。虽然这种改变居住用途的绅士化(gentrification)更新颇具争议，但作为特殊的个案，并未成为一种普适的模式。其积极意义是保存了所在街区的里弄空间肌理，活化了其中早已衰败不堪的生活形态。[14]在如今城市地价飙升、保护与发展相冲突、各利益攸关方博弈趋于激烈的现实面前，旧城改造的运作愈来愈举步维艰，而"有机更新"如何适应这些新的情况，是国内外都在关注和探讨的焦点问题。

从上述分析中可以得出几点基本的结论：现代性促成了城乡改造中的物质现代化，也造成了历史空间存弃的失衡和失控，忽视甚至去掉了其所承载的民族、地域历史身份和文化多样性(diversity)。在经济和文化全球化的当下，传统城乡改造有必要坚持反思现代性的历史主义观念，保持各地文化多样性的地域主义立场。城乡改造的本质是文明转型进化的方式，而传统与现代的关系实应转化为保护与创新的权衡。这里所谓的"保护"，从广义的城乡建设领域看，其实就是对现代性激进改造的制衡，因而这些问题必然体现于传统与现代、保护与创新，以及全球化与本土化如何相互融合，并转化为"全球在地"(glocalization)的思考与行动。笔者以为，这应是发展中国家文化(包括建筑)演进的价值观所系和策略选择。

参考文献

[1] RIEGL A. The Modern cult of Monuments: Its Character and Its origin[C] // Opposition 25. New Jersey: Princeton University Press, 1982: 21-50.

[2] JOKILEHTO J. What is OUV? [R]. ICOMOS Study. Berlin: Hendrik Babler Babler Bäβler Verlag, 2008: 11-14.

[3] FEILDEN B M. Conservation of Historic Buildings[M]. Burlington: Architectural Press, 2003: 9.

[4] VINNAS S M. Contemporary Theory of Conservation[M]. Oxford: Butterworth-Heinamann, 2005: 213-214.

[5] MADSEN ST TS. Restoration and Anti-Restoration[M]. Oslo: Universitetsforlarget, 1976.

[6] PEVSNER N, FAWCETT J, et al. The Future of the Past[M]. London: Thames and Hudson Ltd., 1976.

[7] RUSKIN J. The Seven Lamps of Architecture [M]. New York: John Wiley, 1849: 161.

[8] JOKILEHTO J. A History of Architectural Conservation [M]. Oxford: Butterworth-Heinamann, 1999: 219-223.

[9] 梁思成. 中国建筑史[M]. 天津: 百花文艺出版社, 2005: 12.

[10] 常青. 历史建筑修复的"真实性"批判[J]. 时代建筑, 2009(3): 118-121.

[11] 常青. 桑珠孜宗堡历史变迁及修复工程辑要[J]. 建筑学报, 2011(5): 1-9.

[12] 芒福德. 城市文化[M]. 宋俊岭, 李翔宁, 周鸣浩, 译. 北京: 中国建筑工业出版社, 2009: 445-446.

[13] 塔夫里. 建筑学的理论和历史[M]. 郑时龄, 译. 北京: 中国建筑工业出版社, 1991: 41-43.

[14] 常青. 旧改中的上海建筑及其都市历史语境[J]. 建筑学报, 2009(10): 23-28.

[15] BYARD PAUL SPENCER. The Architecture of Additions: Design and Regulation[M]. New York: W. W. Nortin & Company, 1998.

[16] 吴良镛. 北京旧城居住区的整治途径: 城市细胞的有机更新与"新四合院"的探索[J]. 建筑学报, 1989(7): 11-18.

历史城市保护方法二探：让地层说话
——以扬州城址的保护范围和特色保护策略为例

Another Discussion of the Methodologies Applied in Protecting a Historical City That Let the Stratum Talk: A Case of Protection Zoning for the Old Sites and Features of Historical City Yangzhou

陈薇 教授
东南大学建筑学院
Prof. Chen Wei
School of Architecture, Southeast University

Stratum, an important archeological term, can be employed to unveil the historical facts lying there. A historical city would have a range of "cascades" that have stored what had happened over time. "Let the stratum talk" would enable history to speak, unveiling what had happened in a historical city. This paper discusses a range of issues concerning the protection of the national heritage Yangzhou old sites (from Sui-Tang to Song Dynasties) and features of historical city Yangzhou using a combined methodology of cascading, revealing, matching and featuring.

一、层叠

中国历史城市通常有一个突出现象和重要特征，曰"层叠"，用考古学的概念说，"地层"十分丰富。如北京，由辽燕京、金中都，到元大都、明清北京，城址有迁，但屡有层叠，紫禁城内外应至少包括有辽代及其以后的历代叠压；如西安，由秦咸阳、汉长安、隋唐长安，到明清西安，城址层叠最丰处，历代多有踪迹；如南京，由孙吴建业到六朝建康，从五代南唐金陵到宋代建康，从明初南京到近代首都，城址从西往东拓展，层叠及错位发展关系十分清晰；如杭州，历史上基本沿凤凰山及西湖东侧呈现自南而北再向东的发展趋势，因而凤凰山和西湖东侧层叠最复杂。

因此，我们在描述历史城市的特色时，其实十分困难。北京的特色是明清的大屋顶？西安的特色是唐风？南京的特色是秦淮风貌？杭州的特色是南宋遗风？当我们在以历史上最辉煌的或者当今留存较好的城市风貌和特色来描述或扩大到一座历史城市时，抑或以此来指导城市的特色发展时，便显得粗犷有余。因为这种大而化之，会抹杀丰富的历史，含糊城市特定区域或场所的微妙，消解历史城市的文化多元，简化城市发展的历史轨迹。那么什么方法可以解忧？唯有"杜康"——让地层说话，因为地层是层叠型历史城市的酒酿。

"地层"来自考古学，即依托地层揭示的器物承载的文化和地层土壤混杂的事件堆积，可以交叉排比建立广大时空范围的人类古代遗存演变的时空体系。对于历史城市而言，让地层说话，就是让地层表达出城市的时空体系和关系；对于历史城市的特色而言，让地层说话，就是针对特定场所，揭示出此地曾经存在的历史信息、功能属性和时间逻辑。因此，让地层说话，就是比较客观和真实地道出历史城市的厚度和范围、多元文化及其定位,从而有助于划定保护范围,并建立历史城市保护尤其是特色保护的策略,是关于历史城市保护方法的一种探索。

本文试以历史城市扬州为研究对象,经过慎重选择。第一,古都尽管历史层叠现象突出,但在变化过程中,人为因素较强,如果按考古学的地层学理论,地层母体裹挟的事件信息遗存较多,比较复杂,寻找出规律非一文可以概括;第二,层叠少、特色鲜明的历史城市(近代型如上海、职能型如自贡、名胜型如桂林、风貌型如平遥、民族型如拉萨),不特别适合和需要采用地层学方法;第三,历史悠久的一般地方城市的特色保护,是我们今天面临的工作重点和难点,其中扬州首当其冲,因为整个"扬州城遗址(隋至宋)"是全国重点文物保护单位①,在地方城市中仅此一例,而在唐代扬州便有"扬一益二"之称②,其保护具有的深度、难度和广度,如果能兼顾好,对一般地方城市则有四两拨千斤的启示意义。

扬州富有历史积淀的城墙

扬州是典型的层叠型历史城市,自春秋建邗城始,经历3 000余年的演变发展,至今在历史城市保护方面,成就突出,尤其在整体管理和控制方面,于全国独树一帜,但在城市特色方面,是当今值得研究推敲和细化完善的重要内容。2007年受扬州市政府委托,由东南大学建筑设计研究院承担"扬州城遗址(隋—宋)保护规划"③,2011年经国家文物局组织专家组评审正式通过。本文以此为平台和依据进行延伸探讨,以便更加有效和直接地推进历史城市保护。

二、拉开

"扬州城遗址(隋至宋)"(以下简称"扬州城遗址")位于今扬州蜀冈上下,范围包括现老城区及西北郊部分,面积约18.25 km²,是超大的保护单位,也是一大遗址。遗址上既有保护甚好的位于北部的蜀冈子城遗迹,又有南部现代的城市生活。只有拉开扬州的层叠,结合文献和考古成果,才可以建立扬州历史城市的时段层在空间上的定位。

1. 第一阶段(春秋至南北朝时期):蜀冈范围建邗城、广陵、都广陵

周武王三年(约公元前1044年)大封诸侯,以其子封于干,遂成为西周的封国属地,称为邗国。周敬王三十四年(公元前486年),吴王夫差为北上伐齐的军事目的,并伴随沟通长江和淮河的邗沟开凿,建造邗城,是扬州筑城之始,位于蜀冈高地。当时长江很宽,紧逼蜀冈。

周元王三年(公元前473年),吴被越所灭,邗归越。周显王三十五年(公元前334年),楚破越,杀越王,邗归楚,置县,称广陵。楚怀王十年(公元前319年),对吴筑邗城加以修筑,为广陵城之始。经考古发现,现蜀冈上存在着的城分为两部分,称之为东城和西城,两部分之和即汉广陵城。

汉高祖十二年(公元前195年),高祖以荆国故地封刘濞为吴王,"都广陵",在封国内开凿盐运河,增筑广陵城,这是扬州第三次筑城记载。刘濞死后,置江都国于广陵。汉元狩二年(公元前121年)改为广陵郡。汉元狩六年(公元前117年)复置广陵国。东汉时先复国后改郡。汉广陵经过刘氏诸侯王400余年的营造,已成为临江大都会。东汉末年黄巾起义,两晋交替,魏人南侵,刘宋王朝内部碾杀,经侯景叛乱使广陵古城尽遭兵火焚毁,成为一座"芜城"。东晋废帝太和四年(公元369年)和刘宋孝武帝大明二年(公元458年)也曾先后筑城,近年来考古也发现在今蜀冈下扬州城内有六朝青瓷出土④,说明六朝时人们已居住

---

① "扬州城遗址(隋至宋)"1996年11月20日由国务院公布为第四批全国重点文物保护单位。
② "富庶甲天下,时人称扬一益二。"《资治通鉴》中唐昭宗景福元年条。
③ 《全国重点文物保护单位——扬州城遗址(隋至宋)保护规划(2010—2030)》,项目负责:陈薇,项目参加:陈薇、钟行明、张剑葳、刘妍、孟超、薛垲、祁昭。
④ 罗宗真,《扬州唐代古河道等的发现和有关问题的探讨》,载《文物》,1980年3期。

于蜀冈下并从事生产活动了。

2. 第二阶段（隋唐时期）：蜀冈上下建江都郡、扬州

隋代文帝时始广陵郡被扬州之名，时人名江都，沿用汉、六朝广陵城故址，并为宫城所在地。继六朝，隋代蜀冈下平原不断发展，最重要的就是隋炀帝开凿大运河，"于扬州开山阳渎，以通漕运"①，交通便利的江都有了面江、背淮、临海、跨河的巨大优势，遂使江都迅速发展繁荣起来，"炀帝巡幸乘龙舟而往江都"以后，"公家漕运，私行商旅，舳舻相继"②，盛世繁华可见一斑。这不仅带来人口聚集和城市范围扩大，也使城市性质产生变化，由军事城市转为商业都市。

此时城市范围扩大。在考古调查中，发现子城下的地带有东西相对的门址，有学者认为其形制与位于蜀冈上的隋宫城南门相近，而与唐罗城内另外一些仅有一门洞的门址存在一定差别，有可能是隋代遗址。③ 在傅熹年先生的《中国古代城市规划建筑群布局及建筑设计方法研究》一书中对隋代江都城做了较详细的复原，书中明确提出隋代罗城的大小。④

唐代罗城继续发展，由于长江泥沙在江北的淤积，平原扩大，加强了蜀冈下的活动和聚落向南部的发展。同时，唐王朝定都长安，经济仰仗于江淮："今赋出天下，江南居十九。"⑤江都位于南北水路交通之要冲长江与运河的交汇点，成为重要的江南物资转运集散港埠，蜀冈下河道两侧逐渐形成市街和码头，并形成了初步的路、桥布局，至中晚唐在罗城修筑城池并规划街道，定名扬州也是在这时期。⑥

这样，唐代扬州遂由子城和罗城组成。子城在蜀冈上，沿用汉、六朝广陵城址⑦，罗城范围比隋代进一步扩大，子罗两城呈"吕"字形布局，其范围经考古探明，四至已经明确。

3. 第三阶段（五代至宋时期）：唐扬州的东南-西北对角线先后成周小城、宋三城

唐末五代扬州城遭战火洗劫，周世宗占据扬州时，认为城大空虚难守，"遂于故城内就东南别筑新垒"，称周小城。⑧

北宋扬州城沿用周小城，称为"宋大城"。宋室南渡后扬州成南宋皇室北门，军事防御地位十分突出。南宋建炎元年（1127年）宋高宗南迁扬州，对原北宋州城进行修筑和加固，淳熙二年（1175年）郭棣知扬州，认为蜀冈上的汉唐故城"凭高临下，四面险围"，可以据以防守来犯之金兵，遂在蜀冈唐子城废墟上修筑"宝寨城"（又名宝祐城、堡城），与作为州城的宋大城南北对峙；不久又在其间筑夹城，疏两濠，⑨从而形成南宋扬州三城——宋大城、宝祐城和夹城的格局，使宋大城的防御能力更加坚固⑩，城门均有瓮城，考古成果证实形制完善，为南方瓮城之先。元兵久攻扬州不下，也说明宋城军事防御能力很强。

4. 第四阶段（元明清时期）：南缩为扬州路、扬州府

元代扬州城袭用宋大城，蜀冈上的宝祐城以及夹城逐渐荒废。元至正十七年（公元1357年），扬州归朱元璋所有，命张德林守扬州，"以旧城虚旷难守，乃截城西南隅，筑而守之"⑪，形成明初的扬州路。嘉靖

---

① 《隋书·卷一·帝纪第一高祖上》。
② 《元和郡县志·五·汴河》。
③ 中国社会科学考古研究所、南京博物院、扬州市文化局、扬州城考古队：《扬州城考古工作简报》，载《考古》，1990年1期：自象鼻桥附近蜀冈南沿经桑树脚向南至扬州市第二人民医院西南角的一道南北向的土岗，另外在唐城考古钻探中，位于双桥乡的杨家庄西和江苏省化工学校校园内发现了东西相对的两座三门洞的城门址。
④ 傅熹年《中国古代城市规划、建筑群布局及建筑设计方法研究》，中国建筑工业出版社，2001年9月第一版，2003年2月第二次印刷。
⑤ 《全唐文·卷五五五》之韩愈的《送陆歙州诗序》。
⑥ 扬州城考古队，《扬州城考古工作简报》，载《考古》，1990年1期："罗城从初步发掘资料来看，未见隋唐以前的遗迹，初步判定建于中唐或晚唐"；又见王勤金，《扬州唐宋城址的发现》，东南文化（2001年增刊）《扬州博物馆建馆五十周年纪念文集》："在解剖罗城北城冈时，城墙基之下发现有唐代墓葬群，表明罗城之始建只能晚于唐早期"。唐罗城的城墙建造最早的文献记载为《资治通鉴·卷二二九》云："唐建中四年（783年）十一月，淮南节度使陈少游将兵讨李希烈，屯盱眙，闻朱泚作乱，归广陵，修堑垒，缮甲兵。"与考古发掘的结论大致相同。
⑦ 南京博物院：《扬州古城1978年调查发掘简报》，载《文物》，1979年9期。
⑧ 《旧五代史·卷一百一十八·周书第九·世宗纪五》，显德五年（958年）二月。
⑨ 王象之：《舆地纪胜·卷三七》扬州新旧城。
⑩ [清]李斗撰，周春东注，《扬州画舫录》，山东友谊出版社，2001年5月，卷七《城南录》：（扬州）"开元（713—741年）以后襟喉要，乾道（1165—1173年）之间城堡兴。"
⑪ 参见：《明太祖洪武实录》。

三十五年(1556年),在明旧城之东扩建新城,两城合并成为明城,称扬州府。清沿用明城,在扬州设立扬州府,以江都县为府治。1916年拆除新旧河的隔墙,使新旧城联为一体。20世纪50年代拆除城墙,建成环城路。

可以发现,扬州城的发展,在时间梯度上基本连续不断,而落实在空间上,则呈现自北而南、由高而低的变化过程。在整个扬州历史上,唐城规模最大,也是公布为全国重点文物保护单位的范围,与扬州历史上的辉煌时期吻合。而在两区域,层叠最为丰富:一为蜀冈,宋代及其以前,历代叠压,宋代以后也有小规模建设;二为东南,即扬州老城部分,唐代以后持续叠压。另两区域发展时间不连续:一是蜀冈下、老城以北、宋代夹城及东西部分;二是宋大城西部。这两部分宋代以后几为废地,除清代瘦西湖建设景观,只是近现代才有比较高密度的发展和层叠。

三、对位

1. 历史对位

将扬州的地层拉开,除凸显扬州城址历史发展的时间梯度和空间关系外,还伴随展现出城市的环境特征和结构特征。对于扬州这样和运河密切关联的历史城市而言,这两者集中表现在水系和道路上:水系主要和运河及城壕有关,道路则主要和沿河或连接城门有关。如此又推衍发现重要的建筑考古遗址均和水系、城址、道路密切关联,如寺庙遗址。它们是一个系统,这很像考古学中的"缀合"式研究(Conjunctive Approach)[①],注重见物见人——环境考古与聚落考古结合。

落实在我们的工作中,并不是条分缕析地运用什么学派,而是让地层说话,即让扬州历史城市最值得保护的遗址遗迹、历史环境、城市结构及其连带的文化信息,通过对位,可以确定保护对象,并由此划定保护范围。

值得一提的是扬州水系。大约东晋、南朝时,广陵附近江岸南移,长江北岸边滩大幅度淤长,蜀冈下形成"土甚平旷"[②]的长江冲积平原。广陵太守陈敏改建了邗沟南端,由西南的欧阳埭引水。欧阳埭在现在江苏仪征市,引水口距广陵城六十里[③],如此将运河联系上长江,以保证有效漕运。

唐代建罗城,原邗沟古道则成为城市内繁华的市河,其西侧还有一条南北向的运河,称保障河,是一条官河,保障城内繁忙交通和商业运输的畅通。这时沟通扬州以南长江和以北淮河的运河绕城市东南而过。

周世宗时新筑的城市比唐城小许多,周小城范围北壕即柴河,南濠、东濠为运河,西侧以保障河作为护城河。[④] 继后周小城,宋三城中的宋大城西侧的护城河,继续利用了唐代保障河的南段。

元末保障河西北颓圯,明嘉靖十八年(1539年)疏浚[⑤],变成水面略宽的保障湖。其实这也是后来著名瘦西湖的主体。清代将保障河(湖)和唐代西护城河的北段进行东西向的联系,遂成瘦西湖。

这使得理解瘦西湖之所以"瘦"的真实缘由——由城市河系利用而来,也进一步明确即使我们保护的对象是扬州隋至宋的城址,但瘦西湖必须纳入。同理,相关的研究经由拉开和对位,便确定了保护对象,包括城墙及城门遗址、河道及其相关水系、道路、重要建筑遗址。

2. 现状对位

扬州在历史城市保护管理方面有比较严格的相关规定,是保证扬州保护做得比较好的根本。但是由于历史的原因,并不重视唐代这样范围的大城市遗址的保护,而主要成就体现在对于老城(明清城)的历史文化街区保护和蜀冈瘦西湖风景区的管理上。对于前者,保护对象比较支离破碎,特别是对该区域整体层

---

① Walter Taylor, 1948, *A Study of Archaeology*. Southern lllinois University Press.
② 参见:《南齐书卷·十四·州郡志上》。
③ "其水上承欧阳,引江入埭,六十里至广陵城",载刘文淇《扬州水道记》。
④ (万历)《江都县志》古迹。
⑤ 参见:《天一阁藏明代方志选刊·嘉靖淮扬志·军政志》,1963年9月,上海古籍书店据宁波天一阁藏明嘉靖残本景印,上海古籍书店影印,1981年11月重印。

叠的历史厚度重视不够,对于明清历史风貌关注较多;对于后者,划线范围比较随意,管理不够严格和细致。这些都是在前面研究的基础上,通过现状对位发现的问题。

同时,扬州城址独具的文物价值、真实性、完整性、延续性,和现状也具有相当大的距离,我们除逐一展开现状评估外,更和历史比对来发现问题和距离,如对城门的评估,包括历史图纸、现状调查、病害分析等,作为进一步建立相关保护措施的基准和平台。

对于被现代建筑叠压的遗址上的建筑,通过层高、基础埋深的判断,逆向推测原有遗址存在的可能性,作为确立进一步保护管理措施的参照。

3. 保护范围

在对扬州历史城市进行了时空对位后,再经由对历史上扬州城址的价值评估和考古对位,可以确定保护对象的构成。进一步地,通过现状评估和具体而落实的对位,形成比较明确的保护范围,并修正和完善原有不同层级的保护范围和管理规定,在更严格、更合理、更完整、更可操作的原则上,统一了原来不同管理部门制定的区划和规定。

譬如,对于扬州城址的东南部分——老城,原有的历史文化街区划定大致以现状可以考察到的明清建筑及其风貌保存为原则,但当拉开城市地层了解到它层叠的厚重和丰富,显然就不应当简单以如今可以看到的现状为保护对象和范围,而是整体地划出保护范围。而对于叠加在城址(隋至宋)上以后的保护对象和历史文化街区,经过重新审定后调整和沿用原来管理规定内容使之合理。

再如,原来子城保护范围划定较早,随着近年考古成果的充实和对位,发现有些城址在范围以外,得不到很好保护,同时原有划定范围没有考虑历史环境,如城河甚少被整体地划入。另外,蜀冈瘦西湖风景区划线缺少科学依据,管理规定中对于文物保护单位的严格性和历史厚重及复杂性的表达也有欠缺。这次均统一调整在保护范围的划定中。

而对于历史上废弃较早、后来已叠压并扰动了历史地层的现代建筑的区域,此次参照历史文化名城的建设控制高度进行控制,但考虑城市视廊,即保证从蜀冈往南观览,可以领略到历史时序的城市变化与层次。

四、特色

中国层叠型的历史城市,其魅力在于一座城就表达了几个朝代的更迭和变化、物质和事件的交错、时间和空间的运转,所以落实在具体的城市特色上会是丰富的,在城市具体场所上会是独特的,扬州更是如此。

从层叠在地层上最有价值和未经破坏的情形看,扬州基本可以划定几个特色区域:(1)蜀冈子城范围:汉唐遗址区;(2)夹城并宋大城北部:宋代遗址及历史环境区;(3)老城区:明清历史风貌区为主;(4)城市结构的存留:城墙沿线、水系沿线、道路沿线。

结合城市的地形和地貌、历史存留和现状、不同时期的特色表达,可以相应确定扬州历史城市保护工作的策略重点:(1)对唐子城范围建议形成遗址公园:进行进一步考古并结合高地的历史环境进行遗址的真实性表达;2. 对夹城及其周边范围建议形成生态湿地公园:对历史上形成的低洼湿地环境进行严格控制,结合风景区规划,对宋代遗址进行适当表达;3. 对明清老城范围建议加强整合:除目前保护较好的明清历史文化街区的风貌外,注重对历代各类型遗址、遗迹、文物单位和历史文化街区的多样性表达,并落实非物质遗产的场所;(4)严格保护城市的结构特色,加强对历史城墙及城门、水系、道路的保护和维护,改善周边环境,选择特色树种。

如此,不仅可以表达出扬州历史城市具有的环境特色、区域特色、多元特色,更重要的还有时空对位和大遗址保护的整体性、真实性及延续性的特点。而通过水系和道路网络,可以沟通历史城市的丰富和特色变化,进行展示,予人感受。

层叠、拉开、对位、特色,是认知历史城市价值和进行保护的一种思维和工作方式,具体到历史城市的某个地段或者某个节点,同样是展开规划和设计的一种恰当的思路和出发点。

比如瘦西湖,如果我们了解它是唐宋城河巧为利用并凿通水系而成的层叠性质,就不应将其简单作为独立的风景区或园林对待和规划,放在历史城市的区位上,拉开、对位,便会了然认识:瘦西湖接近蜀冈段的旷野开阔趣味,是以唐代的城市背景为底色的;而"虹桥"毗邻酒家,附近码头商业活动频繁,是由于此段位于元明旧城的城壕西北拐角处使然,此段为原来的唐宋保障河,市井繁华;真正造景的主要是清代连接唐宋城河的东西向段,如"白塔晴云"和"五亭桥"等。如此对于瘦西湖在今天的保护及规划,各段的定位就会了然于胸。

又比如扬州南门遗址,经文献记载及考古发掘,唐、宋、元、明、清,历代层叠,历史信息十分丰富,其考古断面的揭示是扬州历史千余年发展的缩影,我们在做南门遗址博物馆时,就运用了拉开、对位的地层学方法,进而将南门的瓮城形制及原有入城通道与博物馆的建筑采光、流线结合,形成呼应和联想,而博物馆建筑特色也不以周围的明清建筑风格为参照,而是本着对本体原有形态整体和真实保护的基本原则,最大可能地进行保护,并和历史环境形成关系,同时为继续考古留下余地。

历史城市保护是复杂但重要和永恒的话题,对于中国历史悠久的层叠型城市,拉开历史,时空对位,便能特色呈现,即从研究出发、从真实落位,以衔接现实的城市多元特色保护为延伸,或许是一条途径。在这一过程中,对历史地层的解读非常关键,因为地层是时段层、文化层、物质层,还是稳定的结构层。

地层是缄默的,让地层说话,历史城市保护思路和工作就会从纷纭繁复的羁绊中轻松起来。

阿巴和加—布达拉—天安门

Afaq Khoja Mausoleum—Potala Palace—Tian'anmen

张之平
中国文化遗产研究院教授级高级工程师
Zhang Zhiping
Professorial Senior Engineer of Chinese Academy of Cultural Heritage

With the cases of Afaq Khoja Mausoleum, Potala Palace and Tian'anmen, the speaker eliminates varied principles applied in different conservation projects, especially concerning the relationship between original and new materials, techniques as well as forms along with historical information.

阿巴和加墓

阿巴和加墓是17世纪中叶建成的,是一个伊斯兰教白山派主教的一家五代72个人的坟墓。这个坟墓是和伊斯兰教的所有的清真寺连在一起的,极具伊斯兰教和新疆特色的。这个建筑实际上是喀什市最老的建筑和最有特色的建筑,也是一个1988年的全国重点保护单位。由于其中埋葬的一个女子,被传说曾经是乾隆的妃子,所以大家也俗称它叫香妃墓,实际上这个香妃和我们熟知的那个香妃并非同一个人。

关于这个建筑,我们找到过1898年一个英国摄影师拍摄的照片,可以看出来这个建筑一直没有大的改变。但是,由于喀什地区是一个地震多发区,所以建筑面临很大的地震威胁。通过1947年的一张照片我们发现,它的穹隆顶曾经发生过坍塌。实际上现在的阿巴和加墓的拱顶是1956年重新建立起来的。但是这个拱顶在建成10多年后,也就是在70年代就开始出现了很多裂缝。20世纪90年代我们做勘察的时候就发现这个裂缝的问题已经严重。这个拱顶是新疆最大的圆拱,它的直径有15米,外径有16米多,高度大概是7.5米,非常高,整个建筑高达20余米。它的内部的裂缝大概的分布情况是每隔1米多就有一个裂缝,已经到了濒危的程度,特别是在地震多发的情况下。

国家文物局经过几个方案的比较,认为必须做一个拆砌。在勘察过程中,我们努力做到在勘察的同时完成物理学分析,看它当时是否已经达到一个临界的状况。在拆砌实施前,我们就认真进行了所有的保护措施。在拆砌的过程当中,我们更清楚地看到了它严重的损坏状况,必须通过工程的措施来进行保护。工程措施主要是结构上的保护,阿巴和加墓的拱顶在1956年修建的时候也是用了一些很巧的方法。因为拱顶下受力最大,所以那里曾经设置了一圈木的圈梁,这个圈梁外面为了防止木头腐朽,还有一个环的两圈铁。但是最后当我们拆的时候,就发现这个木头已经完全脱开了,腐朽严重,这就像桶没有了箍,一定会发生巨大的变化。

在这拆砌的过程中,我们希望采用原始材料,因为按照我们文物保护的原则,应该尽量保持原来的形制、原来的结构、原来的材料以及原来的工艺。在此过程中,我们也要做一些加固的措施,也采用了一些新材料。有一些是实在不行的,比如这两个环梁就不能再用木头的,于是我们在里面加了一些新技术,包括钢筋混凝土,但是还是尽可能地用原来的材料、原来的砖,但是仍然需要保证安全的强度。另外,我们特别重要的一个措施是要当地的民族工人来和我们一起来砌筑。我觉得我非常幸运,在做前期调查的时候就了解到,我们看到当地有一个老先生,他是唯一幸存的参加过1956年砌筑工作的老工人,当时他已经七十岁了,从头到尾参加了我们的砌筑。尽管我和他在语言上不太好沟通,但是我们还是成了非常好的朋友,最后把这个顶封上了以后,结构的问题都解决了。

原来的琉璃花砖是用当地的石膏材料粘贴的,石膏的粘贴力遇水以后会有很大的变化,所以我们想了很多办法来解决这个问题。凡是不了解的东西,我们都提前做了实验。大家一块用传统的方法修护文化遗产,是希望在我们的遗产中更多地保留原来的东西,并真实地留给后人。我们维修的这个屋顶在完工的第二年就经历了一个地震群的群震考验,即经历了7次6级以上的地震,并在三个月不到的时间里,经历了2000多次余震的考验,一直完好无损。这说明我们的方案合理,说明我们砌筑质量合格。更让我们欣慰的是,通过这个过程,我们培养了一支很好的队伍,这些人都有民族的手艺,而且他们又通过这个项目做了很多实验,保持了很多传统,那么大家就更加确信我们应该怎么样去修文物,所以文物保护的理念也越来越科学、越来越完善。

布达拉宫

布达拉宫既是我们国家最重要的历史建筑之一,也是世界文化遗产。所以对这样的遗产,我们就是希望能保持它所有的历史信息和它的价值,尽可能地少改变。因为布达拉宫由红宫、白宫和其他所有附属建筑组成,建在红山之上。建筑利用山,好像长在了山上,山就是它的基座,它就是山的顶部,因此特别好地利用了地形,天设地造地突出了布达拉宫在拉萨河谷的高尚地位。同时,布达拉宫也是历代达赖喇嘛政教合一的办公场所和他们的冬宫。但是布达拉宫比较大的问题就是和山的交接以及西藏地区的地震。它从1642年重新建起来到现在,也已经400年了,所以也有着很大的危险,特别是雨水和自然灾害。

我们常说布达拉宫是一个建筑奇迹,为什么呢?因为在3 700米的高山上建这么大的宫殿,非常不容易,因此对布达拉宫现有的残损状况的勘察和我们对它的维修都是非常大的挑战。首先要把勘测做清楚,大家知道其实布达拉宫在"文化大革命"中周周总理亲自下指示,被完全保护起来,所以它没有受到"文化大革命"的冲击,但是由于它的年久失修,那么它还存在着很多问题,还有很多问题是我们不了解的,所以我们把它分成很多个单元,一个一个地重新去做测绘、做保护。

首先,它的地基基础有比较大的问题。红宫很高,底下有一半以上是基础,基础是建筑稳定最重要的地方,但是因为我们做了施工设计以后,施工队不太懂如何用一些新设备做修缮。这个基础墙是石头和黄泥砌筑的,但是黄泥逐渐松散以后里面空隙很大,为了保证它的安全,我们就配比了适当的黄泥加白灰的砂浆做一些灌注,但由于施工队不会灌注,最后用喷墙的东西乱喷一气,最后搞得包括业主单位和我们的甲方对设计方案都有一些怀疑,所以这个项目是我们做了最多次数施工交底的一个项目,一共做了五次,不断地交换意见。此外,更重要的是我们还需要做一个现场的实验。我们在布达拉宫下面的老城里找到了裂缝来做修补的实验,同时请布达拉宫的工人给我们砌筑了一个试块——一个带裂缝的试块,看看我们到底应该怎么样做好裂缝的修补。在获得了经验之后,我们才开始实行。经过我们的处理,布达拉宫的基础稳固了。而且,我们经过了这个培训学习以后,原来还对这个灌浆技术非常怀疑的人也都接受了它。经过了培训,很多布达拉宫的小工掌握了我们的这种技术,他们也把这种技术用到了平时的修补与保养之中。

天安门

天安门的案例和我们刚才用新的材料所做的有一点不同。天安门是北京城的重要的一个南门,建于明永乐十五年(1417年)。因为城门楼的年久失修,在1970年城楼重建了,留下了重建的标记。它的所有瓦当用的都不是龙纹而是葵花,这个也是典型的"文化革命"的痕迹。当时有些老的、年纪大的希望我们把它恢复成原来皇家的形制,也就是龙的纹饰,但是我们觉得这个信息应该保存,因为它就是"文化大革命"

时建的，所以就把我们城楼的信息保存了。

  但是天安门的主要问题是城台的问题。城台在1970年，为了防水，当时采用了新材料，打了一个大概五六十厘米的混凝土，上下还做了防水，然而这个城台从第二年开始就一直有渗漏。我们终于把它给打掉了以后，一直看到了明代的城墙砖。这样我们把现代的不合理的东西恢复到了传统的做法，当然还增加了一些新型的无机防水。总的来说，现代的人文干预还是要尽量少一点。通过我们和施工队不断的磨合，他们也越来越提高了对传统工艺的一个信任，其实我们很多传统的东西不能轻易否定，凡是传统的，存在到今天的都是合理的，而有时候你觉得不合理是因为我们自己没有认识到它的合理性。

城市发展与遗产保护二元架构的思考

Reflections on the Duality of Urban Development & Heritage Conservation

郭粤梅 教授
联合国教科文组织工业遗产教席持有人
Prof. Guo Yuemei
Holder, UNESCO Chair on Industrial Heritage

This paper analyses the duality of urban development and heritage conservation using the case of the inventory and conservation planning of post-1949 heritage buildings in Jiang'an District, Wuhan. It elaborates the dual juxtaposition of the monumental and the everyday, the governmental and the non-governmental, the municipal and the intramural, and theoretically international and the practically domestic.

一、总述

保护与发展是一个大的"二元"的架构。笔者认为,在这个大的架构下,在资源认定、组织架构和展示利用方面,都有一些相辅相成的所谓二元结构。

本论文以"江岸区1949年后优秀建筑资源调查和保护规划"为例进行阐述。在资源认定方面,认定的对象开始从经典建筑向社区认同的日常建筑转变,从文物系统主导的文物保护单位拓展到建设系统主导的历史建筑和工业遗产建筑;在组织架构方面,从单一的政府组织向政府组织与非政府组织共同参与的转变,从大学与城市割裂的状态向大学与城市合作并逐步走向深度合作状态的转变;在展示利用方面,也开始从单纯的博物馆式保护向保护与利用并重转化,并开始引入历史性城镇景观和国际建筑展等国际理念在中国的实践。

图1 江岸区1949年后优秀建筑资源空间分布

二、江岸区新中国成立后优秀建筑调查

对于武汉而言,截至2016年,武汉共有优秀历史建筑175处,相较于上海的1 058处,天津的910处,这样的建筑遗产数量与超大城市和文化之城并不相称,武汉作为中国近代重要的城市,其建筑遗产数量应远远大于现公布的数量。

从2014年起,武汉市国土资源和规划局率先在全市范围内进行1949年后优秀建筑资源调查,业已完成了武昌、江岸、江汉、硚口、青山、汉阳等7个中心城区的调查工作,其前瞻性、敏锐性和学术性在全国范围内首屈一指。下面以江岸区为例,重点阐述本文的观点。

江岸区是武汉市中心城区之一,位于长江以北,周边与江汉区、黄陂区、东西湖区相连,与武昌区、青山区、洪山区隔江相望。

江岸区城市建设活动最早可追溯到1861年汉口开埠,之后历经了1911年辛亥革命、1927年武汉国民政府成立、1938年武汉沦陷、1949年武汉解放,以及1952年正式设立江岸区,再到1978年十一届三中全会召开等6个重要的时间节点。从江岸区现有的历史建筑保护级别和数量来看,自1861年汉口开埠,城市活动正式开始到1949年武汉解放,历经88年,共产生优秀历史建筑171处,从1949年武汉解放到2015年,总计66年,共产生优秀历史建筑10处。

为最大限度地保证资源调查的完整性和准确性,本次资源调查的整个过程可分为文献研究、现场踏勘、行政复核和专家访谈四个阶段。在对优秀历史建筑调研过程中从武汉城市建设出发,以武汉市城市发展为研究背景,以江岸区城市发展为研究对象,以江岸区城市拓展区为重点区域,以新中国成立后重点建设项目为主要调研点进行调查。

武汉市新中国成立后城市建设中在"一五"和"二五"期间共布置有13处重点项目,其中在江岸区重点建设了堤角工业区(以武汉市肉类联合加工厂为代表),也正是在"一五"期间,武汉市开始由一个商业比重很大的消费型城市,转变成为我国内地重要的社会主义工业城市。

江岸区的城市发展也随着工业的发展进行了拓展,从1950年原汉口租界区范围逐渐拓展到堤角,东侧直抵长江,南侧以江汉路与江汉区相邻,西侧跨过解放大道逐步向外拓展。从1952年武汉市江岸区行政示意图中可以看到,除了工业项目建设,江岸区内另外一个较大的建设类型为军工类项目的建设,从空军医院到总后基地的建设,江岸区的军工类建设主要围绕解放公园向西北方向拓展。

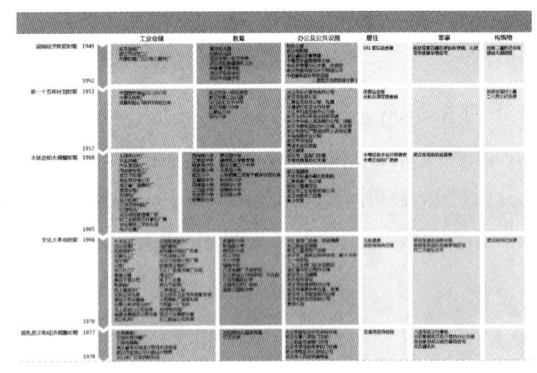

图2 江岸区优秀建筑资源时间分布

通过对比1955年和1987年的地图,可清晰地看出江岸区的主要建设区域位于解放大道及丹水池至堤角一带两大片区。

通过对城市发展的解读,结合实地踏勘,本研究对江岸区的新中国成立后优秀建筑进行了空间及时间总结。

从空间分布来看,教育及科研设施主要分布在建成区内,这一时期的教育及科研设施建筑体量较少,主要服务周边居民。

工业与仓储建筑分布在沿长江及中山大道带,呈带状分布,其中位于丹水池至堤角区域的建筑规模较大,特别是丹水池处的仓储建筑与铁路相结合,形成规模宏大有铁路转运的仓库群。

居住类建筑在这一时期较少,新中国成立后至1978年,社会生活围绕着"先生产后生活"的观念进行,住宅主要围绕工厂建设。其中单独建设的居住建筑主要为市委住宅楼等一些政府部门或无生产职能的国有企业宿舍。

军事建筑为保密性建筑,在本次调研中无法进入,但从文献资料和地图上可以看出该类建筑基本上还是以解放公园为中心,向后湖方向发展。该类建筑也是本次调研过程中碰到的建筑质量较好、建筑艺术较高的一类。

办公、医疗及其他建筑主要分布在建成区及解放大道以北两处区域,该类建筑体量一般都不大,特别是在建成区内的建筑,主要以拆除原建筑并以原建筑为基地进行建设,在解放大道以北区域建设了体量较大的建筑,如长江勘测设计院办公楼、武汉市青少年宫、武汉剧院等建筑。

三、思考

资源认定:文化遗产保护的研究与实践经历了一个漫长的发展演变过程,早在古罗马时期,一些经典的希腊庙宇类建筑，就被认定为需要被保护的对象。直到"二战"前，建筑遗产保护的对象都集中于著名的"经典建筑单体"，譬如古建筑废墟、中世纪宗教建筑、古堡等。而自1964年《威尼斯宪章》出台后，"历史纪念物"的概念则由"伟大的艺术作品"拓展到"随时光流逝而获得文化意义的过去一些较为朴实的作品"即大众建筑领域，通俗地说也就是"日常建筑"。放眼国内，遗产的认定也由最初文物系统所管理的文物，逐步拓展到住建部门在全国范围内所开展的针对一系列历史建筑、工业建筑的遗产认定与保护。

"江岸区新中国成立后优秀建筑资源调查和保护规划"的核心体现了资源认定的二元架构，即从纪念性经典建筑到社区认同日常建筑的并立。

组织架构：遗产保护的架构首先是政府主导自上而下的，正如我刚刚所说，针对的仅是很小范围的"经典建筑"，而对于"日常建筑"保护的推动则更多的来自社区运动所产生的自下而上的方式。一些具有价值认同和相同城市记忆的人群逐步集聚，成立非政府组织，在他们的努力下实现了一些最为经典的城市发展与遗产保护案例，譬如我们所熟知的纽约"高线公园"，正是在纽约FHL（高线之友）组织的大力保护下，免于拆毁，实现重生（建成空中花园走廊），最终为纽约赢得了巨大的社会经济效益，成为创意设计与遗产保护的典范。

我们一直在思考，武汉可以怎么做？2015年，在武汉市政府的支持下成立了"武汉共享遗产研究会"，这是一个兼具学术性和专业性的非营利性社会团体，由积极投身于本地文化遗产保护与发展的专家、学者和相关设计单位、科研院所、高等院校、行业研究会及其它相关企事业单位自愿组成，在长期的积累中持续研究，建立本地专家智库，逐步完善地方遗产保护的法律法规。

另一方面，我们也在探索，武汉的高校资源可以为武汉做什么？2016年，中信建筑设计研究总院与华中科技大学联合，成功申报了"联合国教科文组织工业遗产教席"，整合大学与城市的资源，将研究与实践相结合，成为武汉与国际对接的重要窗口。

研究会的成立、教席的成功申报，实现了从政府组织到非政府组织以及大学与城市的融合促进。

展示利用：遗产保护并不是为保护而保护。2010年上海世博会提出"城市，让生活更美好"。同样，遗产，也应当是让我们的生活更加美好。联合国教科文组织所提倡的"可持续发展"，不仅是环境、经济，还包含有文化，而遗产便是作为文化传承最好的物质载体。去年"无界论坛"的主题是"创意城市与文化遗产"，讨论的就是如何更好地理解、运用国际理念，在中国的实践中尝试、创新，从而实现文化的诠释与延续，让我们少走弯路。

2005年，联合国教科文组织在世界遗产与当代国际会议上首次提出"历史性城镇景观HUL"的概念，并于2011年正式通过《关于城市历史景观的建议书》，这是一种面对当代城市历史地段保护与更新的城市遗产管理办法，试图将保护与发展相结合，探索一种更加可持续的城市发展途径。

HUL认为城市是一个不断进化的有机体，是历史分层积淀的结果，以动态的视角来看待历史的"过程"性和"层次"性，强调从更加广泛的城市背景与地理环境中看待价值，将城市遗产保护目标与社会和经济发展目标相结合。

它提出六大具体方法步骤，全面整合了原有遗产保护研究与管理的各类方法，既强调遗产保护真实性与完整性，同时也适应现代城市发展，试图寻找保护与发展的创新路径。

联合国教科文组织连续十多年一直在进行历史性城镇景观概念的推广与试行，目前在全球范围内已有多个试点，它们遵循HUL的理念，结合自身的文化特色与遗产资源进行不同尝试。

"遗产化"：一个发展中的复杂进程
"Heritagization": A Complex Evolving Process

高曼士 教授

比利时鲁汶大学雷蒙德·勒迈尔国际保护中心

Prof. Thomas Coomans

Raymond Lemaire International Conservation Center, KU Leuven, Belgium

Heritagisation is the process whereby a relic that is not heritage gradually becomes heritage. This process is based on the awareness of heritage values, which could vary according to the contexts and result in different kinds of protections and uses.

"遗产化"是一个比较新的概念,体现的是一个不断发展不断变化的复杂过程。现在许多建筑不能被人们认定为建筑遗产,一些建筑正在经历申报、评定等程序,被定义为建筑遗产,甚至是世界遗产。因此,我们就需要了解是什么样的运作机制使得建筑被认定为建筑遗产。建筑遗产按照不同的价值认定分为几个层级,一些是一般的历史建筑,一些是市级省级的,在某种情况下它同样会变成国家级。还有一种情况,就是更加杰出的遗产会被我们称之为世界遗产。

所以,遗产化是建筑被认定遗产甚至不同级别遗产的一个过程。在一些地方的遗产变成更高级的遗产或者说是世界遗产这个变化过程中,到底是谁在决定这个变化,为什么会有这样的一个变化,又是在什么时间决定的这样一个层级的变化。总结起来,即三个非常基本的问题,即"what""who""why"。第一个问题是 what,什么是遗产化,通过什么样的方式来评估文化遗产价值。第二个问题是关于人的,它关注的是哪些人参与了文化遗产认定的过程。最后一个问题是为什么,即为什么我们要做这样一个文化遗产化的过程?

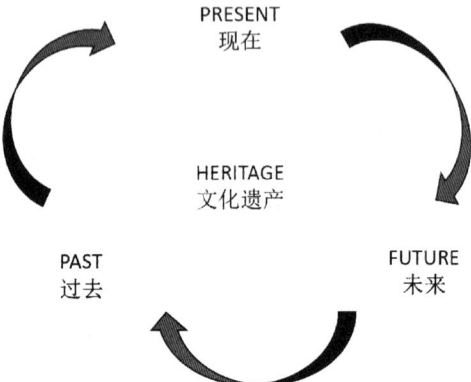

"Heritagization": a Complex Evolving Process
"遗产化"：一个发展中的复杂进程

1. What——什么是遗产化

遗产化的过程是一个相当复杂的过程,也是一个永远不会停息的动态过程。每一个新生时代下的人们,会有自己对文化遗产的理解和认识,他们会用自己的眼光衡量过去,他们也会用这样的模式不断来创造"遗产化"这样一个过程。因此我们现在所做的关于文化遗产保护工作都是与我们现在的语境密切相关的,我们知道我们现在在保护什么,但是我们不知道的是我们现在保护的东西,五十年后或者一百年后会处于一种怎样的境地。

这里提到一个概念,即"遗产时间",它和一般人在现实生活中理解的时间是不一样的,要比现实生活中的时间慢很多,因为建筑遗产本身承载着历史记忆,伴随着时间记录着过去、现在甚至未来的信息。

案例——布鲁塞尔歌剧院,在修复的过程中,各相关方都参与到了这个工作,因为剧院本身对技术要求很高,在建造设计甚至后期改扩建的过程中,不仅需要对应景观视线,同时要考虑到声学,建筑考古学家通过不同的资料来源能够判定这座建筑在历史上发生过的改变或者修复工程的痕迹。因此，不同时间所经历的改造特征是十分重要的，需要结合当时的社会背景进行深入研究。比如在对整体的通风系统进行研究时，有些学生发现这座建筑的通风系统在历史上曾经过很大的变化，刚开始整个通风系统的流向是从上至下的，后来在某一个时期又改成从下至上的模式，但是现在人们发现后来改造的通风系统不是很好用，所以现在又要重新使用最初的通风方式；又比如照明系统，现在的照明系统和之前的照明系统已经发生了很大的变化，因此需要对这样的一些变化进行研究；再比如空间信息也是考虑的重要对象，2000年蓝色部分显示的屋顶铺面、观众席列入受保护的部分，但是我们看到大量空间标记为空白，因为考虑到舞台随着时代的变迁，它会有更多新的技术材料加入，为以后的改建留出一定的空间。我们不允许在没有深入研究建筑时空语境基础上对其进行修复工作，我们不允许部分的修复或者是边修复边改这样随意的过程的出现。

2. Who——谁在参与遗产化

参与到文化遗产化进程中的人都有哪些？这些参与者不仅仅包括我们的专家学者，也有来自社会各个方面的具有不同角色的人们。参与建筑遗产化，认定保护建筑遗产，更应关注的是保护的遗产状态，一座建筑是否受保护是相当重要的。通过确立其保护地位，使得建筑成为了遗产，这些遗产就从私有权属变成了社会大众需要共同保护的遗产，这同样是遗产化的一个过程。不同的国家都有自己对于保护或者保护地位的界定，都有一套法律法规，这些法律法规中规定了谁需要对建筑遗产保护行为有发起的职责，哪些类型的保护可以被实施，保护工作需要设立哪些标准，等等。但是不同国家的法律法规不同，在保护政策在资金支持上、在保护对象建成时间上、在价值认定上等等，保护工作所产生的结果差别很大。

那么我们在这里就需要讨论到底是哪些人会发起或者是实施对建筑遗产的保护行动。通常保护建筑遗产职责都是由政府或者是某个相关的部门发起的，但有些国家是由公民们自下而上发起的。遗产到底是谁的遗产，它是这些国家领导人的遗产还是人民大众的遗产。政府的保护是自上而下的，大众的保护是自下而上的，人们都可以通过网站表达自己的遗产观点，或者进行一些申诉，或者是通过这样的一些平台对文化遗产进行一个自下而上的保护。因为人们已经清晰地认识到文化遗产是他们生活的一个部分，所以社会大众对于文化遗产的议题是保持着高度关注的，通过这样一个过程形成了一个自下而上、自上而下的保护文化遗产的过程。自上而下就是来自我们的相关政府机构、文化遗产保护专业人士，自下而上就是来自于我们的公民或者是文化遗产的所有人。两者之间的这种不同形式的运动并不矛盾，而是共同发挥了更强大的力量，使得文化遗产能够成为他们提升生活质量的重要组成部分。不同的遗产化手段不仅不会相互矛盾，而且可以相互融合，朝着一个方向推进文化遗产的保护。

案例——布鲁塞尔的文化遗产保护活动，在活动开展前，邀请所有的市民参与到这个小规模的文化遗产保护当中，这些小的遗产就是城市建筑立面上的小部件或者组成部分，比如建筑装饰细部、彩色玻璃、壁画等，它们都是建筑的重要组成部分，但是同时也很容易被损坏。这些建筑遗产尺寸小而且数量繁多，它们可能无法成为官方意义上的文化遗产，但是由于它们都位于建筑的主要立面上，是城市生活和城市公共空间的组成部分。因此文化遗产保护机构的负责人就决定开展这样的一些活动，让社会大众能够关注这样一些小遗产的保护，继而拨给一部分的资金专门用于这些小遗产的修复工作。人们就开始和这些工匠一起合作编写一些项目建议书，然后把这些建议书交给一些相关的文化遗产保护机构，当这些项目建议被采纳之后，他们就能够获得一些保护这些小遗产的资金。这是一个自上而下遗产保护过程，充分证明大众参与到文化遗产的保护中的作用，也正是这样的遗产保护运动从而带动了自上而下的遗产保护。这样的运动也是关于公众对于文化遗产的保护义务和责任的教育。

3. Why——为什么进行遗产化

还有一个问题就是为什么要这么努力地保护这些遗产。因为不知道未来会发生什么，现在所做的这些工作会不会是完全无意义的。如果我们知道今天花了这么多精力为遗产而战,我们的子孙后代是可以从中获益的,是不是对我们后代在文化认同这方面是有益的呢?我们必须认识到的一个现实是,关于文化遗产的历史也是在不断变化的,每一个不同年代的人都以自己的方式书写着关于遗产的故事。

在意大利,很多小朋友在学校就有关于遗产保护的教育;同样在英国各个遗产保护地有一些专门针对儿童设计的文化遗产保护活动,从小开始普及文化遗产教育。与学校教育相一致的活动还有一些民间组织的自下而上的文化遗产保护工作。除此之外,文化遗产的保护者还面临的一个挑战就是全民参与的文化遗产,同样在文化遗产的公共空间里面为残疾人士提供相应的设施,使得大家都能参与到文化遗产的保护行动之中。

遗产化是一个过程,这个过程复杂且在不断地变化发展之中,它包含了很多层面的因素。文化遗产恰巧位于过去和未来的交叉点,遗产所处的这个中心位置来源于即使现在对未来一无所知,依旧能够从过去获取相关的知识,能够更好地管理现在,避免发生一些不应该发生的状况。从过去吸取经验避免犯错,创造又一个更好的未来——这就是遗产的意义之所在。当然我们也会说历史不是也在做相同的事情吗?但是我们现在所说的文化遗产尤其是我们的建筑遗产,以一种可视的方式在我们的公共空间里提供了一个可以被我们感知的事物。这就是为什么我们说文化遗产尤其是建筑遗产那么重要,以至于我们要花很大的心血去保护它们。

从 Loft 到社区：上海中心城区"城中厂"
居住化更新的特征研究

From Loft to Community: A Study on Characteristics of Residential
Regeneration of "Downtown Factory" in Shanghai Central City

李振宇 教授
同济大学建筑与城市规划学院院长
Prof. Li Zhenyu
Director of School of Architecture & Urban Planning, Tongji University

With the promotion of industry and stock planning, a large number of "Downtown Factories" in the central city of Shanghai are in need of regeneration. After the three phases of "bulldozer-style demolition", "creative industrial park" and "waterfront new town", the mixed residential function is becoming a new trend in the transformation of "Downtown Factory". In this paper, 20 projects are included in the case study, and are divided into five stages: worker dormitory, loft studio, low-rent housing, affordable housing, and community. Through the research of the residential regeneration strategies, the paper sums up six characteristics: fuzzy legal boundary, cautious administrative promotion, price polarisation, messy & dull cityscape, small & monotonous scale, and spatial convergence. Furthermore, this paper puts forward community development as the inevitable trend of the regeneration of "Downtown Factory". By choosing successful international cases for comparative study, it sorts out the feasible methods in Shanghai. Finally, the paper points out the barriers to the residential regeneration of "Downtown Factory" in Shanghai central city, and puts forward strategies as references and inspirations for the widespread implementation of the residential regeneration mode of "Downtown Factory".

1 引言：居住化是上海中心城区"城中厂"更新的重要方向

上海的近代工业在全国起步最早，1865年江南制造局的成立是洋务运动的开端，标志着中国工业化的开始。长达150年的发展中，上海涌现了大量具有时代特征的工业厂区，集中于杨浦滨江、苏州河畔、原南市区和肇嘉浜沿线以及吴淞口地区。20世纪90年代，上海开始推行"退二进三"政策，将中心城区生产功能迁至周边，留下大量废弃的工业用地及附属建筑。据统计，上海总面积6 340 km²，其中工业用地761 km²，占比12.00%；中心城区即外环线内总面积660 km²，现状工业用地面积91 km²，占比13.79%（2011年），远超纽约的2.88%（2002年）、东京都的1.67%（2007年）。① 2015年4月通过的《上海市城市更新实施办法》明确提出上海进入存量规划阶段，即未来城市发展将以城市建设用地的功能置换为主要方向，尤其涉及大量工业用地。

---

① 郑德高，卢弘旻. 上海工业用地更新的制度变迁与经济学逻辑[J]. 上海城市规划，2015(3)：25-32.

上海的"城中厂"产生于城镇规模化扩张进程中：曾经的城市边缘区变为中心区，废弃的工厂成为内城中心的飞地。第12届国际工业遗产保护联合会（TICCIH）发表的《下塔吉尔宪章》中，强调工业场所是工业遗产的主要体现形式。因此，"城中厂"的经济和文化价值是更新中应当关注的重点。本文在对上海中心城区"城中厂"的研究中得出其具有的8点特征：位于内城中心，生产功能退化，规模差异巨大，土地划拨为主，海派工业遗存，建筑低龄化，基础设施较差，以"单位"为结构。由于区位、规模、土地性质等因素影响，"城中厂"更新持续时间长，牵涉利益关系繁杂，更新模式多元且具有相当的随机性、临时性和不稳定性。

图1　伦敦泰晤士河南岸既有城市肌理的保留

上海的"城中厂"更新始于20世纪90年代后期，分为4个阶段。在经历了10年"推土机式"的1.0阶段后，2004年上海市经委挂牌18家"城中厂"改造的创意产业园，开启了"创意产业园"的2.0阶段。2010年世博会开启"滨水新城"的3.0阶段，带动了虹口北外滩、徐汇滨江、民生码头等一系列更新实践，亦开始重视厂房的再利用。然而3.0阶段依然停留在传统规划思路上：办公、商业、住宅多为新建，厂房以"建筑"为单元保留改造，既有城市公共空间基本被重构。因此，以成片工业用地为基础、以融入城市和遗迹"存续"①为原则、强调文化增长和符号消费的理念、以混合型居住社区为目标的4.0阶段，应当成为上海中心城区"城中厂"更新的新常态。本文对上海中心城区内既有或曾有的20个居住化案例进行研究，分析居住功能在更新中出现的5个阶段、居住化的策略及其6点特征，尝试探讨"城中厂"居住化更新的新思路和新方法。

2　"城中厂"居住化更新的5个阶段

"城中厂"是低龄的工业遗存，同时作为人类文明和城市发展的见证，亦是承载人类历史的重要媒介和人类历史遗留的文化景观②，如何平衡保护和再利用的关系是重点。《下塔吉尔宪章》中强调赋予工业遗产新功能是可接受的，且有利于可持续发展和经济复兴。③避免静态保护，"空间绩效"④成为更新的重点目标。上海中心城区的"城中厂"更新再利用存在五种典型模式：办公导向的创意园、文化导向的展览馆、旅游休闲导向的公园、购物导向的商业、居住导向的社区。而社区模式在上海无疑是最具有发展潜力的。究其原因，首先，作为人口导入性都市，上海中心城区

图2　维也纳煤气罐住宅

的居住需求压力巨大，同时上海作为全球城市，社区营造的多元性和文化特征成为吸引人和资本的重要因素，因此"城中厂"改造的社区可以兼顾功能使用和符号消费⑤的双重需求；其次，居住围绕生产的混合模式在20世纪80年代开发区经济启动前一直是上海城市发展的主要模式。在产城融合新背景下，三产替换二产，强化居住功能就成为"城中厂"融入后工业城市的重要思路。最后，上海在过去30多年间兼具国有经济中心和市场开放前沿两大特征，各类不同诉求的主导力量对"城中厂"居住化进程影响巨大。本文

---

① 常青. 创刊词[J]. 建筑遗产，2016(1).
② 刘伯英. 工业建筑遗产保护发展综述[J]. 建筑学报，2012(1)：12-17.
③ The Nizhny Tagil Charter for the Industrial Heritage[S/OL]. Nizhny Tagil，2003[2016-10-10]. http://ticcih.org/about/charter/.
④ 杨帆. 大城市地区工业用地存在问题的初步分析及思考：以上海市为例[J]. 城市发展研究，2016(4)：80-86.
⑤ 张希，徐雷. 消费逻辑下的建筑神话：从符号学角度分析消费社会的建筑发展驱动力[J]. 建筑师，2013(6)：20-26.

通过类型学的方法将居住化的形式分为以下五类：

2.1 企业主导——职工宿舍

上海传统经济支柱是国有劳动密集型产业，住宅、学校、医院等依附生产存在。自1978年知青返沪以及市场经济带来大量人口流动之后，上海中心城区的居住和生产比例出现失调，部分厂房通过内部空间分隔、增加开窗面积、通入煤气等方式，被临时改造成职工宿舍。这类厂房居住化成本低、配套有限、目标固定、游走于法律边缘，多出现在大型生产企业的园区内。典型案例有浦东新区在2006年由60余栋、2万余平方米闲置厂房改造而成的服务外来务工人员的"灰领公寓"。

2.2 个人主导——Loft工作室

"退二进三"政策推动了上海文化产业和"城中厂"的结合。1998年，登琨艳将苏州河畔原杜月笙仓库改造成Loft工作室，自下而上开启"城中厂"的创意园更新阶段。① 在M50创意园区，部分厂房2～3层，高度8～10 m，进深10～15 m，接近居住建筑尺度，艺术家遂将其改造成"下商上住"的工作室。此后该模式被应用到多个创意产业园中。然而由于基础设施差、行政监管严以及居住和办公租金回报差异巨大，在经历10年拉锯战后，居住功能最终从大多数园区中消失了。

2.3 资本主导——廉租房

1992住房改革以来，上海居住成本不断攀升，市场化运作的由厂房改造的廉价公寓产品不断出现。如高阳路114号的东方公寓，原为良工阀门厂一栋3层厂房，紧邻黄浦江并遥望陆家嘴。改造时将3层隔成5层，且每层被划分为90多个单间，最小不到6 m^2，通道狭窄，管线乱布，存在严重消防隐患。廉租房模式一定程度缓解了中心城区低收入人群的居住困境，具有正面意义；但同时安全隐患大，易受法律行政干预影响，是"城中厂"居住化更新的过渡阶段。

2.4 政府主导——保障房

2008年全国开始大规模建设保障性住房，上海中心城区逐渐出现政府主导的厂房改造保障房项目。居住化更新的主要障碍在于用地性质变更，政府主导可以避免产权和使用权出现冲突，此种方法在丹麦、挪威等存在土地公有制的国家亦较为常见。上海黄浦区瞿溪路原豆制品厂，通过加层、内挖阳台、架空通道、按柱距划分套间等方式将进深13～18 m的"U"字平面厂房改造成单元式保障房。保障房模式将改造后的建筑本体空间纳入社会福利体系，但并未涉及社区环境的营造，对城市风貌保护的态度亦较为模糊。

2.5 文化主导——居住社区

随着上海对于规划工业区块外、集中建设区内的现状195 km^{2}工业用地商业化转型的许可，出现了一批强调工业文化特征的"城中厂"居住化更新项目。其中以陕西南路历史风貌保护区里的嘉善坊涉外公寓为代表：一个由9栋建筑组成的针织品厂被改造成功能混合、利于交流的社区。居住、办公、商业建筑面积比为4：3：3，完整保留了老厂房之间狭窄的道路并进行景观设计，建筑外挂露台，屋顶改造成居民活动场所，庭院则成为公共集市，立面选用深浅两种暖木色涂料拉毛面，一方面较好延续了既有工业文化特征，另一方面形成了具有归属感的社区氛围。

综上所述，上海中心城区的"城中厂"居住化更新是指将位于外环高架路以内的工厂及其附属建筑和构筑物，改造成以社区为结构、居住为目的的宜居空间，同时混合植入办公、商业、休闲等功能的更新模式。从类型和时间的对应关系上可以得出，最初的无序、被动的居住化改造并不能称为更新，职工宿舍仅是生产单位内部资源的临时性转换。Loft工作室、保障性住房是自下而上和自上而下居住化更新的主要形式

---

① 刘成，李泓. 浅论上海工业遗产再生模式：世博背景下的工业遗产的昨天、今天和明天[J]. 华中建筑，2011(3)：179-181.

和两个起点,是对个人和政府在这一进程中的作用的一种探索。廉租房是阶段性产物,对于盘活废弃工业用房和缓解底层居住压力起到正面作用,同时验证了"城中厂"更新为居住社区的经济可行性。近年来,随着上海住宅建设的重心从数量效率转向综合效益,住宅类型已出现多元化趋势[①],而承载工业文明的"城中厂"能够提供极具特色的新型居住体验。30 余年间,上海中心城区"城中厂"居住化更新呈现三大趋势:从建筑改造转向厂区更新,从追求经济产出转向体验工业文化,从空间消费转向符号消费。

3 "城中厂"居住化更新的 6 个特征

上海中心城区"城中厂"居住化更新的背景不同于西方国家,其各发展阶段出现较早,城镇化和城市更新并行;土地权属单一,政府掌握主导权;开发机制自上而下,民间话语权微弱;遗产保护意识淡漠,更多考虑短期收益。以下通过对 20 个案例的居住化策略研究,总结出上海中心城区"城中厂"居住化更新在法律、行政、经济、文化、规划、建筑等层面体现出的 6 个特征:

3.1 法律——边界模糊

上海中心城区"城中厂"居住化更新的主要困境在于法律认定:一方面工业用地和居住用地间转性困难;另一方面市场需求促生徘徊于法律边缘的项目。部分厂房改造的住宅出现"贫民窟"倾向,卫生、安全问题丛生,因此又受到法律行政干预,形成恶性循环。如半岛 1919 东端廉租房,是由一栋平面尺寸 72 m×30 m,6 m 高的单层大跨厂房改造而成,房间根据 6 m 的柱距划分为 8 排东西向隔间,走道狭窄,多数房间没有直接对外的通风采光口,条件极为恶劣。归根究底,过去城镇规模化扩张阶段的法律体系不再适用于"存量规划",随着更新项目不断增多,亟须在法律层面予以明确定义,达到规范更新行为、形成良性循环的目的。

3.2 行政——谨慎推动

上海"城中厂"更新源自文创产业和废弃工厂的结合。居住功能多为相关从业人员服务,而文创产业的发展依赖行政行为和文件的推动。2004 年以来,上海市经信委共挂牌市级创意产业园 89 处,其中 78 处改造自中心城区的"城中厂",占比 87.64%,总建筑面积达百万平方米,涉及研发设计、文化传媒、建筑设计、策划咨询、时尚消费五大方向。[②] 2016 年颁布的《关于本市盘活存量工业用地的实施办法》中开始认可工业用地转型为研发总部、商业、办公、教育、医疗、科研、养老等功能的用地,但同年颁布的《关于加强本市工业用地出让管理的若干规定》明文禁止在工业用地上建设住宅类建筑布局和形态。此外,各级政府主导的少量厂房改造的保障房,亦在步步谨慎地推动着"城中厂"的居住化更新。

3.3 价格——两极分化

"城中厂"的居住化更新源于稀缺性:一方面其区位较好、租金低廉、空间适应性高,适合在中心城区工作却无法负担房价的人群居住;另一方面其代表工业文化,可以提供不同于普通住宅的居住体验。因此基于经济稀缺性,加之政府禁止厂房改造成可出售住宅,促使上海中心城区"城中厂"更新呈现两极分化:如作为廉租房的东方公寓,月租金每平方米只有 50~70 元;而代表高端居住的 Base 公寓租金高达每平方米 300~350 元(数据来自作者 2016 年 5 月 21 日的现场走访调研)。前者着眼物质空间产出,强调满足基本需求;后者着眼居住文化体验,强调文化资本的价值。

3.4 文化——风貌杂乱

"城中厂"是重要的工业文明物质文化遗产。上海市规土局划定的 32 块工业风貌保护区中包含大量

[①] 李振宇,常琦,董怡嘉.从住宅效率到城市效益:当代中国住宅建筑的类型学特征与转型趋势[J].时代建筑,2016(6):6-14.
[②] 上海市经济委员会,上海创意产业中心.创意产业[M].上海:上海科学技术文献出版社,2005:97.

厂区。然而改造的临时性和不稳定性导致缺乏对城市风貌的保护协调，缺乏具有约束力的城市设计导则和尊重历史的建筑设计，为了满足居住需求随意分隔和加建空间，进行不可逆的墙面开窗及粉饰、随意布设管线和空调机位等；社区管理的不力甚至缺位造成生活垃圾堆积，路面坑洼不整，严重影响居住质量。整个社会缺少对工业遗存的保护意识，是造成这一切的文化背景。

3.5 规划——尺度小微

上海中心城区"城中厂"更新中居住多为辅助功能，规模较小，且多位于厂区角落、里弄深处或厂房的二层及以上。在个人主导的 7 个案例中，居住空间面积一般不超过 10%，且多由小进深厂房、厂区办公、宿舍楼改造。而独立居住化更新项目则受到工业类型、平面尺寸、采光通风、建筑层高等多重条件约束，改造为居住的厂房以原纺织和食品加工产业为多（进深约 12～16 m，层高 10～15 m，改造后 3～5 层），建筑面积较为有限（如 Base 公寓 2 000 m²，龙恒和迪凡公寓各 2 500 m²，嘉善坊涉外公寓 4 500 m²）。

3.6 建筑——布局趋同

类型的两极分化，导致上海中心城区"城中厂"居住化更新的建筑空间呈现 2 种主要类型，即分层通廊式和跃层单元式。前者基于大进深和大层高的特征，以柱距为模数，纵向将一层完整分为两层，横向则通过单廊或中廊，形成类似酒店的布局；后者源自纽约苏荷区的 loft 模式，横向形成独立入户的单元，内部将 4.5～6 m 层高上下分隔，首层为艺术工坊或商业，二层为居住空间，典型案例有田子坊、M50。但空间布局类型总体趋同，居住体验感较差。

4 国外成功案例分析

"城中厂"居住化更新在西方国家已成常态。如纽约苏荷区、伦敦沙德-泰晤士地区、阿姆斯特丹东港区等，按照更新机制的不同可分为"自下而上""自上而下""多方混合"三类。苏荷区位于下曼哈顿地区，占地 0.44 km²，曾是纽约的钢铁生产和仓储基地，拥有大量铸铁建筑。20 世纪 60 年代起大批艺术家进驻区域并对厂房进行修缮改造，同时结成"艺术家租户联合会"与各利益团体抗争，最终促使政府和社会通过建立历史文化保护区、放宽银行贷款条件等方式认可区域的保护更新。"自下而上"模式原动力弱，效率低下，缺乏法律和行政的支持，从而造成苏荷区的更新周期长达 30 余年，其间火灾频发，治安混乱，环境恶劣，基础设施和生活配套匮乏。[①] 但另一方面，由于资本介入少，苏荷区既有街道风貌得到较好保护，城市形态相对均匀，110 m×60 m 和 150 m×60 m 的两种街坊结构被完全保留，街道宽度维持在 12～20 m，街坊以围合式为主，建筑通过 1～2 个东西向的条状内院串联。空白地块采用"补缺"手法，改造成契合原有风貌的建筑或绿地，整个更新过程中大拆大建现象鲜有发生，居住类型多元，社区富有活力。

伦敦沙德-泰晤士地区是典型的"自上而下"更新模式，强调统筹和效率。这片仓库区位于泰晤士河南岸的萨里码头，占地约 0.2 km²，更新由中央政府成立的伦敦道克兰开发公司（LDDC）统一筹划，充分利用老建筑的经济和文化价值，形成居住主导，办公、零售、旅游和展览等功能混合的城区。[②] 沙德-泰晤士地区拥有近 300 年历史，水道纵横，街道曲折，街坊大小从 140 m×80 m 到 70 m×40 m 不等，街道宽度约为 12 m。整个区域呈现圈层结构，内部为围合式街坊，沿河则是条状建筑（伦敦最为完整的维多利亚风格建筑群被基本保留，并植入现代化的居住配套和基础设施，创建极具吸引力的居住环境。同时在中心广场新建文化地标——蓝色"圆"住宅（The Blue Circle），其建筑在尺度、风格、材质设计上遵循既有风貌，新旧建

---

① 李振宇，常琦，董怡嘉. 从住宅效率到城市效益：当代中国住宅建筑的类型学特征与转型趋势 [J]. 时代建筑，2016(6)：6-14.
② Brian Edwards. London Docklands: Urban Design in an Age of Deregulation[M]. [S. l.]: Butterworth Heinemann, 1992: 94-95.

筑得以较好地融合。[①]

阿姆斯特丹东港区采用"多方混合"的更新模式,更加关注社会公平及利益相关者的诉求。东港位于阿姆斯特丹伊日河(IJ River)和阿姆斯特尔河(River Amstel)河口东北侧,占地 1.25 km^2,更新持续 25 年。一方面政府成立"新增住房管理委员会"主持更新,一方面倡导"公私合营"和多方协商,努力实现本地安置,建立社会住宅和商品住宅混合的社区。[②] 由于兼顾多方利益,更新拆除部分仓储建筑,新建一些高密度、高容积率的保障性住房。同时基于港区线性形态形成新的单层带状城市肌理,街坊尺度从 150 m×50 m 到 80 m×50 m 不等,并建设具有地标特征的大型建筑。尽管社会保障工作很完善,但阿姆斯特丹东港区更新对工业遗存的关注明显不够,对街区整体风貌保护显得较为无力。

5 居住化更新对策

上海中心城区的"城中厂"居住化更新具有特殊的历史背景,形成了特殊的法律、行政、经济、文化、规划和建筑特征,在更新中应基于城市法律和行政体系、经济发展阶段、文化认同、技术水平寻求合适的方法。本文根据前述研究与分析,提出相应的以下 6 点对策:(1)法律上建立针对"城中厂"居住化更新的相关法规,制定灵活的土地制度,逐步放开在居住功能介入下对所有权和经营方式的各种可能性;(2)行政上仿效伦敦道克兰更新,创建政府背景的公司平台,减少沟通审批流程,建立多方协商机制,兼顾各方利益;(3)经济上鼓励混合产业和银行贷款的引入,建立以工业遗存更新为对象的税收抵免政策,重视保障性住房和既有厂区的有效结合,同时设立"毒地"治理专项基金,做到"先治理再改造";(4)文化上通过建立工业旅游区、工业风貌保护区等打造极具工业文化特征和示范意义的居住社区,从而提升社会认可度,使保护街坊风貌和更新使用得以统筹发展;(5)规划上打破厂区围墙,混合多种功能,将居住社区的各类设施公共化,保持历史肌理,增加建筑密度、容积率和层数,避免局限于建筑内部的静态改造;(6)建筑上采用"负面清单"管理模式,在规划和城市设计控制范围内,鼓励具有类型学贡献的居住建筑形式,强调建筑风格和使用人群的多元混合。相信通过以上途径,最终将形成上海中心城区风貌优良、具有高度适应性、能够自我发展的新型城市居住社区。

[①] 史蒂文·蒂耶斯德尔,蒂姆·希思,塔内尔·厄奇. 城市历史街区的复兴[M]. 张玫英,董卫,译. 北京:中国建筑工业出版社, 2006:125-127.

[②] 程晓曦. 阿姆斯特丹东港码头改造:城市复兴中的多重平衡[J]. 世界建筑, 2011(4):102-106.

从历史风貌保护到城市景观管理
——基于城市历史景观(HUL)理念的思考

From Historical Features Preservation to Urban Landscape Management: Based on the Historic Urban Landscape Approach

张松 教授
同济大学建筑与城市规划学院
Prof. Zhang Song
School of Architecture & Urban Planning, Tongji University

This paper analyzes the conceptual difference of "Landscape" and "Fengmao" (features), and then discusses the cognitive otherness on urban landscape between China and Western countries, and its implications in international commendations. On the basis, it analyzes the instructiveness of historic urban landscape concepts and approaches on the urban heritage conservation. The article proposes that it is necessary to shift the paradigm from historical features preservation to urban landscape management. In addition to strengthening the integrated conservation of the urban heritage, the relevance, integrity and diversity of the urban landscape should also be considered including the protection and utilization of landscape resources, change management of urban landscape.

1 "景观"与"风貌"概念的差异

1.1 不断延展的"景观"内涵

景观(landscape)一词,在西方社会从最初的"放眼所见之地表"到特指"风景画",进而发展到视觉美学的含义,经历了漫长的历史时期。20世纪初,景观一词获得文化和生态的意义,到20世纪末,其可持续性的内涵与价值得到关注。早期的景观研究专注于自然风景的艺术审美特征或"如画性(picturesque)",多采用静态研究方法。20世纪以后,文化地理学将人类学、社会学理论引入地理学研究领域,在文化与景观之间建立起了联系。文化不再是抽象的存在,文化对景观的塑造体现在政治、经济等社会因素与环境之间的相互作用上。"文化是动因,自然是载体,景观则是呈现的结果。"① 近年来,景观研究领域关注景观的社会属性高于其物质属性。因此在文化地理学研究过程中,"景观"在传统的视觉意义之上增添了社会、文化、生态等多重含义。

不同的学科领域对"景观"研究有不同的偏好,地理学以整体观分析自然地形、地物在空间上的分布和时间上的演化,将景观作为一个完整的空间体系

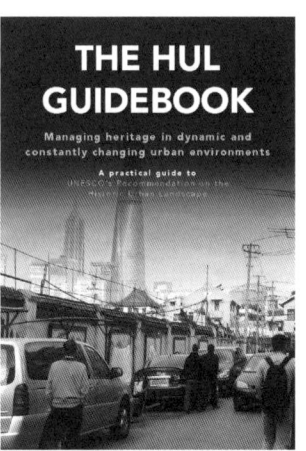

HUL指导手册

---

① Carl Ortwin Sauer. The Morphology of Landscape [J]. University of California Publications in Geography 2, 1925, 2(2): 19-53.

探讨景观形成的过程；生态学研究景观的结构、格局和功能，分析景观动态变化以及相互作用的机理，关注景观的系统性。在英国，"to landscape"指环境美化，比如通过重新配置植被和改造地形来提供令人愉悦的美景，显然今天很少有人会在理论上认为景观是仅与视觉有关的事物。[①]

受生态学思想影响，景观都市主义（Landscape Urbanism）将城市理解成一个生态体系进行重新阅读、再现和设计，以景观作为重新连接（reconnecting）城市空间秩序的手段，其目的并不是要使城市看起来像一幅风景画，而是从强调"图—底"（figure-ground）关系的城市肌理构成，转向将城市表面设想成一个能促进与组织其各项环境条件之间动态联系的、有生命力的载体。[②]

随着景观含义的不断丰富，景观研究的对象也从自然风景和唯美景观，转向多数人共享的、朴素的地域景观，促进了城市景观范畴的扩展。[③] 城市景观是人的生活方式的表现，是城市社会政治、经济发展的记录。无论是从景观形成的结果，还是从景观形成的过程看，城市景观都具有深刻的文化意义和社会意义。

1.2 时常被误解的"风貌"特色

在国内的城乡规划学科领域，"景观"似乎还不是一个特别重要的专业用语。例如，在1998年发布的国家标准《城市规划基本术语标准》（GB/T 50280—1998）中就没有"景观"一词。只是在定义"绿地"和"城市绿化"这两个用语时，有"美化景观""美化城市景观"的描述；在"竖向规划"这一词条下，有"为满足道路交通、地面排水、建筑布置和城市景观等方面的综合要求……而进行的规划设计"的解释，"城市景观"被列在多项实用功能之后。

"景观"一词，在风景园林学科使用较为普遍，在城市设计及其相关分析研究中也有较多使用。而在历史保护专业领域，较常使用的一词是"风貌"，在国家《文物保护法》《历史文化名城名镇名村保护条例》等法规中使用的是"历史风貌"一词，有"保持和延续其传统格局和历史风貌"等相关规定；在《城乡规划法》中使用的是"传统风貌"一词，规定"制定和实施城乡规划，应当保持地方特色、民族特色和传统风貌"，"旧城区的改建，应当保护历史文化遗产和传统风貌"。

"风貌保护"一说，大概是从"历史文化风貌区保护规划"这样的专业说法中简化形成的，旨在强调与"文物保护"的区别。但"风貌"一词的定义并不严谨，也较少单独使用。在《历史文化名城保护规划规范》（GB 50357—2005）中，"风貌（townscape）"术语的定义为"反映历史文化特征的自然环境与人工环境的整体面貌和景观"，因在历史文化名城保护中所关注的风貌主要为历史城区的整体格局、传统肌理和街巷景观。

而在2012年住建部发布的《历史文化名城名镇名村保护规划编制要求》（试行）中对"传统风貌建筑（traditional style building）"的定义为在历史地段内，除文物保护单位、历史建筑、登记不可移动文物外，"具有一定建成历史，对历史地段整体风貌特征形成具有价值和意义的建筑物"。在多数情形下，所谓"传统风貌建筑"给人的景观意象往往指向坡屋顶形式建筑，甚至是所谓的"明清风格"建筑。

由于对"风貌"等专业术语缺乏科学明晰的定义，在实际操作中则会出现误读、曲解，甚至是有意歪曲的现象。如违背原真性和完整性原则的所谓古城"复原"重建；按某一时期、某一建筑风格所进行的历史文化街区"修复"打造；或者对沿街建筑采取"穿衣戴帽"等方式统一协调风貌的美化工程等。在一些地方的保护实践中，历史文化街区保护的"完整性"原则，常常也会被误解为由决策者或设计师等少数人士通过"设计"确定的"完美"形象再现。

1.3 欧洲景观政策的启示

欧洲国家和城市是在立法保护城市遗产和维护历史景观方面开展最早、做得最好的地区。在各国大

---

① [英]麦琪·罗.《欧洲风景公约》：关于"文化景观"的一场思想革命[J]. 韩锋，徐青，编译. 中国园林，2007(11)：10-15.
② 葛舒眉，张京祥. 优雅地存在：景观都市主义视角下的河流复兴[J]. 国际城市规划，2012 (3)：113-117.
③ 张丹. 欧盟景观政策发展研究[J]. 城市规划，2011 (12)：58-59.

量卓有成效的实践基础上,2000年,欧盟成员国为了保护、管理和规划共同的景观资源,形成了欧盟的景观政策文件《欧洲景观公约》(简称《公约》)。《公约》中对"景观"的定义为"被人们感所知的一个区域,其特征是自然因素和/或人为因素作用和相互作用的结果"[①],涵盖自然的、农村的、城市的和城郊的地区,包括土地、内河和海洋地区。在关注杰出景观的同时,也关注日常或不太好的景观。《公约》强调:景观是人们所处环境的基本构成,是欧洲共同的文化遗产和自然遗产多样性的表达,也是人们身份认同的基础(foundation of identity)。

《公约》注意到景观在文化、生态、环境和社会领域具有重要的公共性作用,是有利于经济活动的一种资源,是欧盟成员国可持续发展的关键因素,应当促进景观保护、管理和规划的可持续性。《公约》强调对所有景观特征(landscape character)的关注,从而取代了传统认识中注重景观美学(landscape aesthetics)的主导观念。景观是文化在人类发展过程中沿着不同的轨迹所产生的结果,城市是欧洲文化的主要载体,文化多样性形成了欧洲多元的城市景观。

同年制定的《欧洲大陆的空间可持续发展指导原则》指出:可持续的空间发展政策与经济和社会需求以及生态和文化功能密切相关,欧洲景观的多样性在欧洲可持续的空间发展中具有不可估量的潜力。在欧洲的发展规划和政策中,景观的价值和意义得到了充分体现,一些国家将历史景观作为国家资产进行保护管理。

2 HUL中景观及城市保护的理念

2.1 国际保护政策中景观观念的演变

"景观"概念的变化,也反映在国际遗产保护政策发展过程之中。1962年,联合国教科文组织(UNESCO)颁布《关于保护景观和遗址的风貌与特性的建议》,提出"人类在各个时期不时使构成他们自然环境组成部分的景观和遗址的风貌与特性遭受损害、破坏,导致世界各地文化的、美学的,甚至是至关重要的遗产趋于贫瘠",呼吁关注文化景观、自然景观及古迹在科学和美学上的重要意义。当然也反映出国际建议的时代局限性,保护领域重点关注于视觉环境的美景(beauty)和建筑遗产的艺术特质。

2011年11月,UNESCO通过的《关于城市历史景观的建议书》(以下简称《建议书》)是一份关于城市保护的新的国际文件。城市历史景观(HUL)理念将城市地区视为具有文化和自然的价值与特征的历史性层积(historic layering)。城市遗产是历史性层积和当前发展的动态叠合,强调文化与自然、物质与精神之间的关联。城市保护的价值评估,已从纪念性建筑,转向更为广泛地关注城市在社会、文化、经济发展进程中的重要意义。[②]

《建议书》倡导采用"景观方法(landscape approach)"重新认知、评估城市遗产,将城市保护融入发展战略。"景观方法"将历史城市作为一个整体来看待,成为一种认识历史城市价值的新思维,通过"景观"在遗产保护和城市发展之间搭建起重要的桥梁。城市历史景观(HUL)理念考虑到更为广泛的地理环境、城市文脉以及无形文化遗产,这与《欧洲景观公约》中将历史城镇在内的整个地域环境作为景观资源,并采取相应的景观管理政策的理念基本一致。

2.2 城市遗产与景观资产

"城市遗产是人类的社会、文化和经济资产,由具有价值的历史性层积所界定,这些价值从持续和现存的文化、传统和经验的积累中产生,并作为其多样性被认可。"[③]历史性城市景观理念试图改变将历史地区

---

① Council of Europe. The European Landscape Convention[R]. [S. l.]:Council of Europe,2000.
② UNESCO. Recommendation on the Historic Urban Landscape[R]. [S. l.]:UNESCO,2011.
③ UNESCO. Recommendation on the Historic Urban Landscape[R]. [S. l.]:UNESCO,2011.

作为特定建筑群进行静态保护的既有方法,指出城市遗产作为重要的社会、文化和经济资源,在提升城市地区宜居性、促进经济发展、增强社会凝聚力等方面具有重要意义。

《建议书》采纳2004年欧盟《通过城镇内部的积极整合实现城市历史地区的可持续发展》报告中有关城市遗产扩展对象的构成:(1)具有突出文化价值的纪念性遗产;(2)没有突出的遗产要素,但以相对丰富的方式呈现;(3)可以考虑的新的城市要素。① 城市遗产既包括那些已经得到广泛认可、代表宏大记忆的重要纪念物和历史地区,也包括承载社会记忆与市民日常生活密切相关的普通建筑、城市街巷及社区。

城市遗产对象的扩展需要调整既有的保护方法,引入景观的方法来辨识、理解和诠释城市的历史性层积。《建议书》提倡通过综合调查,绘制历史城市的自然、文化和人文资源分布图;采用参与性规划方法以及与利益攸关方进行磋商,就保护价值达成共识;评估在面对社会经济压力和气候变化影响时遗产价值特征的脆弱性;将城市遗产价值及脆弱性状态纳入更广泛的城市发展框架。2016年6月UNESCO亚太遗产中心发布的《历史性城市景观方法实施指南》(简称《实施指南》),提出应基于每个历史城镇的本土语境,调查和评估其自然、文化和人文资源,在形成价值共识的基础上将城市遗产保护整合到城市整体发展战略框架。②

2.3 景观保护与变化管理

英国历史地理学家伊恩·D. 怀特认为"景观是重写本(palimpsests)",它们构成了集体记忆的载体,记载了人类在地球表面上连续不断的各阶段的活的历史。他强调:变化一直是景观的特征。随着圈地活动、工业化、城市化以及高速公路和运河系统的扩大,景观变化的规模和速度不断增大。在20世纪,景观变化成为了一个全球化的过程,并受到了全球的关注,导致人们对现存的、有价值的景观及其特征在过去的发展变化产生越来越大的兴趣,人们期望保护这些景观,使之免受不利变化的影响。③ 这一观念与《建议书》中强调的"城市是经过岁月累积在环境中形成的多重层积(multi-layers)"的理念高度一致。

美国著名城市设计理论家凯文·林奇,在《此地何时》(What Time Is This Place?)一书中针对城市规划应对变化的重要性和变化管理(managing change)的设计策略做了系统分析和哲学思考。他认为:时间意象的质量对个人幸福感至关重要,也决定了我们是否能够成功管理环境变化。一个理想的意象必须既颂扬和扩充现在,又与过去和未来取得联系。变化管理(managing change)的艺术必须考虑转型过程的累积效应。它必须理解时间安排和策略的作用、物理变化和社会变化之间的纽带,以及物理变化如何有时被用作实现社会变化的杠杆。④

今天,城市是现代性神话观念(the myth of modernity)的主角,然而城市化并不意味着高楼大厦的"堆砌"。进入存量发展时代,需要高度重视空间的社会性和空间形式的多样性,而"如何管理变化"将成为城市设计范式转型(shifting paradigm)必然面对的重要课题之一。

3 名城保护与城市设计的范式转型

3.1 历史景观与日常生活世界

《建议书》推荐各国在城市保护过程中藉由动态演进、历史性层积和景观方法来认识历史城市,识别城市遗产,并将城市遗产保护积极融入城市总体规划中。城市历史景观保护的本质不在于展示或重现某一

---

① Dupagne A, Ruelle C, Teller J, et al. Sustainable Development of Urban Historical Areas through an Active Integration within Towns[R]. [S. l.]:European Commission,2004:11-15.
② UNESCO. The HUL Guidebook: Managing Heritage in Dynamic and Constantly Changing Urban Environments[R]. [S. l.]: UNESCO, 2016.
③ [英]伊恩·D. 怀特. 16世纪以来的景观与历史[M]. 王思思,译. 北京:中国建筑工业出版社,2011.
④ [美]凯文·林奇. 此地何时:城市与变化的时代[M]. 赵祖华,译. 北京:北京时代华文书局,2016.

时期的历史风貌或氛围,而是要通过真实的历史景观激活集体记忆,保持社会情感再生产的力量,维护社会文化环境的连续性。

长期以来,相关专业领域和社会各界对历史景观保护的认识局限在重要文物古迹或传统风貌的视觉特征,依靠保护规划等进行静态的风貌维护。有些城市,将历史地区作为文化消费对象简单地进行旅游开发。也有为了追求所谓的"传统风貌"舍本逐末,置真实的历史建筑和社区居民诉求于不顾,开展得不偿失的所谓"复原""复兴"工程。这些以保护的名义所进行的开发行为,往往会损害城市遗产的真实性、完整性和多样性,破坏社会稳定的物质网络,导致地区的历史文脉断裂和人文内涵丧失。

因此,需要全面理解城市保护的多重意义,突破单纯以时代风貌和建筑外观特征为标准识别城市遗产的局限性,能够发现和认识更多的遗产资源及潜在资源,通过城市保护,提升环境品质,促进城市的可持续发展。[①] 城市遗产保护,既要保护历史景观的视觉环境特征,更要维护与之关联的历史文脉和场所精神。要实现这一目标,改善和提升居住环境质量以保持历史地区的活力,通过环境改善和功能引导维护社会网络结构的稳定性等政策措施不可或缺。

3.2 城市更新中的景观保护

城市的历史城区汇聚了前人的努力和社会财富,是具有文化底蕴的场所,正是那些体现地方传统和富有生活气息的、看似平凡的日常景观,丰富了城市肌理的多样性。事实上,由于对城市遗产的认知出现了较大的偏差,历史城区长期疏于保护和管理,导致建筑外观破损、环境质量下降。一些看上去破破烂烂的老城区正被当作棚户区进行大改造,为了追求存量用地的经济效益,往往简单粗暴地抹去了一个地区的集体记忆。

近年来,在中央城市工作精神指导下城市更新正成为各地城市规划的热点。一方面,城市有机更新符合城市生长的新陈代谢规律,有助于维护城市历史景观的连续性;另一方面,实施有机更新必须认识到蕴藏在城市建成环境中的资源价值,从历史文化、社会情感以及生态美学等角度,对历史城区的潜在资源进行全面科学的评估。[②] 上海在创新发展和转型发展背景下提出了城市更新的全新理念,要从"拆、改、留并举,以拆为主",转换到"留、改、拆并举,以保留保护为主"的政策方向。在城市有机更新过程中,应当运用景观特征评估方法将历史城区作为一个整体对待并保持其空间特色,强化其有价值的特征和整体属性(attributes),在保护历史景观视觉特质的同时,维持城市能够正常运转的良性功能。

3.3 上海的风貌保护与景观管理

2003年1月1日,《上海市历史文化风貌区和优秀历史建筑保护条例》在上海市正式施行。2005年,市政府在中心城区划定12片历史文化风貌区,合计占地面积近27 km²。在正式批准的《历史文化风貌区保护规划》中确定了144条道路(街巷)为风貌保护道路,其中64条为"一类保护道路",即通常说的"永不拓宽的街道"。2007年9月,市政府批准了规划局《关于本市风貌保护道路(街巷)规划管理若干意见的通知》,这个规范性文件使得风貌道路的保护管理有了执行的基本依据。但是从全市范围的规划管理体系看,目前还只有历史文化风貌区的景观控制管理规定,其他地区几乎没有环境品质和景观管理的规划工具。由于土地财政等因素的主导和影响,不仅是在历史文化风貌区建设控制范围之外,就是在其范围内往往也是高强度的开发建设,缺乏有效控制引导再开发行为的具体措施。

武康路是位于衡山—复兴历史文化风貌区内的风貌保护道路,作为上海市历史风貌保护整治的试点项目,在2007—2009年期间,徐汇区对武康路实施了综合整治工程,并以风貌保护道路规划和实施为契机,在区级层面探索风貌保护的长效管理机制,以历史街道景观和街道空间为重点对象,提出风貌道路沿

---

① 镇雪锋. 历史性城市景观控制引导策略研究:城市保护思想理念的解析及启示[D]. 上海:同济大学,2013:175-176.
② 张松. 历史城区的整体性保护:在"历史性城市景观"国际建议下的再思考[J]. 北京规划建设,2012(6):27-30.

线保护、控制、引导和管理等方面的技术规定,将风貌区保护规划向精细化管理方面推进。①

同样位于衡山—复兴历史文化风貌区核心区的永康路的命运就出现了较大的波折。这条曾被称为"上海最具风情的酒吧街",曾因无证经营、跨门营业等原因被强制关停的事件成为2016年媒体报道的热门话题。自发形成的商业人文景观,因酒吧深夜经营造成的"噪声扰民"或手续不全等实际问题该如何管理? 是简单地"回到从前",还是采取适应市场需求的业态调整? 事实上,"恢复历史建筑和街区功能形态",往往只是迅速处理事态的一个简单做法。

历史风貌保护是历史文化名城保护的基础,城市有机更新或城市修补可以更加积极有效地促进历史地区环境品质的改善和提升。因而应当由城市遗产保护规划引导城市有机更新的有序开展,而不是不顾原有的法定规划,随意进行旧区更新,或是简单开展市容环境整治。城市设计在建成环境区域,应当更多地承担历史景观维护管理的责任,而不是作为一种新的手段来简单否定历史性层积或法定管理程序。武康路和永康路这两条风貌保护道路的现实案例说明:风貌保护和景观管理不是形象美化(beautiful)工程,所谓的风貌整治也不应是面子工程,而是涉及日常生活和场所精神的城市设计与景观管理的重要课题。针对历史文化风貌的控制引导和日常管理,既需要主管部门的精细化管理,也需要多元主体的社会参与。

4 结语:迈向景观管理的城市保护

"景观"的视觉美学有着源远流长的历史,传统的以视觉美学思维认识城市的方法是景观管理的基础。近年来,国内外学者均注意到,景观处于持续变化的过程中,一种长期稳定的文化景观是可持续土地利用的结果。因此,考虑到其历史特征和美学价值的景观保护与可持续管理具有重要的意义。②③

国际遗产保护政策中所提倡的城市历史景观(HUL)方法对城市遗产保护和景观管理的重要启发在于:景观的价值不局限在视觉美学层面,应当关注促使景观形成的经济、社会因素和物质环境"变化",需要重视那些普通的日常景观对于城市生活的意义,需要了解和重视社区居民在景观形成和保护管理中的作用。

总之,历史文化名城和历史风貌保护需要从消极控制向积极保护(active conservation)方面主动转型;城市设计应当从全面设计未来愿景方案向建成环境的变化管理方面积极转型。城市景观保护、营造和管理,需要在城乡规划体系中逐步充实完善。通过城市设计维护城市景观的延续性,欧盟的景观政策和景观管理经验值得我们学习借鉴。

无论是城市设计、景观管理,还是历史保护、环境整治,都应当尊重自然之造化、前人之成就、现存事物之特性,并能够从中发现美好的特征和元素。正如《实施指南》所指出的,应在可持续发展框架下通过一系列传统的和适应本地情况的创新性工具,为城市保护提供保障。不断扩展对城市遗产价值和意义的认知,有助于识别那些构成城市场所魅力的特征与元素。通过对历史景观及其背景环境的评估、监测和管理,才有可能避免城市景观的碎片化现象,维护城市景观的可持续性,并在保护和传承的基础上不断创新,塑造更具魅力的人居环境。

---

① 沙永杰,伍江. 上海市徐汇区历史街道保护规划探索[J]. 时代建筑,2013(3):34-39.
② [德]约翰尼斯·穆勒.(重新)塑造景观:中国的人类干预景观遗产[J]. 张阁,陈航,译. 风景园林,2016(8):16-26.
③ 林箐. 乡村景观的价值与可持续发展途径[J]. 风景园林,2016(8):27-37.

城市空间的时间性研究

A Temporal Study on Urban Space

何依 教授
华中科技大学建筑与城市规划学院
Prof. He Yi
School of Architecture & Urban Planning, Huazhong University of Science and Technology

This speech analyzes the existing form of time in urban space based on the Marxist concept of time. Taking historical relics as annotation and elements cycle as scale, it projects time onto urban space. With two relevant cases, further research is carried out to study the different process of historical accumulation in urban space, then obtains synchronic and diachronic context configuration, and builds up an intrinsic connection for urban historical environment.

时间周期的缩短,必然导致空间发展过程的压缩。近20年,中国城市持续快速发展,使城市空间产生分异和嬗变,新旧对峙,二元拼贴,历史环境零散化、模糊化成为现阶段城市的普遍现象,与此同时,也切断了历史文脉的传承和延续。城市的发展不仅有空间的延伸,还有时间的延续,由于时间维度的缺失,使城市空间的历史内涵和文化特征无法被理解和阅读。面对这一特殊的发展时期,本文从城市空间的社会本质特征出发,以时间为视角,以历史累积为对象,研究城市空间的时间化现象;并通过时间的连续性来构建空间的完整性,将那些因为空间断裂而失去意义的历史要素统一起来,为城市遗产的整体性保护,提供一种新的思维方式。

1 城市空间的时间存在

讨论时间就不能回避时间观。关于时间,亚里士多德定义在运动的基础上,时间是运动和静止的尺度;奥古斯丁从内在的时间观出发,将时间看作是意识的回忆、思索和期望,而不是外在的客观物;黑格尔把时间解释为事物存在的形式,正是现实事物本身的历程构成了时间;柏格森则认为时间就是生命的存在,是不断的创造与生成。马克思从时间、空间、客体、主体的四维视野,考察人类社会发展的历史进程,提出了"时间是人类发展的空间"这一著名的论断,并明确了"时间是以活动的形式存在着",活动是易逝的,当过程告一段落时,时间并没有化为乌有,而是转换了形式。过程消失在产品中,"劳动物化了,而对象被加工了,在劳动者方面曾以动的形式表现出来的东西,在产品方面作为静的属性,以存在的形式表现出来。"因此,对象化是马克思主义时间观的前提(刘奔,1991)。

城市空间作为人类社会实践活动的载体,总是寻求在空间形式中的最佳表现,由此形成了精神追求向物质环境的连续转化。获得一定寿限的人们,拥有一定气数的朝代,把自身所持续的一段生命和时间,物化为一系列"对象",从而取得了空间的形式。或者说,当一个阶段的营造活动结束时,人类的精神和智慧就转化为城市空间的物质形式,因此,城市空间同时也是社会实践活动的结果。人类社会发展过程中的制度文化、美学思想、宗教信仰、民间习俗和科技水平等都将在城市空间中留下印迹,正如法国地理学家夏保所言,"城市是一个自我形成的整体,其中的所有元素都参与了城市精神的塑造。"(阿尔多·罗西,1995)。

人类文明的这种物化过程赋予了城市空间历史和文化,体现了人类的思想和价值,形成了一种独特的空间现象。事实上,这种"独特现象"就是由历史累加及文化积淀所表述的"活动的形式",由于活动是连续的,反应在空间上就组成了一系列的时间注记。

2 城市空间的时间注记

人类的历史时间包括时序、纪事和变迁三层涵义:"时序表明了人类历史活动先后顺序的区别,纪事标志了人类历史活动具体内容的记忆,变迁则反映人类历史活动所引发的社会变革。"(龙先琼,2011),下面把历史时间的三层涵义放在城市空间中进行讨论。

首先,时序作为时间的基本属性,是城市空间演变进程的参照系,表现为不同空间要素产生的前后顺序。城市空间中的历史建筑物及构筑物,是时间在空间中的投影,代表不同时期的社会关系、经济发展和技术水平,使逝去的时间得以可数。例如在晋南的中国历史文化名城新绛古城中,隋朝的园池、唐代的大堂、宋代的文庙、元代的鼓楼、明代的钟楼、清代的安子巷、民国的天主堂,将城市发展的历程清晰地勾勒了出来。时序使城市空间发展具有时间矢量,城市文脉之所以连续,就因为有各时期典型的空间要素作为时序中的刻度(图1)。

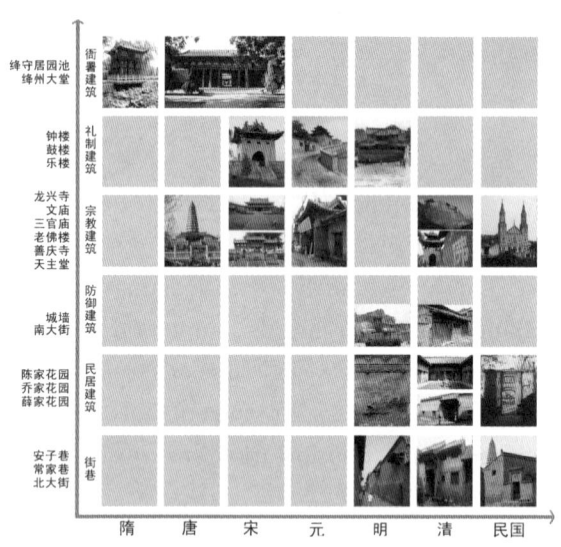

图1 新绛古城的历史建筑时序

第二,纪事是时间的本质内容,它标明城市空间各要素是能够识别的历史记忆,为已经消失的文化提供一种独特或特殊的见证。例如太原府城中的南华门历史街区,南华门、精营街、阎公馆旧址、赵树理故居等,固然标识了"年代"这种时间先后顺序,更重要的是承载了其中的历史事件:南华门纪录了明代晋王府270年的历程;精营街纪录了清代"精骑兵"军营的存在;阎公馆见证了民国时期阎锡山对太原统治的历史阶段;赵树理故居纪念了20世纪50年代中国文学史上的"山药蛋"流派。特定历史的注记,也成了城市历史阶段划分的识别,南华门街区也因为汇集了明代王宫、清代军营、民国政要、现代文学等诸多相关的历史要素,成为太原府城发展的缩影。城市空间因为不同时期的历史要素而有时间性,一个具体的历史要素因为纪事功能而有意义。

第三,变迁形成了时间的外部特征,城市空间演变在较长一段时间内的整体性变化是变迁,变迁构成了城市发展的阶段。在时间的视角下,讨论城市空间中某个朝代的古城墙与护城河、街道与里坊、古建与民居,不仅是指某个历史时间,也反映出这个时间城市空间的阶段性特点。例如,古城墙与护城河作为防御设施是冷兵器时代城市的显著标志,城墙在历史意义上代表了封建社会的制度文化,城墙的消失是城市空间进入近现代社会所发生的整体性变迁;狭小的里弄或胡同反映的是步行时代的城市尺度,城市道路的普遍拓宽是工业化时代的发展要求;而城市肌理的转换更是全面折射出城市社会经济的阶段性。变迁表明城市空间发展不断由量到质的积累过程,城市空间的历史属性得以真正确立。

3 空间要素的时间周期

"历史不外是各个世代的依次交替"(马克思,恩格斯,1995),人类文明发展的周期性现象意味某种时间的循环往复。时序、纪事和变迁作为城市空间发展的时间注记,在时间轴上是有规律的,表现为空间要素的节律性变化。城市空间的各种要素,包括城池、街道、建筑等各种物态形式,不可避免地受到时间背景的制约,有着不同的生命周期。由于要素具有连续性,它不断地被转换或替代,有着自我调整及更新的能力,因此,城市空间发展的历史是前后相承的,后者就必然包含着前者的部分内容及质素,形成了一种"如此类推,以致无穷"无限伸展的时间现象。

3.1 空间要素的自然周期

自然周期指城市空间要素受到自然因素影响衰减后,所进行修复、改造、重建等一系列循环往复的活动,是一个不间断的过程,这一持续性的活动,将过去延伸到现在。由于城市空间中不同要素的周期性不同,所反映的物态形式变化也有各自的时间规律。民居建筑的变更与人的平均寿命基本同步,约为75年左右;公共建筑由于民间组织的定期修缮,其生存周期相对较长,约为200年,但一些有象征意义的标志性建筑,时间更为长久;街巷肌理受城市总体格局的控制,具有一定的稳定性,周期可长达300～500年,因此,今天仍然能够看到一些城市明清时期的历史街区;山水格局是一个长期、稳定的存在,对城市空间的影响是整体性的或终极性的,一般以世纪为计量单位。

自然周期是一种基于"天地钟"所显示的节律性"测度时间",是一个渐变的新陈代谢过程,因此,在城市空间发展中,要素的新旧交织成为一种常态。尽管由于各要素周期的长短不同,出现不同时期的要素并置在同一时空的现象,但整体上却呈现出一种自然规律下的均质或统一状态。这种时空形态反映在许多历史悠久却空间完整的古城中,如土耳其的伊斯坦布尔古城区,在博斯普鲁斯海峡两岸有君士坦丁堡的古城墙、拜占庭时期的清真寺、奥斯曼帝国的王宫,但是,民居作为城市空间的大背景却处于持续更新的状态,由于在更新中始终维护着原有的物态形式,包括尺度、色彩与空间关系,历史肌理得以延续。和谐的城市空间展示的是完整时间过程,自然演化的结果。

3.2 空间要素的人工周期

人工周期指城市空间在强大的人为干预下,所进行的大规模改造、重建、新建等一系列构建性活动,是一个短时间内突变的过程。纵观中国历史上的城市空间演化,在新旧政权的交替时,一些激进的变革者出于革故鼎新的传统,发生了一些包括"堕城"在内的城市空间结构性转换。人工周期在时间维度上表现为一种中断的或间歇的特征,是"变迁"的内在因素,也是"纪事"的重要线索,但却使"时序"变得模糊,并在城市形态中形成了对比和拼贴的效果。

不论是大规模的旧城改造,还是局部的建筑更新,人工周期均以要素的"非正常死亡"为前提,构成一系列"历史事件"。而每一个历史事件留在城市空间的"印记"就成为时间"刻度",时空的关联耦合组成了城市空间密码。关于这点,英国建筑师库哈斯(Rem Koolhaas)曾研究柏林城市形态背后所暗示的各种力量及事件,认为柏林的丰富性在于那些激动人心的历史片断:新古典主义城市、早期现代大都市、纳粹首都、现代主义的试验床、战争的牺牲品、死而复生的拉撒路、冷战英雄等。现实的柏林充满着断裂、冲突和自发性,隐藏着无数等待发现的多义空间。

用马克思主义的历史发展观分析人工周期:"每一个阶段都是必然的。因此,对它所发生的时代和条件来说,都有它存在的理由,但是对它自己内部逐渐发展起来的新的、更高的条件来说,它就变成过时的和没有存在的理由了,它不得不让位于更高的阶段,而这个更高的阶段也同样是要走向衰落和灭亡的……"(马克思,恩格斯,1965)。人类文化的价值观作用于城市空间,自上而下地形成理性的城市空间秩序,因此,可以认为人工周期是超越自然限制的城市空间本质。

4 城市空间的历史文脉

"建成环境中任何时期和类型的建筑或其他要素,总是传递出当时的思潮或'精神'。因此,每一个城市都能当作多层次的'文本',以及符号和象征的叙事来'阅读',……建成环境记载了城市的变迁。"(伊塔洛·卡尔维诺,2006)城市空间是一部史书,文脉是城市空间的叙事方式,历史要素之间存在的关联性,使城市文脉可以通过物质形态被阅读和理解。

在语言学中文脉用来表达上下文的关系,著名的瑞士语言学家索绪尔(Ferdinand de Saussure)提出了语言共时性和历时性的研究方法:"前者是在同一个时期内存在的要素之间的关系,后者是在时间之中一个要素为另一个要素代替。"如果将文脉引申到城市空间,则是介于不同要素之间的内在联系。由于城市文脉是在一个特定的空间内形成的历史范畴,并在时间中有上下延伸的作用,因此,建立在时间矢量上的城市空间文脉,便成为研究城市特定历史环境的重要方法。本文借助两个案例,将语言学的逻辑关系用于研究城市空间中历史累积的不同方式,作为学术观点与大家商榷。

4.1 历史文脉的共时态

共时语言学(synchronic study,synchronie)又称静态语言学,从一个断面研究语言在某个历史时期的状态和发展。笔者进一步引申,认为共时的叙事方式在一定意义上包含了蒙太奇效果。"蒙太奇"原本是一个建筑学的术语,意为构成与装配,即将独立的建筑元素根据总体设计加以处理,使它们比原来个别存在时具有更高的效用(李敏泉,1989)。在中国古典诗词中就存在蒙太奇思维,如马致远的小令《天净沙·秋思》:"枯藤老树昏鸦,小桥流水人家,古道西风瘦马。夕阳西下,断肠人在天涯。"其中一系列不同时空存在的名词跳跃组合,但知觉的整体性却将各个意象关联为一个统一体。共时态在城市空间中,表现为不同历史时期的要素在同一个空间单元内的共时存在状态,要素之间存在着明显的时间差异性,使得城市空间具有"间歇"和"断裂"的痕迹,反映出城市空间发展过程的分异性和嬗变性。

图 2　太原府城中南华门街区的历史变迁

南华门曾是晋王宫的南门所在,朱棡在宋城外的杏花岭高地修建晋王府成为明太原城统治的象征;清顺治年间晋王府却被一把火化为灰烬,街区空间经历了一次跳跃性的转换,王府旧址成了清兵的精骑营,用于控制汉人反满,日后"精营"一词逐渐成为清太原城的符号;清末精骑营废除,街区空间再一次整体嬗变,演化为社会上层达官贵人的宅第,民国时期修筑正太、同蒲铁路时,德、日工程师建造的数栋别墅及山西军阀阎锡山、省长徐永昌故居成为这一时期的代表;新中国成立后新生的政权又将此作为行政中心,现在五一路的大药房曾经是政府礼堂的旧址。随后,街区空间为适应新的功能,又经历了一次次更替和转化,成片院落式民居,被各单位宿舍楼取代。南华门街区经历了明朝晋王府、清代精骑营、民国官宅、新中国成立后的行政中心,政权不断更替,城市空间也在不断重构,并构成一系列"历史事件"成为城市文脉中的"纪事"(图2)。

南华门历史街区的遗存状况反映了某些共时态的特征:街区地名是明代晋王宫城门的记忆;街巷骨架在清代兵营的结构上局部叠加明代宫城的巷道,并延续了"南华门"和"精营"的二元命名方式,如南华门东二条巷、南华门东四条巷、精营南横街、精营中横街等;历史建筑以典型的民国时期风格为主;而街区肌理则是传统民居院落和单位宿舍楼的二元拼贴。从街区历史要素的组成关系,可以看出共时态空间文脉的普遍存在:一方面,要素本身呈零散化或片断化;另一方面,在整体结构上却互为一体,体现出城市空间复杂性、多样性的本质特征。

4.2 历史文脉的历时态

历时语言学(diachronic study,diachronie)又称演化语言学,主要研究语言在一定的时间跨度内所经历的种种变化，历时态在城市时间形态上表现为同一要素的演化或变迁现象，如城市中轴线的生长、城市中心的转移、城市边界的拓展等，是在一个时间流程中叙述事件的始末。

位于山西省南部的新绛古城坐落在汾河北岸的二级阶地上，历朝历代的建设均随形就势、因地巧构，将自然地形与礼乐秩序完美结合，建城理念从隋唐建城至清末民国一脉相承，延续千年。城中的凤凰岭居高临下，集中了不同时期的城市标志物：隋朝的宴节楼、唐代的龙兴塔、元代的鼓楼、明代的钟楼、清代的老佛楼、民国时期的天主教堂……。标志物不断涌现，历时千年，成长为一条凸显的天际轮廓线，主从有序，错落有致，将空间关系化作时间艺术。其中的文脉是通过一定的阅读顺序而显现的，其中时间的"序"和空间的"位"是叙事的关键。

按照时间顺序，新绛古城的轮廓线起自衙署花园的宴节楼，这座隋开皇十六年(596年)由梁轨开挖修筑的绛守居园池作为衙署的一部分，位于城西北的衙坡上，循礼卜地而筑，《新绛县志卷八》(民国)载："县署即旧州署在城内西北崖上，高敞宏壮，甲于列郡……"隋开皇十六年为"序"，于西北高崖为"位"，组成衙署时空注记。城市空间的文脉以"王权至上"为开端，随后的鼓楼、钟楼均在衙署高阜先后修建，晨钟暮鼓，王权空间进一步得到强化。

唐初，龙兴寺高居在南大街一端，寺中宝塔43 m高，弋指蓝天，古城因此形势夺人，气象非凡，城市空间叙事达到高潮。宗教中心如此突显，使衙署建筑群谦恭地寄居在佛塔的身影之下，这在中国古代州城中也很少见。在这里，唐高宗咸亨元年(670年)为"序"，择城中而要为"位"，组成龙兴寺时空坐标。清时，二层高老佛楼与龙兴寺同地基而建，进一步巩固了佛教的中心地位。

民国二十六年(1937年)，荷兰籍主教孔照明主持修建新绛天主堂，再一次沿凤凰岭高崖选址于衙署与龙兴寺两组标志物之间，并与上海天主堂用同一图纸。高大的天主堂雄踞黄源，于城中三关五坊之上，是这条轮廓线"异质同构"。教堂西边为传统四合院组成的修道院，两座建筑紧紧相依，注释了民国时期中西合璧的时代精神。

从新绛古城天际线的演化，可以看出城市历史要素的历时态特征：首先，要素的发展是持续不断的，并有一条清晰的叙事主线。新绛历史上长期为州治所在地，领晋南五县，作为权力的中心场所，标志物彼此并置，说明了"天际线是在协商与交涉中达成的象征，那些影像之所以出现在城市天际线是因为它们获得了出场资格。"(斯皮罗·科斯托夫，2005)是权力"制造"了城市，制度"安排"了城市的空间结构；而标志物彼此对立，又暗示着各方权势对城市空间的争夺。其次，要素的发展是"因时而变"的，显示出对时间的依附性质，不同时代的特征相互关联，集结为城市空间文脉，是时间因素最直白的表现。

5 结语

本文从城市发展的历史进程出发，将城市空间视为时间化的空间。芒福德(Lewis Mumford)在《城市发展史》一书中将这样的城市空间称为"容器"："城市从起源时代开始便是一种特殊的构造，它专门用来贮存并流传人类文明的成果。"其中，贮存是空间属性，是历史积累在三维概念中的"广延"性存在；流传是时间属性，是历史积累在四维概念中的"持续"性存在。因此，只有建立包括时间在内的"四维城市"概念，才能真正把握城市发展过程中的历史文脉，对城市遗产进行更为有效的保护。

参考文献

[1] [美]刘易斯·芒福德. 城市发展史：起源、演变和前景[M]. 宋俊岭，倪文彦，译. 北京：中国建筑工业出版社，1989.
[2] [美]斯皮罗·科斯托夫. 城市的形成：历史进程中的城市模式和城市意义[M]. 单皓，译. 北京：中国建筑工业出版社，2005.
[3] [意]阿尔多·罗西. 城市建筑[M]. 施植明，译. 台北：尚林出版社，1995.
[4] 刘奔. 时间是人类发展的空间：社会时—空特性初探[J]. 哲学研究，1991(10)：3-10.
[5] 龙先琼. 试论区域史研究的空间和时间问题[J]. 齐鲁学刊，2011(1)：40-43.

[6] 王富臣.形态完整:作为城市设计的一种策略[J].同济大学学报(社会科学版),2004,15(3):69-74.
[7] 马克思,恩格斯.马克思恩格斯全集:第2卷[M].中共中央马克思恩格斯列宁斯大林著作编译局,编译.北京:人民出版社,1995.
[8] 马克思,恩格斯.马克思恩格斯全集:第21卷[M].中共中央马克思恩格斯列宁斯大林著作编译局,编译.北京:人民出版社,1965.
[9] [意]伊塔洛·卡尔维诺.看不见的城市[M].张宓,译.南京:译林出版社,2006.
[10] 徐思益.论语言的共时性和历时性[J].新疆大学学报(哲学人文社会科学版),1980:81-88.
[11] 李敏泉.蒙太奇思维与城市文脉中的环境设计[J].新建筑,1989(2):50-60.

文化·城市·未来：
文化遗产在城市可持续发展中的角色

CULTURE, URBAN, FUTURE: ROLE OF CULTURE IN SUSTAINABLE URBAN DEVELOPMENT

《文化·城市·未来:文化促进城市可持续发展全球报告》节选

全球半数以上人口目前生活在城市地区,世界各地的城市为此纷纷踏上可持续发展之路。联合国致力于落实《2030年可持续发展议程》以及《新城市议程》,因此务必要汇集各方最佳政策,让我们的城市充分发挥出全部潜能。

前途有艰难险阻,教育、粮食安全、水资源管理、建设包容社会和有效机制等可持续发展问题首先给城市带来冲击。但城市也是人类历史上最璀璨的发明创造之一,可以为人类探索出一条通向未来的出路。最重要的是,城市集中了具备创造力和生产力的民众,并且协助他们从事最擅长的工作:交流、创造、创新。从美索不达米亚平原的古城,到文艺复兴时期的意大利城邦,再到活力四射的当代大都会,城市始终是推动人类发展的最强大动力。如今,我们必须再次寄希望于城市。

文化是实现城市复兴与创新的内核……文化作为一项战略资产,在提升城市的包容性、创造力和可持续性方面显示出了力量。创造力和文化多样性历来是城市发展的重要动因。文化活动可以促进不同社区实现社会包容,支持它们开展对话。物质及非物质遗产是塑造城市特性、形成归属感和社会凝聚力的必要因素。文化是一座城市灵魂的象征,有助于城市繁荣发展和建设人人享有尊严的未来。教科文组织近几十年来正是围绕着这一观点开展工作,特别是制定了"创意城市网络"等计划、提出"学习型智慧城市"倡议和保护城市历史景观。明确承认文化是促进可持续发展的动力,也是实现可持续发展目标11("建设包容、安全、有抵御灾害能力和可持续的城市和人类住区")的重要条件之一,为这种观点注入了新的活力。

以人为本的城市,同时也是以文化为本的空间。我们必须将这一现实转化为更有效的政策和可持续的城市治理。城市已然成为天然实验室,人们在这里研判如何磋商、管理和经受最迫切的挑战。我们必须强化城市的文化资产、遗产和创造机会;城市居民在遗产中寻得了意义和身份,而创造机会成就了更加充满活力、宜居和繁荣的城市……

联合国教科文组织

Culture · Urban · Future: Global Report on Culture for Sustainable Urban Development (Excerpt)

With over half of the world's population now living in urban areas, the road to sustainable development passes through cities in every corner of the globe. As the United Nations works to implement the 2030 *Agenda for Sustainable Development* and the *New Urban Agenda*, it is critical to bring together the best policies to make the most of our cities.

The challenges we face are steep and cities are on the frontlines of sustainable development issues such as education, food security, water management, the development of inclusive societies, and effective institutions. Yet cities are also one of humanity's most brilliant inventions for crafting solutions for the future. Fundamentally, cities bring creative and productive people together, helping them to do what they do best: exchange, create and innovate. From the ancient cities of Mesopotamia to the city-states of the Italian Renaissance and the vibrant metropolises of today, urban areas have been among the most powerful engines of human development. Today, we must once again place our hope in cities.

Culture lies at the heart of urban renewal and innovation... Creativity and cultural diversity have been the key drivers of urban success. Cultural activities can foster social inclusion and dialogue among diverse communities. Tangible and intangible heritages are integral parts of a city's identity, creating a sense of belonging and cohesion. Culture embodies the soul of a city, allowing it to progress and build a future of dignity for all. This reflection has been at the core of UNESCO's work over the last decades, notably through the development of programmes such as the Creative Cities Network, the Learning and Smart Cities initiatives and the protection of historic urban landscapes. This vision has received new energy with the explicit recognition of the role of culture as an enabler of sustainable development, and as one of the key conditions to achieve Sustainable Development Goal 11 to "Make cities and human settlements inclusive, safe, resilient and sustainable".

A human-centred city is a culture-centred space. We must translate this reality into more effective policies and sustainable urban governance. Cities have become living laboratories for determining how some of the most pressing challenges we face are negotiated, managed and experienced. We must strengthen the cultural assets of cities, the heritage that provides a sense of meaning and identity to their inhabitants, and the creative opportunities that enhance the vitality, liveability and prosperity of our cities...

UNESCO

中国历史文化名城制度建立 35 年的回顾与思考

Reflections on the 35 Years of Establisment of the System of
"Famous Historical and Cultural Cities" in China

赵宝江

原建设部副部长

Zhao Baojiang

Former Vice Minister, Ministry of Construction

This speech introduces the establishment and development of the system of "Famous Historical and Cultural Cities" in China. Referring to those achievements as well as shortcomings and problems, the speaker shares his reflections and propositions.

我国 5 000 多年的悠久文明,城市是一个主要载体。我国古代城市建设,蕴藏着极为丰富且极具智慧的思想观念、理论原则和技术手法。早在周代就形成了营城制度,并把城邑总体布局纳入礼制轨道,形成特有的空间秩序。中国建筑自古以来在世界上就具有重大影响,同欧洲建筑、伊斯兰建筑并称为世界三大建筑体系。相对于另外两大体系,中国建筑历史更加悠久、体系更加完整、更加注重自然和生活。时至今日,我国古代城市建设思想仍然具有重要借鉴意义。

自 1982 年国务院公布第一批国家历史文化名城至今已经 35 年了。35 年来,国家历史文化名城的数量从 1982 年设立时的 24 座,增加到现在的 132 座,同时还公布了 252 个中国历史文化名镇和 276 个中国历史文化名村。国家历史文化名城制度的设立,对于保护我国珍贵的历史文化遗产、继承我国悠久的传统文化、树立文化自信、建设美丽中国,实现中华民族伟大复兴具有重要意义。

下面简要回顾一下 35 年来中国历史文化名城保护工作的情况。

一、国家历史文化名城制度的建立

1. 历史文化名城制度的建立

1981 年,在北京大学侯仁之、建设部郑孝燮、故宫博物院单士元三位先生的提议下,全国政协起草了一份专题报告,要求尽快公布一批文物古迹丰富的历史城市。该报告很快得到中央的批复,时任国家建委主任谷牧随即把具体文件起草的任务交给了建委和文物局。

1982 年 2 月 8 日,国务院直接批转了《国家建委等部门关于保护我国历史文化名城的请示》,公布了首批北京、承德等 24 个国家历史文化名城。

1982 年 11 月,全国人大常委会通过了《中华人民共和国文物保护法》,规定:"保存文物特别丰富、具有重大历史价值和革命意义的城市,由国家文化行政管理部门会同城乡建设环境部门报国务院核定公布为历史文化名城。"这是第一次明确定义历史文化名城的概念并写入国家法律。

1983 年 2 月当时的城乡建设环境保护部、城市规划局和文化部文化局召开"历史文化名城规划与保护座谈会",发布了《关于加强历史文化名城规划工作的几点意见》(简称《意见》)。《意见》指出:"历史文化名城这一基本概念,反映了城市的特定性质,作为一种总的指导思想和原则,应当在城市规划中体现出来。"这个文件还从规划角度提出了历史文化名城的概念,关于名城的条件和应该保护的内容。

公布国家历史文化名城的措施,在各地引起重大反响,保护历史文化名城的思想逐步推广开来,许多城市纷纷提出申请,希望能成为历史文化名城。建设部和国家文物局在1984年开始着手第二批名城名单的审定工作,研究名城的条件、标准、制定申报程序,要把历史文化名城的保护制度化。

1986年国务院在公布武汉、上海、天津等第二批36座历史文化名城的《城乡建设环境保护部、文化部关于请公布第二批国家历史文化名城名单报告的通知》中确定了历史文化名城的审定原则:"不但要看城市的历史,还要着重看当前是否保存有较为丰富、完好的文物古迹和具有重大的历史、科学、艺术价值。"

1994年,国务院公布了第三批历史文化名城的名单,共计37座,此后,名城的审批按照成熟一个公布一个的方式进行。本次公布的历史文化名城共有正定、邯郸等37座。

2002年10月,第九届全国人民代表大会常务委员会第三十次会议通过了修订后的《中华人民共和国文物保护法》(简称《文物保护法》),其中第二章第十四条规定"保存文物特别丰富并且具有重大历史价值或者革命意义的城市,由国务院核定公布为历史文化名城",对历史文化名城的概念再次进行了法律意义上的表述。2008年4月,国务院第三次常委会议通过了《历史文化名城名镇名村保护条例》。该条例对历史文化名城仍延续文物保护法的概念,但对具体的申报条件有了进一步细化,并具体指出具备下列条件的城市、镇、村庄可以申报历史文化名城、名镇、名村"①保存文物特别丰富;②历史建筑集中成片;③保留着传统格局和历史风貌;④历史上曾经作为政治、经济、文化、交通中心或者军事要地,或者发生过重要历史事件,或者其传统产业、历史上建设的重大工程对本地区的发展产生过重要影响,或者能够集中反映本地区建筑的文化特色、民族特色。申报历史文化名城的,在所申报的历史文化名城保护范围内还应当有2个以上的历史文化街区。"

2. 历史文化名城概念的拓展

1985年3月,正值第二批历史文化名城评选材料的上报期,建设部城市规划司开始对部分申报材料进行实地调研。建议除了历史文化名城,再定一个"历史性传统街区"的名目,实事求是地缩小范围,可能会更有助于抢救保护。

1986年国务院转批《城乡建设环境保护部、文化部关于请示公布第二批国家历史文化名城名单报告的通知》对"历史文化保护区"的概念有了正式的确认。

1997年8月建设部发出《转发〈黄山市屯溪老街历史文化保护区保护管理暂行办法〉的通知》(简称《通知》)。《通知》指出"历史文化保护区是我国文化遗产的重要组成部分,是保护单体文物、历史文化保护区、历史文化名城这一完整体系中不可缺少的一个层次,也是我国历史文化名城保护工作的重点之一",明确了历史文化保护区的特征、保护原则与方法,并对保护管理工作给予了具体指导。

2002年《文物保护法》正式提出历史文化街区的法定概念,规定了"保存文物特别丰富并且具有重大历史价值或者革命纪念意义的城镇、街道、村庄,由省、自治区、直辖市人民政府核定公布为历史文化街区、村镇,并报国务院备案"。2005年国家《历史文化名城保护规划规范》明确了"历史文化街区"的概念,并规定历史文化街区的用地面积不得小于1公顷,文物古迹和历史建筑的用地面积宜达到保护区内建筑总用地的60%以上。2008年国务院颁布的《历史文化名城名镇名村保护条例》明确了"历史文化街区"的法律地位。

"在历史文化街区范围内除了文物古迹,应当分布有大量历史建筑和其他未列及的文物资源。历史文化街区的划定与保护,既要考虑历史遗迹的真实性,街区风貌的完整性,还要考虑居民生活的连续性。"将历史街区保护有机地融合到城市规划之中,有利于摆脱过去在城市环境中孤立对待文物建筑保护的做法。福州"三坊七巷"的保护是一个很好的案例。"三坊七巷"已成为福州的名片,凡是到福州去过的人必去"三坊七巷"参观。

3. 历史文化名城的国际化

随着文化遗产保护的不断深入、保护理念和内容的不断拓展,到20世纪90年代末我国应联合国教科文组织世界遗产中心的要求开始申报可以反映我国人居环境的历史城镇和历史村落的遗产项目,其规模开始由原来的点状或单一项目发展到作为人类聚居地的历史城镇或村落。1997年12月3日,在意大利那不勒斯召开的联合国教科文组织世界遗产委员会第21届大会上,我国的历史文化名城平遥、丽江及苏州古典园林被列入《世界遗产名录》,这标志着我国名城保护工作已经得到相关国际组织的肯定。

4. 特有的历史保护理念

历史文化名城是我国特有的历史保护理念:①它是一项措施,不只是一项荣誉;②它要保护城市,而非城市中的一个个文物;③历史文化名城保护的内容可以归纳为保护文物古迹和历史地段、保护和延续古城的格局和风貌特色、继承和发扬优秀历史文化传统,也就是是说,除了文物古迹外,包括名城中的历史文化街区、古城的整体格局和风貌,还包括优秀的传统文化、非物质文化遗产;④历史文化名城要制定保护发展规划并纳入城市总体规划,明确界定保护范围,制定有效的保护管理措施。

历史文化名城是一个与城市行政管辖有关的历史文化遗产概念,其保护范围和具体内容在历史文化名城保护规划中确定。正如《历史文化名城名镇名村保护条例》所指出的:"历史文化名城应当整体保护,保持传统格局、历史风貌和空间尺度,不得改变与其相互依存的自然景观和环境。"

二、我国历史文化名城保护法制体系的演变

历史文化名城保护法规体系的演变,是伴随着新中国成立后城镇历史文化保护而发展变化的。

新中国成立后,我国城镇历史文化保护法制建设首先从文物保护开始;改革开放后,随着历史文化名城名镇名村保护工作的深入开展,我国城镇历史文化保护的法律法规体系也日趋完善。从保护的法规层次来看,主要分为全国性保护法律、法规和规范性文件,地方性法规及规范性文件。

1994年9月,建设部、国家文物局印发了《历史文化名城保护规划编制要求》为历史文化名城保护规划明确了技术要求。

文物保护、城乡规划法规的制定。2003年建设部令第119号发布《城市紫线管理办法》,进一步提出了在编制城市规划时应当划定保护历史文化街区和历史建筑的紫线。2007年颁布的《城乡规划法》,提出历史文化名城、名镇、名村的保护以及受保护建筑物的维护和使用,应当遵守有关法律、行政法规和国务院的规定;2008年颁布的《历史文化名城名镇名村的保护条例》对历史文化名城、名镇、名村的申报、批准、规划、保护提出了具体要求。

2014年建设部第20号部令发布了《历史文化名城名镇名村街区保护规划编制审批办法》。2016年建设部印发了《历史文化街区划定和历史建筑确定工作方案》要求用5年时间全面完成历史文化街区划定和历史建筑确定工作,对历史文化遗产应保尽保。

三、我国历史文化名城保护的内容和方法

1. 历史文化名城保护的基本内容

从1961年颁布《文物保护管理暂行条例》到1982年开始建立历史文化名城保护制度,中国历史文化遗产保护制度一直是以文物保护为核心的单一体系,直到1982年,历史文化名城的提出使得我国遗产保护制度形成双元结构,1986年又提出的历史文化街区概念使得我国的中国文化遗产保护制度形成了包括文物、历史街区和历史文化名城3个层次在内的多层次体系。"保护文物古迹及历史地段,保护和延续古城的风貌特色,继承和发扬城市的传统文化。"前三点为物质要素,最后一点为非物质要素。

历史文化街区的概念也经历了一个从模糊到清晰,范畴从大到小的过程。1986年公布第二批国家历史文化名城的文件中,最早提出了"历史文化保护区"的概念,当时的历史文化保护区不仅包含了城区中有传统风貌的历史地段,也包含不在城区范围的历史文化村镇、建筑群。在2002年《文物保护法》修订中,"历史文化街区"成为法定名词取代了"历史文化保护区",在历史文化名城中历史街区的保护有着极其重要的现实意义。于是从2003年开始,中国历史文化名镇名村保护制度单独设置。

历史文化风貌区目前并非法定概念,也没有统一的定义。

2. 历史文化名城的保护方法

历史文化名城的整体保护方法。在整体保护方法中,首先要强调从城市整体发展角度协调保护和发展的关系,具体来说应当做到以下几点:在城市性质中体现名城的特点;合理地确定城镇发展战略,优化历史城区的产业结构;采取合理的城镇用地布局,疏解旧城人口,调整旧地用地功能;改善历史文化名城、名镇、名村的基础设施、公共服务设施和居住环境。总的来说,名城保护不能就保护论保护,应当把名称保护和城市的社会经济发展结合起来。在整体保护中应当从山水环境、传统格局、历史风貌和非物质文化遗产四个方面进行保护。

历史文化街区的保护方法。历史文化街区的保护方法目前主要包括:①保护历史遗存的真实性,反对拆真建假,保护好现存各类历史文化遗存,确保历史信息的真实载体不受到人为破坏和自然损毁;②保护历史风貌的完整性,避免擅自改变和侵占历史环境保护街区的空间环境;③维持社会生活的延续性,应保持一定比例的原住民,延续生活,继承文化传统,改善基础设施和居住环境,保持街区活力;④划定核心保护范围和建筑控制地带界线,制定相应的管理规定;⑤对保护范围内的建筑物、构筑物和环境要素进行分类保护;⑥保护街区内的非物质文化遗产和传统文化。

历史文化名镇名村保护方法。历史文化名镇名村的保护方法目前主要包括:①保护好镇、村现存的历史文化遗存和整体风貌特色,确保历史遗存的真实性,保护历史信息和真实载体;②镇域、村域的总体保护,明确镇域、村域内需要保护的历史文化遗存,对镇域、村域内的景观环境、空间布局提出控制与引导措施;③保护与名镇名村密切相关的地形地貌、河湖水系、自然生态等景观和环境,制定相应的管理规定;④划定核心保护范围和建设控制地带界限,制定相应的管理规定;⑤对保护范围内的建筑物、构筑物和环境要素进行分类保护;⑥改善基础设施、公共服务设施、生产生活环境;⑦延续传统文化、保护非物质文化遗产。

3. 保护认识的深化和内容的拓展

数百年来,人们对于文化遗产保护的认识不断深化,保护内容不断封堵,正确理解历史文化名城保护内容的外延,是关系到历史文化名城保护工作发展全局的重大课题。新时期历史文化名城的拓展主要包括工业遗产、文化线路、20世纪遗产和文化生态保护4个方面。其中对于工业遗产的保护越来越受到重视。

从英国"工业考古学"的兴起到《下塔吉尔宪章》的出台,工业遗产保护理念日趋完善。在新的文化遗产保护理念的指引下,工业遗产的保护日益得到国际社会的关注,众多国家已经通过制定保护措施、合理利用等方式使得工业遗产得到最大程度的有效保护和利用,许多地区的工业遗产保护与产业结构转型、环境整治、社会经济复苏等内容统筹协调,取得良好的效果和成功的经验。

我国近代工业起步较晚,但是工业化与中华土壤相结合,产生了众多类型丰富、特色显著地工业城市和工业遗产,拥有丰富的空间形态和特色,具有重要的遗产价值和文化意义。

在目前,我国对于工业遗产的保护实践案例主要分为三种类型:改造为博物馆、展览馆的模式,如上海世博会的中国船舶馆、乐山嘉阳小火车;文化创意产业植入模式,如北京198艺术区、上海苏州河沿岸仓库;城市开放空间的塑造,如中山岐江公园等。

工业遗产是具有历史学、社会学、建筑学和科技、审美价值的工业文化遗存,包括工厂、车间……以及工艺流程、数据记录、企业档案等物质和非物质文化遗存。

4. 保护情况概述

35年来,我国相继建成了以名城为主体的保护体制,完善了历史文化名城保护法律法规体系。以《城乡规划法》《文物保护法》为基础,出台了《历史文化名城名镇名村保护条例》,促进了我国历史文化名城、历史文化遗产保护与国际接轨。各地各级政府也制定了一系列地方的名城、名镇、名村保护规章。各地也认真地贯彻执行国家的名城、名镇、名村保护规定。名城、名镇、名村得到了较好的保护。

2010年12月,住房城乡建设部和国家文物局开展国家历史文化名城、中国历史文化名镇名村保护工作检查。两部委联合检查组对31个省市的54个国家历史文化名城进行了重点抽查。检查主要内容包括：名城名镇名村保护范围及数量变化，历史文化街区、历史建筑、文物保护工作情况，保护规划制定，保护规划实施，地方法规制定，国家专项补助资金使用等几个方面。通过检查，两部门对聊城等8个保护工作不力的名城予以通报批评。

5. 历史文化名城保护工作中存在的问题

应当注意到，随着社会经济的快速发展，历史文化名城保护工作仍存在不少问题。一些历史文化名城的文化遗产遭到了破坏，主要表现：

（1）城市建设缺乏特色。随着城镇化进程的推进，一些城市历史风貌丧失、历史文脉断裂、城市特色消失。空间秩序混乱，存在"千城一面，万楼一貌"的现象。

（2）历史城区的格局被破坏。由于一些城市忽视了城市布局的整体调控，在历史城区已经十分拥挤的情况下，依然利用古城的地理位置优势开发建设，拆古建新，对古城格局与风貌造成了严重破坏。

（3）历史文化街区环境品质下降。大多数历史文化街区建造年代距今时间较长，人口密度过大，市政基础设施落后，建筑年久失修，居住环境差。

（4）开发性破坏日渐突出。一些城市急于发展经济，对历史文化资源进行过度开发，甚至以景区建设、旅游开发替代历史文化遗产和城市风貌保护，甚至出现了拆除真实历史遗存、建造假古董的情况，对历史遗存造成了不可挽回的损失。

四、对名城名镇名村保护工作的几点思考和建议

保护好历史文化名城，不仅有利于历史文化遗存的保护，而且对于传承历史文脉、发展先进文化，满足人民群众精神生活需求，增强中华民族的凝聚力具有重要作用。可以从以下几方面做好历史文化名城保护工作。

（1）进一步要求地方政府落实对历史文化名城的保护责任，提高各级政府和公众的历史文化遗产保护意识。同时，加强全社会的保护意识，鼓励群众参与、支持保护工作。

（2）完善法制，加强监管。完善配套法规建设，形成完整的历史文化名城名镇名村保护管理法规体系。逐步建立健全历史文化名城监督检查制度、定期评估机制和保护动态监测平台，加强对保护工作的日常监督。

（3）科学规划，严格实施。加强历史文化名城名镇名村保护规划编制工作，提高保护规划的质量和水平。严格按照批准的保护规划开展工作，坚决制止和纠正违反保护规划的行为。

（4）完成所有城市历史文化街区划定和历史建筑确定公布工作。用5年左右时间，将保存文物特别丰富、历史建筑集中成片、能够较完整和真实地体现传统格局和历史风貌，并具有一定规模的区域核定公布为历史文化街区，并划定保护范围；将具有一定保护价值、能够反映历史风貌和地方特色的建、构筑物确定公布为历史建筑。提出明确的保护要求，制定切实可行的保护整治措施。

（5）加强名城保护工作检查。今年是国家历史文化名城制度设立35周年，将开展历史文化名城保护工作检查。通过保护工作检查，表扬先进并推广保护工作经验，通报批评保护工作开展不力的名城，并限期整改。

当前，我国城市进入新型城镇化发展时期，历史文化名城保护工作得到了党和国家领导人的高度重视。习近平总书记多次指出，历史文化是城市的灵魂，要像爱惜自己的生命一样保护好城市历史文化遗产。我们将和各国同仁一道，努力探索和实践历史文化遗产保护的方法，处理好城市改造开发和历史文化遗产保护利用的关系，切实做到在保护中发展、在发展中保护。

古民居保护的思考

Reflections on Conservation of Historic Vernacular Dwellings

阮仪三 教授
同济大学国家历史文化名城研究中心主任
同济大学建筑与城市规划学院 教授、博导
Prof. Ruan Yisan
Director, Research Center on National Famous Historical & Cultural Cities,
Doctoral Supervisor, School of Architecture & Urban Planning, Tongji University

The tangible bearer of Chinese traditional culture, historic vernacular dwellings and their setting is subject to conservation. Meanwhile, voluntary reconstruction and construction of dwellings in traditional style as well as the tolerance of local government present an inspirational case in Yangzhou.

今天我在这里讲中国古民居保护的思考,为什么谈这个问题,因为古民居还没有得到大家足够的重视。我到欧洲参观过马克思故居,他的孙女一家四口依旧居住在里面。我看到了马克思过去的生活场景,心里非常温暖,这就是西方保护的方式。我们有自己的民居,也有自己的保护方式,如武汉的民居——汉口附近的大土楼。民居保护方面,目前上海提出了申报世界遗产。

中央城镇化工作会议提出"望得见山,看得见水,记得住乡愁",对于民居来讲,这是很有文化、很科学、很有人情味的要求。乡愁是包含着家乡祖祖辈辈人与人之间的亲情关系,而这些关系又凭借着那些故乡的古老建筑及建筑所形成的场景风光特色而存在,建筑承载了人与人之间的亲情。

传统民居中的礼仪空间

中国民居创造了阖家团聚的礼仪空间格局,营造了温馨的家庭氛围。无论是北京四合院,苏州、扬州的厅堂式住宅,徽州的四水归堂,云南、贵州的三合一照壁、四合五天井以及福建客家的土楼,到了上海近代就演变成中西合璧的石库门,这些房子核心全是合院式的。合院就有天井,与天地相通。房子围合起来安全、保温、遮风、避阳,但不能离开天地,上通天下通地,强调人的居家礼仪,敬天地、拜祖先、阖家团聚、和睦相亲,并且长幼有序,内外有别。北方四合院组成的胡同、江南房子组成的街巷、上海石库门组成的里弄,都由于居住在这些房子里的人,不分贫富、职业、地位,相互关心,互相帮助,讲礼貌,懂情分,也就出现了"青梅竹马""过门亲家"等充满亲情的故事,这就是中国式的传统文化留给我们的物质遗产。

而现在大规模的建设,各地采取的都是彻底的改造,拆掉旧房建新房,把老的这些中华优秀文化传统——和睦、礼让、尊老爱幼、有礼有序的空间格局依存的物质基础全都丢弃了。保护老房子也就是保护中华传统文化,而提倡礼仪,重振中华礼仪文化,就要保护老建筑和它所形成的传统场景和氛围。

在扬州,我看到在古城里有一些老居民在改建新房子或是营建着古式的新房子。有不少人家在自家的天井、院子里栽种了适宜的花草树木,有的堆了半壁假山,有的开了个池塘,更有的围了廊子,盖了亭子,俨然是一个居家的小园林。住户摒弃了干巴巴的方盒子、冷冰冰的瓷砖,而用自己的双手恢复了老祖宗留下的诗情画意的环境。有人做统计,这样的古典民宅有100多处。他们在用自己的力量保护着历史文化,用自己的行动在找回乡愁。

我想,从现行的城市房屋管理法制上说这些行为都是违章搭建,而扬州市政府允许他们去做,没有大的干涉,说明政府也有明智的政策措施。其中还有复杂的房产权、租用权的政策问题,想必是因扬州政府有一定的对策,民众改建的积极性才能不被扼杀。我认为扬州市政府是有所作为的,作为著名古城的领导者站在了保护的前列。特别是扬州市的老百姓,因为只有实际的居住者,才对自己的喜爱和厌恶最有发言权,对于古建保护与拆毁,扬州老百姓已经用行动给了明智的答案。

在发展中守护城乡遗产,留住乡愁是中国走向现代化的同时,又不失去本民族文化传统的必由之路。我们现在建的房子,千城一面,粗俗的建设设计,哪里有中国味?哪里有地方味?哪里有民居味?希望大家认真地思考。我企望各地政府都能学学扬州的做法,使历史建筑有一个更新的动作,迎合老百姓的需求。

UNESCO 历史性城镇景观建议：面向可持续城市的理论与实践
The UNESCO Recommendation on the Historic Urban Landscape (HUL): Theories and Practice for Sustainable Cities

迈克尔·特纳 教授
联合国教科文组织城市设计与保护研究教席持有人
联合国教科文组织世界遗产中心主任特使
联合国教科文组织世界遗产委员会前副主席
Prof. Michael Turner
Holder, UNESCO Chair in Urban Design and Conservation Studies
Special Envoy to the World Heritage Centre Director
Former Vice-President, UNESCO World Heritage Committee

《历史性城镇景观建议》的通过是对城市整体规划中文化遗产角色的一次里程碑式的认识与肯定。HUL 也越来越被人们理解为一种方法，而非一种遗产门类。全球范围内的一系列试点项目显示出它在激励各地的主动性以及方法创新中具有的重要作用。本文旨在探究 HUL 如何可以成为 2016 年《新城市议程》中关于城市可持续发展相关内容的理论基础，以及如何有助于实现联合国可持续发展目标中的相关目标（条款 11.4）。城市的层次是塑造城市认同、认识文化多样性、建立社会包容性的重要因素。《新城市议程》中也强调了"物质遗产与城市景观的其他要素在反映地方认同"中所具有的重要性。河流都市文明（River Urbanism）即为一个具有意义的主题类型而 HUL 的重要功能就是为实现可持续性提供理论与实践工具。

1 Background

1.1 Urbanism

a. From the *World Heritage Convention* to the *New Urban Agenda*

In less than fifty years, between the *World Heritage Convention* of 1972 and the *New Urban Agenda* of 2016, cities multiplied from 2 to 28 mega-cities with population above ten million inhabitants while overall, nearly half of the world's 3.9 billion urban dwellers now reside in relatively small settlements with fewer than 500,000 inhabitants.[①] This has been accompanied by political changes from socialism to neo-liberalism, speculative growth to sustainable development and the revisiting our appreciation of urban heritage. This has generated new challenges and opportunities including the socio-economic transformations and the impending digital revolution. A number of milestones have been passed together with

---
① United Nations (2014). World Urbanization Prospects: The 2014 Revision.

seminal texts that have evidenced these changes.

There have been two concepts, sometimes diverging, sometimes merging, underpinning planning processes—the collective right of "doing good" and individual rights based on the principle to "do not harm"—*primum non nocere*. These concepts also highlight the differences between the sources of US planning through tort and that of the UK city fathers of the 19th century "doing good" translated into top-down and bottom-up actions.

Although the concept of public use and public interest was paramount—there was little knowledge as to how the public use and interest can be assessed. Heritage emerged only much later as an amenity when the values became to be recognized by the wider community.

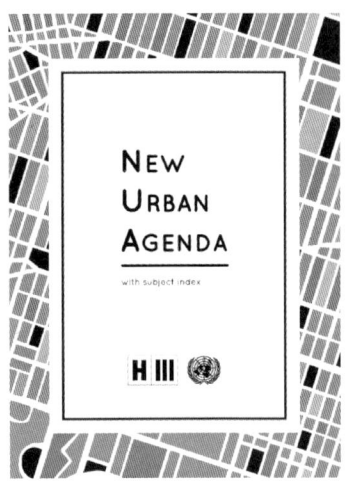

《新城市议程》

Questioning, planning concepts, public values and human rights, the dramatic political changes in the Eastern bloc, from 1989, sent ripples around the world. However, these changes were also tempered by cultural norms affected by Buddhism, Hinduism and Shintoism and twentieth-century communism. The 21st century opened into a global swamp.

The speed of political changes in the governance of our cities is in sharp contrast to their physical manifestations. Anachronisms appear, buildings outlive their owners and in a similar way we see that texts outlive their authors, and become part of a set of cultural habits equal to, if not surpassing, the importance of authorial intent. Supporters of Jacques Derrida have read this insight into "the layered meanings and incompleteness of language subverting reason and rationality, stripping centuries of assumptions from words and allowing fresh ideas to emerge". *Shakespeare in Modern Dress* clearly being an acceptable interpretation of the well-known plays and with trans-cultural version in Lin Zhaohua's innovative direction of the *Tragedy of Coriolanus* at the 2013 Edinburgh Festival. Modern functions inserted into the historic urban fragments and forms provide for similar expressions.

Recent global processes and trends suggest that a deep critical review of assumptions and paradigms currently used to analyse and explain urban processes, and hopefully to solve them is urgent and necessary. Many concepts, value systems and design principles are inadequate to understand and explain new conditions; they must be changed. Various countries that for a long time have been strongly influenced by Western culture are rediscovering the relevance of their traditional cultures. Traditional notions, concepts, methods are increasingly used to tackle and solve nowadays situations and issues. The success of some of these efforts suggests the opportunity to further develop research and invention in this field. [1]

Much emphasis has been laid on the definitions of the "Non-Western City". Zeynep Çelik[2] notes that urban spaces and social structures feature at the core of new investigations while a noteworthy consequence is the gradual reversal of the isolated position of the non-Western cities as exotic case-studies.

b. Urban heritage

The city can no longer be seen as a single entity; it is now construed as a series of urban fragments[3]

---

[1] Paolo Ceccarelli, *Past Is Not a Frozen Concept: Considerations about Heritage Conservation in a Fast Changing World*, Volume 1 No 3, September 2017.

[2] Zeynep Çelik: *New Approaches to the "Non-Western" City*; Journal of the Society of Architectural Historians, Vol. 58, No. 3, tember, 1999, pp. 374-381.

[3] These fragments have been well defined in European urban research projects as SUIT, URBACT and HerO.

and overlays breaking down boundaries with woven textures of warp and weft, with seams and hems sometimes fraying at the edges. Moving from monuments to living cities and from statements to narratives, the role of culture as a driver and/or an enabler for sustainable development in facilitating this change has become important. This was underscored in 2011 with the adoption of the UNESCO Recommendation on the Historic Urban Landscape (HUL) approach, highlighting the correlation of culture with nature and the tangible and intangible, in the opening paragraph:

"Urban heritage is for humanity a social, cultural and economic asset, defined by an historic layering of values that have been produced by successive and existing cultures and an accumulation of traditions and experiences, recognized as such in their diversity."…. extending beyond the notion of "historic centre" or "ensemble" to include the broader urban context and its geographical setting…. This wider context includes notably the site's topography, geomorphology, hydrology and natural features, its built environment, both historic and contemporary, its infrastructures above and below ground, its open spaces and gardens, its land use patterns and spatial organization, perceptions and visual relationships, as well as all other elements of the urban structure. It also includes social and cultural practices and values, economic processes and the intangible dimensions of heritage as related to diversity and identity. (UNESCO, 2011)

The focus must surely be on the rights to, and the role of, urban heritage, especially as this single type represents over a quarter of all inscribed on the World Heritage List. The term "urban heritage" is used to provide a more inclusive definition than, for example, town centres, historic quarters. Moreover, the unpublished report[①] of the World Heritage Centre based on the research of Professor Ana Pereira-Roders and Dr. Loes Veldpaus (Pereira-Roders & Veldpaus, 2010) indicates that there are over 1600 sites of urban heritage encapsulated in the World Heritage List, and a dramatic increase since 2010 due to the larger number of serial nominations and the greater application of cultural landscapes.

Based on the decisions of the World Heritage Committee, in December 2015, the World Heritage Centre commissioned a study that focused on the taxonomy and understanding of urban heritage in the context of the *World Heritage Convention*. The study revisits urban heritage definitions, terminology and types, as well as the threats to urban heritage, based on the state of conservation reports and particularly through the applying of the approach of the 2011 UNESCO Recommendation on the Historic Urban Landscape (HUL). The outcome of this research and assessment positions urban heritage as a type and organized into three categories:

(i) *Urban Archaeology* being sites which provide exceptional evidence of the past;

(ii) *Urban Area* being sites which, by their very nature, have developed and will continue to evolve under the influences of cultural, social, economic and environmental change;

(iii) *Urban Form* being sites demonstrated by planning or design concepts that have shaped and organized the city and remain evident.

In-depth knowledge of cultural resources can lay the foundations for a "place-based" approach to planning, while the cultural approach, relying on "layering the city over the city", can assist in rethinking planning models, particularly in the face of the growing variety and complexity of urban frameworks.

---

① O'Donnell, P. and Turner, M., *UNESCO Report on Urban Heritage*, December 2015.

2. Culture—the tool for sustainable development

Three critical milestones were in 1987 with the *Brundtland Report*[①] on sustainable development, the fall of the Berlin Wall in 1989 and the Earth Summit in 1992 with the recognition of Cultural Landscapes in the *Operational Guidelines of the World Heritage Convention*.

2.1 HUL for sustainable urban development with the cultural aspects

Essentially it was the debate in the *World Heritage Convention* that triggered the need to address the issues of urban heritage, beyond the listed monuments and away from the still current urban definitions: uninhabited cities, cities inhabited and cities of the twentieth century.[②] The large-scale developments outside the buffer zone of the Old City of Vienna affecting the inner city monuments brought about, in 2005, the *Vienna Memorandum* addressing contemporary architecture in historic contexts at the same time that the first EU-URBACT proposals were published to foster sustainable integrated urban development in cities across Europe. What was common to all these initiatives was the need for a more integrative approach in considering urban heritage, and the recognition that heritage could provide added value and identity to urban development.

a. The concept and approach of HUL

The HUL followed on from the *Vienna Memorandum* and was finally approved in 2011, travelling for six years between cultures and countries as needed for a UNESCO mechanism. It defined that the "integration of historic urban area conservation, management and planning strategies into local development processes and urban planning, such as, contemporary architecture and infrastructure development, for which the application of a landscape approach would help maintain urban identity".

"Historic Urban Landscape" does not refer to a heritage category to be protected, but rather to a perspective and an approach, which can be applied to deal with "a balanced and sustainable relationship between the urban and natural environment, between the needs of present and future generations and the legacy from the past".

b. Managing change

The HUL approach aims to recognize the dynamically changing identity and character of cities through the identification of the structures, places and other traditional cultural elements of historical significance in cities and through the analysis of their historical contexts and evolution. This approach, by taking into account local context, provides a positive path to urban conservation and development through a series of steps in order to effectively manage changes.[③]

The evolution of management systems for urban heritage has been slow albeit with spurts in the 1970s with the UNESCO Nairobi Recommendation and the UK creation of Conservation Areas. The subsequent ICCROM Integrated Territorial and Urban Conservation Programme (ITUC) 1994 to 2004 was a beacon of its time which came with the greater recognition of Sustainable Development in 1987 and in the wake of the 1992 definition of Cultural Landscapes in the *World Heritage Operational Guidelines*.

---

① *Our Common Future*, United Nations World Commission on Environment and Development (WCED) 1987

② 40th session of the World Heritage Committee Side event organized by the UNESCO Culture Sector: Urban heritage conservation for sustainable development, Istanbul-16 July 2016.

③ Shanghai Agenda for the Implementation of UNESCO Recommendation on Historic Urban Landscape (HUL) in China, 2014.

These new challenges will need to be met by a more humanistic and integrative approach in which the role of urban heritage is better defined and valued particularly in the light of social transformations, and in order to facilitate the safeguarding of the heritage on one hand and its contribution to sustainable development on the other.

The contentious issue of the HUL approach centred on the interpretation of "development" where in paragraph 18 it indicated that "many economic processes offer ways and means to alleviate urban poverty and to promote social and human development. … When properly managed through the historic urban landscape approach, new functions, such as services and tourism, are important economic initiatives that can contribute to the well-being of the communities and to the conservation of historic urban areas and their cultural heritage while ensuring economic and social diversity and the residential function". This also provided the link to the upcoming 2030 Sustainable Development Goals (SDGs) and the accompanying 2016 *New Urban Agenda* (NUA).

2.2 UN 2030 Sustainable Development Goals

The turn of the millennium generated a renewed interest in urbanism together with the 2000 UN Millennium Development Goals (MDGs) and the ratification of the EU Landscape Convention, though it became clear very quickly that the problems of tomorrow could not be solved with the tools of yesterday.

The 2030 Agenda for Sustainable Development with the Sustainable Development Goals approved in September 2015 at the United Nations have fairly and squarely put sustainability at the forefront of the world agenda. However, the efforts to improve the visibility of culture and cultural heritage do not seem, at a first glance, to be successful. The debate on a fourth pillar of culture as indicated in Agenda 21 for Culture, which was adopted by United Cities and Local Governments (UCLG, 2010), or more preferably, in my opinion, a brace to the existing three pillars seems to have now inadvertently been resolved in favour of the latter as culture does not appear as an independent heading in any one of the seventeen goals. In hindsight, this might be a more vital role for culture as permeating sustainability in all its forms.

While a closer look at the texts might reveal the paucity of the role of culture in the SDGs, it is still a major change from the MDGs where culture and heritage were not even mentioned. The direct references are simple and can be summarized as a total of nine culture/ cultural mentions.[①] The introductory chapter of the SDGs outlines the concepts of the strategy and refers to culture in its broader context. It acknowledges the natural and cultural diversity of the world and recognizes that all cultures and civilizations can contribute to sustainable development.

Successively in the texts, four of the goals have more specific references including education, economic growth and local cultures.[②] Notwithstanding, the most direct reference is in Goal 11 *making cities and human settlements inclusive, safe, resilient and sustainable* detailed in target 11.4 which should be read as a complete sentence: *To strengthen efforts to protect and safeguard the world's cultural and natural heritage in order to make cities and human settlements inclusive, safe, resilient and sustainable*. Protecting cultural heritage is not a target in itself but as a means to achieving Goal 11 of the SDGs. This may be achieved with the engagement of other mechanisms as the UNISDR Sendai Framework with the Resilient City Campaign and the UNFCC.

---

① Turner, M., *Challenges for the World Heritage Convention in adopting the UN Sustainable Development Goals*, Heritage Series, De Gruyter, 2017 (in press)
② Turner, *Culture in the Sustainable Development Goals*, 2017

UNESCO had branded "culture as an enabler for sustainable development" in 2011 within its midterm strategies. However, efforts to formally adopt culture as a driver or an enabler for sustainable development within the SDGs were not entirely successful and were countered with culture being recognized as a contributor.

2.3 New Urban Agenda

The *New Urban Agenda* adopted at the UN-Habitat III congress in Quito, October 2016 has also underscored this integrative approach. Our built environment, its urban form and architecture are the evidence of this past, and is an irreplaceable component for the sustainable urban development of our future.

Following the SDGs and specifically, Goal 11, the NUA sets global standards and guidelines to help governments achieve these goals, especially regarding policy, social, economic, health, cultural and security factors. With these important documents, there is an urgent need to integrate the UNESCO texts thus providing for a combined methodology for implementation, evaluation and reporting.

How new is the *New Urban Agenda*? This is definitely debatable since the answer depends from one national and local context to another. However, the question itself indicates the relevance of the Agenda as for some signatories this may be a break-through, for some others this vision and principles are considered as given.

a. UNESCO Global Report

The UNESCO Global Report *Culture | Urban Futures* (September 2016) prepared for UN-Habitat III, examines the contribution of culture to urban sustainability, includes case-studies from all over the world, and indicates the importance of culture as an integral component of sustainable development. Towards the UN-Habitat III in Quito, October 2016, an inter-disciplinary workshop was convened in December 2015 with the resulting Hangzhou Outcomes[①] that recommended establishing a global network focusing on three major strands:

(ⅰ) People-centred cities are culture-centred spaces;
(ⅱ) Quality urban environments are shaped by culture;
(ⅲ) Sustainable cities need integrated policy-making that builds on culture.

These outcomes were intended as a policy framework document summarizing in twelve-paragraph guidelines to assist governments in the implementation of the 2030 Agenda for Sustainable Urban Development and the *New Urban Agenda*.

While the Dossier in the UNESCO Global Report indicated the many cultural programmes, the comparison focuses on the seven UNESCO cultural Conventions and 34 UNESCO Recommendations.

From the seven conventions of UNESCO, the three conventions having most direct urban connections are the 1972 "Convention concerning the protection of the world cultural and natural heritage", the 2003 "Convention on safeguarding of the Intangible Cultural Heritage" and the 2005 "Convention on the Protection of the Diversity of Cultural Expression". Mention should also be made of the UNESCO Recommendations focusing on urbanism, landscapes and national heritage. These soft law standards setting for the development of national laws and practices have been identified, notably the 1976 Nairobi Recommendation, concerning the Safeguarding and Contemporary Role of Historic Areas and the 2011 Recommendation on the Historic Urban Landscape.

---

① UNESCO, Hangzhou Outcomes, December 2015

b. "Cultural" and "culture" analyses

The textual engagement of "cultural heritage" was considered as the common denominator for the comparative analysis and the development of synergies between the NUA and the UNESCO cultural mechanisms. As a result, in the final draft of the *New Urban Agenda* that was unanimously adopted, there are 30 references to culture. It is referred to as a noun in seven instances where it may be interpreted as a driver for sustainable development and 23 references as an adjective being an enabler for sustainable development.

c. Action Framework for the Implementation of the New Urban Agenda (AFINUA)

Conditions for effective implementation are also outlined as the setting-up of policy frameworks at national, regional and local levels; participatory planning; international cooperation; capacity-building and sharing of practices, policies and programmes amongst governments at all levels, but without any operational plan, targets or indicators to which Member States and other policy-makers are accountable. The *New Urban Agenda* already calls for a follow-up and review of the commitments made by the Member States linked with the review of the 2030 *Agenda for Sustainable Development*. It invites the General Assembly of the United Nations to report on the progress of the implementation of the *New Urban Agenda* every four years.

Based on the overarching SDGs, it is important to note that in the opening paragraphs of the New Urban Agenda, Member States are committed to work on

—social inclusion and ending poverty;

—urban prosperity and opportunities for all;

—environmentally sustainable and resilient urban development.

This can be a challenging process considering the different commitments of the Member States and the lack of targets and harmonized indicators across countries. While the document is meant to be universal in scope, it is not binding in terms of implementation. The latter depends on the voluntary commitments Member States and urban stakeholders are willing to take and make visible in the Quito Implementation Plan.

The New Urban Agenda also guides the work and reporting of international organizations in paragraph 82, inviting relevant international and regional organizations and bodies and paragraph 167 in providing a qualitative and quantitative analysis of the progress made in the implementation of the New Urban Agenda.

This translates into coordinating and integrating approaches to sustainable urbanization in the UNESCO system and the first reporting in the year 2020 to the UN General Assembly.

UN-Habitat, in preparation of the Action Framework for the Implementation of the *New Urban Agenda* (AFINUA), is reviewing the content of the *New Urban Agenda* (NUA), in order to facilitate the conversion of the NUA into a pragmatic and efficient framework of implementation. For this purpose, the contents of the NUA have been analyzed in fifteen categories, including the four cross-cutting principles of the strategic plan of UN-Habitat.[①]

The fifteen pillars[②] constitute an ordered framework that begins with a dedicated pillar on UN Prin-

---

[①] Available in the UN-Habitat website http://nua.unhabitat.org/list1.htm#.

[②] 1. Principles and Values (PV); 2. Urbanization and Sustainable Development (USD); 3. National Urban Policies (NUP); 4. Rules and Regulations (RR); 5. Urban Planning and Design (UPD); 6. Financing Urbanization (FU); 7. Urban Basic Services (UBS); 8. Housing and Slum Upgrading (HSU); 9. Risk Reduction (RiR); 10. Research and Capacity Development (RCD); 11. Human Rights (HR); 12. Climate Change (CC); 13. Gender (GE); 14. Youth (Y); 15. Local Implementation (LI).

ciples and Values. The NUA refers in many occasions to the principles and values of the United Nations seen not only on the general framework of the human rights but also including the 2030 *Sustainable Development Agenda*, the *Paris Agreement on Climate Change*, the Sendai Framework for Disaster Risk Reduction, the World Humanitarian Summit, the Migration Conference and of course, the Habitat I, II and III conferences.

The Action Framework for Implementation of the New Urban Agenda (AFI-NUA) also highlights the importance of "local identities reflected in material culture and other formal elements of the urban landscape".

(ⅰ) National urban policies;
(ⅱ) Urban legislation, rules and regulations;
(ⅲ) Urban planning and design;
(ⅳ) Urban economy and municipal finance;
(ⅴ) Local implementation.

2.4 The Asian scene

Local identities bring us to the examples of the Asia and Pacific Region.

The Chinese way of appreciating a painting is often expressed by the words *du hua*, "to read a painting" being the discipline that derives from the practice of calligraphy. Traditionally, every literate person in China learned as a child to write by copying the standard forms of Chinese ideographs. [1] It does because the artist has managed to distill his observations, achieving this with the most economical means: brush and ink on paper. The aim of the traditional Chinese artist is to capture not only the outer appearance of a subject but its inner essence as well—its energy, life force and spirit. To accomplish his goal, the Chinese painter more often than not rejected the use of colour, relying on line—the indelible mark of the inked brush. Linking calligraphy, poetry and painting, Wang Wei (c 700-761), as a polymath, created a poem as part of a sequence of twenty "landscape painting poems" (shanshui shi). [2]

This is the essence of the Historic Urban Landscape approach.

At the urban level of management, the "Machinami Charter", the Japanese ICOMOS Charter for the Conservation of Historic Towns and Settlements in Japan, 2000, gave the following definitions: "Machinami, usually translated as 'Historic Town', is a Japanese word that includes a nuance of the historic core, in both its tangible and intangible factors, its physical and spiritual aspects, that would be created by a 'bond of spirits'. It also contains the tone of making a line, hand-in-hand, that applies both to buildings and to people. Shuuraku, the Japanese word for 'settlement', is often translated as village. In this Charter it also contains an idea of a community's surrounding natural and cultural environment."

In today's globalizing and urbanizing world, cities are of great importance to the protection of human welfare and health, the development of social creativity and cultural diversity, as well as the conservation and sustainable use of tangible and intangible cultural heritage. Urban cultural heritage in China has been greatly affected by its rapid urbanization and the unsustainable development process. Its conservation is being challenged in different grounds today, including the pressures of urban transformation, the needs at heritage sites to develop tourism, the competition among local governments, to name

---

[1] Hearn, Maxwell. *Chinese Painting*, in *Heilbrunn Timeline of Art History*, New York: The Metropolitan Museum of Art, 2000. http://www.metmuseum.org/toah/hd/chin/hd_chin.htm(June 2008).

[2] Lichtung in Correspondence with 'Lu Zhai': Five Ways of Reading Octavio Paz's Translations of Wang Wei, Toming Jun Liu pp. 38-66 *The Willow and the Spiral: Essays on Octavio Paz and the Poetic Imagination* edited by Roberto Cantú, 2014.

but a few. How can we deal with the relations between protection and development, the new and the old, as well as the past and the present in different situations?

During the expert meeting on Historic Urban Landscapes, in October 2012 in Shanghai, HUL was seen as a significant mechanism in localizing urban texts,[①] so with the intensive activities of WHITR-AP and the personal commitment of the late Dr. Ron van Oers, the *Shanghai Agenda for the Implementation of UNESCO Recommendation on Historic Urban Landscape in China* was accepted in 2014.[②] It recognized that cities and their development were a key factor to human welfare and that there were new challenges for urban cultural heritage conservation in China. It concluded that the HUL approach considers that contemporary architecture has positive effects on revitalizing historic settings and thus increasing their attractiveness. Therefore, rather than opposing the interventions of those contemporary buildings or elements in historic settings, the HUL approach seeks to establish a harmonious continuity between the two based on a thorough consideration of the type of interventions that fit the character of specific historical contexts.

Three basic objectives were identified for the implementation of the UNESCO Recommendation on the Historic Urban Landscape in China:

(ⅰ) the management of "change",
(ⅱ) the improvement of living conditions for local populations and communities, and
(ⅲ) the creation of a virtuous cycle in urban conservation.

This was to be supported by collaboration and innovation including interdisciplinary research, involvement of stakeholders and local practices.

3. Urban landscape—case study—river cities

River urbanism is an example of a significant thematic pattern and HUL has a major task to play in applying the relevant tools to achieve sustainability.

Historic cities developed near a source of income and possible growth, as water sources and important crossroads. For the mobility and agriculture development, important water sources were and still are a major attribute to the develop ment of cities and urban areas in different variations. The historic area of Wuhan started to develop more than 3,500 years ago, and until 100 years ago comprised three independent cities—Wuchang, Hankou, and Hanyang. Those three cities were known as "Jiusheng Tongqu"—the nine provinces' leading thoroughfare, of great importance in China. While the first bridge of Wuhan was opened in 1957 as an outcome of combining the three cities into one. When looking at the development of the Wuhan, like other river cities the HUL recommendations have a great influence on observing, understanding and for the future development of the city, the urban area, and of course the historic landscape of the area.

3.1 Types of river cities

There are different types and forms of river cities, like Wuhan, two or three cities around the same place on a river on different banks as Budapest on the Danube and Mostar on the Neretva River; similarly, cities as a border between two countries as on the Congo River with the two capitals of the Democratic Republic of the Congo and Republic of the Congo, Kinshasa and Brazzaville. A river can also be a nat-

---

① Based on a Historic Urban Landscape Action Plan, UNESCO General Conference Resolution 36 C/23.
② Shanghai, China, December 2014; 1st revision January 2015; 2nd revision April 2015; 3rd revision May 2015.

ural boundary, with cities straggling on either side, as the Mekong river border between Thailand and Laos and where Vientiane, the capital, is located on the Lao side of the river.

"One-bank river cities" is a place for differences and time and political develop ment and natural and landscape options, one—side cities can be located on borders like Vientiane, Varanasi on the Ganges, or Manaus in Brazil located on one side of busy Amazons River. "Two-bankment river cities" that developed in harmony over time need a "smaller" river and more time, on the Italian landscaper the city of Verona on the Po River and the historic and imperialistic the city of Rome on the Tiber. Those cities started their first human settlement on one bank but with time the city developed in harmony around the two sides of the city with a system of bridges and roads that continued from one side to the other.

For negotiable rivers and estuaries, the harbour city developed as a trade centre, however with changes in navigation and the industrial revolution most of these cities, as London on the Thames had to change while others like the St. Lawrence River and the Great Lakes adapted themselves being a natural border between USA and Canada.

The attributes in those cities included not only the city bridges but also the memories of the ferries, the old waterbeds and the years of floods and droughts. The bridges were recognized as important centres for trade, Ponte Vecchio on the Arno and Pulteney Bridge on the Avon for the city or as engineering achievements as Firth of Forth, Sinan's Bridge of Višegrad across the Drina, while others become themselves symbols as the Rialto in Venice and the fictitious bridge over the River Kwai.

3.2 Applying NUA and HUL

The HUL approach extending beyond the notion of "historic centre" or "ensemble" includes the wider context, notably the site's topography, geomorphology, hydrology and natural features. To this is added the social and cultural practices and values, economic processes and the intangible dimensions of heritage that have made the city.

The *New Urban Agenda* detailed in various ways the importance of water and water use in sustainable urban development, and there are two paragraphs that we should analyse for water inside the city. The first, paragraph 72:

"We commit ourselves to long-term urban and territorial planning processes and spatial development practices that incorporate integrated water resources planning and management, considering the urban-rural continuum on the local and territorial scales and including the participation of relevant stakeholders and communities."

This shows the importance of water use and its continuity in the city, and when looking over river cities, as historic cities that developed around the river, the river is the most important resource for urban development. The river gave the city life and the reason for continuity. The second, paragraph 114(c).

"We will promote access for all to safe, age- and gender-responsive, affordable, accessible, and sustainable urban mobility and land and sea transport systems, enabling meaningful participation in social and economic activities in cities and human settlements, by integrating transport and mobility plans into overall urban and territorial plans and promoting a wide range of transport and mobility options, in particular through supporting:

…

(c) better and coordinated transport-land use planning, leading to a reduction of trave and transport needs, enhancing connectivity between urban, peri-urban, and rural areas, including waterways and transport and mobility planning, particularly for small islands developing States and coastal cities;"

The contribution of the river to the historic city not only for transportation, but also for addressing mobility, including the movement of peoples and cultures, ideas and knowledge and languages was essential. The agriculture areas spreading out from the urban to the rural provided a sustainable hinterland and integrative use of water sources. The future development of river cities will provide a continuum as a place of mobility and change.

3.3 Challenges for growth and change

The first cities and civilizations were situated on the banks of the rivers like the Tigris and Euphrates, the Nile, the Indus and the Yangtze, which gave the people the opportunities to move and to pass on their knowledge, traditions, culture, religious theory and goods. Although our cities are growing, water transportation is losing its function and harbour cities are slowly stagnating with abandoned buildings, a shadow of their glorious days, as in Liverpool. However, the reuse of the river as an important water source for agriculture, cultural heritage and identity, environmental quality and recreation are putting back new life and the HUL tools are an instrument for providing sustainable development of a city.

River cities challenges—city growth, transportation, work

a. Mobility and development—people movement, trade and economy, knowledge and ideas.

b. Water use—down and up the stream, water-power context, agriculture around the city, religions, nations and government.

4 Future Ahead

The habitation of place is essential for culture, giving a key role to UNESCO in engaging the *New Urban Agenda* of UN Habitat. To be responsible for culture, to respond to it, to attend to it caringly needs tools and mechanisms which may be applied through ten major UNESCO themes in culture and which can be engaged in the recommendations for Urban Futures. However, the major UNESCO mechanism for urban planning and design is the 2011 Recommendation on the Historic Urban Landscape and this has a reporting mechanism to the World Heritage Committee in 2018 and to the General Conference of Members States in 2019. It becomes clear that there is a need for a coordinative approach which may be achieved in paralleling, mainly, the texts of the HUL and NUA.

The implementation of the Recommendation on the Historic Urban Landscape will be a key leverage for the activities of the newly launched UNESCO Urban Network for Culture promoting an integrated territorial approach for urban areas, incorporating assessment, monitoring and reporting mechanisms.

HUL Forum is a networking initiative to raise awareness and constructive dialogues amongst researchers, institutions and practitioners who engage with the timely and multifaceted problematic of the historic urban landscape; the first HUL Forum was held in London in March 2017, at the Bartlett School, University College London. The NUA-HUL approach needs further case-studies, guidance manuals and research, including annual thematic meetings, to recognize different typologies of urban settlements supporting the proposed Urban Knowledge Platform.

Where do we go? The dissonance between Urban Heritage Assessment and the planning systems is growing and integration should be supplemented with harmonization. In evaluating emerging approaches to integrated appraisals in the UK, Richard Eales, et al. (2005), point out "the challenges for the integrative approach given inevitable resource limitations will be a risk that the depth of impact investigation may be sacrificed for the breadth of coverage. Furthermore, the risk of integrated appraisals being 'captured' by a dominant set of interests leading to the neglect of particular types of impacts".

An exegesis has yet to develop and we are currently seeing some confusing and even conflicting situations, as we have witnessed in Liverpool with three heritage appraisals—each pulling in different directions. On the bright side, we are finding that the HUL Recommendation is being used extensively and UNESCO is preparing a survey and report to internalize these case studies in formulating an acquis-culture.①

Specifically, there needs to be a greater effort to develop "the application of a range of traditional and innovative tools adapted to local contexts". The tools identified include:

(i) Civic engagement tools;

(ii) Knowledge and planning tools;

(iii) Regulatory systems;

(iv) Financial tools.

Applying HUL-NUA, is it a burden or a blessing? The evolving terminology between an approach and a category highlights the need for harmonization with the Sustainable Development Goals, the UNESCO Global Report on Culture | Urban Futures and specifically the *New Urban Agenda* through, for example, the Strategic Environmental Assessment (SEA). The 2005 SEA Directive's requirements identified significant effects on the environment and incorporated "cultural heritage including architectural and archaeological heritage, landscape and the interrelationship between the above factors" as an integral part of our environment. These meetings may be expanded with the engagement of the UN Habitat New Urban Agenda and the UNISDR Resilient Cities programme.

High on the agenda are the effects of societal changes and the speed of transformation which is prioritized for the coming years and which is being understood through the digital revolution. The potential of crowdsourcing as a key tool for democracy is being developed by many players for the SDG awareness programmes and will be a major contributor for change. Being the marching orders for the coming 15 years, it is imperative to identify where and how the associations with cultures can give added value to sustainability.

Linking culture and nature will be echoed with the merging of the city and landscape and the main achievement will be with the acceptance and implementation of *Culture as an Enabler for Sustainable Development*.

It is vital to address the inter-dependence of two parallel issues—the tangible and intangible and linking culture and nature. The tangible and intangible follow the relevant conventions, programmes and mechanisms. Linking nature and culture may be referred to through the IUCN urban alliance, based on the Hawaii 2016 congress resolution 29 and the ICOMOS-IUCN joint paper② where two major recommendations were given:

(i) to explore, learn and create new methods that are centered on recognizing and supporting the interconnected bio-cultural character of the natural, cultural and social values of highly significant landscapes and seascapes; and

(ii) to improve outcomes for conservation and recognition of cultural diversity through the implementation of new working methods and organizational cultures, including through the specific advisory processes that support listing and monitoring through the World Heritage Convention.

The HUL decision included seven actions:

---

① Michael Turner, *UNESCO Chair in Urban Design and Conservation Studies*, February 2017.

② From "Connecting Practice Project: Final Report" IUCN and ICOMOS

(ⅰ) Create a special website;
(ⅱ) Establish a working group;
(ⅲ) Develop technical assistance packages;
(ⅳ) Encourage scientific research;
(ⅴ) Organize conferences and symposia;
(ⅵ) Support the development of didactic materials, curriculum design and teacher training;
(ⅶ) Organize a review exercise—2019.

中国古代礼制与城市空间设计①

Traditional Chinese Ritural System and Urban Design

杨华 教授

武汉大学中国传统文化研究中心主任

Prof. Yang Hua

Director of Research Center of Traditional Chinese Culture, Wuhan University

Symbol of the origin of Chinese Civilization, the traditional ritual system played an important role in blueprinting ancient cities. Different functions and importance of certain ritual space reflected social changes, which bear inspirations for today's design of urban space.

一、礼仪建筑是中国文明起源的标志

礼制是中国文明起源的一个重要特点。关于文明起源的标志,一直存在争论。一般认为文字、青铜器、城市、国家是一个社会进入文明的基本要素。

在东亚中国,所有这些文明要素,都跟礼仪制度有关。中国最早的文字(如甲骨文、金文),记载的正是祭祀的内容。中国最早的青铜器,并不是生产工具,而是祭天、祭祖的礼仪法器。中国早期的文字和青铜器,都是为了"敬天法祖"。越来越多的学者相信,中国早期文明的直接推动力,并不是生产技术的突破,而是以祖先崇拜为核心的礼制活动,这也是中国早期文明区别于世界其他文明模式的特点之一。从礼制的视角,可以重新谱写西周以前近万年的中国早期历史。②

城市是中国进入文明阶段的一项标志,如何界定中国早期的城市?进入文明初期的中国城市,不是商业中心,而是政治中心和宗教中心。其最大的标志,就是礼仪性建筑。这些礼仪性建筑,主要包括三类:一是朝堂,即宫殿;二是陵墓;三是祭祀场所。这三样东西,也是古代王权合法性的标志;换言之,也是文明的另一个要素——国家——成立的标志。

每个王即位,都预先决定这三样东西;每个都城的选址和建造,都预先决定这三样东西。今天的夏商周考古,要寻找一个王朝的都城,都必须满足这三项条件。

以陵墓为例。修筑陵墓,亦是王权的象征,历代统治者即位伊始便着手修陵。③每个城池和聚居点,都有族墓,在城池的北面。《墨子·备城门》说,战争中要让将士们死守被围困之城,必须具备有十四个条件,其中之一就是"父母坟墓在焉"。若守城将士的父母坟墓在此,必然不会弃城他逃。

再以祭祀系统为例。"国之大事,在祀与戎",④祭祀的内容相当广泛,包括天神(包括日月星辰、风雨

---

① 本文是教育部人文社会科学重点研究基地重大课题"民间日用类书与中国古代礼制研究"(批号 15JJDZONGHE018)的阶段性成果。
② 张光直:《从商周青铜器谈文明与国家的起源》《连续与破裂:一个文明起源新说的草稿》,载张光直著《中国青铜时代》,北京三联出版社,1999 年。卜工:《文明起源的中国模式》,科学出版社,2007 年。
③ 参见拙文《中国古代礼仪制度的几个特点》,《武汉大学学报》(人文科学版)2015 年第 1 期。
④ 《左传·成公十三年》。

雷电之神)、地祇(包括土地、山川之神)和人祖(包括远祖和直系亲祖、历代先王)三大系列。它们分别都有自己的祭祀场所。

祭祀祖先的场所,称为宗庙。祭祀、战争、册命、盟会、日常生活人生礼仪等都在祖庙中举行。所以,首先,它是一个跟祖先沟通的宗教空间,通过祭祀求得祖先的庇佑;其次,是一个政治空间,很多重大的国家政务(如战争和盟会)和家族事务,都在这里商议决定,并以祖先的名义举行;最后,它是血缘宗族的人口聚集空间,起到所谓"收族"的作用。

所以,关于古代都城营建时的规划设计,都特别重视其礼仪性设施:

凡邑,有宗庙先君之主曰都,无曰邑。邑曰筑,都曰城。(《左传·庄公二十八年》)

君子将营宫室,宗庙为先,厩库为次,居室为后。(《礼记·曲礼》)

凡帝王徙都立邑,皆先定天地、社稷之位,敬恭以奉之。将营宫室,则宗庙为先,厩库为次,居室为后。(《三国志·魏书·辛毗杨阜高堂隆传》)

杜预《春秋释例》谓:"若邑有先君宗庙,则虽小曰都,尊其所居以大之也。"也就是说,具有宗庙、其中供奉着先祖神主牌位,这样的人口聚居点,才称为"都",否则只能称为"邑"。在古文献叙述方法(春秋笔法)中,再小的聚居点,只要有宗庙,都用"都"来尊称它("大之")。在2 000多年前的上古中国,人们对于因商业贸易而聚集的居民点并不重视,重视的是礼仪性建筑设施。

在先秦,实行宗法制度和分封制度,大宗(嫡长子)世代继承并坚守着宗庙,而庶子则在自己的远方封地中复制祖庙,当然这种复制具有严格的等级限制——天子建造七代祖庙,诸侯建造五代祖庙,大夫建造三代祖庙,上士建造二代祖庙,下士建造一代祖庙,庶人不允许建造祖庙。到秦汉时期,皇帝将自己家的祖庙有计划地扩大到全国,强制全国各地者认同自己的祖先,通过这种方式来加强皇权。这一点已在最近出土的秦汉简牍中得到证明。

二、中国古代都城设计中的礼仪制度

中国古代的都城建筑有其内在的礼制规定。这种规定表现在两个方面:一是都城规模的规定,二是都城内部建筑布局的规定。

关于都城的规模,即都城的面积大小、城墙高低厚薄,都有礼制规定。例如,《左传》记载,鲁隐公元年(公元前722年),郑庄公的弟弟共叔段被分封在京这个地方,但是他的城池规模巨大,当时人认为这已逾越礼制,并将招致祸害:

都城过百雉,国之害也。先王之制,大都,不过参国之一;中,五之一;小,九之一。今京不度,非制也。君将不堪。①

分封诸侯的都城规模与宗主国的首都规模之间存在固定的比例关系,最多不能超过首都的三分之一,中等的是其五分之一,小的是其九分之一。东汉许慎所著《五经异义》说:"天子之城九仞,公侯七仞,伯五仞,子男三仞。"如果超过这些规定,将成为谋反动乱的实力基础。

一直到帝国的后期,这种规定仍然起作用。在历代正史的《礼志》中往往有此类规定,例如明燕王朱棣在北京建燕王城时,便逾制违规。建文元年(1399年),他上书南京朝廷,对于朝野关于他逾制的物议,做了一番辩解:

……谓臣僭侈,过于各府,此盖皇考所赐,自臣之国以来二十余年,并不曾一毫增益,其所以不同各王府者,盖祖训营缮条云,明言燕因元旧有,非臣敢僭越也。②

虽然有此辩解,但燕王朱棣觊觎王位的野心不容否定。礼仪制度实际上就是政治规则。

---

① 杜预注:"方丈曰堵,三堵曰雉。一雉之墙,长三丈,高一丈。侯伯之城,方五里,径三百雉,故其大都不得过百雉。"不合法度,非先王制。

② 《洪武实录》附建文帝事。

关于古代城市的结构,最常见的描述见于《周礼·考工记》:

匠人营国,方九里,旁三门。国中九经、九纬,经涂九轨。左祖,右社;面朝,后市。市、朝一夫。

东汉的郑玄注云:

营谓丈尺其大小。天子十二门,通十二子。国中,城内也。经纬谓涂也。经纬之涂,皆容方九轨。轨谓辙广,乘车六尺六寸,旁如七寸,凡八尺,是谓辙广。九轨积七十二尺,则此涂十一步也。旁如七寸者,辐内二寸半,辐广三寸半,绠三分寸之二,金辖之间三分寸之一。王宫所居也。祖,宗庙。面,犹乡也。王宫当中经之涂也。

意思是说,上古的都城是九里见方,每面城墙开三个门。城中有东西向、南北向各九条大道,每条大道可容九辆车并行,按照今天的尺寸计算,每条路约 16.5 米宽。① 古代城市坐北朝南,那么,城里王宫的左边(东边)是宗庙,右边(西边)是社稷坛;王宫路寝的前面(南边)是朝堂,后面(北边)是市场。朝堂和市场都大约长宽一百步。《考工记》的成书年代争论很多,最晚不晚于西汉。这说明了 2 000 多年前中国人对于都城的设计模式。

从西汉开始,儒家思想成为中国传统的官方意识形态,儒家关于城市建筑的理念也得以推广和实施,中国历代大致都按照《周礼·考工记》的这种设计理念来建筑都城。汉唐时期的礼仪建筑不一定完全遵循此制,但圜丘、方泽、南北郊、明堂、辟雍、灵台、社稷、宗庙这些要素,则是各代建都时都必不可少的。例如,《考工记》中的一门三道,"方九里"的崇方传统,在历代都城都得到继承。② 目前,其中的不少遗迹都已得到发掘,相应的研究也已有不少。③ 不过有学者认为,《周礼·考工记》"匠人营国"记述的所谓西周都城布局规划,既与西周都城的考古发掘不合,也与春秋战国诸侯国(如鲁国都城)的布局不合。它描述的所谓西周都邑布局规划,实际上是根据西汉长安城的布局事实附会而成的。④

现在看来,真正与《周礼·考工记》最为接近的,是元代所建的大都城,即今天的北京城。明清两代,又沿袭并完善了这座城市的诸多礼仪建筑,形成今天所知的北京城的格局:太庙在东(今北京市劳动人民文化宫),社稷坛在西(今中山公园),天坛在南(正阳门外),地坛(方泽)在北(安定门外),日坛在东(朝阳门外东郊),月坛在西(阜城门外西郊)。此外还有先农坛、先蚕、山川百神等祭祀场所。⑤

三、近千年来中国城市空间的雅俗二元格局

《吴越春秋》说:"筑城以卫君,造郭以居人,此城郭之始也。"⑥中国上古和中古时期的城市功能,以拱卫君主,安置贵族为主。其政治功能和军事功能居于首要地位,而经济功能居于其次。宋代以后,中国出现了市民社会,等级贵族制受到挑战,个人的存在和意义越来越受到重视。就城市布局而言,迎来了"城市革命",里坊制度解体,城市聚集商品交易的经济功能大大提升。例如,上古以来"面朝后市"的格局,到汉代基本得到继承,但是自北魏时已不复如此。⑦ 同时,因商业功能而兴起的中小型城市在各地普遍出现。

那么,近 1 000 年来,在这些市民化的城市中,礼仪性建筑的形态是怎样的呢?

有一个前提必须了解,经过司马光、朱熹等人的倡议,士大夫从宋代开始建立自己的家庙。尤其是明代中期允许平民建立始祖庙之后,各地平民便普遍建立祠堂。士大夫和平民们分别在自己的祠堂中举行

---

① 钱玄:《三礼通论》,南京师范大学出版社,1996 年,第 157 页。在郑玄所著《驳许慎〈五经异义〉》中,有《天子、公侯、伯、子、男之城高》一篇,专论城池大小。
② 中国社会科学院考古研究所编著:《中国考古学·秦汉卷》,中国社会科学出版社,2010 年,第 223—225 页。
③ 参见姜波:《汉唐都城礼制建筑研究》,文物出版社,2003 年。中国社会科学院考古研究所:《西汉礼制建筑遗址》,文物出版社,2003 年。刘庆柱:《汉长安城考古发现所反映的礼制文化》,《文史知识》2013 年第 4 期。徐卫民:《秦都城中礼制建筑研究》,《人文杂志》2004 年第 1 期。
④ 李锋:《〈考工记〉成书于西汉时期管窥》,《郑州大学学报》(哲学社会科学版)第 32 卷第 2 期(1999 年 3 月),第 106—111 页。
⑤ 朱士光:《初论我国古代都城礼制建筑的演变及其与儒学之关系》,《山西大同大学学报》(社会科学版)第 12 卷第 3 期(1998 年 9 月)。
⑥ 《太平御览·卷 193·居处部二十一·城(下)》引。参见周生春:《吴越春秋辑校汇考》,上海古籍出版社,1997 年,第 261 页。
⑦ 中国社会科学院考古研究所编著:《中国考古学·秦汉卷》,中国社会科学出版社,2010 年,第 226 页。

礼仪活动,对皇家宗庙的崇拜大大削弱。城市按照自身的发展规律和地域特点,形成一套内在的礼仪空间结构。在一般的城市,出现了两个礼仪中心:

一是文庙。儒学在西汉成为国家意识形态之后,儒学的创始人孔子成为中国的文化神,指导着中国人的精神世界和日常生活。历代都祭祀孔子,孔子获得很多封号(如宋代加封至圣文宣王,元代加大成至圣文宣王),孔门后裔代代奉祀。东晋时孔庙正式进入国家最高学府,北齐时将孔庙推广到各郡国的学校,唐贞观四年(630年)令各地州县一律建造孔子庙。从此,孔庙便遍及各地,成为城市礼制活动的中心之一。尤其是科举制度之后,它更成为中国的学校神,各级州县学校都设有孔庙以奉祀孔子,故又称"文庙"。19世纪中叶,全中国有学校孔庙1 730多所,东亚的朝鲜、越南和日本也有不少。①

古代孔庙在城市中的选址,经历了由城外转入城内的演变。历代都城的孔庙,一般设在皇城的东南方(北京的国子监孔庙在紫禁城的外东北部)。地方州县的文庙选址,一般也以城市中心的东部或东南部为多。文庙居东,武庙居西,"左文右武"成为后来各地城市的基本格局。② 文庙与学校一般呈左右布局(左庙右学,或左学右庙),也有前庙后学的布局。

从中央朝廷到地方政府,从中原王朝到"蛮夷"政权,都要拜谒文庙,祭祀孔圣,以之作为自己文化正统性的标志。围绕着文庙,各地每年都会举行很多礼仪活动,如开笔仪式、释菜礼、乡饮酒礼、鹿鸣宴,以及祭祀孔圣、祈祝文运的各种活动。为了补扶风水,很多城市的文庙附近都建有文峰塔、魁星楼,这些塔、楼也成为这个城市的文化活动中心。总之,围绕文庙,形成一个精英文化的礼仪空间。

二是城隍。中国历代统治者在建立政权之初,都必须制礼作乐。而"明有礼乐,幽有鬼神"的原则,则普遍影响到他们的制礼活动。也就是说,人世间的礼仪制度,与鬼神祭祀的秩序、空间、时间等完全可以打通。

城隍神是城市的守护神。它最初的功能是守护城池、保障治安,在被纳入道教的神仙体系之后,又兼有了治国安邦、祛恶除凶、调和风雨、忠义教化、管领亡魂等职能。孙吴时期开始为城隍立庙,南北朝时开始流行。从唐代开始,统治者为城隍神封爵封王,明代大封城隍神,为全国的城隍神定级别,首都城隍神级别最高。各地的城隍神往往被人格化,大多是当地的贤臣勇将、历史英雄。在城市普遍发展和佛教、道教等高级宗教进入中国人的生活秩序之后,城隍信仰又成为融合儒、释、道三教于一体的城市文化符号。

城隍与上古早就存在的社稷神并不相同,"社稷所以养人也,而城隍所以卫人"。③ 然而随着中国城镇化的加速,城隍信仰获得了广泛的民众基础,各级市镇乃至乡村,都广修城隍庙,其庙宇规模和香火之盛,超过了社稷祭祀。④ 明朝洪武三年(1370年),朱元璋改革礼制,取消了岳镇、海渎和城隍的各种封号,使城隍神脱离人格神序列,列入国家祀典,成为与山川、岳镇并列的自然神。⑤ 皇权神授,人间的政治管理与阴间的区域神对应,皇帝与下面各都、府、县的政治管理,通过都、府、县各级城隍神而得以展现出来。每个地方官员上任伊始的法定首务,便是"进香谒庙",即朝拜本地的城隍神。所以,城隍神既是民间的信仰,也是官方的信仰,城隍庙是纳入国家祀典系统的礼仪空间。后来,土地神信仰更多集中到乡村,而城隍信仰随后也从城市扩张至乡村,出现"乡村化"趋势。⑥

因为中国的佛寺、道观多居于深山名胜,再加之城隍信仰兼具有儒、释、道合一的功能,所以,城隍信仰在城市获得了更多的发展空间,城隍庙也在市民文化中发挥了更多功能。各地祭祀城隍分别有自己的祭祀时间和祭祀频率,如明初以后,除京都为"二祭",各地城隍于每年清明、七月半、十月初一共三次例祭,此

---

① 孔祥林等:《世界孔子庙研究》,中央编译出版社,2011年。
② 沈旸:《东方儒光:中国古代城市孔庙研究》,东南大学出版社,2015年,第172-200页。
③ 秦蕙田:《五礼通考·卷45·社稷篇》。明朝初年,曾有礼官上奏说:"城隍之祀,莫详其始,先儒谓,既有社矣,不应复有城隍。"《明实录》洪武元年正月戊申条。于志斌:《祭城隍民俗考》,《苏州大学学报》1998年第1期。
④ 滨岛敦俊著,沈中琦译:《明清江南城隍考:商品经济的发达与农民信仰》,《中国社会经济史研究》1991年第1期。黄怀忠:《从土地到城隍:明清华北村落社区演变中的庙宇与空间》,《清史研究》2011年第4期。
⑤ 滨岛敦俊:《朱元璋政权城隍改制考》,《史学集刊》1995年第4期,第7-15页。
⑥ 赵世瑜:《庙会与明清以来的城乡关系》,载赵世瑜著《狂欢与日常:明清以来的庙会与民间社会》,三联书店,2002年,第162-186页。

外还有城隍庙主诞日祭,国有大灾告庙,城隍出巡,等等。各地的城隍庙市,都是当地最大的商业、宗教、民俗节日,到时迎神赛会、商贾如云、娱乐并作。各地城镇的庙会,几乎成为当地的狂欢节。① 所以,城隍庙一带的街区往往又是当地最大的商场和游乐场,那里茶肆商铺林立,江湖百技充斥。这里成为百姓进香、品茗、看戏、购物、会友和游乐的中心所在,"市"的功能超越了"庙"的功能。② 无疑,这里也是近代城市市民文化的中心所在。

总之,近一千年来,中国传统城市内部的礼仪空间发生了较大变化。原来作为中心的儒家礼仪建筑和宫殿建筑,虽然仍然存在,但是科举制度和市民文化催生了两个新的礼仪中心,一是文庙,二是城隍庙。前者是精英文化的聚集地,后者是民间文化的聚集地。

四、传统城市礼仪空间对当代城市规划的启示

进入现代社会,人们的生存方式发生巨大变化。首先,皇权统治被打破,宫殿和朝堂的崇高的中心地位。其次,宗教信仰被解构,城中庙宇的功能也基本被消解。再次,科举制度废除后,文人精英与大众文化之间等级落差弱化了。最后,也是最重要的,文化传播手段发生根本变化,获取信息易如反掌。那么,现代城市是否还需要中心?需要什么样的城市中心?

关于城市空间的思考,在今天尤其具有现实意义。随着中国的经济腾飞,中国的城市越来越大,出现了很多国际化的大都市;同时,乡村城镇化步伐正在加快,越来越多的农村人口聚集到城镇。在这个过程中,传统的城市礼仪空间对今天的城市规划是否还有些许借鉴意义?

第一,现代城市需要怎样的城市中心?一般来说,现代城市以商业中心(CBD)为中心,或者是围绕若干个商业中心展开的。虽然商业模式发生变化,但这一点与前现代社会的城市模式并无区别。但是,一个城市的中心如果仅限于商业,很容易造成空心化,到夜晚成为无人居住的"鬼城"。如何在商业中心嵌入文化的元素,值得深入思考。在这方面,前现代的城市空间布局大有可取之处,市民的商业活动与礼仪活动、文化活动相联进行,而且与官员的政治活动也不冲突,这才令城市充满活力,彰显出城市有别于乡村的特点。

第二,现代城市建设理念强调弱化城市中心,加强社区、小城镇建设。然而,今天中国城市的社区设计很不令人满意,人口密集,高楼林立,缺少人情味。在基督教和伊斯兰世界,直至今天,城镇的日常生活中宗教仍然占有重要地位,教堂还是很多城镇的活动中心。教堂的钟声和教堂广场虽然已失去了中世纪以来的诸多功能,但它们仍然有助于平和与宁静,有助于消解职场竞争导致的身心疲惫。如果在中国的大城市社区和小城镇建设中,吸收传统礼仪空间的元素,将人与土地、人与神灵、人与自我内心的关系采用更加宁静、舒缓、亲切的建筑语汇表达出来,换言之,将市民的人生礼仪活动在社区得到妥贴安置,这无疑会营造出更加宜居的环境,增添城市的魅力。

---

① 参见赵世瑜著《狂欢与日常:明清以来的庙会与民间社会》。
② 苏智良、姚霏:《庙、信仰与社区:从城隍信仰看近代上海城隍庙社区》,《社会科学》2007年第1期。

聚落认知与乡建误区

Misdirections of Rural Construction Based on Settlement Cognition

李晓峰 教授
华中科技大学建筑与城市规划学院副院长
Prof. Li Xiaofeng
Deputy Director of School of Architecture & Urban Planning, Huazhong University of Science and Technology

Elaborating on the definition of different types of settlements, this speech proposes access to a better assessment of their value and criticises various ideas and practices in misdirection during the process of rural construction in China.

当下中国,乡建活动如火如荼,从国家层面到地方政府都高度重视,政府机构各部门积极响应,规划师、建筑师、景观师、工程师参与其中。这几年我们乡村建设变化很大,问题也凸显。

那么,当代乡建运动存在哪些误区?

要寻求问题答案,我们应该先从聚落认知开始。

山地聚落

一、聚落认知

聚落就是村落,由相互依存的社会性生存方式所决定,简单地说就是人类各种形式的聚居地的总称。

1. 作为风景的聚落

乡村在当代为城市人所关注,为投资商所青睐,为旅游部门所重视,很大程度上是因为在很多人眼中,乡村是一道道不同于城市环境的美丽的"风景"。于是人们从审美角度研究乡村价值,从景观视角分析乡村环境,从旅游角度营建乡村风貌,风景建设一度成为当代乡建运动的主流目标。

2. 作为遗产的聚落

建筑群遗产是指从历史学、艺术或科学的观点看,在建筑风格、分布或在环境景观中的地位等方面,具有突出普遍价值的独立的或连续的建筑群。

聚落遗产应属建筑群类遗产。部分独立的乡土建筑单体被文物部门列入保护名录的则是文物类遗产(文保单位);暂未列入保护名录的可称为聚落与乡土建筑遗产资源。

3. 作为社区的聚落

聚落和社区既相互区别又相互联系。共同点:都以一定的地理区域为基础,都包含有一定的人群;不同点:两者所暗含的重点不一样,聚落所强调的是一定人群的自然和居住属性,而社区所强调的是一定人群的社会经济属性。

二、认知视野

从规模上,认知聚落的视野有宏观、中观、微观,有村、乡、城、地方城市、大都市,形态上有三点式、集中式、阶梯状聚落等等;从内涵上,主要是自然地理视野和社会人文视野。

1. 自然地理视野

这实际上就是关注聚落与山水环境的关系。平地聚落,对环境的干扰比较小,所以是发散型的;山地聚落,在山水之间,山底、山脚、山坡上都有;滨水聚落,强调水与环境的关系,如吊脚楼、洞庭湖船民聚落;水上聚落,如南国水上村庄、秘鲁的浮岛。

2. 社会文化视野

血缘型聚落:在湖北中南部地区非常多,他们共同有一个姓氏,有共同的公共建筑——家族祠堂;业缘型聚落,如:生意之家,集中在一起,很多古镇基本上都是这种聚落,像黄龙古镇;地缘型聚落:由于各种限制,大家住在一起,他们没有祠堂,但有一些公共中心,如庙宇,有共同的信仰;戍防型聚落,如:堡寨、关隘;神缘型聚落,如:藏族聚落、维吾尔族的清真寺、以寺院为核心的傣族村寨。

三、价值认知

要认识聚落的价值,我们还必须了解两个命题——"缘"与"分"、"居"与"业"。"缘"与"分"为聚落发生条件,缘是聚的关联前提,分是落的逻辑制约,因"缘"形成不同聚落类型,因"分"存在聚落秩序;"居"与"业"为聚落的发展机制,业是聚落的运转基础,居是居民的生活方式,因"业"形成不同聚落类型,因"居"形成不同的聚落特征。

基于聚落的特征,我们可以看到聚落的综合价值:

审美价值——乡村景观;遗产价值——历史信息积淀;使用价值——适应性;认识价值——建筑是生活的舞台;情感价值——历史记忆,情感寄托;借鉴价值——民间智慧。

四、当代乡建的几个误区

从聚落的特征和价值认知,我们可以看到在建设社会主义新农村、美丽乡村等宏大战略目标下,乡村变新了,但也丢失了许多东西,我们的乡村建设存在很多误区:

1. 乡建方向:唯美主义主导,观赏性讨论过多,生活性探讨不足,重视视觉审美,忽略价值本源;
2. 乡建受益者:乡外人多于乡里人,乡建投入与产出基本与村民无关;
3. 乡村建设:安居与乐业分离,从旧的空心村到新的空心村,尚未乐业、无从安居;
4. 聚落遗产:保护重于利用,保护第一,忽略利用,持续投入,维持艰难;
5. 乡村规划:城市经验移植乡村,自上而下,难接地气。
6. 乡建目标:景区与社区倒置,纸上的景区,消逝的社区。

我们要留存聚落的情感以及留住朴实的乡村景象,既要保护物质文化,也要保护非物质文化。我们的乡村,首先是个社区,其次才是景区。

中国城乡遗产的未来：现场工作坊、国际交流与分享式学习

The Future of Urban & Rural Heritage in China: On-site Workshops, International Exchanges & Learning Through Sharing

兰德 教授
著名中法建筑文化活动家
法国当代中国建筑观察研究所负责人
Prof. Françoise Ged
Prominent Activist in Sino-French Exchanges on Architectural Culture,
Chief of the Observation of Architecture of the Contemporary China

如何界定未来城乡可持续发展中文化遗产的角色？中法之间的一系列合作通过现场工作坊的形式推动与居民、地方政府、专家及技术人员的面对面交流与跨学科合作以及经验的分享学习。为了最终实现以文化创意为核心的城乡可持续发展目标，需采取正确的战略与行动。

Heritage is a subject that is more and more open to new discussion and conceptualisation throughout the world, and China has experimented with very different practices for the past two or three decades. Schools of urban planning and architecture have opened new training courses. For local authorities, it is a hot topic: is heritage preservation a good way to attract tourism and to develop a solid economy for the area under their management, or is it a means to achieve better financial value and development for business?

工作坊现场

How should heritage, with its derelict buildings, be dealt with? What is the place of heritage, both urban and rural, in our daily lives? Which methodology is appropriate?

It has become ever clearer to everyone that a demolished building cannot be reconstructed as it was. Heritage is linked to emotion, with invisible roots, and building a similar urban or architectural entity cannot replace what has been demolished.

Earth, wood, stone and bamboo, which have been the local resources that have made possible "smart" building strategies using the incredible know-how from the past centuries, are now seen through the lens of sustainability. We are able to learn from the past and develop new strategies for the future through the detailed description and analysis of the skills of past generations.

The "Observatoire de l'architecture de la Chine contemporaine" (OACC), in "La Cité de l'architecture et du patrimoine", is engaged in a long-term cooperation process with Tongji university, and is also active within certain schools of architecture in Paris which have academic exchanges with Chinese Universities. I would like to share some of the working procedures and results that we have engaged in through the "joint workshops" organized with the Ecole de Chaillot, a specialised school for graduate architects on heritage preservation and restoration, with the ENSA (National Superior School of Architecture) Paris Malaquais, the ENSA Paris Val de Seine, and the ENSA Nancy.

Faced with 21st-century challenges, and the presence of virtual exchanges in our daily lives, I am convinced that we have to look for more face to face opportunities to share talents, embrace interdisciplinary processes of learning and put students and professors "in real life" (IRL) situations with the active participation of local authorities and public services. We need to decide what heritage to preserve for future generations and why, and determine the best practices and share them. This process also involves learning by doing, sharing the competences and the challenges of each local situation and studying the different dimensions, including the historic and cultural, the urban and rural landscape. How can we change our ways of thinking about this? I would say that we could practice more transdisciplinarity (with universities, local authorities and services, inhabitants, etc.) and interdisciplinarity (history, geography, culture, urban planning, economy, architecture, fine arts, etc.).

1. A strategic goal: to promote cultural creativity from a comprehensive perspective

In 2016, for World Cities Day, launched on October 31 by the UN, Shanghai Municipality published the *Shanghai Manual* 2016.① The role of culture is more and more important for this Chinese metropolis in acquiring an outstanding international position, and maintaining a balance in the economic development of the city.②

The *Shanghai Manual* adopts an attitude promoted by UNESCO③ in their last report—*Culture for Sustainable Urban Development*. According to the Shanghai Manual, "from a macroscopic perspective, the development of cultural creativity can not only bring economic benefits to a city but also produce social benefits. All cultural practices and cultural participation can bring power to social groups (especially vulnerable groups on the margins of society), and help them integrate into local social life more naturally and even improve their well-being. However, in many places, cultural creativity is still regarded as an industry only, and the output value or amount of employment is used as the main indicator of the evaluation, of cultural and creative industry development while ignoring the importance, exploration and excavation of its social value. Particularly, the creation of creative milieus has been neglected for a long time. A city should be regarded as a cultural 'container' and cultural creativity is like the air in the container which helps culture infiltrate into every aspect of economy, politics, culture, environment, and pluralistic society innovation".

Chinese cities try their best to be included in networks such as UNESCO's Creative Cities Network,④ and to follow UNESCO recommendations, in particular the one on the Historic Urban Land-

---

① 〈http://www.urbanoctober.org/downloads/ShanghaiManual2016EnglishVersion.pdf.
② In 2015 we organized a study trip to Paris and the surrounding areas on this topic for Tongji University researchers.
③ http://www.unesco.org/culture/culture-for-sustainable-urban-development/pdf-open/global-Report_en.pdf.
④ http://en.unesco.org/creative-cities/home.

scape[①] especially since the implementation of the UNESCO Bureau WHITRAP (World Heritage Institute for Training and Research, Asia-Pacific Region). The UNESCO Creative Cities Network was created in 2004 to promote cooperation among cities that have identified creativity as a strategic factor for sustainable urban development. Their common objective: is the first such instrument on the historic environment issued by UNESCO in 35 years. It is an additional tool for integrating policies and practices of conservation of the built environment into the wider goals of urban development while respecting the inherited values and traditions of different cultural contexts.

2. How to attain the goal?

a) Identifying appropriate places, in different cities, for the launch of research and innovation actions in collaboration with Chinese partners:

—in close relationship with Chinese partners previously involved in academic and professional exchanges or symposiums (i.e. the urban planners and architects from the French Presidential program). The partners have committed themselves:

1. to working with local authorities in undertaking concrete urban projects related to cultural, societal and urban redevelopment;

2. to taking charge of students and young researchers from the colleges of Architecture and Urban Planning, as well as the colleges of Sociology and of Heritage;

3. to taking an interest in developing and managing experimental projects on cultural and sustainable urban development.

b) Local authorities are the key actors in implementing sustainable development policies.

To pursue our goal in developing innovative research and working procedures, we try to serve as a link in the chain that initiates and ensures good relationships between local authorities, local representatives (committees of inhabitants, local associations) and the technicians, such as urban planners, architects, engineers, sociologists and cultural directors.

Identifying these different links in the urbanization process is the first condition for implementing innovative action (see, for instance, the report *Rencontres de Shanghai* 2014,[②] a unique collective experience in Shanghai involving the Xuhui Urban Bureau, Tongji University, the Cite de l'architecture & du patrimoine, WHITRAP, the Shanghai Urban Bureau, OACC). The aim is to improve the daily living environment, including work, travel, education and social life, in order to bestow greater value to the cultural and social mix in urban and rural areas.

Promoting strategic planning that will preserve the environment and the "commons" 7 is a major issue, which requires the involvement of the inhabitants in order to fight against the degradation of the local, cultural, climatic and sanitary environment. Therefore, a global approach, with the local authorities, the local inhabitants and the technicians is a key requirement.

3. Forms of action to be implemented

Different forms of action could be implemented: workshops, including the production of video-films

---

① http://whc.unesco.org/en/activities/638.
② https://we.tl/3Z0a9gAWry.

about the process and the results for wider distribution (WeChat, YouTube, etc); short term missions by researchers and decision-makers on specific topics; interdisciplinary seminars; teaching and research residencies organised through exchanges.

References

[1] Gaël Giraud (2016), "The Commons, a Key Concept for the Future of Development", http://ideas4development.org/en/commons-development/.

[2] New Urban Agenda-Habitat III, https://www2.habitat3.org/bitcache/99d99fbd0824de50214e99f864459d8081a9be00?vid=591155&disposition=inline&op=view.

[3] OECD and CDRF (2010), "Trends in Urbanisation and Urban Policies in OECD Countries: What Lessons for China?", Organization for Economic Cooperation and Development (OECD) and China Development Research Foundation (CDRF), Paris. http://www.oecd.org/urban/roundtable/45159707.pdf.

[4] Rencontres de Shanghai 2014, french version to download: https://we.tl/3Z0a9gAWry.

[5] Shanghai Manual 2016, http://www.urbanoctober.org/downloads/ShanghaiManual2016EnglishVersion.pdf.

[6] UN-Habitat (2014), "The City We Need, United Nations Human Settlements Programme (UN-Habitat)", https://sustainabledevelopment.un.org/content/documents/733FutureWeWant.pdf.

[7] World Bank and DRC (2014), "Urban China: Toward Efficient, Inclusive, and Sustainable Urbanization", The World Bank and the Development Research Center of the State Council, the People's Republic of China. www.worldbank.org/content/dam/Worldbank/document/EAP/China/WEB-Urban-China.pdf.

[8] The UNESCO Creative Cities Network, http://en.unesco.org/creative-cities/home;
Historic Urban Landscape Recommandation: http://whc.unesco.org/en/activities/638.

历史性城镇景观视角下历史文化街区的保护与复兴

Conservation & Revival of Historical & Cutlural Blocks in the Perspective of Historic Urban Landscape

邵甬 教授
同济大学建筑与城市规划学院教授、博导
联合国教科文组织亚太地区世界遗产培训与研究中心上海分中心主任

Prof. Shao Yong
Doctoral Supervisor, School of Architecture & Urban Planning, Tongji University
Director, World Heritage Institute of Training & Research for the Asia & the Pacific Region under the auspices of UNESCO, WHITRAP (Shanghai)

The case of Yuehu Historical & Cultural Block in Ningbo epitomizes the general situation of many such blocks across China. "Protective demolition", commercial development and uncontrollable implementation of site plan all pose challenges to the well-being of those blocks, while HUL approaches point out a way out based on the continuity in time and space.

一、中国历史文化街区的普遍状况

1. 历史文化街区的物质衰败和功能衰退

物质性衰败：历史建筑的年久失修，居住拥挤、房屋承载力较差，街区环境质量变差，基础设施、公共设施不能满足现代需求。

功能性衰退：历史功能、地位的消失，文化气质的湮灭，从传统居住社区变为租户集中区，老龄化、贫困化、社会问题众多。

2. 历史文化街区的消极维系与突变再生

消极维系：缺乏资金、产权复杂，历史建筑进一步衰败，居住环境持续恶化，社会问题进一步加剧。

突变再生：由开发商和市场主导的大规模改造，非文物保护单位被拆除，历史环境破碎，原住民大量搬迁，生活氛围不再，商业化开发，背离真实性、完整性原则。

二、宁波月湖历史文化街区案例的探索

1. 宁波千年历史住区的独特价值

唐代：府城内的蓄水库；宋代：月湖十洲初成、宅院始建、人文始盛；明清："诗意的栖居"、宁波文化学术教育中心；民国：近代化城市社区；新中国成立后：社会主义改造后的城市社区。

月湖街区经千百年之涵养，融自然与人文于一体，物化于民居院落、书院花园中，在中国的历史文化名城中独树一帜，具有重要的历史文化价值；"书藏古今、港通天下"更道出了月湖街区对宁波人文精神的重要意义。

2. 从千年住区到"无人区"

2008—2011年年底宁波海城公司对月湖(西区)历史文化街区的核心部分开始以商业开发为主导的实施计划,聘请美国波士顿设计集团设计,采用"保护性拆除"＋"商业化开发"模式,结果造成"月湖无人区"。

2011年开始,住建部和国家文物局等专家及社会各界对波士顿与宁波街区更新方式的反对迫使月湖工程叫停,但月湖"无人废墟"已成事实。

3. 破釜沉舟的《保护规划》

2012年同济大学正式接手月湖历史文化街区保护规划:

遗产保护:基于历史文化价值,确定保护对象,从"文保单位"扩展到"历史街区"。

街区复兴:复兴思想为"以文化为导向的街区复兴计划",注重体现公共性和公益性,彰显宁波传统文化精神和空间特征的历史文化街区;功能定位为人文博览、文化交流、居住、商业休闲和创意旅游等;复兴目标为增加具有公共利益性质的文化博览和文化活动等功能,成为宁波中心城区的特色文化空间集聚区。

整合滨河绿地、街坊绿地等开放空间,成为宁波中心城区的核心生态和人文景观区。强化文化休闲、文化旅游等特色功能,成为宁波中心城区的特色文化旅游区。

4. 修补弥合的《修建性详细规划》

城市界面的修补和城市公共空间的营造,街区肌理的修补和新旧的可识别性和共存对话,最后街区建筑修缮与设计的问题突出。

5. 不可控的实施阶段

由于新建筑退街过多,尽管红线宽度为4米,实际尺度失衡。新增规划道路同样尺度过大,破坏了历史街区的整体感觉;月湖街区2016年入选省级特色小镇后,最终转型为金融与文化旅游融合发展的金融小镇,街区的公共性缺失。

宁波对历史文化街区突变式发展的惯性操作思维导致了实施结果仍较大程度脱离了规划。

三、HUL视角下历史文化街区的保护与复兴

1. HUL的概念内涵

历史性城镇景观是城市保护思想和方法发展到一定阶段的产物。

"文化和自然价值及属性在历史上层层积淀而产生的城市区域,其超越了'历史中心'或'整体'的概念,包括更广泛的城市背景及其地理环境。"——《HUL建议书》

2. HUL的工作方法

价值层积:HUL方法的核心是对历史层积(Historic Layering of Values)过程的分析,包括有形与无形的各方面,且必须以物质肌理和社会结构的真实性为前提。分析价值层积的关键在于厘清层积背后的关联性,即结构与脉络。

整体保护:HUL方法包含整体性保护思想,不同于关注旧城及建筑风貌、形态的物质性整体保护,而是充分考虑社会、经济发展情况和改善居民生活环境的综合政策措施的整体性保护。

持续有效的管理:HUL方法的关键在于整合城市遗产保护目标与社会经济发展目标。拥有良好的顶层设计,建立针对性的合作机制,寻求多方参与,构建良好的管理框架。对不好的变化实施有效的控制引导,让正面效应不断累积。

因地制宜:借鉴当地传统,关注社区的需求,帮助本地居民提升生活品质。

实施关键步骤:完整调查、绘制城市自然、文化、人文社会资源——通过参与性规划和问询,就核心价值属性达成共识——评估各属性在社会经济发展和气候变化下的脆弱性——将遗产价值保护纳入城市发展战略框架——优先制定保护与发展的行动计划——建立针对性合作机制和地方管理框架。

主要实施工具:公众参与、知识和规划、监管体系、财务手段。

3. 从"消极维系"和"突变再生"走向"历史性城镇景观管理"

历史文化街区的突出特性是地域文化是重要载体，必须融合保护与发展，共同寻求未来经济社会复兴的路径。HUL视角的转变，从文物保护到地域文化的保护与发展，上下结合，多方协同，社会合力，避免突变再生。

在不断变化的社会文化及经济影响下的发展，更重要的是解决居民和物质空间之间的关系，我们要保持真实性、完整性。但最大的矛盾就是历史建筑有一定的持久性，不符合现在人们的生活。居民，一方面是街区的创造者，另一方面也是这里的保护者。在这种情况下，我们要把握历史建筑和居民之间的关系，也就是使公共利益和私人利益达到平衡。

我们在平遥古城做了一个这样的尝试。我们当时做了两个规划，一个是保护规划，一个是管理规划，最关键我们还做了一系列行动计划以及民居保护修缮的导则。导则的目标针对平遥古城内未列入文物保护单位和未登记为不可移动文物的传统民居院落修缮、保养等日常行为进行引导，建立传统民居修缮和环境治理的申报，还有设计和施工的管理机制。我们的观念是只要政府设立保护修缮资金，每年几百万就可以，由房屋的主人申请这个基金，有时候修的是整个房子，有的时候是门头，政府审核以后给予补贴，再加上自己的一些资金，就可以进行保护修缮，从而使房产得到升值。在历史建筑里面，把怎么提升新能源、新技术纳入改善过程当中，使老百姓自己生活的环境得到改善，如果老百姓有传统技术还可以在其中与一些非物质文化遗产结合起来。

HUL视角下的历史文化街区的保护与复兴，我们可以看到很多绿色的空间，如社区活动空间、社区服务中心，还有新能源等等技术融合的公共空间，使得整个街区可以恢复得比较体面、饱含文化又生态宜居。我们很希望在更广的范围推广历史文化街区，使我们街区走一条既不是消极维系，也不是突变之路，而更多的是对环境的管理，这个就是HUL历史景观强调的，在空间、时间上有一种延续性，使得历史的环境既保存文化的特质，同时又能满足现在人民的生活和需求。

扬州可持续的古城保护

Sustainable Conservation of the Historic City of Yangzhou

郑路

江苏省扬州市古城保护办公室前主任

Zheng Lu

Former Director of Conservation Office of the Historic City of Yangzhou

This speech introduces the conservation work carried out in Yangzhou, a famous historic city which is famous for the Grand Canal, the Slender West Lake as well as its classical gardens. The work includes the compilation of guidelines, the founding of specified governing bodies, issuance of relevant regulations as well as the establishment of pilot projects.

一、扬州历史文化名城保护概况

扬州是首批公布的全国24个历史文化名城之一。扬州保护的框架,其实就是"一条线,两大片":"一条线"就是古运河,特别是2014年成为世界遗产以来,扬州在古运河两岸的文化遗迹得到了很好的保护;"两大片",一个是明清古城,在20世纪90年代初,扬州市政府为了保护扬州老城,采取了老城建新城的做法,建设了新城西区,之后有了规模,形成了新的商业文化中心,另外一个区就是瘦西湖风景区,1988年被评为国家级风景名胜区。

二、明清古城

扬州明清古城指的是5.09平方千米的老城区。古城的传统格局保护完好,具有传统风貌的老街区还有262公顷,主要特色有:

(1) 独特的城市格局:逐水而城、历代叠加;双城街巷体系并存;河城环抱、水城一体。
(2) 古朴的城市风貌:"平缓型"的城市空间;匀质细腻的城市肌理;集"南秀北雄"于一体的建筑风格。
(3) 秀丽的城市园林:扬州园林自成一派,风格典雅秀丽,清秀中见雄健;绿杨城郭是扬州。
(4) 多元的城市文化:文学、书画、戏曲、民间工艺、宗教、商业多元并存,雅俗共赏、南北交汇、东西兼融。
(5) 丰富的历史遗存:文保单位168处,有价值的传统建筑约900处。

但明清古城也存在很多问题,如:人口面临老龄化,低收入人群比重较大;建筑自然老化问题较严重,尤其是一些传统民居;基础设施较差,大部分民居无单独厨卫设备,地下给排水系统不完善;缺乏小型公共绿地和休闲娱乐场所;交通矛盾相对突出;历史文化遗产未能得到很好的保护和利用。

三、近些年所做的保护工作

1. 明确保护理念

坚持谨慎的可持续的保护更新理念,明确提出将老城保护与改善居民居住条件和居住环境相结合,以改造和修缮为主——居民少量搬迁,以完善和提升为主——基础设施配套,以环境改善为主——拆除违章,建设绿化。树立构建"和谐城市"和"社会包容城市"的保护目标,充分考虑原居民的利益,不断改善他们的居住条件和居住环境,尽量使现有的邻里结构和社会经济联系不受破坏。制定了全面的和多元化的保护战略,通过市民、社区、商业和政府开展多方面合作,确保居民生活质量有明显的改进和提升。

2. 规划研究编制

《扬州老城区历史文化街区消防专项规划》《扬州传统建筑特色调查和传承研究》《扬州市历史建筑修缮技术导则》。

3. 成立专门机构

2004年成立扬州市古城保护与利用、改造与复兴工作领导小组,2009年成立扬州市古城保护办公室,2010年建立扬州市古城保护联席会议制度,其间还成立了扬州市名城建设有限公司、扬州历史文化名城研究院、古城保护专家库。

4. 出台相关政策

《扬州古城保护条例》《扬州古城传统民居修缮实施意见》《彩衣街公有住房产权出售试行办法》《扬州老城区民房整修与保护技术导则》《扬州古城区街巷综合整治技术导则》。

5. 实施项目重点

历史遗迹修缮,修缮文保单位35处;传统街道整治;传统民居修缮;环境风貌提升。

四、关于古城保护的思考

(1)经济提升的手段单一,重旅游、轻风险;
(2)文化弘扬的根基肤浅,重展示、轻传承;
(3)居住环境改善的措施不力,重政府、轻民众。

五、公众参与在扬州民居修缮工作中的实践

1. 机构代理型

2006—2007年,德国技术合作公司(GTZ)与扬州市政府合作,提出了设立"古城保护办公室"、制定"民居修缮补贴办法"等构想,推行实施了扬州市文化里民居修缮示范工程。

2. 政府引导型

扬州市彩衣街项目自2011年7月开工整治,社区动员、政策支持、补贴发放,至2012年4月底全面完成。

3. 政策支持型

2010年起,扬州市出台了《扬州古城传统民居修缮实施意见》和《扬州老城区民房整修与保护技术导则》,累计修缮传统民居105户,建筑面积约8 470平方米,共发放修缮补贴近156万元。

4. 民间自发型

扬州新"传统民居"、新"私家园林"是近几年在老城区更新中出现的一个新现象。已有570户居民对老房子进行修缮。它丰富了城市文化的内涵与特色,确保了历史古城风貌的整体性。更重要的是,居民普遍增强了城市历史文脉的记忆。2015年11月10日《文汇报》以《留住乡愁——扬州老城民居改造新意探

究》为题,介绍了扬州的做法。

古城保护与更新是一项时间长、要求高、标准严、程序复杂的艰巨工作。我们将遵循体现历史文化名城"历史的真实性、风貌的完整性、生活的延续性、文化的可读性"的原则,努力把扬州建设成为"古代文化与现代文明交相辉映的名城"。

文化·大众化·数字化：
新时代的文化遗产保护与公众参与

CULTURE, MASSIFICATION, DIGITIZATION: CULTURAL HERITAGE PRESERVATION AND PUBLIC PARTICIPATION IN THE NEW ERA

文保社会组织在新时代文化遗产保护中的实践与思考

Practice and Reflections on Social Organizations in the Protection of Cultural Heritage in the New Era

梁钢
中国文物保护基金会副理事长、秘书长
Liang Gang
Deputy Chairman and Secretary General, China Foundation For Cultural Heritage Conservation

Culture is not only a macroscopic concept but also a broad perception with the sense of humanities. As a country with a history of 5,000 years, China has profound cultural heritage. In this new era, Chinese people need to be confident with our own heritage and to enhance the traditional culture of China, which can be fused with digital technology, in order to revitalize the ancient culture. Social organizations play important roles in helping the government to promote cultural development and in connecting the folk and the government. As a public welfare social organization, China Foundation For Cultural Heritage Conservation has broken through some conventional restrictions in its past work and has made some contributions to cultural heritage protection, such as the "Saving Old Houses" project and the "Great Wall Protection Plus Me" project, which have been highly appraised by the society. Yet with the trend of digitization, we still need to strengthen the cooperation with the public and improve the social promotion to involve more young people into traditional culture.

一、新时代文保社会组织参与文化遗产保护的背景

中国文物保护基金会始终致力于中国传统文化的保护利用与传承推广,在过去的几年中做了一些与文化遗产保护与推广相关的项目。关于文化遗产保护,先做两点阐述:

(一)新时代文化遗产保护的背景。党的十九大以来,以习近平同志为核心的党中央一直强调"文化自信"。习近平总书记在中国文联十大、中国作协九大开幕式上的讲话中指出:"坚定文化自信,离不开对中华民族历史的认知和运用。历史是一面镜子,从历史中,我们能够更好看清世界、参透生活、认识自己;历史也是一位智者,同历史对话,我们能够更好认识过去、把握当下、面向未来。"中华优秀传统文化是我们最深厚的文化软实力,也是中国特色社会主义植根的文化沃土。汲取中华优秀文化并与当代价值文化相结合,有利于建设中国特色文化自信意识形态体系;当国际社会面临

"保护长城,加我一个"项目箭扣段修缮

重大问题时,能够提供中国智慧、中国方案,有利于提高中国的国际地位,早日实现中华民族伟大复兴的中国梦。

(二)物质文化遗产与非物质文化遗产相互依存,密切联系。物质文化遗产的形成、保护与修复,都离不开非物质文化遗产的传统技艺,大部分非物质文化遗产的成果也以物质形态体现,即便是艺术表演、乐曲演奏等非物质形式的成果,也依托一定物质形态的载体。两者的存续与集成都归结到人,特别是非物质文化遗产独特的"非物质"特性,注定了它的存续是以人为载体的,所以,关于非遗保护这样一个命题,核心是要调动人的积极性与关注度。我们应把文化遗产自身具备的独特历史渊源、人文情怀、艺术价值充分唤醒,并为之注入新的生命与活力,使之在当下焕发出新的光彩,这也正是文化遗产保护的意义所在。

二、文保社会组织在新时代文化遗产保护中的作用

新时代背景下,中国文物保护基金会作为公益性公募基金会,在充分认识自身的角色定位的基础上,主要从以下几个方面参与文保事业。一是承担政府和其他社会主体不能做或者不愿做的事;二是与各地文物保护部门、有关社会组织、公益慈善社会组织以及其他社会力量积极联络,探索社会力量参与文物保护和利用的新的方式和途径;三是积极向社会募集资金,对文化遗产和非物质文化遗产进行专项保护;四是开展各项活动促进文化遗产的展示、宣传、价值研究与传播。具体来讲就是做好文化遗产的传承者、守护者和文化遗产保护的开拓者。

(一)文化遗产的传承者。截至2019年7月良渚古城遗址被列入《世界遗产名录》,中国已有55项世界遗产,其中文化遗产37项、文化与自然双遗产4项、自然遗产14项,世界遗产总数居世界第一。据《国家文物事业发展"十三五"规划》统计发布,我国共有不可移动文物766 722处,加上刚刚发布的第八批国保单位762处,目前共有国保单位5 058处,另有省保单位17 298个处。全国以文物和各类遗址为依托建立起来的博物馆、纪念馆有4 692家。全国国有博物馆馆藏文物约5 000多万件,民间收藏的文物尚不明确。虽然国家在逐年加大文物保护力度,但文物资源浩若烟海,保护任务仍然重如泰山。2007年,中国文物保护基金会创办了"薪火相传"宣讲活动,旨在表彰社会各界在文化遗产保护中做出的突出贡献及文物系统基层工作者的奉献精神,至今已成功举办了十届。第十一届以"寻找红色基因传承者"为主题,即将在杭州举行。宣讲活动开展以来,先后有100多位文化遗产保护杰出人物和杰出团队通过宣讲先进事迹,产生了广泛的社会影响,成为基金会推动全社会积极参与文物保护的一个品牌项目。我们坚持弘扬先进,讴歌奉献,宣扬应该宣扬的,关注未被关注的;我们坚持体制内体制外、系统内系统外并重,为形成社会力量共同参与文物保护的大格局助力;我们坚持公益属性,公开公平公正,突出事迹优先,始终不搞有偿评选和暗箱操作;我们坚持围绕文物保护利用的主题,有所创造创新,每年确定一个重点方向,常搞常新。十年的薪火相传,见证了我国文物保护事业的加强与发展,见证了社会力量参与文物保护由涓涓细流到激流澎湃的过程,见证了中华优秀传统文化创造性转化和创新性发展的历史趋势。"薪火相传"宣讲活动已经成为文化遗产保护领域"更好传承中国精神、中国价值、中国力量"的有益实践。

作为广泛动员社会力量参与文物保护的成功范例,2016年9月,中国文物保护基金会与腾讯公益合作发起了"保护长城,加我一个"公募项目。项目以河北喜峰口,北京箭扣、北京八达岭等地长城点段为实施地,通过线上公募+线下募集的方式进行,截至2018年底公募筹款5 300多万元。成为中国文化遗产保护事业进程中规模较大、科学技术投入较多、社会公众参与较广的一次成功尝试。2019年7月箭扣南段通过竣工验收并取得示范性效果,成为明代砖石类长城修缮的样本工程,为今后国内同类长城修缮提供了模式与经验。

(二)文化遗产的守护者。首先,基金会利用社会组织的公益属性,可以开展一些政府部门不方便直接出面开展的文物保护修复活动。2016年,我们受财政部、国家文物局委托,组织实施了"拯救老屋行动"项目。项目以习近平总书记新时代中国特色社会主义思想为指导,紧紧围绕乡村振兴和脱贫攻坚国家战略,按照国家七部委局关于保护传统村落的工作部署,资助范围为中国传统村落内各级文物保护单位和第

三次全国文物普查登录的一般不可移动文物中的个人产权文物建筑。项目资助修缮资金的50%，带动产权人出资和地方政府整合其他项目资金解决另外50%的修缮资金，同时还吸引设计研究团队无偿为传统村落提供智力支持、志愿服务以及社会捐赠，构建了以财政资助为推动、房屋产权人为主体、社会力量广泛参与的传统村落保护新模式。2016年至2018年三年时间，我们实施了4个县的"整县推进"项目和12个村的"特色村落保护"项目，资金总规模达到3亿元以上。中央电视台多次予以报道。作为古村落古民居保护利用的重点实施项目，"拯救老屋行动"被写入党中央国务院发布的《乡村振兴战略规划(2018—2022年)》，成为落实乡村振兴战略、保护乡村文化遗产、传承乡村文化根脉的一个重要举措。

其次，承担一些政府尚未关注或暂时顾及不到的文物保护项目。2016年我们启动了基金会首个海外公募项目"英国北洋水师水兵墓修缮项目"。1881年和1887年清政府曾两次派北洋水师官兵赴英国纽卡斯尔造船厂接收超勇、扬威及致远、靖远军舰。两次远航中共有5名水兵不幸客死他乡。一百多年过去，这五座墓碑断裂、风化、倒塌，景象残破凋零。经英国当地政府相关部门同意，基金会面向海内外发起公众募集项目，同时也是为了让全世界华人知道，120多年后，海内外中华儿女并没有忘记他们，让他们在异乡安息。该项目得到社会各界和海外华人华侨的广泛关注和响应，BBC等很多外媒对项目进行了报道。2019年6月项目顺利竣工。

此外，围绕习近平总书记"让文物活起来"的总体要求，我们还开展了"价值研究与传播""红色记忆V计划"等项目。通过这些实践，基金会作为政府部门委托的项目实施监督方，在角色上更加专业，方式上更加灵活，实现了"政府主导、社会组织参与"的文物保护路径与方式的创新。

(三)文化遗产保护的开拓者。我们处在一个变革的时代。现代科技成果的广泛应用使我们的生活发生了翻天覆地的变化。中国文物保护基金会与时俱进，不断探索应用现代信息技术推动文物保护与利用发展的手段和方法。敦煌石窟是多元文明交融发展的重要载体和结晶，敦煌石窟壁画具有脆弱性和不可再生性，2018年我会与中国敦煌石窟研究保护基金会、敦煌研究院、腾讯公益共同发起敦煌"数字供养人"公募项目。项目旨在宣传、传播中华文化遗产的保护意识，引导公众，特别是年轻人了解中国灿烂文化遗产，并参与到文化遗产的保护中来。项目将莫高窟第55窟壁画以数字形式真实完整地永久保存下来，为文物保护、考古研究、美术临摹等方面提供数据支持，让观众进行多角度、深层次、全方位的艺术欣赏和体验，使不可移动的敦煌文物突破物理空间，通过互联网和移动终端实现了全球共享。

三、文保社会组织参与文化遗产保护前景展望

中国是拥有5 000多年悠久历史的文明古国，中华大地上灿若星辰的文化遗产不仅是承载灿烂文明、传承历史文化、维系民族精神的重要载体，也越来越成为构筑时代创新动能、促进社会高质量发展、提升人民生活幸福感的载体。党的十八大以来，以习近平同志为核心的党中央高度重视文物工作，习近平总书记对文物保护工作发表了一系列的重要讲话，国家出台了多项法律法规，如《关于实施中华优秀传统文化传承发展工程的意见》《关于加强文物保护利用改革的实施意见》等。展望未来，在继续做好文化遗产保护这项重点工作外，文保社会组织在文化遗产保护领域将会发挥越来越大的作用。

(一)宣传普及推广。引导全社会参与文化遗产保护是文保社会组织的基本职能，我们可以通过组织论坛、讲座、沙龙等，普及文保知识，传播文化遗产的历史文化内涵，联络和发展更多的文保志愿者，为文物保护和利用奠定群众基础。新的时代更要重视利用互联网的手段，通过朋友圈、微视频、公众号等方式，宣传普及推广文化遗产资源。

(二)推动文旅融合发展。近年来，文创产业发展迅猛，文化遗产发挥了重要作用，很多文创产品是以文化遗产创意为灵魂设计开发出来的。特别是有些地方利用非遗资源开发的突显地方文化特色的广播影视、戏曲艺术、美术工艺、视觉传媒、环境艺术等产品，都是文化遗产保护利用的表现形式。当前，科技数字文旅的新时代已经开启，催生出了很多新的业态、新的模式和新的产品。文旅融合成为文旅产业发展的主要路径。文保社会组织要抓住机会，发挥资源优势，推动文旅融合创新发展。

（三）坚持调查整理与研究。发挥文保社会组织的强项，继续做好文化遗产资源的调查，组织开展有关研究文章的撰写，为专业机构和主管部门拾遗补缺，推出更多的专业成果。

（四）参与制度设计。文化遗产保护利用方面的制度性安排，当前还不十分完善，国家层面的有关制度、规范、导则的形成要以各地的规范性文件为基础，在有关地方制定这方面规范性文件的过程中，我们文保社会组织应该主动反映群众意见，提出建议，同时，做好社区群众的宣传解释工作，这是社会组织的独特作用。

谁的遗产？国际古迹遗址理事会视野下的文化遗产保护与公众参与

Whose Cultural Heritage? Cultural Heritage Conservation and Public Participation—from the Perspective of ICOMOS

彼得·菲利普
ICOMOS 秘书长
Peter Phillips
Secretary General of ICOMOS

ICOMOS 是一个由一万多名文化遗产专业人士组成的组织，他们都是各自领域的专家。公众在 ICOMOS 的工作中起什么作用？ICOMOS 专家又在扩大文化遗产领域这一工作中起到什么作用呢？如果社会群体不重视文化遗产，他们就无法生存。保护遗产的政治意愿最终来自社群的支持。不过，公有部门和私营机构都可能有将遗产推倒重建的计划，而这种重建计划亦得到一定程度的公众支持。有时，公众对遗产的支持只是在大量遗产消失后才得到激发。ICOMOS 的专业人员有两个重要的角色：为保护那些已被重视的地方提供专家意见；识别和保护那些可能还没有被充分重视的地方，以便在它们的价值被公众认可之前能够保护它们。在这两种情况下，ICOMOS 都需要与社群合作，以取得成功的遗产保护成果。

Firstly, may I thank the city of Wuhan and the forum for inviting me here today for their hospitality and their generosity. I am very grateful. And on behalf of ICOMOS, I extend my thanks to you. This morning is devoted to the relationship between the public and the conservation of their cultural heritage.

I will be discussing this relationship from the viewpoint of ICOMOS. So what is ICOMOS? ICOMOS is the International Council on Monuments and Sites. It was founded over 50 years ago in Warsaw. It's dedicated to conserving and promoting the world's cultural heritage. Most people know ICOMOS as one of the three advisory bodies to the UNESCO world heritage committee.

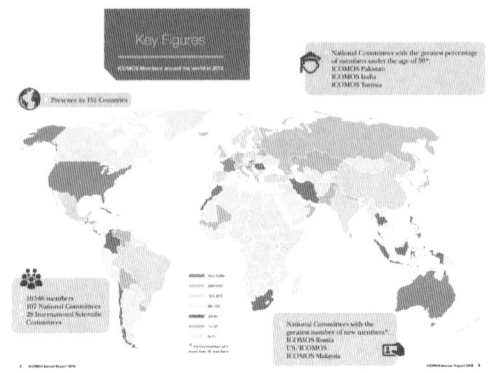

ICOMOS 在全世界的分布（截至 2018 年）

But this is only part of our role. We have a secretariat based in Paris. And much of what we do is to develop theoretical and practical guidance on best practice or conserving cultural heritage. One of the most public events that we organize is the International Day for Monuments and Sites, which is held every year on April 18. The theme this year was rural heritage, of which China has an immense amount.

This is what ICOMOS looks like within the world. As you can see, our representation is not at all even. There are many places in the world where we would wish ICOMOS to be stronger. But you can also see that China is one of the strongest places where ICOMOS is active. And we have a great many good experts in China who are helping to further the cores of ICOMOS.

We have 10.5 thousand members worldwide. We have 107 national committees as in 2018 and more are being formed. We have 28 international scientific committees. And again, more of those are in the process of formation, particularly one on the heritage of water, which I hope will be established in Sydney at the ICOMOS General Assembly 2020.

So where does the community fit into all of this? This is a slide of the community trying to fit into the Forbidden City on a Chinese National Holiday. As you can see, there are great many more of the community than there are of ICOMOS.

So the relationship between ICOMOS and the community can be explained if we go back to basics and think about what heritage is. If you take the word heritage literally, it means what we inherit from the past. But that includes everything, the good and the bad. So it is not a very useful definition. What we prefer to do is to say that heritage is what we value of what we have inherited from the past and what we wish to pass on to the future.

This creates some difficulty because heritage is a moving target. Because we are talking about values and about people, we have different people who value different things at different times. So it is very common, for example, that the heritage of the recent past is not well valued until a certain period has gone by. And then the community comes to realize that perhaps it is heritage that should be valued. In the end, it is the community, all of you who decide whether heritage will be valued and protected.

So many people, lawyers in particular, would prefer heritage issues to be black and white. In other words, it is a very easy line between what is heritage and what is not. Unfortunately, this is not the case. This is the real picture. It is shades of grey. And heritage is towards one end of the spectrum, what is not heritage is towards the other end. And how we decide on this, whether we decide and when we decide depends very much on community attitudes. And in this case, a majority of community attitudes.

And this is not only the case for cultural heritage, we are increasingly coming to realize that there is a spectrum between nature and culture. So that in almost all cultural heritage, there is an aspect of natural heritage, and the same applies in the other direction. Sometimes, however, the community prefers to rebuild rather than to preserve. This is a photograph of Wuhan taken in about 1915. As you can see, the city wall still survives, and it is a very low-scale development. This is the city approximately 100 years later. Great changes, you can see.

Sometimes, and this is certainly true in my own country, heritage may be valued only when it is in danger of disappearing, or has actually gone. Clearly in Wuhan, much has gone, but also much has survived and is valued. So what is the role of the expert from ICOMOS in all of this?

This, by the way, is an unintentional self-portrait taken while I was recording a little rural building on a remote property south of Sydney. So the first and most obvious role for the ICOMOS expert is to help the community by providing expert heritage advice on the conservation of cultural heritage that the community already values. That's the easy part. The more difficult part is identifying and defending cultural heritage that is not yet adequately valued by the whole of the community. Sometimes only a small section of the community will find things that are valuable. But in both cases, ICOMOS needs to work with the community.

And ICOMOS has laid down a set of guidelines within its ethical principles for how it relates to the community. Like most professional organizations, ICOMOS has a code of ethics, and this is Article Three or a summary of Article Three that deals with the relationship between ICOMOS members and the general public. Firstly, we acknowledge that all ICOMOS members have a moral duty and a moral obligation to transmit cultural heritage values. Secondly, we need to take the public interest into account in everything we do. In other words, it is not just experts preserving heritage for other experts. Thirdly, we need to acknowledge and to value the community involvement and collaboration. So again, not taking the community for granted, but involving them at every step of the way. Fourthly, we need to recognize that there is a co-existence of cultural values, and that needs to be recognized in the context of human rights. And this is particularly the case where values are contested as sometimes shared in an amicable way, sometimes shared in a less amicable way. So ICOMOS members need to take these considerations into account and to deal sensitively with all parts of the community. And the final thing of course is to promote cultural heritage within the community to encourage access to and support for cultural heritage in every possible way, including financial.

In all of this, there are a number of challenges for ICOMOS experts. One of the first challenge is identifying who the community actually is. Because in many cases, the community is many communities, and many of which will have an interest in a particular aspect of cultural heritage. Identifying these people and taking account of their wishes and desires and opinions is all part of what ICOMOS needs to do.

So for this purpose, we have established a working group on rights-based approaches. This group is also called our common dignity. One of the many things that it does is to look at the role of indigenous communities in relation to cultural heritage, especially in relation to world heritage. Indigenous communities are sometimes not consulted by their state parties when a nomination is proposed. Even though those indigenous communities are the primary caretakers of the cultural heritage, and their protection and management is what keeps the place. It keeps its outstanding universal value.

The second one, as I've mentioned earlier, is dealing with places where values are contested. In other words, not everybody agrees on what the values are or should be. One recent example of this is the world heritage nomination of the Meiji Industrial Sites in Japan. So this, as you probably know, was inscribed for its outstanding universal value relating to the industrial development of Japan in the late 19th and early 20th centuries. But the nomination was challenged because it failed to recognize the role of forced labor from other countries during subsequent decades. So this was an issue for ICOMOS in how it evaluated the property. And the conclusion it came to was that all aspects of the history of the Meiji Industrial Sites should be interpreted on the site.

The 3rd one, not just for ICOMOS experts, but for experts of every color and creed, is lack of trust in experts, which seems to be growing in the world. An American author, Tom Nichols, has recently written a book called The *Death of Expertise*: The Campaign against Established Knowledge and Why It Matters. And he argues that with the rise of the Internet, all of us know everything. Or at least we think we do. And this dramatically affects our respect for experts in any particular field, medicine being a particular case in point. This view is reinforced every time an expert opinion is shown to be in error, regardless of the fact, for example, that most of us get into an airplane with a blind trust in the expertise that keeps the airplane up in the air. This is what might be called the democracy of expertise. In other words, we all know what should be done? So it is a challenge for the expert within this environment.

Finally, of course, there are always differences in expert opinions. Sometimes these differences are genuine because the subject matter is not decided. Sometimes, however, there are suspicions that expert opinions may be affected by political interests or by financial interests. So again, this tends to color the public's view of the expert opinions. These are all challenges for ICOMOS experts.

So how does ICOMOS deal with those? The way that ICOMOS deals with expertise, particularly in its institutional view, is to form its community of experts. So this brings the theme of the public or the community and the experts together. When ICOMOS expresses an institutional opinion in particular about World Heritage. That opinion is based on the collective view of a substantial group of expert members who have taken deliberate steps to avoid political or financial bias and who have taken the rights and the views of all sections of the community into account.

These are the people. A sample of the 10.5 thousand who can help the public value and preserve its heritage. We look forward to an ever more fruitful partnership between ICOMOS and many communities that care for their heritage.

文化遗产与公众同在

Heritage with the Public

冯天瑜 教授
武汉大学
Prof. Feng Tianyu
Wuhan University

The people are the creators of culture and, of course, the protectors, appreciators and inheritors of culture. The cultural heritage, as a relic of cultural history, should be treasured by the society and studied by specialists, but should never be put on the shelf and become objects in an ivory tower away from the public.

文化遗产所拥有的公共属性以及文化遗产保护的公共性,决定了公众参与文化遗产的保护、传承的必然性。

我们谈到文化遗产的保护,首先想到的是国家级、地区级的那些重要的博物馆。譬如我们湖北的湖北省博物馆、武汉市博物馆,它们承担着保护、利用、传播文化遗产的功能。除了这样一些建制性的博物馆、纪念馆以外,要发挥文化遗产的公众性,我们还要关注、发展一些栖息在民间的各种专题的、专门的、有特色的民间博物馆、展览馆。

我在日本讲学了多年,注意到日本除了大型的博物馆以外,还十分注意发展专题的、民间的、小型的博物馆和展览馆。譬如东京的街头有人力车博物馆,丰田市有专门的丰田汽车博物馆。如果把人力车博物馆和丰田汽车博物馆对比来看,它们将19世纪二三十年代一直到当下的最先进的最现代化的汽车,整个地进行了展览。如果我们把它们贯通起来看,人类的出行这个问题上的文化遗产,就有了一个非常完整的、生动的、形象的一个展现。

汉口里分

武汉市在这方面也做了很多的工作。汉口的文体中心虽然是以足球场为主,但里面也设置了一个荆楚金石博物馆。金就是青铜器,石就是石雕,这个博物馆中设置了金石全形拓的展览。很多人没有注意到它的价值,其实这个是非常重要的文化遗产。拓片技术在中国隋唐已经出现,但限于平面。从十九世纪三四十年代清代的道光年间开始,出现了全形拓片的技术。全形拓片又叫立体拓片,这是一个很了不起的创造,在人类发明摄影技术之前,能够立体地把青铜器、雕刻的石器等器物立体地呈现。这个技术发明的时间,恰恰跟法国人达盖尔发明摄影技术同时。后来,这一技术慢慢地中断了,也被很多人遗忘了,现在我们又重新把它发掘出来。荆楚金石博物馆将全形拓的技术重新展开,这对于文化遗产的保存以及在民间发挥其文化传播作用是非常重要的。

我们的文化遗产,不仅仅指最著名的几个点,诸如河姆渡遗址和安阳的殷墟。我们借用美学家的一句话,美是无处不在的,问题是我们要有发现美的眼睛。我们也可以说文化遗产是无处不在的。有价值的遗产深藏在我们的生活的很多地方,我们要善于发现。

其他城市的一些做法很值得我们参考。比如当你走在维也、彼得堡的普通街道上,只要留心观察,就会发现很多建筑物上面都有标牌,注明此为某某作家、工程师或医生的住所,并简单介绍了他们的文化贡献。我们在这样一种街道当中行走,我们就如同行走在历史的图层上、行走在文化遗产的展览群当中。像这样的工作我们应该多做。在彼得堡涅瓦河畔,我曾经发现过非常重要的碑文。其中有李鸿章给当时沙皇送的一个碑文,但是这么重要的一个东西呈现在那些地方,很少看到国内的介绍。这样的工作我们也应该多做。

对城市的文化遗产的发掘、保护和传承而言,我们应该有选择地特色存留、修整一些街道里分。目前,极具中西交汇特色的汉口里分亟待保护,这些老街巷中都包藏着许多很值得弘扬的文化价值,这些文化遗产都是我们留给后人的历史的实物见证。从这些文化遗产中,我们可以看到我们的先辈是怎么生活的,也能够留存传统式的人际关系。

这样一些街道里份的建筑当中,可以说包藏着文化的四个层面:物质文化、制度文化、行为文化(生活方式)和观念文化。如果我们把它们都毁掉了的话,就会把很多重要的历史遗迹、有价值的历史遗产都埋葬了,这是很不应该的。在这方面我们有很多的工作可做。

我们武汉还有着非常丰富、相当完整的近代以来的工业遗产。清末,张之洞在武汉建成了亚洲第一家现代化的钢铁联合企业——汉阳铁厂,也建造了中国近代最重要的陆军兵器的制造中心——汉阳兵工厂。铁厂和兵工厂的主要设备在抗日战争期间都已经迁移到大后方四川去了,但是在武汉还有遗迹。汉阳铁厂和兵工厂的有些设备,现在还在重庆某些工厂里面也使用。武汉要把这些记录下来,以丰富和还原汉阳铁厂的情况。汉阳铁厂比日本的第一个现代化的钢铁联合企业早七年,但是我们现在的保存以及对它的价值的开掘和张扬都还不够。

民国的工业遗产,就更为丰富:汉口有南洋烟厂,武昌有第一纱厂、裕华纱厂。这都是在整个中国乃至亚洲都非常有地位的纺织工业的基地。现在这些厂,因为设备更新、厂房转移,也在慢慢地拆毁,现在可能还保存了一点。

第一个五年计划期间,中国有 156 项最重大的工业建设,其中武汉有武钢——武汉钢铁公司、武重——武汉重型机床厂,还有武锅——武汉锅炉厂,还有武昌造船厂也都是第一个五年计划时期建的。武汉可以说是中国当时最先进、最重要的重工业基地。由于厂房的迁移和企业的发展,这些工业遗产的保护,也要更加重视。

这一点我们要向德国的两个重要的工业遗产基地学习:一个是鲁尔工业区,一个是萨尔工业区。这些地方的工业遗产保护可以展示出工业革命的初期和中期的工业发展状况,不是仅仅在书籍当中所看的能够取代的。工业遗产的保护至关重要。

我们是个文明古国,因此中国的考古界甚至于觉得唐宋以后都不算什么了,因为中国的文化太古老了。其实我们谈文化遗产不能仅仅只把古代的看成我们的文化遗产,近代文明、现代文明的遗产离我们今天的生活更切近,里面包含的东西更有值得我们今天借鉴、思考的地方。近现代遗产的保护与考古工作一样至关重要。

最后,关于非物质文化遗产的保护问题,非物质文化遗产其实是物质和非物质结合的东西。比如武汉的汉剧、楚剧、湖北评书。这些遗产的保存还有弘扬的问题也同样至关重要。

文化遗产和我们的公众是一体的。文化遗产与公众同在,与我们的生活同在。

新时代文化遗产保护与公众参与

Cultural Heritage Preservation and Public Participation in the New Era

杨相卫

武汉市文化和旅游局局长

Yang Xiangwei

Director, Wuhan Culture and Tourism Bureau

Attaching importance to and expanding public participation is an important content of urban cultural heritage protection in the new era. In recent years, Wuhan has actively promoted the construction of "historical city", forming a new pattern of cultural heritage protection led by the government and involving the society. The main practices have the following three aspects. First, attach great importance to the protection of cultural heritage the social publicity and promotion of. Second, constantly improve the system of encouraging public participation in the protection of cultural heritage. Third, actively explore ways for the public to participate in the protection of cultural heritage. Based on this, we propose several thoughts on public participation in the protection of cultural heritage. First, the relationship between the government and the public should be properly handled in the protection of cultural heritage. Second, we will further arouse the enthusiasm of the public to participate. Third, we will give full play to the role of all parties in the protection of cultural heritage.

一周前,第七届世界军人运动会在武汉胜利闭幕。这既是一届精彩、非凡、卓越的军事体育盛会,也是一场文化的盛会。尤其值得一提的是,军运会的35处比赛场馆中,共有17处是在旧有场馆的基础上,通过维修改造再利用的。军运会既彰显了文化中国的辉煌成就,也体现了"精致武汉"在保护文化遗产、推动"老城新生"方面的不懈努力。今天,是明天的历史。目前,我市正筹划设立武汉世界军运会博物馆。借此论坛机会,我想就城市文化遗产保护与公众参与,从一名城市管理工作者的视角,谈一谈个人的体会,与大家商榷。

一、重视和扩大公众参与是新时代城市文化遗产保护的重要命题

城市是文化的载体,文化是城市的灵魂。丰富的历史文化遗产,既是一个城市区别于其他城市的标签,也是这个城市个性魅力的源泉。习近平总书记指出:"历史文化是城市的灵魂,要像爱惜自己的生命一样保护好城市历史文化遗产。"重视和扩大公众参与,以更好地保护好城市文化遗产,越来越成为中外城市管理者的共识。

城市文化遗产的公共属性和文化遗产保护的公共责任,决定了公众参与文化遗产保护的必然性。城市文化遗产是城市的宝贵财富,也是全体市民的集体文化记忆,是城与人、古与今割舍不断的精神纽带。参与文化遗产保护是市民的权利,也是应尽的义务。实践中,越来越多的市民对城市文化遗产产生浓厚兴趣,公众参与文化遗产保护意识不断增强。

城市文化遗产的稀缺性和不可再生性,决定了公众参与文化遗产保护的紧迫性。受保护意识薄弱、自

然灾害、人为损坏等不利因素影响,历史文化遗产保护形势仍然严峻。一方面,虽然文保专家、规划师、文化遗产使用人和普通市民越来越多地参与到文化遗产保护中来,但尚未形成全社会共识。另一方面,城市文化遗产的保养、维护和修缮需要大量资金,仅仅依靠公共财政的投入存在不足。引导公众参与文化遗产保护的激励机制、监督机制需要进一步健全完善。

公众的文化自觉和新时代保护渠道的多样化,决定了公众参与文化遗产保护的可行性。新中国成立特别是改革开放以来,随着我国综合国力的提升,人民群众有了更清醒的文化自觉和文化自信,越来越多的人以各种方式参与到文化遗产保护工作中来。同时,信息化条件下,人们了解文化遗产的途径增多,参与文化遗产保护的平台和渠道也更加通畅,政府与市民更容易在文化遗产保护过程中进行意见沟通、形成价值共识。

二、公众参与城市文化遗产保护的武汉实践

武汉具有3 500年建城史,1986年被国务院公布为第二批国家历史文化名城,历史文化资源丰富。目前,全市共有市级以上文物保护单位275处,其中全国重点文物保护单位33处;优秀历史建筑208处。近年来,武汉积极推进"历史之城"建设,启动武昌古城、汉口历史文化风貌街区、汉阳归元片区生态修复、老城复兴、文脉复归工程,形成了政府主导、社会参与的文化遗产保护新格局。概括起来,主要做法有以下三个方面:

国际古迹遗址日志愿者活动

一是高度重视文化遗产保护的社会宣传推广。我们积极培育市民的文化遗产保护意识,通过举办"文化和自然遗产日"特色主题活动,发挥文博单位社教功能,深入社区、学校举办流动展览等方式,宣传文化遗产保护法律法规;加强盘龙城国家考古遗址公园、明楚王墓群等文化遗产保护、展示项目建设力度和优质文化资源供给,让公众在参观中感受文化遗产魅力,增强文化自信和文化遗产保护意识,公众参与文化遗产保护的积极性日趋增强。2012年,无界论坛永久落户武汉,至今已连续举办七届,为扩大文化遗产保护的社会教育发挥了重要作用。今天,我们也很高兴地看到,通过举办"青少年无界论坛",文化遗产保护的理念已经开始向青少年群体传播。

二是不断完善鼓励公众参与文化遗产保护的制度。比如,《武汉市文物保护若干规定》就明确鼓励组织和个人以捐赠等方式,支持和参与文物保护事业;《武汉市历史文化风貌街区和优秀历史建筑保护条例》确定了历史文化风貌街区的保护改造,必须遵循政府主导、企业开发、市场运作、社会参与的原则,并规定了表彰和奖励公众参与的情形。再如,武汉市人民政府《关于加强历史文化名镇名村保护和可持续发展工作的意见》提出,建立社会力量投资历史文化名镇名村保护和利用的机制。

三是积极探索公众参与文化遗产保护的形式。我们鼓励社会力量通过研究、宣传、收藏、展示、传承、捐赠等方式,参与非物质文化遗产、历史文化风貌街区和优秀历史建筑保护工作;鼓励单位和个人对历史文化遗产保护规划、方案等提出意见,依法依规对破坏历史文化遗产的行为进行监督。在实践中,产生了很多成功的案例。比如,武汉大学早期建筑群是全国重点文物保护单位,武汉大学对其进行了很好的保护和利用,使建设最美大学校园与保护城市文化遗产相得益彰。武汉设计之都客厅——翟雅阁博物馆,是企业和社会力量参与保护历史建筑并建成博物馆的优秀范例。中国历史文化名村黄陂大余湾,是民间资本保护名村名镇历史资源的典范,已经成为市民乡村休闲旅游的好去处,实现了保护和利用的双赢。

三、创新公众参与文化遗产保护的几点思考

近些年来,我们在城市文化遗产保护方面做了不懈努力,也取得了一些成绩,但保护工作中面貌趋同、建设失调、管理错位等问题仍然或多或少地存在。要解决这些问题,真正实现科学保护,必须解放思想、创新机制,其中的一个方面就是进一步激发广大市民参与文化遗产保护的积极性和创造性。

一是要正确处理文化遗产保护过程中政府和公众之间的关系。在城市文化遗产保护过程中,政府和公众有着共同的目标,这个目标就是留住城市的记忆,共同建设一个特色鲜明的历史之城。在文化遗产保护中,政府和公众是一个有机整体,并因各自的角色不同,发挥相辅相成的作用,形成保护文化遗产的强大合力。政府应始终居于主导地位,在城市规划、政策制定、宣传发动等方面充分发挥引领作用,同时,充分利用高等院校、科研院所专家学者的专业和智力支持,社会公众则应积极参与,为城市的文化遗产保护献计献策、出资出力。

二是进一步调动公众参与文化遗产保护的积极性。只有当大多数人欣赏、珍惜、享受文化遗产,它才会受到有效的保护。政府可通过多种渠道的宣传和推广,拉近城市文化遗产与广大市民的距离,让公众理解、接受和欣赏文化遗产的历史价值、美学价值和社会价值,进而将文化遗产保护融入到自己的生活方式中来,努力形成"保护遗产,人人有责"的社会共识。

三是充分发挥社会各方在文化遗产保护中的作用。各级政府应切实履行属地管理主体责任,及时研究解决文化遗产保护工作中的突出问题,充分发挥规划引领、政策引导作用。文化、规划、房管等政府主管部门应切实履行好监管责任,依各自职责统筹指导全市文化遗产保护工作。文物保护单位、优秀历史建筑的所有人或者使用人,要进一步增强责任意识,切实履行好共同保护文化遗产的社会责任,积极引导企业、社会团体和广大市民,主动参与到文化遗产保护工作中,为建设国家历史文化名城做出自己的贡献。

文化遗产是人类的共同财富,保护好、利用好文化遗产是每一个人的责任。只有扎根群众沃土、吸引公众参与,才能更好地实现文化遗产的保护传承和深厚滋养,获得更绵长的生命力。我相信,随着保护意识和参与意识的增强,将会有越来越多的人加入传承人文精神、延续城市文脉的行列中来,文化遗产保护的明天会更加美好!

公众参与和城市遗产的物质与非物质价值
Community Participation and the Tangible and Intangible Values of Urban Heritage

迈克尔·特纳 教授
联合国教科文组织城市设计与保护研究教席持有人
联合国教科文组织世界遗产中心主任特使
联合国教科文组织世界遗产委员会前副主席
Prof. Michael Turner
Holder, UNESCO Chair in Urban Design and Conservation Studies
Special Envoy to the World Heritage Centre Director
Former Vice-President, UNESCO World Heritage Committee

在《世界遗产公约》发布40周年之际,地方社群在可持续发展方面的作用愈发突显,以应对城市格局变化方面的挑战,特别是那些因日益增加的人口和发展压力而受到影响的城市。这篇文章概述了城市社区不断变化的特点,以及为讨论它们的作用而需要的相关词汇和通用语言。通过技术革命,我们对社群和利益相关者的理解在时间、地点和空间上都得到了扩展,以涵盖社会的虚拟维度。社群的新角色根据一系列的价值和解释重新定义了社会分组的身份。这座城市不再只属于那些"创造了它"的人,它接纳了移民社群,通过他们自己的眼睛重新诠释了它的原始价值——这也引出了旧城重生或再生的概念。城市属性是对真实性和完整性的检验,需要重新审视,从而更广泛地接受"他者"。犹太教喀巴拉主义中的"退隐"(tzi mt z um)和日本的"間"(Ma)可以创造精神和物质的城市空间。联合国教科文组织关于历史性城市景观的建议呼吁使用新的工具来翻译思想,以达成城市生活的共识,而不是单一的叙述。

Introduction

While cultural and urban continuity is being debated, the revolutions affecting the city have multiplied exponentially, creating a dissonance between people and places. These revolutions have included the industrial revolution of the eighteenth century, the social and economic revolutions of the nineteenth century, the environmental revolutions of the twentieth century, and the technological revolutions of the past decade.

At each point in time, these revolutions have impacted the city with figures that are sometimes mind-boggling. The various projections from the current statistics indicate that some 50 percent of the world's population is living in cities and will escalate to a figure of over 75 percent that will be living in cities by 2050 (Seetharam, 2010), a doubling of urban neophytes in the developing world. Whether it is a decade before or after 2050 is irrelevant; it is more than poignant to view the changes in Shanghai during the twenty years 1990—2010—a view that speaks for itself.

These transformations have created a changing context, losing tradition and continuity, with old and new pressures on the urban landscape changing the setting. This has, in terms that have been identified in the UNESCO Recommendation on the Historic Urban Landscape,[①] changed the mindset of conservation from the objects of the monuments to the subjects of the living cities.

Who are the urban communities in this dramatically changing scene? How are their voices heard in order to generate an enriching symphony rather than a cacophony of sounds? The urban complexities challenge the single client-user in the managing of the site, as the multiplicity of stakeholders, including the custodians, has now to develop tools for managing not only the site but the people living and working in our cities. But, it is the first subparagraph of Article 5 in the *World Heritage Convention* that outlines the obligations of States Parties to the *Convention*. The article determines that States Parties adopt a general policy that aims to give the cultural and natural heritage a function in the life of the community and to integrate the protection of that heritage into comprehensive planning programs (UNESCO, 1972).

However, community is loosely defined in the *World Heritage Convention* and the *Operational Guidelines*. Many terms are used interchangeably and include "International community" "Stakeholders" "Site managers, local and regional governments" "present and future generations of all humanity", and "local communities, non-governmental organizations (NGOs) and other interested parties and partners, general public, civil society, local people"[②].

Further references are made in the *Nara Document*,[③] where it is indicated that all cultures and societies are rooted in the particular forms and means of tangible and intangible expression that constitute their heritage and that these should be respected; and that the management of cultural heritage belongs, in the first place, to the cultural community that has generated it, and subsequently to that which cares for it.[④]

The idea of a "community" implies that there are certain prerequisites, where all people are of the same "kind," with very similar ideas, similar backgrounds, do not have outward mobility and are influenced by their peers. This does not occur in the real urban world and is not always an ideal situation. If this does occur then it can isolate neighbors who are "different", but it can also exhibit social closeness (McDowell, 1999). Therefore a community is not always an ideal term when we analyze local areas. In many instances the word "neighbor" might be more relevant, highlighting the fact that most areas are not communities. They are places where neighbors live—a "neighborhood".

The more generic term of "stakeholders" might be better for indicating the multiple choices and the multifaceted associations based on the dynamic past and present circumstances.

Levels of participation

It was in the mid-1960s that citizen participation reached the public agenda, receiving formal acclamation in 1969 with the *UK Skeffington Report* (Skeffington, 1970). It was during this period that Sherry Arnstein wrote her seminal paper on a Ladder of Citizen Participation in which she identified a wide spectrum of participation ranging from manipulation to citizen control (Arnstein, 1969).

Arnstein essentially divided participation into three groups with degrees of nonparticipation, tokenism, and citizen power. Using this ladder it would be safe to say that the text of the *World Heritage Convention* supports actions somewhere between placation and informing; this is probably a safe and conservative rung to be at on the ladder.

The current Strategic Objectives (also referred to as the "Five Cs") are the following (UNESCO 2011):

1. Strengthen the credibility of the World Heritage List;

2. Ensure the effective conservation of world heritage properties;
3. Promote the development of effective capacity-building in States Parties;

1. Manipulation→2. Therapy→3. Informing→4. Consultation→
5. Placation→6. Partnership→7. Delegated Power→8. Citizen Control

Fig. 1 The ladder of citizen participation indicating the level aimed for in the implementation of the *World Heritage Convention* (Arnstein, 2007:236).

4. Increase public awareness, involvement, and support for world heritage through communication;
5. Enhance the role of communities in the implementation of the *World Heritage Convention*.

While the fifth "C" was added in Christchurch, 2007, to the first four "Cs" of Budapest, 2002, it is apparent that the Strategic Objectives are a comprehensive whole which can be construed around the public actions for the protection of heritage also indicating the points of participation within the processes. On a closer examination of the *Operational Guidelines*, nine points of participation can be enumerated that relate to community involvement with different actions. These can be grouped within five subject headings: (1) Public awareness, support, and education in all spheres; (2) National Inventories and Tentative Lists; (3) The listing of world heritage properties; (4) Management; and (5) Monitoring and reporting—the state of conservation.

It is clear that within the wide range of activities, greater emphasis will need to be given to NGO involvement. While this might range from empowerment-engagement to consultation and informing, there has been a reticence to engage NGOs, in the fear that it would invite troublemakers and rabble-rousers and extend processes of approval. It is now generally accepted that this is not necessarily true and in many cases the opposite is valid. It should be emphasized that the participation of the public in the workings of the *World Heritage Convention* is an essential component and should be seen as an inherent part of heritage protection—not just as a means to an end, but an end in itself.

Dealing with the heritage of past, present, and future questions the responsibilities and representations of the two communities identified in the *Nara Document*—those who created the heritage and those who should be currently caring for it. This simplistic formula is acceptable for a monument or a site, but the urban complexities need clearer guidelines. The creation of such guidelines would need to include the changing social patterns that adapted, hijacked, or ransomed the original fabric, while the structure of urban responsibilities lies in a web of stakeholder connections between central and local government on one side and the residents, neighbors, and visitors, pilgrims, or tourists on the other. An urban *Nara Document* is urgently needed that might build on the new UNESCO Recommendation for Historic Landscapes.

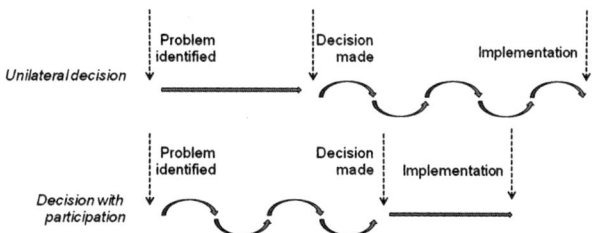

Fig. 2 Comparison of the length of time: Unilateral decision versus public participation (Creighton, 2005:18).

These situations can be seen and possibly redefined as compromise or co-existence. Is a compromise a watering down of our values? Not if the layering and evolution of the city are the essence of the value. The dimensions of culture, place, people and time provide us with a matrix to cross-reference these urban reactions.

The relationships of the various situations have been identified and include the "same place at different times" and "same time in different places". Focusing on the former and at the level of the building, the simultaneum mixture developed after the counter-reformation (Spohnholz, 2011) can still be witnessed in the Lutheran and Catholic altars in St. M. Kozal Church in Gniezno, Poland, or the Französische Friedrichstadtkirche in Berlin, Germany, which was reinstituted in 1985. At the urban level, the changing uses of the Brick Lane communities in the East End of London are evidence of the migrants and ghettoes in the port areas of cities around the world with their cultural diversity. Originally built for the eighteenth century Huguenot silk weavers, they quickly became a center for the nineteenth-century Methodist community, while the influx of European Jewish migrants of the twentieth century working as tailors⑤ has now given way to a vibrant twenty-first century Bengali center for art and fashion. The central building, built in the 1740s as a Huguenot chapel and schoolroom, became a Methodist chapel in the early nineteenth century, a synagogue in the 1890s, and a mosque in the 1970s (Gard'ner, 2004). It really does reflect the changing demographics that have helped make this area such a rich and culturally diverse neighborhood.

A lucid example of the latter situation at the same time in different places can be seen in the Chinatowns that have sprung up around the world, some more successful than others. Community transplants,⑥ a xenograft, or contemporary architecture in historic areas have been similarly compared to their medical associative achievements and failures. The participation in urban dialogues can create new forms, either through syncretism⑦ or symbiosis.⑧

And while the European Chinatowns are somewhat "lighter" than their American counterparts, it is the Paris banlieue or faubourg that provides the negative experiences that should be evaluated in the relationships of people to place.

Research on migrant communities is demonstrating a more complex relationship linking minority groups to the society they live in and their places of origin. The common perception of immigrant and ethnic clusters characterized by segregation fails to deal with the complexity of these phenomena. A discussion of the concepts of segregation and community shows that in such complex societies it is incorrect to assume a correspondence between space and society (Vaughan, 2007). While the key issue of "minority space" is that of urban space that were socially, architecturally, or culturally formed and shaped by the presence of migrants and foreigners, we will need to ask "How is such space perceived by the local population?" as well as "What is the role played by urban space as a stake within broader patterns of social coexistence or exclusion?" Vaughan notes that individuals can be members of several communities simultaneously and that the urban environment can be structured to enable encounters between a diverse set of social groups. This is the challenge and potential in a multi-cultural society, for the stakeholders of today are the custodians of tomorrow.

We are fooling ourselves with a single idyllic image of the European city. In this context, how many people live in the city where they were born? In confronting changing societies, there is a need to transcend time and place. If the newcomers might embrace place, then the old-timers will need to provide space, in recognition of the changing heritage of today. Are we willing to accept syncretism or symbiosis, coexistence, or compromise? Will a North African living now at Notre Dame claim this as his or her heritage? Would the displaced French living in their manors accept this? Similar situations can be seen with the Albanian community in the historic center of Naples and the Turkish communities in Berlin. All this puts a new perspective on the meaning of "local communities".

Increasing public awareness of this fundamental dimension of heritage is an absolute necessity in order to arrive at concrete measures for safeguarding the vestiges of the past. This means developing a greater understanding of the values represented by the cultural properties themselves with their urban attributes as well as respecting the role such monuments and sites play in contemporary society.

Parallel to this, the conceptual debate on the paradox of universalism and particularism can be understood within the definitions of *Outstanding Universal Value of the World Heritage Convention* on one side and the renegotiating of values in the *Burra Charter* on the other.

Values and beliefs (standards), which have significance for a cultural group or an individual, often include, but are not limited to spiritual, political, religious and moral beliefs. Places may have a range of values for different individuals or groups, and values are continually renegotiated (ICOMOS, 1999).

In a world that is increasingly subject to the forces of globalization and homogenization, and in a world in which the search for cultural identity is sometimes pursued through aggressive nationalism and the suppression of the cultures of minorities and the essential contribution made by the consideration of authenticity in conservation practice is to clarify and illuminate the collective memory of humanity.[9]

We need to reflect not only on the changing social structures but also the evolving interpretations of the values and political opinions of the populace. The values that have been identified within the past, present, and future are dependent on interpretations and the cultural connections through time, place and people.

It is not enough to agree on the values, which strangely enough might be quite unproblematic, but to debate, the interpretations of these values are many times the casus belli. The existentialism of Jean-Paul Sartre (Sartre, 1985) and the historicism/ empiricism of Francis Bacon are to be seen in the light of the liberal universalism developed from the *U.S. Bill of Rights of* 1791 and the *Declaration of the Rights of Man and Citizen of* 1793 and propagated by Kant. Each approach dramatically changes our understanding of our physical environment. Later philosophers, such as Gilles Deleuze and Emmanuel Lévinas, have added much to our understanding of interpretation, while the *ICOMOS Ename Charter* (ICOMOS, 2008) has focused on translating these concepts to practical reality. In the urban scene, the Judeo-Christian ideas for resurrection might be dramatically opposed to the Hindu concepts of reincarnation in debating the values of new lives in old cities. The urban metamorphosis needs to be appraised as part of the evolving approach to protecting the values of the city by a polyglot society.

It is not just the inanimate physical object of still life, of the monument, but also the integration of the spirit of place, the context and setting as the physiognomy through the palimpsest of intangible traditions and tangible urban fabric. For the intangible, it is the *Convention on the Protection and Promotion of the Diversity of Cultural Expressions* (UNESCO, 2005) that has extended our understanding of criterion (5) of the *Operational Guidelines* and provided a more structured format for understanding the components of cultural continuity and diversity. These might include typologies, chronologies, topologies, anthropologies, philologies, and themes.

The diversity of cultures and heritage in our world is an irreplaceable source of spiritual and intellectual richness for all humankind. The protection and enhancement of cultural and heritage diversity in our world should be actively promoted as an essential aspect of human development,[10] which can be achieved through participatory processes. This is not restricted to any one culture; the community participation in the Japanese town in the concept of Machinami,⑪ the pillow of poetry in Uta-makura, and the climate and culture in Fudo are all evidence of these values.

Cultural heritage diversity exists in time and space and demands respect for other cultures and all aspects of their belief systems. In cases where cultural values appear to be in conflict, respect for cultural diversity demands acknowledgment of the legitimacy of the cultural values of all parties.⑫ After the *Nara Document* opened new vistas on cultural diversities, it was the Burra Charter (ICOMOS, 1999) that generated the next debate, focusing on the assumptions that:

1. The healthy management of cultural difference is the responsibility of society as a whole;

2. In a pluralist society, value differences exist and contain the potential for conflict; and

3. Ethical practice is necessary for the just and effective management of places of diverse cultural significance.

Conflicts should be seen in a wider significance and perceived as challenges; in modern Hebrew, the three-letter root word "a'm t" refers to a colleague or a friend. However, it has a synonymic meaning of conflict, in which a true friend will come in positive conflict for castigation.

Not all factions of the public have a voice; the past and the scars of history have, in many instances, been eliminated or disinfected, reducing their implications in the narrative. These can be witnessed in many situations but could include the Märzrevolution in Berlin, the May Day demonstration at the Winter Palace in 1918, and, more recently, Sandy Row in Belfast. The voices of those taking the Bastille depicted by Jean Pierre Houël, les barricades of Victor Hugo, and the current Parisian banlieue are all part of the public realm and past, present, and future communities will all have a stake in the determination of the urban landscape. And how might the 2002 destruction of the Bamiyan Buddhas in Afghanistan be recorded by the different stakeholders? Restore the monument as if nothing had happened or leave the evidence as it was?

While it is simple to consider sites post factum, there are issues that are part of an ongoing debate as to the public pressures for the protection of the panorama of Saint Petersburg from Palace Bridge (UNESCO, 2012) and the pristine sites of the Western Caucasus, where Greenpeace demanded a discussion on the environmental implications of development for the Winter Olympics. The concerns of the various public interests are commendable, while the issues need to be resolved in real-time.

Authenticity and Integrity

The tests of authenticity and integrity accompany cultural properties in their evaluation as indicated in the mapping sentence:

The values as defined by the criteria through a comparative analysis are expressed by the attributes and qualified by their authenticity and integrity; the conservation policy consists, inter alia, of management practices and integrative approaches with added layers of protection (buffer zones) sustainably balancing the external constraints, risks and resources.⑬

Integrity is defined in the *Operational Guidelines* as "a measure of the wholeness and intactness of the natural and/or cultural heritage and its attributes." And the examination of: the conditions of integrity, requires assessing whether or not the property:

a) includes all elements necessary to express its value;

b) is of adequate size to ensure the complete representation of the features and processes which convey the property's significance;

c) is free from the adverse effects of development and/or neglect (UNESCO, 2011).

It might be concluded that urban integrity demands a policy of the "minimum necessary and the maximum possible" to be applied to the evaluation of the attributes of each urban value. This approach will allow for space in the future layering of the city for new generations or for social transformations. Furthermore, greater emphasis needs to be given to the context and setting as a part of the buffer zone,⑭ providing an added layer of protection rather than battle lines and no-man's land. These areas should also provide for economic and environmental sustainability and allow for a more comprehensive view of the challenges of the city.

This minimalistic approach can be understood within the Lurianic Kabbalah concepts of tzimtzum, where the infinity, or En Sof, and the angelic hierarchies (universes or olamot) are contracted to create a void, thereby defining the human space (Schochet, 1988). In Japanese thought, the idea of Ma gives a space or hiatus between activities allowing for thoughts and reflections (Pilgrim, 1986), while the Chinese Wu Wei leaves space for future activities (Loy, 1985). Even Le Corbusier, in his influential book *City of Tomorrow*, indicated a page "left blank for a work expressing modern feeling" [Le Corbusier, 1987(1929)].

But it is the authenticity that is critical to the discussion. Essentially, the *Nara Document* was born out of the debate on the monument and object and its "authenticity" based on "originality," while the urban contexts will require a more developed application of this definition. Already in 1996, just two years after the *Nara Document* was drafted, the debate on historical heritage and living cultures emerged with Professor Bertrand Hirsch⑮ advancing the hypothesis that the definition of cultural heritage is at the crossroads of two processes: research and the relationships maintained between societies and states with regard to their past. He highlighted the tension between "the revindication of historicity and the acknowledgement of the dynamism, complexity and specificity in the diverse societies" (UNESCO, 1996). This debate continued in the meeting on Authenticity and Integrity in an African Context, which took place in 2000 in Zimbabwe (UNESCO, 2000). The *Nara Document* was seen as a first step toward moving from the exclusively "monumentalist" vision to a more anthropological and global approach; from the world of stone to the world of wood.

The ability to understand the value attributed to heritage depends on the degree to which information sources about this value may be understood as credible or truthful. Knowledge and understanding of these sources of information, in relation to original and subsequent characteristics of the cultural heritage, and their meaning, are the requisite bases for assessing all aspects of authenticity.⑯

One of the first recorded instances of the term "authenticity" was probably at Session IV of the Council of Trent that was celebrated on April 8, 1546, under 194 MICHAEL TURNER AND TAL TOMER Pope Paul III. At this moment in time a decree concerning the edition and use of the sacred books was given (Brownlee, 1857):

Moreover, the same Holy Council considering that not a little advantage will accrue to the Church of God if it be made known which of all the Latin editions of the sacred books now in circulation is to be regarded as authentic, ordains and declares that the old Latin Vulgate Edition, which, in use for so many hundred years, has been approved by the Church, be in public lectures, disputations, sermons and expositions held as authentic, and that no one dare or presume under any pretext whatsoever to reject it.

Everyone realized that the original *Old Testament* was in Hebrew and the original *New Testament* in Greek. Here the Latin Vulgate was authenticated as the official translation, authenticating the values of the *Testaments*. It thus should be noted that the word authenticity might be used in the meaning of original, but also in the meaning of the authentication of the value.

To underscore this, we can "authenticate the value" of the staircase to the Church of Araceli with documents showing the views of the Roman Capitol by Giovanni Battista Piranesi and the spirit of the intangible with the dialogues of Petrarch (Cevat, 1986) with the Roman Caesars in conjunction with Cola di Rienzo and the "parlanti ruine" of Piranesi with the drawings of Nolli.

The UNESCO Recommendation on Historic Urban Landscape is the approach that should now be harnessed to develop a new language for community participation and urban heritage.

The state of conservation of Cologne Cathedral, Germany, 1996 (UNESCO, 1996) and the Historic Centre of Vienna, Austria, 2001 (UNESCO, 2001) are evidence enough for the winds of change. While certain monuments and even specific urban fabrics will be seen as monuments, most urban situations result from a patina and layering that is its inherent value.

The value of the layering of space (Tuan, 1979) of the urban fabric has been discussed viewing Hopi space and time through the subjective and objective realms and the northern city of Peking as an axis mundi. Within this layering the city is rebuilt by, over, instead of. It is absorbed, occupied, and even hijacked. It is the difference between the concepts of the seven cities of Delhi with New Delhi, each built by the other, and the layering of the archaeological mound as the famous Tel Megiddo, with each city stacked above the water source.

How can these situations be evaluated through participatory processes? The Environmental Impact Assessment (EIA) has gone a long way in developing a body of knowledge in these fields with participation and responsibilities, while the addition of the Heritage Impact Assessment (HIA) (ICOMOS 2011) can bring together an integrative approach by defining the problems and stakeholders and developing a process that includes:

Screening→Scoping→Alternatives→Assessing→Reviewing→Decision→Monitoring[17]

Lingua franca

The *Himeji Recommendations* provides a clear light, not in just reviewing the definition sof authenticity but also in emphasizing the importance of the continuing debate on the need for the involvement of communities.

The *Himeji Recommendations* of 2012 states that:

"The attribution of values to heritage is a social rather than a scientific or technical process involving multiple individuals and groups. Further discussion is needed on the relationship between values and authenticity, and specifically on the way in which the integration of local and global values can inform the authenticity and significance of heritage; also, on how to understand the range of communities that are relevant to the identification and management of heritage, and how best to involve them in this process." (Japanese Agency for Cultural Affairs and Himeji City, 2012)

This reaffirms the need for greater emphasis to be placed on developing processes, tools, and frameworks that can enable community participation in the negotiation of integrated heritage management strategies and the development of an Esperantopromoting dialogue.

The Rosetta Stone at Memphis in 196 BC on behalf of King Ptolemy V at the British Museum is surely the epitome of how we might develop a local language and meaning and share particularistic ideas in a universal context. It also embodies the needed transparency that all local vernaculars were respected.

"The proverbial wisdom of the populace in the streets, on the roads, and in the markets, instructs the ear of him who studies man more fully than a thousand rules ostentatiously arranged."[18]

References

Arnstein, 2007. A Ladder of Citizen Participation// R L Stout. The City Reader New York: Routledge Taylor & Francis Group: 233-244.

Brownlee C, 1857. The Doctrinal Decrees and Canons of the Council of Trent. New York: American and Foreign Christian Union.

Cevat, 1986. Our Architectural Heritage: From Consciousness to Conservation. Translated by P. A. Bakklcioglu. Paris: UNESCO.

Creighton L, 2005. The Public Participation Handbook: Making Better Decisions through Citizen Involvement. San Francisco: Jossey-Bass.

Gard'ner M, 2004. Heritage Protection and Social Inclusion: A Case Study from the Bangladeshi Community of East London. International Journal of Heritage Studies, 10(1):75-92.

ICOMOS, 1999. The Burra Charter: The Australia ICOMOS Charter for Places of Cultural Significance. [2013-04-12]. http://australia.icomos.org/wp-content/uploads/BURRA_CHARTER.pdf.

ICOMOS, 2008. ICOMOS Ename Charter for the Interpretation and Presentation of Cultural Heritage Sites [2013-04-012]. document, http://icip.icomos.org/downloads/ICOMOS_Interpretation_Charter_ENG_04_10_08.pdf. 196 MICHAEL TURNER AND TAL TOMER.

ICOMOS, 2011. Guidance on Heritage Impact Assessments for Cultural World Heritage Properties. [2013-04-012]. http://www.icomos.org/world_heritage/HIA_20110201.pdf.

Japanese Agency for Cultural Affairs and Himeji City, 2012、2012 Himeji Recommendations from the Meeting of Experts on Heritage and Societies: Toward the 20th Anniversary of the Nara Document and Beyond. Electronic document, http://nara2014.wordpress.com/himeji-recommendation, accessed April 20, 2013.

Le Corbusier, 1987 [1929]. The City of To-morrow and Its Planning. Mineola: Dover Publications.

Loy, 1985. Wei-wu-wei: Nondual Action. Philosophy East and West 35(1):73-86.

McDowell, 2000. City Life and Difference: Negotiating Diversity// Allen J, Massey D, Pryke M. Unsettling Cities: Movement/Settlement,: 95-135. London: Routledge.

Pilgrim B, 1986. Intervals ("Ma") in Space and Time: Foundations for a Religio-Aesthetic Paradigm in Japan. History of Religions 25(3):255-277.

Russell, Harry S, 1900. The Jew in London: A Study of Racial Character and Present-day Conditions. New York: Thomas Y. Crowell & Co..

Sartre-P, 1985. Existentialism and Human Emotion. New York: Citadel Press.

Schochet, Jaocb I. 1988 Mystical Concepts in Chassidism: An Introduction to Kabbalistic Concepts and Doctrines. Kehot Publication Society, Brooklyn.

Seetharam, Kallidaikurichi, 2010 Developing Living Cities: From Analysis to Action. World Scientific, Singapore.

Skeffington, A. M., 1970 People and Planning: Report of the Committee on Public Participation in Planning. Her Majesty's Stationary Office, London.

Spohnholz, Jesse, 2011. A Companion to Multiconfessionalism in the Early Modern World. In Confessional Coexistence in the Early Modern Low Countries, edited by Thomas M. Safley, pp. 47-75. Brill, Leiden.

Tuan YF, 1979. Space and Place: Humanistic Perspective// Gales, Olsson G. Philosophy in Geography Dordrecht, Springer: 387-427.

UNESCO, 1972. Convention Concerning the Protection of the World Cultural and Natural Heritage Adopted by the General Conference at Its Seventeenth Session. [2013-04-12]. http://whc.unesco.org/en/convention text.

UNESCO, 1996. Convention Concerning the Protection of the World Cultural and Natural Heritage. [2013-04-18]. http://whc.unesco.org/archive/1996/whc-96-conf201-21e.pdf.

UNESCO, 2000. Authenticity and Integrity in an African Context. [2013-04-18]. http://unesdoc.unesco.org/images/0012/001225/122598mo.pdf.

UNESCO, 2005. Convention on the Protection and Promotion of the Diversity of Cultural Expressions. [2013-04-12]. http://unesdoc. unesco. org/images/0014/001429/142919e. pdf.

UNESCO, 2011. Operational Guidelines for the Implementation of the World Heritage Convention. [2013-04-12]. http://whc. unesco. org/pg. cfm? cid=57.

UNESCO, 2012. Convention Concerning the Protection of the World Cultural and Natural Heritage. Electronic document [2013-04-12]. http://whc. unesco. org/archive/2012/whc12-36com-19e. pdf.

Vaughan, 2007. The Spatial Foundations of Community Construction: The Future of Pluralism in Britain's "Mutli-Cultural" Society. Global Built Environment Review, 6(2): 3-17.

Notes

① Approved by the UNESCO General Conference in November 2011.

② These terms appear in the *Operational Guidelines of the World Heritage Convention* as follows: International community (para 6, 15, 49, 269), Stakeholders (para 3, 12, 40, 64, 111, 117, 119, 123, Annex 5,6,9), Site managers, local and regional governments (para 3, 12, 64, 123, 168, Annex 6), present and future generations of all humanity (para 7, 15, 49, 109, 170n, Annex 5,7)local communities, non-governmental organizations (NGOs) and other interested parties and partners, general public, civil society, local people (para 12, 38, 40, 64, 90, 123, Annex 3,6).

③ Appearing as Annex 4—*Authenticity in Relation to the World Heritage Convention*.

④ *Nara Document on [Diversity] Authenticity*, 1994.

⑤ Russell and Lewis's maps of Jewish East London in 1900 show street by street the density of Jewish settlement (Russell and Lewis, 1900).

⑥ Turner, M: Historic Urban Landscapes—Synoecism et al, Keynote Lecture presented to the UNESCO Forum—Universities and Heritage, 5th April 2009, Hanoi, Vietnam.

⑦ Syncretism is "the combination of different forms of belief or practice." It can take place through debate and the dialectical enrichment of diverging opinions. (Encyclopædia Britannica Online, s. v. "religious syncretism", accessed April 12, 2013, http://www. britannica. com/ EBchecked/topic/497438/religious-syncretism).

⑧ A (symbiotic) mutualism is the association between organisms of two different species in which each is benefited. (Encyclopædia Britannica Online, s. v. "mutualism", accessed April 12, 2013, http://www. britannica. com/ EBchecked/topic/399884/mutualism).

⑨ Para 4, The Nara Document on [Diversity] Authenticity, 1994.

⑩ Para 5, The Nara Document on [Diversity] Authenticity, 1994.

⑪ The '"Machinami Charter"'—A Charter for the Conservation of Historic Towns and Settlements in Japan (adopted by Japanese ICOMOS Committee in 2000) gives the following definitions: "Machinami, usually translated as '"Historic Town"', is a Japanese word that includes a nuance of the historic core, in both its tangible and intangible factors, its physical and spiritual aspects, that would be created by a 'bond of spirits'. It also contains the tone of making a line, hand-in-hand, that applies both to buildings and to people. Shuuraku, the Japanese word for 'settlement', is often translated as village. In this Charter it also contains an idea of a community's surrounding natural and cultural environment."

⑫ Para 6, The Nara Document on [Diversity] Authenticity, 1994.

⑬ Herb Stovel and Mike Turner (2011).

⑭ Buffer Zones, World Heritage Paper Series 25, M. Turner.

⑮ Professor Bertrand Hirsch, the Centre for African Research, University of Paris 1, participated in the Global Strategy of the African Cultural Heritage meeting in Addis Ababa, Ethiopia, 1996.

⑯ Paragraph 80, Operational Guidelines of the World Heritage Convention.

⑰ Flowchart of key steps in the environmental impact assessment procedure (from UNEP/ CBD/SBSTTA/7/13 and Ramsar Wise Use Handbook 11).

⑱ Source: Proverbs, or the Manual of Wisdom, on the title page, printed for Tabart & Co., London (1804).

科技＋文化·腾讯的长城文保实践

The Practice of Great Wall Cultural Heritage Protection under Tencent Technology ＋ Culture Integration

葛燄

腾讯云副总裁

中国文物保护基金会长城保护公益专项基金主任

Ge Yan

Vice President, Tencent Cloud

Director, the Great Wall Protection Special Fund of China Cultural Relics Protection Foundation

长城小兵 IP

32年前,长城被联合国教科文组织列入《世界遗产名录》,是中国首批入选的世界遗产之一。那时,我们还是青少年。如今我们作为世界遗产的守护者,相信这些珍贵的世界遗产会在一代又一代人的坚守下,为这颗星球留下最美好的故事。

在座很多人都知道,腾讯是世界上最大的互联网公司之一。我们拥有中国最大的社交平台和用户规模,我们有能力、有义务通过平台去连接亿万网友,让善意变得触手可及。我们相信当善行与文化叠加在一起时,当善行与科技融合在一起时,所散发出来的力量是超乎想象的。如今,腾讯从消费互联网迈入产业互联网,一个全新的数字文化生态正在形成。

2017年7月,腾讯正式发起"长城你造不造"计划,围绕长城保护与激活两个维度展开:用最新的科技手段最大限度地留存文化遗产本身应有的风貌与气质;与此同时,借助腾讯的技术平台,将历史悠久的文化遗产,与当今每一个个体的生活,尤其是年轻群体的生活连接起来,让长城成为当代文化的重要组成部分,以此激活长城在用户心目中的魅力。

因为我们相信,年轻一代是守护和传承传统文化的中坚力量,传统文化与文化遗产保护的传承需要争取到年轻一代的热爱与探索,于是我们做了以下这些尝试。

在IP孵化与打造的探索方面,为拉近长城与年轻用户之间的心理距离,我们发布了3个能够代表长城又具有年轻元素的IP形象"长城小兵",借助公众号与互动小程序的形式,用有趣实用的内容向用户讲述长城的故事,每个小兵其实都是代表了长城上的一座知名关隘,比如关小偏代表的是偏头关,关小小代表的娘子关,而关小山代表的是海边的山海关长城。这些形象可以很容易地与各种新媒体形式进行结合和呈现。

2018年,三个长城小兵形象被孵化成文创产品在长城文创体验馆小程序上售卖,所获得的收益将捐赠给长城保护基金会助力长城的保护。

在激发青年创造力方面,我们在2017年举办了Next Idea腾讯创新大赛,联合了国内六大区域媒体集团,发起围绕长城的文创设计大赛,并在2018年举办了长城遗产标志征集。大赛选中的标志会在长城保护联盟中优先使用,而产生的长城文创作品通过创意的助力,对于古老长城是传承,更是创新。

另一种年轻人最喜欢的生活方式就是在线游戏了,在当今社会,电子游戏可以以其独特的方式去记录和诠释中国的传统文化。腾讯旗下的游戏《王者荣耀》推出长城守卫军系列游戏角色、《QQ飞车》推出游戏内仿真的著名长城段赛道,这些游戏在长城上的特别设定卷入了上亿用户深度参与,它们都是"长城守护计划"的一部分。

更值得一提的是,微信小程序还为长城保护打造了一款"一起修长城"的小游戏,并在联合国教科文组织2019年度世界遗产大会上亮相,吸引了国家文物局局长刘玉珠在内的多位领导现场体验,并对腾讯长期发挥数字手段保护长期给予高度评价。

在长城知识科普与传播方面,我们希望将长城背后的历史、建筑、人文、艺术、自然等故事和知识讲述出来,用更深度的内容去唤起用户的情感共鸣,于是有了长城人、长城专家问答、长城星空摄影联盟的出现。

在其他长城文化传播、研究和创新探索方面,目前已经有科学绘本《长城绘》得以面世,《长城绘》填补了国内同类图书的空白,获得了文化遗产保护与青少年教育等领域的广泛好评。由腾讯影业出品以长城修缮工程为背景的纪录片《筑城纪》,也计划于2019年12月正式上线。

中国文物保护基金会通过腾讯公益发起"保护长城,加我一个"项目,也让所有人都有机会"一块做好事",保护长城。今年中秋佳节,双方共同推出的《长城万里共婵娟》数字体验。用户只需举起手机,瞄准现实中月亮的方向,便可绘制长城月景。目前"保护长城,加我一个"项目已经成为腾讯公益平台有史以来吸引最多公众参与、捐款量最大的文化遗产类项目。

在腾讯公司新文创战略下,我们不仅针对长城实施落地了一系列文保实践工作,通过创意与科技助力古老的长城继续传承与创新。与此同时,腾讯还从线上延展到线下,在其他文化遗产保护领域拓展出了很多新的应用场景。

由腾讯与敦煌研究院共同合作研发的"敦煌诗巾"文创轻应用小程序,汇集了九色鹿、三兔共耳等敦煌最具代表性的文化元素。通过专业设计师的精心设计,每个用户都可以设计出漂亮的丝巾,并一键下单定制购买。这款小程序上线不到一个月,就有280万用户参与互动。这个模式不仅打通了从用户设计到线下定制生产的产业链条,还邀请用户参与到敦煌的数字化艺术创作与建设中来,将敦煌的文化符号得以更广泛的传播。

从这里,我们推出腾讯文创云插件,它可以通过不同的组合与更多的文化机构和城市合作,根据不同的文化元素组合来实现个性化定制和生产,以便捷的方式快速接入场景化应用,通过场景化和多平台渠道释放腾讯线上和线下能力。

今年,我们在文创文保工作上还做了很多科技与数字创新实践。9月16日,腾讯和故宫博物院再次"官宣"共同签署深化战略合作协议。过去合作的三年里,双方通过不断探索,共同打造出了数字文博的新标杆。未来三年双方将聚焦科技应用与学术创新,通过"数字化+云化+AI化",在文物数字化采集与文化研究等领域深入助力"数字故宫"建设。腾讯将负责10万件故宫文物的高清影像采集、精修工作,为故宫建设数字文物库,更好地对文物进行信息保存和管理展示。基于腾讯的科技能力和新文创思路,腾讯将携手故宫,形成一套面向未来的数字解决方案。

同时,我们也在联合社科院等业内专家,围绕数字文物库的云存储、运维等需求,制定"文博行业云服务标准",并共同申报国家科技部课题,探索数字文物基于云服务的前沿合作范式。为此,我们开发了文化云平台和IP综合服务平台,以"一云一平台"的架构,通过腾讯的云能力在文化标识、数字化、内容传播、AI人工智能等方面致力于文化遗产的活化,并激活当地相关产业的发展。

因为科技的进步,我们身处在一个"人文"能在公共生活中发挥广泛创造性的时代,这就是数字人文时代。我们要做的是将连接和技术创造性应用到不同场景当中,线上线下深度融合,创建数字生态共同体,打造出更多丰富多彩的产品与服务,不仅丰富国人的文化生活,也能提升社会服务的效率,解决社会问题。

文化是一个国家、一个民族更基本、更持久、更深沉的力量。中华文化历久弥新,生命力恰恰在于开放与创新。接下来,我们还将和更多国内外文化机构、地方政府展开合作,构建一个连接能力更强、共享度更高的数字生态共同体,推动文化产业高质量发展,实现与践行腾讯公司的愿景和使命"科技向善,提升人类生活品质"。

赖特"流水别墅"的数字化
Digitization of Frank Lloyd Wright's Fallingwater

帕梅拉·杰罗姆 教授
ICOMOS 执委
Prof. Pamela Jerome
Executive Committee memeber of ICOMOS

自1988年以来,建筑保护工作室的专业人员参与了弗兰克·劳埃德·赖特的杰作流水别墅的保护工作,该作品最近被列入世界遗产名录(2019年)。别墅位于宾夕法尼亚州的米尔润。它的主楼和宾客楼建于1935年至1939年,是考夫曼家庭的周末住宅。它从1963年后作为家庭博物馆,目前每年大约有18万人参观。经过五年的研究和原型修复,以及一份两册的总体规划,我们设计和实施了一个分阶段的外立面修复项目,完成于1999—2003年。我们测量并用AutoCAD绘制了建筑的各个立面及残损状况,作为1999年时的建筑状况评估。在为了修复工程而拟备的建筑图纸中,我们以每块石头为精度绘制了每一块需要加固及/或重新防水处理的石板地及露台。这些是使用重叠照片的照片马赛克达到的。2016年,我们被邀请回到现场检查情况,并就日常维护提供建议。当时,我们建议重新记录结构。这次使用激光扫描。这一次,我们在2016年5月完成了外部、2017年3月完成了内部的记录。本报告将以流水别墅的经验为基础对手工和数字的记录技术进行比较。

Fallingwater and its conservation have been a work of many years for me personally. I was the project manager for about 15 years during the period when it was being restored. This summer, it became a World Heritage site as part of a serial nomination of Frank Lloyd Wright's 20th-century heritage.

The Outstanding Universal Value comes from Criterion II. It is about the fact that he had a significant influence on 20th-century architecture and Modernism. The site itself is kind of remote. It is located in Pennsylvania, as you can see in the United States, in the mountains, about 60 miles southeast of Pittsburgh. It was the vacation home or weekend home of wealthy Pittsburgh citizens Edgar Kaufmann, Sr. and his wife, Liliane. They owned a department store in Pittsburgh. And their son, Edgar Kaufmann, jr. [sic], had met Frank Lloyd Wright by becoming one of his apprentices at Taliesin West. Frank Lloyd Wright designed a masterpiece for the Kaufmann family. Fallingwater was incredibly daring from the structural perspective for a house built in 1935 through 1939. In plan, it consists of the main house, which is at the bottom part of the slide. Later, there was also a guest house added. So the main house was built between 1935 and 1936, and the guest house was finished by 1939.

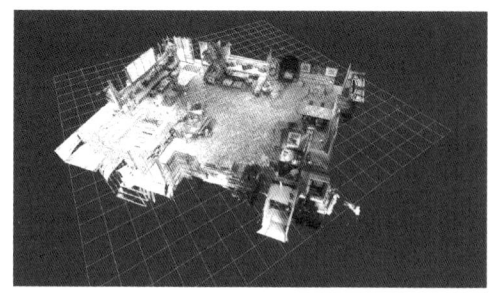

流水别墅数字建模

It is an iconic building. It is incredibly well known. It receives about 180,000 visitors per year. The tours are allotted six minutes per room. It is very, very well organized. Its significance is of course important. And considering it is a World Heritage site, it is the embodiment of Frank Lloyd Wright's organic architecture. It was declared a National Historic Landmark. And now it is one of the World Heritage sites that is the serial nomination of Frank Lloyd Wright's 20th-century heritage. The design is well known for its unusual setting and the fact that it cantilevers over a waterfall. It also has unique elements like a 3-story steel window. The restoration, which occurred between 1999 and 2003, followed many years of studies. We first started working on the site in 1988. I became the project manager in 1992. So there was a lot of experimentation on this building. I also produced a master plan in two volumes. The first volume was the existing conditions assessment with 179 CAD drawings. And the second volume was the actual master plan. We had to reconstruct some of the elements that were failing.

For instance, we needed to understand certain things about the building. What we have discovered was that the concrete was poured and then a topping was added that is a very different mix. And that created continuous cracks. We also looked at the paint on the interior of the building to understand what the original finishes were. We have been gradually restoring the interior as well, in terms of the paint finishes. And then we did a bunch of tests to resolve the painting of the exterior, which by the way, is still not resolved. It seems like paint want to stick to this building.

So we are going to go back and do some more testing now. The documentation that was done in 1999 was hand measurements, overlapping photo-mosaics, which were then hand-sketched and rasterized and then imported into CAD. And the reason we needed to do stone by stone drawings of the floors- and you are looking at the living room with its east and west terraces-was because we were going to lift all of this stonework, and then remedially reinforce the structure, because the cantilevers were failing from under-reinforcement.

In addition, we were going to re-waterproof all of the terraces and roofs. So this is the point where we have removed everything. And we are actually post-tensioning the concrete beams to give the proper strength so that the building would not collapse. And it was literally in danger of collapse at this point. So shoring was installed as a temporary measure. All of the living room furniture had to be removed. You are seeing in the bottom left-hand corner, the naked living room, and above the post-tensioning cables.

Same with this photograph. These are the main cantilever beams while they were being post-tensioned. The living room, I might add, is the premier space in the house. So imagine that photograph before when the living room was naked. And this is what it looked like after restoration.

We still have issues at Fallingwater. So we are now back at the site for the last three years working on the maintenance of the restoration. We are still experiencing cracks and we have problems with the concrete.

Frank Lloyd Wright used river pebbles which have a lot of chert. We think we have an alkali-silica reaction going on as a result. There are a lot of different issues with this building. But we continue to do the repairs. The maintenance staff on site has been trained to do these types of repairs. And we are also testing out new waterproofing systems, newer generations of better products. So, one of the things we did when we got back to the site is proposed it be re-documented. Our documentation was 20 years old. The existing conditions are always important at various points in time. To understand what is going on, we did over 400 laser scans over 10 days. Now we have laser documentation. You are all very familiar with this I am sure. It is a much better way to document a site. And we also scanned the interior with all the furnishings in place. You can see the target points here. This is normal when you are doing a laser-scanning project.

The staircase to the stream, by the way, is one of the elements we had to reconstruct. The steel straps constantly corroded. We ended up replacing them with stainless steel. But reconstruction was just reconstruction because the stairs had been knocked off in the 1960s by debris during a flood. So we felt like this did not impact authenticity as it was already a reconstruction. This is my colleague Douglas Emilio, who is a partner at my firm. He is doing the laser documentation himself. During this laser documentation, we still had to deal with a new tour group coming in every six minutes.

So it is a site that never stops, except for in the winter for two months when it is closed. And this is the living room. So laser-scanning captures millions of data points. This is the living room we are looking at, and this one as well. And you also capture very accurate photography.

So what are the next steps? Completing the registration of the scan data and modeling, and by the way, when we were back at the site last year, we did more scans. We are now working to review photos, maintenance records, curatorial information, etc. because naturally, this will end up on their website. Also, there are potential end uses. We have a new digital record that can be compared later on in 10 years, 20 years to another digital record. We now are comparing it to the documentation we made 20 years ago. It is a way to record maintenance and it is also a method of public interaction with the data and the subset of the data, especially once it goes on the website.

认同与参与——节日文化景观中的大众参与和文化传承

Identification and Participation: Cultural Inheritance in Festival Cultural Landscape

李松

文化和旅游部民族民间文艺发展中心前主任

Former Director of Center for Ethnic and Folk Literature and Art Development, Ministry of Culture and Tourism

As part of the civil time regulations, festivals are events for people with same cultural recognition to take part in. They are in everyone's life and have accumulated profound cultural wealth. They are the carriers of cultural diversity and intercultural communication. The festival cultural landscape, composed of time, communities, ritual belief, public space, food supplies, art games, rules, and taboos, stories and legends, is the most important field with social vitality for the representation and application of cultural heritage integration. The social mobilization ability of festivals and the bearing capacity of excellent traditional culture provide a solid social foundation for the production and reproduction of culture. The systematic record and study of the traditional festival culture of all ethnic groups in China's territory provide common cultural matters for interdisciplinary cooperation and combined innovation of history, sociology, art, anthropology, ethnology, folklore, imaging and other related disciplines, and also provide space for cooperation in the protection of tangible and intangible cultural heritage.

作为国家文化部的一个学术机构,我们近十多年来,对中国的传统节日进行了较为系统全面的研究工作。它也是文化遗产保护当中的一个面向。

首先,节日作为一种时间制度,是全人类都有的一个文化存在。从参与的角度来说,节日可以说是社会参与的一个最为广泛和频繁的公共文化事项。而且它是一个任何社区、族群、国家、民族都不会中断的文化事项。

每个人在生命过程中,作为组成社会的生命个体,都会与节日相伴。不同年龄的人有不同的文化感受,我们的节日为不同年龄的人设置了很多的环节。

节日文化景观

节日文化与人的个体生命和群体的发展密切联系。中国有句老话叫"以文化人",实际上节日就是这样一个载体。当然我们在文化保护的意义上,在中国的传统社会里,我们所说的民俗、习惯、价值观念和公序良俗,实际上都是在节日这个系统中得以传承的。因此说,节日本身就是一个活态的文化事项。

节日的这种文化事项,有一个基本的存在的基础,就是文化认同。对历史文化、社区文化、民族文化、区域文化,甚至国家文化的认同,使得节日成为大众的一种社会的集体的行为。

建立在文化认同基础上的节日文化习俗,是在公共利益最大原则下,以"民主协商"的方式固化和内化而成的传统,是连接历史和维系生活秩序的重要"纽带"。

节日不是私人时间,节日是公共时间。节日从来都不是为自己的,一定要尽社会的义务。从家庭开始、进而到社区、进而到整个社会,这样的节日制度安排,在中国的传统节日体系当中,尤为突出和明显。

节日也可以整体作为文化景观。

我们将文化保护分为物质文化和非物质文化,但是总体作为文化遗产而言,在节日当中,物质文化和非物质文化在节日中是综合运用的。这里所说的国家意志和地方知识的相互发展,也是说明我们大传统和小传统的互动,或者叫礼俗互动,在节日当中,通过老百姓的生活实践得以实现。

不同文化间的交流,尤其是进入现代社会以来,由于旅游的发展,使得节日已经成为越来越多的交流的文化平台。在历史上,节日的区域性、共享性是非常明显的,很多节日都是不同文化间互相交流的节点。在我们的传统节日体系里边,大量的存在多民族、不同信仰的人共享的节日。

作为国家记忆的节日文化研究是历史文化研究的一个重要面向,《中国节日志》的研究作为国家哲学社会科学的重大委托项目,从 2008 年开始展开。在这一研究中,有社会学、人类学、民族学、民俗学、艺术学、影视学等各个学科的介入。研究从历史文献研究、田野工作、影像记录、数据库建设等方面着手,据不完全统计,大概有 3 000 到 4 000 硕博研究生参与,工作共历经 11 年,目前还没有最终完成。这一项目形成的众多研究成果,为文化遗产保护的不断优化提供了学术支撑。

非物质文化遗产,这个概念我们还要有一些更多的思考。从文化保护的角度来说,节日本身就是一个综合载体。大量的节日空间当中老百姓的生活实践,实际上就是一个传统文化在不断演进的这样的一种过程。

在现代社会,我们的节日和假日被混淆了。目前我们传统节日面临的重大考验就是,我们在城市化和工业化的条件下,以农耕文明为主要土壤养育出来的节日传统,基本上被异化为假日。但节日是社会公共时间,假日是私人时间。在这一点上我们当今社会在文化传承上,是面临着最大的挑战。社会上说我们的节日没有味道,是因为节日越来越个人化,时间越来越私有化了。

真正中国的传统节日,所有节日的安排,都是全社会总动员,做一个公共文化的事项的设计,例如是一个重大的祭祀和礼仪事项的组合。节日都是这样安排的。因此这样的文化传统、文化载体,在现代社会当中面临重大的考验。

节日文化对全人类来说,也是一个重要的文化载体,而且它时时刻刻都焕发着创造性的能力。我们的节日文化演绎到近现代社会,奥运会、世界杯等都可以成为节日。我们的日历上也有越来越多的纪念日,这些都是由国际社会经过讨论,在达成广泛共识的基础上,构成的文化传承和文化交流的一种平台。

其实节日的本质就是处理关系。中国的传统节日在节日当中处理人与天的关系,处理人与人的关系,并且规范着人的伦理。节日文化,追求多样性文化之间的相处之道,是全球化条件下的一个世界性话题。在保护、参与、交流的语境中,文化遗产保护工作的本质,就是为了构建人类命运共同体,奠定坚实的文化基础。

波尔多月亮港的公众参与反馈
Public Participation in Bordeaux, Port of the Moon: Feedback

西尔万·肖恩巴尔特 博士
法国波尔多国立建筑景观设计学院
Dr. Sylvain Schoonbaert
Architect, Doctor in Urbanism, Historian, Project Manager at Bordeaux Métropole
Teacher-researcher at the National School of Architecture and Landscape of Bordeaux

波尔多月亮港是一片城市居住区,它在2007年被评为世界遗产。在认定过程中,公众扮演了什么角色呢?市民们是怎样了解以及参与到项目中的?我们如何评估他们在参与过程中为遗产增加的价值?我们可能会想知道现有的监管和立法工具是否充分以及满足需求。在这些监管框架之外,还有一些公众的声音。这样证明了,在一个地方成为世界遗产之前,就存在着真正的集体居住的需求。

Public paroticipaotioon

Je me contenterai donc d'évoquer ici aujourd'hui ce que je connais: Bordeaux et le port de la Lune, site inscrit en 2007 sur la liste du patrimoine mondial, pour vous parler de l'importance de la concertation et de la participation publiques dans la gestion de ce site.

Mais pour vous présenter Bordeaux, puis-je introduire une comparaison avec Wuhan? Wuhan fait à peu près la superficie du département de la Gironde. Et Bordeaux est comme vous le savez, et comme aimait à le rappeler son ancien maire Alain Juppé, un village comparé à Wuhan.

En revanche, Bordeaux comme Wuhan sont deux villes nées d'un fleuve et du commerce: la Garonne et le Yangtsékiang leur ont donné une économie prospère et des patrimoines culturels matériels et naturels remarquables.

Ces deux villes sont attractives et cultivent chacune à leur manière modernité et héritage. Elles revivent et se modernisent depuis une trentaine d'années de façon notable. Wuhan a conscience de la nécessité de préserver son patrimoine. Bordeaux a aujourd'hui un temps d'avance sur cette question: comment s'est faite cette prise de conscience?

Comment évaluer la plus-value de la participation du public à cette reconnaissance? Les outils règlementaires et législatifs existants sont-ils suffisants et satisfaisants (1.)? Les formes d'expression du public ne se manifestent-elles pas au-delà et en dehors de ces cadres règlementaires (2.)? Ne démontrent-elles pas, en effet, l'existence d'un véritable besoin collectif d'habiter un site du patrimoine mondial (3.)?

Pour répondre à ces questions, je rappellerai d'abord les textes légaux qui régissent la participation du public dans la règlementation française. J'aborderai ensuite l'élaboration d'un des outils de planification qui en assure la gestion au titre de son inscription sur la liste du patrimoine mondial, à savoir le plan de sauvegarde et de mise en valeur (PSMV) de son site patrimonial remarquable (SPR). J'évoquerai enfin des modalités plus ou moins informelles, de la participation citoyenne pour la préservation de ce bien.

1. Ce que dit la loi

En France, une règlementation spécifique concerne la conservation du patrimoine culturel et de nombreuses institutions publiques et parapubliques participent à sa préservation et sa mise en valeur. Paradoxalement, le Code du patrimoine qui est le premier texte à s'intéresser à la conservation du patrimoine culturel matériel depuis la loi sur les Monuments historiques de 1913, elle-même issue de la règlementation instaurée au XIXe siècle, ne comporte aucune mesure spécifique liée à la participation et la concertation citoyennes.

Et pourtant, elle place l'intérêt public au-dessus du droit privé, allant jusqu'à considérer que si la valeur d'un bien culturel le justifie, il n'est pas nécessaire d'obtenir l'accord de son propriétaire pour le protéger au titre des Monuments historiques.

Cette loi porte également qu'une personne publique, un maire ou une association par exemple, peut demander la protection d'un bien culturel sans l'avis de son propriétaire.

Cette fonction régalienne mais aussi démocratique est typique de la préservation du patrimoine en France. Elle est complétée par des évolutions récentes du Code de l'urbanisme créé en 1954 et du Code de l'environnement (initié en 1930 et confirmé en 1976). Ces deux codes fixent les modalités de l'information et de la concertation règlementaire du public dans les projets ou les opérations d'aménagement susceptibles de porter atteinte à l'environnement en général et à la valeur d'un bien culturel en particulier.

Je m'en tiendrai ici aux fonctions du Code de l'urbanisme.

Dans ce Code, la participation publique relative aux opérations d'aménagement et de planification est principalement règlementée à l'article L. 103-2 qui stipule:《Font l'objet d'une concertation associant, pendant toute la durée de l'élaboration du projet, les habitants, les associations locales et les autres personnes concernées:

1° L'élaboration ou la révision du schéma de cohérence territoriale ou du plan local d'urbanisme (...)》

Les plans de sauvegarde et de mise en valeur tiennent lieu de documents d'urbanisme et entrent donc dans cette catégorie.

Dans ce cadre règlementaire, la récente loi sur la Liberté de la Création, l'Architecture et le Patrimoine (dite loi LCAP promulguée le 7 juillet 2016) a introduit notamment:

—L'obligation que les SPR soient dotés d'outils de médiation et de participation citoyennes (article L. 631-1), ceci ne marque pour le moment qu'une intention mais c'est une nouveauté.

—Une avancée encore timide pour la gestion des sites du patrimoine mondial: son décret d'application du 29 mars 2017 dispose notamment à l'article R. 612-1:《Pour assurer la préservation de la valeur universelle exceptionnelle des biens reconnus en tant que biens du patrimoine mondial, l'Etat et les collectivités territoriales ou leurs groupements protègent ces biens et, le cas échéant, tout ou partie de leur zone tampon par l'application des dispositions du présent livre, du livre III du code de l'environnement ou du livre Ier du code de l'urbanisme. 》

—Une représentativité accrue des associations du patrimoine dans le collège des commissions locales des sites patrimoniaux remarquables. La loi LCAP fixe à un tiers le nombre de leurs membres (article D.

631-5).

Avec cette loi, les anciens secteurs sauvegardés, les zones de protection du patrimoine architectural, urbain et paysager (ZPPAUP) ainsi que les aires de mise en valeur de l'architecture et du patrimoine (AVAP) ont été transformés en sites patrimoniaux remarquables (SPR) qui sont désormais gouvernés soit par des plans de sauvegarde et de mise en valeur (PSMV) qui existent depuis 1962 ou des plans de valorisation de l'architecture et du patrimoine (PVAP) qui ont remplacé les ZPPAUP et les AVAP. Ce sont des changements de pure forme. Dans les pratiques, cette loi ne change pas les comportements des citoyens qui réagissent peu, et légitimement, nous allons le voir, à ces glissements sémantiques.

2. Ce que dit le public

A Bordeaux, le plan de gestion du port de la Lune (1810 ha) présente trois outils urbanistiques principaux qui en garantissent la préservation de la valeur universelle et exceptionnelle:
—près de 360 monuments historiques inscrits ou classés et dont le nombre augmente régulièrement,
—un plan local d'urbanisme intercommunal (PLUi) patrimonial de près de 1 000 ha et 40 000 parcelles,
—enfin, un plan de sauvegarde et de mise en valeur (PSMV) de près de 150 ha (3 500 parcelles et 7 000 immeubles).

Je vais m'attarder sur la participation du public dans la révision de ce dernier plan qui a commencé en 2013 et qui est à présent achevée.

La participation du public à la révision de ce dernier document s'organise légalement grâce à la mise à disposition de registres papier et d'un registre électronique. Ces outils peuvent s'avérer efficaces pour recueillir l'avis des citoyens, notamment en ce qui concerne de grandes opérations d'aménagement et de travaux.

Mais il s'avère qu'ils n'ont pas été efficaces pour cette concertation règlementaire. En effet, le registre électronique de cette opération n'a recueilli que sept observations alors qu'il a été ouvert durant près de trois ans et les registres papier n'ont reçu aucune observation.

Comment donc alors trouver les moyens d'attirer, d'informer le public et le faire participer et partager davantage à ce type de projet?

L'organisation de balades thématiques en petits groupes, avec des questionnaires papiers, dans les quartiers du site patrimonial remarquable, puis autour de thématiques particulières (espace public, logement, activités économiques, architecture...) a en revanche connu beaucoup de succès.

Les participants à ces promenades, assez peu nombreux mais très fidèles (environ 400 personnes ont communiqué leur adresse mail et se sont inscrits et sont venues à plusieurs promenades thématiques-certaines presque à toutes), se sont montrés très actifs. Chaque fois, ils ont, en grande majorité et malgré leur petit nombre, rempli des questionnaires manuscrits pour montrer à la fois leurs réactions face au projet qui leur était présenté, mais également exprimé leurs désirs et leurs propres projets pour le site patrimonial remarquable de Bordeaux.

Les conclusions du bilan de cette concertation légale mentionnent, de 2016 à 2018, 544 participants et 252 contributions écrites, dont la plupart lors des promenades publiques organisées durant ces deux années. C'est très peu si l'on considère que le centre historique de Bordeaux compte 20 000 habitants. C'est beaucoup si l'on sait qu'au contraire le public ne s'exprime pas en général sur la mise en œuvre des documents d'urbanisme.

A titre de comparaison, une nouvelle concertation est ouverte depuis le 30 septembre 2019 sur le devenir des boulevards et de leurs barrières: les entrées dans la ville historique du site Unesco sur la rive gauche de la Garonne. Celle-ci a recueilli pas moins d'une centaine d'avis des citoyens en à peine une semaine. On voit donc la relativité de l'importance de l'outil numérique pourrecueillir l'avis du public en fonction de l'intérêt qu'il porte au sujet même sur lequel on l'interroge. Ici, contrairement au sujet précédent, la circulation, la pollution, les conflits d'usages sont au cœur d'un sujet pour lequel les citoyens réagissent de façon épidermique. Quoi qu'il en soit, il convient de se demander également comment le public peut aussi s'exprimer au-delà et en dehors de ces cadres règlementaires. Il existe en effet d'autres formes de participation.

3. D'autres formes de participations

2007 est la première année où l'UNESCO a rendu obligatoire la présentation d'un plan de gestion pour tout nouveau site candidat. Et Bordeaux a donc répondu à cette demande. Mais Bordeaux, contrairement à Lyon par exemple, n'a pas concerté spécifiquement pour sa candidature. En revanche, la Ville a mené et continue de mener une série d'actions et de projets très partagés qui ont largement participé au succès de son inscription et continuent à contribuer à une bonne gestion du site. Ces projets ont d'ailleurs toute leur place dans le plan de gestion du site.

Du côté privé, parmi les milliers d'associations créées en France chaque année, il est impossible de connaître exactement lesquelles sont réellement actives dans le domaine du patrimoine, car mis à part leur enregistrement en préfecture, on ne connaît pas toujours le nombre de leurs membres et leurs activités exactes. Certaines sont pourtant très anciennes et réelles, actives et bien connues.

Elles ont pour origine les sociétés savantes, issues du pouvoir royal et maintenues pour la plupart au XIXe siècle par les régimes politiques: une loi de 1901 sur la création des associations leur a donné toute leur légitimité.

Au XXe siècle, elles ont pris un essor considérable. La Société archéologique de Bordeaux (SAB), figure ainsi parmi les plus anciennes et l'une de ses valeurs premières a toujours été de veiller et d'alerter la collectivité des dangers potentiels liés à la disparition du patrimoine face à des projets d'aménagement peu scrupuleux. D'éminents membres de la SAB ont largement contribué à l'inscription du port de la Lune en 2007.

L'association Renaissance des cités d'Europe bien plus confidentielle, est non moins active. Ses «nuits du patrimoine» et ses visites de chantier sont réputées pour attirer de nombreux visiteurs et sensibiliser de nombreux publics aux actions entreprises en ville pour la mise en valeur du patrimoine et sa préservation durable depuis la création du secteur sauvegardé de Bordeaux.

L'association Sites & cités remarquables de France, basée aujourd'hui à Bordeaux, a une influence et une considération nationales. Cette association réunit près de 260 villes et villages dotés d'un patrimoine remarquable et elle travaille avec les collectivités qui obtiennent son label à créer des CIAP (Centre d'Interprétation de l'Architecture et du Patrimoine). Ces CIAP ont pour mission de sensibiliser tous les publics, et plus particulièrement les habitants et les jeunes, à la valorisation du patrimoine.

Du côté public, force est de constater que les obligations règlementaires ou les incitations à faire se multiplient. Les collectivités qui en ont la responsabilité investissent donc de plus en plus pour la participation du public lorsqu'elles engagent des opérations d'aménagement et leurs efforts pour la valorisation du patrimoine méritent d'être soulignés.

Les concertations organisées dans le cadre du projet urbain Bordeaux 2030 ont largement ouvert, à partir de 2006, une série d'échanges où des opérations d'aménagement d'envergure, dans les quartiers des Bassins à flot au nord, de La Bastide à l'est et de Belcier au sud, ont conduit à de nombreuses réunions publiques où les citoyens ont non seulement exprimé leurs désirs et leurs besoins, mais ont aussi dû se confronter à la dure réalité des investisseurs et de leurs projets. Chacune de ces réunions a donné lieu à la publication de carnets où la parole des habitants était notamment retranscrite dans des verbatim.

Le CLUB (Comité local Unesco Bordeaux), a été créé en 2008 face aux menaces de déclassement de la ville qui prévoyait la construction d'un pont monumental reliant des quartiers en développement au nord de ses deux rives. Ce pont risquait de porter atteinte à la valeur universelle et exceptionnelle du site inscrit. Il a donc fallu démontrer à l'expert de l'Unesco envoyé sur place puis à la Commission du Patrimoine mondial que ce projet garantissait au contraire une mise en valeur pérenne du site, en permettant notamment le passage et l'accès des navires de toute sorte au cœur du port de la Lune. Depuis 2008, le CLUB qui est composé de personnalités de la société civile, d'experts et de représentants des institutions publiques-il est important de souligner qu'il ne comporte pas d'élus-a examiné des dizaines de projets sensibles susceptibles de porter atteinte à la valeur universelle et exceptionnelle (VUE) du site inscrit ou, au contraire, de la consolider. Le CLUB n'a pas de pouvoir décisionnaire mais il donne un avis aux élus et ses rapports sont transmis au Centre du patrimoine mondial. Son rôle de veille est donc essentiel à la garantie de la VUE du port de la Lune.

Agora, biennale d'architecture, d'urbanisme et de design, a connu un succès grandissant à travers ses sept éditions organisées de 2004 à 2017. Cette biennale a été conçue pour partager avec le grand public des questions réservées aux spécialistes au moment où les travaux liés à l'implantation du tramway et à la rénovation des espaces publics majeurs du centre-ville historique et de sa périphérie créaient des inquiétudes et des désordres d'usages légitimes. En 2012, cette biennale a spécialement été consacrée au patrimoine et son commissaire, l'architecte Marc Barani, a mis en valeur la pérennité de ses infrastructures et de ses tracés, au-delà des objets architecturaux qui composent son patrimoine traditionnel.

Lors de la dernière édition d'Agora, en septembre 2017, Alain Juppé maire de Bordeaux a lancé une vaste enquête prospective dénommée Bordeaux 2050. Cette mission a été une expérience originale de prospective qui s'est achevée en 2019 et a permis à des milliers de citoyens de s'exprimer et de participer sous des formes diverses et variées à la réflexion sur ce que pourrait être la métropole de Bordeaux dans trente ans. Je ne citerai que deux exemples des manifestations mises en œuvre à cette occasion: le《camion du futur》et le serious game de la métropole du futur.

Le camion du futur a sillonné à 42 reprises l'agglomération pour recueillir l'avis du commun des mortels, des habitants《ordinaires》, mais vus comme des experts de leur territoire. Ils aiment avant tout leur commune, mais s'approprient volontiers un morceau de la carte postale de Bordeaux. Bien sûr les questions de transport et de logement sont au cœur de leurs préoccupations, mais au cœur de ces dernières ils interrogent avant tout la densification de la métropole, pour laquelle ils souhaiteraient être davantage consultés.

Le serious game #BM 2050 a recueilli près de 200 000 visites et près de 50 000 joueurs en ligne, dont je fais partie. Les participants, essentiellement locaux, ont contribué à dessiner parmi 109 《pépites》, des sites repérés pour leur potentiel évolutif, un projet urbain plébiscité particulièrement autour de 11 d'entre eux.

Quatre grands scénarios dessinent ainsi la ville du futur: la métropolisation continue et s'autorégule, l'exigence décarbonée règle la ville, la nature redessine la ville et enfin, l'équilibre des territoires fait la vie. C'est vers cette dernière exigence que s'oriente aujourd'hui le développement urbain de Bordeaux et l'on aura compris que si ces participations peuvent porter à sourire, elles montrent et nourrissent le véritable engouement des publics dès lors qu'une certaine qualité de contributions leur est proposée.

4. Conclusion

Je n'ai parlé ici que de quelques exemples de participations publiques que je connais et auxquelles j'ai participé de près ou de loin à Bordeaux durant un peu plus d'une dizaine d'années. Mais, vous l'aurez compris, elles sont bien plus nombreuses que le bref inventaire que je viens d'en dresser et j'aurais pu en citer bien d'autres.

Les outils règlementaires de concertation, de planification et de gestion des sites du patrimoine mondial en France sont sans doute ceux sur lesquels peut se fonder une connaissance et une reconnaissance solides pour leur avenir et leur bonne gestion. Cependant il ne faut pas négliger les multiples actions entreprises hors des cadres règlementaires qui, bien souvent, témoignent d'une appropriation pérenne de ces sites alors qu'elles n'ont pas une reconnaissance officielle.

En ce sens, l'évaluation de la plus-value culturelle apportée par la participation publique dans la mise en place d'outils de gestion d'un site du patrimoine culturel matériel doit absolument tenir compte de l'existence d'une représentation collective de ces forces sociales qui sont essentielles afin d'apprécier une véritable appropriation du public pour conserver-c'est-à-dire habiter-les sites du patrimoine mondial.

Dès lors que des initiatives individuelles se répètent et se transmettent, elles deviennent collectives et publiques. Ces participations protéiformes démontrent l'existence d'un besoin collectif d'acculturation et d'appropriation du public pour conserver-c'est-à-dire habiter-un site du patrimoine mondial. On l'aura compris, ces participations publiques dépassent largement le cadre de la gestion d'un site du patrimoine mondial. Elles n'ont, pour ainsi dire, pas besoin de lui pour s'exprimer, même si l'existence de ce dernier en révèle toute l'importance.

5G 时代下的文物保护公众参与

Public Participation in Protection of Cultural Relics in the 5G Era

刘爱河 博士
中国文化遗产研究院副研究员
Dr. Liu Aihe
Associate Professor, Chinese Academy of Cultural Heritage

The 5G era will bring a far-reaching social change. The digitalization, intelligence, socialization and popularization trend of it will deeply change people's life and production pattern of the society, and will also create many new industries. 5G's super high speed, low delay, massive connection, ubiquitous network and other features make information collection, storage and acquisition more convenient. The data analysis, matching, and push of information are more accurate, which is conducive to fully mobilize all kinds of resources and to realize more effective interpersonal communication. They also greatly improve the efficiency of organization and management, so as to provide more power and possibilities for the public participation in cultural heritage protection. In 5G era, the main body, contents, and channels of information communication will be more diversified, and the communication efficiency will be significantly improved. By means of visualization, immersion, and interaction, the public can more intuitively and conveniently perceive cultural heritage and experience cultural heritage conservation and maintenance, and participate in relevant activities, which can not only improve public awareness of heritage conservation but also increase their initiatives of it.

5G时代下的文物保护主要包括两个方面的内容：一个是5G时代下将产生的变革，一个是新的互联网时代的社会组织募资。

首先说说5G，这两年各个国家都高度地关心5G：我们国家是把5G作为国家战略来部署；而美国可能更加关心，它把5G作为其称霸世界的一个重要的基石，所以也把我们的华为作为一个重要的打压对象。因为5G会带来信息领域的一个重大的变革，它会改变互联网的规则，甚至会在某种程度上改变世界的格局。我觉得这个5G将给我们带来非常大的影响：它堪比蒸汽机、堪比工业革命、堪比核爆炸。

这两年我国也在全面快速地推进5G：比如说已经在武汉，发出了全球第一张自动驾驶车辆的商用牌照；比如说我们的湖北省博物馆，已经建成了全国第一家的数字智慧博物馆。那5G到底有多厉害？它不是简单地在4G上面加1G。它有三大特点：就是超高速、低时延、大连接。它的速度能够达到4G的几十倍甚至上百倍，它的连接能力可以达到4G的一千倍。4G实现了人和人的连接，但是5G将会实现人和物、物和物的连接，真正实现了万物互联、人机深度交互。

将来我们的生活场景可能就是这样的：所有的东西特别的智能、特别的聪明，会给我们提供大量的信息，而且也会在这个基础上，会催生好多新的产业、新的业态。其实现在5G已经显现出它的优势，比如在工业农业、教育、城市管理、医疗等等方面，已经显现出来了。那5G会给我们文物领域会带来什么呢？其实在国家文物事业的"十三五"规划中，已经提到了"互联网＋中华文明"，提到了物联网，也提到了智慧博物馆、智慧故宫、智慧敦煌这样的概念。但是由于4G的能力相对有限，所以这些发展还相对比较缓慢。

前不久习总书记在敦煌研究院座谈的时候,提出要运用先进技术加强文物保护和研究。现在应该说5G就是非常重要的一个先进的技术,所以我觉得文物行业也应该及时地关注5G、研究5G、拥抱5G。

那5G能够给文物保护利用带来哪些方面的影响呢?我觉得至少有这几个方面,我也是大胆地设想了一下。因为在我们现在云计算的基础上,5G会有一个更先进的一个计算方法,它叫边缘计算。有了这个方法,我们对文物信息的采集,及对观众、游客等的信息的采集会更加的智能,而且也更安全。有了这些信息的话,我们就是可以给我们的文物管理带来很大的便利,大大地提高文物保护利用管理的效率、效能。

而且就是5G条件下,超高清视频会非常的普及。有了超高清视频,文物的安防监控会迎来一个新的时代。而且远程作业也很容易实现,现在已经有医院可以远程做手术了,将来远程修复文物,我觉得也是完全有可能实现的。

而且VR和AR大家可能也都比较熟悉,也是5G时代非常典型的应用。因为4G条件下速度比较慢,这个体验不是很好。但是在5G条件下,它就完全没有卡顿,会很流畅,所以我们带上相关设备真的就是身临其境。所以将来VR眼镜会很轻薄,也会渐渐地就会变成无线的。现在我见到的还都是有线的。有了无线的VR眼镜,我们就可以随时随地虚拟感受文物的现场,感受各种的文物场景。而且也可以远程教学,它一个很大的好处就是能够做到优质资源共享,而且可以大大降低成本。

湖北省博物馆已经建成了全国首家的5G智慧博物馆。昨天下午我也专门去体验了一下,因为我没有5G手机,所以有的功能我没有体验到。但是我只体验了两个场景,一个就是敲击编钟,一个就是拿上越王勾践剑,体验一个战争的场景,确实是比前几年的效果要好很多。昨天重庆的好多朋友也去了,我不知道他们有没有体验这个。

接下来我讲一下社会组织的募资,因为对于社会组织来说,它资金的募集是一个非常重要的内容。应该说,现在社会组织迎来了一个非常好的一个机遇:一方面法律法规越来越完善;另一面就是互联网发展得非常之快。2018年的时候,我国的微信用户已经超过了10亿,而且5G离我们越来越近了。从目前的情况看,募资主要有三个渠道:一个就是向企业募捐;一个就是互联网的募捐;一个就是理财加公益。

现在企业是我国公益捐赠的第一主体。从我国慈善蓝皮书和各个基金会的募资情况来看,确实也是这样的。而且一般来说就是大企业是喜欢捐钱给大机构,国内国外都是这样的。比如说巴黎圣母院,在火灾以后的很短时间内就筹集到10亿欧元的资金。相反巴黎有80多座教堂的经费非常的欠缺。

互联网公益这几年发展得非常之快:一方面是理念发生了变化;一方面技术也带来了巨大的驱动力。现在我国已经形成了全球最大的互联网公益捐赠平台。民政部公布了20家互联网平台,其中尤以腾讯公益和阿里巴巴公益的募捐能力最强。

比如说腾讯公益这几年已经募集到55亿元的善款,能力还是非常强的。而且腾讯发起的"九九公益日",已经是全国乃至全球最具有影响力的一个公益日了。无论是参与捐赠的人次,还是收到捐赠的金额,每年都会有大幅度的提升。还有阿里巴巴公益,它的募资能力也是比较强的。截至2018年,入驻这个平台的慈善组织已经有250多家。但很遗憾的是,我没有发现一家文物保护领域的社会组织入驻阿里巴巴的平台。

有了互联网的平台,就是好多个社会组织,它一方面是资金的结构发生了变化,另一方面就是量也有大幅度的提升。所以可以说,互联网推动中国的慈善事业实现了弯道超车。墨卡托基金会的中国代表阿克曼对此也给予了高度的评价,他说中国的互联网公益在世界范围内都具有样本性。

"一个公益组织能吸引多少善款,最重要的是什么?"这是腾讯公益的内部会议上的一个问题,是催泪指数?感人指数?明星效应?都不是,而是透明度。所以说有效的合作是从了解开始的,募资能力和透明度密切相关。从满天星公益、从抗战老兵基金的实践,都可以得出这个规律。我在中国社会组织网上查了一下,文保领域社会组织历年的工作报告,我只查到三个组织的,而这三个组织也正好就是募资能力最强的三个基金会。所以说长期的合作,我觉得还需要持续地关注。

比如说美国有一个网站,它做得特别好,它长期追踪9 000多个家庭和个人的捐赠行为,用可视化的方式来展示出来。大概就是这样一个画面:它可以选择地区,也可以选择州,可以选择年份,可以显示捐赠的金额,也可以显示服务的小时,还可以显示所占的比例,而且它还可以显示不同类型组织接收到捐赠的情况,也可以显示不同类型人群捐赠的情况,我觉得这样的研究特别有价值、有意义。

这个是最近深圳的一个新尝试。它就是发行理财产品,然后理财产品将部分收益捐赠给文物保护项目。就现在发行了几个效果还不错,也是一种新的探索。

捐赠人最关心什么呢?比尔·盖茨基金会每个月都会收到300多个项目的申请,但是只有1‰能接受到捐赠,可以说是百里挑一。而且他们特别重视项目的预算,而且他们会经常派人到各地去跟踪,看看这个项目实施的怎么样,还要保证他们的捐赠能够落到实处。

所以我总结了一下募资要做到五好:政策学习好,项目策划好,资金募集好,项目执行好,客户维系好。现在有一个大家都比较认同的方法,或者说是一个理念:就是用商业的手法来做公益。就是做公益的时候,一定要把捐赠者当成是参与者,要及时向他们反馈信息,要做到公开透明,这样就会有比较好的募资的效果。

下面简单介绍几个国内外的案例:

比如说,"给予星期二"跟咱们那个"九九公益日"差不多,是一个互联网的公益日,它通过Facebook和Twitter也产生了强大的传播效果,募资能力也还不错。而且20年也开始和腾讯公益合作。

还有襄阳的"拾穗者"。他们今天也来了好多朋友。刚才励部长致辞的时候也提到,他们这么多年做了特别多卓有成效的工作。他们这个读城活动,前段时间基金会的刘广军主任也去考察过,对他们这个评价也比较高。这是李秀桦大哥在给大家讲会馆,而且他们最近也出版了一本会馆的专著。《襄阳晚报》对他们的相关的活动也做了很多的报道,而且他们也在开展互联网众筹来建博物馆。这么多年他们获得了无数的奖励,市长对他们评价非常高。特别难能可贵的是,他们得到了市财政资金的资助,我觉得这对于一个社会组织来说是非常不容易的。虽然钱不多,就十多万,但是对他们来说,我觉得简直就是救命钱。对于一个高校对于一个科研院所来说,这点经费不算什么,但是这些经费能够让他们做很多很多的事情。市文明办也把他们作为一个荆楚楷模重点来打造。

接下来还要简单介绍一下这个重庆的保护志愿者服务团队,他们在互联网众筹方面也做得非常好,可以说可圈可点。比如说公益日之前他们就会发布消息,他们会对他们组织做一个详细的介绍,包括即将发起什么项目,具体怎么捐,还准备了爱心伴手礼,很贴心。就"九九公益日"结束后,他们会及时地总结和真诚地答谢,有完整的链条,所以他们这个募资效果还是挺好的。

还有古村之友的"濒危文物撑伞行动",现在有大量的偏远贫困地区的低级别的文物没有资金保护,所以他们就通过互联网众筹来给大家筹集资金,保证在这些房子上面先撑一个伞,保证它们暂时不塌不漏。他们在山西已经做了20多个项目,而且这些项目也得到了山西文博之家李强先生的很多帮助。他们在深圳、在广州也都开展了很多的项目。而且我觉得这个项目重要的是,它把当地的力量给激活了。

刚才我介绍的其实还是4G时代下的一个资金募集,那5G时代这个资金募集会有怎样的变化呢?我觉得将来技术会更先进,信息的传播会更及时;所以人们关注、亲近、参与文化遗产或者文物保护会更加的便捷;而且将来会有更多的终端,有更大的数据量,有更智能的计算方式,社会组织有这些数据的话,就可以更准确地找到目标人群;而且将来信息会更透明,人们可以随时随地的关注项目的进展,关注资金的使用,所以就要求社会组织管理要更加规范,更加专业。当然,也可能带来用户信息隐私的泄露问题,所以我觉得还是要加强立法,也需要加强行业的自律。

将来的生活场景我觉得有可能这样,我们坐在无人驾驶车上,可以浏览一下智慧博物馆,也可以关注一下中国文物保护基金会的箭扣长城保护和现在进行的喜峰口长城保护,也可以关注一下人文武汉的扫街活动,也可以带上VR眼镜,身临其境地感受一下今天这个无界论坛和社会力量参与文物保护的论坛,也可以顺手做一点指尖公益。

5G的应用其实远不止这些,而且5G之后还会有6G,6G会给带给我们更大的惊喜。

遗产与社群——来自亚洲的范例

World Heritage and Communities: Examples from Asia

西蒙尼·里卡
联合国教科文组织亚太地区世界遗产培训与研究中心上海分中心副主任
Dr. Simone Ricca
Deputy Director, World Heritage Institute of Training & Research for the Asia and the Pacific Region under the auspices of UNESCO, WHITRAP (Shanghai)

在过去的20年中,在近期许多世界遗产的概念演变中,"社区"已成为遗产话题的中心。这强调了社区参与和支出在城市、文化景观和自然遗址等方面的保护和发展策略中出现的必要性。然而,确定"有关"社区及其实际参与保护的过程——尤其是在鉴定和管理世界遗产时——是一个极其复杂的问题,不应简单地加以处理。"社区"不是"给定的"实体,也不是"固定的、传统的",相反,它们就像遗产一样,在不断演变,并以多种复杂的方式与周围的自然和建筑环境相互作用。三个亚洲的案例(叙利亚、越南和阿拉伯联合酋长国)强调了一些利害攸关的问题,指出《世界遗产公约》通过阐述能够与不同群体和敏感性相关的包容性叙述而提供的机会。遗产,尤其是世界遗产的原则,可以提供积极的知识与文化框架,有助于推动地方发展和保持地方特性的完整性。

The role of communities in heritage preservation and management is a key factor today in World Heritage, but this has not always been the case in the past.

The growing role of communities is related to the change of approach to what is heritage, and the perception that it is a social construct, an element that is not fixed and immutable, but that evolves in time. Our understanding of what makes heritage has changed dramatically in the past twenty years and will continue changing in the future. We know that there is not a clear-cut, black and white, separation between what "is" and what "is not" heritage, that there is not a rigid divide between cultural and natural heritage, nor between tangible and intangible heritage, but instead a continuous overlapping and shifting of all these components.

This is related to the radical change in the understanding of what is heritage that has taken place in the past twenty years, a process that is commonly referred to as a "paradigm shift". This relates especially to the appropriation of heritage by communities, to an expansion of the values to include its use by communities and the economic value of heritage, to the emergence and understanding of the relevance of intangible heritage values that make a place heritage, and to the idea that the protection of heritage actually has to come to terms with the fact that heritage is changing and evolving, shifting from static protection to a new approach capable to address the dynamic changes heritage is confronted with.

When we ponder what this "shift" implies at the practical level, we realize that it implies much wider obligations in the protection of heritage, including recognizing the fundamental role of communities. Therefore, heritage protection today is related to the promotion of cultural diversity(brought by communities), the protection of larger ecosystems, the interaction between human communities and natural sites, the integration of intangible assets, cultures and local knowledge (intimately connected to communities), and to the idea that heritage protection should also aim at providing vitality to communities and at defining compatible uses. All this is possible only through the involvement of local communities.

UNESCO has defined a series of "Strategic Objectives" for the implementation of the 1972 *World Heritage Convention* commonly known as the "5Cs": Credibility, Conservation, Capacity-building, Communication, and Communities. The last two key words—Communication and Communities, are obviously particularly relevant to our topic today.

The *Operational Guidelines for the Implementation of World Heritage Convention*, Article 119, underline that "*World Heritage properties (…) should promote and encourage the active participation of the communities (…) as necessary conditions to its sustainable protection, conservation, management and presentation*". It is important to understand that the *Operational Guidelines* evolved in parallel to the development of the 2003 *Intangible Heritage Convention*, which obviously focuses on communities.

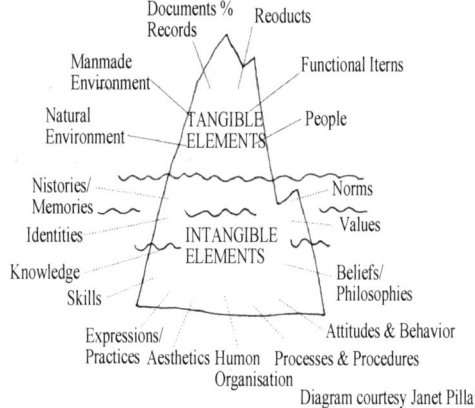

制作文化地图

Community participation is achieved through a series of tools and practical field methodologies, like the "participatory approach", aiming to involve the ensemble of concerned stakeholders in this process. Mr. Philips has already talked about rights-based approach, which essentially means to implicate communities, especially native communities and minorities, into the management of a site, taking into consideration human rights and culture to avoid developing mistrust and mismanagement.

ICOMOS, IUCN, and ICCROM have prepared a booklet on rights-based approach that presents a series of cases that seem relevant. I just point out very briefly two examples: a case in Norway, and one in Peru. In both these cases, at the moment of inscription, the perception of the role of communities was not yet obvious and evident. These nominations were prepared in a traditional top-down, expert-driven manner. But in fact, both urban sites and archaeological sites are connected to communities, and now this principle has been acknowledged and is being integrated into the new site management strategies.

Another innovative tool, which is recognized by UNESCO as a crucial technique, is the concept of "cultural mapping", that is done through a series of tools and techniques, but that aims to involve communities in activities and projects to record, conserve, and use cultural elements in order to support the cultural diversity. Cultural mapping is an approach that integrates both tangible and intangible elements that contribute and define heritage for communities.

There are also other tools like the Historic Urban Landscape Recommendation (HUL). This is an example taken from the small city of Ballarat in Australia, a typical example of HUL application that shows how community participation is now at the centre of the heritage discourse.

But the reality of the work in the field is not so simple… We know these rules, we know these tools, but the reality is more complex. There are issues that are not always dealt with so easily, like the fact that "communities" are not a given, stable entity, but change as much as our perception of heritage has changed.

How to deal and integrate communities in a pattern, for instance, of rural depopulation and rapid urban growth? How to integrate immigrant communities and their heritage and their background coming from different regions of a country or from different countries of the world? What is the role of the community when new generations are completely detached from what was the traditional know-how and logic? How to integrate multiple ethnic groups and diverse religious communities?

These are just some of the examples that make working with communities so complex. And, finally, which memories are we preserving? How can we integrate complex issues like colonial heritage?

I will try to address these issues through three examples, showing how the World Heritage nomination and the discussions around it, might contribute to overcome these problems.

The first example is a bit sad, because now in these areas a civil war is raging. The Ancient Villages of Northern Syria were listed on World Heritage in 2011, and in the *World Heritage List in Danger* in 2013, because of the war.

The problem here was that the communities living on the site were only very marginally concerned by the protection of this heritage, which was perceived as distant in time and not related to their cultural and religious background. There was a distance between the government's approach to preserving this heritage as a tourist resource, as part of the multilayered narrative of "Arab identity", on the one side, and the actual feelings of the community that perceived it as an opposition to their agricultural and urban development, as distant culturally and historically, and therefore irrelevant for them, on the other.

This is an issue related to the connection between heritage and identity, to the dichotomy between the community living today in these areas and the vestiges of the past. This is Saint Simeon Church in Northern Syria.

What could World Heritage do in this case? And what was the role played by the nomination file? The driving idea was that in the long-term, community participation could help integrate cultural multiplicity and contribute to raise people's tolerance and respect. We don't have to be naive though, because sometimes local communities are myopic or are sectarian. It is not just because initiatives are developed "bottom-up" that they automatically integrate a multiplicity of values… This is an example where the local community would have probably destroyed this heritage. And the work of World Heritage nomination was to explain and mediate through finding ways to integrate the local community in the discourse. This was achieved in three ways: 1) trying to distance the heritage from its exclusively Christian connection, as opposed to the Muslim one, showing that it actually represented a transition from the Pagan culture of the Roman Empire up to the monotheistic Byzantine Empire; 2) focusing on the idea that we are talking about a "cultural landscape" where communities and life are as relevant as the ruins and we are not talking about simple archaeological ruins; 3) and then, of course, through management practices and strategies that involve local residents, integrating this heritage in the life of the community in a more effective way. Tragically, today this area is under war and I don't know exactly what has happened to these places in the last years.

Another example that relates to the integration of multiple layers of history and the role that World Heritage nomination could play is the *Citadel of Thang Long, Hanoi* in Vietnam that was inscribed in 2010.

Hanoi Historic City was, as you know, the capital of the French colony of Indochina. You can see three areas in the map: in brown the military citadel, in blue the colonial city, and in red the mercantile area of the city. The military area was a citadel that grew up on the same place where successive layers of citadels were created: 11th-century citadel, 15th-century citadel, 1802–1805 Nguyen Citadel, then the stronghold of the French colonial army, and then, later, also the headquarters of the Vietnamese revolutionary fight against the colonial occupation with bunkers created under the citadel from where the war against the French before, and the Americans later, was directed.

The communities do not perceive these multiple layers in the same way. And one of the issues was the preservation of the colonial military heritage. In Vietnam, the value of French colonial civil architecture, urban villas, urban neighborhoods, and city plans, is acknowledged and integrated in to the national discourse. But military heritage is so much related to the darkest part of the colonial power that it has a much harder implication for being preserved. The nomination is permitted to launch a process of community appropriation of the space through a number of activities organized by the central and local governments, aiming to re-integrate the citadel area in the city. Now, the former citadel is a park where people go and enter in, appropriating the site in a different way. And this confrontation, this new perception of this urban sector, both by authorities and communities, progressively allows a different interaction also with the more difficult parts of the history of the site. World Heritage nomination has favoured the definition of a richer and more multiple preservation strategy.

The third case is a city that has failed the application process to become a World Heritage site: Dubai. But this case permits us to introduce other issues that are relevant to our discussion.

When we think about Dubai, we generally tend to think about a modern city, a city with no heritage, a post-modern city par excellence. Dubai, like most of the United Arab Emirates, is inhabited at 90 percent by foreigners and many of these foreigners are transient, they are not staying for all the life in the city. How can heritage help to creat a community out of this complex social reality? Of course, Dubai is composed of an elite of Arab merchants, but it is also composed of a large Indian community with its religious Hindu temples, and this is not just a recent phenomenon with the massive immigration of workers but is part of the trade history of this city.

It is a city of merchants and traders that attracts people from Iran to Pakistan, India, and far beyond. It is also a city where you have a large Western ex-pat community and a growing tourist presence. All these people can be part of the heritage of the city. All these groups can contribute to imagining a city where residents have a better interaction among them and a better relationship with a multiplicity of "histories". This can be done through a "national" Arab/Emirati appropriation of heritage, but also through sharing and teaching children from many different backgrounds about the history of the city and its values.

The preparation of the World Heritage nomination, albeit unsuccessful, was an opportunity to develop heritage-focused initiatives for both Emirati and foreign residents aiming at reinforcing their sense of belonging and mutual understanding among communities. Multiple stories, multiple languages, multiple religions, and diverse food, create the unique heritage of the city, to which also new residents can connect and can contribute. This is why I think it is an interesting example of the positive role World Heritage can play even when it doesn't work out at the end.

Can we say that World Heritage brings something to the debate on the role of communities? Indeed, to whom belongs this heritage? World Heritage says these outstanding sites belong to the entire humanity, but what are the links? What is the connection between the modern inheritors and the ancient creators of that heritage? How can we reinforce this link? How can we present this link?

Probably the idea is that we need to accept that there is a "dissonance", an absence of agreement on what are these values. An absence of agreement that depends on the different values of different social groups, different ethnic groups, different generations, and different gender groups may have. This is probably inevitable, and we need to consider it as a richness, not as a problem. The involvement of communities, besides experts—as Philips reminded us we should not minimize the relevance of experts, but "we" should not be the only players in the game—permits to bring multiple versions of history to the fore, and therefore to preserve multiple versions, multiple parallel stories and histories. Such an approach also permits to limit ideological misuse of heritage that can sometimes lead to its deliberate destruction when heritage becomes a target, as we have seen so often in Syria, in Afghanistan, or in former Yugoslavia. The participation of the communities in the definition of heritage values is probably a way to imagine a way forward. Where this approach is followed there are fewer risks of destruction.

This last point relates to the very idea at the heart of UNESCO Constitution: *Since wars begin in the minds of men, it is in the minds of men that the defense of peace might be constructed*. It is the idea to privilege the dialogue among people, among communities, that lies at the heart of the mission of UNESCO, and the *World Heritage Convention*.

信息时代的文化遗产保护：数字监测技术的应用与发展

Cultural Heritage Protection in the Information Age: Application and Development of Digital Monitoring Technology

李晓武

上海建为历保科技股份有限公司 副总裁

Mr. Li Xiaowu

Vice President of Shanghai Jianwei Cultural Heritage Conservation Tech. Co., Ltd.

Risk is everywhere in the process of cultural heritage protection. The risk factors affecting the safety of the cultural heritage include material risk, man-made risk, environment risk, project risk, biological risk and disaster risk, and so on. In the application of digital monitoring technology, we put forward the concept of intelligent digital monitoring and established a monitoring evaluation and early warning system, which has achieved good results in practice. With the development of modern science and technology and the improvement of cultural heritage protection concept, digital monitoring of cultural heritage will surely usher in new development opportunities.

一、数字化监测技术的应用背景

（一）文化遗产保护过程中风险无处不在

数字化监测技术的应用背景，首先与文化遗产保护过程中的风险因素有关。围绕文化遗产的风险是多样的，既有当前的也有潜在于未来的，既有内部的也有外部的，既有静态的也有动态的。文化遗产风险评估的任务就是要从错综复杂的环境中找出其安全所面临的主要风险，结合科学的评估算法，进行量化评估。

安全评估一方面可以通过感性认识和历史经验来判断，另一方面也可通过对各种客观的量化资料和安全监测数据来分析，经过归纳和整理，结合专家智慧，从而找出影响文化遗产安全的各类风险因素及其破坏规律。因为风险具有可变性，因而安全评估是一项持续性、系统性、动态化的工作，要求文物行政管理单位密切关注、动态评估。

总的来看，影响文化遗产安全的风险因素主要包括六个方面：本体风险，包括倾斜、沉降、开裂、空鼓、风化、断裂、残缺、剥落、起翘等等；人为风险，包括非法拆除、非法建设、城市开发、人为破坏等等；环境风险，包括温度、湿度、光照、水力、风力、重力及冻融等等；项目风险，包括技术不当、维修过度、破坏文物、损害文物、影响风貌等等；生物风险，包括植物风险、微生物风险、动物风险等等；还有灾害风险，包括地质灾害、气象灾害、水文灾害、火灾等等（图1）。

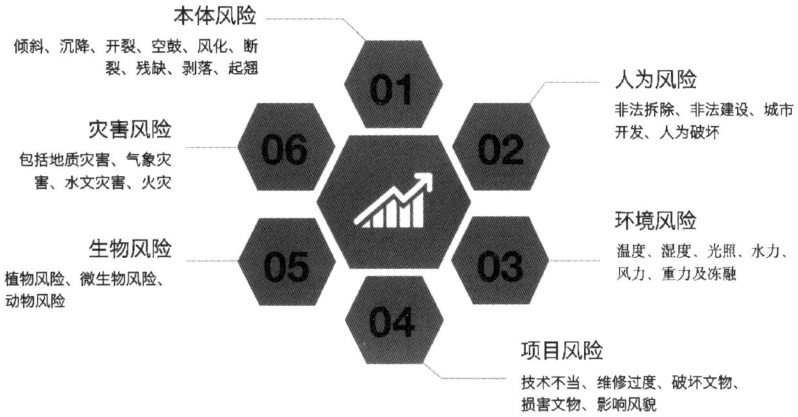

图 1　风险因素构成

1. 本体风险

本体风险方面,主要是结构和本体的一些物质载体上面体现出来的各种劣化或者它的结构方面的威胁,这些都会对遗产造成直接的价值损失。以木结构建筑为例,其本体风险可表现在以下方面:结构病害风险,包括木构件的应力与强度、沉降、倾斜等等;局部变形风险,包括柱、梁枋、斗拱的弯曲、变形、断裂、劈裂、移位等等;附属设施病害风险,包括抱鼓石、石狮、浮雕、踏跺、垂带石的缺损、破裂等等;装饰病害风险,包括木雕的材质老化、腐朽、虫蛀、霉变、劈裂,砖雕与石雕的酥碱风化、劈裂、潮湿、霉菌生长,彩绘的起甲、粉化、颜料层脱落、酥碱、龟裂、裂隙、划痕、涂写、烟熏、空鼓、地仗脱落、褪色变色、水渍泥渍等等。

2. 灾害风险

灾害风险方面,主要包括了地质灾害风险、气象灾害风险、火灾风险。这些灾害往往对遗产安全影响巨大,一旦发生,就可能会对文化遗产造成灭顶之灾。

1) 地质灾害

2008 年的汶川地震对文化遗产造成了灾害性的影响,共有 169 处全国重点文物保护单位(其中 2 处已列入《世界遗产名录》),250 处省级文物保护单位受到不同程度损害,共有 2 766 件馆藏文物受损,其中珍贵文物 292 件。2017 年 08 月 08 日,四川省九寨沟县发生 7.0 级地震。那次地震中,各级文物保护单位 24 处,近现代重要史迹及代表性建筑类 21 处、古建筑类 2 处、古遗址类 1 处,均遭到不同程度损坏。公元 79 年,庞贝古城遇到维苏威火山爆发,整个城市被埋在火山灰中。目前发掘出的遗产中,围绕市政广场,有朱庇特神庙、阿波罗神庙、大会堂、浴场、商场等,还有剧场、体育馆、斗兽场、引水道等罗马市政建筑必备设施。作坊店铺众多,都按行业分街坊设置,连同大量居民住宅。这些都成了研究罗马民用建筑的重要实物。山体滑坡、泥石流等其他地质灾害,对遗产也会造成巨大的损失。

2) 气象灾害

台风、雷电、暴雨、冰雹、暴风雪、酸雨等气象类灾害因素也会对文化遗产造成很大的破坏。2014 年 7 月 15 日,凤凰古城沱江水位上涨,导致古城部分被淹,建筑受损。2016 年 9 月 15 日,受第 14 号台风"莫兰蒂"的影响,鼓浪屿多数历史性建筑受到不同程度的破坏,灾后进行了抢救性保护。

3) 火灾

火灾方面,包括 2019 年 4 月 15 日巴黎圣母院的火灾,2019 年 10 月 21 日意大利都灵市中心皇家马厩与马术学院火灾以及 2019 年 10 月 31 日日本冲绳县那霸市的世界文化遗产首里城火灾,对文化遗产都造成了令人痛心的损失。

3. 人为风险

人为风险方面,包括非法拆除、非法建设、不当施工、城市开发或者破坏文物的其他行为,这些对文化遗产的保护也会产生很大影响。人为风险强调的是人类活动(如生产、生活、旅游等)可能对文物安全产生的影响。值得注意的是，城市开发过程中的重大工程，如地铁、高架、隧道、桥梁、高楼等建设，在其开发过程中及开发完成后都可能会对周边文物产生大的扰动，影响文物安全。

4. 环境风险

环境风险，指文物所处的大环境和小环境可能对文物安全产生的风险。主要反映在外界的风力、雨、温度、湿度、有害气体、光照、水力、重力及冻融等对文物的劣化（如风化、起鼓、开裂、生物霉菌等）产生的影响。

5. 项目风险

项目风险，又可称为技术风险，主要体现在技术方面，如文物保护过程的技术使用不当、过度维修、保护措施不当等原因，造成的文物损毁、破坏及风貌改变等状况，这些对文物本身来说也是一个重大风险源。

6. 生物风险

生物风险方面，主要是植物、动物、微生物方面的风险。例如植物根系对建筑造成的直接破坏；细菌、真菌对岩画、壁画影响巨大；动物如皮蠹、拟裸蛛甲、衣蛾、书虱、尘虱、白蚁、土蜂等害虫是造成历史建筑结构损毁及构件破坏的重要原因。

（二）预防性保护理念的发展与实践

监测技术应用在文化遗产保护方面的前提是预防性保护理念的发展。预防性保护是通过长期监测、科学记录，以科学监测数据积累为基础，研究文物的变化规律，达到制定和实施科学的保护控制措施的目标。

随着时代的进步，中国的文物保护工作理念也发生了重大变化，由原来抢救性保护为主的方针向抢救性与预防性保护、文物本体和周边环境保护并重转变。

国家文物局《国家文物保护科学和技术发展"十二五"规划》中明确指出："推进文物的抢救性保护与预防性保护文物的有机结合，加强文物的日常保养、监测文物的保护状况，改善文物的保存环境。"预防性保护的特点是：可监测、可预警、可预控、可预防、低成本、可持续。

目前，预防性保护理念已经在包括故宫、敦煌、庐山、九寨沟、大理三塔、宝光寺塔等遗产地或文物保护单位上得到成功应用。

（三）风险管理理论的成熟与应用

在文化遗产保护工作中应用风险管理理论和方法已经得到了国际、国内有关组织的重视。目前，国际上已经开展了大量与风险管理有关的实践工作，对我国文化遗产的风险管理工作提供了重要的指导作用。在对文化遗产的风险管理中，对自然灾害的研究较多，而对自然环境变化、人类活动给文化遗产带来的影响的研究相对较少，对这两方面进行的风险管理研究主要针对博物馆。文化遗产风险管理发展理念的提出，也是希望利用数字化监测技术，为文化遗产保护提供相应的帮助。

风险管理理论的提出，有利于我们利用现代物联网技术等现代科技技术加强对文物风险的提前预知，或者应用一些预防性保护技术来进行相应的干预。

此外，物联网、大数据、云计算、人工智能、5G等技术的发展，都在数字监测方面为文化遗产的保护提供了很好的技术支撑。

二、数字化监测技术的应用实践

（一）关键支撑技术应用

监测技术方面，我们应用了一些关键的技术，包括云计算、大数据、人工智能、物联网、3S（GIS、GPS、RS）、3D扫描、无人机等，为我们整个文化遗产物联网监测方面提供了一些基础的技术支撑。

在数字化监测技术应用方面，我们提出智能化数字监测的概念。智能化数字监测应该具有自主感知、自主学习、自主评估、自主表达、自主防范及自主调控能力。

在监测智能感知设备方面，在监测应用实践过程中，根据不同文化遗产类型及其面临的风险的不同，我们充分运用了结构类传感器、气象类传感器、环境类传感器、视频图像类传感器、消防类传感器、水文水质类传感器、地质灾害类传感器、游客分析类传感器、生物探测类传感器等感知设备，力求远程、实时、全面、持续、准确地获取到影响文化遗产安全的各指标要素数据。

（二）监测评估及预警体系的建立

数字化监测实践过程中，我们首先建立了一个综合性的监测评估体系。这一体系的建立包括五个环节：（1）评估因素的确定；（2）评估体系层次结构的确定；（3）确定评估因子权重；（4）制定评分标准；（5）评估体系实施。

评估体系又分为客观评估体系和主观模糊综合评估体系。客观评估体系的评估因素主要是指可用工具直接测量并可量化的遗产监测指标要素，如建筑的倾斜、沉降、整体结构的稳定性等。客观评估体系量化评价方法是利用科学测量的方法收集遗产本体状态及影响因素的数据，应用层次分析法及相关的数学分析方法进行计算，最终得到结果。

主观模糊综合评估体系的评价因素是遗产保护中不能用工具直接测量的指标，如安防、消防系统是否完备，保护规划是否制定，周边建设是否侵犯了文物的建设控制地带等。其量化评价方法是结合层次分析法和模糊数学进行分级评价，建立相应的监测评估体系。主观模糊综合评估体系的评分原则对遗产的各个因素进行定性的主观评价，将评估分值作为原始数据，结合多层次的模糊综合评价方法对原始数据进行处理，从而最后得到遗产保存状态的主观评价分体系的得分。

对于监测过程中采集各风险指标要素数据，通过智能算法、大数据分析模型的运用，再结合行业标准、专家智慧、趋势分析、关联分析、风险评估，运用预警模块，进行多方位风险预警信息的发布和风险处置。

（三）数字化监测技术应用实践

在数字化监测实施过程中，我们首先需要对遗产的现状进行调研和评估，包括收集相应的遗产基础资料，从现状着手了解遗产面临的主要的风险，从而制定出详细的、针对性的监测方案。

1. 案例一：外汇交易中心大楼

外汇交易中心大楼位于上海中山东一路15号。这栋建筑建于1902年2月，具有典型的巴洛克风格，由德国倍高洋行的倍高和宾午设计，原为华俄道胜银行大楼，其东立面和北立面均为重点保护对象。它是外滩第一幢大量采用花岗岩建造的石头房子。在此之前外滩的建筑都是二三层高的体量较小的砖木结构房子。大楼的基础首次采用现场拼焊的钢桁架整体吊置于沉砂垫层的地基上，使整个大楼的荷载通过整体钢桁架均匀地传递到地基上。这幢大楼也是外滩建筑群中第一个使用白色瓷砖做外墙贴面的建筑。它也是"国内最早安装电梯""上海最早使用钢骨混凝土混合结构""上海最早使用釉面砖贴面、卫生设备的建筑"之一。建筑正立面装点着三种古典柱式——方形爱奥尼克壁柱、半圆形爱奥尼柱和塔司干双门柱，庄严而典雅。室内的装饰也十分精美。

在外汇交易中心大楼的保护过程中，发现了潜在的各种风险。由于它地处外滩沿线，地铁的运行、马路上交通设施的和周边建筑的施工，还有本体各方面的结构的问题，都对它现状的保存构成很大威胁。具体包括：近年来该房屋出现了不同程度的沉降、变形现象，大楼横向发生了极大的不均匀沉降；根据2012年的地基承载力检测结果，大楼一层轴C/1-3和轴8/B-C墙体基底压力标准值约为140 kPa，大于上海地区地基承载力标准值100 kPa；个别承重墙体出现结构性裂缝，屋面阁楼木屋架出现明显的变形，原有钢构件普遍锈蚀，外立面板材面层少量裂缝、钉孔、缺角和沾垢；大楼结构整体性较好，墙体分布基本均匀，部分竖向承重墙体不连续，采用转换梁结构体系和悬挂结构体系，钢梁和砖（石）柱之间、转换钢梁和型钢木搁栅之间以及四层木柱与主体结构之间等的连接部位较薄弱；参考《建筑抗震鉴定标准》（GB 50023—

2009),按 A 类建筑评估大楼抗震构造,其未设混凝土圈梁、转换结构体系和悬挂结构体系抗震不利及连接节点薄弱等三项不满足 A 类建筑抗震要求。

我们从它的潜在主要风险着手,制定了相应的监测方案,针对每一个楼层,包括建筑周边可能面临的一些风险因素,通过设置了智能感知设备,建立了一个综合性、立体监测体系。纳入监测体系的主要指标包括建筑整体沉降、局部位移、结构应力变化、火灾、微环境、大环境、渗水、白蚁等方面的内容。监测系统构建完成后,一方面可以进行单项指标的异常预警,另一方面可以综合相关数据进行整体风险评估。不管是单项的异常预警还是综合性的风险评估,能够给文物管理单位提供及时的、预防性的决策依据。让管理单位提前感知到在文物的保护过程中,存在哪些问题或者哪些风险因素,并告知其应采取什么样的预防性或干预性措施。

系统建成运行过程中,发出过好几次有效的渗水预警、白蚁活动预警及相关结构指标异常的预警。证实了系统的有效性。

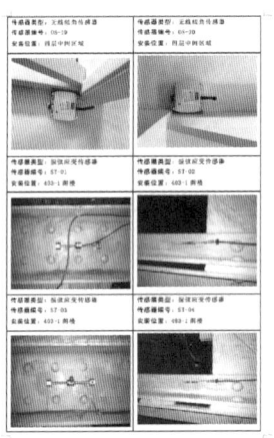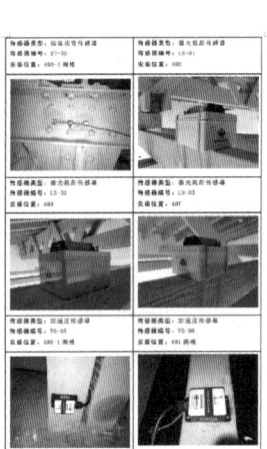

图 2　外汇交易中心大楼监测设备布设

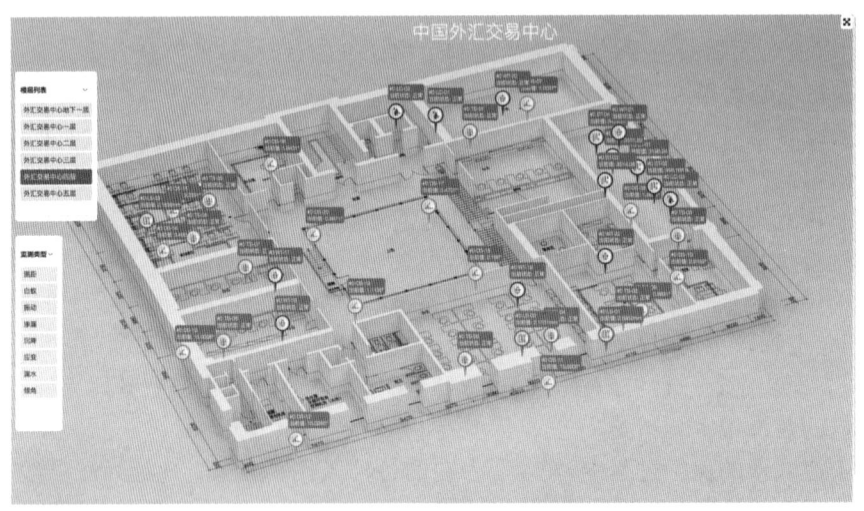

图 3　外汇交易中心大楼监测预警平台可视化界面

2. 案例二:上海市旧政府大楼

上海市旧政府大楼——绿瓦大楼为传统复兴风格的四层宫殿式建筑,外型处理变化多样,平面为左右前后对称式布置,斩假石外墙面、绿琉璃瓦单檐庑殿屋顶、红圆柱、彩绘斗拱、月台栏杆、麻石台阶、丹陛等等,整个建筑气势宏伟,美观大方。建筑原为旧上海特别市政府大楼,今为体育学院办公楼。1989 年 9 月

25日被上海市人民政府以"旧上海特别市政府"名义列入上海市第五批文物保护单位。

在监测项目实施过程中，我们首先也对它的保存现状进行了分析，全面了解它潜在的风险威胁。我们经分析认为该文物的结构风险是其目前首要关注的风险。通过前期的勘察和结构建模，对建筑相应的结构风险进行了相应的计算，从而了解到它结构层面上的载荷变化和安全方面存在的风险隐患，找到了应该重点关注的部位（图4）。

在具体实施过程中，通过采用应变计、静力水准仪、倾角仪、水浸传感器、振动传感器、温湿度传感器等智能感知设备，对大楼的结构变形、漏水、微环境、振动情况进行了全面监测，实时感知。采集的数据会通过无线网络实时汇聚到文物云平台，通过云平台的智能分析模块，对与单项数据的变化趋势进行分析预测，对于不同类型数据进行关联分析，对于整体保存状况进行综合评估。一旦发现异常变化和风险威胁，系统通过短信、微信、App、监控大屏等多种模式向相关责任人发布预警信息，并联动应急预案。

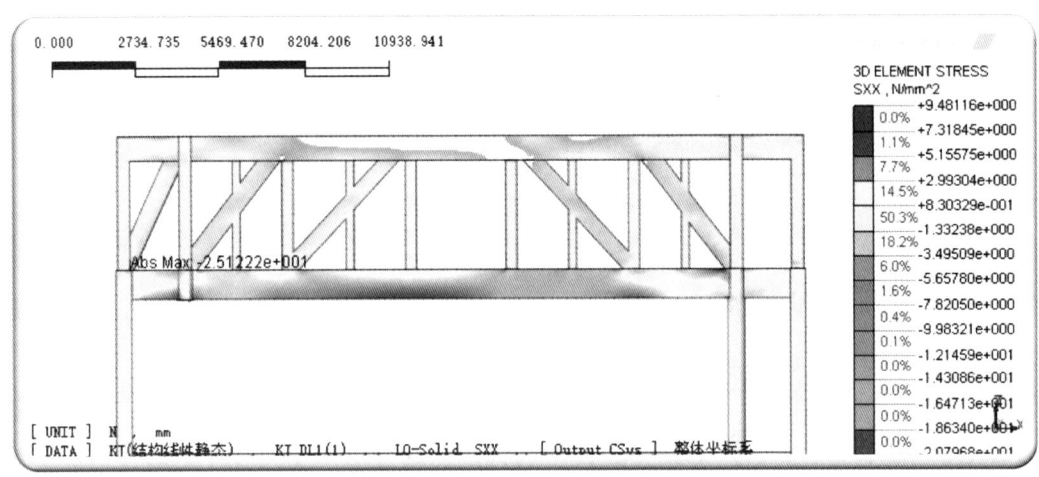

图4　绿瓦大楼结构建模分析

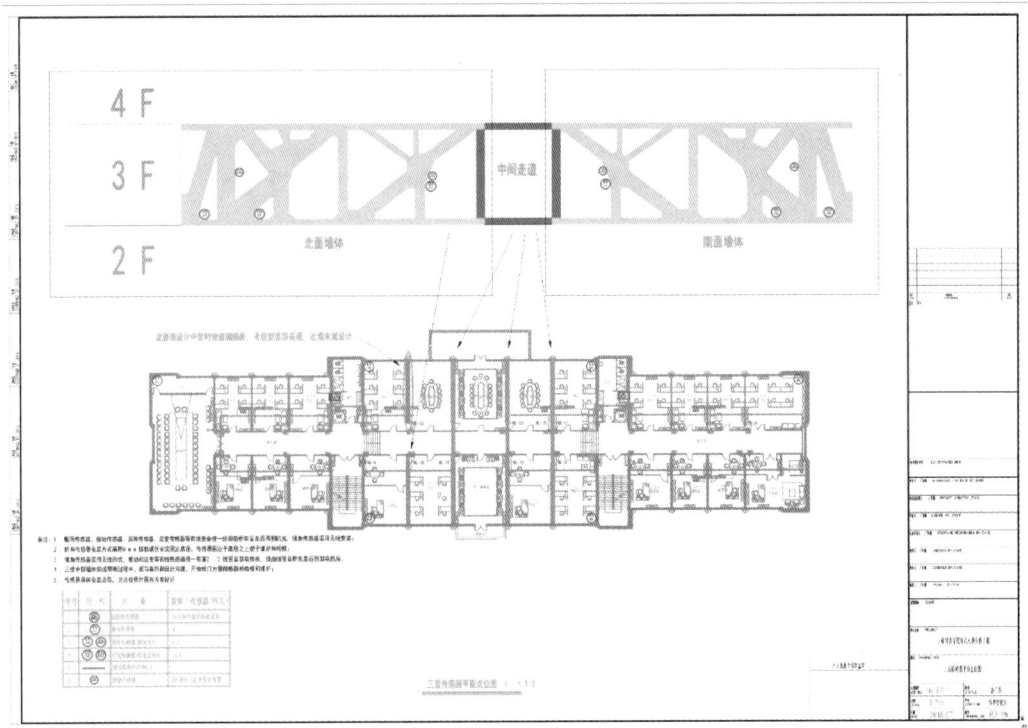

图5　绿瓦大楼监测设计方案

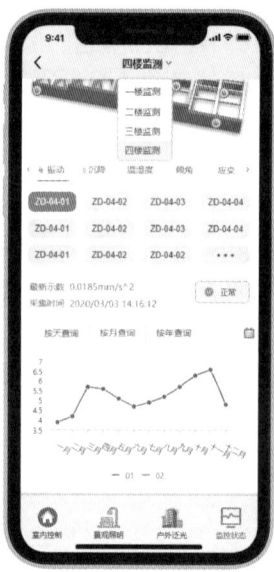

图 6　绿瓦大楼监测预警系统移动端

三、数字化监测技术的发展与展望

随着现代科技的发展和文物保护理念的提升，针对文化遗产的数字监测必将也会迎来新的发展机遇。未来，文化遗产保护领域的数字化监测技术有望朝着以下几个方向发展：

第一，数字化监测技术朝着标准化和规范化方向发展。现在国家文物局和各地方文物局都在纷纷制定相应的监测规范和标准，例如《古建筑结构安全性鉴定技术规范》、各地的地方规范，还有国家文物局颁布的《古建筑木结构维护与加固技术规范》和预防性保护相关的一些规程。未来，将出台更多针对文化遗产数字化监测的国家、地方、行业标准，指导行业的发展。

第二，完善的文化遗产风险评估体系建立。在数字化监测方面，结合现在的一些风险管理理论和风险管理的办法，应该建立一套完整的风险评估和管理体系。国家文物局要求各文物行政管理部门要及时了解文物保护的现状，进行及时的评估。但是在评估层面目前却缺乏量化的一些标准和依据。数字化监测技术的应用以及风险评估体系的构建，能够为文物保存现状的评估和风险预警提供支撑。这些潜在的应用需求又会反过来促进文化遗产风险评估体系的建立。

第三，文化遗产监测体系会朝着多样性方向发展。当前，我们针对文化遗产（包括世界遗产地、文物保护单位）的监测更多是关注文物本体（例如建筑结构方面的风险和威胁），却没有对引起它本体变化或者劣化的周边环境或者其他影响因素进行过多关注。下一步在监测方面上会朝着多样性方向发展，包括遗产的本体、自然环境、自然景观、社会环境、灾害风险、城市建设，甚至游客行为方面，都会全面纳入监测体系中。

第四，文化遗产数字化监测技术会朝着智库化的方向发展。现在很多世界文化遗产、文物保护单位都陆续建立了监测系统，但是在监测系统建设完成后，对数据怎么应用，通过数据怎么给遗产的管理、遗产的安全提供什么样的决策依据，却缺乏后续的支撑。很多单位完成监测系统建设后，由于没有相应的专家体系的支撑，对于采集的数据到底能够反映什么样的风险问题以及如何进行干预和应对，未能形成闭环。因此，文化遗产数字化监测技术未来的一个发展方向，应该是建立完整的专家智库体系，为监测、分析、应急处置提供支撑。

第五，文化遗产数字化监测技术更趋智能化。随着人工智能技术的发展，为监测体系的智能化也提供了很好的支撑。在具体的应用上面，包括人工智能语音语义识别技术、人工智能图像视频识别技术、人工智能大数据分析技术和智能化感知技术等的广泛应用。这些技术为监测体系朝智能化方向发展提供了很好的支撑。

第六，文化遗产数字化监测设备实现跨越式发展。5G时代将能够给监测设备的发展提供很好的通信支撑。加上其他如电子技术、机械技术、材料技术等的发展，智能感知设备将在低功耗、高稳定性、高可靠性、高适应性、高寿命、轻型化、小型化、远距离传输、智能化方面都会取得更大的发展。而随着监测设备的发展和技术提升，监测设备的品类将日趋丰富，将能更加便捷地获取各种在遗产保护过程中对文化遗产产生威胁的直观量化指标数据。

第七，新技术将得到广泛性、综合性应用。拥抱新技术可以加速文化遗产数字化监测行业的发展。比如物联网技术方面，已经从传统的物联网技术（IoT）过渡到人工智能物联网技术（AIoT）。结合AI技术、5G技术、机器人技术、卫星技术、大数据和图像技术，将能够加速文化遗产数字化监测行业的发展，也为文化遗产的风险评估、风险管控提供很好的技术支撑。

第八，文化遗产数字化监测朝集成化、多级化管理发展。当前的文化遗产的监测管理更多的是单个的、孤立的模式，各自为政，未能形成数据共享和大数据效应。未来的发展趋势，会把各监测系统横向的、纵向的打通，解决信息孤岛问题，实现数据共享，实现大数据的价值效应，实现国家、省级、市级、区县级、文物保护单位多个层级的集成管理模式，实现全产业链、全价值链、全要素的融合。

第九，文化遗产数字化监测物联网服务实现平台化。未来，在物联网平台发展方向上将更多的是以物联网服务平台（PaaS）的模式来提供服务。一些大型平台商如阿里巴巴、华为等正在构建各自的物联网服务总平台，然后将各个行业的物联网应用接入平台，后续通过各自行业的专家或者行业的相关人员进行数据分析，实现物联网的云服务模式。

城市建设中的本地声音与公众参与
——以法国的小城市为例

The Local Politician and Participative Democracy in Urban Project, in Small French Cities

西格罗尼·查尔斯　博士
法国建筑师
Dr. Ségolène Charles
French Architect

  法国领土的特点是社区分散,小城市数量众多,人口密度低。通过去中心化的改革,中小城市的地方政治家占据了中心位置,所以他们不得不拥有许多技能,如城市规划。因此,城市项目是由一个复杂的参与者网络组成的,不同参与者有着不同的期望和作用。自 2000 年以来,这些技能都变得专业化和多元化,城市项目也越来越倾向于公民参与:在法国当地政治环境下,公民参与正成为一条不可避免的道路。"公众参与市场"不断扩大。同样,"参与专家"的数量也在增加:从通信办公室到设计师或建筑和城市设计者。数字媒体是公众参与中"创新"的关键。本文的案例是一个法国西部小城市的城市规划和公民参与任务。作为法国建筑与城市设计者,我们旨在分析有公众参与的农村环境中城市项目的过程,也旨在阐明部分地方政治家代表合同方时的此过程。

  My presentation today is going to focus more on public participation than heritage. But we can, in a way, apply to heritage projects.

  I'm an architect and urban designer. I work half time as an architect in an architecture and urban design office named Atelier du Lieu, and worked part-time as a last year Ph. D. student with two research laboratories, Paris-la-Villette School of Architecture and Sorbonne University. My research is based on the collaboration between actors and researchers.

  It's an operational questioning: the difficulties in the urban project appear when the politician was absent from the debate and not playing his role of the regulator by re-placing the project and our intervention in its context, said by Nolwenn Dulieu, manager of Atelier du Lieu.

  And it's a research questioning as well. Because we feel that in France researches on public participation mainly focus on the citizens and there are not so many researches on the local politician, particularly into rural context.

  I'll present a case to the analysis. Our office is an architecture and urban design office specialized in citizen participation projects. If you use the typology of French designers and toward public participation, we have first of all a reluctance, which is totally against participation. We have the strategists who see participation as a way of winning projects. And we have the pragmatists who see public participation as a way of enriching the projects. And we have activists who see participation as a way to empower people. Our office has a more pragmatist and activist position towards urban projects and public participation. It's been the witness of the growth of citizen participation in France in post May 1968 events in

1996. Today there was a new deal of co-constructing architecture and urban project in France. Then it went down and went up again with the environmental crisis.

In the beginning of 2000, they had what we call in France a new deal for public participation, which there is a development of the public market, an increasing number of laws in favor of public participation. More and more experts developing from diverse domains participated, from architects to designers to urban planners, even communication offices. And we see that in that politician crisis, the local French politician loses legitimacy. But what we see in France is that it has citizen who wants to influence the way of living.

So there are not only counter-proposals to urban projects, heritage projects and architecture projects, but also an increase in bottom-up initiatives. Today the thing is that public participation is so developed that it is kind of industrialized, having methods or proposed by designer in kits. Innovation today in France in public participation means digitalization and tools for the majority of the local politician. So what I'm going to ask today is that is digitalization the main answer to involve the inhabitants in urban or heritage projects?"

Paris has 2.1 million inhabitants. Nantes, in the west of France, has 400,240 inhabitants. And I'm going to bring you today a very small French city of 6,000 inhabitants, which is kind of quite common in France because the territory is very fragmented and made of all parishes who become this kind of small city.

So this case is that municipality who has been calling us for doing an urban project. And we say yes, but you have to involve the inhabitants. The goal of this mission was to imagine the city center of tomorrow. In this little city, the population is still increasing, but there have been conflicts for 15 years in the municipality around the development plan of this inner city. Every five years, the mayor changes. There is no coherence in the city center. There is no development plan to enhance and preserve heritage. The new mayor in 2014 wants to continue and conclude the previous plan development with the architect from our office's proposition to corporate with inhabitants.

The first diagnosis we've been working on was identity and dreaming workshop. We asked inhabitants what they wanted to do for the city center. They said a green city, a secure public space where children can play far away from the cars and identity of the inner city by reinforcing local shops using the ground floor. They wanted to preserve the existing architecture, enhance old and beautiful houses and give more space to the church for the court. Because historically the church was kind of stuck between buildings. So we did this diagnosis and we proposed several scenarios to the citizens.

We first went on an urban stroll, walking around the city and showing our first proposition. We did then two site plan workshops each time we've been adjusting the development plan little by little. In the end when the development plan was quite fixed, we said that maybe we had to adjust in very small details and sectors. So we did on-site experimentation. That's the first phase of our mission.

We've been working with the inhabitants on different sectors who had needed to be adjusted. For example, site number two was a car street before. The experimentation was to pedestrianize it for 2 months and see how we were going to go. Site number one was a nice square near the church but has no practices in the court in the square. They were just like nobody was going to disappear even though there was a very nice potential.

Because it's a very small city and we are in a sustainable way of practicing urban planning, we've been trying to use existing materials and to experiment and draw on site with removable painting. So we went to the technical services with the mayor, with inhabitants. And we've been seeing how much we could use. And then for two months, there was experimentation that we asked inhabitants their opinions about this new pedestrianized street of this new square. We've been like putting a little thing to develop practices and through a paper and digital survey, we've been asking for the opinions. And actually we had kind of a petition because the people who were using the street didn't want one of those streets getting pedestrianized. So the red line you see on the picture had been adjusted because of the experimentation.

In terms of analysis, this is a very interesting mission. If you use the Ladder of Public Participation, which has been created by the American sociologists who have been developing the French context in 2011, we can say you have information from very below till codecision, where citizens are associated with the decisions.

Here we can say that we have been doing co-production. Citizens are not only invited to discuss the issues or the proposition made by designers. They are also involved in the research of solutions for the projects.

But we still face difficulties. First, the diagnosis phase has been done without the population's opinion. During the scenarios phase, many of the workshops which should be planned initially with the population were postponed by the city. Because of this last-minute change of date, many of the inhabitants could not take part in the planning workshop.

During the experimentation phase, our office had to do many things which were not included in the initial budget: communication graphic, documents to help the city build the experiments. And we had this strong petition not to pedestrianize streets.

We used to understand the difficulties we're going to face today. The indicator is used to evaluate the degree of participation. They are the results of 15 years of research on public participation in France. First, you have your left argumentation on how the project was presented an argument in front of everyone. We had exhibition panel installed in the public space to inform day after day what the decision was, why we chose this solution over the other. In terms of inclusion, we tried to create a citizen panel to be as more representative as we could and we've been using different discussion mediums to interest and to mobilize people who cannot read or understand the plan properly. In terms of transparency, we had reports done by every workshop put on the website, so every decision was being publicized into the public space.

The main difficulties were continuity and articulation. In terms of continuity, the date initially planned were postponed after we left this small city. The city did not continue to work with inhabitants. And in terms of articulation, the occupation is how the participatory plan is articulated to the project. We see it was not properly articulated. For example, the urban stroll aiming at inventorying the urban situation was organized after the diagnosis was done.

So we could think maybe there was a lack of choices on methods. But actuallys, the research shows that is more about actors' system, unofficial interest putting pressure on the urban project. We had the municipality and the architecture office, which are working on the official project. But actually what we did not realize for the first time is that powerful landlords who did not want any development on the plan were putting pressure on the municipality. Private and individual interests were confronted. But in official decision processes like former local politicians, former economic actors, or even the parish, what the public participation permitted is to contribute to stabilizing a more transparent decision-making system. One of the worst things we're done because we try to be transparent argumentation decision-making was that the exteriors pressure could not influence that much on the urban project decision. Our research shows that the mayor in those small French cities is a key person for the new urban project system.

So in terms of conclusion, what I want to say today is: who governs? Because in urban or architecture or heritage project with public participation is strongly linked to the decision. In the French context, we see the new offices specialized in public participation are up for it as well as the citizens. And innovation in French public participation process is often understood as digitalization.

Designers have the ability to contribute to public participation in urban and architecture projects. They understand the urban and architecture issues, and they can be the relevant facilitators between the politician and inhabitants.

So, talking about participation in architecture and urban project is talking about decision-making. Who governs? Who arbitrates the decision? For what purpose?

It's very important to integrate tools as a metho to guarantee transparency, argumentation, and inclusion. The use of digitalization is complementary.

But what appears to be fundamental in the French context in urban and architectural projects is understanding the management process. It's fundamental to guarantee the participation process in urban or heritage projects, whereas the local politician of a small city is willing to use public participation. He needs to be accompanied. Public participation in a French context supposes raising new issues for French architects or designers, which are beyond their initial design competences.

中国文化遗产数字化

The Digitization of Cultural Heritage in China

贺艳
北京清城睿现数字科技研究院院长
Ms. He Yan
Dean of Beijing Qingcheng Ruixian Digital Technology Research Institute Co., Ltd.

非常高兴能跟大家分享这个话题,这个话题非常呼应论坛主旨。我们更加关注中国文化遗产数字化在新应用、新场景和新产业的发展。从我的观察来看,文化遗产数字化的上半场集中在行业应用方向上,更多的是技术服务。一方面是文化遗产的管理机构需要更多的新技术来解决其在研究和管理中存在的问题;另一方面是测绘技术,包括科技保护,很多跨界的成熟技术被应用到文化产业领域,帮助解决文化遗产的相关问题。

文化遗产具有某些独特属性,诸如真实性和脆弱性等,但这也给数字技术和文化遗产的结合应用提供了很好的界面。因为数字技术具有的可逆性和非接触化等都非常有助于解决与文化遗产相关的问题。中国的文化遗产数字化技术发展水平,与世界上的同行们基本同步,主要应用于文化遗产数字化的记录、阐释、应用,以及部分消失遗产的数字重建。

这几方面在中国都有非常多的实践案例,其中数字敦煌、数字故宫和数字圆明园是最典型的综合应用案例。我们所用的技术与国际同步,包括测量测绘技术和输出的产品。例如,云冈石窟研究院对云冈石窟进行了完整的数字建模、数字点云的测量,并将数字监测应用到记录石窟的风化过程之中,有效地改进了文化遗产保护的工作精度。数字勘察等技术还被运用到了山西双林寺。诸如采用多光谱的技术对部分浅藏壁画的研究,有效提升了文化遗产保护的科技化程度。中国传统村落数字博物馆也是基于航拍建模的,然后基于互联网应用,把大量的传统村落进行了数字化的记录并在网络上传播。

下面基于这些技术点的应用,再举几个重要的案例。如数字敦煌,历时数十年。最初,工作人员对石窟类的脆弱遗产进行了监测,开始数字化的记录和采集。后来,敦煌研究院完成了大量在洞窟内的采集工作,形成了一些高清影像。近年来,他们也开始把一些数字影像用于展示和分享。如敦煌莫高窟前面的数字球幕电影,包含很多小展览,有很多基于VR的应用,让大家可以远程感受敦煌石窟。而且用这种方式可以有效减缓人们大量进入石窟对壁画造成破坏。敦煌将AR技术应用于移动展览,可以把壁画上的部分静态画面给予动态的表达,让人们更好地去理解佛教故事所潜藏的内涵。

类似的还有数字故宫。故宫也是中国的重要文化遗产,与石窟相比体量更大,以建筑为主体。数字故宫工作也始于十几年前,工作人员对故宫的可移动文物和古建筑进行了一系列的数字化采集。在此过程中进行了大量的测量、测绘、建模工作,包括精准的颜色匹配,这是对现存记录尽可能贴近真实的技术处理。同时,这几年也走向一些最新的应用。比如在养心殿的展览中运用VR技术、环幕影院、数字触摸屏等方式,让大家可以感受到故宫曾经的使用场景和辉煌状态,而不是现在的老旧状态。工作人员还开发了很多关于故宫内涵的App,比如对12美人图进行了深入阐释,包括对其所藏的文物等。这些App进入了很多普通观众的日常生活之中,让他们可以用很亲近的方式去接触故宫里的大量文化,其中包含针对儿童的"卡通皇帝的一天"等。

再如数字圆明园。与前面几个案例不同的是,圆明园是一个已经消失了的遗产。法国作家维克多·雨果把圆明园等同于希腊的雅典卫城。在中国人的心目中,对圆明园的重建等同于欧洲人对古罗马的重建,一直抱有很高的热情。但对于这样一个废墟,不可能做到原址复建,这样也不符合文化遗产保护的原则,那么数字重建就成为解决困难的一个出发点。这项工作最早从1930年代的中国营造学社开始,那时清华大学就开始介入到整个研究之中,历经几代人,他们完成了海量的数据采集和数字建模工作。对残存的遗址,也运用数字测绘技术进行了详实地记录。同时基于对历史文化遗产的研究,对其残存构件,进行了虚拟归案的研究,不但完成了数字模型,还直接服务到了遗产地的修复之中。

另外,根据相关的档案。如,当时圆明园的西洋楼用的是法国的一套机械水利系统,所以工作人员就查到了当时法国的相关图纸,完成了一整套机械系统的复原。同时结合探地雷达等技术,探清了圆明园没有进行考古发掘的区域,明确了地下铜水管等的位置。除对遗存和档案的研究之外,更主要的是把遗存信息、档案信息,包括中国传统古建筑的一些营建方法结合到一起,去重新构建、reconstruction它原来的样貌。

在完成设计之后,所有的数字模型被精准地按照图纸进行了完整地复建。可以把它理解为我们是在数字世界里面构建了一个一模一样的建筑。所有的东西都匹配图纸,而不是臆想的、预测的结果。包括其中假山的堆叠,也是将一块一块的假山石堆在一起。瓷器及其他家具,也都是完整地按照实物建模。还对残存的构件建立了相关的数据库,我们可以在里面检索到每一个现存构件的相关信息。

这是最后完成的。右边是整个考古遗址的现状,左边是其历史样貌。在这个虚拟现实系统里,它可以不同角度地同时旋转,观察它不同时期的完整考古遗址和历史场景的对比。我觉得非常重要的一点是,我们完成的所有数字模型,最后都会给出准确表达。在这个图上,红色的部分是完全基于遗存和实物所存留的。蓝色部分是通过实物复原的。比如说它是中轴对称结构的,只要左边还存在,右边就可以复制。还有一些是依据老照片和铜版画构建的。我们会随着它所依据的准确度的级别变化进行打分。同时,用数字模型的方式记录,也有助于在找到更充分的资料之后去进行修正。这个原则是完整匹配文化遗产所要求的真实性和准确性原则的。

这是完成之后的遗址盛景呈现,包括对其室内的数字还原。这是最后要完成的工作,至今已经10年了,但只完成了2/3。这一系列工作也取得了相关的发明专利和软件著作权。整个圆明园的数字资产包现在估值是5 000万元,被中国版权保护中心授予了中国10大著作权人之一的称号。其数字模型的构建,因为是一个完整的工作流程,是我们在工作中所建立的一整套的科学方法,包括对其准确性的坚持,所以最终形成的数字模型具有相当高的价值。结项时,国家科技部给了非常高的评价,认为这个方法为解决中国多达33万处的古遗址、古墓葬开辟了一条全新的途径。同时我们也得到了国际同行们的认可。希腊古奥林匹亚遗址(奥运会的起源地)邀请我们团队把数字圆明园的范式带到希腊,去协助他们完成数字奥林匹亚的复原。

刚才讲到的其实还只是科研,下面要讲产业应用。我们要将完成的部分文化遗产的数字化记录、保存、重建之后所形成的数字资产,跨界推向市场,走到人民中去,通过文化赋能去形成更多文化产品。这些文化产品的最终对象是广大消费者和公众。这可以打破文化遗产行业的市场容量壁垒,获得更广阔的未来。这是一个大的背景形势。现在,文化已成为越来越重要的影响因子,而且数字创意经济本身就是一个国际新兴战略产业,这两者就是一个政治意义和经济方面的结合,会带来非常广阔的市场。

大家可以看到,面积巨大的遗址区和众多的文化遗产,虽然很宝贵,但在实际生活中或多或少地会让地方政府官员感到有些头疼,会成为珍贵的包袱。但同时,基于历史传承和科技的跨界融合创新,给我们带来了文化消费的升级产品。这些新型产品可以很好地被运用到遗址地中,而不会对遗址造成破坏。我们不是要通过重建等方式去解决文化遗产的保存和利用问题,而是要加入新产品,带来新应用。所以,我提出我们认为很重要的一个观点:基于文化遗产去构建城市新型消费场景和商业模式,是未来的一个重要发展方向。大家试想,如果在圆明园350公顷的园区里面,活跃着十几款应用、展厅,以及大量的文创产品,其背后带来的是多少产业机会?多少家企业会在里面获得生存空间?所以我们提出,以文化遗产本身的文化赋能为出发点,所带动的后端产业正是基于新消费和新场景,可以带来新产业和新业态。

综上所述,文化遗产数字化可以有效地促进科学研究,对考古文博工作产生激励,实现数字测绘、信息管理，因为我们所有数据的根本来源来自对遗址的精准解读。其最终的数字创意、数字制造及文化艺术等相关部分，都可以融合进来，形成一个真正具有感染力的产品。当其形成新的消费场景后，基于人工智能、数据服务的大量后端应用，都可以加入。整个产业化链条的形成，就是文化遗产数字化的下半场。我们已经非常惊喜地看到，有很多跨界的合作伙伴已经开始关注这一领域，并做出了有效尝试。比如说腾讯、英特尔。这也是和基金会的合作，用机械手结合皮影戏。百度也做了兵马俑的一些 AR 场景应用。这都是非常专业的国际、国内著名企业，他们已经开始介入这一领域。

同时我们也可以发现，虚拟现实（VR）、增强现实（AR）、混合现实（MR）、感映现实（ER）、交互现实游戏（ARG）等一系列 5R 技术，可以有效应用到文化遗产之中。我们基于圆明园的实践经验梳理出了三个大的类型：第一种基于遗址地本身在园区内的运行，我们称之为"瑞游"；第二种是基于文化艺术和科技所形成的展览性、展演性产品——"瑞秀"；第三种是衍生出来的数字文创小礼物——"瑞礼"。

下面我们简单介绍一些应用。

这是一款基于遗址地增强现实的导览。它可以在原地进行历史信息的虚拟推演。你可以看到各个场景废墟对应的历史场景，包含时间转轮，就是其在不同历史时期的变化，这个产品在 App store 上获得了非常大的下载量。这是基于智能手机全员 LBS 的智能服务，提供不同的游线。这个产品在园区运行了将近 4 年，用户反馈非常好。这是青少年活动与教育结合的 ARG 游戏，在地图上不同颜色的游线，是根据其文化遗产地内涵所整理出来的不同的文化线路，孩子们通过不同的分组抽签可以获得不同的线路指引。基于 iPad 上的答题引导，基于位置的打卡服务，都需要到达每一个特殊地点，去 get 相关信息，获取得分，最终形成了一场比赛。这个产品非常受欢迎，已经服务了大概 600 名参与者。

同时，相关产品也直接进入了教育系统。如我们在圆明园的课程已经覆盖了北京最著名的几所中学——清华附中、101 中学、人大附中，等等。还有展览产品，其特点是可以脱离遗址地本身而存在，可以在遗址地内，也可以在遗址地外展览。这是一个小型展览，运用了增强现实、虚拟现实、眼镜等方式，最终获得了当时整个北京的"周末去哪儿"的推荐前端。中国园林博物馆也做了一系列基于圆明园主题挖掘的展览，包括结合展陈布景去完成一些青少年的教育活动。当时，青少年活动站 200 人的名额一天就售罄了。还有这种全沉浸式展厅，这家 2017 年开馆，到目前为止已经接待了 16 万以上的观众。它通过全身心的方式去感受当时圆明园的园林盛景，吸引了大量集体组团参与，在节假日更是所有人都席地而坐的满场状态。

还有更高配的 360 度全沉浸式秀场。这是我们 2018 年 12 月在北京开办的秀场，是一个超尺度的全域 360 度环。全程建设的环境让人有一个更好的代入感，同时它还运用了非常多的艺术化手法，包括情感的、戏剧化的表达，将一个非常科学的原始素材进行了非常艺术化的表现，包括情感的调动。很多观众在现场会观看三四遍，而且很多人看完出来就是流着眼泪，当时也让我们非常受鼓舞。在 17 天里，这个 1 000 平方米的展厅空间接待了来自 15 个省市自治区、超过 2 万的观众。人们在网上看到新闻后，坐着火车、飞机前来看展，在现场留下了 2 215 条留言。让我们非常感动的是，包括孩子们在内，都是跪着或站着写。我们觉得他们读懂了我们，或者说他们的反馈让我们觉得自己的努力非常值得。他们感觉到，科技让一切成为可能。孩子们很喜欢他们看到的文化和科技，更重要的是他们都获得了文化自信，觉得我们曾经的历史是如此美好，今天的科技是如此强大，这一点让我们感到文化遗产数字化产品未来可期。

就对圆明园的理解来看，在看展览之前，大部分人觉得它是一片废墟。看完展览之后，感到自豪的百分比提高了 40%；对文化遗产的理解，也在短短一两个小时的参观之后有了极大提升。这充分说明这种方式对于文化遗产内涵价值的阐释是非常有帮助的。这是当时一条新华社当天就过了百万的转发，包括公众们的评价，纷纷说获得了新的认知。在这场展览之后，北京市政协收到大量的代表提案，将其服务于城市建设。其中，海淀区已经决定要建设三山五园、数字展、艺术展示中心。新首钢的高端产业区也要在冬奥广场（也就是 2022 北京冬奥组委的旁边），建设一个瑞国际创意馆，将这些新的应用场景落地，包括让我们去做光影夜宴之类的更加跨界的合作。

在整个后端的三个正在运行的新项目之中，我们的产业模式和合作模式更加宽广。我们集成了国际软硬件的一个头部企业,来共同完成这些场馆的建设,包括最新的人脸识别AR云、松下、京东方、阿里、商汤科技等一线企业,提供他们的技术,共同来服务于整个应用场景的建设,同时去拓展更广阔的产业化边界。

在拥有流量之后,就会产生大量文创消费的空间,有各种各样的授权方式。最后,我给国际专家和国内嘉宾们推介我们CIPA2021的一个会议。菲利浦先生应该很了解,CIPA也是ICOMOS下属的一个专业委员会,我也是CIPA的国际执委。CIPA2021的全球双年会将在北京举行,我们这次探讨的议题是Great Learning and Digital Emotion,也就是我们要把更多的智慧学习服务于文化的表达。

综上,我演讲的主旨是文化和科技需要深度融合,最终形成的是能够真正提供给公众、打动人心的产品。

美国的遗产保护与公众参与

Cultural Heritage Conservation and Public Participation in the United States of America

詹姆斯·瑞普 教授
ICOMOS 法律、管理与财经问题委员会秘书长
美国佐治亚大学教授

Prof. James Reap
Secretary General, ICOMOS International Committee on Legal, Administrative & Financial Issues
Professor, University of Georgia

本文将简要概述公众参与美国历史建筑和历史街区的规划和登录过程,并以佐治亚州为例。它将从州、区域和地方的角度集中讨论这种参与的法律和实际方面。本文还将讨论在信息时代发展起来的较新的公众参与工作、工具和技术。

This paper provides a brief overview of public participation in the planning and listing processes for historic properties and districts in the United States with particular examples from the State of Georgia.[1] It will focus on both the legal and practical aspects of this participation from a statewide, regional and local perspective. Finally, examples will highlight newer public participation efforts that have developed in the information age.

Public participation is difficult to define because of the many forms it takes. Viewed broadly, it can involve such activities as political party participation, lobbying and protest, public advocacy, solicitation of comments, review and reaction, interest group involvement, and service on advisory or review boards. Even litigation has been suggested as an example of public participation.[2] We will primarily examine administrative agency decisionmaking but also look briefly at some other types of participation.

Direct public participation in administrative agency decisionmaking seems to reflect the strains of individualism and political egalitarianism that run deep in the American character.[3] During the past 70 years, public participation has achieved something of a venerated status in the United States.[4] This was not always so. At the turn of the twentieth century, when public administration began to develop into a

---

[1] The State of Georgia was established in 1733 as a colony of Great Britain. It achieved its independence during the American Revolution and was one of the 13 original states to become part of the United States of America. Its landmass comprises 59,441 square miles, making it the largest state east of the Mississippi River. Its population of over 10.5 million makes it the eighth largest US state by population. The state is subdivided into 159 counties, each with its own local government.

[2] Nancy Perkins Spyke, *Public Participation in Environmental Decisionmaking at the New Millennium: Structuring New Spheres of Public Influence*, Boston College Environmental Affairs Law Review, 26(2): 1999, 263-267.

[3] Jerry L. Mashaw, Due Process in the Administrative State at 23 (1985).

[4] Jim Rossi, *Participation Run Amok*, Northwestern University Law Review 1997, 92: 174. These concepts are not unique to the United States. ICOMOS has asserted that cultural heritage right includes the right to participate in decisions affecting heritage and the cultural values it embodies. *Declaration of ICOMOS Marking the 50th Anniversary of the Universal Declaration of Human Rights* (Stockholm, 1998).

distinct field, its theorists suggested that administration be left to professional administrators. The public's role, in this view, should be confined to voting in elections and lobbying elected policymakers. Under this scenario, the public would elect officials who would set policy through legislation and provide only general oversight of professional administrators. This would enable administrators to exercise "neutral competence" insulated from the direct interference of party politics. The oversight role was not to be shared with the general public. ①

By the 1960s public administrators were viewed as servants of the "elite", neither neutral nor competent, and out of touch with the public. As the federal government tried to grapple with the increasing complexity of modern life, a proliferation of new programs came into being. The line between policy-making and administration became difficult to draw. Congress sought the advice of administrators in developing policy, which was then filtered through federal, state and local bureaucracies before being implemented in the community. Problems were so complex that Congress could not anticipate all of the policy implications, and administrators were left to fill in the blanks. That complexity, along with the power of technical expertise and specialized knowledge, tended to prevent effective oversight of administrators by elected officials. Increased public participation in both the planning and implementation of public programs was seen as a solution to this problem by enabling citizens to influence policies as they were being developed and implemented. This approach had the additional benefit of giving voice to previously neglected constituencies. ② In addition to informing decision-makers, public participation was seen as a way to educate citizens on policy issues and contribute to the understanding of different viewpoints by different segments of the public. Ideally, it also could help form consensus on issues and even produce better citizens by inspiring civic responsibility. ③

There are also a number of drawbacks to increased public participation. It is often non-representative. Those who choose to participate are frequently not a cross-section of the public in terms of income or education and generally represent pre-existing organized groups which advocate special interests. Their involvement may not serve the broader public interest. Citizens who do not understand scientific or professional quality standards also may challenge them. Public participation can increase the cost of programs and the time necessary to implement them as more individuals and groups try for a piece of the action. Innovation, too, can become a casualty to veto or compromise when many parties with divergent interests are involved. ④

Whatever the positives and negatives of public participation, it has become a regular part of the planning and designation processes in the preservation field and appears to be here to stay. The extent to which it is used depends upon the legal and regulatory requirements of each program and the administrator's determination of its usefulness in a particular case. ⑤There are different approaches to the use of public participation in formal agency decisionmaking, including those where the administrator

1. makes the decision alone (no participation);

---

① John Clayton Thomas, Public Participation in Public Decisions at 16 (1995). President Woodrow Wilson asserted that "Directly exercised in the oversight of the daily details and in the choice of the daily means of government, public criticism is, of course, a clumsy nuisance." *The Study of Administration*, Political Science Quarterly, 1887, 2(2): 210.

② See id. See also Nancy Perkins Spyke, *supra* note 2 at 269.

③ Rossi, *supra* note 4, at 187-188.

④ See Thomas, *supra*, at 25-29. See also Spyke, *supra* note 2, at 273.

⑤ Thomas suggests that where the need for high-quality decisions is greater (e.g. consistency with standards, legislative mandates), there is less reason to involve the public. Where the need for public acceptance of a decision is high, there is an increased need for public involvement. Where both are significant, a balance must be struck. See id. at 36.

2. solicits ideas and suggestions from different segments or groups of the public and makes a decision that may or may not reflect group influence;①

3. solicits ideas and suggestions from the public assembled as a single group (e. g. public hearing②) and makes a decision reflecting group influence; or

4. attempts to reach an agreement on an issue with an assembled public. ③

Assuming one accepts that public participation on a particular issue is desirable (or required), securing an acceptable level of participation or an adequate cross-section of the public can be a challenge. Most citizens choose not to become involved in most issues. Individuals tend to be involved only when they are affected directly, either financially or in an area where they have strong feelings. ④ Even where they are directly affected, many individuals prefer that their interests be represented by groups such as, in the preservation context, business groups, neighborhood associations, churches, non-profits, and professional groups. Administrators are put in the position of brokers or harmonizers among the different interests while seeking to include input from underrepresented groups and furthering the general public interest. This interest group model is probably the dominant model of administrative action in the United States today. ⑤

In the balance of this paper, I will explore the issue of public participation in the State of Georgia. To a large extent, Georgia is typical of other states, although there are differences among states in the federal system. Even in programs such as the National Register of Historic Places, there is some flexibility in how states involve the public.

One way governments can enable public participation is "passive"—ensuring that its records, and meetings of its officials, both elected representatives and administrators, are open to the public. On the federal level the *Freedom of Information Act*⑥ and the later *Sunshine Act*,⑦ passed following the Watergate scandal during the Nixon Administration, guaranteed access to government documents and processes.

Georgia has two significant pieces of legislation which reflect the "passive" approach to public participation, the *Open Meetings Act*⑧ and *Open Records Act*.⑨ The *Open Meetings Act* is designed to ensure the people's business is not conducted behind closed doors, and the public has a written record of

---

① An example of the second approach is the review and comment mechanism used by many public agencies. It involves developing a proposal internally, presenting it to the public and soliciting comments, revising the proposal (or not), and publishing the final version. While capable of producing meaningful public input, the process is often characterized as "decide, announce, and defend," a cliché for the failure of administrators to truly take into account the public's views. John S. Applegate, *Beyond the Usual Suspects: The Use of Citizens Advisory Boards in Environmental Decisionmaking*, Indiana Law Journal, 1998, 73(3): 904. A number of techniques can be employed to improve the effectiveness of this approach in achieving broad-based participation including public surveys, workshops and advisory boards or review panels.

② *Id.* at 904. Applegate asserts an inverse relationship between the hearing's size and its communicative effectiveness. Well-attended meetings occur in response to controversial issues and are subject to "venting" and defensiveness. Smaller hearings, where real dialog can occur, are generally routine meetings attended by "regulars".

③ Thomas, supra, pp. 40-41.

④ Thomas, supra, p. 56.

⑤ Applegate, supra, pp. 906-908.

⑥ 5 U. S. C. § 552.

⑦ The declared purpose of the act is to increase public oversight of federal agencies, improving the decisionmaking processes "while protecting the rights of individuals and the ability of the Government to carry out its responsibilities." Pub. L. 94-409, § 2, 90 Stat. 1241 (1976).

⑧ O. C. G. A. § 50-14-1 to § 50-14-6.

⑨ O. C. G. A. § 50-18-70 to § 80-18-77.

action taken at the meeting. ①The law was later strengthened by adding the requirement that the agenda of public meetings be published up to two weeks in advance to let citizens know what will be discussed or acted upon. ②Violations of the law are grounds for a court to void any actions taken at the meeting and award costs and attorney fees to the complaining parties. Officials shown to have willfully violated the law face more than a lawsuit, they can be criminally charged and forced to answer for their action in court. ③Georgia's public administrators must also be as open with their records as they are with their meetings. The *Open Records Act* requires public officials to produce records or documents within three business days of receiving a request to review or copy them. If a technical problem prevents meeting this deadline, they must state in writing when they will be produced or spell out why the particular records are exempt. (In fact, very few documents, such as medical records, are protected from disclosure.) While these legislative provisions do not guarantee citizens', input into governmental decisionmaking, they do provide the public access to information about what their government is doing.

Another "passive" approach provided by government is the protection afforded those individuals who do actively participate from being targets of "strategic lawsuits against public participation" ("SLAPPs"). These suits are brought for the purpose of silencing citizens who are exercising their constitutional rights to participate in public discussions, such as by opposing the plans of a land developer or urging the designation of a property as a landmark. The suit may lack merit but can succeed in eliminating the opposition of individuals who cannot afford to defend themselves in court. ④ Half of the states have enacted legislation to discourage SLAPP suits, including Georgia. ⑤If a court determines that a lawsuit has been filed for an improper purpose, such as to suppress the right to free speech or petition government, to harass, to cause unnecessary delay or increased costs, a court can dismiss the suit and award the injured party costs, including attorney's fees. ⑥

Turning to more "active" means of facilitating public participation, I will examine first the opportunities offered in the planning arena. This is the area in which citizens can have a substantial and long-range impact on preservation programs.

As one of the conditions for state participation in the federal preservation program, the *National Historic Preservation Act* (*NHPA*) mandates the provision of "adequate public participation."⑦In addition, each State Historic Preservation Officer (SHPO) is required to "prepare and implement a comprehensive statewide historic preservation plan"⑧. Regulations issued by the National Park Service pursuant

---

① The law provides that meetings of every public agency (or any special or standing committees thereof) must be open whenever there is a gathering of a quorum of members pursuant to a schedule, call or notice, at a designated time and place, at which official business or policy is discussed or presented or action taken. O. C. G. A. § 50-14-1. Meetings can be closed only under very limited circumstances. Those that might be encountered by preservationists include discussions of future real estate acquisitions or considering personnel actions involving a public employee. O. C. G. A. § 50-14-3.

② O. C. G. A. § 50-14-1(e).

③ O. C. G. A. § 50-14-6.

④ The U. S. Supreme Court has stated, "A lawsuit no doubt may be used… as a powerful instrument of coercion or retaliation… Regardless of how unmeritorious the… suit is, the [target] will most likely have to retain counsel and incur substantial legal expenses to defend against it." *Bill Johnson's Restaurants v. NLRB*, 461 U. S. 731, 740-741 (1983).

⑤ Daniel A. Kent and Douglas M. Isenberg, *Georgia's New Anti-SLAPP Statute: Protecting the Right of Free Speech Against Meritless Claims*, Georgia Bar Journal, 1996: 26-28.

⑥ O. C. G. A. § 9-11-11.1.

⑦ Title I, Section 101(b)(1)(C), codified at 16 U. S. C. 470a (current version at 54 U. S. C. § 302301).

⑧ *Id.*, at Section 101(b)(3)(C). Information on the Historic Preservation Planning Program of the National Park Service can be found at https://www.nps.gov/preservation-planning/. Electronic copies of full plans or plan profiles for all states and territories can be found on this site.

to *NHPA* clarify what the planning process entails.① The Park Service has also promulgated the *Secretary of the Interior's Standards for Preservation Planning*, which includes specific guidance for public participation. The preamble to the Standards asserts, "Early and continuing public participation is essential to the board acceptance of preservation planning decisions."② The Park Service also provides for a "rigorous" periodic evaluation of the state program focusing on a wide range of activities under *NHPA*, including comprehensive preservation planning and public participation.③

In fulfilling its requirements under this federal legislation, the SHPO and his staff in the Historic Preservation Division (HPD) of the Georgia Department of Natural Resources prepared *New Vision: The Preservation Plan for Georgia's Heritage* in 1996.④ To produce the first plan, the SHPO sought two rounds of public participation prior to drafting and after review of the draft. Several techniques were used to reach the public prior to drafting, including public questionnaires, local forums, soliciting views on historic resources, and in-depth interviews with a selected group of Georgia's preservation leaders.⑤ As the plan was developed, HPD sought the reactions of the Georgia National Register Review Board, Georgians for Preservation Action, and selected preservation leaders. The second phase of public participation involved soliciting review and comment from a panel selected to represent a broad cross-section of opinion, regions, professional expertise and area of interest in preservation. The completed plan was adopted and is implemented through annual action plans. Since the implementation of the initial plan, Georgia has revisited its historic preservation plan every five years.⑥

The development of Georgia's most recent state plan involved three periods of public comment beginning in 2015.⑦ For six months, the HPD distributed a ten-question survey via its website, digital newsletter, Facebook page, and emails to regional planners and certified local governments. The survey was further spread by local governments, universities, and nonprofits. The survey received 400 responses, four times as many responses as in 1996. Over 75% of these respondents found out about the survey through the email newsletter, website, or Facebook. Based on responses from the surveys, the HPD

---

① "[C]arry out a historic preservation planning process that includes the development and implementation of a comprehensive statewide historic preservation plan that provides guidance for effective decisionmaking about historic property preservation throughout the State." 36 C. F. R. § 61.4(b)(1).

② These standards are a component of the *Secretary of the Interior's Standards and Guidelines for Archaeology and Historic Preservation* and are available through the National Park Service. The guidelines suggest involving the following: historians, architectural historians, archaeologists, historical architects, folklorists and persons from related disciplines; interested individuals, organizations and communities; and prospective users of the preservation plan. The recommend coordination with other planning efforts at local, state, regional and national levels. *The Secretary of the Interior's Standards*, National Park Service, https://www.nps.gov/tps/standards.htm (last visited Sept. 22, 2019).

③ 36 C. F. R. § 61.4(d)(1).

④ *New Vision: The Preservation Plan for Georgia's* Heritage, Georgia Dept. of Natural Resources (1996).

⑤ *Id.*, Ch. 7. Despite using several techniques to solicit input, the public participation obtained is consistent with two points made earlier: people tend not to participate unless they are directly affected by the issues involved and that they tend to be represented by groups. Fewer than 100 responses were received to the questionnaire, although the plan characterized that response as representing "a broad spectrum of organizations, areas of the state, professional disciplines, volunteer activities, and perspectives". The forums were attended by only 411 people in a state with a population of more than seven million at that time. Again, the plan stated that these participants represented "many communities and organizations" and that they "brought into focus the widely varying viewpoints on preservation and historic places, and the widely varying needs for preservation services throughout Georgia". When asked by this writer, who attended the Decatur forum, how many individuals were not preservation professionals, only two raised their hands. In fact, the largest group of those in attendance were professional archaeologists.

⑥ *State Historic Preservation Plan*, Georgia Dept. of Natural Resources, https://georgiashpo.org/statepreservationplan (last visited Sept. 23, 2019).

⑦ *Id.* at 81.

compiled a draft set of goals which was then released for a one month public comment period.[1] The HPD received ten responses and incorporated marked deficiencies into its draft plan.[2] During this one month period, the draft plan received three comments which were incorporated into the plan, unless outside of the SHPO's role.[3] The resulting plan, called "Integrating Innovation with Preservation" was enacted in 2017 and will serve as Georgia's historic preservation plan through 2021.

One source of information for the development of Georgia's state plans was the preservation plans developed by local communities.[4] Many communities throughout the United States have developed formal written preservation plans, reconciling in one document all of the policies and procedures regarding the community's historic resources.[5] The Georgia law and regulations, for example, outline a model process for developing a local preservation plan,[6] incorporating the Secretary of the Interior's Standards for Preservation Planning. The Georgia model suggests that a broad cross-section of the public be included in the process.[7] One segment of the public, the residents of historic towns and areas, warrants particular consideration. The *US/ICOMOS Preservation Charter on Historic Towns* states that "residents... should be actively and continuously involved in the planning process. ... Their reactions and comments to all public and private proposals for the area should be actively sought".[8] While it is important to have a stand-alone local preservation plan to articulate the preservation goals and objectives of the community, it is even more important that those goals and objectives are incorporated in broader community planning. This helps ensure consideration by other programs such as land use, transportation, and development. The *US/ICOMOS Preservation Charter* supports this approach, declaring that the preservation of historic towns and historic districts or areas must be an integral part of every community's comprehensive planning process.[9]

Georgia was one of the first states to adopt growth management legislation with the passage of the *Georgia Planning Act of* 1989.[10] This law requires each local government in the state to prepare a long-range comprehensive plan. The plan is intended to identify community goals and objectives as well as determine how the local government proposes to achieve them. Ideally, it is to be used in government decision-making on a daily basis. Failure to have an approved plan can result in the loss of state funding for a range of activities. While the scope of growth management is much broader than historic preservation, almost all such legislation includes historic preservation as a goal and/or a required planning element.[11] By including preservation with other key elements, comprehensive planning fosters better coordination

---

[1] *Id.* at 82.
[2] *Id.* at 86.
[3] *Id.* at 87.
[4] The Georgia Constitution, Art. 9, § 2, Par. 4, explicitly grants authority to plan and zone to local governments, but also permits the General Assembly to limit this power by generally applicable statutes.
[5] Bradford J. White and Richard J. Roddewig, Preparing a Historic Preservation Plan, (American Planning Association, 1994), p. 4.
[6] The Georgia Constitution, Art. 9, § 2, Par. 4, explicitly grants authority to plan and zone to local governments, but also permits the General Assembly to limit this power by generally applicable statutes.
[7] *See*, *supra* note 32.
[8] *A Preservation Charter for the Historic Towns and Areas of the United States of America*, Committee on Historic Towns US/ICOMOS (1992).
[9] *Id.*
[10] O. C. G. A. 50-8-1 to 50-8-12.
[11] David Listokin, *Growth Management and Historic Preservation: Best Practices for Synthesis*, The Urban Lawyer, 1997, 29: 202.

between preservation and other land use controls such as zoning.① The Georgia law requires that historic resources be considered along with land use, economic development, community facilities, population, housing, and natural resources.②

The Georgia Department of Community Affairs, which oversees compliance with the *Georgia Planning Act*, has established rules and regulations requiring local governments to hold at least two public hearings prior to submitting the plan for review. At least one hearing must be held prior to developing the plan to inform the public of the purpose and process and elicit community input on needs and goals. A second hearing is held after a draft plan is prepared to allow residents to make suggestions, additions or revisions. Finally, the local governing body must take official action to approve the draft plan and certify that public participation requirements have been met before submitting it for regional and state review.③

Another area in which there are opportunities for public participation is in the listing of historic properties in an official register or their designation as landmarks or historic districts by government authorities. The nation's basic inventory of significant historic properties is the National Register of Historic Places, a listing of properties that have been nominated and accepted as having historic, architectural, archaeological, engineering or cultural significance, at the national, state or local level. The criteria for inclusion and process for listing are provided by the *National Historic Preservation Act of* 1966 and regulations adopted by the National Park Service for its implementation.④ Although it is a federal program, it depends heavily on its state and local partners. The National Register is one of the most popular preservation programs among Georgian citizens. There are some 2,000 listings representing more than 80,000 historic properties, and new nominations are requested in record numbers.⑤ Public participation has been a hallmark of this program.⑥

All nominations must be consistent with the approved state historic preservation plan (which is developed with public participation), and the state is required to consult with local authorities in the nomination process.⑦ The state must specifically notify affected property owners and elected officials in the jurisdiction where the property is located at least 30 days before the State Review Board considers a nomination.⑧ Copies of the nomination must be provided to anyone requesting it or made available at public places such as libraries or courthouses so that comments may be prepared prior to its review. For nominations containing more than 50 properties, notice may be published in the newspaper and it is suggested that a public information meeting be held in the immediate area.⑨ After approval by the Review Board,

---

① Such coordination, while dictated by logic, is frequently absent. There are other advantages. By being part of a comprehensive community plan, preservation can blunt criticism that it is part of the NIMBY ["Not in My Back Yard"] process to stop growth. *Id.*, at 206 and 210.
② O.C.G.A. §§ 50-8-1 to 50-8-12.
③ Rules and Regulations of the State of Georgia, Chapter 110-3-2.06(4).
④ 54 U.S.C. §§ 302101-302108; 36 C.F.R. § 60.
⑤ *National Register of Historic Places*, Georgia Dept. of Natural Resources, Historic Preservation Division, https://georgiashpo.org/sites/default/files/hpd/pdf/National%20Register%20FactSheet.pdf (last visited Sept. 23, 2019).
⑥ The Historic Preservation Division also has responsibilities under the Georgia Register of Historic Places. All properties listed in the National Register are automatically listed in the Georgia Register, which was created primarily to facilitate the provision of state grants and tax incentives and ensure that historical resources affected by state projects are considered under the *Georgia Environmental Policy Act*. Public involvement requirements for the National Register satisfy requirements for Georgia Register listing.
⑦ 54 U.S.C. § 302303; 36 C.F.R. § 60.6.
⑧ 36 C.F.R. § 60.6(c).
⑨ 36 C.F.R. § 60.6(d).

all comments received by the state and any objections from property owners① must be submitted to the Park Service with the nomination. ②The rules provide for additional publication in the *Federal Register* and a final opportunity for any person or organization to petition the Keeper of the National Register to accept or reject a nomination. ③In communities that have been designated as Certified Local Governments (CLGs) under *NHPA*, there are additional opportunities for public participation. The state may delegate some of its responsibilities for the National Register process to CLGs. ④ Among other requirements, Certified Local Governments are required to provide for adequate public participation, including recommending properties for the Register. ⑤There are 98 CLGs in Georgia which provide increased opportunities for local citizens to become part of the National Register as well as other planning and protection programs. ⑥

An area in which public participation is even more crucial is the designation of historic properties and districts by local historic preservation commissions. There are over 2,300 local commissions in the United States, many with the power to regulate changes in the appearance of historic properties and delay or deny requests for demolition permits. The implications of designation can be significant for property owners. While their rights in this area are protected by provisions of the federal Constitution as well as the constitutions and laws of every state, they are nonetheless subject to legitimate restrictions on their use of designated historic properties. One concept that underlies these legal protections is that every citizen is entitled to "due process"—basic fairness in making, administering and enforcing laws. A key due process principle is that individuals affected by government action have a right to notice and an opportunity to be heard. ⑦Among the most common challenges to government action in the context of local preservation, ordinances are situations where owners are not given adequate notice of a proposed designation or hearing procedures that do not provide adequate opportunities to present testimony or evidence or rebut the testimony of others. ⑧

The Georgia Historic Preservation Act established a framework for local governments to create historic preservation ordinances and institute a process to designate historic properties and districts. Public participation is specifically mandated at two different points: when specific properties or districts are being designated, and when a property owner of a designated property or a property in a designated district

---

① Properties will not be included in the Register if a private property owner or a majority of owners of private properties within a district object to inclusion or designation. 54 U.S.C. § 302105. This process is under revision, however. The proposed rules would allow the landowner or landowners owning the majority of land within a district within a district to object to a nomination. *See*, *National Register of Historic Places*, Federal Register, https://www.federalregister.gov/documents/2019/03/01/2019-03658/national-register-of-historic-places (last visited Sept 23, 2019). However, the environmental protections afforded by the act extend to properties *eligible* for the Register as well as those actually listed.

② 36 CF. R. § 60.6(k).

③ 36 C.F.R. §§ 60.6(q) and 60.6(t).

④ At a minimum, CLGs in Georgia review local nominations prior to their presentation to the Georgia National Register Review Board. 54 U.S.C. § 302504. CLGs are also eligible to apply for federal preservation grants set aside for them and participate in additional training opportunities. 54 U.S.C. § 302505.

⑤ Id. at § 61.5. Requirements may include open meetings, published minutes, and published procedures.

⑥ *Certified Local Government Program: Preservation through Local Planning*, Georgia Dept. of Natural Resources, Historic Preservation Division, https://georgiashpo.org/sites/default/files/hpd/pdf/CLG/CLGFactSheet.pdf (last visited Sept. 23, 2019).

⑦ A full treatment of due process is far beyond the scope of this paper. However, a useful discussion for preservationists may be found in Bradford J. White and Paul W. Edmondson, Natl. Trust for Historic Preservation, Procedural Due Process in Plain English (1994).

⑧ James K. Reap and Melvin B. Hill, Jr., Law and the Historic Preservation Commission: What Every Member Needs to Know, National Park Service Cultural Resources Partnership Notes (2007).

applies for a permit to make a "material change" in the exterior appearance of a property.[1] In the first instance, the historic preservation commission and the local governing body are required to hold a public hearing on the proposed ordinance. Notice of the hearing must be published at least three times in the principal newspaper of general circulation within the jurisdiction and written notice mailed to all owners and occupants of properties within the area nominated.[2] Some local ordinances provide for more public notice than required by state law. The DeKalb County preservation ordinance mandates written notice to owners and occupants of properties adjoining nominated properties or districts and posting signs on individually nominated properties or on public streets wherever they intersect the boundaries of historic districts.[3] These measures are clearly designed to maximize public participation. At the public hearing, those in attendance are afforded an opportunity to comment orally on the proposed designation and are allowed to submit written comments to be incorporated in the record. Following the public hearing, the local governing body must adopt a formal ordinance of designation, also at a public meeting. Local governments routinely provide additional opportunity for citizens to address these and other issues at their meetings.[4]

Another initiative, which focuses on a long under-represented group in preservation, is the Georgia African-American Historic Preservation Network (GAAHPN). Established in 1989, the first one of its kind in the country, the network has become a means of garnering input from this segment of the community as well as connecting persons who are working to preserve the significant physical and cultural legacy of the black community throughout Georgia.[5] This effort has resulted in the inclusion of African-American preservation initiatives in the state preservation plan and an increase in both National Register listings and local designations for sites related to African-American heritage.[6]

One must consider the role of non-profit preservation organizations, particularly the Georgia Trust for Historic Preservation. Founded in 1973, the Georgia Trust is one of the largest statewide nonprofit preservation organizations in the United States and serves as a model for similar organizations around the country.[7] With a paid professional staff and numerous volunteers drawn from its membership, the Trust serves as an advocate for the interests of its members. It played a key role in developing the state's preservation plan and other public planning efforts. The Georgia Trust also coordinates Georgians for Preservation Action, a statewide council that mobilizes grassroots preservationists across the state to advo-

---

[1] O. C. G. A. § 44-10-26.

[2] Notices must be published or mailed not less than 10 nor more than 20 days before the public hearing.

[3] Dekalb County, Georgia Code of Ordinances Sec. 13.5-8.

[4] O. C. G. A. § 44-10-26. For further commentary on the Georgia Historic Preservation Act, see John C. Waters, Maintaining a Sense of Place, A Citizen's Guide to Community Preservation (1983).

[5] *Historic African American Resources*, Georgia Dept of Natural Resources, Historic Preservation Division, https://georgiashpo.org/africanamericanresources (last visited Sept. 23, 2019).

[6] Integrating Innovation with Preservation, Georgia's State Historic Preservation Plan 2017—2021, Georgia Dept/ of Natural Resources (2017), p. 13.

[7] *FAQs*, Georgia Trust for Historic Preservation, https://www.georgiatrust.org/about/faqs/ (last visited Sept. 23, 219). Today there are statewide preservation non-profits in most states. The combined membership exceeds 55,000 and there are more than 136 staff members working full time for these organizations. David J. Brown, *Statewide Preservation Organizations and NHPA*, 19 CRM no. 6, 1996, at 35. In 1998, the Georgia Trust received the Trustees' Award for Organizational Excellence from the National Trust for Historic Preservation. 24 *The Rambler*, (Georgia Trust for Historic Preservation) # 14, p. 2 (November/December 1998). The Georgia Trust maintains a site on the World Wide Web at www.georgiatrust.org.

cate for preservation laws, programs and policies. ①

Public participation techniques and media have evolved rapidly in the age of the Internet. Looking back at a presentation I gave at a conference in the late 1990s, I noted that "with these tools available, we are likely to see calls for even greater access to government information and public participation." In 2000, nearly half of American adults were not using the Internet; in 2019 that number dropped to ten percent. ② The Internet offers Americans a more convenient, and sometimes more interactive, way to engage in preservation efforts and with preservation efforts. The Georgia SHPO's office noted the importance of internet-based resources to provide up to date preservation information to a wider audience. ③ Broadly categorized, these innovations include digitization of prior public participation mechanisms, online training modules, and online exploration of historic sites and museums.

First, digitization of prior public participation mechanisms brings preservation procedural requirements to the Internet. Some local historic commissions, like Washington, D.C., are live-streaming their meetings and making videos of past meetings available. ④ Interested residents in Athens, Georgia can sign up for the Neighborhood Notification Initiative (NNI) to receive notices by text and email for upcoming meetings of the Historic Preservation Commission. ⑤ Availability of the NNI helps to fulfill the notice requirement that due process mandates. The Internet has also changed the way that Americans can submit public comments to federal agencies regarding federal rulemaking. When federal agencies propose changes to their rules the agencies are required to receive and consider public comments. ⑥ Regulations.gov provides an online mechanism for the public to make their comments heard. For instance, the National Park Service recently considered changing rules related to the listing of properties on the National Register. The agency posted the proposed changes on regulations.gov for 60 days, ⑦ resulting in the submission of over 3,000 public comments. ⑧ Similarly, the Cultural Property Advisory Committee of the Department of State utilized regulations.gov to allow submission of comments regarding requests from other countries to enter into cultural property agreements with the United States. ⑨ The committee also holds virtual public sessions using the Zoom web conferencing service. Anyone may observe without reservation or participate by prior email request. ⑩

Second, online training modules are offered for the public, local historic commissions, and preser-

---

① *Advocacy*, Georgia Trust for Historic Preservation, https://www.georgiatrust.org/our-programs/advocacy/ (last visited Sept. 23, 2019). GAPA has played a role in many hard-won advances for preservation including creation of the Heritage 2000 grant program, property tax incentives for historic buildings, the Georgia Register of Historic Places, an inclusion of preservation concerns in the *Georgia Comprehensive Planning Act* and the *Georgia Environmental Policy Act*.

② *10% of Americans Don't Use the Internet. Who Are They?* Pew Research Center (Apt. 22, 2019) https://www.pewresearch.org/fact-tank/2019/04/22/some-americans-dont-use-the-internet-who-are-they/.

③ *Georgia's State Historic Preservation Plan*, Georgia Dept. of Natural Resources, Historic Preservation Division, at 13 (2017) https://www.georgiatrust.org/our-programs/advocacy/.

④ *Live Video-Historic Preservation Review Board Meeting*, DC.gov, https://planning.dc.gov/node/905332 (last visited Sept. 10, 2019).

⑤ *Neighborhood Notification Initiative*, Athens Clarke County Unified Government, https://www.accgov.com/nni (last visited Sept. 10, 2019).

⑥ 5 U.S.C. § 553.

⑦ The time period was eventually extended.

⑧ *National Register of Historic Places*, Regulations.Gov, https://www.regulations.gov/docket?D=NPS-2019-0001 (last visited Sept. 10, 2019).

⑨ Cultural Property Advisory Committee: Notice of Meeting, Regulations.Gov, https://www.regulations.gov/docket?D=DOS-2019-0031 (last visited Nov. 27, 2019).

⑩ https://eca.state.gov/highlight/cultural-property-advisory-committee-meeting-october-29-30 (last visited Nov. 27, 2019).

vation professionals. The Advisory Council on Historic Preservation is a federal agency tasked with promoting preservation of the United States' cultural heritage and advising the president and Congress on preservation policies. Under the *NHPA*, the ACHP is responsible for "encourag[ing]... training and education in the field of historic preservation"①. The ACHP offers courses on compliance with the *NHPA* to federal, state, tribal, and local preservation practitioners, federal agency staff, and students. ② These courses are available both in person and online. The National Park Service is also responsible for preservation education under the NHPA. ③ NPS offers online technical training videos and webinars. NPS offers online training for sustainability, rehabilitation, preservation tax incentives, historic property maintenance, and local historic districts. ④ The National Center for Preservation Technology and Training, a division of NPS, also offers some online training. ⑤(NCPTT also offers in-person conferences for professionals). NCPTT's website features videos about preservation stories and interviews with preservation professionals.

Third, the Internet age offers additional ways to interact with historic sites and museums. Electronic media can enhance historic site visitation with additional features. The Historic Cobbham Foundation, a historic district in Athens, Georgia, offers a "walking tour" of historic homes in the historic district. Their website features a Google Maps overlay that allows visitors to view the history of each building as they walk through the neighborhood. ⑥ Some historic sites offer phone apps to enhance visitors' experience, such as 360° views of historic sites and other enhanced features. ⑦ Mount Vernon, for example, offers a GPS-enabled plant finder to see the history of nearby plants on the site. ⑧ For those who cannot physically visit historic sites, the Internet offers an alternate view of museum collections. The Library of Congress, the United States' oldest federal cultural institution and largest library in the world,⑨ is attempting to digitize millions of items in its collection. ⑩ In 2017 alone, the museum digitized 7.1 million objects. ⑪ The Library of Congress further engages the public in their preservation efforts by recruiting virtual volunteers to transcribe the digitized documents. ⑫ Georgia's FindIt program combines education efforts with the web availability of historic resources. ⑬ The FindIt program trains students in GIS capa-

---

① 54 U.S.C. § 304102.

② Section 106 Classroom Courses, Advisory Council on Historic Preservation, https://www.achp.gov/training/classroom (last visited 26 August 2019).

③ 54 U.S.C. § 303903.

④ *Online Training*, Nat'l Park Service, https://www.nps.gov/tps/education/online-training.htm(last visited Sept. 10, 2019).

⑤ *Videos*, Nat'L Ctr. for Preservation Tech. & Training, https://www.ncptt.nps.gov/blog/category/videos/ (last visited Sept 10. 2019).

⑥ *Walking Tour*, Cobbham Historic District, http://www.historiccobbhamfoundation.org/walking-tour-4/ (last visited Sept 10. 2019).

⑦ *See, e.g., Permanent Exhibits*, Nat'l Museum of Nat. Hist., https://naturalhistory2.si.edu/vt3/list-1-NMNH.html (last visited Sept. 15, 2019); *Virtual Tours of Monticello*, Monticello, https://www.monticello.org/house-gardens/virtual-tours-of-monticello/ (last visited Sept 10. 2019); *Learning from the Past: Revisiting the Abiel Smith School* 1835-1855, Museum of Afr. Am. Hist., https://www.maah.org/online_exhibit(last visited Sept 10. 2019).

⑧ *Mount Vernon*, GooglePlay, https://play.google.com/store/apps/details?id=org.mountvernon.app&hl=en_US(last visited Sept. 10, 2019).

⑨ *Fascinating Facts*, Library of Congress, https://www.loc.gov/about/fascinating-facts/, (last visited Sept. 10, 2019).

⑩ Marguerite Reardon, *Carla Hayden Has An Audacious Plan To Make Library of Congress Available To You Online*, cnet, (Apr. 10, 2019) https://www.cnet.com/news/carla-hayden-has-an-audacious-plan-to-make-the-library-of-congress-available-to-you-online/.

⑪ *Id*.

⑫ *By the People*, Library of Congress, https://crowd.loc.gov/?loclr=blogloc (last visited Sept. 15, 2019).

⑬ *FINDIT*, University of Georgia, College of Environment and Design, https://ced.uga.edu/pso/findit/ (last visited Sept. 15, 2019).

bilities, allowing them to map Georgia's historic resources and make their findings available on the Internet. One excellent example of a public engagement tool for the cultural resource database is the Austin Historical Survey Wiki. Citizens are able not only to access information through interactive maps and query tools, they can contribute to the database by uploading their own photographs and information to the site. This approach adds valuable local knowledge to professional contributions. [1]

Citizen participation has become an important component of public programs focused on cultural heritage conservation in the United States. This reflects a widespread belief that decisions incorporating community interests and values through well-managed public participation are better decisions and create an ongoing relationship that facilitates smoother implementation. Technological innovations continue to provide additional opportunities to enhance the traditional forms of participation that have developed over the past seven decades.

---

[1] https://soa.utexas.edu/programs/historic-preservation/work/austin-historical-survey-wiki (last visited Nov. 27, 2019).

国际视野下的文化遗产保护与公众参与
Heritage Preservation and Public Participation, from an International Perspective

对话人：菲利普先生、杰罗姆教授、里卡博士、肖恩巴尔特博士、查尔斯博士、巴里奥努艾奥教授

主持人：许颖博士

Mr. Peter Phillips, Prof. Pamela Jerome, Dr. Simone Ricca, Dr. Sylvain Schoonbaert, Dr. Charles, Prof. Barrionuevo

Host: Dr. Xu Ying

Xu Ying: Thank you very much for your presentations today. We have learned a lot. We need further discussions on public participation from an international aspect because we are from different countries. Even when we are facing the same problem, we will have different solutions. And sometimes with the same situation, people may react differently.

My first question is: sometimes when we are doing urban renewal, we meet some newcomers to the city, who come from a distance to live and work in the city. Sometimes they cannot afford better quality housing and end up in the so-called "urban village". And sometimes the urban village is heritage. When we are doing urban renewal in these kinds of areas, we are thinking of two different groups—the people who live there for all their life and the people who just come for maybe one year or even one month. When faced with urban renewal, they will have different attitudes. Do you have any suggestions?

Peter Phillips: Australia proceeds urban renewal in one of these two ways. It is either government-directed, what I might call wholesale. In other words, it deals with large areas at once. Or it is privately directed, it is piecemeal. That is to say, it occurs little by little. So the issues are generally different. Little by little urban renewal is known as gentrification. And it usually means that people with a lot more money than the original inhabitants move into an area, and often because it's close to the city, it's well located and sometimes even environmentally desirable, but has become run down, perhaps because of industrial processes that were formerly in the area, but now closed down.

So these areas then become more desirable. Urban renewal takes place almost without any government intervention at all. I think in fact the way of introducing a whole lot of people into an area, who are quite different from the traditional inhabitants occasionally such as an area in Sydney called Miller's Point was originally developed for private housing, was very close to the walls, then it became came very noisy and dirty. The wealthy people moved out and their place was taken by workers on the docks who needed to live close to where they were employed. So it started as a rich person's area. It became a less rich person's area. And it's now turned around. And it's going to be a rich person's area again.

The other problem, of course, is where you have the wholesale intervention, where the government would actually move in and do what was called slum clearance and completely renew the area. And in many cases, the inhabitants were displaced many kilometers from where they have grown up and they used to live and work and that is very unfortunate.

Pamela Jerome: In the US, when we talk about urban renewal, it is about demolition and rebuilding. However, in New York, where I am from, there's no space left. So what they've been doing is building new parts of the city over the railroads and over areas that were previously not used for construction. They can do this because the technology now can be used to expand these areas. So we just got a whole new part of the city on the west side, over the Hudson Yards, of course for the wealthy. Because nobody can afford to live in Manhattan anymore unless they've been there for a very long time and still have the old rent. On the other hand, the historic areas were actually abandoned from the 1950s onwards after WW II, and the returning soldiers all wanted to have their own houses so everybody moved to the suburbs. This increased the race riots of the 1960s. And then finally, in New York City, there was the bankruptcy of 1975, which made it even worse. The city was essentially abandoned by the wealthy, and the artists moved in. And whenever the artists show up, eventually the wealthy come back. Because the artists pave the way for everything else. And so that's exactly what happened in the 1960s. You could have rented an apartment at 60 dollars in New York City. The same apartment now will cost you three to four thousand dollars a month. And things have really turned around in New York, which was so unsafe and now it is so safe. You can go out at any time of the day and night. But are the original inhabitants around? Rarely, very rarely. And that's because they were priced out of their neighborhood.

Simone Ricca: I think your question has two different aspects: the community moving in and the process of urban renewal. I will say something about the issues related to the presence of newcomers. Modern cities are made of newcomers. It is a myth to say that the communities "were there", when the city grows from two hundred thousand people to two million. Obviously, even if everyone remains, there are one million eight hundred newcomers. How to integrate newcomers from rural areas or even—this is not the case in China, but the case in many other countries—from other countries? Foreign communities will often take over very poor and dilapidated areas. This is a key issue. And that is what I was trying to demonstrate before with the example of Dubai which is a rich city. But I also worked in the old city of Jeddah in Saudi Arabia where the core of the city has been squatted by poor foreign Muslim pilgrims who settled down in Saudi Arabia more or less legally. Now there is a renewal project and restoration project of the historic centre of the city. The issue is: can this population, and the multiple perspectives they bring for the vitality of this area, be integrated into the project?

I think this is an issue that is relevant also for China. Thinking about cultural events like the Carnival in London brought in by Caribbean communities. It is now part of the heritage of London, but it has nothing to do with "British" London; it is something else that adds to the quality and the multiplicity of a great city. So I think this is an area to be considered and to be developed even for China. There are a number of knowledge, skills, and heritage values brought by newcomers to an area. It is a fascinating challenge to find a way to integrate them into urban and conservation policies.

Ségolène Charles: I'm talking about urban renewal in France. We have all these periods after the war when we had built high-level buildings outside the city. In the beginning, it was a mix of more rich than poor people. But then there was the problem of maintenance. And so they were only relatively poor people left. Today in those neighborhoods since 2014 in France, there will be a whole policy in the public participation to take those people into consideration, because we all know that usually, the more the poor people are, the less influence they express. In France, we call them the low voice people, because they don't express themselves.

So there is all system of getting back to why they won't. What are their traditions? Because usually those people are immigrated. I'm thinking of an example. We've been working in a Muslim community. And they used to picnic on the grass. But the new renewal idea was to give them benches, but they're not using them. So when you're talking about heritage, like having those people using public space to have a picnic is kind of heritage for them. And we were giving them the chance to be out there in the way of using the space. And so we trying more and more and are doing more researches on those people to keep them back somedays.

Lorenzo Barrionuevo: In my country, the main problem that we have when we make a plan of renovation of the city is that the major only works for four years. They make a master plan and the ideas do the renovation, but after four years they will be changed.

We have a large industrial development area called 22@ in Barcelona as a regeneration example, which was built at the beginning of the 20th century. And now with the new major, she wanted to change all the ideas that were agreed by the people of the city when we wanted to change this old industrial area to the new technological district, at the beginning of 21st century. In China the master plans will be carried out for much longer they will not change due to the change of the municipality officials.

Pamela Jerome: I am now thinking about my other country, Greece. In Athens, we had a mayor who proposed the unification of the archaeological sites, which are scattered around central Athens but were never really connected to each other in an urban way. The idea proved so popular with the public, and it was carried through over twenty years under several mayors. They never stopped it from happening because it was political suicide to stop it. So no matter what party and what mayor was in power, they continued with the unification of the archaeological sites, which ended up removing major boulevards, pedestrianizing them, introducing parks, so that all the archaeological sites were connected.

Sylvain Schoonbaert: In fact, from Bordeaux where I came, the historic center where the traditionally lived by students. In Bordeaux where I teach, I saw some students sleeping in the car in the university campus. It is a problem with the historic center that it is so attractive yet not affordable.

Xu Ying: Thank you very much. My next question is about generations. Sometimes the older generation likes to preserve their heritage because the city center or the heritage sites are places they have lived for a long time, maybe for their whole life. But the younger ones want to be moved out and paid a lot of money by the government so that they can have better housing, affordable transportation, and all other things. So sometimes they don't agree with the same urban renewal or heritage conservation project. They may have different attitudes, between grandfathers and grandsons. So how do we involve the young people in heritage preservation?

Lorenzo Barrionuevo: What happened here in China is different from ten years ago in different universities where I worked. One of the things that are important about the generation gap is that the old people and young people need to understand that they need to be proud of their heritage. In China, you have millenniums of culture and sometimes you prefer to demolish a heritage old building to make a new modern building. Here in Wuhan, you are lucky because you preserved all the concession areas. In other cities, they demolished some beautiful old areas and made new developments. I think the main problem is education.

Ségolène Charles: Public participation in a way is one of the qualities, which helps to symbolize the older people. When you're going on the urban walk with these people, while using your architecture or urban planning competency, like, look at this, this is beautiful. The perspective is nice and it helps people to know their neighborhood better. They will understand your perspective that they need to preserve.

And then through discussions and debates, what we call empowerment, you give power to people to discover what they have into their hands. So I don't work that much of heritage. But today I was very impressed that public participation and preserving what you have are strongly linked.

Xu Ying: Yes, you need to let them know first to love it.

Pamela Jerome: It's all about awareness building. And then it's about capacity building. It's not the foreign experts who are doing the work. It's local participation. I worked for many years in Yemen, and I used to bring my students there. For them, it was the most exotic place they had ever been to. For the locals, we were the exotic people. We were exotic, not their surroundings.

What we were doing was documentation training. And we were using the documentation training to raise public awareness and to do capacity building. So we paired each American student with a local professional or an architecture student. And the act of documenting a series of buildings developed their appreciation, the local appreciation for those buildings, which had mostly been sidelined because they were so foreign to that environment. They were viewed as the mansions of the rich, and the local people didn't care about them.

But once they started to look at them closely, realizing that it was their grandfathers who were the carpenters, the masons, the lime craftsmen. Then they started to respect those sites, not as the houses of the wealthy, but as the products of their ancestors.

Simone Ricca: If you allow me, and this is a bit ambitious, I will try to say something about Chinese life and society: my feeling is that this is not any more the case. The young generation is actually much more attentive to heritage and pays more attention to its preservation than their parents' generation. The grandparents were part of this tradition, and now there is a growing attention in the youth. It is the generation in between, that lived the transition to "modernity", that has been detached from tradition. But I think that the young generation does not need to go back only to the grandparents' heritage. It is also about what they see and what they perceive in a city that hosts one million students (like Wuhan). You have one million people who look for different ways of living, who look for different spaces to be in. I think that heritage and historic neighborhoods have the chance to provide a very exciting environment for many youngsters, young artists, young architects, but also for other categories of students. So, maybe, we can be a little bit optimistic. Even if I am not knowledgeable enough about Chinese society, I have the feeling you're entering a new phase in China, a phase in which the new generation is bringing a different perspective.

Peter Phillips: I don't think it's necessarily a generational thing. As Pamela said, I think it's all about awareness. I have encountered many older people who are totally dismissive of the heritage, and many young people who are extremely enthusiastic about it. One of the interesting things though is the associations of built heritage with certain types of activities or people. Houses for the rich, for example. I encountered this a few years ago in China. We were doing a research project on the environmental performance of traditional Chinese housing and comparing it with modern housing that was built in the same pattern with modern materials. In fact, the traditional Chinese housing was just as environmentally sound as the new building. But when we talk to people about the fact that these houses could easily be renovated and made well, a number of people said, but these are houses for the poor, we want to live in new houses for the rich. And a number of these were older people who were keen to move up in the world.

The other comment I want to make is from my first visit to China, we were being shown around a number of your world famous-heritage buildings, Forbidden City and Summer Palace, and so on. And we were told that in the very early days of the Chinese Communist Revolution, they were keen to sweep away all of the trappings of previous imperialist China. But they were persuaded not to by the same argument that Pamela was just using, which is to say these places might have been built for the imperial masters, but they were built by the Chinese people, so the buildings here are celebrating the wonderful work of Chinese craftsmen. And that persuaded the Red Army to preserve many of these buildings. So very valuable a lesson, I think.

Xu Ying: Thank you very much. Now we will give some time to the audience. We will let them ask one or two questions.

A gentleman from Jingzhou asked a question about how communities may help the government to improve the cultural heritage preservation. Because sometimes the preservation work is not efficient. The communities can help the government.

Lorenzo Barrionuevo: Sometimes they need to encourage the government from the people. I'm going to tell you about a special case. We are designing a primary school in Nanchang. We had an agreement with the municipality that they take consideration of the students and the teachers. So we were asking them what kind of school they wanted. And they, especially the older teachers, are very happy because it's the first time that somebody asked them about what the school will be like, and what is the necessities of them. You have to find ways to promote the relationship between the citizens and municipalities.

In my personal opinion, I think that the main problem is that officials from municipalities in all countries who used to work in one way, don't want to change the way that they had to work. It happens here in China, in my country, in Europe and USA.

Pamela Jerome: I'm going back to the example of my work in Yemen, where I served in the role of coordinator between the NGOs that was on the ground and the government. Because the government would not listen to the NGOs, but they would listen to a foreign expert, so I became the mouth of the NGOs. I would go to them and say, "What do we want to do here?" "What is it that you desire?" "What do you consider important?" And then I'd relate that to the government. And they listened to me, but not to the NGOs.

Silvain Schoonbaert: I think heritage is a choice. And it depends on how we chair this choice. In France, we have a lot of debates about the heritage of the 20th century. And many, many people think that these buildings must be protected, although others don't understand why these buildings were protected as the historical monument of France. So this is really a question of share, we had heritage to share, to look at what we want to be the heritage of tomorrow.

Simone Ricca: I would say that the answer is the inclusion of heritage into urban development and renewal. The idea is not to keep preserving heritage as a separate thing "next" to urban development and the new world but integrating it into a different path. Imagining—through community participation and a number of tools we were discussing—a kind of development that is capable to assess the values for the community of these places, to keep and preserve the heritage, and imagining a new city that has a scale that guarantees a better human community life. It's a very hard job. There are no perfect cases anywhere. It is the idea of the Historic Urban Landscape Recommendation that relates to a different way of thinking about the future of cities more than looking backward only about the preservation of the past city. So that might be a kind of pathway to follow, or an approach capable to give some ideas about the future imagination of the city. But it's a very complex task.

Ségolène Charles: I'm gonna again take the French context. And what we see on a small, local scale is that the elected representatives are afraid of public participation. Even if it's a tendency today, they have to do it. But they're very afraid. Why? Because what we see is, a public participation process creates needs to have a back and forth process. And this back and forth process is creating uncertainty. It's not a big thing. Yet for a politician, for elected representatives, this is the worst thing that can happen. And for the French elected representatives of the small city, they need to be accompanied by experts, by architect, by experts specialized in participation to show them that even if there are unfixed things in the process, they're still having a place in the decision process. Once they realize that, usually they want to do it again, and work again with the population and listen to the population.

Peter Phillips: Two things I would say. One is that politicians like to be popular. So if the community can come up with a scheme that the politician can take forward, then the politician will be popular with the community. So that's something worth doing. The other thing is that supporting what Simona was saying about the Historic Urban Landscapes process. Much of that process at the beginning is cultural mapping and working out exactly what kind of place you have at the moment, what you like about it, what you don't like about it, what is your vision for different places. This is something that people can do for themselves. It is certainly useful to have professional guidance, but it is not necessary. If the people of the city can actually get together themselves and start working on these things and then take them to the politicians and say, here is our plan for the city. You might be surprised at how readily that would be adopted because as I said, adopting the people's plan for the city is a show far away to be popular.

Xu Ying: I think it is time to conclude this dialogue and thank you for all your opinions and all your examples. It has been a very nice time having you here. And thank you very much for the audience to listen to us. Thank you all.

视频篇

精选摘要

工程·文化·景观

ENGINEERING, CULTURE, LANDSCAPE

白鹤梁古水文题刻原址水下保护研究与工程实践

Design of Underwater In-situ Protection Works for White Crane Ridge Inscription in Three Gorges Reservoir Area

葛修润

中国工程院院士

Ge Xiurun

Academician of Chinese Academy of Engineering

三峡水利工程建成后,水库正常蓄水位将提高到 175 m,库区有大量的文物需要保护。白鹤梁题刻既是国家级文物,也是三峡工程文物保护的重点,然而由于其特殊的地理条件和保护要求,保护方案几经论证才最终形成。本文主要介绍了用"无压容器"概念修建白鹤梁题刻原址保护工程方案的设计理念及主要设计成果。工程于 2003 年 2 月开工建设,2009 年 5 月建成开馆。这一极具创新设想的工程实践,成为世界上唯一的遗址类水下博物馆,为水下文化遗产的原址保护提供了成功的工程范例。

After the completion of the Three Gorges Project (TGP), the normal storage level of the reservoir will be raised to 175 m and a large number of cultural relics need protection in the TGP reservoir area. Due to the special geographic conditions and protection requirements, the protection schemes are formed finally after repeated proof. We describe the design idea and main design result of in-situ protection scheme of White Crane Ridge Inscription with the concept of Non-Pressure Vessel. The construction began in February of 2003 and the museum opened in May of 2009. It becomes the only relics-type underwater museum in the world and provides an example for the in-situ protection of underwater cultural heritage.

高速铁路选线与古遗迹保护
——以京沪高速铁路安徽凤阳段选线与明皇陵保护为例

High-speed Railway Line Selection and Protection of Historical Sites
Taking Selection of Anhui Fengyang Section of Beijing—Shanghai High-speed Railway and Protection of Imperial Tombs of Ming Dynasty for Example

王玉泽
全国工程勘察设计大师
中铁第四勘察设计院集团有限公司总工程师

Wang Yuze
Master of Survey & Design
General Engineer, China Railway Siyuan Survey and Design Group Co., Ltd.

本文重点阐述京沪高速铁路安徽凤阳段选线过程中正确处理好铁路线位与全国重点文物保护单位——明皇陵的关系的过程及其绕避方案,并就如何处理好铁路建设与各类保护区、古迹、文物等的相关关系进行讨论。

This paper puts emphases on how to deal well with the relationships between selection of Anhui Fengyang Section of Beijing-Shanghai High-speed Railway and protection of Imperial Tombs of Ming Dynasty, a key national cultural relics protection site, and how to determine a bypassing scheme. It also discusses on how to deal well with the relationships between railway constructions and various nature reserves, historical sites and cultural relics, etc.

三峡工程文化遗产保护与利用

The Protection and Application of the Cultural Heritage of Three Gorges Project

徐麟祥
全国工程勘察设计大师
长江勘测规划设计研究院总工程师
Xu Linxiang
Master of Survey & Design
General Engineer, Changjiang Institute of Survey, Planning, Design and Research

  三峡工程是当今世界最大的水电站,被誉为中华民族伟大的标志性工程。三峡工程在创建了一系列世界水利工程的纪录的同时,也保留了大量珍贵的文化遗产和建设文化遗产。本文全面回顾了三峡工程中文化遗产保护和利用的典型案例,石宝寨、白鹤梁、张飞庙、大昌古镇,以及三峡工程的相关保护展示区和三峡博物馆等。

Being the largest hydropower station in the world, Three Gorges Project (TGP) is known as the great landmark project of Chinese nation. During the long construction period, it has created a series of world water conservancy project records, at the same time, it retained a large amount of precious cultural heritage and construction heritage. The paper reviews the typical cases and the protection of the cultural heritage of the TGP, Shibaozhai, White Crane Ridge, Zhang Fei Temple, the Dachang Ancient Town, as well as the related conservation and display areas and the Three Gorges Museum, etc.

桥梁工程与文化环境协调统一的设计实践

Designing Practices on the Harmonious Relationship between Bridge Construction and Its Cultural Environment

徐恭义
全国工程勘察设计大师
中铁大桥勘测设计院集团有限公司副总工程师

Xu Gongyi
Master of Survey & Design
Deputy General Engineer, China Railway Major Bridge Reconnaissance & Design Institute Co., Ltd.

　　本文简要介绍了世界知名桥梁如何融合景观环境,将工程演变成为世界文化遗产的相关实例,并通过新建桥梁工程与文化环境协调统一的设计实践,阐述了桥梁工程设计需因地制宜,尊重文化环境,保护自然原生景观,做到工程、景观、文化的有机融合,有利于打造城市名片,进而形成文化遗产。最后提出倡议,保护武汉长江大桥,争取尽早成为世界文化遗产。

　　This paper briefly introduces engineering practices where well-known bridges integrate into the landscape environment and change themselves into world cultural heritages. Through design practices of harmonizing cultural environment with bridge projects, this paper concludes that bridge engineering design should be tailored to the environment, respect the cultural environment, protect the natural landscape, and realize the integration of the project, landscape, and culture. This effort in engineering design can help to build urban business cards and then change into cultural heritages. Finally, a proposal for the protection of the First Yangtze River Bridge is raised, which can help it become a well-known cultural heritage.

活态桥梁遗产及其在我国的发展
Living Heritage Bridges and Their Development Trends in China

万敏
华中科技大学建筑与城市规划学院
Wan Min
School of Architecture & Urban Planning, Huazhong University of Science and Technology

提出桥梁遗产概念,并从活态遗产与桥梁遗产的结合中领悟活态桥梁遗产的内涵;阐述了开展活态桥梁遗产研究具有直面需求、填补空白、弘扬文化的重要意义;并从(1)古桥价值研究奠定的基础,(2)我国文保体制产生的重要作用,(3)工业遗产、文化景观、历史城镇与古村落等其他遗产领域对活态桥梁遗产研究的贡献,(4)新闻媒体的推波助澜等四方面阐述了活态桥梁遗产在我国的理论与实践发展线索。

This paper proposes the concept of bridge heritage, and comprehends the connotation of living heritage bridges from the combination of living heritage and heritage bridges. It explains the significance of carrying out living heritage bridges research, such as facing the demands, filling the gaps, promoting the arts and culture and then explains the development clues of Chinese living heritage bridges in theory and practice from four aspects: (1) laying the foundation of the value study of Old Bridge, (2) the important role of China's cultural relic protection system, (3) the contribution of the industrial heritage, cultural landscapes, historic towns and ancient villages to living heritage bridges study, (4) the catalytic role of the media in promoting living heritage bridges value found.

南水北调大型水利工程与文化遗产保护
——武当山遇真宫保护工程

South-to-North Water Transfer Project & Cultural Heritage Conservation

Yuzhen Palace Protection of Wudang Mountain

邓东生

长江勘测规划设计研究院

Deng Dongsheng

Changjiang Institute of Survey Planning Design and Research

南水北调是缓解中国北方水资源严重短缺局面的重大战略性工程。本文以位于水源地的遇真宫保护工程为实例,介绍了如何对水利工程中所遇到的文化遗产进行保护,并通过多种方案比较,得到因地制宜的最佳保护方案,在实施中采取了整体顶升的核心技术,有效地解决了工程建设和文化遗产保护之间的矛盾,对于类似文物的保护具有一定的借鉴意义。

This paper takes Yuzhen Palace protection of South-to-North Water Diversion Project as an example, and introduces how to protect cultural heritage in water conservancy project. The best plan is chosen by comparing protection plans. The upraise technology is adopted in the construction plan, which is useful to other cultural relic protection of analogous project.

城市轨道交通设计与文化遗产保护

Urban-track Design and the Protection of Cultural Heritage

吕晓应

中铁第四勘察设计院集团有限公司副总工程师

Lv Xiaoying

Deputy General Engineer, China Railway Siyuan Survey and Design Group Co., Ltd.

城市轨道交通线路和站位的设置及施工方案经常与地下文物、古迹发生交叉干扰,如何保护这些文物和古迹?本文以郑州轨道交通紫荆山站为例,通过合理的线路站位选择、平面布局、竖向设计并结合可行的施工方案,说明城市地铁的选线、站位设置对保护文物古迹的重要性。

It is normal that the construction of urban track lines and stations discords with the underground cultural relics and monuments. How to protect these cultural relics and historical sites? The author is taking Zijingshan Station of Zhengzhou Rail Transit as an example to go through the reasonable line station location selection, layout, vertical design, and construction scheme. The urban subway line, chosen according to the importance of protecting cultural relics and monuments, should be taken into the design in the very first stage.

工业废弃地,明日城市的宝贵资源
——国际最佳实践对中国的启示

Derelict Industrial Land, a Valuable Resource for the City of Tomorrow
Some International Best Practices of Potential Consequence to China

皮埃尔·拉孔特 博士
城市环境基金会主席
国际城市与区域规划师协会(ISOCARP)前主席
Dr. Pierre Laconte
President, Foundation for the Urban Environment
Former President, ISOCARP

就工业工程遗产来说,对适应性再利用的需要是更加明显的,因为它在工业的变迁以及加速技术的变革当中有很大的应用。本文拟通过实例来阐述工业工程遗产在当代背景下是如何被保存和再利用的,同时让后代记住它的过去。在德国的恢复当中,它将大型的工业荒地变成湖泊或公园;在捷克共和国,为了教育的目的,它把一个复杂的重工业废弃地保存下来;在布鲁塞尔,把对工业遗产的处理作为市区重建计划的一部分。欧盟工业工程遗产委员会(IEHC)每年都会评选出一些年度的欧盟文化遗产奖。其中的一个奖项颁给了布鲁塞尔的一个啤酒厂,它是一个从装饰艺术的啤酒厂改建为艺术和文化相结合的啤酒厂,同时它还尽力去为了教育的目的而再利用一些19世纪早期的机器。此外,还有荷兰的电力和天然气发电厂、历史性的防洪给水工程,还有蒸汽机的重新利用。一个反复性的问题就是内部空间的重新利用。

Nowhere is the need for adaptive reuse more evident as in the case of industrial and engineering heritage, which is in very large supply as a result of industrial delocalization and accelerated technical obsolescence. The paper intends to show through examples how industrial and engineering heritage has been saved and reused in a contemporary context, while allowing future generations to keep the memory of its past. It examines among others the reconversion of German large industrial wastelands into lakes or parks, the saving of a derelict heavy industry complex for education purposes in the Czech Republic, and the handling of industrial heritage as part of an urban renewal program in Brussels. It takes as examples a number of Europa Nostra's Annual Heritage Awards following the action of Europa Nostra's Industrial and Engineering Heritage Committee (IEHC). One of the Grand Prix was given to a Brussels art-deco brewery reconverted into an art and cultural complex while in addition endeavoring to reuse an earlier set of machines from the 19th century for educational purposes. Other examples include electricity and gas plants, historic flood control waterworks in Holland, and reuse of steam engine rolling stock. A recurring issue is the reuse of the inside space.

关于"工程·文化·景观"的思考

秦顺全
中国工程院院士
Qin Shunquan
Academician of Chinese Academy of Engineering

工程是人类文明史上的特定艺术。许许多多人类历史文化遗产本身就是有工程特征的,从埃及金字塔到万里长城都是人类文明和智慧的结晶。在新的工程建设中,特别是大型工程建设中所遇到的文化遗产保护问题特别需要我们认真的思考。我们需要整合社会各界力量,实现遗产保护与发展的并行,实现工程与艺术的相互融合,让这个时代的伟大工程成为未来的文化遗产。

Engineering is a special kind of art in the history of human civilization. Many historical and cultural heritage sites have engineering features. From the pyramids of Egypt to the Great Wall, they are all the results of human civilization and wisdom. In new project constructions, especially in large project constructions, cultural heritage protection problem needs serious consideration. We need to integrate the forces of all sectors of society, realize the fuse of heritage protection and development, and realize the mutual integration of engineering and art. Thus, we can make the great projects of this era become the cultural heritage of the future.

传承与发展：汉正街历史风貌区的城市更新研究

Inheritance and Development:
Research on Urban Renewal in Hanzheng Street

段飞　博士

联创国际设计集团武汉顾问公司总经理、总规划师

Dr. Duan Fei

General Manager and Chief Planner, United Design Group Wuhan Consulting Company

在复兴大武汉背景下，从汉正街面临的机遇与挑战入手，提出汉正街历史风貌区传承与发展的问题。通过优秀案例的经验分析，总结城市更新中城市历史风貌区保护与利用的策略，从街道尺度、街道肌理、街道界面、建筑造型、建筑材质及建筑组合六个方面论述汉正街历史风貌区有机更新的方法。

Starting with the opportunities and challenges, the question of protection and development of the Hanzheng Street historic area was asked in the context of the renaissance Wuhan. On the basis of strategies of protection and utilization of the historic area in urban regeneration, which come from the excellent experience through case analysis, the question of protection and development of the Hanzheng Street historic area was answered from streets scale, street texture, street interface building style, building materials, and building combination.

人文·人居·新时代

——文化线路在城乡可持续发展中的角色

CULTURE, HABITAT, NEW ERA
ROLE OF CULTURAL ROUTES IN SUSTAINABLE URBAN AND RURAL DEVELOPMENT

从"建广厦"到"兴家园"
From House Construction to Home Building

武汉地产集团
Wuhan Real Estate Group

武汉是中国历史文化名城、国家中心城市,其城市格局的形成与变迁十分具有代表性。新中国成立后,武汉进行了四次城市规划,但直到改革开放以后,武汉的城市建设才出现质的飞跃。从住宅统建到商品房及城市的综合开发,武汉的人居理念逐渐形成。进入新世纪以后,"建设国家中心城市,复兴大武汉"的目标成为武汉城市建设的发展方向。城市价值的发现,包括地标的打造和人居环境的改善等,都离不开"以人为本"。从"建广厦"发展到"兴家园",武汉城市建设的理念越来越具有开放性、包容性和亲民性。其中,东湖绿道的规划、建设和使用,已被列入联合国人居署改善城市公共空间示范项目,成为当代城市建设的"武汉样本"。今天的武汉正朝着现代化、国际化、生态化的目标奋进。

As a famous historical and cultural city in China and a national central city, the formation and change of Wuhan's urban pattern are very representative. After the founding of the People's Republic of China, Wuhan carried out its urban planning four times, but it was not until the reform and opening up that the urban construction of Wuhan took a qualitative leap. From the systematic construction of housing to the comprehensive development of commercial housing and the city, the concept of habitation in Wuhan has gradually formed. After entering the 21st century, "building a national central city and rejuvenating Wuhan" has become the development direction of Wuhan's urban construction. The discovery of urban value, the building of landmarks and the improvement of the living environment, are all people-oriented. From house construction to home building, Wuhan's urban construction concept is becoming more and more open, inclusive and accessible. For example, the planning, construction, and use of the East Lake Greenway have been included in the UN-HABITAT demonstration project to improve urban public space, becoming the "Wuhan sample" of contemporary urban construction. Today's Wuhan is forging ahead toward the goal of modernization, internationalization, and ecologicalization.

联合国人居署的文化、人居、线路思考

Thoughts on Culture, Habitat and Routes from the Perspective of UN-Habitat

张振山
联合国人居署驻华代表
Mr. Zhang Zhenshan
Representative in China, UN-Habitat

文化因人而产生,使人类的生活丰富多彩,为人类的发展做出贡献。文化是城市发展的动力和灵魂,而城市则是文化的载体和传承者,二者相辅相成。因此,在城市的发展过程中,需要重视文化的传承和保护。回顾中国过去40年城市化的经历,既有很好的经验,也暴露出不少问题。城市包括城市文化在内的可持续发展问题成为当今的重要问题。联合国分别在2015年和2016年通过了《2030年可持续发展议程》和《新城市议程》,对城市文化的发展和保护作出了很明确的阐述和要求。其中,《新城市议程》是一个以行动为导向的,并为国家、地区和地方政府提供指导的文件。它包括了文化和遗产的内容,承认文化和文化多元性是人类精神给养的来源,并为推动城市、人类住区和公民可持续发展作出重要贡献。

Culture is created by people, and it makes life colorful and contributes to human development. Culture is the driving force and soul of urban development, while the city is the carrier and inheritor of culture. They complement each other. Therefore, in the process of urban development, it is necessary to attach importance to the inheritance and protection of culture. Reviewing China's urbanization experience in the past 40 years, it reveals both good experience and many problems. The sustainable development of cities including urban culture has become an important issue. In 2015 and 2016, the United Nations adopted *The 2030 Agenda for Sustainable Development* and *The New Urban Agenda*, which clearly stated and required the development and protection of urban culture. *The New Urban Agenda* is an action-oriented document that guides national, regional and local governments. It includes the content of culture and heritage, recognizes culture and cultural diversity as the source of human spiritual sustenance and contributes significantly to the sustainable development of cities, human settlements, and citizens.

丝绸之路的文化线路思考与实践

Thoughts and Practice: The Silk Road as a Cultural Route

陈同滨 研究员
中国建筑设计研究院总规划师
Prof. Chen Tongbin
Chief Planner, China Architecture Design & Research Group

文化线路因 1993 年西班牙朝圣之路提请申遗而开始讨论,之后越发受到重视。它强调跨区域、国家的互动与交流,且必须具有时空上的连贯性和整体上的文化意义。"长安—天山廊道的路网"是丝绸之路中的一条廊道,东起长安,西至塔拉斯河谷,涉及中国、哈萨克斯坦、吉尔吉斯斯坦三国,共 33 个遗产点。线路可分为中原、河西走廊、新疆和七河四个地理文化单元。其空间关系完整,各单元各自的生业、民族特征、文化特征鲜明,且互有区别。遗址按照历史功能可分为中心城镇、商贸聚落、交通防御设施、宗教遗迹、关联性遗迹五大类。通过这种分类可以建立起该线路的整体遗产价值。该线路促进了人类文明、亚欧大陆间的交流,又见证了很多历史的阶段,展现了人地关系,即人们如何在长距离的交流中利用自然的地形、气候进行一些创造。

Since Routes of Santiago de Compostela was listed on the World Heritage List in 1993, cultural routes have been discussed and become increasingly important. The term emphasizes the interaction and communication between different regions and countries and must have the coherence in time and space and the overall cultural significance. The Routes Network of Chang'an-Tianshan Corridor is a corridor in the silk roads, starting from Chang'an in the east and ending in the Talas River valley in the west. It consists of 33 heritage sites in China, Kazakhstan, and Kyrgyzstan. The route can be divided into four geographical and cultural units: the central plains, Hexi corridor, Xinjiang, and Qihe Area. Its spatial relationship is complete, and each unit has its own distinct characteristics of life, nationality and culture, which are different from each other. According to the historical functions, the sites can be divided into five categories: central towns, commercial settlements, traffic and defense facilities, religious relics and related relics. This classification can clarify the overall heritage value of the route. The route has promoted exchanges between civilizations in Eurasia. It has also witnessed many historical stages and demonstrated the human-earth relationship, that is, how people make use of the natural terrain and climate to create something in long-distance communications.

北京的城市复兴
Renovation of Beijing

吴晨　博士
北京市建筑设计研究院有限公司(BIAD)总建筑师
全国人民代表大会代表,北京市政协常委
Dr. Wu Chen
Chief Architect, Beijing Institute of Architectural Design
Deputy, the National People's Congress
Member, the Standing Committee of the Beijing Municipal Committee of CPCC

　　2002年,吴晨在国内率先提出了"城市复兴"的理念。此后从2004年开始,吴晨及其团队在北京和其他城市围绕此概念,进行了一系列理论与实践的工作,如北京老城的修复工作、首钢遗址的复兴工程、通州副中心和北京CBD的中国尊等。团队参与的北京老城的修复工作,主要包括皇城周边整治、南锣鼓巷管控疏导、什刹海人行步道疏通以及隆福寺的复兴工作,其中天安门广场附近一个历史街区的复兴工作现已完成,被誉为"北京老城复兴的金名片"。北京首钢工业遗产复兴已取得阶段性成果,已于2016年被确定为北京市2020年冬奥组委会总部的基地,还设计了一个高线公园——首钢天际。于2018年竣工的中国尊,重新书写了北京CBD的天际线,是目前北京最"网红"的建筑之一。首钢现在尚未对外开放,但很可能将是北京下一个最"网红"的点。

In 2002, Wu Chen first proposed the concept of "urban renewal" in China. Since 2004, his team has carried out a series of theoretical and practical work based on this concept in Beijing and other cities, such as the restoration of the old city of Beijing, the revival project of Shougang, the Tongzhou sub-center and the Zhongguozun in Beijing CBD. The team participated in the restoration of the old city of Beijing, mainly including the renovation of the surroundings of the Imperial City, the control and guidance of Nanluogu Xiang, the dispersion of Shichahai pedestrian walkway and the restoration of Longfu Temple. Among them, the restoration of a historical district near Tian'anmen Square has been completed, which is known as "the golden name card of the revival of the old city of Beijing". The revival of Beijing Shougang's industrial heritage has achieved staged results. In 2016, it was identified as the base for the headquarters of the Beijing 2020 Winter Olympic organizing committee, and a high line park named Shougang Tianji was designed. Completed in 2018, Zhongguozun has rewritten the CBD's skyline and is one of the most web-craze buildings in Beijing. Shougang is not yet open to the public, but it is likely to be Beijing's next most web-craze point.

汉江流域文化线路上的城乡聚落研究

Study on Uban and Rural Settlements along the Cultural Route of the Han River Basin

李晓峰　教授

华中科技大学建筑与城市规划学院副院长

Prof. Li Xiaofeng

Deputy Director, School of Architecture & Urban Planning, Huazhong University of Science and Technology

　　汉江流域自然条件复杂,是东部平原通往中部盆地和西部高原的自然文化走廊。它既是航道、商道、隘道,又是移民通道,用"遗产廊道"的概念来形容它非常贴切。流域内的聚落类型,可从自然环境视野和聚落主体视野,分别分为滨水聚落、平原聚落、山地聚落、船民聚落,以及农耕型、商贸型、戍防型、治所型。城市和聚落的变迁动力机制有外在、内在两种。外在动力涉及河湖环境自然、行政决策和军事战争,内生动力包括经济发展和人口变迁。聚落遗产的保护和发展目前面临很大挑战,如大量传统聚落消失、单一化和空心化等。贯穿汉江流域的聚落遗产廊道,应该成为研究流域聚落的独特视角。聚落的保护应该从水环境的保护入手,并兼顾聚居者的基本权益,先乐业再安居。

　　The Han River basin, with complex natural conditions, is a natural and cultural corridor connecting the eastern plains to the central basin and the western plateaus. It is a waterway, a commercial route, a narrow pass, and a passage for immigrants. The concept of "heritage corridor" is very appropriate to describe it. The types of settlements in the river basin can be divided into waterfront settlements, plain settlements, mountain settlements, boat settlements from the perspective of the natural environment, and agricultural settlements, commercial settlements, garrison settlements and administrative settlements by the main body of settlements. There are two driving forces of urban and settlement change: external and internal. The external driving force involves the river and lake environment change, administrative decisions and wars, while the internal driving force includes economic development and population change. At present, the protection and development of settlement heritage are facing great challenges, such as the disappearance, simplification and hollowing of a large number of traditional settlements. The heritage corridor in the Han River basin should become a unique perspective for the study of settlements in the basin. The protection of settlements should start with the protection of the water environment and take into account the basic rights and interests of people living in settlements.

ICOMOS 的文化·人居·线路的经验与思考
——以纽约高线公园为例

Experiences and Reflections on Culture, Habitat and Routes from ICOMOS
Take the New York High Line Park as an Example

詹姆斯·瑞普 教授

ICOMOS 法律、管理与财经问题委员会秘书长

美国乔治亚大学教授

Prof. James Reap

Secretary General, ICOMOS International Committee on Legal, Administrative & Fiancial Issues

Professor, University of Georgia

虽然文化线路的定义强调了各种有形和无形的问题,但它是由运动、交流、对话等形式表现出来的活力来赋予文化线路特征的。文化线路不仅可以是一段时间内存在的一条线路、一条实际存在的线路,也可以由一系列的文化和历史上的重要因素共同组成,它可能从未在历史、空间和时间上存在过。

在美国,与文化线路最接近的概念应该是国家步道系统,景区步道和高速公路都非常重要。纽约的高线公园,最初开通于1934年,是纽约西区的一条货运高架铁路。1999年,"高线之友"创立,他们受到了围绕着老线路生长起来的美——自然之美与风景之美的启发。2009年,新的高线公园作为一种文化环境体验开放,每年都有新的艺术、景观和产品,每年吸引超过700万的游客前来。景观是这条交通廊道成功的关键因素之一,艺术设计是其发展的核心。它融合了纽约的历史和文化,使纽约市民和世界各地的游客都能接触到它。在每个地区和国家,文化路线的概念都需要适应自己的具体情况,以适应自己的文化和场所。

While the definitions of cultural routes emphasize various tangible and intangible issues, its dynamism in the form of movement, exchange and dialogue characterizes the cultural routes. A cultural route can be not only a route that exists over a period of time, a physical route, but also a series of culturally and historically important elements that can be a perceived product. It may never have existed in history and space and time.

The closest concept to cultural routes in the US is the national trail system. Scenic trails and highways are important aspects. The Highline Park was opened in 1934 as an elevated freight railway in West New York. In 1999, the Friends of the High Line was founded. And the founders were inspired by the natural and landscape beauty that had grown up around the old line. In 2009, the present Highline Park opened as a cultural environmental experience with new art, landscape, and productions that are having annually, attracting more than seven million visitors a year. The view is one of the key aspects of the success of this transportation corridor. Art is a key concept. It blends the history and culture of New York, making it accessible to New Yorkers and visitors from all over the world. In each region and each nation, the concept of cultural routes needs to be adapted to their own particular circumstances, their own culture, and their own venues.

从文化线路中阅读欧洲历史
——以克吕尼修道院及其欧洲网络为例

When the Cultural Routes Provide a Reading Grid That Allows to Understand the History of Europe
The Example of Cluny Abbey and Its European Network

克里斯托弗·沃罗
欧洲克吕尼修会古迹联盟主任
欧洲文化线路法国联盟主任
Mr. Christophe Voros
Director, European Federation of Cluniac Sites
President, French Federation of European Cultural Routes

克吕尼是10世纪初建于法国勃艮第的本笃会修道院。在中世纪,克吕尼成为欧洲文明的主要中心之一,留下了跨越整个西欧的1800多个遗产地。因其超越政治边界,对欧洲在封建时期的形象构建做出了贡献,并在构建欧洲各地区的共享文化上发挥了重大作用,所以,克吕尼网络被欧洲理事会正式认定为欧洲文化线路。这种方式区别于联合国教科文组织和世界遗产的评定。UNESCO在全球范围内行动,其基础是识别和保护被认为是特别的遗产,而欧洲理事会则致力于遗产网络的活化和价值,以进一步加强欧洲认同。克吕尼的案例促使我们迅速使用新技术以起到修补建筑和重建的作用。我们还开展了欧洲青年文化教育交流项目,通过共同的文化遗产和当地的文化艺术实践来激励年轻人,发展文化旅游,整合那些可能离得很远的历史遗迹,使这些遗产地之间产生共鸣,成为对彼此有意义的地方。

Cluny is a Benedictine abbey founded in the early 10th century in Burgundy, France. During the middle ages, Cluny became a major center of European civilization, resulting in the emergence of the development of over 1,800 sites across Western Europe. Because its reaching out behind political frontiers contributed to the imagines of feudal Europe and played a major role in the establishment of a shared culture that was common for several European regions, this federation of Cluniac Sites is officially recognized as a European cultural route. This approach is very different from that of UNESCO and the World Heritage. UNESCO acts on a global scale founded on the identification and protection of heritage considered exceptional, and the Council of Europe acts for the animation and the value of a networked heritage to promote European identity. The story of Cluny fosters us to quickly use new technologies to rebuild and recreate. We also had cultural and educational exchange projects for young Europeans, and inspired young people through their common heritage and also contemporary cultural and artistic practice. The cultural route gathered historical sites or places far from each other, working with a lot of sites from different countries, to make the sites resonate with others to be a place that makes sense to them.

河流与遗产
River and Heritage

卡尔·万增　教授
法国图尔大学教授
联合国教科文组织"河流与遗产——大河文化"教席持有人
Prof. Karl M. Wantzen
Professor, Universite Francois Rabelais at Tours
Chair Holder, UNESCO Chair on River Culture-Fleuves et Patrimoine

　　文化,意味着对多变的自然的适应。在河流文化的概念里,我们把生物和文化多样性的这些要素结合起来。河谷是文明的摇篮。在低地中,河流的干流扮演了文化传送带的角色。文化是人类不同生活方式的信息传递者,会对景观的多样性产生影响。从相反的角度来看我们现代的生活方式,你会看到各情境中的压力源之间日益加剧的相互作用,使生物的生存更加困难。如今,河流面临着严重的污染问题,造成了生物多样性的下降,我们也正在失去那些依赖于河流文化与生物多样性相互作用的文化。我们必须创建人类与河流相遇的场所,以维持生态系统的功能。我们必须通过河流恢复前后对我们自己和生物多样性在生态系统功能中的表现的测量来检验恢复措施的有效性。

　　Culture means adaptations to a variable nature. In the river culture concept, we have put together these elements for both biological and cultural diversity. River valleys are the cradles of civilizations. In the low land main channels, they act as a conveyor belt for culture. Culture is the transport of information about different ways of living of humankind and also effects on landscape diversity. If our modern way of life was seen from the reverse perspective, you'll see an increasing interaction between stressors in various situations that make the survival of biological species more difficult. Today, rivers are facing serious pollution problems, resulting in a decline in biodiversity. We are also losing all the cultures that are depending on culture on the interaction between the river culture biodiversity. We have to create siles where humans and rivers encounter, to maintain ecosystem functions. And we have to check the efficiency of our restoration measures by measuring ourselves and the biodiversity's performance in the ecosystem functions before and after river restoration.

文化遗产与城市发展
——澳门历史城区面临的挑战

Cultural Heritage and Sustainable Urban Development:
Challenges in the Historic City of Macao

弗莱塔斯

ICOMOS 共享遗产委员会委员

(澳门)建设工程有限公司,首席建筑师/CEO

Arch. Maria José Freitas

Member, ICOMOS International Scientific Committee on Shared Built Heritage

Principal Architect/CEO, AE TEC-MO Architecture & Engineering Ltd.

　　澳门是由东西方两种文化共同塑造的。从葡萄牙殖民统治时期开始,遗产就在中国政府的特殊安排与特殊协议下得到了保护,当地的遗产保护工作一直做得不错。到了2005年,澳门历史中心成功列入世界遗产名录。城市历史中心的价值需要得到尊重,并保持其完整性,所以澳门政府在2014年出台一项新的保护遗产的法律。但随之而来的是新的挑战。新的挑战基本上与博彩业有关。虽然赌场为政府提供了充足的资金来保护遗产,但也带来了过多的游客,有些超出文化遗产的承载力。为此,澳门政府遵循了ICOMOS提出的对文化遗产的HIA(遗产影响评价)的指导和《巴拉宪章》,通过对文化遗产的保护和适应性再利用项目实现遗产的活化,来增强遗产的文化价值,保持遗产与城市的可持续发展。

　　Macao was built including two cultures, the occidental culture and also oriental culture. Since the Portuguese administration, under special arrangement and special agreement with the Chinese government, the heritage was protected. The local heritage has always been preserved well. In 2005, the historic center of Macao was successfully inscribed on the UNESCO World Heritage List. The value of the historic city center needs to be respected and we need to keep their integrity. So in 2014, a new law protecting heritage was put in place by Macao Government. But then there are new challenges. The new challenges are basically related to the gambling situation. Although the casinos bring money and the government has money to protect heritage, but having too many tourists is beyond the capacity. Macao is now doing heritage impact assessment (HIA), and following the *Burra Charter* process. They are doing revitalization through heritage conservation and adaptive reuse projects, strengthening the cultural value and guaranteeing the sustainability of the heritage and the city.

特别篇

面向未来的共享遗产

共享遗产：文化的声音，交流的力量

SHARED HERITAGE:
THE VOICE OF CULTURE, THE POWER OF COMMUNICATION

再生：建成遗产的活化途径
Regeneration: A Rebirth Approach of Built Heritage

常青 教授
中国科学院院士
同济大学建筑与城市规划学院
Prof. Chang Qing
Academician of Chinese Academy of Sciences
School of Architecture & Urban Planning, Tongji University

  对于建成遗产而言，建筑师大多既不会是极端的保护主义者，更不应是极端的激进创新者。而是应以敬畏和批判的态度，对其进行适应性的修旧、利废、活化、再生。在建成遗产保护与经济社会发展之间寻求平衡点。

  总之，保护是前提，再生才是目的。建成遗产再生不仅仅是简单生硬地将新旧分开、各自作为，而是要探求规则管控下的新旧共生，真正将建成遗产变成经济社会发展的一种文化驱动力。

  "再生"指对既有的或历史性的建造物进行保留再造，或在功能废弃后对其进行活化复兴，其概念有五个要点。(1)意涵：指修旧、利废及活化、复兴，而非大拆大建或平地新起。(2)逻辑：保质期一般为50年至百年，但可以再生方式循环使用。(3)原则：建造本体尚存，文化价值仍在，或可赋予新的内涵。(4)策略：留、改、拆、添并举，特别以保留为首要。(5)辩异：更新或改造与之不同，尤其不适合历史环境及建成遗产。

  建成遗产及其历史建成环境再生是一个复杂的再造过程，需要恰当处理新旧关系以及存量与增量的关系。对于历史建成环境，尤其需要积极地保护和适应性创新，也就是恰当处理好保存、修复、翻建、加建和新建之间的关系。

让文化遗产成为武汉疫后重振的重要力量

Let Cultural Heritage Become an Important Force in the Revitalization of Wuhan after the Pandemic

杨相卫
武汉市文化和旅游局局长
Yang Xiangwei
Director, Whuan Culture and Tourism Bureau

习近平总书记强调,"让收藏在博物馆里的文物、陈列在广阔大地上的遗产、书写在古籍里的文字都活起来"。武汉是国家历史文化名城,丰富的文化遗产是城市的宝贵财富。我们将更好地保护和利用文化遗产,让文化遗产"活起来"。

一、整体谋划,规划引领,更好彰显提升武汉的文化魅力。一是精心组织实施《武汉历史文化名城保护规划》。二是制订完善盘龙城国家考古遗址公园、明楚王墓群、湖泗瓷窑址群等大遗址保护规划。三是加快编制《武汉革命文物保护利用规划》。

二、挖掘资源,举办展览,为疫后重振提供精神文化养分。围绕鉴往知来,弘扬优秀传统文化,守护武汉城市文脉;记录城市百年变迁,见证武汉大城崛起的绝代风华;守正创新,传承红色基因,彰显武汉英雄城市精神;充分发挥各类博物馆的功能。

三、深化文旅融合,充分发挥文化遗产的经济价值。一是加强资源转化利用,让文化遗产成为旅游资源。二是改造提升,将文化遗产密集区打造为文化旅游消费聚集区。疫后重振的武汉,再一次迎来蝶变与"新生"。道阻且长,行则将至。我们将加强文化遗产保护利用,为武汉疫后重振、浴火重生提供坚实的文化力量支撑。

重塑老汉口历史风貌，传承大武汉城市文脉
Restore the Historic Landscape of Old Hankow, Inherit the Cultural Context of Wuhan

董志向
武汉旅游体育集团董事长
Dong Zhixiang
President, Wuhan Tourism & Sports Group Co., Ltd.

汉口历史风貌区的改造提升要围绕提高城市品质、体现城市特色、展示历史文化名城风貌来推进改造工作，真正让老旧街区"变活"，焕发新的生命力。

一、聚焦历史建筑保护，留住武汉人共同的情感记忆

汉口历史风貌区内拥有武汉市最为丰富的历史文化资源。但伴随着城市的不断发展，曾经的"大武汉"中心出现了产业小散化、文化边缘化、人口老龄化、设施老旧化等不同程度的问题，特别是疫情发生以来，基础设施和环境卫生"结构性"短板突出，迫切需要结合疫后重振，呼应民生诉求，活化历史资源，提高城市品质。

二、聚焦城市功能提升，造福武汉人寻常的百姓生活

将集中精力把汉口历史风貌区打造成为凝聚城市精神的世界级滨水空间，作为武汉疫后重振的典型模式、对话世界的文旅地标片区、未来健康生活的全球样板。形成"两轴引领、六片联动、网络织补、节点示范"的总体空间结构。

三、聚焦城市文脉传承，共享武汉人百年的城市遗产

我们希望通过对风貌区的保护与修复，延伸大武汉的文化脉络。同时我们更希望通过对风貌区的改造与提升，讲述我们这个时代的故事与精神，使风貌区成为我们留给子孙后代的共享遗产，我们将通过这份共享遗产，进行一场跨越时空的文化交流。

作为资源的文化遗产——源流运动的实践

The Practice of Yuanliu Movement—as Cultural Heritage Resource

杭侃 教授
山西大学副校长
Prof. Hang Kan
Vice President, Shanxi University

文化遗产是一种特殊的资源,所以应该利用、可以利用。其作为资源的难点则是古今之间的隔膜。考古学科往往需要有专业训练之后才能读懂。虽然考古的材料是巨大的物质文明基因库,但是考古报告往往像医院病历,以学术的形式一丝不苟地写成,让人无从下手了解。

我们现在经常讲让文物活起来,可是"活"了以后,收益却是有限的。工艺美术界去做文创设计的时候,往往又沉迷仿古、妄自出新,因为文化积淀有限,只会"提取符号"、生拼硬凑。我们觉得要在这中间培养一些能够搭桥的人,所以我们发起了"源流运动"。

发起"源流运动",首先因为考古学科掌握着丰富的古代物质文化资源,当前中国的考古学科,也已从构建时空框架阶段发展到了解释阶段,成了一个美学、设计、艺术的"富矿"。"源流运动"区别于一般考古科普平台,而是做"考古·艺术·设计"交流平台做的一些事情。

"源"是面向过去,"流"是面向未来,讨论如何把知识体验带入日常生活,把古典美好和当代社会有机地进行结合。宗旨是"考镜源流,以故为新"。希望能够解放古物,唤醒创造力。

文化遗产与城市可持续发展——上海的实践与思考
Cultural Heritage and Sustainable Urban Development: Practice and Reflection of Shanghai

邵甬 教授
同济大学建筑与城市规划学院教授、博导
联合国教科文组织亚太地区世界遗产培训与研究中心上海分中心主任

Prof. Shao Yong
Doctoral Supervisor, School of Architecture & Urban Planning, Tongji University
Director, World Heritage Institute of Training & Research for the Asia & the Pacific Region under the auspices of UNESCO, WHITRAP (Shanghai)

城市面临一些普遍问题：千城一面、万屋一貌，城市品质"五大三粗"现象，"消极保护"的历史街区，方兴未艾的"仿古"热潮。在城市中，这些模式和做法都不符合"可持续发展"目标。

2016年，联合国教科文组织《文化·城市·未来：文化促进城市可持续发展全球报告》指出：文化具有使城市更繁荣、更安全和更可持续的力量。2016年国际古迹遗址理事会提出"要让文化和文化遗产积极地融入城市发展规划和政策中去"的观点。联合国教科文组织于2011年开始推动的历史性城镇景观的方法兼顾了文化遗产的保护与发展，是有利于实现可持续发展的，值得推广。

文化激发的思南路历史街区复兴和遗产引领的杨浦滨江再生，都是这方面上海的优秀案例。在现在经济全球化、世界文化趋同的浪潮中，文化的多样性和环境的多样性所造就的历史空间显得弥足珍贵。文化与遗产，能够让城市环境更可持续，更包容的社会发展，更包容的经济发展，能够带来更多和平和安全。

武汉：城市文本与当代阅读

Wuhan: Urban Texts and Modern Reading

何依 教授
华中科技大学建筑与城市规划学院
Prof. He Yi
School of Architecture & Urban Planning, Huazhong University of Science and Technology

武汉的历史街区与现代城市不断地融合和交融的过程当中，要解决这样几个问题：在碎片的历史城区当中如何实现保护发展的整体关联，在刚性的保护框架下如何实现文化资源的合理利用，在孤立的文物语境下如何实现历史文脉的阅读体验。

城市文化遗产迫切需要探索创新性保护方法：从保护城市遗产走向保护遗产城市。历史之径实际上是对零散的历史信息通过线路进行重新组构的一种方式，是一种时空的叙事方式。

历史之径的方法，第一步是由点到线，确定文脉的认知方式。第二个过程是线段相连，是城市特色的体验之路。第三个是由线串圈，最终的目的是要把沿线的历史街区活化起来。从点到线再到圈的过程，实际上也是从阅读到利用的一个方式。

具体的做法，第一是为武汉的四区域分别制定对策：汉口原租界——近代遗存丰富中的主题彰显；汉口汉正街——大规模更新中的记忆缝合；汉阳旧城区——山水文化层积中多元组合；武昌古城区——蛇山南北连接中的事件再现。第二是"一线贯通"，选择出一条历史之径，经江岸沿江一线—汉正街、跨两江一湖、走龟蛇一线，承载"名城武汉"历史文脉，集合"最武汉"特色地标，营造"魅力武汉"城市品牌。具体的活化模式则有节点活化、线性活化和网络活化三种模式。

当代遗产价值的保护与阐释

The Conservation and Interpretation of Modern Heritage Value

陈曦 副教授

苏州大学金螳螂建筑学院历史建筑保护与发展研究所所长

Prof. Chen Xi

Director, Institute for Conservation and Development of Historic Buildings, Gold Mantis School of Architecture, Soochow University

传统的遗产从历史的纪念物到要被活化利用为文化资产的过程中,它的价值应该得到怎样的认知、保护以及阐释?衔接它们两者最重要的是价值。价值像一个桥梁,将过去、今天和未来连接起来。

以苏州大学为例,其前身东吴大学是中国13所近代的教会大学之一。它最早的教学楼是钟楼,也被称为"林堂"。东吴大学见证了中西文化的交流,校园建筑也是中西合璧,英国的建筑师和中国的工匠之间产生了很多微妙的碰撞。除了历史、艺术、科学等几大价值以外,苏州大学其实还承载着更多维度上的价值,有一张"意义之网"。对于遗产社区的人来说,校园细微的、每天都能够接触到的、触摸到的地方,让他们能够留下更加深刻情感的联系。

那么,我们要保护什么?学校的钟楼——"林堂",是学校最早建立的教学楼,是学校的精神象征。1950年代,"林堂"两个字被抹去,至今也没有得到恢复。但在其南部新建的王健法学院新教学楼采取了非常巧妙的办法来呼应"林堂"的价值特征。所以对遗产的价值的认识在不同的时代并不相同,不同的时代、不同的人群面对遗产的对话会选取不同的对象。

我们如何来保护这些遗产?面对遗产,不仅专家学者和社会的管理者可以展开讨论,真正的遗产的所有者、权益者——这些遗产社区的人们,他们的意见、他们的观点更加重要。

网师园的传统与现代

The Tradition and Modernity of Master-of-Nets Garden (Wang Shi Yuan)

吴琛瑜 博士
苏州市网师园管理处主任
Dr. Wu Chenyu
Director, Master-of-Nets Garden (Wang Shi Yuan), Suzhou

1997年和2000年,先后有拙政园、留园、网师园、环秀山庄、沧浪亭、狮子林、艺圃、耦园、退思园9座苏州园林,作为"苏州古典园林"的典型例证,被联合国教科文组织批准列入《世界遗产名录》。苏州古典园林是明清时期江南地区士大夫阶层文人写意山水住宅园。

网师园是宅园一体保存完整的一座苏州园林,是"小园极则,以少胜多"的典范。1979年到1980年网师园的殿春簃作为中国改革开放之后第一个外经贸项目、第一个对外文化交流项目出口到了纽约大都会博物馆。今年(2020年)是大都会博物馆"明轩"建成40周年。网师园也曾经在苏州城市发展历史上起到了重要的作用,20世纪90年代初期,中国和新加坡两国政府曾在网师园小姐楼内谈判苏州工业园区项目。

40年间,在明轩也发生了很多的故事,有很多人到明轩里面去了解中国的传统文化,殿春簃也迎来了很多海外的游人。网师园既有传统的一面,同时又有国际性和当代性。今年因为疫情,很多的华人留在美国回不来,大都会的明轩反而成为他们思念家乡、思念中国的一个途径。

40年前的人给我们留了这么好的一段渊源,40年后的今天我们这一代人的所思所做所想,都将成为网师园、殿春簃和明轩未来的一段历史。

疫情之下文化遗产价值的思考
Reflection on Cultural Heritage under the Pandemic

施春煜先生
联合国教科文组织亚太地区世界遗产培训与研究中心(苏州)副研究员
苏州市世界文化遗产古典园林保护监管中心监测部主任
Mr. Shi Chunyu
Associate Researcher, World Heritage Institute of Training and Research for the Asia and the Pacific Region under the auspices of UNESCO(Suzhou)
Director of Monitoring Department, Suzhou Conservation and Monitoring Centrefor the Classical Gardens of World Heritage

在这次疫情当中,各地文化遗产的处境都非常艰难。很多遗产地过度地依赖于旅游经济,疫情一来之后,就完全切断了它的经济来源。但保持了原来的传统产业,或其他附加产业的村庄、古镇,生存受到的影响就比较小。

所以在遗产地的保护中,一定要遏制单纯旅游业态的野蛮生长,还要促进产业的多元化,尤其是发展传统的地方特色的制造业、手工业、农产品加工业,开发出特色的产品、高附加值的商品。在这种条件下,如果疫情来临,人流虽然切断,但物流还没有切断,我们通过网络可以把这些商品售卖出去,那么这些地方就很容易生存下去。

如果说若干年以后,火神山医院也成为一种遗产,我们去这个地方看的话,应该要关注什么?应该是他们的医护制度、医疗水平、当时是怎么去抢救病人的一系列制度与方法。我们需要加强对于软遗产的关注,关注文化遗产中无形的部分,这样会对后人产生更大的启发。

地标建筑的复活

Renaissance D'un Batiment Emblematique

拉尼奥先生
国际古迹遗址理事会法国国家委员会主席
法国建筑科学院院士
Mr. Jean-François Lagneau
President, ICOMOS France
Fellow of Ecole nationale supérieur d'Architecture

巴黎莎玛丽丹(Samaritaine)百货公司位于巴黎的腹地——西岱岛旁新桥附近。这个建筑群由4栋楼构成,于1870年至1934年由法国的一对企业家夫妇建造。当时是19世纪下半叶法国工业革命大发展的时期,城市的发展也产生了重大的变革,出现了新的销售模式——百货商店。

这对夫妇最早的门店很小,然后他们逐渐把周围的楼都买了下来,进行改造和施工。最初的大楼为金属结构,外立面进行施工的时候,内部已经开始使用。它有一个非常大的玻璃顶棚,外观是新艺术风格,颜色和细节都非常丰富。随后,这对夫妇一直对建筑群进行改造和扩张,直到他们离世后,百货公司被出售给了LVMH集团。2005年,百货公司因为消防、年久失修和业态变化的原因关闭。我们现在正在对其进行改造。

根据法国历史建筑保护的政策,(对)建筑的保护、修复与新建有严格的规定。最后经过讨论,百货公司的1~3号楼的主体将进行保护和修复,4号楼则拆除重建。此前,为了不分散顾客购物的注意力,楼内的壁画曾一度被白石灰覆盖,陶瓷装饰也被遮挡。如今,移除白石灰和遮挡物后,20世纪初叶的壁画和装饰又重见天日。虽然修复中使用了新材料,但也尽量力求恢复往昔的风格,被破坏的装饰也都进行了修缮。新建的4号楼建筑的玻璃立面也能够在映照周边历史风貌的情况下,达到与老建筑的和谐统一。

遗产网络与遗产地

Networks and Places of Heritage

弗莱塔斯
ICOMOS 共享遗产委员会委员
(澳门)建设工程有限公司，首席建筑师/CEO
Arch. Maria José Freitas
Member, ICOMOS International Scientific Committee on Shared Built Heritage
Principal Architect/CEO, AE TEC-MO Architecture & Engineering Ltd.

在过去，在我们的脑海中，物质遗产永远是一个有故事的地方，我们参观纪念物的内部和外部空间，也在记忆中保持对我们参观过的纪念物的精神重建。在某一时刻，这种精神重建可以被恢复出来。如今，借助新技术，我们可以重新创造空间，我们可以在古迹中穿行，可以参观它，体验过去不可能的体验。我们还可以想象现在它与未来的情况互动。疫情之下，博物馆打开大门让我们参观，这在过去是不可想象的。技术和遗产在今天紧密相连，可以帮助我们探索遗产新的情况并揭示新的潜力。

澳门的城市规划中也使用了这些技术工具来进行可视化，方便公众参与，这也有利于保护澳门并于2005年被联合国教科文组织列入《世界遗产名录》的历史中心。在规划新建筑的时候，遗产影响评估非常重要。澳门在氹仔岛和路环岛的中间规划了大片的填海区用于建造新建筑，从而更好地保护了位于老城区的文化遗产。

共同未来，共享遗产

Shared Future, Shared Heritage

对话人：西格弗里德·安德斯教授、艾希特博士、詹姆斯·瑞普教授、兰德教授、弗莱塔斯女士、
查尔斯博士、燕海鸣博士、朱海俊先生、施春煜先生

主持人：丁援博士、许颖博士

Prof. Siegfried Enders, Dr. Claus-Peter Echter, Prof. James Reap, Prof. Françoise Ged, Ms. Maria José de Freitas, Dr. Ségolène Charles, Dr. Yan Haiming, Mr. Zhu Haijun, Mr. Shi Chunyu

Hosts: Dr. Ding Yuan and Dr. Xu Ying

Hosts: Good morning, good afternoon and good evening! It is a bit strange to say greetings like this, and we are really thankful for your coming to join us in this online event. Welcome all of you! Today is the International Day on Monuments and Sites, and this year the theme is Shared Cultures, Shared Heritage, Shared Responsibility.

As you might have known, we have been organizing Crossover Forums and Dialogues ever since 2012, and we started with discussing cross-cultural heritage. These years, with the guidance of ISC SBH and the help of experts from all over China and all over the world, we are pushing forward our research on Shared Built Heritage.

共同未来，共享遗产

This year, the coronavirus pandemic has made the discussion of Shared Heritage even more important. Facing the ongoing global health crisis, we are now thinking of the legacy that the pandemic is going to leave us. As you might have seen, here in Wuhan, two emergency hospitals were built in ten days to contain more patients. Three days ago, they have finished their missions and were shut down. Prof. Ruan Yisan just said in the video that the two hospitals are the modern heritage. I wonder what you think about it.

We have four topics to discuss today. First, Let's discuss these questions: What exactly does "Shared Heritage" stand for? What is the difference between "Shared Heritage" today and the Shared Built Heritage that we have been used to?

Siegfried Enders: Dealing with COVID-19 shows us, particularly in a frightening way, the withdrawal to national and private areas worldwide, delimitation and exclusion instead of common ground and sharing. It is therefore all the more necessary and of the greatest importance if on the International Day for Monuments and Sites initiated by ICOMOS we look to the future, to a common future of a common shared cultural heritage and, in my opinion, to the opportunities of a common cultural heritage.

The International Day for Monuments and Sites 2020 is under the ICOMOS motto "Shared Cultures, Shared Heritage, Shared Responsibility", so it builds on the motto "Sharing Heritage" of the European Cultural Heritage Year 2018 and wants to get in the mood for the ICOMOS General Assembly, which unfortunately has to be postponed.

The experiences that many ISC SBH members gained from conferences, study trips and symposiums around the world and have had in dealing with shared cultural heritage over the past 11 years have shown how important it is for them to deal with and understand the common, shared cultural heritage for International understanding and mutual understanding.

It is necessary that this work is continued through the well-known activities carried out by the ISC SBH and its partners and colleagues in the past. The chances of a close scientific, cultural and thus also economic cooperation may help to overcome the increasing nationalism and the demarcation.

In the past, the work of the ISC SBH was mainly related to the built cultural heritage (MONUMENTS and SITES). I think it should stay that way. Working with the intangible cultural heritage should be left to others. In my opinion, focusing on the conservation of monuments and sites is useful when it comes to preserving them.

In this way, I see a common future for responsible handling and ultimate preservation of the shared built heritage.

James Reap: Good morning for me, and good evening to you. It's a pleasure to be with you. I want to begin by thanking our colleagues in Wuhan for organizing this meeting. I think it shows the kind of leadership that they've exhibited for the past nine years in organizing conferences, celebrating the idea of shared heritage and coming out of this international crisis taking the lead in having this conference today. So I think that's very important. I do want to say briefly that I somewhat disagree with my colleague Siegfried Enders, although we may actually have more agreement than it first appears. I think perhaps the shared built heritage is actually much wider than buildings. And I'd like to give you a very brief look at a concept that's relatively new here in the United States. I'd like to highlight the Cane River National Heritage Area in the United States. We have 49 of these in the country and it's a large agricultural area in the state of Louisiana that has a culture developed from the Spanish, the French, the Native American, the African American, and then the English and German settlers who came there. So it is an area of shared heritage. The built heritage is an important part of it. There is a national park, 7 national landmarks, 3 state historic sites, historic plantations, homes and churches. But the importance of this area goes beyond that—it's the agricultural tradition, the agricultural landscape patterned after the French colonial landscape, the unique language, the unique cuisine, the unique culture represented in this area. So taking the "built heritage" to the "built landscape" and "cultural landscape" is important because certainly the buildings don't exist alone. They exist in this cultural mix of building tradition, language and culture. So I really welcome the idea of expanding the concept of shared heritage. I don't want to forget the built heritage because ICOMOS focuses very strongly on monuments, sites, districts and buildings. But as we all know, the world heritage program has embraced the idea of cultural landscapes, and that combination of nature and culture, which I think is very important. So I think this is a wonderful opportunity to have this kind of dialogue to talk about where we may go with this concept in the future and I thank my colleagues in Wuhan for undertaking this.

Maria José Freitas: Thanks for the opportunity. I want to congratulate you all for organizing this web conference. It's also my first time in a conference like this. Hopefully, I've been working here in Macao, which is now in a very safe situation. Nowadays we are working, and we are always wearing masks. Life keeps going on. I didn't prepare any special thing to say tonight, but really I'm embedded in the shared heritage. When I work to recover old buildings and so on, I work with shared heritage. And nowadays, when I build new buildings and do new projects, it is again shared heritage, because I'm working with people from different nationalities. And really here in Macao, we can feel this kind of atmosphere. When you visit the city, you can see it is multicultural. But I really want to go behind multiculturalism. I want to say that this is inter-culturalism. And what we have here is because the things and all the encounters between Occident and Orient are really mixed in the inter culturality. It is for me even more important. And also you can understand this when you read the city, the urban planning, and also the intangible heritage. They, in my point of view, are connected. Even when you think about what is built, you have a concept, you have an idea. And this idea can be shared or you can get it from other persons, or even the governments can impose some different ideas on you. The mixture here is really very strong. And I would say that the architecture and the urban planning and so on are the stages where everything happens. After all this situation that we are living in all the countries now, we still can understand this. I think the city now step by step is recovering. We can see more freedom in people when they walk along the streets and have meetings and conferences. And I think this is very important to keep this inter-cultural atmosphere. That's why my personal feeling is following this situation. When I see this, what we are doing now, different people in different countries in different continents, talking about the heritage, sharing ideas about cultural landscape, about HUL, about the effort that the people of Wuhan is done to recover from the situation, which is a lesson for all of us. And this is sharing: sharing our knowledge, sharing our experiences, sharing our past, and also sharing our future.

Françoise Ged: Thanks to the Wuhan team for this organization. And thanks for this first meeting via different continents. I think the first silver lining of this shared pandemic situation may be this opportunity to work now through videoconferencing. I would like to share with you some reflections from Bruno Latour, a French sociologist and philosopher: "If everything is stopped, everything can be questioned, inflected, selected, sorted, interrupted or on the contrary accelerated." (at the end of the message, the phrase I try to translate, or in the enclosed doc.) In a lot of media, the main concern is how to recover the production as before the epidemy. According to Bruno Latour, maybe the last thing we have to do is just to do the same as what we were doing before. It is also difficult to talk about during the crisis period because so many people are personally concerned with the material difficulties of the situation. Maybe we could just share these two things. The first is the sanitary crisis, which is a worldwide crisis. The second is the ecological mutation. If we know we could go out of the sanitary crisis, maybe we have to share more about the ecological mutation. And this could be the next step for the "shared built heritage" program. We could use this sanitary crisis, as you are doing now, with this conference, through America, China, Europe and talk about the new tools to enter this ecology mutation. The text from Bruno Latour is available on his website with different translations (http://www.bruno-latour.fr/news_and_logs.html) and I would like to share them for the future.

Claus-Peter Echter: My friend Siegfried Enders is also here and we have been for a long time participating in the shared built heritage group of ICOMOS International Scientific Committees. We had a change in this concept. It was in the last 10 years, when Siegfried together with Dutch friends initiated this international scientific committee, it was about colonial architecture, sharing architecture between colonial powers like the Dutch and the people in the colonies. For the Dutch, it was in Suriname. But then we changed the concept of shared heritage because of the changing of borders like in Europe after WWII. We have shared built heritage monuments like churches, which have been before belonging to Russia or Germany and now it's in Poland. And this is shared built heritage we have to cope with. And it's the same situation with monuments in Russia, which is now? The monuments there had been belonged to a German cultural heritage before and after the war. I just have told you about practices and examples of shared built heritage in Europe, especially in Germany, Russia and Poland.

Hosts: So the first round seems to have ended here. We have two different sides. The first insists that the concept of shard built heritage focuses more on the transcultural or inter-cultural built heritage, which we have been using for a long time. And there are other people who are talking about a greater concept of the sharing. So here come my second round of questions. I heard that the social distancing strategy is going to last longer. So these days we have seen a lot of "sharing" of heritage, especially using digital techniques. What do you think of this kind of sharing? Is this the future of heritage, or the future of the interpretation of the heritage? Or the future of getting to know the heritage?

James Reap: I'm happy to hear from some of our Chinese colleagues about their thoughts. I think we have an opportunity to build on what we have done so far and to the ex and the scope of our studies. And perhaps this kind of international crisis that focuses so much on national issues, narrow issues, will provide us an opportunity to talk about how important this shared culture is to all of us.

Siegfried Enders: That's a very difficult question. I can talk only out of my experience. And for me, it might be very difficult if I think of preservation and conservation of monuments and sites cutting out the face to face issue. If you have to do it all virtually, to discuss issues when you can't see the texture or can't feel the material or can't experience the skills. And all these traces are very important for the monuments. Actually, I can't think of ways to conserve and survey like we did before, according to our principles and so on. I don't know the kind of way to get into this new technology of virtual communication. In this very specific case of conservation, you can talk about philosophy and you can talk about theories and so on. This is possible. But if it comes to conservation issues, I doubt it. I'm afraid.

James Reap: I think we do have some new tools that we can apply, although it's certainly not like being there. Some of the things that I've seen recently in virtual reality and 3D video scanning and using drones can allow you to see some materials in a way that have been difficult before. So I think it's not ideal, we need to touch and feel places and buildings and that sort of thing. But I think there are some tools that we can use better, and maybe this kind of crisis is helping us use some of these new tools to expand our tool box. And when things improve, we all have not only traditional tools, but these very new tools.

Maria José de Freitas: I think this is all part of the scientific knowledge nowadays. We also have when we study the buildings, when we do the heritage impact assessment, we always like to go there. Even the smell is important. Through the smell, the people around you can feel just being there. But as in any other things, we have new tools in drawing, and we have the 3D and x-rays of buildings. We have a lot of technologies that can help us do the complete screening of the building. So all of this can work together in a way that we can have a better experience, a better knowledge of the building, even we can try and can exercise some kind of situation. If we do this, what will happen? If we do that, what will happen? At all these kinds of situations, you can do by simulation. In 3D, virtual reality, you can experience the result. So all of these work together. And then we can make use of the tools we have. But of course, we need to experience, we are still human, we still need to understand by ourselves what the situation is. I think it's a kind of interwork in their knowledge also that is necessary to go ahead with it.

Siegfried Enders: It is of course very useful for technology and for the scientific approach of doing research about conservation things and learning about the material and so on. But as a whole, it might be difficult without having the face to face experience of the monuments and sites. I think if we wouldn't have been to the places and meet all the people involved in the treatment of the heritage, we would have it all only on the screen, it would be a completely different experience or impression. Don't you think so?

Claus-Peter Echter: I totally agree with Siegfried because it is really dangerous now in this only virtual coping with the monuments. I had the same feeling as Siegfried when I accompanied him 10 times looking at shared built heritage in different countries. We went to this monument, which has been shared built heritage in Suriname, the capital city of which is world heritage. We saw it, we discussed it with our friends there. I think if you only do it virtually, it's something different and I think it's really a danger.

Françoise Ged: I work with students at university with these new tools, giving lessons with "zoom" or similar platforms that we didn't have a few weeks ago. And I have been very impressed by a session between teachers, which talked about new examination processes and examples. The crisis could be an opportunity to reflect upon a new system for exams. For instance, to engage students in collective work, for a limited time, where they have to share common knowledge. During our webinar, there has been a complete change in the way of thinking about sharing knowledge. As in the last century when I was a student, is the question to know what is the level of knowledge of the students? Maybe it could be to learn how to be confident in our collective thinking, in what we could do all together in the same collective projects, and how to be able to go further and to make these collective processes. So I think it's linked with what we are discussing now about shared heritage. To share heritage is also to share results. And how to share results is also how to work together. And maybe we don't all have the same vision of what results are and what we could share all together and how we could work all together. For me, it's a very new experience and an opportunity to think about how to go further for the next steps. For instance, what we could share with virtual platforms and what we really need to do all together when we are face to face. Because there are so many specific situations and sites, as we already said, where we have to be face to face. But there are other exchange possibilities where we don't need to be face to face. To be on-site, for direct comprehension of people and situation is also important to avoid fake information, especially in this period where there is so much fake information. This is also our responsibility, how to give opportunities to young generations to know better what is fake information and what is not fake information.

Ségolène Charles: I really do agree with what Françoise Ged just said, as a young architect, I has beer already deeply believing that the human should have been in the center of our projects. As I am working a lot about citizen participation, I really do believe collective action. Sharing something needs to be construct need to be think about need to be together people around to create this shared heritage. And I really did believe in it even more today that we need to create architecture and urban projects. Like I'm talking about what I'm working on without the people who have been directly concerned, even though is the digital age that we were talking about last November and all these digitalized tools. They can be very useful. And they can be a very interesting way to get to create, get to construct, get to think all together. But we should not, I think we should be taking into consideration and be careful about it in a way that it's only tools. And the more important about all this collective action is the process. And how we will be a deliberating, constricting sharing and all these digital tools should remain and be kept in our head just as tools. And in this context of crisis, I really do believe and I did believe it before as well that the new generation, for example, in my work of architect of urban designers, of local politicians; of technical services in France, in the different cities, will bring and I hope they will bring and think about how we should keep making common sense together.

Hosts: What will the outstanding universal value be of the shared heritage next stage?

Siegfried Enders: I think the value of shared heritage is considered to be very high. Because it gives a kind of common sense, which is quite important in our world. And as I had already said in my introduction. This crisis now creates a lot of separation and nationalism and so on. So sharing is very important for the future and sharing cultural heritage is very important. Otherwise, I wouldn't have been working with this committee for many, many years. And I think this kind of idea of sharing will also have a future. Because people are looking for their roots, where they are from. They want to know the history to identify themselves within the society. And this shared aspect is a very important one because it gives the links to other parts of the world to other people, which is in from my point of view in this world, very important. It also gives understanding of internationally living together. So I think this will have a future and it's kind of our task to look for ways to carry on with our ideas and activities to improve the knowledge and the treatment and the awareness of shared heritage. Coming back to my first statement, I think of course the intangible part is very important. But it's a question whether it should be done all together, or could be shared in different sections. Some are taking more care of focusing more on this part and others focusing on the other part.

James Reap: A part of this conversation brings to mind the topic of the forum two years ago, and that was partially focusing on cultural routes. And the idea of cultural routes was expressed in the ICOMOS and the UNESCO motto is based strongly on the flow of exchange between along a cultural route. And that is what gives in the minds, I think of those who focused on the UNESCO and ICOMOS mottos, the outstanding universal value of cultural routes, the importance of exchange, not just the fact that you have a physical route, but you have an exchange of ideas of culture along it. So I think that it certainly gives strength to the argument that shared cultural heritage is an important aspect of intangible cultural heritage. The World Heritage Convention itself, along with the Hague convention, is a very internationalist document. Talking about the culture of one is important to the culture of all. So that there is this idea of shared world heritage. So I think that the shared aspect is of it growing importance in world heritage and the concept of an outstanding universal value. So I think our focus on this committee and the focus of the center in Wuhan is very appropriate now, because of this growing emphasis on sharing.

Claus-Peter Echter: I think about your question of the outstanding universal value of shared heritage, it's very important. I'm totally of the opinion of James Reap that the outstanding universal value of the shared heritage will be more important in the future. And I think he had his right point when he quoted about the World Heritage Convention and I think the criterion II there about the exchange of ideas is really important. So what about the exchange? What ideas are in the exchange? What is the degree of exchange? Is it outstanding? And I think so because we have a shared built heritage which is on a regional level, on a national level or a worldwide level. And I think we should always look at this and I think this criterion II is always one of the most important criteria in world heritage, which is not only important for world heritage, but for heritage in general.

Maria José de Freitas: I think that in this global world where we live now, a world of globalization, the routes are important to understand who we are, and what are we doing here. So, I think everything is important related to our personal lives and related to heritage. Also, the experience that we can have by ourselves, I'm talking especially about people more related to the architectural field, or the urban field and also the social field, because when we do architecture, we are doing it for people. So, when we feel architecture, when we feel the cities, when we try to understand the cities, we need to be there. It's always a question of sense and sensibility. And in the globalized world, it is so important for us and for everybody to understand the routes, to understand who we are and what our role is. Architecture and heritage in this aspect can have an important connection and attachment. That's why I think that is important to experience by us. It is important to keep the outstanding values. Because this is what can link things and people together. And this is something that we can understand and proceed. Talking again about the tools, they always help us to understand the real thing, and even sometimes to understand the pathologies and so on, to go ahead trying to make it better, but is always important for us to focus and to understand what the role of the humanity is. Nowadays, talking about so many people moving from one country to another country is very important to keep the traditions and to keep the immaterial heritage. I always think that if there is some material heritage connecting together, it can also help the attachment of the people and the feeling of a place—The Sense of Place. I think this important concept is something that is pointing out in the heritage and in shared heritage. The understanding of the Sense of Place is an outstanding value. In our time, this is really important.

Françoise Ged: Already a lot of things have been explained by each of us, and especially as said Maria, the feeling of the place is the most important, for the comprehension of outstanding universal value. It is what we could share: What sort of different feelings? And these feelings could be the first material to deal with in urban projects, the common basis which to elaborate an urban project and to be involved in the future of our cities and places.

Ségolène Charles: When I think about universal value, I think about the project we've been dealing with in urban projects or architectural projects, working with the inhabitance. Usually, at the beginning of our missions, people do not agree or have different views about the project. And what I like about citizen participation regarding architecture or heritage context is that the main objective is that we don't talk that much about is to construct this universal value. I don't know if I could define it properly. But what I think about is that in a way, when working and producing with the inhabitants, we are trying to tend to a value that we can't define properly, but that is kind of becoming in a way universal. The most different the inhabitance who are taking part in the citizen participation process are the more difficult they are, the more interesting it is. Because we don't agree, because we are different, because we have different interests to defend, little by little having an engineering of participation, trying to adjust the process. We are creating this universal value. I think we are trying in a way. And that is why in part I think it is particularly interesting. And then we are doing what Maria José was saying about the sense of place.

Yan Haiming: Thank you for inviting me to share my opinion on the 3rd question. Actually the theme of this year ICOMOS Day is shared culture, shared heritage and shared responsibility. And I think the outstanding universal value, which is tightly associated with the world heritage system, is on the very basis of the world heritage convention, which stresses the importance of shared responsibility of all human beings for protecting heritage sites. So it's not what shared heritage may have the universal value. But on the other hand, the basis of world heritage that should be shared by all human beings, should be shared heritage. And according to the semantic article just published today written by the president of ICOMOS China, Mr. Song Xinchao, we are living in the world that is losing our vision that has been shared in the past decades that we are going to have a globalized world. We are going to break down all the obstacles and all the barriers between different nations and different people. Now we're in the world of more and more nationalism, segregation, isolation, hatred, disbelieves and dis-communications between each other. So this is very important that this year's theme is and should be paid a lot of attention by heritage professionals. To make it simple, all shared heritage is associated with the very basis, the very basic principle of world heritage. And we look forward to having you more and more sites and buildings of shared heritage on the world heritage list. This should be the principle of the World Heritage Convention and also for all the heritage sectors, professionals, preservationists and all people that are engaged in this kind of cause. That's my personal opinion.

Hosts: Our last questions today are how we preserve the shared heritage in the future and what our shared responsibility is. We need to clarify it more.

Siegfried Enders: I think they're very essential questions. How do we preserve the existing shared built heritage or shared heritage. First of all, I think it is important to raise the awareness about the importance of this kind of heritage. And this could be done by all means of communication. And if awareness is around and the importance of this issue is known, then there are a lot of different ways to preserve it. And of course, it depends on the legal system in one country, the economic situation and so on. But I think the most important part is really that people understand. They need to know why this shared aspect is so important for them, for their culture and for their heritage.

James Reap: I do think that we have an opportunity now to move forward strongly, not to stand on the sidelines of talking about the importance of shared heritage and shared built heritage. This is the time to do that during the aftermath of this crisis. We have been concerning about surviving day to day and I know we will be looking towards the shortages of funding for heritage in the phase of the need to support humanitarian issues. But heritage is a humanitarian issue. And I think the shared aspect of that fact is what brings us all together. So I think that we need to continue to communicate among ourselves and with other colleagues in the heritage field, about the importance of this. So I think this is a good start today in doing that.

Maria José de Freitas: In my point of view, I think each one of us has a lot of responsibility in this field, because we are professionals, because we also share our ideas about shared heritage in this kind of conferences and forums and so on. So in my point of view, each one of us should be always paying attention to what's going on around, and be in a way in contact with people, raising their attention to this. Recently I teach about conservation to some students in a university. It was a master's degree course, and they came from different areas: journalism, sociology, anthropology and so on. They are not so aware of architecture, urban planning and so on. Then I started discussing with them and nowadays they are sending me pictures about situations they don't find so well, about shared heritage. I think if each one of us takes care and has a proactive view instead of keeping on the sidewalk, making it part of our daily life, being more enthusiastic, we can share the enthusiasm. This plan is something important even with the students, with the young generation. Then this will be a kind of a movement. This kind of movement is good because it makes things happen. So I'm really very positive about this situation. And I think this movement, especially here in Macao, is quite interesting, and Macao plays with Mainland China and plays with the world. So we keep going on and we keep moving and we want to do more. That's my goal and the strategy I think that should be followed. We need to find synergies between all of us.

Claus-Peter Echter: I think you asked about the future of shared heritage and how we can preserve, I think Siegfried has told us the really important aspect to raising awareness. According to the participation of the people of the examples told by Ségolène, I think this is participation. And civic society is a really important aspect now for cultural heritage and I think one of the best ideas for future heritage is one of the best ideas is called sustainable development plan from the UN, the 17 SDGs. And I think if we look at these different aspects, we have to solve this big problem to manage this sustainable development of this and of the heritage. But I think in the SDGs, we will have really important tools to do it.

Françoise Ged: To respond to your questions of how to preserve shared heritage in the future and what could be our shared responsibility, I want to share also with you the tool proposed by Bruno Latour, the French philosopher, who I talked about at the beginning. According to his suggestion about the process of description, the first step could be to describe what we think is shared heritage. Then, during the common discussion, we could discover that the result will not be the same for everybody for the same place. For instance, regarding the heritage of the 20th century, there are a lot of things we really don't want to have again. So in this shared heritage, what we really want to preserve, and why it's important or why it's not so important. To add some concrete issues, for instance, what about shared heritage and tourism? What sort of tourism do we want to have in the cities? If I pursue the links between urban and rural resources, what sort of things would we like to have as shared heritage? The work of description could be the first responsibility we could have in the tasks we have together, and in the tasks we have individually as teachers, professionals and so on. The points of views are always quite different in society and in the different parts of the world.

Ségolène Charles: I will repeat once everyone has been saying so far, talking about the heritage that I'm now working on especially on the heritage in my practice or my research. But when I was in Wuhan with you last Crossover Forum, I was struck how both citizen participation and heritage could be and should be linked together. When you're working about citizen participation, you put together what we so-called experts and citizens. And everyone's got the expertise to share. And in a way, what we learned is that it's raising awareness while we are talking together on some subjects, experts and citizens. I will be illustrating my word with a citizen convention on climate which is happening today in France, 150 inhabitance has been randomly chosen to work on this issue. And actually, for two weeks, they've been listening and hearing about experts, international experts in the climax. Now they are working together on this issue, not only they are raising their own awareness. But what we have been observing through this process is how everyone is understanding the limits that we needed to face in order to go through for example this climate subject. But this example could be applied to the heritage subject.

Zhu Haijun: As to the question of how to preserve the shared built heritage, I do agree with the opinions of Siegfried. That first of all, we should have the awareness of preserving this kind of unique heritage that showed the evidence of cultural exchange, the coexistence of different cultures and different civilizations. That is the outstanding universal value of this kind of shared heritage. It shows the fact that different cultures and different civilizations can co-exist harmoniously. People in the past years have been promoting this kind of cultural exchange. And it also give suggestions for our generation and even the generations in the future that we should agree that the trend of globalization and culture exchange can happen in future days. So the past and the solutions to that done by the people of the past days can give us good suggestions on how to deal with the different cultures and civilizations. And we can not only preserve the cultural heritage, but also create more cultural heritage for future generations. We are the generation that makes history.

Yan Haiming: I would like to say maybe it's a bit related to the second question. Shared heritage online is always an alternative. It's not the central or the core of the vision of shared heritage concept. I hope the COVID-19 could be contained in a short fashion. And we can not only share our culture online, but also share the heritage physically and also share our responsibility face to face in near future. That's the last words that I would say also on behalf of ICOMOS China.

Hosts: Thank you all for the support for Wuhan. I believe everyone will get through this. We can get through the global crisis. And we hope someday we will see each other face to face. We received greetings from all over the world at the beginning of the pandemic. Everyone was greeting us and everyone was caring for us. It was very warm-hearted of you and thank you very much.

共享遗产：从认知到方法

Shared Heritage: From perception to method

许颖、丁援

中信建筑设计研究总院 ICOMOS 共享遗产研究中心

Dr. Xu Ying and Dr. Ding Yuan

ICOMOS Research Center on Shared Built Heritage,

CITIC General Institute of Architectural Design and Research

"共享遗产（Shared Heritage）"是一个仍在不断发展的概念，"共享建成遗产（Shared Built Heritage，或译作'共享建筑遗产'）"是其重要的源头，也是其主要的组成部分。1995 年，荷兰国家保护局（Netherlands Department for Conservation，NDC）和斯里兰卡建筑、规划和遗产方面的管理机构合作，举办了一个关于"斯里兰卡的整体城市复兴和遗产"的研究和培训班，主要关注了其殖民地时期的遗产。与此同时，荷兰政府也启动了一个技术援助项目——"加勒遗产项目"，并于 1995 年 2 月 24 日至 28 日在斯里兰卡的科伦坡举行了一次关于"欧洲以外的欧洲建筑和城镇规划（荷兰时期）"的国际研讨会。这次研讨会发布了《关于保护荷兰与亚洲接触产生的物质遗产的科伦坡宣言》。作为宣言的一部分，与会学者提出了关于在国际古迹遗址理事会成立一个关于殖民地（Colonial Settlements）/双源建筑（Buildings of Dual Parentage）/共同遗产（Mutual Heritage）建筑的国际委员会的建议。

"共享遗产"从这时起，正式进入了全球遗产学界的研究视野。

一、从"共同遗产"到"共享遗产"

在 ICOMOS 荷兰和 ICOMOS 斯里兰卡成员的共同努力下，一个新的 ICOMOS 国际科学委员会——ICOMOS 共享殖民建筑与城镇规划委员会（ICOMOS-SCAT）于 1998 年成立。委员会成立之初有 10 位成员，来自荷兰、斯里兰卡、英国、澳大利亚、美国、葡萄牙与西班牙等国。委员会的目标主要有：

- 识别和评估/重估属于共同遗产的纪念物、遗址和景观；
- 激励和开拓保护和修复/更新项目；
- 鼓励融入规划和发展项目；
- 发布和展示研究、设计和咨询工作的成果；
- 参与共同遗产领域图书馆、档案和文件服务的发展
- 在相关地区和场所提供技术支持。

在这一时期，对于"共享遗产"的认识还较为粗浅。从委员会的章程来看，当时将这一类遗产称为"共同遗产"，其代表内容主要是历史上殖民地的遗产——双源建筑。

成立之后，委员会发展迅速，成员从 1998 年的 10 人发展到 1999 年 ICOMOS 成员大会时的 35 人，到 2000 年时就已经有 53 名成员，其中 10 人来自亚洲和澳大利亚，16 人来自欧洲，11 人来自非洲，15 个来自美洲和加勒比地区。不幸的是，2001 年 11 月，委员会主席弗里茨·范·沃登教授意外去世，委员会的所有活动都告一段落。

花了将近一年的时间，在 2002 年 12 月 4 日于马德里举行的国际古迹遗址理事会成员大会上，委员会

终于选举出了一位新的主席。在这次会议上,委员会的名称改为了"共享殖民建筑遗产国际科学委员会"。在当时,委员会内就已经有人反对"殖民遗产"一词,特别是来自印度尼西亚和南非的成员。

2003年,在荷兰政府的要求下,委员会将名称从"共享殖民建筑遗产"改为了"共享建筑遗产"。这一戏剧性的更名没有经过委员会成员的同意,完全是为了获取荷兰政府的资助而做出的被动性更改——"殖民"这一词汇已经被敏锐的政治界(荷兰外交部)弃之不用,遗产界不得不做出相应的反应。

"共享建成遗产"与之前的名称相比,去掉了政治性,用"建成遗产(Built Heritage)"指代建筑、城镇规划等遗产要素,更易被来自不同地区的研究者所接受。而正是因为去掉了"殖民"一词,更多类型的"共享遗产"开始不断进入研究视野,"共享遗产"的价值也有了根本性的转变。

二、从"共同"到"多元"

2005年,对"共享遗产"的研究和讨论进入第二个十年。在这一时期,科学界和政治界也出现了"共享遗产"的思想。显然,寻找可以"共享"的共同议题、共同价值观和共同责任是20世纪诸多战争(包括冷战)带给所有国家的一个教训。欧洲一体化也被视为祛除欧洲大陆的极端民族主义的解药。也正因为如此,"共享遗产"的研究视角发生了变化——"共享遗产"不再只是殖民者与殖民地人民需要共同面对的过去,在全球化的背景下,"共享遗产"成为了一个新的遗产类型,它见证了多元文化的交流、融合与冲突,成为不同民族、不同地区的人们了解自身历史的重要纽带。

由于20世纪90年代中东和东南欧冷战后政治形势的变化,苏联和东欧的遗产引起了建筑师、规划师和艺术史学家们的注意,他们开始寻找与邻国同行合作的新方式。他们必须面对从邻国继承的建成遗产的保护问题,这种"共享遗产"的保护,也亟需国际合作。2005年,欧洲委员会在《法罗公约》(《关于文化遗产对社会的价值的框架公约》)中提及了许多"共享"的内容,以及如何处理由于边界变化等原因从其他国家继承的遗产的问题。以波兰为例,它需要在所有的边境地区处理与立陶宛、白俄罗斯、乌克兰、摩尔多瓦、罗马尼亚、斯洛伐克和德国"共享"的建筑遗产。因此,国际古迹遗址理事会波兰国家委员会设立了一个"共享(联合)遗产科学委员会"以满足日益增长的研究需要,他们也与国际古迹遗址理事会取得联系,要求将这一问题落实到委员会在国际一级的任务中。随后,国际古迹遗址理事会波兰、乌克兰、白俄罗斯、立陶宛和德国等国家委员会开始密切合作,开展了许多研究和专家交流活动。

2006年,ICOMOS共享遗产科学委员会终于给出了"共享建成遗产"的定义:"共享建成遗产包括有历史意义的城市与农村结构或要素,这些结构或要素是多元文化影响的结果。"

三、从"共同价值"到"普遍价值"

从2006年起,ICOMOS共享遗产委员会参与了ICOMOS对各国申遗文本的审查。2008年,马来西亚的马六甲与乔治城的申遗成功,是"共享遗产"研究的一个里程碑。它们"突出普遍价值(OUV)"的重要内容,就是其亚洲多元文化遗产和传统中的"共享"因素。

马六甲是一个著名的港口城市,历史上曾经被马来人(1396—1511)、葡萄牙人(1511—1641)、荷兰人(1641—1795和1818—1824)、英国人(1826—1941和1941—1957)和日本人(1941—1945)统治。在城市中,葡式、荷式与英式的建筑都留有遗存,建筑又多带有伊斯兰、印度与中国的特色。马六甲和乔治城独特的遗产展现了东西方之间已经发展了500多年的贸易和文化交流。源自亚洲和欧洲的影响赋予了这些城镇鲜活的、有形的和无形的多元文化遗产。马六甲的政府建筑、教堂、广场和防御工事展示了这段历史的早期阶段,它起源于15世纪的马来苏丹王朝,始于16世纪初的葡萄牙和荷兰时期。乔治城则代表了18世纪末的英国统治时代,以住宅和商业建筑为特色。这两个城市构成了东亚和东南亚独一无二的建筑和文化景观。

马六甲与乔治城的申遗成功的一个示范意义,是让"共享遗产"研究的关注点从遗产对利益相关方的"共同价值",转换到了遗产对于人类的"普遍价值"。"共享遗产"不仅仅属于创造遗产的群体,而且这类遗产体现的人类文明的交流与交融,具有普遍意义。

在马六甲与乔治城申遗成功之后,又有一些以"共享遗产"为突出普遍价值的文化遗产被列入了世界遗产名录。其中,2017年鼓浪屿申遗成功,成为中国首个被世界广泛了解的"共享遗产"。

表1 ICOMOS共享遗产委员会参与的世界遗产评审项目

	时间	项目	国家	ICOMOS意见	推荐标准	世界遗产大会结果	列入标准
1	2006	阿普拉瓦西·加特地区	毛里求斯	退回重报	—	成功登录	(vi)
2	2008	马六甲海峡的历史名城——马六甲与乔治城	马来西亚	补充材料推荐列入	—	成功登录	(ii)(iii)(iv)
3	2009	旧城,大里贝拉历史中心	佛得角	补充材料推荐列入	—	成功登录	(ii)(iii)(iv)
4	2009	历史城镇大巴萨姆	科特迪瓦	退回重报	—	补充材料推荐列入	—
5	2010	蒙巴萨的耶稣堡	肯尼亚	退回重报	—	补充材料推荐列入	—
5-2	2011	蒙巴萨的耶稣堡(再次申报)	肯尼亚	退回重报	—	成功登录	(ii)(iv)
4-2	2012	历史城镇大巴萨姆(再次申报)	科特迪瓦	补充材料推荐列入	—	成功登录	(iii)(iv)
6	2012	拉巴特:现代都市与历史古城	摩洛哥	登录	(ii)(iv)	成功登录	(ii)(iv)
7	2013	莱武卡历史海港城镇	斐济	登录	(ii)(iv)	成功登录	(ii)(iv)
8	2015	圣安东尼奥布道区	美国	登录	(ii)	成功登录	(ii)
9	2017	姆班扎刚果:前刚果王国的首都遗迹	安哥拉	登录	(iii)(v)(vi).	成功登录	(iii)(iv)
10	2017	鼓浪屿:历史国际社区	中国	登录	(ii)(iv)	成功登录	(ii)(iv)
11	2018	孟买的维多利亚哥特式和装饰艺术建筑群	印度	登录	(ii)(iv)	成功登录	(ii)(iv)
12	2018	贸易时代:雅加达古城和四个离岛	印度尼西亚	不予登录	—	撤回	—
13	2018	长崎地区隐藏的基督教遗址	日本	登录	(iii)	成功登录	(iii)

在上表所列出的ICOMOS共享遗产委员会参与评审的13个项目中,有12个最终被列入世界遗产名录。其中,ICOMOS给予"登录(Inscribe)"建议,并在当年的世界遗产大会上直接进入名录的有7项;ICOMOS认为需要补充材料(Refer)再予登录,在当年的世界遗产大会上直接进入名录的有3项;ICOMOS对4个项目给与了"退回重报"(Defer)的建议,但其中2项在当年的世界遗产大会上成功进入名录,另外2项则在当年的世界遗产大会上被认为需要"补充材料",并在随后的申报中进入名录。

这12个项目中,6项来自非洲、4项来自亚洲、1项来自大洋洲、1项来自美洲,没有来自欧洲的项目。这固然与各国遗产申报策略相关,但如果以"共享遗产"为视野重新审视欧洲文化遗产,能够体现"共享"这一突出普遍价值的遗产仍亟待挖掘阐释。

四、从遗产到视野

从2009年开始,ICOMOS共享遗产委员会组织了一系列的会议与学术考察,极大地拓展了"共享遗产"的内涵。这些会议与考察正在推动"共享遗产"从一种遗产类型转变为研究与保护这一类遗产的视野。

从内涵方面来看,"共享遗产"不仅包括一般意义上的遗产建筑与城镇景观,还包括工业遗产、军事遗产等特殊类别的遗产。而综观这些"共享遗产"的遗产点可以发现,"共享遗产"的来源有殖民、边境变更、战争等政治原因,长距离贸易等经济原因和宗教传播、主动学习等文化原因。

表2 ICOMOS共享遗产委员会学术活动表

	时间	地点	事件	关注内容
1	2009年	格但斯克(波兰)	学术会议	欧洲共享遗产
2	2010年	苏里南	学术会议	欧-非共享遗产
3	2011年	开普敦(南非)	学术会议	非物质的共享遗产
4	2011年	首尔(韩国)	学术会议	亚洲现代工业遗产
5	2012年	鼓浪屿、武汉、北京、天津(中国)	学术考察	中国近现代共享遗产
6	2012年起每年	武汉(中国)	学术会议	跨文化遗产保护等
7	2013年	武汉(中国)	学术中心成立	共享遗产研究与保护实践
8	2013年	古巴	学术会议	美洲的军事遗产
9	2014年	佛罗伦萨(意大利)	学术会议	反思共享遗产
10	2015年	日本	学术考察	日本近现代共享遗产
11	2016年	德国-法国-卢森堡	学术考察	欧洲共享遗产
12	2017年	里斯本(葡萄牙)	学术会议	跨文化遗产保护
13	2017年	埃武拉(葡萄牙)	学术考察	欧洲共享遗产
14	2017年	西孟加拉邦(印度)	学术考察	印度共享遗产
15	2018年	爱沙尼亚-芬兰-俄罗斯	学术考察	北欧与苏联的共享遗产
16	2019年	摩洛哥	学术考察	非洲共享遗产

从2012年开始,ICOMOS共享遗产委员会联合武汉市人民政府,每年在武汉主办一次"无界论坛",在汇集国内外专家对文化遗产进行多角度的探讨的基础上,不断推进"共享遗产"的研究。2013年,ICOMOS共享遗产研究中心落户武汉,成为ICOMOS共享遗产委员会在全球范围内设置的唯一一家分支机构。研究中心成立之后,立足共享遗产的研究与保护实践,结合武汉的"共享遗产"遗存,依托"无界论坛",还开展了"无界对话""青少年无界论坛"等活动,将"共享遗产"的研究与工程实践、城市可持续发展、文化线路、公众参与等主题结合,推动了"共享遗产"这一遗产研究视野的扩展。

表3 "无界论坛"及"无界对话"主题

	时间	论坛主题	对话主题
1	2012年	跨文化遗产的保护与发展	—
2	2013年	工程·文化·景观	—
3	2014年	大学与城市	"80后"对话"90后"
4	2015年	创意城市与文化遗产	当东方遇见西方
5	2016年	时间与空间:城市更新中的文化遗产	女性与文化遗产
6	2017年	文化·城市·未来:文化遗产在城市可持续发展中的角色	全球遗产教育网络的建设
7	2018年	人文·人居·新时代:文化线路在城乡可持续发展中的角色	文化线路与长江大保护、遗产保护与城市发展
8	2019年	文化·大众化·数字化:新时代的文化遗产保护与公众参与	全球视野下的文化遗产保护与公众参与

武汉的文化遗产是否可以申遗？如何申遗？在2019年"万里茶道"列入中国世界遗产预备名录之后，这两个问题都有了答案。从遗产形态上来看，"万里茶道"是一条文化线路；从遗产价值来看，它的诸多遗产点，都具有"共享遗产"的特征。在武汉市内，除了"申遗"的遗产点外，还有众多文化遗产都需要从"共享遗产"的视野重新认识。除此之外，还应将"共享遗产"与"文化线路"作为两种方法，应用在遗产阐释、管理、展示与保护的实践之中。

五、从物质到非物质："共享建成遗产"到"共享遗产"

2020年，ICOMOS会员大会和国际古迹遗址日都将主题定为了"共享文化、共享遗产、共享责任"。其中，"共享遗产"的表述为Shared Heritage，与"共享建成遗产(Shared Built Heritage)"相比，这一表述将建成遗产仅作为"共享遗产"的一部分，"共享"内涵中的非物质因素得到彰显。

从这个角度反思上文提到的ICOMOS共享遗产委员会参与评审并最终列入世界遗产名录的12个项目，显然，它们并不是世界遗产名录中全部的"共享遗产"。有一些遗产在共享遗产委员会成立之前就已经列入，有些则在"突出普遍价值"的阐释中更加强调其他的特征。单体建筑、历史城区、文化线路，都可以体现"共享遗产"的特征，许多跨国申报的"系列遗产"也明显具有"共享"的特性。

以中国为例，2005年申遗成功的澳门历史城区，就是典型的"共享遗产"，而且是活态的共享遗产。在这一历史城区内，历史建筑与传统街区，以及美食、语言、生活方式、审美眼光，都体现着东西方文明的交流与交融，而且直至今天，仍然保持着充沛的活力。如今，欧洲人、土生葡人、亚洲人在澳门共同生活与工作，共同承担传承当地独特的多元文化的责任，这正是"共享文化、共享遗产、共享责任"的鲜明写照。

以欧洲为例，2004年申遗成功的斯特鲁维地理探测弧线，是目前跨越国家最多的世界遗产。它自北至南由挪威、瑞典、芬兰、俄罗斯、爱沙尼亚、立陶宛、拉脱维亚、白俄罗斯、摩尔多瓦和乌克兰的265个测量点组成，目前被列入世界遗产名录的有34个，从北极圈到黑海，总距离2 820千米。这一系列测量点由俄罗斯科学家瓦西里·雅可夫列维奇·斯特鲁维创建于1816—1855年，当时分属挪威－瑞典联盟及俄罗斯帝国两个国家，由于地缘政治的变革与边境的变更，这一跨越10国的系列遗产，虽然从建筑风格等方面并不具有多元共享的特征，但从其体现的"共享文化"与"共享责任"来看，应该属于"共享遗产"。

六、从认识到方法："共享遗产"向何处去？

在新冠肺炎疫情肆虐全球、全球化进程受到极大阻碍的今天，对"共享遗产"未来的思考变得更加必要。推动"共享遗产"这一研究领域发展的关键，在于将"共享遗产"从一种对遗产的认识，转化为研究、保护文化遗产乃至创造未来遗产的方法。

以20世纪遗产为例，目前，以建筑师为中心的"作品集"正在逐渐成为申遗的热门。2016年，为了纪念勒·柯布西耶对现代主义运动的杰出贡献，将其17个建筑列入了世界遗产名录，成为建筑界的首例。这17个作品分布在法国、瑞士、比利时、德国、阿根廷、日本和印度，世界遗产大会的决议中指出，这些作品"在三个大洲的七个国家，在半个多世纪的时间里，在建筑史上第一次证明了全球建筑实践的国际化"。其突出普遍价值的表述中，也提到这些建筑"展示了半个多世纪以来，在世界范围内前所未有的人类价值观的交流，关系到现代运动的诞生和发展"。

将这一组遗产列入世界遗产名录也给我们留下了新的思考——在全球化的今天，人类文化、技术、价值观的广泛交流，将会为世界留下大量的"共享遗产"，保护勒·柯布西耶的17座建筑，也是为保护未来的"共享遗产"提供示范。

从语义学角度来看，汉语中的"共享遗产"一词可以从两个层面理解。偏正结构的"共享遗产"对应"Shared Heritage"，动宾结构的"共享遗产"则对应"to share heritage"。而后一语义正是实现"共享遗产"由认知到方法转换的关键：在全球化的今天，主动沟通与交流、共享遗产，才能够更好地展现世界遗产及各类文化遗产的价值,也才能更好地通过保护遗产,实现可持续发展的目标——2012年,联合国可持续发展会议发布了《2030年可持续发展议程》,包含17项可持续发展目标(Sustainable Development Goals),其中第11个目标是:"建设包容、安全、有地域灾害能力的可持续城市和人类住区",这一目标的第四项具体要求正是"进一步努力保护和捍卫世界文化和自然遗产"。

2020年初,新冠肺炎疫情肆虐全球,疫情将全世界人民联系在了一起,但也造成了物理上的隔阂与文化上的紧张,这都对文化事业尤其是文化遗产保护视野产生了巨大的影响。联合国教科文组织文化助理总干事埃尔乃斯托·奥托内·拉米雷斯(Ernesto Ottone Ramirez)表示:"在这个数十亿人在空间上彼此分离的时期,文化将我们团结在一起,让我们保持联系,缩短了我们的距离。在这个令人焦虑和充满不确定性的时刻,文化提供了慰藉、鼓舞和希望。然而,虽然文化对于我们度过危机至关重要,但是我们不能忘记文化本身也在受到冲击。"教科文组织因此在全球社交媒体上发起了一场名为"共享我们的遗产(Share Our Heritage)"的活动,向所有世界遗产地管理者征集视频故事,再通过UNESCO向全球分享遗产价值和遗产地应对疫情并坚持保护遗产的故事。可见,将"共享"作为理解与保护遗产的方法,已经体现出了一定的作用。

综上所述,21世纪的"共享遗产"将以三个不同的维度存在:其一是传统意义上的"共享遗产",体现着人类历史上多元文化的交流与交融;其二是方法论意义上的"共享遗产",通过遗产共享促进全球文化的进一步交流;其三是"遗产化"意义上的"共享遗产",即在"共享遗产"视野下建成的新建筑、新地景,它们将成为未来的"共享遗产。"

后 记

一个成功的学术论坛最重要的是什么？我们觉得，是要提出一个"好的问题"。

无界论坛每年都努力向世界提出一个好的问题，这些问题来自文化遗产保护和发展的理论与实践的难点和痛点，这些问题可以引导和激发专家、官员、市民、师生去思考、去实践——

对这些问题，论坛不设标准答案，可能也没有标准答案。台上的"大家"坐而论道，台下的"大家"静心倾听。在全球化和逆全球化的宏大背景下徐徐展开的中国新一轮城市更新的实践中，大家等待这些问题答案的水落石出。

2012年至2020年，无界论坛和无界对话提出的问题包括：

如何评价、保护与利用跨文化建筑遗产？

如何在大型工程中更好地保护文化遗产？

如何促进工程与文化协调发展？

如何促进大学与城市的和谐共振？

如何定位城市更新中的"时间与空间"？如何处理好"创意城市"与文化遗产保护的关系？

如何在城乡发展和遗产保护中更多地利用"公众参与"？

女性与文化遗产的关系？

如何建立文化遗产教育的全球网络？

如何把文化作为未来城市发展的引擎，在新时代使人居更加人文？

如何用"文化线路"的视野去思考城乡发展和遗产保护？

如何在遗产保护领域更多地运用数字技术？如何更好地实现文化与科技的融合？

后疫情时代，文化遗产如何成为推动社会重振的动力？如何共享文化遗产，推动文化交流？

……

无界论坛的成功举办，要感谢远见卓识的领导和专家，要感谢直接参与组织无界论坛的国内外机构，它们是：

武汉市人民政府；

ICOMOS共享遗产委员会；

中共武汉市委宣传部；

华中科技大学；

武汉大学；

华中师范大学；

法国驻武汉总领事馆；

中国文物保护基金会；

武汉市城乡建设局；

武汉市文化局（现武汉市文化和旅游局）；

武汉市江岸区人民政府；

武汉市社会科学院；

武汉市社会科学界联合会；

中信建筑设计研究总院有限公司；

武汉地产开发投资集团有限公司；
武汉旅游体育集团；
中国古迹遗址保护协会（ICOMOS-China）；
联合国教科文组织亚太地区世界遗产培训与研究中心苏州分中心、上海分中心；
UDG联创新锐设计顾问（武汉）有限公司；
上海建为历保科技股份有限公司；
《中国名城》杂志社；
《建筑遗产》杂志社；
《Built Heritage》杂志社；
《新建筑》杂志社；
武汉共享遗产研究会。

丁　援
2020年12月15日
于中信建筑设计研究总院